Douglas Bennet was born in 1916 to a Cheshire farming family. He was to form a close attachment to the last trading coastwise schooners and joined the *Alert* in 1934 and the *Brooklands* in 1939. After the War he always maintained his close interest in the few remaining craft and never missed an opportunity to record their finer details in his meticulous drawings.

David Clement, who has carefully edited Bennet's work and prepared the list of schooners to be found at the end of the book, has nurtured a deep interest in ships and the sea since an early age. He was a founder of the Southwest Maritime History Society, and is editor of its journal. Amongst other maritime associations he is a council member of the Society for Nautical Research, and Chairman of the Topsham Museum.

Schooner SUNSET

The Last British Sailing Coasters

DOUGLAS BENNET

List of Schooners by David Clement

In association with The National Museums and Galleries on Merseyside

CHATHAM PUBLISHING
LONDON

First published in Great Britain in 2001 by Chatham Publishing,
99 High Street, Rochester, Kent ME1 1LX

Distributed by Gerald Duckworth & Co Ltd,
61 Frith Street,
London W1V 5TA

British Library Cataloguing in Publication Data
A catalogue record for this book is available from the British Library

ISBN 1 86176 176 7

All the photographs are from the collections of Terry Belt and David Clement. Every effort has been made to establish their provenance and acknowledge the photographer where known.

Typeset and designed by Roger Daniels

Printed and bound in Great Britain by Bookcraft (Bath) Ltd.

Frontispiece: Charlestown in Cornwall in the heyday of the schooner.
PHOTOGRAPHER NOT KNOWN. DAVID CLEMENT COLLECTION.

CONTENTS

FOREWORD

By Michael Stammers,
Merseyside Maritime Museum

It's one of my lasting regrets that I never got to meet Douglas Bennett. He lived in Swansea and I worked in Liverpool and, although we corresponded frequently, we never actually met. Duggie, as everybody knew him, was a fund of information about coastal sailing craft and, unlike later enthusiasts, like me, he had lived and worked on them and knew them from keel to top. I personally owe him a debt of gratitude for his excellent pair of articles on Mersey Flats and that particular piece of scholarship was one of the factors that stimulated me to attempt to write an overall history of these interesting and neglected local sailing barges.

Douglas also made a very important contribution to the history of coastal sailing craft by writing *Schooner Sunset*. Unfortunately, in his lifetime, he was frustrated by the inability of publishers to understand the value of his work and, in the end, he entrusted the manuscript to the archives of Merseyside Maritime Museum because he felt that we, as a national museum concerned with mercantile affairs, would ensure its preservation. I am delighted to have the honour of writing the Foreword at long last.

The Merseyside Maritime Museum has its own coastal schooner. As is often the case with preserved vessels, she is slightly unusual because the *De Wadden* was built in Holland in 1917 with an auxiliary diesel engine but she also carried a lofty three-masted rig with a single square sail on the foremast. Since we acquired the vessel in 1984 we have gradually been restoring her to her condition when she worked under sail – mainly between Ireland and the Mersey. She arrived, having been sold by her Arklow owners for use as a sand barge and latterly as a fishing charter vessel, in a somewhat dilapidated condition and most of the original fixtures and fittings for the mast and the rigging had long since disappeared. This would have been a problem to our ship keepers but for the fact that they could find many detailed drawings and descriptions in *Schooner Sunset*. So this work has not only an historic interest, but also has a practical value and I hope it will be well received throughout the maritime history community, whether the readers are practical sailors or armchair ones!

M K Stammers

PREFACE

That this book has appeared is in no small measure due to the efforts of a number of friends of the late Douglas Bennet who always wanted to see his efforts in print but were put off by editors who wanted to cut large chunks to make the book 'commercial' – in so doing they would have ruined the intention of this book, which is to provide an overview of the last coastal sailing merchantmen to ply these shores; to detail their design and construction and identify those nuances of change one to another and give the reasons 'Why'. During those years of meticulous observation and recording Douglas was assisted by his wife Marian, also sadly no longer with us.

Douglas sailed in these vessels and later became a most competent engineer and draughtsmen, as is evidenced from his superb line drawings crafted to the most meticulous detail, and which will be of interest to historian and modelmaker alike. Whilst Douglas had moved to Swansea he deposited his manuscript in the area of his youth, with the Merseyside Maritime Museum and we are indebted to the interest and support of Michael Stammers, Keeper of the Maritime Collection, which has made possible the publication of this unique work. We are also indebted to Chatham Publishing for having the courage to publish the complete and 'unexpurgated' version.

The editing and the collecting of the photographic illustrations has been a labour of love for the writer and for that band euphemistically known as the 'Schooner circle' whose interest in these unique craft helped to keep alive a tradition of sail which, until the latter part of the 1960s, was still to be seen around our coasts. That many of the circle such as H Oliver Hill, Grahame Farr, Dan MacDonald, Owen Wickstead and others have now passed on, including Douglas Bennet, means that this work, which is frankly the compilation and assembly of information from all of these and many other sources, is a fitting tribute to the memory of those who were in a position to record the very unromantic and financially impecunious final days of commercial mercantile sail in Britain, as indeed Douglas Bennet does in describing the strictures when sailing under Captain Creenan in the *Brooklands*.

A few, very few, of these vessels survive as charter boats carrying fare-paying passengers, but as time passes even these diminish in number. Some are 'preserved' such as the *Result* in Ulster, and the *Garlandstone*, though to see them is to appreciate that perhaps those vessels would have been better broken up, living on in memory, rather than as the sad specimens of dereliction that they are today. *Garlandstone* has recently been restored at Calstock.

Laudable efforts have been made with the *Kathleen & May* at Bideford, which one hopes will be successful, as she also was almost beyond repair after her laying up on the Thames under the curtilage of financiers who knew nothing of her background, rapidly tired of their 'toy' and left her to rot! The writer sailed on her as a small boy with Captain Tommy Jewell of Appledore in the 1950s when she was in trade to Spillers Mills at Pembroke and some may still remember the lady stevedore – Annie – who humped the sacks of flour on the quayside opposite and under the walls of Pembroke Castle. She was an awesome being for a young 12-year-old and probably for most men as well.

Terry Belt, is another one of the 'Schooner circle' hailing from Pembroke and a friend of Douglas Bennet. He was able to pass me copies of photographs taken by Douglas whilst aboard the *Brooklands* under sail in 1939 which are included in this book. Terry knew the *Brooklands* well when he lived at Burton, near Milford Haven. He writes:

"She used to come up the Haven and usually anchored off Pembroke Dock for a few days before sailing up river past Burton to the quay at Hook, about five miles further on. There used to be an anthracite colliery at Hook and she carried pitprops from Ireland and took coal back. I remember walking to Hook with a couple of friends when I was about twelve years old, just to get a close-up look at her. The last time I saw her was on a bright day in June 1935 [I think], drifting down river on the ebb, all sails set, including her flying squaresail, but with hardly a breath of wind. She anchored off Pembroke Dock, lowering her jibs, squaresail, and upper topsail, clewing up her lower topsail, but keeping the heavier canvas set. At about 6.00pm, a breeze sprang up, she weighed anchor and I watched her sail down the Haven until she disappeared round the Wear Point, but enough of nostalgia..."

DAVID B CLEMENT

I

INTRODUCTION

This book contains no gripping dramas of the sea, no wild adventures nor daring feats of seamanship, nor is it directly concerned with the pleasures or hardships of life under sail. It is an attempt to record the humdrum details of life on board the British schooners of nearly seventy years ago, at a time when they were making their last stand as purely wind-driven vessels against the inroads of the internal-combustion engine. It is written in the hope that it may be of interest to marine historians in general, although it is primarily intended for the use of ship modelmakers who are often confronted with a lack of information on small items of equipment that seldom show up well on photographs. In reverse the things that do show up well in photographs, often, in their inanimate state, provide no clue of the purpose for which they were used.

Much has already been written about the schooner so that its story is fairly well known in broad outline: how it was financed, built and owned; the trades in which it sailed in its heyday as well as in its years of decline; how it was managed and insured; and there is a great deal of information on many aspects of the economic background against which it operated. Up to the present, however, no one has dealt in any great detail with gear and fittings; how they were worked by the crew and why they were worked in one particular way as against another. Nor have the various changes which took place down the years and which were still taking place to the very end, ever been recorded except in the barest outline. Today many of these petty details of the life are in danger of being lost. In the past anyone interested in such matters had only to go down to the quay to see them for himself, but the almost complete lack of any reference to them in literature, except in very general terms, gives the impression that they were not considered to be of very great importance.

This book is an attempt to fill in some of the gaps, which must, by necessity, be left by those painting a broad canvas, and deals with the commonplace details of life on board, which have little power to fire the imagination but without some knowledge of which, the broader canvas may one day become only partially intelligible.

Owing to their simplicity of rig, small fore-and-afters were the last commercial sailing vessels to remain in existence around the British coasts. Today they are all gone and so are most of the men who sailed in them. Those who are left are no longer young and all the signs indicate that in less than twenty years great amounts of the remaining language and way of life, which stretch back in an unbroken line into the remote past, will be severed one by one – utterly and forever. This may sound exaggerated and over dramatised and the objection will immediately be raised that the sailor's ancient language and craft are still enshrined in the heart of every yachtsman and very much alive and kicking; while despite the tremendous changes which have taken place in ships, a great deal of past practise is still commonly in use by both naval and merchant seamen. Before proceeding further it must be emphasised that it is not the use of fid, marline-spike, serving-board or palm and needle that is being referred to, as all these tools of the sailor's trade are still being widely used. There exists, too, such a fascination in rope work, both plain and fancy, that numerous books have already been written on the subject so that there is very little danger that this side of sailoring will ever be lost.

The areas where the same certainty of survival cannot be guaranteed are much more diverse. Because he alone still uses the wind as a means of propulsion, the yachtsman is the only person left in the direct line of succession. In the past, when his vessel had a gaff mainsail, a bowsprit, fidded topmast, and much of the other impedimenta common to the fisherman and the small cargo carrier, his language could not help being the same as theirs. The similarity could become very marked when splicing wires, especially if the splicer managed to get a strand stuck under his fingernail!

However, the modern yacht differs tremendously from these heavily sparred vessels of the past and it would be very surprising indeed if changes in terminology had not, in consequence, also taken place. As would be expected it is in the yachting press that the signs of broken threads show up today. They appear from time to time and in isolation none of them seems to be of any great consequence but the sum total shows a trend which will obviously increase as the years go by. A few examples sufficiently surprising to stick in the memory are probably worth quoting. One is a photograph of some men on the mainyard of a brig, the caption to which stated that they were furling the 'crossjack'! The word was spelled 'cro-jick' to show that the writer knew how it was pronounced! It is also interesting to note that while this treatment is nearly always meted out to the 'forecastle' and 'topgallant', it is never applied to 'keelson', nor to the one word which more than any other sorts out the true sailors from those who have learned it from books – the pronunciation of the word 'tackle' with a long 'a'. To return to the brig, another writer in another article stated that she was blessed by the possession of a 'sparker'!!

A group of enthusiasts on the west coast of Canada built themselves a small barque in which they made the, to them, surprising discovery that if the sheets of a topgallant were let go before the halyard, there was a danger of losing the mast. Had they lived in the days of hemp standing rigging the danger would no doubt have become a reality.

The foregoing examples of broken threads are concerned with square-rigged vessels. There are plenty of examples in the realm of fore-and-aft sail as well and one of the most peculiar has existed in British yachting circles for many years. Its origins are clearly traced in Frank G.G. Carr's *Vanishing Craft*, in which he gives an account of the evolution of the fishing lugger. It appears that most British luggers were originally three-masted, like the French Chasse-Marée, but at some time in the 19th century the middle mast was discarded and the size of the foresail increased to compensate for the loss. In spite of the fact that this modification had promoted the foremast to be the mainmast, force of habit caused the fishermen who used it to persist in referring to the forward mast as the foremast, its sail as the foresail and its stay as the 'forestay' – in some manner, which no one has yet explained, this name for the stay finally managed to get itself transferred to the Thames barge. Even though the vessel wearing it manifestly has no foremast it remains the forestay to this day and there seems little amiss with this usage if one assumes that the name differentiates it from a 'backstay' which does its work in the opposite direction. The Thames barge was a splendid example of a highly specialised vessel and it is not surprising that she spread her influence over many generations of yachtsmen. To an ever-widening circle of people therefore, the stay from the main hounds to the stem head is the forestay. The inconsistency of this usage only comes to light if one tries to apply it to a square rigger. From this standpoint a full-rigged ship

Irish Minstrel at Falmouth 29th July 1927.
Photograph by David E. Smith

would have a fore forestay, a main forestay and a mizzen forestay. The reader can work out the rest for himself. This would be a great joke were it not for the fact that down the years it has given rise to endless and often quite acrimonious arguments in the yachting press, as to the correct name for the headsails in a cutter or ketch, or – the one really in question – that sail which in cargo-carrying schooners and ketches was invariably referred to simply as 'the staysail'. Some have claimed that it was the foresail, others the fore-staysail, which it was, of course, in a schooner, while a third school has managed to have the best of both worlds by proclaiming it the stay-foresail. In spite of the inherent contradiction in their standpoint the fore-staysail foresail school appears to be gaining ground; there can be little doubt that ultimately their usage will replace the older one, which had the full-rigged ship for a yardstick.

An example of the same break in continuity nearer to the subject matter of this book is shown in the much reproduced photograph of the schooner *Sir Winston Churchill* in which she is seen going to windward under fore-and-aft canvas only with her yards squared to a tee. It is possible that the *Churchill* does not always sail like this but that she does so at all comes as rather a surprise. Past generations of seamen would have either sent the yards down or braced them up. This subject is considered further when the repercussions caused by the installation of auxiliary engines are discussed.

A final difference in terminology must be dealt with because it, too, has to do with the schooner rig. In North America square topsails in schooners were probably making their last stand at about the same time as General Custer was making his, and long before this they must have been something of a rarity. To the Americans therefore the unprefixed word 'schooner' came to mean a purely fore-and-aft rigged vessel while those with topsails were called 'topsail schooners' to differentiate them. In the British Isles the case was exactly the opposite, the schooner with topsails being in the overwhelming majority, it was described simply as a 'schooner' while the one without topsails was referred to as a 'fore-and-aft schooner'. This point was made many years ago by Sir Alan Moore in *Last Days of Mast and Sail*, in which he also pointed out that both terms, unless further qualified, meant specifically a two-masted vessel. The point has been made since by other writers, and yet, without abating one iota, we still witness the constant use of the prefix 'topsail' by the bulk of contributors to the yachting press and by those responsible for television programmes, most of whom seem vociferously certain that theirs is the one true faith. The men who sailed in schooners were, of course, quite well aware that they were 'topsail schooners' and they would use the expression themselves when they wished to specify what particular variety they were referring to. Most earlier schooners had a single topsail with topgallant set flying above it but by the 1880s the most popular rig was a standing topgallant set above double topsails. Unless explaining something like this, however, the schooner hand of the past never used the expression 'topsail schooner' at all. He took it for granted and saved his breath.

From the foregoing the reader may have already deduced that anything unqualified by a seaman was the old original whilst the use of a qualifying word implied a later variation. This rule is invariably correct and can be applied with certainty to practically anything to do with sailing vessels. The word topsail, for instance, meant specifically a 'square' topsail, a fore-and-aft topsail being a 'gaff' topsail. This point has been laboured somewhat because many unnecessary expressions like 'three-masted barque' are frequently seen in print although 'one-masted cutter' and 'two-masted brig' are fortunately not yet with us! In this book the common usage of the past has been adhered to as far as possible but, in those cases where this could lead to ambiguity, expressions such as 'square topsail' and 'two-master' have been used.

Despite its wonderful ingenuity the human race has not yet managed to prevent languages from slowly changing their meaning and usage. It is only when the changes are not clearly understood that confusion eventually arises. Thus, the foregoing rather boring definitions should be construed as an attempt to point out the direction in which things are proceeding, rather than as a last stand, or sit, of some linguistic Canute. The purpose of this book is also to prevent future misunderstanding, by recording as much as possible about life in schooners in the years of their decline. It was born out of two brief experiences in youth, and out of the five years which separated them, during which time the writer lived and worked in a schooner port and rubbed shoulders with the men who manned them, dug out their cargoes or trimmed them in, repaired them, caulked them, made their sails or provided them with their provisions. Much of the information then gathered was random and haphazard and often not even sought. It was during the forty years and more that have since elapsed that many of the pieces of a complex and fascinating puzzle finally dropped into their proper places.

The characters in this book are, unfortunately, anything but fictitious. Many, if not all, must now be dead. The writer can only hope that if the mention of any person arouses sad or unhappy memories in the mind of some reader the passage of years will have softened the bitterness and that he will be reminded much more vividly of the humorous or happy incidents of a way of life that now seems almost as remote and unreal as the outer spiral-nebulae.

II

'SHOES AND SHIPS AND SEALING WAX'

The 19th century was a period of tremendous change. By its end the steamship was in the ascendancy, the sailing ship definitely on its way out – though in its last years it underwent greater changes than had occurred over many centuries. The transition from wood to iron and steel construction, which affected both steam and sailing vessels, has been well documented and much publicised. Two other factors that, in their own way, had almost as much influence on the changes taking place have been practically ignored.

The first, a negative sort of factor with a positive result, was that by about 1850 buccaneers, privateers, pirates, Sallee rovers, and suchlike gentry, had almost completely gone out of business except for a few isolated pockets in the Far East, so that for the first time since the collapse of the Roman Empire the yardstick by which a vessel was manned could become the number of men required to work her, not to fight her. This came too late in the day to have much effect upon the size of sailing ship's hatches, which for centuries had been limited by the necessity to carry guns; the steamship, however, profited by it fairly rapidly. Had the sailing vessel also gone in for larger hatches, the big square-rigger might have finished up with a lot of small but fairly powerful dolly winches near her bulwarks, something after the manner of the Humber keel instead of the deck capstans which became the standard equipment.

The second factor was steel standing rigging. If it had been invented in any other century it would have been hailed as one of the greatest triumphs of human ingenuity but coming as it did in the midst of tremendous change its full significance, although not lost on those who were shipmates with it, was never really appreciated by a public which had its eyes firmly fixed on steamships, railway trains, bridges and all the other wonders of the age. After a preliminary period in which it was treated with a certain amount of mistrust, it became popular in the 1860s, and it is safe to say that it, more than any other factor, allowed the sailing ship to continue to grow in size and efficiency until it culminated in the 5,000-ton giants *Preussen* and *Thomas W. Lawson*. These huge sailing vessels would have been a sorry pair with hemp standing rigging and their steel masts would obviously have had to be strong enough to carry the bulk of the load alone. It is fairly obvious that had laid-up wires not been produced, chains or solid bars would have been pressed into service.

Compared with steel, hemp standing rigging was at best a makeshift. It left its mark for centuries not only on the countless generations of seamen who spent much of their time tightening it up, but on the ships they developed as well. When wet hemp's fibres swelled up causing an increase in diameter and a contraction in length resulting an overload on strands already in tension. When it dried out, again it was slightly longer than before and this slack had to be taken up. Even the hemp lanyards in the deadeyes of steel standing rigging suffered from this disadvantage and it was not until the introduction of the bottle screw that a really satisfactory arrangement was arrived at. Hemp under load also stretched considerably so that before it could provide its full support to a wooden mast, the mast itself had to bend. To drive a clipper so rigged really hard must have been a much more nerve-wracking business than it later became with steel wire. In the light of these manifest limitations it is not surprising that for centuries seamen felt that the only part of the mast they could really rely upon in a crisis was the lower mast. They therefore stepped the heaviest lower masts that the size of their vessels would permit and then proceeded to erect upon them light topmasts and absolutely spindly topgallant masts. As soon as a royal was stowed the yard was sent down to lighten the load and, at the slightest provocation, topgallant yard and even topmast would follow it. The evolution of the reefing topsail – when close-reefed the yard was just above the cap of the lower mast – is not without some significance in this connection. A heavier topmast would have been desirable in many ways, but its increased weight would inevitably have thrown a greater strain on to the lower mast in heavy weather. Such was the uneasy balance between conflicting tendencies which seamen had to put up with for centuries. It is not surprising that royal and topgallant yards were very short compared with the lower yards and that centuries passed before the topsails took over from the courses as the main working sails of the vessel.

The main effect produced by steel standing rigging was to make the topmasts and topgallant masts much heavier and stronger and their yards much longer so that the sail plan lost its tapering look and became a great deal squarer. Studding sails and other kites were finally abandoned partly because of the longer yards in use but mostly, it must be admitted, because the sailing vessel was slowly but surely being driven out of the racing trades by steam. In a less spectacular way the same forces were at work on the small schooners of the British Isles. There is ample pictorial evidence that schooners built up to about the 1860s had rather shorter lower masts than later became the fashion, whilst topmasts tended to be longer and more 'spindly'. The flying topgallant, which was almost universally used, owed something of its popularity to its simplicity of gear but also had the advantage that when stowed above the close-reefed topsail it was down near the cap of the lower mast where it would put the least strain upon the standing rigging. It could also, of course, be sent down very easily. The sail plan of the schooner's foretopmast had the same tapering look as that of the contemporary square-rigger. By the 1880s the standing topgallant set above double topsails had become the fashionable rig. It was much squarer than the flying topgallant set up; the topmasts, especially the fore, were heavier and the lower masts slightly longer. It never completely ousted the flying topgallant and was itself discarded in favour of the plain double topsails, before the auxiliary engine finally put an end to topsail yards of all kinds. Its memory lingered on; to the humble men who manned these small vessels it came to have something of the same aura as the skysail had to those in square-riggers; if not the crown of a queen, at least the tiara of a high-born lady. No one ever thought to pass on the information that such-and-such a schooner had once possessed a flying topgallant, but the older men were at great pains to point out any vessel that had once been a double-topsail, standing-topgallant schooner. Sailors always seem to have been fond of tall ships.

Trades and Rigs

The relative merits of square- or fore-and-aft-rigged vessels depended a great deal upon the sort of trade in which they were engaged. It was the schooner's superior performance to windward that caused it to be used for the carrying of mails and perishable cargoes but even if it had sailed like a bathtub it had one trump card that endeared it to the hearts of ship owners: it could be worked by a smaller crew than almost any other rig except the ketch. Becoming popular in the British Isles about the middle of the 19th century, it rapidly ousted the brig from many trades where the latter had been predominant, but was not quite so spectacularly successful against its near relatives the brigantine and barquentine. Small crews, of course, were not a feature of the packet schooners nor of those engaged in the Azores fruit trade in which the vessels were out-and-out racers for the returns on a fast passage were high. The fruit trade had in miniature all the features of the China tea trade: the gambler's chance of making a really handsome profit by being among the first few vessels to arrive in port; the financial involvement of skippers and crews, to the point where they probably felt grievously hurt when forced to reduce sail and perhaps even argued about it before doing so. There was also the final spur that the tea trade did not possess: if the passage lasted too long the cargo could not be sold at even rock bottom prices – it went rotten. There has been talk of rotten oranges being thrown overboard but it could only have been from the top of the load as, even when the western ocean was kind enough to allow the hatch covers to be lifted, it would have been impossible to pile much of the cargo on deck while rooting down for rotten fruit at keelson level. Consideration for the stability of the vessels would not have allowed it.

The fruiters were engaged in a luxury trade to provide delicacies for the wealthy. In contrast the Newfoundland stockfish trade, in which so many of the schooners were engaged in the 1860s, was one which provided cheap food for the working people of Europe and its economic background was, in consequence, of a much more stringent nature – as, indeed, was its watery arena. No doubt a good case could be made for the inclusion of the southern latitudes as well, but the gentlemen who fixed the load lines on a vessel's sides were suffering from no illusions when they decreed that ships using the north Atlantic in winter were not to be loaded so deeply as they could be in any other ocean. It was upon this stormy background that the schooners finally ousted their rivals, the barquentines and brigantines, but their victory was never conclusive. The trade involved a hard, long, drawn-out slog to the westward against the prevailing winds and, after loading, a fast run home to Europe. For the former the fore-and-aft rig was by far the best, but for running the square sail was unbeatable. The introduction of the schooner, the brigantine and the barquentine were all attempts to arrive at a compromise to suit these varying conditions, but the latter two, with their fully square-rigged foremasts, were ideal for the homeward leg; whereas the schooner's lower topsail was too high up the mast to run with comfortably beyond a certain point, while her square sail was too big to carry in anything but moderate winds. Gaff and boom sails were uncomfortable to run under in strong winds and high seas as they produced a side thrust as well as a pushing force. This tended to encourage the vessel to broach and the further aft the sail, the worse the tendency became. Evident enough in the broad mainsails of schooner and brigantine, it became aggravated in the narrow mizzens of the three-masted schooner and barquentine since, having no vang, the sheet could not be eased beyond a certain point or the gaff would begin to lever with tremendous force against the lee swifters. For this reason the mizzen was usually stowed when running in bad weather.

In *The Merchant Schooners*, Dr Basil Greenhill points out the disadvantage the barquentine was under in its struggle against the schooner, owing to its being classed as a 'square-rigger'. He also mentions the attempts to produce a vessel with low topsails for comfortable running but which could be commanded by a man with a fore-and-aft ticket that gave rise to the partly staysail schooners known as the Portmadoc 'jack barquentines'. The brigantine also suffered obliquely from the same problem. Both the schooner and the brigantine had a large mainsail, which in the days of point reefing must have been a handful for the crew. In the interests of easier handling, large schooners were often converted into three-masters by cutting down the size of the mainsail and stepping a third mast, but had this been done to a brigantine it would have made her into a barquentine and she would then have required a skipper with a 'square-rigged' ticket. Conversion of brigantines was therefore nearly always to a three-masted schooner. One of the last vessels afloat, which had received this treatment, was the *Irish Minstrel*, launched in Dundalk in 1879 and cut down to a towing flat on the Mersey in 1934.

Ellie Park

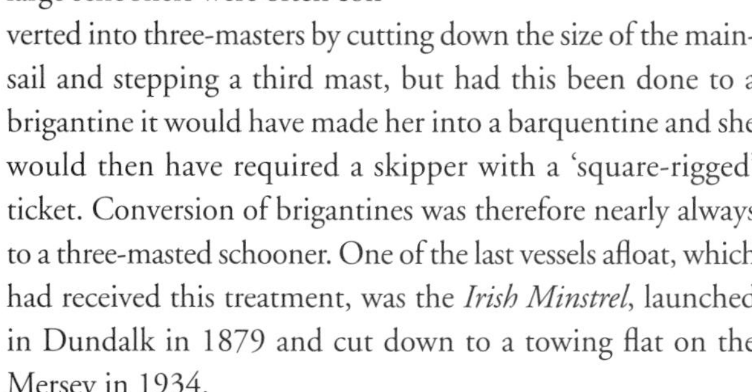

Skippers and Sisterships

Judging by the early age at which many of them got a command, there must have been a chronic shortage of skippers in the second half of the 19th century. This worked most unfavourably against small square-riggers of any kind as it may well have crossed the minds of a lot of promising young men that there was little point in remaining the skipper of a small barque or barquentine when, with a little extra effort, they could finish on the poop of a big steel vessel. Behind the big square-riggers there was the constant demand from the expanding steamship companies for more and more steady-going officers to man their vessels. The drain of manpower must have been enormous. Since very few European schooners reached the size even of the North American three- and four-masters, the owners of the fore-and-aft rigged vessels suffered very little from this problem. These factors had some bearing on the slow elimination of the more fully square-rigged types. But in the end a comfortable run home was not all there was to the stockfish trade. The low topsails of the barquentine, jack barquentine and brigantine were of no comfort during the long beat to windward, when all three of these rigs provided at least two more pairs of staysail sheets to be handled time after time as the vessel went about. The schooners could work lighter-handed than any of them; the three-master, owing to the smaller size of her mainsail, was often handier than the two-master, although nearly always a bigger vessel, and it was the three-masted standing-topgallant schooner, that finally became the most popular rig in the latter days of the Newfoundland trade.

Fruiter and fishbox, schooner and ketch, brigantine and barquentine, deep-water man and coaster; the survivors all finished up in the home trade – a tiny remnant of fleets that had once run into hundreds. Superficially so very much alike as to be monotonous, they were, underneath, all different in small details in which the sailor took a pride and delight in recognising from a great distance. As with the ships so with the men – all manner of men who had sailed in all manner of vessels. Unambitious men mostly, as the bulk of humanity must always be, who saw no reason to change a way of life to which they became accustomed and which, despite their growling, must in the secret recesses of their hearts, have provided them with some degree of inner satisfaction.

The two vessels in which the writer sailed as a young man, *Brooklands* and *Alert*, belonged respectively to the beginning and end of the period discussed. Launched in 1859, the fruit schooner *Susan Vittery* received her second name of *Brooklands* and a change of rig to three-masted schooner sometime in 1918 when she came under the ownership of the Creenan family of Cork. She was also given an extensive overhaul, which almost amounted to a partial rebuild. Just under 100ft [30.48m] long, she was both narrower in the beam and deeper in the hold than most vessels of her length and, when down to her marks, her heel drew a full 13ft [3.96m]. An out-and-out racer she had a tremendous deadrise to her floors, was fined away almost to nothing at each end, and could never aspire to be anything but a very wet ship. Although it could hardly be said that schooners came in stock sizes, a great many were about 88ft [26.82m] long; 22ft [6.71m] beam and about 10ft [3.05m] depth of hold. At 99ft [30.17m] long, 11ft [3.35m] longer than this popular size, *Brooklands* could only load the same amount of coal as they could – about 220 tons [22,353kg]. The bulk of her hold space lay under her main hatch and in the middle of the hatch it was possible to stand on the ceiling alongside the keelson with some degree of comfort. Abreast of the two stanchions supporting the beams under the hatch ends the deadrise had increased to a point where a woman, used to wearing six-inch high-heeled shoes, might have made a stab of standing on the ceiling in her bare feet but to a man it was far easier to stand with one foot on the top of the keelson and the other on the ceiling at the same level, and this involved a great stride. Further forward or further aft she was little better than a wedge. In these features of big deadrise and deep heel, she had much in common with the Breton schooners and barquentines, which once fished on the Newfoundland banks, but since she was a product of the opposite side of the same stretch of water this is not very surprising. If not originally fitted with hemp standing rigging she was at least built under the influence of it, at a time when it was still a thing of the present and, as would be expected, her lower masts were somewhat shorter than later became the fashion. This also owed something to her fine lines as she was definitely on the tender side. Possibly her original rig was a flying topgallant over a single topsail; later she seems to have had a standing topgallant and she finally finished up as a three-masted double-topsail schooner.

In contrast *Alert* was built when steel standing rigging was already well established and her length of slightly over 100ft [30.48m] was the limit reached by the wooden three-master. She was a fair example of the later Newfoundland three-master, built to carry a standing topgallant over double topsails, with powerful bows, a clean run and bulwarks a good 6in [15.24cm] higher than those of *Brooklands*. Her sheer forward was tremendous and from her bowsprit end one could see the full length of her deck and felt oneself almost halfway up to the foreyard. She was the last of four sisterships all from the same model, the other three being *Sunbeam*, *Fox* and *Elizabeth Bennet*. Of this quartet, *Sunbeam* was considered by those who had known them to be the pick of the bunch, kept up like a yacht, with a gold streak on her bulwarks and white-painted anchors. Like the *Brooklands*, *Alert* was a bit on the tender side, in fact some went so far as to say she was cranky, but this was due more to the loftiness of her masts than to the extreme fineness of her lines. She was no sluggard, however, and during the years when she was under the command of a dashing Danish skipper, Peter Mørtensen, she made quite a reputation for fast passages. Those who knew him often referred to Captain Mørtensen as 'Mad Peter', but his lunacy seems to have been of the kind that produced results.

It is debatable whether a cargo of oranges on top of ballast would have put *Brooklands* down to her marks if she had had any, and, with her low sheer and bulwarks and her yacht-like lines one would somehow have expected her to be daintily constructed. In actual fact she was massive; everything about her hull was as heavy and strong as could be in a vessel of her size. In contrast *Alert*, although built to batter her way to windward across the western ocean when loaded down with a cargo of salt, was considered, as were all the other Runcorn-built vessels, to be rather on the weak side. The fact that she and the *Snowflake*, which also spent years in the Newfoundland trade, both managed to survive to be over fifty years old would indicate that this opinion, held by many schooner men, contained a certain element of exaggeration. It would probably be nearer the truth to say that the *Brooklands* was built for racing, in which high profits could be made, and had been constructed almost regardless of expense, whereas the *Alert* was intended for the harsher economic arena of the stockfish trade and had to have first cost taken into account.

The average life of a wooden schooner could not have been very long and the owners obviously had to work upon the assumption that their vessels would have paid for themselves and provided a reasonable profit before they reached this average age. Whatever latent deficiencies lurked in her hull, *Alert* was a well-preserved vessel and, up to the end, no expense was spared to keep her sails and rigging in first class condition. Of tar, paint, oil, rope, wire, spun yarn and canvas, she had more than enough for her wants, while paint, brush, fid, marlinespike, serving board, and palm and needle were in constant use to ensure that her gear was in good working order. In contrast, by the end of the 1930s, the poor old *Brooklands* was definitely 'down on her uppers' – 'parish-rigged' being the old-fashioned expression used to describe her condition.

When the fruit trade declined, the proud *Susan Vittery* had to go into the stockfish trade so that she, too, like the *Alert*, knew the rigours of the rough Newfoundland run, one of the few things they had in common. One cannot help feeling that in this hard-bitten trade she must have been classed as one of the few schooner-rigged submarines that had ever been built!

One final difference existed between the two vessels. *Alert* was still working as a 'round the lander' on the long passages, which often involved doubling the Longships Light – the coasters' Cape Horn – so that as soon as she was at sea and everything in order the crew went on 'watch and watch'. Life aboard was therefore very much as it had been in the days of

Alert in the Mersey. Her 'drooping' yard can be clearly seen.

Photographer not known. David Clement Collection

the Newfoundland trade and, unless something unusual happened, the meals were at regular times and a definite effort was made to avoid calling out the watch below. In the *Brooklands*, confined by the ripe old age of her skipper more than her own, to the short passage work of the Irish Sea, life was much more unpredictable. No one coming on deck had any clear idea of when he would get his next meal or when he would go below, as this was subject to the vagaries of the passage and of the skipper. There did not appear to be any regular tricks at the wheel so that the man in possession of it frequently wondered when he would be relieved. After a fairly long period it could be detected that everyone was on deck all day and that at night some sort of half-baked 'watch and watch' was supposed to prevail. Lest it should be thought that this had something to do with the Irish temperament, real or imagined, it should be stated here that this seems to be the way of life aboard all short-passage vessels of all nationalities in all seas; the very shortness of the passages ensuring that the show will be over before the crew finally succumb to the effects of fatigue and starvation.

Both vessels made tremendous impact on the writer's mind and both were very interesting in completely different ways. The *Alert* was one of the last few vessels in which it was possible to see how schooners had been run in their palmy days. The experience in the *Brooklands*, however, showed far more of the reverse side of the coin.

III

ALERT

When I was young I did not particularly want to sail in a three-masted schooner. To my youthful imagination there was something much more dashing and romantic about the big mainsail of the classic rig and it was under such a piece of canvas, with its long heavy boom and large gaff topsail, that I aspired to sample life as a jolly jack tar under sail. Had I lived in Canada or the United States I should have been able to gratify this somewhat irrational desire without reference to the number of masts the vessel carried, as the North American schooner, having evolved along a different path from that of the European, consisted of a row of foremasts followed by a mainmast; but in any one of these vessels my romantic tendencies would have been thwarted in another way; she would have crossed no topsail yards.

In the early 1930s the installation of auxiliary engines in British schooners was already well into its stride, and as soon as the machinery was running properly the topsail yards were sent down, although the lower yard was nearly always retained. For this reason, when in the early summer of 1934 I started to look for a vessel, I was extremely conscious of the fact that owing to my foibles the number of schooners which I considered eligible was rapidly diminishing. I was disgruntled therefore when, after hanging about Runcorn Docks all one Saturday afternoon waiting for the skipper of the *Mary Sinclair* to return to his vessel, I found that he had just taken on an AB and a cook. I had already discovered that another two-master, *Flying Foam* and the small three-master *Fanny Crossfield*, both of which were lying under the coal tips, had each got a full crew, but although I did not know it, I should have been even more disgruntled had I succeeded in joining the latter vessel, as she had just had an engine installed and her topsail yards were down on deck before she had even left the Mersey.

A week later, after another unsuccessful attempt to foist myself onto a two-master, this time the *Snowflake*, I was told that the three-master *Alert* was short of a cook. I had to wait about as usual until the skipper returned, but when he did I found there were no competitors for the job, so that it was as good as mine; the wages were ten shillings a month plus my keep. I joined her on the Monday morning as she lay under the coal tip and in no time at all I was as black as the ace of spades and peeling potatoes for dinner. A couple of days later *Snowflake* and *Alert* both towed down the Mersey estuary together, behind the Salt Union tug *Waterfly*, the *Snowflake*, being the smaller of the two, was astern of *Alert*. This must have been one of the last times that two Runcorn-built vessels left their port of origin in tow together, as, by the end of 1935, *Snowflake* had been fitted with an auxiliary engine and sold to Italian owners. We could have done with a good shower of rain to get the last of the coal dust out of the rigging, but as we towed down the estuary the sun shone with great brilliance and heat and we coiled down all the heavy mooring ropes on the after hatch, and generally made the vessel shipshape. *Snowflake* seemed to be sheering about a lot, first on one quarter, now on the other, but as Captain Humphreys probably could not see much of the tug for the *Alert*'s high bows, and his vessel steered by the old fashioned tiller and chains to the wheel drum, this was perhaps not surprising.

Abreast of the Rock Ferry pier, the tug started to swing us around in a wide semi-circle and, having brought all three vessels around to face the still ebbing tide, and slowed down to allow them to drift still closer together, the tug skipper asked where his tows wished to anchor. Captain Thomas was adamant that he wished to be back towards Bromborough Dock, and after one or two pungent remarks, Captain Robinson set off back the way he had come; *Snowflake* was duly cast off and we returned once more to our original point below Rock Ferry pier, where we let go our anchor. As things turned out Captain Humphreys had the best of it.

We were a trifle overcrowded in *Alert* as there were seven of us aboard a vessel whose normal complement was five. The afterguard consisted of Captain and Mrs Duddridge, Frank, the mate, and an ancient dog called Sailor, while forward there were two ABs, Chris and Paddy, and myself. At the time George Duddridge had owned the *Alert* for about twelve months, his previous vessel, *Englishman*, having foundered the year before. Mrs Jessie Duddridge sailed often with her husband, although it was fraught with some peril for her as she was very susceptible to seasickness. She was a Runcorn woman and, according to Frank who had sailed as mate with them for some years, the Duddridges had done their court-

Alert undergoing repairs in Falmouth Harbour, 1937.

Photograph by David E. Smith

David Clement Collection

ing in the galley of the *Emily Warbrick*. Their home was in Truro; perhaps on this occasion, Mrs Duddridge had come north to visit old friends in her home town, or perhaps on the chance of seeing her son, but whatever it was she was to pay dearly for it on the long rough passage back to Cornwall. Her son did come aboard briefly while we were in Runcorn, a handsome clean-cut young man in a smart uniform who, after exchanging salutations with Frank, disappeared below to see his parents. At the time I wondered idly whether they had booted him out of the schooner into a reputable shipping company, or whether he had booted himself without waiting for them. The latter seems the more likely.

Frank was a Shropshire man of indeterminate age who seemed to have been in every port in the world and in all sorts of vessels. He had a stomach ulcer of some kind, possibly because of too much short-passage work, where snatched meals at irregular intervals are almost invariably the rule. He had also been boot-legging on the United States coast in the days of prohibition – a highly lucrative and well-paid trade that would have been equally unlikely to help his innards! On various occasions he passed remarks about a long passage *Irish Minstrel* made the year before, and said that she had nearly gone aground at Holyhead 'on her own ashes'. Be this as it may, if the ferocious tides of the Mersey had not swept them away *Alert* would have gone aground on Frank's stomach-powder bottles after a few days at anchor! Frank was very proud of having sailed in the barquentine *Frances & Jane* and never tired of telling us that her decks were as wide as a street, although she was only about 200 tons. Most of the inhabitants of Weston Point must also have known that he had been in her because 'Frank Poole, *Frances & Jane*, 19-something or other' was painted on the dock wall there in black varnish and remained legible for many years. He belched frequently and loudly by day and night to relieve his stomach and, for this reason, I suspect, had elected to come forward and live in the fo'c'sle whilst Mrs Duddridge was aboard the vessel.

Chris, short for Christian, the older of the two ABs, was a liegeman to The Dane, who had married a West Country woman. Like Frank, he was profusely tattooed above the waist and like him, too, he had been almost everywhere in all manner of vessels. Whatever he did, he did tremendously quickly and superlatively well. He wore a moustache and a blue jersey, had a twinkle in his eye and looked like a benevolent Italian organ grinder of about fifty.

Paddy, the other AB, was an apprentice pilot who was obliged by his calling to put in a certain amount of time in sailing vessels, preferably square-rigged. He had been in *Waterwitch* and was now finishing off in the *Alert*. His real name was Maurice and, like Mrs Duddridge, he was prone to seasickness, but only at the beginning of each passage. The final member of the crew, the old sea-dog, had once belonged to Peter Mørtensen. At the time I assumed he had come aboard since his allegedly mad owner had left the vessel, but I discovered many years later from an article in *Yachting Monthly*, May 1940, written by a man who had sailed in *Englishman* that he had been aboard that vessel as well. A dog's hearing, one gathers, is highly sensitive and the vicious 'knock' of a diesel engine falls far from sweetly, even on a human eardrum, so possibly Peter was forced to part with Sailor because the poor old hound could not stand the racket of the engines aboard the *Mary Barrow*. The same article also solved another problem, which had puzzled me for years. When Chris, whose English was at times a bit beyond us, George Duddridge and Frank would look at each other and say 'Peter' I had always thought they were referring to Peter Mørtensen, but could not imagine why because I had found his English very good; he never 'yumped of de yibboom vit his yacket on' or did any of the other things which betray those races collectively lumped together by the English-speaking seaman under the general title of 'square-heads'. The article revealed that there was yet another Dane, an AB also called Peter who had sailed in *Englishman*. Of course, all these Danskers didn't come by accident; the Danes also were in the Newfoundland trade. They stayed in it after the English had given it up and their vessels, still crossing standing topgallant yards were to remain in deep water until the outbreak of the war.

July, in the year of 1934, was hot and the good weather continued into August; what winds there had been were very soft and balmy, but when we arrived in the Sloyne, (a bay on the Cheshire side of the Mersey where the tides are said to run less fiercely than elsewhere), they went on strike altogether, and for several days the sun shone with great intensity while a flat calm blew from all directions. Our days were not spent in idleness. Everything inside the bulwarks was painted from stem to stern, all the standing rigging was set up, the anchor chains were hauled out on deck and chipped and tarred from end to end, a set of fenders was made and fixed to the boat by Paddy, who also put a couple of Turk's Heads on the ends of the mainsheet horse to cushion the thumps of the lower block in stays. Our evenings were spent in a variety of ways: reading, talking and mending clothes; Paddy was working on a model of *Waterwitch* while Chris was making mats like a madman: square mats, round mats, oval mats, flattened out Turk's Heads and figure-of-eights – he made the lot, manufacturing the necessary sennit at what seemed like sixty miles an hour. They were about the only 'perks' or 'fringe benefits' that the sailing-ship seaman ever had; their sale ashore might raise an honest copper or two, and obviously Mrs Neilsen was not going to get very fat on three pounds a month, even though her husband spent little of it on himself and she did not have to keep him in food.

While we were in Runcorn Frank had obtained an ancient wireless set, complete with accumulators, which he referred to as 'the bottles', and one evening we set to and rigged up an aerial on the foremast. The skipper, who had his own radio in the cabin with a brush aerial at the mizzen topmast hounds, came forward and gave us the benefit of his technical advice on how to get a lead down into the fo'c'sle and how to earth the contrivance. This wireless was to give us a good deal of entertainment in the days to come when we were lying windbound, until of course, 'the bottles' finally gave up the ghost. On this first evening when we tried it out we heard Stanley Holloway singing 'With her head tucked underneath her arm..' This tickled Frank no end and for days afterwards he kept referring to the lady of the song as Ann Bowline, in the belief I suspect, that she was related to the well-known Tom, who lay a sheer hulk.

On another evening Frank and Chris had a bug hunt in the fo'c'sle. Chris armed himself with the traditional weapons – a candle and a knife – while Frank went into battle with the blow lamp. The slaughter was terrific, but we were still well-bitten by next morning, the bereaved relatives out for blood and thirsting for revenge, making up with sheer ferocity for what they now lacked in numbers. A couple of days later we painted out the fo'c'sle, the deckhead white and the walls a light buff, and this, far more than our safari, reduced the numbers of our unwanted guests to something with which we could reasonably cope. Not wishing to get paint on their blankets or to be breathing the smell all night, Frank and Paddy elected to sleep in the sail and rope lockers. Chris and I, who did not have donkey's breakfasts, turned into our bunks and, by carefully tucking in our blankets managed to get through the night without wiping much of the paint off and onto ourselves. The result of this was that the next morning the starboard watch was in fine fettle but the port watch was rather grumpy. *Alert*'s tremendous sheer forward, while intended primarily to give her powerful bows and ample reserve buoyancy, as a side result produced a fo'c'sle that was high, light, airy, and a pleasure to live in, far removed from the dark and dripping holes which are so much a feature of the literature on the subject. By day, light came in through the scuttle and two glass prisms, one on each side over the bunks, while at night it was lit by a lamp in gimbals on the pawl-bitt.

Nobody liked being at anchor in the Mersey. There was too much traffic about. From time to time, as the tides served, day or night, the locks at Eastham let out a drove of vessels of all sorts and sizes, a good many of which passed fairly close to us. To make sure that those blundering about in the dark knew which way we were lying we had two white lights showing at night, the normal one on the forestay – where by day we had a pudding fender hoisted – and another one on the mizzen topping lift. The strong tides also made it necessary to give the vessel a sheer with the rudder to stop her from swinging about on her anchor chain, a process which is liable to assist dragging. The philosophy behind this action was to give the vessel a sheer towards any danger, in our case the Cheshire shore and the fleet of shrimpers lying between 'us' and 'it', so that, if for any reason she broke her sheer, she would swing away from the danger and not towards it. As a result this meant that whenever the tide changed direction the wheel had to be shifted and re-becketed which, coupled with the ever-present danger of dragging and the potential menace of all the other vessels careering about, made an anchor watch necessary. The last anchor watcher roused the cook at 6am and, from then until 8am when all hands were called to breakfast, he had the vessel to himself.

The information had been passed on down the years that before the Rock Ferry pier was built, schooners at anchor in the Sloyne frequently had to be steered to prevent them from dragging; furthermore the source of consternation could not be reduced by lying to two anchors as, in all but a very few tides, their chains would become hopelessly entangled. The schooner mariners were therefore only too eager to get away from the place, even if it was no further than Holyhead, where at least they could have two anchors down and all night in. Thus, it was with a certain amount of envy that we watched *Donald and Doris* and *Fanny Crossfield* go off one day under power, just before high water. There was a semi-fictitious wind blowing from the east at the time and shortly afterwards *Snowflake* got the gaskets off their jibs, topsails and boom foresail, overhauled their yard ropes, got their squaresail on deck, and proceeded to heave short on the chain.

Snowflake was that oddity amongst sailing ships, a ghoster, a vessel that you could get steerage way on with a pair of bellows. This does not seem to be a function of fine lines, however – although she had a good clean run despite her Irish Sea stern, her lines were nothing out of the ordinary. The year before, 1933, there had been a small fleet of schooners and the barquentine *Waterwitch* all lying in Mount's Bay and pointing in every direction except the right one. With her fore- and main-sheets slack and her canvas hanging limp, *Snowflake* crawled slowly through all of them, with steerage way on her the whole time. A photograph taken from one of the other vessels appeared in the press at the time and a copy of it now hangs in the National Maritime Museum. For all

her extreme clipper lines, the old *Brooklands* could not have done it; she too could get becalmed and drift about.

At any event, as soon as the tide started to swing *Snowflake* around they broke out their anchor, set their jibs, topsails, foresail and squaresail and were off and coming towards us. *Snowflake* must have been the only schooner left without a motor winch – at least I can recall no other – and with its halyards on the dolly winch it took them quite a time to set their mainsail, but it was set before she was abreast of us, and the gaff topsail above it. She came slowly past with her crew exchanging the usual pleasantries, and she went on crawling down the river, speeding up as the ebb tide got into its stride, until the evening when, the tide turning, she was forced to bring up off New Brighton, where we could still make her out with the 'glass'.

A couple of days later, when I came on deck at six in the morning, it was very dark and overcast and soon a fine drizzle was falling. An hour later it was blowing hard and we started to drag. Moored not far from the *Conway*[1] was another training ship called *Indefatigable*[2] with three masts and two yellow funnels and, as the wind settled down in direction and blew with increasing force, it became evident that we were dragging on a collision course with her. We let go the other anchor and paid out chain on both, but by the time she finally brought up our stern was less than 100ft [30.48m] from her stem, both vessels being dead in line with each other. Here we remained for hours while the wind blew with tremendous force. In the afternoon it moderated slightly, although it was still blowing hard and, as the tide started to swing us around, the immediate danger of dragging into the *Indefatigable* was removed. Finally the wind showed signs of having blown itself out and we spent what remained of the afternoon clearing our hawse.

The business started under Frank's directions, with the skipper as an interested bystander offering suggestions, but it was Chris who finally and in a completely unassuming manner, took control of the operations. He was down under the bowsprit, putting on stoppers and taking them off, telling us when to knock out the shackles, when to heave in or to let out, until finally the tangled mess was clear. All attempts to break out the starboard anchor failed so the port anchor was hove up to the hawse pipe, fished and catted. While we were engaged in this interesting pursuit *Snowflake* came past with nothing set but her standing jib and about a third of her mainsail – the rest of the sail being around the boom – and brought up in her old berth near Bromborough Dock. It was obvious that our starboard anchor was foul of one of *Indefatigable*'s moorings, so late in the afternoon the skipper hailed a passing tug and after slipping and buoying 15 fathoms of chain, we were towed back to a new anchorage further up the river not far from where *Snowflake* was lying. By the time we had eaten our tea, the wind had dropped completely and it was in the sunshine of a summer evening that we dragged out the spare anchor from beneath the mainsheet horse, and moved it forward by means of the reef tackles and throat halyards. The end of the chain was hauled out through the hawse pipe, around the bowsprit shrouds and inboard, and shackled onto the anchor, after which we put a strop around the shank, hoisted it up with the burton and, by heaving in on the chain and coming up on the burton, finally got the heavy brute of a thing over the bows. When the ring stopper and shank painter were made fast it was time for the evening ritual of pumping out, hoisting riding lights, and retiring in preparation for anchor watching or springing out at the crack of dawn.

The next day was a real sizzler with absolutely no wind at all. About the middle of the morning the 'Snowflakes' hoisted their foresail for us to see. Apart from the bit below the reef band, the complete luff of the sail had blown away. Quite a number of the schooners still had point reefing on the foresail, the popular sails for roller reefing being the main and the mizzen. While they were hard at it with palm and needle, Paddy and I were chipping and tarring our new anchor which, if anything, was even heavier than the one it replaced. Apart from this spare anchor, which had probably been obtained from a vessel being broken up, the *Alert* had two smaller kedge anchors, which Frank said had been used in the past for easing her around the bends in the Truro River.

The brief but vicious little gale was followed by several more hot days which were completely windless and, after hanging about for a time, two jigger flats and the pole-masted auxiliary schooner *Eilian* departed under power. The optimistic skipper of one of the flats set his mainsail, and the other, not to be outdone, set his staysail and jigger, but the crew of *Eilian* did not bother to remove so much as a gasket. In the morning of one of these hot days a mist suddenly descended. It was absolutely dense and seemed to have been

[1] *Conway* was a shore-based Training school-ship anchored off Rock Ferry, Birkenhead, and established in 1859 where sons of professional and business men, naval, army and mercantile marine officers were trained over a period of two years for careers as officers in the Merchant Marine. In 1935 the fees were £120 per annum for a cadet to attend.

[2] The former HMS *Phaeton*, built by Napier in 1883 as a Dispatch Vessel (2nd. class cruiser), 4,300 tons, armed with ten 6in guns; sold in 1913 for use as the Training Ship *Indefatigable*. Renamed *Carrick II* in 1941 she was broken up in early 1947. The Training establishment was founded in 1864 taking orphans and sons of Liverpool seamen for training as deck seamen, for the engine-room and as stewards. In 1935 they had approximately ninety boys supported by voluntary contributions and grants from the Liverpool Board of Education.

Alert in the River Mersey c1938.

PHOTOGRAPH BY KEITH P LEWIS. DAVID CLEMENT COLLECTION

organised to coincide with the release of the Manchester Ship Canal traffic. For an hour all was bedlam, the deep-throated, menacing blasts of the big stuff mingling with the nervous high pitched 'pips' of the smaller vessels, while from all around came the vociferous clanging of bells, to which we added our quota. There seemed suddenly to be dozens of vessels anchored all over the place, and the clanging became positively frenzied at times as various vessels deemed that the blasts and pips were getting uncomfortably close. Once we saw the vague shadow of a weekly steamer groping her way slowly down river, then a second later she was gone. The mist melted away in the end just as rapidly as it had come, leaving the sun shining with even greater intensity than before.

One evening *Snowflake*'s crew came aboard to scrounge some wood to make new sidelight screens as they had lost both of them in the gale. They had got under way at about 5am, presumably by their usual method of all puffing into the mainsail at once! But when the wind did get down to business it freshened up so fast that in less than an hour they had taken in their main gaff topsail, flying jib and fore upper topsail, and were beginning to reef their 'fore and afters'. It was not long before their boom jib came in as well and they took more turns in the mainsail and, at some unspecified point, they also stowed their staysail as they felt it was a bit on the elderly side. They were about halfway to Holyhead when the luff of the foresail blew away, forcing them to stow the remnants and after this the vessel began to sag away to the north and, as she got further from the land, to ship heavy seas. The wind was still increasing in force and more and more of their mainsail was being rolled around the boom when the mate, a cheerful and thirsty character by the name of Joe, turned to Captain Humphreys and said, 'Hey skipper, what about that lower bloody tops'l.' 'Do you think it ought to come in?' asked Captain Humphreys, 'Well, then we'll have it in.' Evidently he had been coming to the same conclusion himself. Their cook, a young Welshman who had been in the ketch *Lady Agnes*, said that he and the other AB were well over half an hour on the yard before they got it fast. Since *Lady Agnes* was one of the few vessels left which still had her main gaff topsail set on hoops on the topmast and since this young man had obviously had to cope with the confounded thing, one would have expected him to find any square sail easy by comparison... it was obviously blowing rather hard at the time. With the lower topsail stowed the schooner was somewhat easier, but what little progress they had been making was reduced to almost nothing, so it soon became clear that if they did not wish to finish up in the Isle of Man they would have to run back to the Mersey. The last few rolls in the mainsail were probably taken in to allow her to run more comfortably, as the standing jib was the only sail still set forward and it was probably during the tricky bit as they turned to run and the vessel was momentarily broadside on to the wind and sea that the sidelight screens were washed away.

The first time that he went ashore after the anchor-dragging episode, our skipper made arrangements for an attempt to retrieve it and on a Sunday morning with a nice breeze which sent *Snowflake* to sea once more, a large gang of men came off in a towing flat a little before high water. They retrieved the buoy and the chain and made fast to a heavy tackle stretched out along their deck. They lay back on the fall until the flat's bows were down and her stern up and they could gain no more. Then followed a wait as the tide rose to its full height. When they judged the moment had arrived and the anchor still showed no sign of coming up, they resolved upon one last almighty heave on the tackle. We heard them sing out, we saw them all lie back on the fall; the flat's bows shot skywards and they all fell on their backsides. The chain had broken!

When the wind finally decided to blow again it came from the southwest, bringing with it the *Waterwitch* and the *Jane Banks* with clay cargoes for Runcorn. After lying briefly at anchor they departed up river behind the tug. On the afternoon of their arrival the wind increased rapidly in force and once again we dragged our anchor, but this time we were able to bring the vessel up by letting out more chain. These violent and sudden little breezes, which marked the opening of the 'gale shooting season' for 1934 were of the 'short notice, soon past' kind. All the rest turned out to be of the long-lasting variety. One of the last acts performed by Chris before we left the Mersey was to shave off his moustache. Gone was the genial Italian organ-grinder and in his place was what the man really was – a damned hard case and ten years younger. Only the skipper's wife commented upon it to him, the rest of us just thought about it.

Shortly after this came a morning when a light but steady wind sprang up from the southeast. The dinner was brought forward (in time) and we were finished and washed up by eleven, and had everything loosed and the chain hove short by noon. Then followed a long wait, as there was a weekly steamer anchored under our port bow and we were still partly tide-rode by the last of the flood. Becoming impatient, two young men sitting on the windlass finally said, 'Why doesn't he swing her around with the flying jib?' 'Aw hell,' said Chris, 'We're a long way from Falmouth.' We were.

Finally came the order to hoist away and with the help of the motor winch, we soon had the fore- and mainsails on her, followed by the three jibs. Then, while the skipper took the wheel, we broke out the anchor and hove it up to the hawse pipe, sheeted home and mastheaded the topsails and swung around till we were heading down the river. After squaring the yards we hoisted the mizzen, followed by the staysail and the main gaff topsail and then proceeded to get the gripes on the boat, lash the small punt down on to the after hatch, and stow, jam off, or fling into the boat all the loose gear lying about the deck. Just below the Pier Head our skipper hailed a weekly steamer coming in to ask what it was like outside. 'Flat as a pond,' came the reply from her bridge, followed after a brief pause by 'Bon voyage, skipper.' This little gesture came undoubtedly from a man whose sea life had also started in schooners, as had the majority of deck personnel in steam coasters at this time. At four, when we sat down to our tea, we were just below Crosby and when we had finished we got the anchor fished and catted, and the bobstay hove taut on the windlass.

All afternoon the wind had been slowly freshening and at the same time veering into the west, so that when we came onto our course for Point Lynas we had the yards on the backstay and the water in the lee scuppers. Towards the end of the first dog watch we took in the main gaff topsail, followed about an hour later by the fore upper topsail and the flying jib. By this time it was blowing hard, but we spent the dog watches in the traditional schooner manner, sitting on the weather rail abreast of the wheel talking about those subjects dear to a masculine heart. Mrs Duddridge, of course, was below. It was one of the few times in the whole passage that we did this; most of the time the deck was unfit for human habitation. At the end of the second dog watch we reefed the three fore and afters down to the first hoop, after which the skipper, Chris and myself went below. By tradition the starboard watch on the first night out had the middle watch, this, no doubt, saving the skipper and the mate the trouble of tossing up.

As most people will have read similar accounts many times before this passage will be kept as short as possible. Sufficient to say that when we got below the noise in the fo'c'sle was deafening, the seas did strike the bows like blows from a sledge-hammer, and every timber in the vessel did creak and groan like the devil's orchestra. We had a smoke and then fell asleep almost immediately but five minutes later Frank came and banged on the scuttle and shouted, 'Now then you sleepers, One bell!' and by some miscarriage of justice it had become midnight. The rest will also be well known. By this time the lamp was gyrating wildly in its gimbals, the noise was even more deafening, the schooner was lying far over to it and every few minutes a sea came aboard over the bows and went sloshing across the deck above our heads. On deck it was blacker than the hobs of hell, and way out ahead was the loom of the Skerries Light which, every time it passed over us, left us dazzled and unable to see the ends of our noses. We proceeded aft by a series of short passages from one solid object to another, the lee rail seemed to be completely under water and over our heads from time to time we could hear the lower topsail flogging horribly as the wind shifted in the squalls. The gale was also screaming, howling and roaring through the invisible rigging in the approved manner.

However, there was hot coffee in the cabin, which acted as an effective reviver, and then we had to reef the fore and afters. As the schooner was on the port tack the reef tackles were on the lee side, and as we swung on the fall of the fore reef tackle we were left from time to time dangling in mid air as the vessel heeled. We took the main and mizzen reef tackles to the dolly winches, and belayed their falls onto the drums, pulling down two more hoops on all three sails. Paddy and Frank then disappeared below leaving Chris and myself to pump her out while the skipper steered.

This reminds me of a peculiar incident which occurred later in the passage. Usually there was so much water washing about the decks that there was no necessity to prime the pump, but for some reason on this particular occasion it refused to function. After one or two strokes, Chris turned to me, and above the clamour of the gale he bawled something that sounded like, 'Vass Drrrrr Buggered!' Not knowing the answer I forbore to reply, whereupon he repeated it more insistently. So, although rather puzzled, I pointed out that I was far from buggered because we hadn't even started pumping. Upon this he disappeared into the night without another word. Seizing the brake I gave it about half a dozen short, sharp strokes, the pump primed itself and soon a steady stream of the Irish Sea was rejoining its friends on the lee side of the deck. After I had been pumping for a few minutes, Chris reappeared out of the encircling gloom and, from the clanking sound it made, I realised that he was carrying the 'draw bucket'.

Surprisingly enough *Alert* was still a tight vessel, the pumping seldom lasting more than ten or fifteen minutes. We spent the rest of the watch leaning against the weather bulwarks, Chris and the skipper each steering a trick, while from time to time I went forward to see if the galley stove and the sidelights were still burning. The four hours seemed interminable and Masefield's famous comparison of the wind to a whetted knife turned out to be one of those masterly pieces of understatement that the British are supposed to be so good at. But all things come to an end and the skipper finally told me to go forward and call the watch.

No lookout was kept from the forward end of these vessels, only from aft. This is not very surprising when one considers that the smaller schooners only carried a crew of four men. Had the two men on deck split up, one forward and one aft, in the dark some mishap could have happened to either of them, which the other would only have discovered when it was too late. Together, aft, they helped keep each other awake and this also removed from the helmsman's mind the nasty suspicion that whilst he was freezing at the wheel, the other bloke was having a snooze in the warmth of the galley. This also accounts for all hands eating in the cabin and congregating aft in the dog watches where, for a brief period at least, they could flatter themselves that they were a fine body of men instead of a few scattered individuals.

The small-town background of most of these vessels must not be forgotten; the crew often knew too much about each other to stand on any great ceremony, the younger men had frequently been to school together and their fathers had been shipmates with the older ones. With so few aboard every man had to pull his weight; there was no room for slackers. There was also no room for any rifts caused by the cabin faring better than the fo'c'sle – if the food was not up to much at least all hands were eating it. My own suspicion is that it must always have been a good deal better than in the big square riggers or these small, lightly manned ships could hardly have been kept battering backwards and forwards across the western ocean

with such regularity.

Coming on deck in the morning we found the schooner still driving along under reefed fore and afters, lower topsail, staysail and two jibs, with the north coast of Anglesey abeam. About halfway through the morning watch the after main chainplate on the port side carried away, leaving the lower deadeye flapping about loosely. *Alert*'s chainplates passed upwards through the boxed-in topgallant rail where they could not be examined, and this one had rusted right through. We quickly put the schooner about. Frank came on deck and the shroud was hove taut by two of the boom tackles, both hooked over the sheer pole with their lower blocks attached to a pair of eyebolts, one on the cover plank and one in the pinrail. We were up to our waists in water most of the time while this was being done and were thankful when the job was finished and we could put her back on the port tack.

Later in the morning one of the lower topsail clewline blocks disintegrated and came down from aloft, probably because of the banging about it had received during the night. Rips were also beginning to appear in the sails as the vessel had only her summer suit of jibs and topsails bent; there was no question of passing Holyhead and, at about two in the afternoon, we came around the end of the breakwater to find the *Snowflake*, *Volant*, and *J. & M. Garrett* already lying there. We let go both our anchors not far from the *Snowflake* and spent the rest of the afternoon bending our winter jibs and staysail, and drying and repairing the summer sails before sending them below. The business of lying to two anchors was not due to fear of dragging, but was done by long tradition so that the harbour could take as many vessels as possible. In the 1930s, of course, the necessity for this had long since gone but old photographs could still be seen in which practically every available inch was jammed with sailing vessels. A vessel lying to one anchor will swing in a circle of a radius equal to her own length plus the length of the chain to which she is riding. With the two-anchor method, if it was intended to lie to 15 fathoms of chain, 30 fathoms was paid out on the first anchor dropped, and the vessel allowed to go astern until the chain was stretched out. The second anchor was then let go with 15 fathoms of chain, and 15 fathoms was hove in on the first. This left the vessel between two anchors so that she would swing in little more than her own length.

That evening the 'Snowflakes' came alongside in their boat and took the skipper, Mrs Duddridge and Paddy ashore with them, while Frank and Joe went fishing in the punt. The punt was actually a small sailing dinghy, which had been built by Peter Mørtensen and was equipped with a mast, a standing lugsail and a centreboard. Left aboard Chris and I improved

Alert lying at Charlestown, 24 July 1937, about to load china clay.

PHOTOGRAPH H. OLIVER HILL. DAVID CLEMENT COLLECTION

the shining hour by reading in our bunks. About nine the fishermen returned having caught nothing and shortly after ten they were joined in the foc'sle by the shore party. Paddy had been to the pictures, whilst Mr and Mrs Duddridge had taken the odd observation 'through a glass darkly'. The cook of the *Snowflake*, a native of Holyhead, said that, while the schooner had been lying there nearly a week, this was the first time he had been allowed to go ashore and see his wife although she had come down to the harbour every day with their baby and pram. After seeing Mrs Duddridge aft, our skipper also came forward and went through the formality of asking permission to come below. From one thing to another, talk finally got around to Holyhead in the old days when with every gale it was jammed with schooners, the tail-enders nearly always arriving with a certain amount of damage. Our skipper recalled one occasion in *Englishman* when he arrived minus a few sails and with a sprung main boom. In some manner this led to Frank telling us how he joined a schooner once in some port or other – shorn of much of its lurid picturesque language the story went something as follows:

'I joined this schooner and the next day it took us an hour to pump her out. I thought, "Frank, if this is it in dock with no cargo aboard it won't do for you", so I went in another one and she had long splices in her gear all over the place, so I thought "this won't do either". So I went in another one and the next day was Sunday and we had salt horse for dinner and I thought, "no ruddy duff", etc., etc. So the day after I shifted into another, and we were turned to bending summer bloody topsails and it was the end of September…' …and the reader can have three guesses what he thought!

He must eventually have found one fit to pass his scrutiny but by the time he had finished we had nearly laughed our socks down. Finally the 'Snowflakes' went back to their own vessel, we pumped ours out, hoisted the riding light – only one this time – and all hands turned in for the night.

The gale continued to blow for several days during which time we repaired various bits of damage: a new wire span for the main gaff, a wire strop for a replacement block for the topsail clewline, various rovings and lashings to be made good, and so on. Chris and Paddy manufactured several miles of sennit, we bent the winter topsails and carted our two water barrels ashore to a spring at the top end of the harbour, from which we filled them and the on-deck tank. It came straight from the limestone rock and, according to Frank, was as hard as a whore's heart. Chris also managed to get a wire clove hitch around the standing end of the broken chainplate; the ends were passed up through the bulwarks, through two holes opened out between the deadeye and its wrought-iron strop, and back down again to be seized to their own standing parts. I noticed that no one got down into the scuppers and reached a hand up the hollow of the bulwarks to see what state the chainplates were in. I imagine that everyone suspected we should frighten ourselves to death if we did but on the many occasions when we were forced to put our helm up and run back for shelter this breakage can hardly have done anything to reassure the skipper that he might hang on to his canvas a little longer.

FIGURE 3-1 *Alert* chainplate

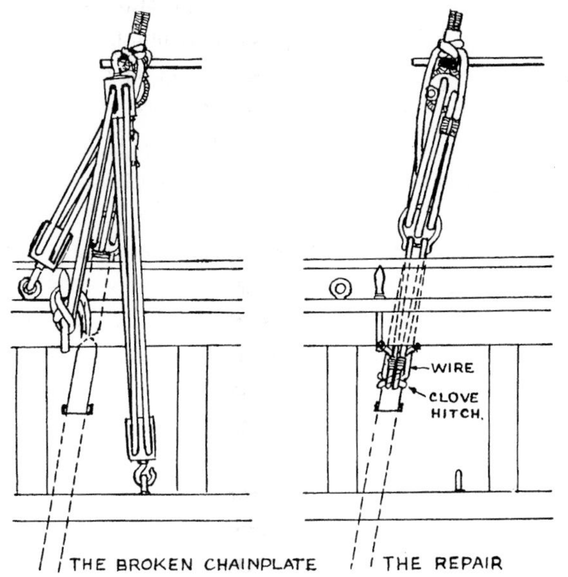

In the afternoon of the second day the sky cleared a bit and the wind seemed to be moderating so *J. & M. Garratt* put to sea, but about two hours later somebody working aloft shouted that she was coming back. The 'Garratts' said that once they got clear of the land they had found the sea and the gale just as bad as ever. The *Garratt* had two 50hp engines in her and was said to be the only schooner using the Chester River that could make Connah's Quay in one tide. What was good enough for her was good enough for everyone else, and no more windlass brakes were shipped!

The gale at last blew itself out and one morning, with a light easterly wind, we put to sea once more. The 'Snowflakes' had got their breakfast over early and had their fore and afters set, one anchor at the hawsepipe and the other hove short by the time we were carrying our food aft. However, they did not break it out until we were ready with ours, no doubt in order to show us their superiority in light winds. We beat down the harbour behind her and as we came outside she set her squaresail, eased her sheets and set up her boom tackles; in a couple of hours she was a small speck ahead of us. We followed on more sedately until about halfway through the morning watch when the sun began to shine fairly strongly and the wind freshened and began to back. Then *Alert* picked up her skirts and started to walk. At noon we took in the gaff topsails and the flying jib, and after dinner the port watch retired leaving us in possession of the deck.

Early in the first dogwatch, with the wind still backing, *Snowflake* ran past us bound back for Holyhead. Captain Humphreys shouted across to our skipper that he reckoned we were in for another southwester so he was going back until it cleared. The dusting they had had on their first attempt to get out of the Mersey was probably still fresh in his mind. As the evening wore on all the signs of more wind to come began to show up – a heavy swell underneath the seas and low clouds flying along before the wind. Below Bardsey, just before dark, *Mary Sinclair* passed between us and the land, going like a racehorse. She had left Runcorn only about a week before us but, while we had been swinging around our anchor, she had made the passage south, discharged her coal, loaded clay and here she was, well on her way back to the Mersey. Needless to say I felt somewhat defrauded. Not only had I missed sailing in a proper schooner with a big mainsail, but I had been done out of a reasonably quick trip south and the fun and excitement of a fast passage back up the Irish Sea. Such trips did occur from time to time, but a lucky vessel required a wind that would get her down to the Longships fairly quickly and then, once she was around the land, shift into the southwest and blow really hard to give her a good shove to the north.

Snowflake was credited with one such fast passage from Cornwall to the Mersey, in 36 hours, while the *Alert,* it was claimed, had once performed the much rarer feat of a fast trip the other way around, from Runcorn to Falmouth, in 55 hours. The *Mary Sinclair*, which was considered to be a fast little vessel, also had one to her credit but I am unable to remember the details. Like many of the famous runs back from Newfoundland they were, in the main, a matter of luck, the east coast china clay traffic standing a much better chance, as one loud and prolonged gale from the southwest would often see them all the way to their destination.

We passed the middle watch in the usual manner, coffee at eight bells and then pump her out, occasional trips forward to see that the sidelights and the galley fire were still functioning, the schooner going all the time full and bye with a strong wind, which, however, still allowed her to carry the upper topsail. Coming on deck in the morning, we found that Frank and Paddy had stowed the upper topsail and, as the wind was still increasing in force, after breakfast we took a couple of turns in each of the fore and afters. The *Alert* had a log, a Walker Cherub, which the skipper streamed from the starboard quarter. There was a mounting for it on each side, but the mate had a similar contrivance in the shape of a mackerel spinner, which he used on his side of the vessel. There were plenty of mackerel and they were a welcome addition to the menu, which by this time was fairly well down to the basic ingredients: salt meat, salt pork, stockfish and potatoes. The fresh meat and cabbages, which we had when we left Runcorn, were long gone although we still had some onions, carrots and swedes and plenty of dried beans. The mackerel were even more welcome to Frank than to the rest of us as they were much easier on his stomach; not only did he scoff his share but he simmered the heads in water on the galley stove for hours to make stock for soup, removed them and boiled up the liquid with a little rice. Rice pudding made with canned milk was about all that Mrs Duddridge could keep down and she rarely appeared at meals except in harbour.

All morning the wind continued to increase in strength. It had long ago backed into its favourite quarter, the southwest, and was now getting down to serious business. At noon, with four hoops down in each sail, the skipper came to the conclusion that since the schooner was no longer making any headway over the ground – in spite of dashing through the water like something gone mad – he might as well put up his helm and run back to Holyhead. Most of the surviving schooners at this period were getting on for fifty years old and were unfit to be driven beyond a certain point, even if there had been any great profit to be made by so doing. The doubtful condition of the chainplates was no doubt lurking at the back of his mind as well. With the yards squared, the boom tackles set up, and the upper topsail hoisted once more, we made good time of it and arrived back at our old anchorage in the evening. Here we found that *J. & M. Garratt*, *Volant* and the *Snowflake* had been joined by the steel ex-Dutchman, *Loch Ryan*, and an old Danish schooner with a straight stem and a flat transom, called *Crest*. One or two small weekly steamers had also had enough. After making all snug we hoisted the riding light, pumped her out and turned in.

The next day was Saturday and in the afternoon I let the galley fire go out so that I could remove some of the clinker and ash produced as a result of burning gas coal from the cargo. It blew hard all day, but in the afternoon the sun shone strongly for a time making life seem suddenly a little more pleasant. Everybody loosed their sails to give them a good drying and in the midst of this a shout went up that the *Waterwitch* was coming in. We all looked down past the end of the breakwater and there she was under two jibs, fore topsails, two main staysails and reefed fore and afters. In a short time the *Jane Banks* also came into view. It could hardly be said that the anchorage was crowded, in fact, compared with the past, it was practically deserted, but Captain Deacon seemed to be in some doubt as to where he wanted to anchor. He stood over to one side of the harbour, then went about and came past our stern on a long reach that took him almost to the inner end of the breakwater, went about and came out again, all manoeuvres being accompanied by a good deal of bellowing from the skipper, while Joe in the *Snowflake* and Frank in our vessel kept up a shouted running commentary of unflattering remarks about his inability to make up his mind, interspersed with imitations of his best quarter-deck manner. While all this was going on, *Jane Banks* was steadily beating up the harbour, but when she clewed up her lower topsail and her headsails started to come down it was evidently too much for Captain Deacon, who put his helm down right away and, without pausing for breath, bawled out to the mate, 'Leggo!' The mate, who was leaning against the cathead with his hammer in his hand, went on leaning against the cathead because he knew that there was still too much way on her. This lack of activity forward seemed to drive Captain Deacon almost frantic and, in tones of rage, he once again bellowed at the mate, 'Leggo!' The mate gave him a long hard look which clearly said, 'All right, if that's the way you want it, that's the way you'll have it.' Down came his hammer, away went the ring stopper, away went the anchor and away went the chain and, before they could even get hold of it to surge some more over the windlass barrel, it came taught as a bar and parted with a bang. There was a hurried shifting of the norman over to port and then a pause as the mate weighed up the vessel's motion through the water and finally, this time without interference from aft, he knocked out the ring stopper and the second anchor brought her up.

Frank recalled two other occasions, which he had seen himself, on which Captain Deacon had lost an anchor through the same silly sort of rivalry in trying to get his hook in the ground before some other vessel. It will be deduced from this incident that unnecessary shouting and bawling aboard schooners, or barquentines for that matter, was not looked upon with any great favour. George Duddridge did not even go in for any 'Stand by' or 'Ready about'; he just nodded to Frank, who set off forward followed by the rest of us. At first, as the only one aboard who did not know the vessel was going about, this took me by surprise, and I was usually in the rear of the party, but in the end I, too, came to recognise the signs, and was ready and waiting to jump to it when the skipper's almost imperceptible nod set us in motion. Apart from the odd bit of singing out as we swigged up the braces, the only other noise made during the entire operation was the loudly-bawled, 'Lee-oh!' by means of which the skipper informed those forward that the helm was actually down.

That same Saturday evening our skipper and his wife went ashore and, when he came off, he told us that they had bumped into Captain Carravick of the *Jane Banks* along with Captain Deacon and that, before anyone else could open his mouth, the latter had said, 'You'll beat us now. We've lost our foresail.' To this George Duddridge and Bert Carravick had replied as one man, 'Aw hell, we're a long way from Falmouth.'

The next day, being Sunday, was the cook's busy day, but the stove was on form after its clean-out and 'schooner on the rocks' followed by a duff was soon polished off by the hungry horde. Then, to our surprise, the skipper's wife produced a cake and gave a slab of it to all hands. Frank, who had a tendency to look for the basest motives, said afterwards that it was probably beginning to go mouldy, but Chris thought it was to celebrate the loss of Captain Deacon's foresail, or possibly his anchor. It tasted all right. We spent a quiet Sunday afternoon reading, repairing clothes and so on, while the crew of the *Waterwitch* were dredging about in their boat in an attempt to locate their anchor and chain. They eventually found it, got the end of the chain aboard and shackled on and by tea time were lying to two anchors like the rest of us. We later found out that they had not been impressed by this as a way of spending Sunday afternoon.

The next morning a large ketch-rigged yacht with jib-headed fore and afters and a professional crew, came staggering into the harbour, well shortened down. A day or so later, when some of them were aboard us, we learned that they had been well down Cardigan Bay when the gale hit them but, being a much newer vessel than the rest of us, and unencumbered by a cargo of coal, they kept slogging on. The owner, a woman, was on board. Finally, after about three days of it, when they were already well to leeward of the point where they started, their skipper had put up his helm in disgust and ran back to Holyhead. They were very popular with the schooner boys as they had a dinghy with an outboard and would go around the fleet to find out if anyone wanted to be put ashore or brought off.

Whenever the sun came out everybody loosed their sails to give them an airing and, at the same time, watched each other like hawks in case someone decided to put to sea. Several days elapsed before the next sortie, which ended, as before, with the vessels one by one straggling back to Holyhead, and the remainder of the passage was a seemingly endless repetition of this well-established routine. In the fullness of time the Irish contingent managed to disappear from Holyhead, while the 'round-the-landers' got themselves as far as Milford, there to repeat the performance. It became monotonous. The pattern was always the same: after a gale had blown itself out a light wind eventually came away from some innocuous quarter. After watching it, and each other, for a time, someone, more foolhardy than the rest, cast off his gaskets and hove his chain short. Others joined in. Others leaned on their bulwarks and smiled cynically. Having got several vessels out to sea and given them an hour or two of reasonable sailing, the wind slowly started to rise and to shift itself around to the southwest. Sometimes it got itself worked up into a frenzy fairly soon, at others more than twenty-four hours would elapse before it really got into its stride. But, one by one, the sails came in: gaff topsails, flying jibs, upper topsails. Then the gaffs started to crawl slowly down the masts, the vessels to heel more and more until those below could

only sleep on one tack with their backs to windward and their knees against the lee side pipe frame of the bunk. If those on deck put the schooner about, those below also went about without even taking the trouble to waken up properly.

Once the gale had really got down to business the seas would come rolling in from the southwest, row after row of them, and for all her sheer, the *Alert* would run her bows deep into them, taking great lumps of water aboard over the weather rail, and sending showers of spray aft as far as the mainmast; at the same time her stern would be high in the air. Since the human eye, or rather the brain which receives its message, is far more impressed for obvious reasons, by vertical distances than by horizontal ones, I got the impression that her counter on these occasions was about twenty feet above the surface of the sea, but if this had been the case, her rudder would not have been in the water at all. As the sea lifted her bows again the stern sank, until one could have used a draw bucket aft without a rope. The clouds were nearly always ragged and low and, from time to time, deposited their contents upon us as they passed over. Occasionally the sun shone briefly, bringing a ray of hope to our sodden hearts, and lighting up with a transient splendour the wild turbulence of the sea around us.

The lee rail amidships occasionally came up for air, but most of the time it was under water. The nights were as black as the inside of a cow and, when things got foul of each other, as sometimes happened, the sorting out was done more by feel than by anything else. Although we were unable to see anything above our heads the orchestra continued to play its loud and discordant music on straining ropes, wire and canvas, while the big three-master staggered on through the inky darkness, with her yards hard on the backstay and one sidelight canted up to high heaven, while the other, at each pitch, tinted with fitful gleams of colour the white water which boiled and surged like a cataract under the thrusting shoulder of the lee bow.

George Duddridge surprised me one night. Chris was steering and we were propping up the bulwarks surrounded by the usual din of screaming winds and breaking seas, when he suddenly turned to me and said, 'Snowball, go down and see if there's something loose in the cabin. A locker door or something like that.' I went below and, sure enough, one of the doors of the little lockers above the horseshoe-shaped shelf was banging about as the vessel heeled and pitched. It had no catch on it so I wedged it with a piece of folded newspaper and went back on deck. I supposed the skipper thought that if his wife were awake it would irritate her. What surprised me was that he had heard it. I hadn't. Having grown up in an engineering family I was familiar enough with the alien noise, which impinges itself first upon the subconscious and then on the consciousness of the engineer, until he receives the message loud and clear. It was quite surprising to me to find this innate ability out of context, as it were, and in a set of circumstances and noises that seemed far more disorderly and difficult to separate mentally than those produced by running machinery. I had been given a vague glimpse, not too clearly grasped at the time, of the differences in our positions. I was quite well aware, of course, that George Duddridge was the captain and owner of the schooner but, while I was standing there thinking how boring and cold it was, and how interminable the watch, he had been listening and watching all the time for his vessel, gauging the feel of her, assessing the strength of the squalls, subconsciously analysing the whole groaning straining fabric of her, so that, finally, when he gave vent to some cryptic remark such as, 'Aw hell. She's sagging away from the land', which announced that he intended to run back for shelter, it was not so much the result of a sudden whim as the end product of a train of thought that had probably been going on for hours.

The point where the skipper decided to abandon the struggle always seemed to arrive. As the wind and sea increased, so did the vessel's pitching, and with the bow and stern alternately half out of the water, the leeway was much greater than normal, so that, despite dashing madly through the sea, the schooner was making little or no headway over the ground. A tack off the land and another on was enough to verify this. Usually we finished up to leeward of our point of departure. The decision having been made, the first thing to be done was to get the mizzen off her. In the dashing and romantic two-sticker in which I had wanted to sail, we should at this point have spent some time reducing the area of the mainsail, whereas, in the handier three-master, all we had to do was to stow a sail of reasonably small proportions. Then followed a pause while the skipper weighed up the approaching seas before putting up his helm. As she came off and the wind came abeam she heeled far over and, as the bows continued to swing, came slowly up again while we squared the yards. Immediately all was peace, except for the helmsman, who now had to work much harder to keep the vessel on her course. All semblance of speed had gone. The seas came rolling up behind her, she threw up her stern and they passed under her, flinging the bowsprit skywards as the stern sank. Although the hard-won miles were now slipping back under the keel at a much greater rate than ever we had gained them, it was only by watching the foam directly overside that any progress could be detected. Having squared the yards the next job was to ease out the fore- and mainsheets and to set up the boom tackles. Sometimes the skipper let her jog back the way she was, at others the staysail was hauled down and the big square-

Fanny Crossfield loading china clay at Par, Cornwall with the *Snowflake* of Runcorn loading ahead of her.

Photographer unknown. Terry Belt Collection

sail dragged up from below and set flying under the foreyard. Sometimes we even set the upper topsail again.

Back at anchor there was always plenty of work to be done. The sails had to be kept dry to prevent them getting mildewed, and repairs had to be made to them, so that they were loosed as often as the weather would permit. There was always something in the running rigging that needed attention, if it was only turning the peak and throat halyards end for end to prevent the wear and tear from being always on the same section of rope. But, in spite of this, the crews began to grow a little despondent and grumpy and to some extent everyone retired into his shell; the growl was always the same: it was as bad as winter, except that it was not so cold. Reading matter was soon at a premium and it was not long before everyone in the various vessels had ploughed through all that was available. Of course, we had other jobs to do; we had our clothes to keep clean and in a state of repair; Paddy was still plodding on with his model of *Waterwitch*, while Chris by this time had abandoned his mat making and was hard at a waterline model of a full-rigged ship. She was a bit of an old timer with a jib-boom and single topgallants, and I noticed with some surprise that he kept heaving away on his bobstay and backropes until he had imparted a downward curve to the jib-boom, such as can be seen in many paintings of schooners

and other small vessels made in the 1860s and '70s, often with Vesuvius blowing off steam in the background. One suspects that this must have been considered the height of fashion before the steel spike boom arrived on the scene and put an end to it.

Alert's windlass bitts were peculiar in that they passed down through the foc'sle to be fayed into the frames somewhere below floor level and, instead of the heavy baulks of fore-and-aft timbers under the deck-head, they passed through two planks about six inches thick bolted to the underside of the deck beams, leaving a gap between themselves and the deck-head which formed a sort of shelf. As I had no sea-boots, the constant immersion in seawater finally caused the soles and the uppers of my shoes to part company, forcing me to stitch them together again. I was doing this sitting on my bunk one Sunday afternoon when Frank spotted me and said, 'Are you repairing your shoes, Horace?' – he had decided early on in the passage that my name was Horace and so Horace it was. When I replied briefly that they were coming unstuck he said in sepulchral tones, like some prophet of doom, 'They're not the only bloody things that'll come bloody un-stuck before we're round the bloody land.' We all laughed but it was obviously getting him down. About half an hour later I needed somewhere to dump various items of gear and, as I occupied the upper bunk, I hit upon the idea of using the shelf already mentioned. By this means I discovered a battered copy of a book by Morley Roberts with some of the front pages missing. I soon devoured it and it went the rounds. If this sounds altogether too reminiscent of another, and much more famous young man, in another *Alert* a hundred years before me, I can only protest that it did happen and would seem to prove, with the sons of Liberty, Fraternity and Equality to back me up, that the more the 'rag-wagon' changed, the more it remained the same.

Alert could be positively identified from miles away by a slightly cockbilled foreyard. It drooped to port. There were plenty of other things aloft that proclaimed her identity even if only her masts were visible, but this foreyard clinched it every time. I have seen photographs of *Elizabeth Bennet* and another unidentified member of the quartet of sisterships, and neither of them had it. Over the years I have seen perhaps a dozen photographs of the *Alert*, and the only one in which the foreyard was not down to port was taken in Fisherow in 1926 by Owen Wicksteed – here it was drooping to starboard.

One day while we were at anchor, Frank decided that he had had enough of this confounded foreyard, which was, he felt, casting a constant slur upon his professional reputation. After squaring the yards, he and Chris went aloft and measured the lifts, and let go and took up the lanyards until they considered they had it right. They then shouted down to Paddy and me to swing the yards a few times, which we did, and it finished up drooping to port once more. This led to more mutterings aloft and more adjustments, which, nevertheless, still produced the same results. Finally, Frank came down and weighed up the yard from directly below; then he went aft and weighed it up from there, and finally out on to the bowsprit end from where he had another good look. When he came inboard he had the plan of campaign all worked out: Chris was to sit on the cap and slacken off to starboard and take up to port. Paddy and I were stationed at the braces, one on each side, to do the swinging after each adjustment while Frank supervised the whole business from aft. It was obvious to all of us that if we continued the procedure long enough we must eventually come to the place where the cockbilling ceased. We did. It was the point at which the yard was so upright that it was leaning backwards and, as soon as we reached it the yard started to droop to starboard. We gave up. Frank decided that, since everybody was used to seeing the yard down to port, it would be better if he restored the 'status quo'. Chris made the necessary adjustments and he came down on deck. How many other mates that yard had defeated is anyone's guess.

I regret that I never asked Tommy Gray whether he had had a go at it. I met him about three years later. He had been mate in her under Peter Mørtensen and, among other things, had come home from Australia in the *Beatrice*. He confirmed what everyone else said about Peter, that he was a damned hard nut, but claimed that on one occasion he had seen him somewhat perturbed when they were 'blown off the church'. I am at loss to explain the origin of this usage as the word 'church' seems to be a substitute for 'coast'. I had heard it before when we towed past the *Fanny Crossfield* in the Mersey and saw that her topsail yards were being sent down. Frank remarked to Chris that they were 'making a fine mess of that little vessel', to which Chris had replied, with some feeling, 'she was the handiest bloody thing on the church'. At the time, youthful diffidence prevented me from asking for an explanation. Like the phrase 'round the land' it seemed to be part of the vernacular.

Everything comes to an end in the fullness of time and, eventually, the weary wanderers rounded the Longships and reached their destinations[3] and, in spite of having lost his foresail, Captain Deacon was the first to reach Falmouth. His bar-

[3] In *Ships & Ship Models*, December 1934 it is recorded "…both *Jane Banks* and *Waterwitch* have made a round trip from Cornwall to the Mersey and back to Falmouth in just over three weeks! In comparison *Alert* took exactly a month from Holyhead to Falmouth, and the *Mary Miller* put into Plymouth 30 days out from Shields…".

Alert towing out of Teignmouth.

PHOTOGRAPHER NOT KNOWN. DAVID CLEMENT COLLECTION

quentine was a powerful vessel even though she was far from being a thing of beauty, her salient feature being a remarkably heavy and ugly-looking stern. As one man put it to me many years afterwards, she had a fine pair of hips on her and was not likely to be pooped when running in bad weather.

The rivalry in trying to reach Falmouth first was not prompted solely by the desire of each skipper to claim that his vessel was faster than the others, the delay in discharging the cargo was considered much more important. For their part, the crews were equally interested as their pay was not due in full until the cargo was out, marking the official end to the passage.

Out of the ruck of those hard-bitten little floating workhouses from time to time came one that, by her seat in the water, her proud sheer and tall tapering masts, possessed a loveliness that, despite her smallness, was breathtaking and had the power to tear at rough men's hearts and cause her to linger in their memories. Such a one was *Alert.* Another was *Mary Barrow. Jane Banks,* the only other three-masted ex-Newfoundland topgallant yarder still working under sail alone, was a horse of a different colour, but an interesting horse at that. She possessed the same bold sheer as the rest but had a rather heavy looking counter stern, which detracted from her appearance. Her yards were set low on her foremast and were the longest and heaviest of any schooner still afloat. For this reason the removal of her topgallant yard had caused her appearance to lose much more than the other two, as it had given her a stumpy and bald-headed look when at anchor or in dock. It was this tremendous square forward which caused her to be almost invariably lumped in with the Portmadoc jack barquentines when she came up for discussion, and, indeed, she was once rigged as such. She was a stiff powerful vessel that could stand up to her sail, and she was also very strongly built and a fitting memorial to the long-defunct Welshman who was her master builder. One small detail of her construction tells more about him than a whole catalogue of her other virtues. In the cap of each of her lower masts was drilled a hole about an inch in diameter and six inches deep, which was fitted with a brass ferrule and a screwed brass cap. The receptacle thus formed was kept filled with oil, which was intended to seep down through the heart of the pitch pine to keep it flexible and preserved far more effectively than ever the occasional slapping of oil onto the outside of the mast could ever hope to do.

In contrast to the *Jane Banks,* the *Mary Barrow* was almost yacht-like in her lines, with a hint of hollowness in her bows, a beautiful run and one of the most nicely-proportioned counter sterns that I have ever seen. Her figurehead was rather on the small side and her trailboards large and long and looking like gratings, which to my conservative eye detracted greatly from her appearance. The whole of the upper part of the stem, figurehead and trailboards projected a long way forward of the knightheads, making her rather short bowsprit look even shorter, and necessitating an unusual arrangement of martingale and bobstay. In spite of this the curve of her stem was very graceful and there was no doubt that when Peter Mørtensen bought her he got one of the finest three-masters still afloat.

Alert had greater sheer forward than either *Mary Barrow*

or *Jane Banks*; her bows were rather full and powerful and her run was a delight to the eye. Her counter stern was semi-circular in plan instead of the more usual ellipse and although not quite as attractive as that of the *Mary Barrow* it had the same long yacht-like overhang that was the height of fashion at the time she was built. Unlike the other two, she bore no immediately visible signs that she had ever crossed a topgallant yard as the original fore topmast had been replaced by one slightly shorter on which she could have set a much deeper upper topsail than she did. Her topgallant backstays had been removed and there were no signs about her bulwarks that she had ever worn the chainplates for them – only the sheave holes in the upper topsail yards were left as direct evidence. Her figurehead had gone before I set eyes on her, lost in a collision in the Downs, but there was about her that indefinable something, said to be mainly in the eye of the beholder, that separated her from the ruck and left me satisfied that, since it seemed I had to sail in a three-master, I had sailed in the loveliest of them all, the one I should have chosen myself had I been given the option.

Down the years I was to find that I was not alone in this opinion. Several years later, whilst on holiday in Anglesey, I got into conversation with a man who had been a schooner skipper in his younger days. After a short time it became obvious that, in the past, schooners must have been forever changing hands. I soon learned that most schooners I knew had been owned in North Wales at some time or another in their careers. I mentioned the *Alert* and his son asked him if she was like the *John Ewing*, a schooner that had gone ashore in those parts a few years previously. I was unprepared for the reply. The father turned on the son, almost fiercely I thought, and said in tones of scorn, 'The *John Ewing* was an "Old Box" to the *Alert*.'

Much more recently, through the Society for Nautical Research, I found that both Owen Wicksteed of Darlington and Dan McDonald of Glasgow had something of a soft spot for her as well. Their photographs of her appear in this book and I am indebted to them for a good deal of information on her past history. I shall never forget a Saturday afternoon in 1933 when I came upon *Alert* and *Mary Barrow* lying side by side in the tide dock at Runcorn, just in from the sea. Both had been freshly painted and, apart from their bobstays which had been tripped, and their anchors which were hanging in the burtons in conformity with dock regulations and long tradition, nothing had been touched; they lay there as clean as new pins, all their gear coiled down neatly and a harbour stow on their sails, while a strong wind, blowing in off the estuary, made music in their taught rigging. I never saw the like of it again. One little thing about these ex-Newfoundlanders was that their crews still picked out in white paint their 'Winter-North Atlantic' marks, although they no longer had need of them nor were they obliged by law to carry them. It was done, I feel, as a mark of respect for the old girls – their battle honours as it were.

Twelve months after I had been in the *Alert* a friend set out along the same wet and windy road in *Jane Banks*. He got no better treatment than I did. They left Runcorn with *Mary Barrow*, which by this time had an engine in her although she still crossed topsail yards. But while Captain Carravick was content to lie at anchor in the Sloyne waiting for a southwest gale to blow itself out, Captain Mørtensen decided to put to sea. The crew said later that the only reason they could find for this decision was that one of them had spat on the deck. What significance this had in Denmark, no one seemed to know; it could possibly have been construed as an omen of good fortune or a gesture of contempt for the skipper but, whatever it was, and despite *Mary Barrow*'s engines, Peter finally had to give up any idea of making Holyhead and returned to the Mersey with his fore and afters well reefed down. When the *Jane Banks* got to sea, she had no better luck. The gale that hit them off the north Welsh coast was from about the south-south-west, and by the time they had decided to retire in good order, they had made too much leeway to return to the Mersey and perforce had to run under the lee of the Isle of Man, coming to an anchor off Ramsey in the shelter of Maughold Head. They had the usual share of setting out and running back from both Holyhead and Milford and, after a long spell of fruitless beating about in an attempt to get around the land, were finally forced to put into St Ives to replenish their provisions. By that time they were down to eating dry biscuits and drinking tea without either sugar or canned milk.

There was a Canadian seaman called Bill in *Jane Banks* and it was from him that we first learned of the horrors of putting about the North American schooner. According to Bill, the crew set off forward, clewing up each gaff topsail as they went; each time a man went aloft on to the cap of the lower mast to dip the sheet under the jumper stay and re-shackle it, to haul up the tack and throw it down on the other side of the gaff, and to lighten up the complicated clewline when the sail was reset. The smartest man had to take the foremast, as he had the least time to get all this done before the remnant on deck had overhauled the jibsheets and let the staysail – their 'payer-offer', come over. If you weren't ready, said Bill, they passed aft to the next mast and didn't come back until they had gone right aft. It was all very pleasant in the summer, but bloody cold up there in the winter. I was to get much the same account myself a few years later on board a big American four-master in Birkenhead.

IV

BROOKLANDS

In 1939 it was 'now or never' if I wanted to sail in another schooner. Not only were the war clouds gathering but also the number of schooners that I considered eligible had dwindled to three. The *Jane Banks* and *Waterwitch* had been sold to Estonia; *Snowflake* was plying the Adriatic as an auxiliary, and *Alert* had been bought by the Marquis of Anglesey for use as a yacht. After spending a lot of money converting her, he decided to have a survey, in the course of which it was found that her frames were too far gone for her to be re-classed[1]. The *Mary Barrow*, after sailing for a time as a fully powered twin-screw auxiliary crossing a foreyard only, had been lost on the Calf of Man in a fog. In 1936 *Mary Sinclair* fell foul of a buoy in the Mersey estuary causing some damage to her headgear and much more damage to the buoy – a figure quoted at the time as around £60 was demanded for repairs to the buoy. As it was not forthcoming *Mary Sinclair* was seized and sold to defray the cost, being bought by Richard Abel & Sons, and cut down to a towing flat. In January 1936 *Flying Foam* was wrecked on Llandudno beach and, one month later, *Nellie Fleming* left Lydney for Youghal and was never heard of again. Some of the auxiliary vessels fared little better. The *Fanny Crossfield* had run aground in Strangford Lough and, along with other damage, managed to unship her rudder, while the smart little Manx-built Chester River schooner *North Barrule* was wrecked in the Menai Strait.

Two of the three vessels still left working under sail alone I knew very well. The *Katie* was one of the first schooners I had managed to see at close quarters. She set a lower topsail only. She had once set a topgallant which, her headstays, proclaimed had been a standing one. According to those who knew, she had had an engine installed in the late 1920s or early '30s, but this had come to grief in some unspecified way and was removed. In a relatively short time she had reverted to sail alone. She was also peculiar in having her staysail fastened to a boom at the foot, in the American manner and as favoured by quite a few ketches, but whether she had a bowline as well so that it could be used to assist the topsail in paying her head off after she had passed through stays, I am unable to say. Because of the one topsail I was not very keen on sailing in her, in spite of the big mainsail to which I had been so much attracted five years before. However, she was there as a possibility and if I failed to get into either of the other two I should have to put up with her.

The other schooner I knew was the handy little three-master *Mary Miller*, which had been a regular visitor to Runcorn from the time she changed hands, and 'Fowey' had replaced 'Dublin' as her Port of Registry painted on her counter. She was one of a number of small three-masters built by Paul Rodgers at Carrickfergus and was a sistership of the *Fanny Crossfield* and the Runcorn-owned *Gleaner*, which latter had once made a passage of thirteen days from Harbour Grace across the Atlantic to Bristol. She was also a sistership of the ill-fated *Nellie Fleming*. I liked the *Mary Miller* and had been aboard her on the odd occasion. The apprentice pilots were still using her to round off their nautical education and in her, from time to time, went other young men who, like myself, wanted to sail in schooners for no other reason than that they were interested in them. One such whom I met was a young Welshman, Gwion Davies, who was sailing in her between bouts of study at Cambridge; while he was on board they seem to have been a happy lot in *Mary Miller*. The skipper had taken his little daughter to bear him company – but she could not have been so little because she went forward to play darts with the lads in the fo'c'sle! I regret that I did not ask him whether they played while they were at sea or only when at anchor or in dock. I thought seriously about *Mary Miller* but at the time felt that I could not afford to let myself in for another long drawn-out slog down the Irish Sea. I was resolved therefore, that if she turned out to be the one, I should try to join her in Cornwall for the passage north.

But there was a third vessel which qualified, one that I had never seen but had heard about. She was Irish-owned, registered at Cork, was an ex-Brixham fruiter and was painted a very light grey. Like *Mary Miller* she was a three-master. Human nature being what it is, it was almost inevitable that this unknown vessel should seem more attractive than the two I already knew and I decided that, if at all possible, she was the one in which I would sail.

[1] See *Brief Glory*, by D.W. Morgan, Brython Press, Liverpool, 1948.

The harbourmaster at New Ross looked long and hard at me when I went into his little office on the quay and asked him where *Brooklands* was. 'Why do you want to sail in her?' he asked, 'Why don't you try for the *M.E. Johnson* or the *Gaelic* or the *Venturer* or one of them vessels?' To this I could only reply, rather lamely, that I wanted to be a painter, a marine artist, and that was why I wanted to sail in a proper schooner with topsails, not in an auxiliary fore and after. I could see he thought this an inadequate excuse, but it turned the conversation to a painting of a full-rigged ship under sail, with which he said there were three things wrong. The first was easy, it was the old usual – no one had overhauled the buntlines. The second one he had to point out to me – the anchor chains were still shackled on; to this I countered that the artist might have imagined himself painting her from the top of Beachy Head, not from the middle of the Atlantic. I forget what the third error was. However, in the fullness of time I found that *Brooklands* was at a place called Passage East on the Waterford River, taking in ballast and that there were no trains or buses to it. A pilot, however, might be going down there in a taxi that afternoon and if I waited about I might get a lift.

Since the alternative seemed to be to walk, I waited and, in due course, the pilot and the taxi arrived and we set off. The scenery in that southeast corner of the Emerald Isle was lovely and, as we got lower down, we could see – through the trees as we whizzed around hairpin bends – the estuary far below us, its waters sparkling in the sunlight. Eventually we came charging over the top of a hill to see a wide expanse of water to port, a huddle of houses ahead, a breakwater sticking out into the estuary and the three masts of a schooner, with a cargo gaff aloft on the fore. I offered to pay my share of the taxi, was smilingly refused, thanked my benefactor and, shouldering my bag, trudged forward down the quay. The harbour was on my left and in it lay the schooner, at a point where the land to the right met the breakwater, forming a little corner into which the sand had been piled high by strong winds and seas. Two of the local lads were shovelling the sand up on to the quay and the crew of the schooner were transferring it in skips made out of sawn-off barrels into the vessel's hold. I dumped my gear in the fo'c'sle, disguised myself in working clothes, and joined in.

Whenever there was a pause in proceedings, I looked hard at the schooner. I knew there was something wrong with her but was at loss to put my finger on it. There were plenty of long splices in her rigging, but she was not the only one and she had come right through the slump, earning her living under sail alone. There were no long splices in her peak and throat halyards nor in the sheets of her fore and afters, while the three sails themselves, from what could be seen, appeared to be in reasonable condition. She had obviously no covers for them, or they would have been on. She had lost the end of her bowsprit and only set two jibs, but the standing jib was a fairly new sail, while the lower topsail had obviously just come from the sailmaker. The fact that they were bent on in summer suggested that she had only one suit of jibs and topsails, but she had what was necessary to fight it out with a gale of wind if she had to. Her deficiencies, whatever they were, were plainly not on the surface. Her starboard side had been newly painted dark green with a yellow streak, a colour scheme I had seen before on the *Windermere* and *Loch Ryan*. The port side was partly green and partly the light grey I had heard of, but the latter was peeling off all over the place. Her deck gear looked as if some paint would do it good as well; her deck could have stood some caulking, but the heavy timbers under her windlass and the tremendously strong chainplates that she wore showed that she was an exceptionally heavily built vessel.

When I got aloft I noticed that she no longer carried her original foreyard. It had been replaced by a long, thin, straight, tree trunk which, on the port side, had merely had the bark taken off and a few knots planed smooth. To starboard it had had to be chopped and planed down to make it symmetrical, but the resulting spar was too small in diameter for the bands of the truss, so that it had been parcelled out in the slings by four-feet long wooden battens, about an inch and a quarter thick. It had obviously never been painted. But although the schooner had a neglected look, there were no 'Irish Pennants'; the mate evidently saw to that. All the same I was left with an uneasy feeling and hoped that we would not run into any dirty weather.

While we had been shovelling the sand I had taken stock of my shipmates and, after we had knocked off, eaten our tea and polished our faces, we had time to get to know each other over a pint. The mate, who was between thirty-five and forty, was the son of the owner, Captain John Creenan, and was a cheerful, likeable sort of man with the 'bells of Shandon' (County Cork) strongly in his speech. Short and powerful, fond of a joke, and a good seaman, it was thanks to his efforts that the old schooner was still going. His name was Christopher, shortened to Christy by the crew. His father was eighty years old and was ashore; he would rejoin the vessel when she was ballasted and in the stream. The senior AB, in fact the only AB, was a young man called Billie, about twenty-three, the same age as myself, and he and Tom the cook were the starboard watch of the vessel. Tom was a cheerful lad in his late teens, although he had little enough to be cheerful about, as he had to cook not only for the crew, but also to prepare

special meals for the skipper, whose stomach, not surprisingly, was no longer able to cope with salt horse and stockfish; it meant double work for Tom every time. The other member of the port watch was Michael, a married man of about forty-five, who was aboard *Brooklands* owing to the lack of any work ashore. He was not a seaman, but was well to the fore in all the heavy graft and pulley-hauley about the decks. To preserve the balance of power, I was put in Christy's watch.

The fo'c'sle of *Brooklands* was low, the deckhead being only about seven feet above the floor. It was tolerably well lit through a square skylight, forward of the pawl-bitt, that had six circular glass bull's eyes in its cover. The companion had a well-worn iron ladder in place of the more usual wooden one. The bunks, as might be expected, were in tandem instead of one above the other, and there were the usual rope and sail lockers in the after corners. When it rained the deckhead leaked a bit, and it leaked a bit more when the vessel was loaded. Crossed Irish flags had been painted on the locker doors, but the rest of the place had not seen paint for some considerable time. The usual bugs were in residence but not in overwhelming numbers and, although it was not a four-star fo'c'sle, it was as good as many another, with slightly more space than average. I suspect that in the palmy days of the orange trade it must have housed a crew of six.

Brooklands from abaft the whaleback, 1939.

Photograph by Douglas Bennet David Clement Collection

The next day it drizzled without wind – a soft day as the Irish call it – and we took in more ballast. The rate at which this happened seemed to be regulated by the locals who shovelled it up onto the quay; we did not get the last of it until the following day – a Saturday. On the Friday afternoon, I got a job that was very much not to my liking. The spider band on the foremast, which took the topsail sheets and the yard ropes and, in *Brooklands*, the standing jib halyard as well, had rusted through and become a constructive total loss. Christy had managed to get a replacement from a schooner that was rotting away on a sandbank at the mouth of the Suir, but it had come off a smaller mast. My job was to cut a groove in the mast so that it would fit. This was bad enough to my mind but to get the bolt in I had to cut rather deeply into the after side of the mast, where it was in tension when under sail. It seemed a sacrilege to me to cut into the good pitch pine, especially as the one and only available chisel was in a deplorable condition. I sharpened it as well as I could on the stones of the quay but was unable to impart the keen cutting edge that would at least have made the job seem a little less like butchery.

Money seemed to be tight aboard *Brooklands*. The crew had still not been paid in full for the previous trip because the skipper had disappeared ashore before the cargo was all out. Having seen Irishmen in action in pubs before I could have deduced their situation from the rate at which they were not drinking, but they made no secret of the matter, which seemed to be rather a sore point. It appeared that Christy was in the same boat, in fact we were all in the boat most of our spare time, pulling upstream and downstream and across to the other side, in search of cheaper forms of entertainment than those on offer in the bar. They were mainly provided by itinerant minstrels who arrived in a lorry, the back of which was used as a stage; they erected frames and a canvas cover to protect the audience from the elements and proceeded to put on a concert. In between the turns, atrocious cheap ornaments were raffled off at a penny a try and, to wind up the evening, boards were put down so that any of the locals who wished to demonstrate their proficiency at Irish dancing could do so. These shows were known as 'gaffs'.

Occasionally something a bit more exciting occurred, such as a race meeting at which horsy looking individuals could be seen in droves, together with the bulk of the population from miles around, while to add to the fun the place was alive with tinkers and their women and children who would pick up and swig generously from your beer if you were daft enough to put it down on the bar. It was vastly superior to a gaff; in fact it probably rated as high as the jackyard on an old-fashioned gaff topsail.

To return, however, to the spider band; while I was getting on with this uncongenial job, some of the locals with nothing better to do, came onto the quay and informed Christy of what he already knew: the vessel that had worn it was much smaller than *Brooklands*; the mast should have been liberally slapped with oil and the band bedded down in white lead putty, and so on.... They obviously knew well enough that Christy had neither the materials available to do the job properly, nor the money to obtain them, and it must have been this constant sniping which caused him, on another occasion, to announce irritably that 'Passage was nothing but a bloody village full of ABs'. From my point of view the most annoying part of the whole job was the knowledge that a chalk circle on a blacksmith's floor, a bit of heat and a few well-aimed swipes with a hammer, would have opened out the half-bands to a bigger diameter, some more thumping would have set the lugs to suit the new size, while a long stud bolt cranked into a curve to clear the back of the mast, would have completed the job. At the time it would have cost less than one pound. I felt vexed for Christy that he should be put in such a position and, although I only got the nut onto the bolt by a couple of threads, I was resolutely determined to cut not another fraction away.

In spite of their manifest drawbacks, I have a liking for the Irish. Their country has little to export except beef, dairy products and jokes about themselves, and for these last, for some reason, they make no charge. Far removed from the cheerful idiots they pretend to be and with as little to be happy about as anyone else in the world, they nevertheless face life with a laugh and a joke and a song. This they share with ordinary working people the whole world over, but centuries of grinding poverty seems to have accentuated it with them. For this reason they make good shipmates. Needless to say we had plenty of singing in *Brooklands*, and it was in her or in the gaffs ashore that I first heard 'Teddy O'Neill', 'Bantry Bay', 'Skibbereen', 'My Irish Jaunting Car' and many others that have long ago escaped from memory. But the song that everyone was singing that autumn was 'South of the Border' which for me and no doubt for many another, will forever bring back memories of the brooding calm before the storm that finally broke over a troubled world. Aboard the old schooner, none sang it more frequently or with more enjoyment than Christy:

Sout' o' deh border, down Mexhico way,
Dat's where I fell in love when stars above came out to play
And now as I wander, m' t'oughts ever stray
Sout' o' deh border, down Mexhico way...

It was on the day after the spider band job that we took in the last of the ballast. At the finish there were 40 tons of it piled up in a big sandcastle sitting square under the middle of the main hatch, with its apex at deck level. We leaned the ladder and the few available planks against its sides, put on the hatch covers and tarpaulins and battened down. That Saturday was a fine warm day, and we loosed all the sails to dry them out after the drizzle of the day before. In the late afternoon it started to rain so that we had to stow them again in a hurry and, while doing this, Christy and Willy both got on the port side of the lower topsail yard, and the footrope broke. They each threw a leg over the yard, came down on deck to recover their equanimity, slacked off the clewline so that they could stand on it, finished stowing the sail and brought the remains of the footrope down on deck with them. Until we had finished dealing with the fore and afters no one had much time to pay any attention to this, but when I finally came to look at the exhibit, I was startled to see that it was made of rope and not served wire. Christy rooted about in the lockers and came up with what looked like a retired boom jib halyard, from which a length was cut, eye-spliced and sent aloft. It was obviously the best that he could do. Having been on the footropes myself without noticing anything about them except that they were there, it all came as something of a shock to me and I made a mental note to tread softly in future when aloft. I was highly successful with this laudable resolution – for at least a day and a half!

The next day was Sunday and while the rest of the crew were making their peace with the Almighty, I was able to get down into the dock, as the tide was out, and have a look at the schooner's lines. The deadrise did not look quite so steep as it later felt when standing on the ceiling after the ballast was all out. Nevertheless, it was quite steep when compared with the normal 10ft-draught home-trade vessels, most of which had fairly flat floors. She was certainly a beautiful model of a vessel.

On Monday morning we turned out at four to catch the tide and, having disposed of breakfast, got the winch started. All schooners had a long rope for warping in docks, usually about five or six inches in circumference and anything up to 50 fathoms [90m] long and, with this taken forward through the bow fairlead and looped over a bollard at the end of the quay, we shot her out stern first into the stream and used the topsails to sail her into the middle of the estuary where we let go the anchor. We spent the rest of the day chipping, scraping and painting, and went gallivanting in the boat in the evening in search of beer and excitement. We sailed the next morning bound for Lydney where we were to load coal. The skipper came off about seven and went below to his cabin.

He was closely followed by the crew who, one after the other, went down to enquire about the money still owing to them from the last passage. All received the same answer, 'What do you want money for now? We're going to sea.' The matter having thus been settled to his satisfaction, if to nobody else's, the skipper came on deck and we prepared to get under way. He seemed to be in a cantankerous frame of mind. It rapidly became obvious that he looked upon Christy as a hot-headed lad who, if not watched, would one day do something rash – he kept interfering in all sorts of little things while we started the winch, got the gaskets off the sails and shipped the windlass brakes. When we broke out the anchor he went aft to the wheel. There was a light wind blowing from the north and we paid her off with the jibs, sheeted home and hoisted the topsails and squared the yards.

As we set off down the estuary we could see, about a mile away on our starboard bow, a screw pile lighthouse of sorts, which obviously marked the extremity of a shoal. We had the fore peak and throat halyards on the drums of the winch, and the gaff was beginning to rise up the mast when Old Johnny left the wheel, came charging forward, gave Christy an order, triggering off a row which proceeded as a running accompaniment to the work being carried out, and in which both parties cursed each other with great fervour and the 'Great Irish

Brooklands on passage eastwards with crew, left to right: Mike, Ordinary Seaman; Christy Creenan, Mate; Tom, Cook; and Willy Furlong, A.B.

Brooklands deck scene with Mike, Dougie Bennet and Tom

Brooklands – the main deck.

Brooklands – aloft on the yard.

All Photographs by Douglas Bennet. David Clement Collection

Swearword' was well to the fore. 'Set the mains'l,' was what he said. 'How dah hell,' said Christy irritably, but at the same time trying to appeal to what little sanity his parent seemed to have left, 'How dah hell d'yeh tink we can set deh -uckun mains'l when deh -uckun fores'ls only half way up deh -uckun mast?' I forget what Johnny replied but it was something fairly idiotic and completely irrelevant.

The debate continued spasmodically as Christy supervised and assisted in setting the fore and afters, the engagement being broken off from time to time as the skipper galloped back to the wheel to correct the vessel's course. It went on while we took the main peak and throat halyards through snatch blocks to the winch and it went on while we set the mizzen by hand. We toiled on, fuming inwardly and feeling solidly behind Christy, wondering all the time whether the skipper would get as far as to tell us to leave the mizzen alone and set its gaff topsail instead. We would have loved to join in and tell him to get on with his steering and leave us in peace. But even in these small vessels where there was precious little ceremony, it was still not the done thing for the crew to join in a row between the skipper and the mate, and in this particular case we would have been butting in to what was, after all, a family quarrel. As we swigged up and belayed the mizzen peak halyard, Christy cast his eyes forward, stood rooted in his tracks and let out a yell, 'She's Lost!'

They were the last words spoken aboard *Brooklands* for what seemed a long time.

We followed his gaze. The screw pile lighthouse was on our port bow and only about two hundred yards away. We were well inside it and plainly heading for shoal water. Old Johnny made a jump for the wheel and spun it hard over to port. Christy shot forward to the port main pinrail and started to let go the braces and, as the rest of us grasped his intention, we made a dive to starboard, grabbed all three braces together, swinging the yards around with a prodigious heave and swigging up each one with tremendous ferocity as though this would have some bearing on the outcome. And then we stood there, all keyed up for violent action, while it slowly filtered through our minds that no more was forthcoming. Slowly she started to swing. I gazed around. The grass seemed suddenly greener. The fair face of the land infinitely more beautiful than it had been before. I found myself repeating inanely and endlessly to myself, 'And having done all, to stand. And having done all, to stand. And having done...aw to hell.'

If I had wanted to do something I could have coiled down the braces, which were lying in the scuppers at our feet, but at the time it seemed a bit pointless. She was swinging now all right. Mike drifted off aft, to port. He said later that if the sticks were going to fall out of her he would rather not have been underneath them. Still she swung, but the gap was closing fast. At 50ft the bowsprit end, like a moving finger, at last began to trace its way across the structure and finally emerged on the other side with nothing but water before it. We were very close now, but the starboard bow edged its way clear until the nearest pile was abreast of the foremast and she could swing no more. We looked up to see if the yards would foul, but they passed clear. As the main rigging came abreast of the nearest pile we could have leaned outwards and struck a match on it. It was no more than four feet away. At the time I was convinced that it was only three! Suddenly she heeled. 'Here we go,' I thought, 'the mizzen cross trees will catch it now', but she only went over so far and then stopped heeling. I looked up at the sails, but they were drawing no harder than before. I looked at the sky, but it told me nothing, and the face of the water showed none of the darkened ripples that betokened extra wind. Just as suddenly she came upright again. The penny dropped and at the same time the transom swept past the piled structure and we were clear. When we got back into the Waterford River one of the 'hobblers' came abreast of us, slowed down his engine and shouted over to Christy about what a near shave it had been. 'It was that squall that saved ye, Christy,' he shouted, 'It was that squall.' Christy grinned and said nothing, and we all thought, 'That was no squall, mate. That was her heel scraping over the bank.'

As we coiled up the ropes and tidied the decks we slowly simmered down. At the tail end of the job I went aloft to make up the gaskets on the topsail yards. I completely forgot that the footropes were not all that they should have been, and I never remembered again whilst I was in her. There were too many other things to ponder on in that vessel. I had already come to the conclusion that the claims of Captain Mørtensen's supporters were grossly exaggerated and that the man was, in fact, little better than an amateur. As I came in off the lower topsail yard, I looked down at the old vessel below me and suddenly remembered the dark forebodings I had been harbouring against her, engendered by what the harbour master at New Ross had failed to say. I could have laughed out loud with relief. There was nothing the matter with the poor old bitch; I should have consulted Joseph Conrad on the subject before jumping to conclusions.

Old Johnny was obviously past it. He was much further past it than Captain Deacon in *Waterwitch*. Many years later when I read *Out of Appledore*[2] for the first time, I arrived at the point where Captain Slade began to wonder whether he was getting too old for the job. I followed his deliberations

[2] *Out of Appledore*, by William Slade, Percival Marshall & Co., London, 1959. The jacket of the book was from the painting *Reefing* by Douglas Bennet.

with intense interest and almost ineradicable bias, but when I came to the place where he decided it was time to step aside and leave the job to a younger and fitter man, I felt a great surge of happiness. Oh, wonderful Captain Slade! In the face of those two silly old sea dogs in maritime mangers, the sturdy common sense of the man shone forth like a lighthouse. I felt like giving him a cheer.

Nobody in *Brooklands* ever mentioned his father to Christy, nor did he pass any comment of his own, but he must have had a fair idea that we all felt his dear old dad was doing him a dirty one. Mike and Willy told me that on several occasions Christy had cleared off in weekly steamers, but always his mother had got on to him about leaving his poor old father in the hour of his need and so forth as well as, I suspect, dangling the eternal bait in front of him that one day the schooner would be his. Christy, I think, had almost given up hope of this ever happening; one day in general conversation he remarked that if *Brooklands* ever got an engine in her, the first thing he would do would be to get a steel rudder, so that half the squirt from the propeller wasn't wasted against a dirty great lump of timber. Now I know that he did eventually get command of her. Somehow I had always suspected the worst; nor did I know until the publication of Michael Bouquet's *Westcountry Sail*[3] that she lasted as long as she did.

***Brooklands* under sail.**

Photographer unknown. David Clement Collection

She was a picture in Old Spanish Lace
And for a tender while I kissed deh smoile upon her face
For it was a fiesta, and we were so gay,
Sout' o' deh border, down Mexhico way.

Off the Hook we passed the auxiliary schooner *Ellie Park* (see page 13) coming in. Like *Brooklands* she was registered at Cork. She had a fore topmast and gaff foresail, and set two jibs, but her mainsail was jib-headed, and the lower mast poled off above the hounds. She was either a ketch-rigged schooner or a schooner-rigged ketch. We slanted off to the southeast with the wind on the port quarter. It backed slowly into the west but never increased in force and we spent the morning washing down the decks and wiping the paint inside the bulwarks with wet cloths. There was no soojee (old ropeyarns bound together and used for cleaning decks, bulwarks etc.) so we achieved very little in the way of removing grime. There was not much sailoring done in *Brooklands*, not because it wasn't there to do, but because there was nothing there with which to do it. All the same, Christy did his best to keep us occupied, but for all the good we were doing we might as well have had one watch asleep below. As it turned out, watch and watch didn't begin until midnight and finished at breakfast time, so that in the first twenty-four hours at sea, everyone got four hours of sleep. Tricks at the wheel and meals seemed to follow no set pattern. When Old Johnny shouted, 'Cook. Get my dinner under way!' we knew that our own would follow in the fullness of time. We ate it in the fo'c'sle, Christy included, with the plates on our knees, as the small table on the pawl-bitt would only accommodate two and in any case it was a bit too far away from the lockers on which we sat.

Since we were on deck all day there were no watches to be called, no shouting of 'One Bell'. Down the scuttle to mark the passage of time, and I wondered idly on that first day whether or not there would be any dog watches either. I need not have worried. As soon as tea was over, the entire crew, except the skipper and the helmsman made a beeline for the windlass and the mate was in the van. If Old Johnny was steering, so much the better, Christy never bothered to send anybody aft as he did when one of the lads was at the wheel. He left the old boy to bellow when he wanted a relief helmsman. It was all very different from normal 'round the land' practice.

I wish I knew more about many of the things I heard on that windlass. We worked our stock of jokes off on each other, sang songs and swapped experiences. From time to time, often to illustrate some humorous incident or as an aside, Christy would make tantalising references to experiences in his youth on the wild West of Ireland coast, to the Blaskets and the Aran Islands, with tales of schooners and even weekly steamers, their anchors out ahead and ropes ashore to trees and rocks on the banks, trapped in narrow inlets, sometimes for weeks on end, while day and night the wind howled through their rigging, and the Atlantic, with a 3,000-mile fetch, thundered and broke in fury against the rocky portals of their

[3] *West Country Sail* by Michael Bouquet, David & Charles, Newton Abbot, 1971.

prison. No wonder Christy was in the habit of referring to his native county as 'County Cork, deh next county to New York'. In lighter vein were stories about other vessels caught, not by the weather, but by the Irish temperament, miles and miles from the nearest post office where the frantic telegrams of the owners could only accumulate dust, so that the skipper could say each morning, 'Sure we'll send ashore for a bucket of porter and we'll sail tomorrow.'

In Christy's youth *Brooklands* had also worked 'round the land'. He recalled one occasion when they were in Newcastle-on-Tyne in company with an American schooner, the skipper of which was something of a raconteur. They had a night ashore together and the American captain told him what must have been the forerunner of the shaggy dog story. It was either a shaggy Irishman story or a shaggy schooner story; it went on and on at great length, and Christy laughed his socks down when he came to the end. In re-telling it I have tried to make it as short as possible…

A small flush-decked American three-master had been loading cargo all day and all night, so that when the morning came on which they were to sail, the crew were absolutely exhausted. The last part of the cargo to come aboard was a consignment of pigs in open-work crates – so that the animals could breath – and these they stowed on deck abaft the galley, lashing them around rather loosely with some rope. They were short of a man and, at the last minute, the skipper managed to engage an Irish farm worker who knew nothing at all about the sea. The crew beat the vessel out of the harbour and, as soon as they were outside, staggered off forward and fell into the sleep of utter exhaustion, while the mate did the same in the opposite direction. The skipper lingered on the deck long enough to give the Irishman a few simple instructions on the art of steering, and then he too retired below, telling him that if it came on to blow he should call him out. He was just getting away into a deep sleep when down came the Hibernian helmsman with the information that it was blowing really hard. Wearily the skipper followed him on deck but, although it was blowing pretty fresh and something ought to come in, he was too tired to really care. 'Aw shucks, Paddy,' he said, 'Sure this is only a capful of wind. Call me out when it really begins to blow,' and with this he retreated below again, hoping that the wind wouldn't freshen any more, and leaving the Irishman with the feeling that he had made a fool of himself.

The next part Christy described at great length: how the wind kept increasing in force; how one after the other the jibs, the staysail and the gaff topsails in haphazard sequence blew out of the bolt ropes, leaving the schooner with nothing but her three fore and afters. And as each sail blew away the narrative was punctuated by the cryptic statement, 'Paddy went on steering'. While all this was going on aloft the pig crates had worked loose and were bashed by the seas against the bulwarks, the masts and the deck gear, until most of them had disintegrated, and crates and pigs and pigs and crates, hurroo, hurroo, were washing about all over the deck in a tangled heap. After some time the pigs managed to extricate themselves from the mess, staggered up to windward, out of the water, and took refuge under the lee of the weather bulwarks. However, a tremendous sea hit the schooner's bows; her stern sank as the jib-boom rose in the air, the pigs staggered and tottered aft, fell over each other or lost their balance, until finally the whole fleet of them came surging aft between the bulwarks and the cabin and, as they came around the end, they slid over to leeward, crashing against the binnacle as they went past. The Irishman could stand it no longer. He rushed below and shook the captain into wakefulness. 'Skipper,' he said, 'her ups and downs are gone, and her ins and outs are gone, but its not that I'm callin' you out for, it's to stop these bloody pigs from bumping into the calculation box!'

Another, much shorter, story from the American skipper concerned a similar Irishman who was sent forward to act as the lookout. On seeing a liner approaching ablaze with lights and with the great glaring eyes of the port and starboard sidelights, he rushed aft and reported that a row of houses and a chemist's shop were bearing down on them! Possibly the American captain was of Irish extraction and was keeping up the tradition of the Emerald Isle. If so he could claim to have been doubly successful in selling jokes about the Irish back to the Irish.

Nothing of any great consequence happened during the first day at sea, nor during the night, and we rolled steadily along with the wind aft for most of the next day as well, until late in the afternoon watch, when we were well up the Bristol Channel and it was time to get the ballast over the side. By now we were running wing and wing with the wind dead aft, the foresail and the mizzen being out to starboard and the mainsail out to port. With nothing but the ballast to hold her in check, the old schooner was doing a nice long steady roll. The guy tackles had been on the booms since we left Hook Head or, to be strictly accurate, they had been on the fore and main. There was no boom tackle for the mizzen, so a piece of elderly rope had been pressed into service to perform this duty. We stowed the foresail, de-mousing and unhooking its halyard blocks as we needed them for the cargo gaff, and hauled it to port as far as it would go, supported by the topping lift. Then we got the gripes off and the burtons on to the boat. We had intended to pick it up and dump it on the sidedeck to port, but when we had hoisted it up and

Brooklands under sail with squaresail set.

Photographer unknown. Terry Belt Collection

kicked the chocks flat, our skipper came charging up on us from aft and insisted that we leave it hanging in the burtons and lashed to the rigging. No doubt this was a more seamanlike procedure and, had we been forewarned, we could have got a couple of lines ready for the purpose. As it was we were left pushing the boat with one hand and trying to grab something off the pinrail with the other. When the schooner rolled to port we all fumbled frantically, but before we could get a line loose we found ourselves being pushed back towards the hatch as she rolled back again to starboard. While we were doing this, Christy was exchanging the usual pleasantries with his father, as well as being to the fore in the pushing and grabbing. We were still going at it with might and main and had almost succeeded on several occasions in getting a half-nelson on it at one end or the other, when Old Johnny suddenly turned and looked aft. We did too, and were just in time to see the mizzen boom give that little curtsy that in a fore-and-aft sail proclaims that the wind has gone out of it. What happened next is best described by a word popularised by an American strip cartoon: 'Wham!'

Round came the boom, hotly pursued by the gaff, the bogus boom tackle parted at the first tug, and the old *Brooklands* was stopped in mid roll as the sail filled again on the port quarter. Fortunately the sheet held or we might have been short of a shroud or two. Christy, realising that with both sails on the same side the vessel was much more skipper-proof than she had been before, called our attention back to the boat, on which we were still dancing attendance and, in a short time, we had it securely lashed to the rigging.

The skipper had started aft at a fast sprint as soon as he saw the boom dip but he arrived to be just in time to be too late, like many a better Irishman before him. While we were knocking out the wedges and getting off the tarpaulins, Christy went aft and dropped the coil of the mizzen throat halyard off the sheer pole so that he could use the end to secure the mizzen boom once more. While he was away we passed the opinion that, with a little extra effort and a little more wind, the skipper might have been successful in his attempt to convert the old vessel back to a two sticker again!! As it was it had been a cheap gybe. One would hope, however, that even a fearless chap like Old Johnny would have hesitated to leave the wheel of a 'wing and wing' schooner in anything like a breeze. It must have quietened him down a bit, because he didn't leave the wheel again until we had

dropped the hook off Portishead, many hours later.

Den she sighed as she whispered, 'Mañana'
Never dreamin' dat we were partin'
Oh, I lied as whispered, 'Mañana'
For dat tomoro' never came

We started the winch, hoisted the cargo gaff, lifted the hatch covers and the fore and after, and got in on top of the pile of ballast. There were three skips. Mike, Willy and I had one apiece and we all shovelled like idiots to see that ours was not the one that held up the proceedings. On deck Christy and Tom hoisted them out with the winch. Tom hauled on the vang to assist Christy in getting them over the side where they were tipped and returned to their owners who, like the pile of sand, were slowly sinking below deck level. About 10pm, when we had already been on the move far too long without sidelights, we came to anchor. There was still about one ton of sand in the hold and we had to get lanterns to see it. We hoisted the anchor light, heard Old Johnny give his famous battle cry, 'Cook. Get my supper under way!' and returned to the hold to sweep it clean. We stowed the sails in the dark and sat down to our meal at eleven. We turned in at midnight. There was still anchor watching to be done, and at four in the morning all hands turned to again so that we could be ready when the tug arrived at six.

It was a beautiful summer morning with the sun shining strongly and not a breath of wind. Anchored not far from us was a weekly steamer, a wisp of smoke from her funnel going straight up into the air. She was no youngster; her long topmasts above the utilitarian lower parts required for the derricks proclaimed that she had been built in the days when the appearance of a vessel still counted. Whoever designed her was an artist as well as a naval architect; her proportions were just right, her sheer finished forward in a proud and defiant forecastle head, and the rake of her masts and funnel set her off to a tee. To me, at any rate, she was lovely as she sat there in the water, her reflection mirrored under her. She was just a bit too far off to make out her name. But there was no time to stand gazing at unknown steamers. We hauled out the towrope, dumped the boat overside and hove the chain short. By the time we had eaten breakfast, the tug was alongside.

I had already gathered from the rest of the crew that our skipper had something of a phobia about Lydney. The bowsprit end had been lost while entering the dock on one occasion, and the figurehead knocked off on another. There was a long split in the heavy, solid oak topgallant rail forward on the starboard side, which stretched from the billboards nearly to the fore chainplates. This, too, had been caused by an encounter with the dock wall at this fearsome place. I had been there the year before and knew the entrance pointed upstream at an angle of about 45 degrees, but why this should make entry difficult for an un-powered vessel, I was unable to imagine. I had also noticed that upstream of the dock was a sort of graveyard where old wooden vessels had been run aground and left to rot.

We passed the towrope to the tug, broke out the anchor and away we went. As our next job would be to haul the heavy towrope back on board again, we remained forward in the knightheads, gazing at the calm still water and the steady foam wash from the tug's counter.

Three times during the tow Old Johnny left the wheel, came forward and bawled at the tug skipper, 'Hey mister! Giver her a good pluck!' If there had been a strong west wind blowing at the time, I could have appreciated his problem. The only other reason that I could see for the demand was that if the tide was still flooding when we swept across it to

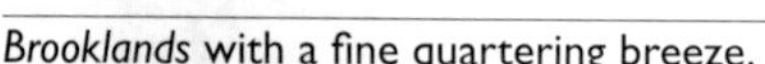

Brooklands with a fine quartering breeze.

Photographer unknown. Terry Belt Collection

line up for the entrance, we might, if we had insufficient way on, get carried upstream on to the aforementioned graveyard. In the event of this happening I could not see why an anchor promptly dropped and a rope out on to the quay when high water was reached would not have saved the situation. But tug skippers usually time their arrival at dock entrances to coincide with high water, so the chances of this happening seemed a bit remote. Each time Old Johnny shouted to him, the tug skipper gave absolutely no indication that he had heard the request or that he intended to do anything about it. Possibly he resented being told how to do his job. The third and last time was towards the end, when the tug had already swung us through our arc and was lining us up with the dock entrance.

For a time nothing happened. Suddenly we heard the tug's telegraph clang and saw the water boil up under her counter; it coincided with her mate coming on deck with an axe in his hand. The most likely explanation for this was that he was going to chop some sticks to start a fire on which to cook their breakfast, but the crew of *Brooklands*, pessimists to a man, immediately jumped to the conclusion that he anticipated some kind of trouble, and if proved right, was going to cut the towrope. At any rate he disappeared with his axe, came back a few minutes later without it, and slipped the rope in the usual manner. The tug gave us a farewell toot and set off at a rate of knots back down the Severn. We gazed as though hypnotised at her departing rear. Somehow the impending doom that we had set our minds upon had failed to materialise and we found the mental shift required by this difficult to make. Finally we tore our eyes away from her and looked ahead to find the dock entrance approaching rapidly.

The dock was crowded with vessels of all kinds and, not very far in, was a weekly steamer with her stern towards us. Our normal gloom returned with a rush releasing springs of action once more and, in a thoroughly pessimistic frame of mind we bent on the heaving lines and waited. One thing was certain: if the tide was still flooding it was having absolutely no effect on the lean racer's hull beneath our feet, which was cavorting towards the dock at a nice steady canter. As the bowsprit end drew level with the quay we had time for a last look round. We observed that the crew of the weekly steamer, who had been congregating aft around their galley door, seeing the good ship 'Creenan's Folly' bearing down on them, had got themselves forward and were getting ashore. Then the heaving lines shot out and each man was in a little world of his own watching the not-so-slow, snake-like crawl of ropes around bitts and heavy horn timbers, as they paid out in tiny jerks and produced, it seemed, no effect at all on the runaway vessel. There were three ropes out, the long warping line and two 10in grass hawsers, the shorter of which was aft; it was the first to come to an end, was duly turned up on the heavy cleat, stretched and went thin until water flew out in all directions, and then it parted with a loud crack. It was followed shortly after by the one forward. This left only the long warping line, the thinnest of the lot, which Christy was holding on the port windlass bitt, and never did fly-fisherman play his catch with more assiduous care, the sweat stood out on his brow as he checked all he dared, while fathom after fathom seemed to be sliding out through the fairlead. The result of his perspiring efforts was that he finally ground the schooner to a stop just as the bowsprit was about to enter the weekly steamer's galley door. To put it in the Irish idiom, if she had still had the end of her bowsprit on, that trip she would have knocked it off again. I will say this for Captain Creenan: from the moment the tug slipped us, he never left the wheel nor did he interfere in what was going on. Perhaps the gybe the day before had rattled him or perhaps even he realised that the slightest move on his part would have precipitated the crisis, which we were trying to avert. The verdict in the fo'c'sle on this little episode was 'Why let your children roam the streets?'

Sout' o' deh border I rode back one day
Dere in a veil of white, by candlelight she knelt to pray
'She was a nun,' said Christy, gratuitously.
An' deh mission bells told me dat I mustn't stay
Sout' o' deh border, down Mexhico way.

When we came down to earth we found that the schooners *Welcome* and *Invermore* and the ketches *Emily Barratt*, *Bessie*, *Bessie Clark* and *Progress* were in the dock with us. *Welcome*

left that same afternoon, her crew rattling up her jibs and staysail in fine style, to show that, despite being an auxiliary vessel, they still did things in a seamanlike manner. They knew, of course, that they were being watched from every schooner and ketch in the dock and by a fairly heavy sprinkling of men in the steamers as well. So did we when our turn came to sail. We found out that no coal was being loaded that day because there was a holiday in the area. Had it not been for this we should probably have been under the coal tip and out again by the next tide, but the delay enabled the crew to go aft and ask for some money so that they could go ashore in the evening. Each man and the mate managed to extract three shillings from the skipper and with this bounty we sallied forth into the town, had a pint, went to the pictures and bought some chips. Willy ate only half of his chips and got Tom to warm up the rest for his tea the next day. He said it was grand tack.

The next morning we turned to at four and, while Tom was cooking the breakfast, we turned the schooner around and warped her across the dock under the tip. We were loaded by ten. As was usual with schooners, our small hatches gave the trimmer plenty of work and, as the coal rose in the hold, they took it in turns to kneel in the square of the main hatch with a steel plate and a shovel with which to fling coal out into the wings. The fore hatch and the one aft were used for access only, so that trimming could be carried out towards the ends of the hold. The three-master *Donald and Doris* arrived with the tide and so did the tug, and at eleven we slid out of the dock behind her, followed by the motor ketches *Emily Barratt* and *Bessie Clark*. As the tug swung us around to the west we set the topsails and did our best to send the jibs up the stays as handily as *Welcome* had done the day before, but ours had single halyards, not double purchase ones like hers – a fact which our audience had probably not failed to note. The wind was blowing fresh from the northeast. We set the fore and afters and the gaff topsails without any interference from Himself, who seemed content to stay at the wheel and leave us to it. The fact that *Bessie Clark* was hanging on to our tail may have had something to do with it. She remained about 100ft astern of us for several hours and we did not seem to be able to shake her off, nor did she gain on us, so I suppose they had sufficient revs on their engine to maintain station, but probably insufficient to pass us. Finally our ways parted.

As we got further down the channel and out into more open water a slight swell began to get up. I noticed that, although the old fruiter was running with her lee scuppers still just clear of the water, each time she pitched her bows into the swell, the water came rushing in through her hawse pipes while, as

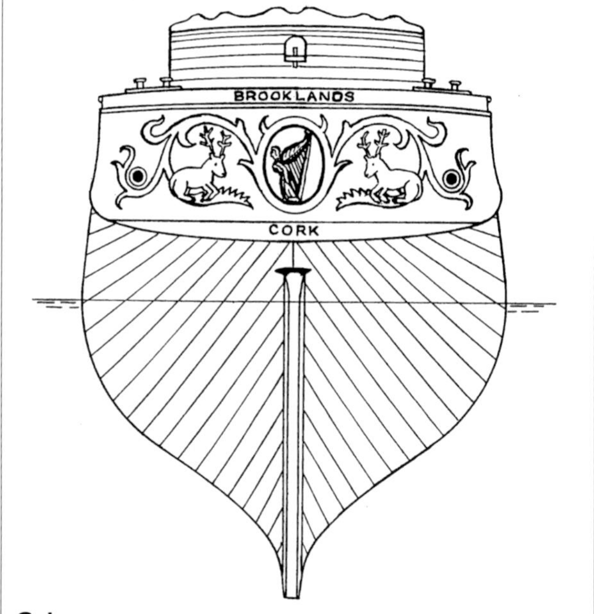

Colours

Boom support: Deep stone.
Sternlight bracket: Dark green.
Transom: to 1939 Light grey after 1939 dark green with yellow lettering.
Harp: Pink, white,red, blue and black.
Background: Light stone (mast colour).
Frame and scrollwork: Reddish-brown.
Stags: Light stone with reddish-brown shading.
All outlined in black.
Sternpipes: Light stone.
Wheelhouse roof: Bright green.
Fairleads: Black.

Note: The general outline of this drawing was taken from a snapshot of the 1930's (photographer unknown). The underwater body is as the camera saw it and does not purport to be the shape of the vessel's midship section.

the stern sank, it did the same through the two pipes in the transom. She must have been a wet vessel in anything like a sea. Fortunately the wind did not increase in force or we should have been swimming in the fo'c'sle! In *Alert* we used to pass the ring stopper chain through the ring of the anchor by climbing out over the knightheads and standing on the anchor stock. Now that the old *Brooklands* was down to her marks, I realised why Christy preferred to fish for it with a hook on the end of a length of wire. I had wondered also whether, once she was loaded, we should be in for long spells at the pumps, but in this I need not have feared. She was tight.

We spent the westbound passage in much the same way as when we were bound east in ballast, cleaning, scraping and painting the winch house, wheelhouse and galley. The paint was thinned down until it was almost watery. I was not the first artist to sail in *Brooklands*. There had been another man before me who had painted the panels in the cabin and adorned the stern with stags and the harp of old Ireland. [See figure 4-2] I wanted to get over the stern in a bosun's chair and have a go at touching up this painting, which was cracked, blistered and very faded, but Christy thought it would be a waste of time in such a sharp-ended vessel. On reflection, I think he was right. I should have been up to my knees in water most of the time and swinging around in ever-decreasing circles. Instead he asked me to paint '*BROOKLANDS – CORK*' on the boat's transom. To be done properly the job should have had the lettering cut into the wood, but I shuddered at the thought of having another bout with the chisel. It was too broad in the blade anyway, so I painted the name as requested.

We sailed on all day with the wind on the starboard quarter and all night too, and were soon back to our normal state of being chronically short of sleep. We were in the track of the south of Ireland traffic and day and night the eastbound vessels in ballast passed by. By the middle of the next afternoon the wind had become lighter and we found ourselves being slowly overhauled by two vessels I had not seen before, the ketch *Ketch* and the three-master *Earl Cairns*. We set the squaresail and, for a time, held our own, but the wind continued to decrease in strength and they finally left us astern. Late in the afternoon, with Hook Head in sight we were passed by *James Postlethwaite*, bound for Passage and, before nightfall, we were becalmed.

For the first and only time in my life I heard a man whistling for a wind. It was Captain Creenan. The noise was made by hissing through the teeth and was more like the sound of wind in steel rigging than a proper whistle. He paced up and down the deck whilst doing it and from time to time snapped his fingers and said loudly, 'Come on. Come on.' Nothing happened. Nothing happened until well after midnight when the tide turned and we had to let go an anchor. Nothing continued to happen until about 4am when a light breeze sprang up from the northwest. It freshened as time passed and we beat up the Waterford River in the morning sunlight in fine style. It was the first time I had seen *Brooklands* up to full and bye, admittedly in ideal conditions, and she was slicing through it like the old thoroughbred she was, leaving barely a ripple in her wake. 'LEE-OH'. Jibsheets and brace blocks rattled and clattered cheerfully as she stood on her heel and swung smoothly off on the other tack. It was the nearest thing to yachting that the poor benighted schooner hand was ever likely to experience. It was real sailing.

We could see the ketch *C.F.H.* at Arthurstown and *James Postlethwaite* at Passage. As we passed across the line of the breakwater, Christy suddenly said 'That vessel's got a twist' and sure enough her mizzen mast was well out of line with the other two. Higher up the estuary the wind became deflected by the hills on either side and blew in turn from all directions, and we worked our way slowly up until we reached the railway bridge over the River Barrow. We blasted long and loud on the foghorn but nothing happened, so we were forced to anchor. We took in the gaff topsails, fore topsails and headsails, but left the fore and afters standing. We must have been anchored for nearly an hour and Christy had finally decided to stow the jibs and topsails when a train rattled over the bridge. Five minutes after it had gone the bridge started to swing. We loosed the topsails once more and sailed through with the wind astern, coming to anchor again some distance upstream. In the afternoon a motor barge arrived to tow us up to New Ross. This barge was used to dredge sand and shingle from the river bed for building purposes and was also a means of transport for people from various places on the Barrow who wished to go down to Waterford on Sunday afternoons.

The scenery in the Barrow valley was as beautiful from the water as it had been from the road, with hills and well-wooded stretches along the banks. Here and there we passed a weekly steamer tied up to the trees at a small pier or jetty, discharging coal into carts. It must never have been very far from the road down which I came in the pilot's taxi.

We reached Ross at 10pm and, as soon as it was possible to set foot on the shore, Willy went off in search of cigarettes as we had all run out. It was 11pm before we got her moored and we all turned in, had a good growl and went to sleep. We were just downstream from a road bridge with a swinging section in it and, in the morning, we warped through the bridge to the coal yard, which was above it. We were unable to get close to the bank owing to our deep draught so a long wide gangplank had to be taken aboard from a double-doored opening in the coal yard. During the day we trundled the coal in barrels down this plank into the yard, but at night the doors were closed and we had to go ashore in the boat. We pulled under the bridge and tied up at the steps on the town quay. The crew thought this was a great joke as we were about twenty miles from the sea although still in tidal water.

The coal was discharged by a gang of men employed by the owners of the yard. The next day, Old Johnny had another of his cantankerous moods and started shouting at them for being too slow in getting the vessel discharged. He said he would put in a claim for demurrage if they didn't get a move on. They were working hard enough and the foreman merely returned him a load of flowery language and told him he would finish up by having to come to him for a price of a candle.

I got the boat across the stern so that I could have a go at repainting the transom but found that the wood was rotten in quite a few places; in order to preserve the artistic work the rest of the transom had gone unpainted for years. Most schooners with transom sterns had the transom itself made of fairly thick slabs of timber. *Brooklands* seemed to be an exception – above the deck it was merely planks about an inch and a quarter thick. Probably this had been done during the rebuild of 1918 as it seemed out of keeping with her strong construction everywhere else. The brushes available for the job were on a par with the chisel and the colours of paint were very limited. I suspect it was a wasted effort – I'm sure she lost it in the end. For this I am sorry as it was a nice job and, in earlier days, would have been done in carved wooden 'gingerbread' work. Christy once passed a comment about the tremendous length of her original main boom and from this went on to remark that, before it was replaced, the wooden bar across the top of her wheel house, which acted as a support for the boom, had been carved with the words, 'Be just and fear not'. Somehow the painting on her transom seemed to fit in with this.

It took about two and a half days to discharge the cargo – not bad going despite the skipper's dissatisfaction; 100 tons per day was considered to be good work. Somehow, whilst we were otherwise engaged, possibly eating in the fo'c'sle, the skipper managed to fold up his tent and steal away once more, no doubt to forestall the inevitable request for the crew's overdue wages.

In a month the schooner had delivered two cargoes of coal for which her owners received about £160. This must have been well above her average earnings over the year and the crew rightly felt that their own small fraction of it should have been paid out at the proper time. It was obvious that the vessel was not getting her share either. What Captain Creenan hoped to achieve by hanging on to it, I am at a loss to understand, but he must certainly have witnessed a large turnover in his labour force. Willy, I could see, intended to be a sailor and, being single, could afford to stick it out until he had learned all that he could, after which I did not doubt that he would transfer his allegiance to a motor schooner or steamer. Tom, the cook, was a young lad and probably cared little so long as he got his money in the end, but I could see that Mike, with a wife and two children, could hardly afford to go on subsidising Old Johnny for much longer. One of the subjects for humorous debate aboard weekly steamers in those days was this: if they did not receive their money promptly on a Saturday night, were the crew entitled to grind the vessel to a stop in mid-passage. This was never taken seriously, but it was obvious to the crew of *Brooklands*, who were paid by the month anyway, that they could not refuse to sail until they were paid without first going through some long-winded and expensive legal procedure that ended up with something or other being nailed to the mast.

The sailing-ship seaman was paid a miserable wage for a life of hard toil, skilled work and exposure to the elements. It was a miserable wage even in a day when miserable wages were all too common everywhere and, although the fires of youthful indignation have long ago burned low, I still think it was absolutely despicable to cheat or defraud or even temporarily withhold the tiny pittance from men who were willing to work such hard, long hours for such a paltry reward.

Captain Creenan had been born in the year 1859, the same year that the *Susan Vittery* slid down the ways. In his childhood the orange trade was still going strong. When he was twenty-one, in 1880, the Newfoundland trade was approaching its peak, but schooners were to be launched in large numbers for another twenty years before the decline really began to show. It is a pity that he was such a cantankerous old man because he must have known much about both of those now-vanished trades – his was a knowledge forever lost. He whistled for a wind. He still persisted in referring to the two sails of the lower foremast as the 'boom' foresail and the 'square' foresail, at a time when to everyone else they had been shortened to foresail and squaresail. He probably went to sea in what today would be considered his childhood. His contemporary, Captain Deacon, had his youth blighted by having to work long hours on a farm. Both men were products of an age when life could, and frequently did, press with unbelievable harshness and brutality upon the working population. It is probably true to say that only those who passed through the same hard times had either the right, or the necessary knowledge, to pronounce the final judgement on what they could or should have been.

Owing to the deep draught, the old schooner was now unable to use the port of Lydney until the tides served her once more, so the next cargo was to be malt for Dublin. Thus, instead of Conrad's famous Falmouth fruiter scenting her wake with oranges and lemons, there would be an ex-Brixham fruiter permeating hers with the sweet smell of old brewery. Having other work to do and being free to go, I left. As I crossed the bridge at Waterford, coming from the station, my bag over my shoulder, I could see sticking up at the far end, the three masts of a fore-and-aft schooner. She was remarkable at that late date in still possessing three full-length fidded topmasts and I suspected she was the *Earl Cairns*, which I had never seen at close quarters. So, indeed, she turned out to be, but she could also have been *Windermere* of Dublin; I was so long gazing at her and wondering in an absent-minded way why I didn't think she was the latter vessel that I com-

pletely failed to notice a man coming in the other direction. I was quite surprised, therefore, when a cheerful voice on the starboard bow asked, 'Are you joining her?' I turned to face a smiling stranger.

'No,' I said, 'I've just left the *Brooklands*.'

'Is she up at Ross?'

'Aye.'

'Some vessel.'

'Too bloody true,' I replied.

Apart from a few small snippets of information, I remained for over thirty-five years in complete ignorance of what had happened to the *Brooklands*, her skipper and her mate, until my attention was drawn to an article in *Ship's Monthly*[4] by Richard Scott of Limerick, who had also sailed in her. Through the good offices of Terry Belt I was able to make contact with Dick, who allowed me to make a short synopsis of his article and was also good enough to correct one or two misconceptions, which I had laboured under ever since I left the old vessel. These I obtained from the crew and from people ashore and I am sure they were given in good faith because, surprisingly enough, I heard the last echoes of them a few years ago from a native of New Ross whom I met in Burnley.

They all proclaimed that Captain Creenan was eighty years old, whereas his real age at the time I was in the schooner was a mere sixty-five. They could be excused from making this mistake; he certainly looked much older, and his behaviour did little to give the lie to it. I had also been told that when loaded the *Brooklands* drew 14ft aft. A photograph in Terry Belt's possession, with the draught marks newly painted, confirmed that 12ft 6in was her maximum.

Captain Creenan remained in command until 1940, although he later did a couple of trips in 1946 whilst Christy was out of action with a shoulder injury. With Christy once more in charge,[5] she took a cargo of clay from Ballinacurra to Weston Point, intending to load salt. For some reason the salt cargo did not materialise but she was chartered for a trip to the West Indies.

David Clement confirmed that after leaving the Mersey at the start of her intended Atlantic crossing *Brooklands* was severely buffeted and returned with damage to her port bow, subsequently repaired with a steel plate. The charter fell through due to the death of the client and she was laid up at Wallasey until January 1948, when she was bought by Captain Ashworth of Courtown, County Wexford, who fitted her with twin engines. She loaded coal at Garston for Youghal, but had engine trouble on passage. After discharging her cargo she proceeded to Wicklow where she was again laid up for two years. In 1952 she was bought by Dublin owners and fitted with new twin diesel engines. German shipwrights, employed by her owners, removed her mizzenmast, reduced her bowsprit to a short stump and re-rigged her as a two-masted fore-and-aft schooner.

She was abandoned in sinking condition and foundered off the Tuskar Rock on Easter Monday, 6 April 1953, after a life of ninety-four years. Her Norwegian master, Captain Arne Drengsrud, and her crew of three were rescued from the Tuskar by the Rosslare lifeboat. The schooner sprang a leak near Saltee Islands that night when an attempt was made to reach Rosslare. Strong headwinds were encountered and, after pumping proved inefficient against the ingress of water, the vessel was abandoned with her decks awash, Captain Drengsrud jumping into the boat carrying his dog as the vessel sank in 20 fathoms. The crew were eight hours pulling to the Tuskar Rock. Prior to this incident she had loaded her first cargo following her refit – 200 tons of fertiliser destined for Dungarven. After leaving Dublin she ran aground off Cunnigar Point, Dungarven on 27 February 1953, flooding her engine-room and crew's quarters. Several attempts were made to tow her off, but it was not until about half her cargo had been discharged that she could be moved on 5 March, only to run aground again about 50 yards from the quayside. She finally reached her berth the following day.

That she survived so long with such Spartan attention during her latter years is a tremendous testimonial to the West Country men who selected and cut her timber so many years ago. She was the last of everything: the last of the extreme clipper schooners afloat and the last of all to cross topsail yards.

Johnny Creenan died in 1952. Christy Creenan was mate of the motor vessel *Marlog* when he was drowned in Waterford Harbour in October 1974 after falling whilst boarding his ship. His wife died just before Christmas 1975. Their son still lives in Ballinacurra and Christy's brother kept a pub in the same town. They have every right to feel proud of two men who showed up well under trying circumstances, who not only upheld the best traditions of the sea, but of their own green island as well. May they rest in peace.

Den she sighed as she whispered, 'Mañana'
Never dreamin' dat we were partin'
Oh, I lied as I whispered, 'Mañana'
For dat tomoro' never came.

[4] *Ships Monthly*, Volume 1, No.11, November 1966.

[5] Christy Creenan was so noted a skipper that the vessel was never known by his compatriots as the *Brooklands*, but would be referred to as the 'Christy Creenan'. Captain Peter Herbert of Bude who well remembers Christy Creenan and, indeed, owned one of the last sailing vessels in trade, recalled that this continued a pattern of his father's where the ship would be referred to as 'Creenan's a'comin'' whenever she arrived somewhere. The master-owner and his son were at least as famous as their vessel.

V

HULLS AND BUILDERS

The foregoing brief accounts of life in schooners have been written in the long and established traditions of nautical literature. They tell the reader all that is likely to be of interest, with a few short explanations here and there where some incident requires slightly more elaboration for its point to be fully grasped. What they do not tell is akin to the submerged part of an iceberg and it is with this material that the rest of the book is concerned.

No attempt will be made here to give an account of how wooden ships were built, as both professionals and amateurs are still building yachts in the traditional way in many parts of the world, so there is no immediate danger of any ancient crafts being lost. The almost universal use of power tools today has taken most of the hard work out of the job but hand tools are still widely used by woodworkers of all kinds and show no sign of ever being completely supplanted. There exists, too, such a copious supply of literature on the subject of wooden shipbuilding that even people with absolutely no previous experience have been able to tackle the job with complete success.

FIGURE 5.1
Bevels

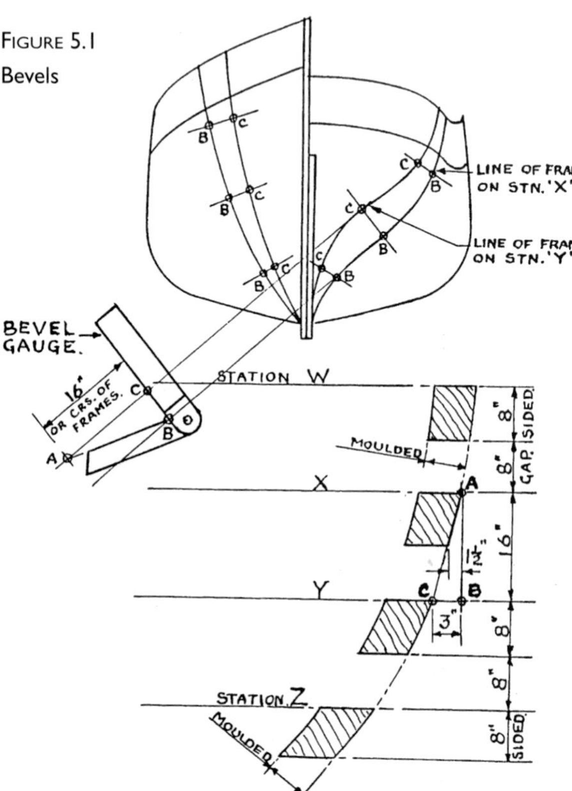

One element, which deserves mention, is the bevel on the frames as many who have not had to deal with this seem to find it rather mysterious. Figure 5-1 shows the lines of two pairs of frames as marked out on the mould loft floor but with the gap B-C deliberately exaggerated. Referring to the sections below it will be seen that the bevel of the frame on station 'x' is the angle of the hypotenuse A-C of triangle A-B-C. With the frames and the spaces of equal dimensions, the amount of bevel to be taken off this particular frame at the point measured will be half the distance from B to C. This assumes that the line A-C is straight, whereas in fact it is a part of a curve, but the error introduced by this assumption is well within the limits to which shipbuilders normally worked. The reason why frames at 16in centres were popular in the past was that the bevel per inch of siding in the timber could be obtained in the units used; eighths, sixteenths, etc., without any very involved calculations. If the dimension B-C was 3in, then the bevel taken off an 8in-sided frame would be 1½in. The bevel per inch would be 3in divided by 16 (ie. 3⁄16 per inch). If it was intended to make the frame out of 10in timber the bevel on it would be 3⁄16 multiplied by 10 – ie. 1⅞in.

The bevel on the outside of any frame also had to come off the inside, to take the ceiling planks and, in view of the laborious job this would have been if using an adze, it is not surprising that in many yards the sawyers sawed the bevel into the frames. One way this could be done was by supporting the work pieces on planks sloping at the angle of the bevel, so that sawing could be done vertically. This involved the sawyer in calculating the bevel per inch so that he could arrange his planks to suit. As the bevel on the frame changed, the angle of the planks would be adjusted to suit and, as it is unlikely the sawyers would have stopped every few minutes to make small adjustments, they must, for some of the time, have sawn at an angle. This, no doubt, was where the real skill lay.

References have been made by other writers to regional differences in schooners, in many cases without being very explicit as to where these differences lay. By the 1930s they

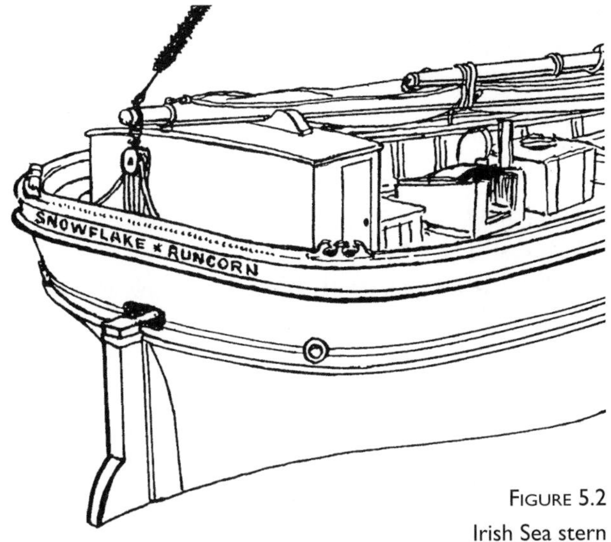

FIGURE 5.2
Irish Sea stern

were confined to the hulls alone, as the simple rigging and gear, without ever becoming as standardised as in the big square rigger, had reached a state of uniformity involving the use of a few popular variations on each well-known theme, which will be dealt with in later chapters.

Probably the best known of the regional hull variations is the Irish Sea stern, often referred to as the 'Flat's Stern' after the type of vessel of that name [Figure 5-2]. The salient feature of this was that the rudder was 'out of doors'; that is to say it did not pass through an overhanging counter as the sternpost was the aftermost part of the hull. The vessels built with this type of stern have been fairly well dealt with in the columns of *Mariner's Mirror*[1] and in Basil Greenhill's *Merchant Schooners*[2] and most readers will be familiar with the slightly more elegant version produced by William Ashburner of Barrow, and one or two others in that same area.

Vessels built in the 'Flat' area often had other things about them which proclaimed the region of their origin. The Flat seldom sported a topgallant bulwark and in consequence its pinrails were intermittent lengths of timber bolted to the bulwark stanchions about 9in below the level of the rail. Both of these features were to be found in *Englishman*, built at Glasson Dock. They were to be found in most iron and steel schooners for other reasons. Intermittent pinrails were also a feature of the 'Barrow Flats', *James Postlethwaite, M.E. Johnson, Useful* and *Isabella*, although all these vessels had a topgallant bulwark.

Another variation, but at this time only partially regional in nature, was the deep heel and raking sternpost of some of the West Country vessels and of the schooners and barquentines of Brittany. It was not confined solely to Europe, being one of the characteristics of the celebrated *Ann McKim* of Baltimore, and was essentially a deep-waterman's hull. Its drawbacks in the coasting trade are hardly likely to have escaped the reader's notice in the chapter on the *Brooklands*.

[1] *Mariner's Mirror* is the Journal of the Society of Nautical Research.
[2] *The Merchant Schooners* by Dr Basil Greenhill, 2 vols, Percival Marshall, London, 1951/1957. New revised two-volume edition, David & Charles, Newton Abbot, 1968. New revised single-volume edition, Conway Maritime Press, London, 1988.

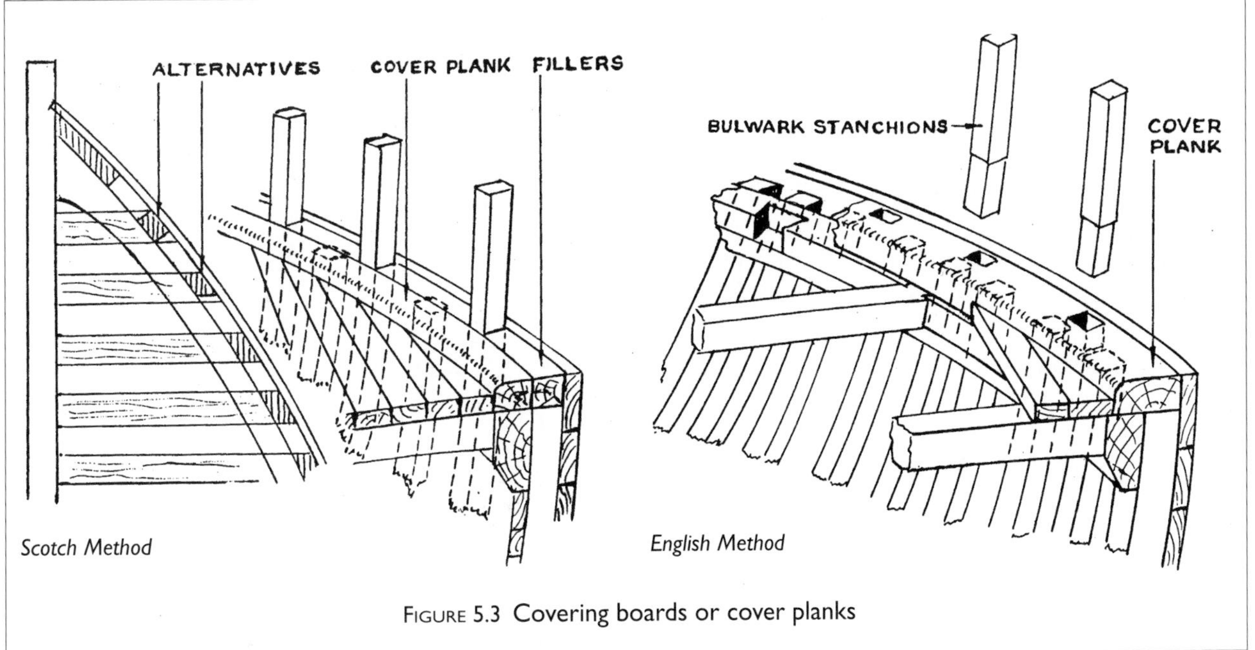

FIGURE 5.3 Covering boards or cover planks

A regional variation which, not being very noticeable, has so far received little attention, was to be found in the different methods used in England and Scotland when dealing with the covering boards or cover planks – the heavy timbers around the edge of the deck which formed the waterways and supported the bulwark stanchions. Anyone familiar with the Scotch[3] fishing vessels will have noticed that it almost invariably has a tremendous number of bulwark stanchions supporting bulwarks, which are seldom much above a foot high. These are the ends of the frames, which have been carried up above deck level. The cover plank proper is inside them and the spaces between have been filled in with short pieces of timber. Even when painted all over, there is a tell-tale line inside the stanchions to indicate that this method of construction has been used [Figure.5-3]. A further confirmation sometimes seen in vessels with parallel frames was that, in the bows, no attempt was made to square up the stanchions, so that they finished up with the cross-section of a parallelogram instead of a rectangle. Schooners and other larger wooden vessels were also built this way, but not all the frames were extended upwards as bulwark stanchions. It was not a feature likely to be noticed by anyone not deliberately looking for it and is perhaps of little interest apart from the fact that it gave a stronger bulwark, especially desirable in way of the chainplates. If the bulwarks were swept away in heavy weather there was also less danger of leakage into the hull.

In the English method, the frame ends were cut off flush with the top of the deck beams; the cover planks were made from broad pieces of timber through which holes were cut between frames into which separate bulwark stanchions were driven from above. When *Kathleen & May* was previously rehabilitated and put on show it was claimed that she was a good example of a West Country schooner. At the time this seemed a rather thoughtless attempt on the part of an area rich in maritime tradition to rob a small, silted-up, and little-used Welsh port of some of its honour and glory. However, since the publication of Tom Coppack's *A Lifetime With Ships*[4] this no longer matters; Connah's Quay is now firmly on the map. But this is not the whole of the story. The *Kathleen & May* was built in the yard of a couple of men called Ferguson and Baird, and those who examine her cover planks will find evidence that these two haggis-eating builders of a Welsh West Country schooner used the method normally found north of the Tweed.

A schooner with unusual cover planks was *Irish Minstrel* built at Dundalk. In most vessels there was a step where the deck planking met the cover planks, the latter being about double the thickness of the deck planks. In the *Minstrel* the cover planks were about 18in wide and were tapered down in thickness from inside the bulwark stanchions to where they met the deck planks, making the scuppers or waterways a shallow vee-shaped trough, into which the lead scupper pipes emerged through oval holes [Figure. 5-4].

Sterns, other than the Irish Sea type, varied considerably in the amount of counter overhang. In general the older the vessel the less the overhang, which seems to have increased slowly until the later 1880s, when it hardened out into the long yacht-like counter, which remained the fashion for both sailing vessels and steamers until the end of the century. Among schooners, *Alert* and *Mary Barrow* represented the end product of this line of evolution. Vessels with the transom type of counter stern were usually older than those with the elliptical type, although *M.A. James*, built in 1900, was one exception at least. But, in these rather vague trends in marine fashion, the idiosyncrasies of individual builders and owners were always there to modify matters to their own liking and to make the issue much less clear cut.

A feature, which could also be used in conjunction with the counter overhang as a rough indication of the vessel's age, was the sheer. Prior to 1850 ships seem to have been almost flat and their bowsprits sprang out of the knightheads at a sharply steeved-up angle. From this time onwards sheer gradually increased, until in the late 1880s it culminated in the tremendous sweeping curve forward that was so much a fea-

FIGURE 5.4
Waterways and scuppers
Irish Minstrel

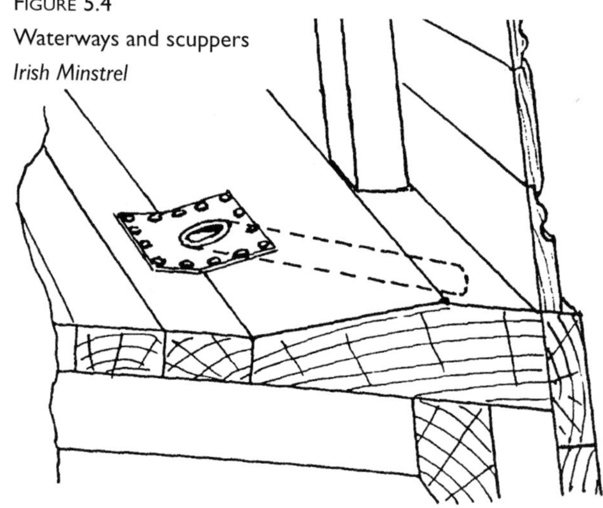

[3] Those who claim that this should be Scots or Scottish and that 'Scotch' is a drink, are referred to the book, *The Non-potable Scotch* by J.K. Galbraith. In support of Mr Galbraith's standpoint the writer wishes to state that his own limited researches, together with those of countless thousands of other engineers, have long ago established beyond dispute the depressing fact that the 'Scotch Boiler' contains absolutely no whisky whatsoever!

[4] *A Lifetime with Ships*, by Tom Coppack, T. Stephenson & Sons, London, 1973.

Bessie of Barnstaple taken at Wrafton in August 1937.

Photographer unknown Terry Belt Collection

ture of the latter day Newfoundlanders and, in the realm of the big sailing ships, of vessels such as Masefield's *Wanderer.*

In the second edition of *The Merchant Schooners* there are a set of lines taken from the half-model of a vessel built at Kingsbridge, which, but for one or two obvious features, could easily be mistaken for those of the *Susan Vittery*. Both vessels had a big deadrise to their floors; both carried their fullest section well forward, between the two masts; both had a beam to length ratio of 1:4.7, and both had a raking sternpost. The features in which the two vessels differed were that the *Susan*

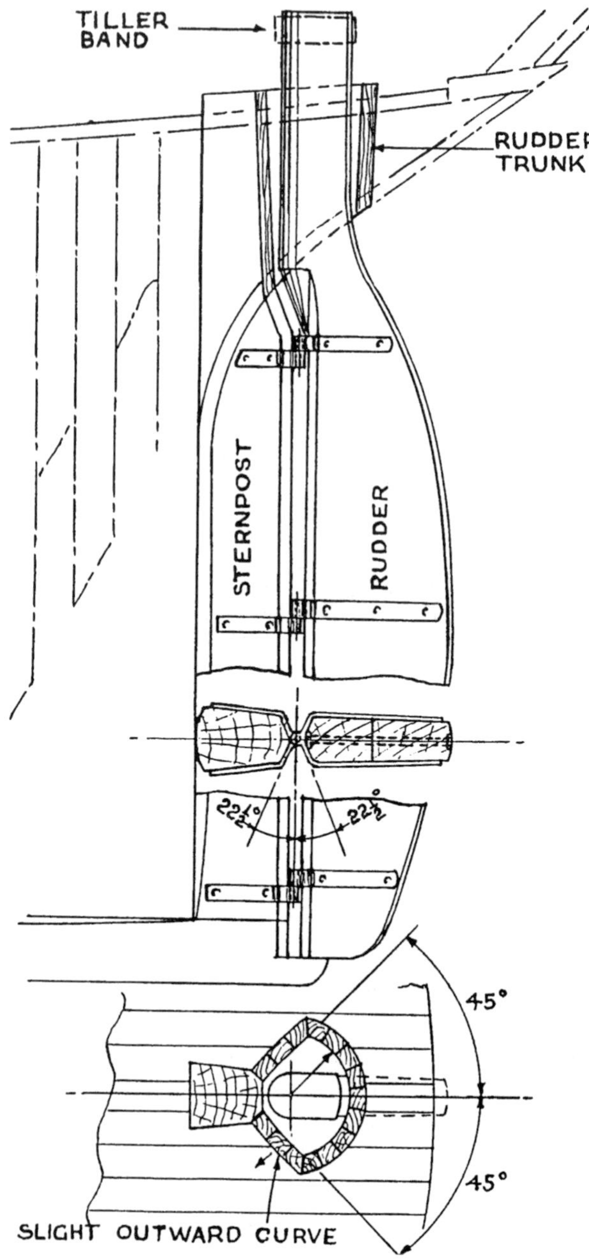

FIGURE 5-5 Rudder

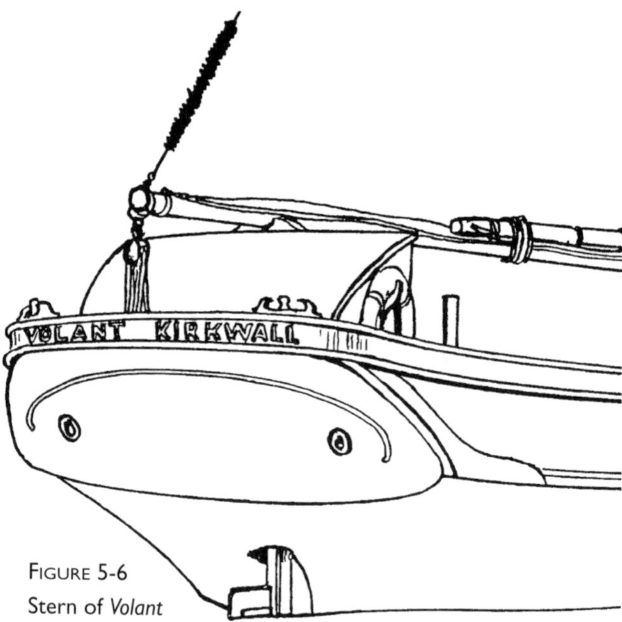

FIGURE 5-6
Stern of *Volant*

Vittery drew less water forward, she had more sheer and slightly higher bulwarks, and her stern had far less overhang than that of the Kingsbridge vessel. This unknown schooner has been tentatively dated at about 1870, but her lack of sheer should make her an earlier vessel than the *Susan Vittery*, while the long overhang of her counter should make her later. The two conflicting tendencies should cancel each other out, making her a contemporary and, in spite of the fact that this kind of 'mad mathematics' can hardly be considered valid, 1860 seems a much more likely date for such an extreme type of racer. The evidence for this comes from Michael Bouquet's *No Gallant Ship*[5], in which he states that this was the year that marked the beginning of the end for schooners in the fruit trade, and that, in less than ten years from this date, the writing was on the wall.

The counter stern was a much more expensive end than the Irish Sea type as the rudder stock passed upwards through a trunk to a point above deck level where the tiller was fastened to it. The rudder trunk had a section like a quarter of a circle [Figure 5-5] but the two forward sides were slightly curved. The trunk was tapered from top to bottom so that the staves, which lined the hole, something after the manner of a barrel, could be driven home from the top until tight. In order to keep the size of the trunk to a minimum, as it was a potential source of leakage, the rudder stock was often joggled forward by several inches, as shown in the diagram. The old-fashioned long tiller, which humorists referred to as 'the rib-tickler', was shipped in a tapered square hole cut in a fore-

[5] *No Gallant Ship*, by Michael R. Bouquet, Hollis & Carter, London, 1959.

Useful at Princes Dock, Glasgow, 23 April 1929.

Photograph by Dan McDonald. Terry Belt Collection

and-aft direction through the stock, but the various short types, to which the force of the steering wheel was applied, were usually secured by iron bands.

There was one variation of the transom type of counter stern, which was definitely regional as far as the British Isles were concerned. It was to be found in schooners built in the northeast of Scotland and was exactly the same as the sterns of many Scandinavian wooden vessels, reflecting the long centuries of trade and mutual influence, which started when the 'front doors' of these islands were on the east coast and continued unabated when the discovery of the Americas caused them to be moved to the west. Also commonly used in the North American vessels it was much the same as any other transom stern, except that the topgallant bulwark was curved around the corners instead of butting in at right angles. The schooners *Volant* and *Minnie* bore the last surviving examples of this type of stern, [Figure 5-6], the latter vessel being also the final schooner in possession of a jib-boom and wooden dolphin striker.

Many more schooners started life with figureheads than finished up with them, as they were very vulnerable in collisions as well as susceptible to rot. Although they received coat after coat of many colours of paint, the areas in which they were faired into the stem were open to attack and the thick covering of paint on the visible parts tended to conceal the rot until it was too late. After the 1914-18 War, during which building had come to an end, the skilled labour required to replace a figurehead either wholly or in part, was no longer available, and it finished up as the one piece of a wooden vessel which, once lost, was gone forever. By the early 1930s, there were about twenty vessels left with figureheads still intact. Many were mundane pieces of workmanship, but one or two

stood out above the rest. Michael Bouquet states that the figurehead of *Lochranza Castle* was a beautiful piece of work, but it was gone before this writer set eyes on that vessel.

Another of the Annalong schooners, *Volant*, had a very attractive figurehead and, by good fortune and the loving care of her owner, Mr L.J. Upton, this lady still survives at Falmouth, where she can be seen outside 'The Bosun's Locker' chandlery. Dan McDonald would have awarded the palm to a lady called *Agnes Craig*, although he rates the *Sunshine*'s figurehead a close second. I am also indebted to him for drawing my attention to what might be classed as an act of piracy, in which the figurehead of one vessel was transferred to another. This, he says, happened in the case of *Uncle Ned* which was laid up at Arklow in 1934 and whose figurehead later appeared on the *William Ashburner*. 'Uncle', he thinks, never looked very happy on the *Ashburner*'s bows. The same thing must have happened in *Brooklands*. The *Susan Vittery* seems to have started life with a figurehead. Later she had a fiddlehead and scroll-work only and, finally, when rigged as a three-master and renamed *Brooklands*, she had a figurehead once more, which must have been the one that came to grief during one of her arguments with the dock wall at Lydney.

Three out of the final handful had male figureheads. These were *William Ashburner* already mentioned, *Mynonie R. Kirby*, which started life as the *Cadwallader Jones*, and *Irish Minstrel*. The *Irish Minstrel* was dressed in an old-fashioned frock coat and his right arm was bent at the elbow, as though at one time he had carried some musical instrument. Before being finally sold and cut down, this vessel lay in the dock at Runcorn for about twelve months, in a thoroughly neglected state, and it is almost impossible for me to separate her in my memory from the old Irish song, 'The Bard of Armagh':

Oh, list to the tale of a poor Irish harper,
Laugh not at the strains from his old withered hand.
Remember, his fingers could once move much sharper
To start up a song of his dear native land.
At fairs and at wakes, I could twirl my shillelagh.
I could slide through a jig with my shoes tied with straw
And all the pretty fair maids from hillside or valley,
Would dance with Phelim Brady, the Bard of Armagh.

The craze for painting figureheads all white was probably inspired by the Elgin Marbles. According to those artistic people of the time, there was a pure classical beauty about them and their sightless eyes, which all good artists and sculptors should take heed of. This school got something of a knock later on when evidence was unearthed that pointed to the fact that the vulgar Greeks had actually had the appallingly bad taste to paint them in lifelike colours! As far as the people in

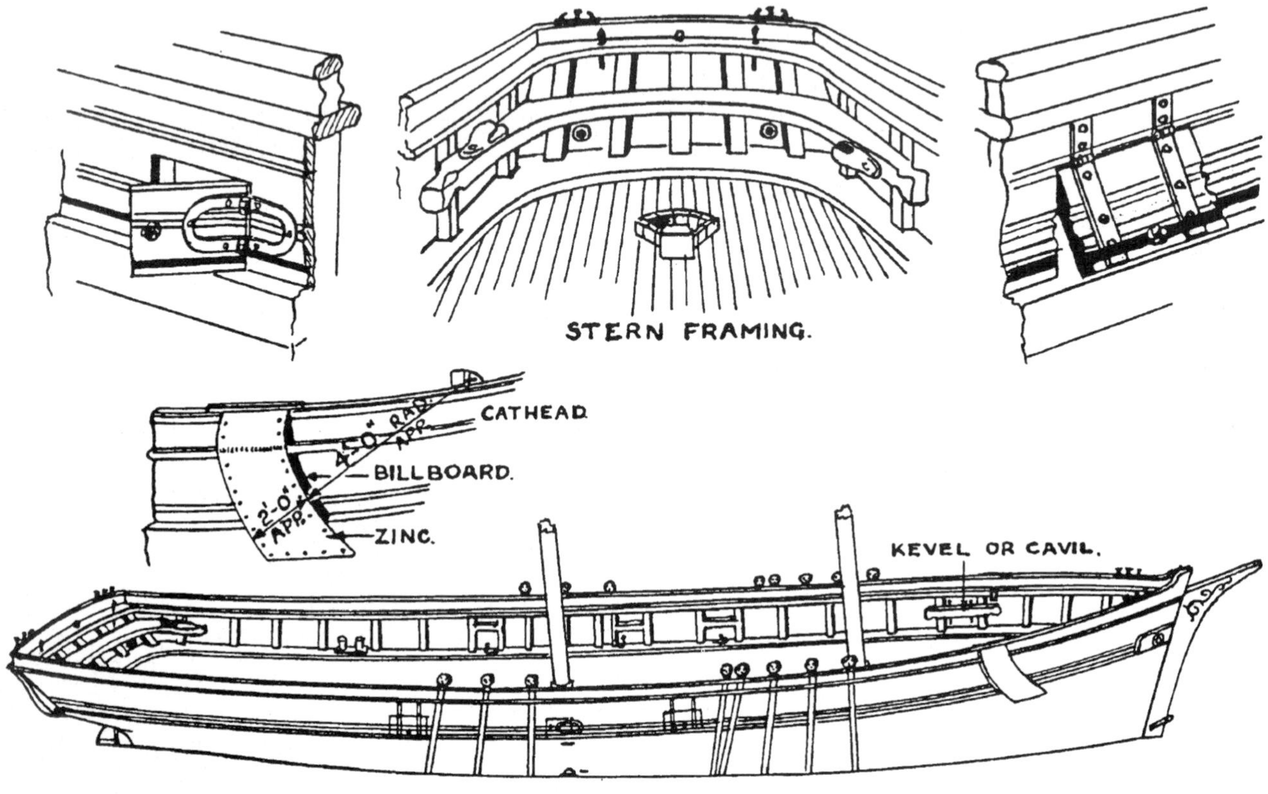

STERN FRAMING.

CATHEAD

4'-0" RAD. APP.

BILLBOARD.

2'-0" APP.

ZINC.

KEVEL OR CAVIL.

FIGURE 5-7 Bulwarks

Mary Sinclair showing her deep narrow hull.

Photographer unknown. Terry Belt collection

schooners were concerned, this particular quirk of fashion seems to have completely passed them by. To the end they clung to the older tradition of getting the figurehead painted as well as possible, with a glow in her cheeks and a gleam of bright colour in her dress. The *Alert*'s figurehead seems to have been one of the few classical beauties adorning a schooner's bows but even she, in spite of her advancing years, does not seem to have got so far as to become a white-haired old lady! And whether she spent the whole of her life in this state of bridal purity is open to debate.

She was gone by the time that the writer sailed in the vessel that bore her, probably lost in a collision in the Downs in 1929. Schooners' figureheads were nearly always smaller than life-size in order to be in keeping with the scale of the vessels that carried them.

To the writer's mind the classic form and colour scheme of the trailboards always looked the smartest, black-varnished, like the hull, and with the scrollwork picked out in white.

Bulwarks and their fittings displayed a surprising uniformity in wooden vessels. Two types of wash port were in use,

My Lady showing details of her figurehead and gingerbread work.

Photograph by Wilfred Sharman. David Clement Collection

Figure 5-8 Chainplates (bulwarks not to scale)

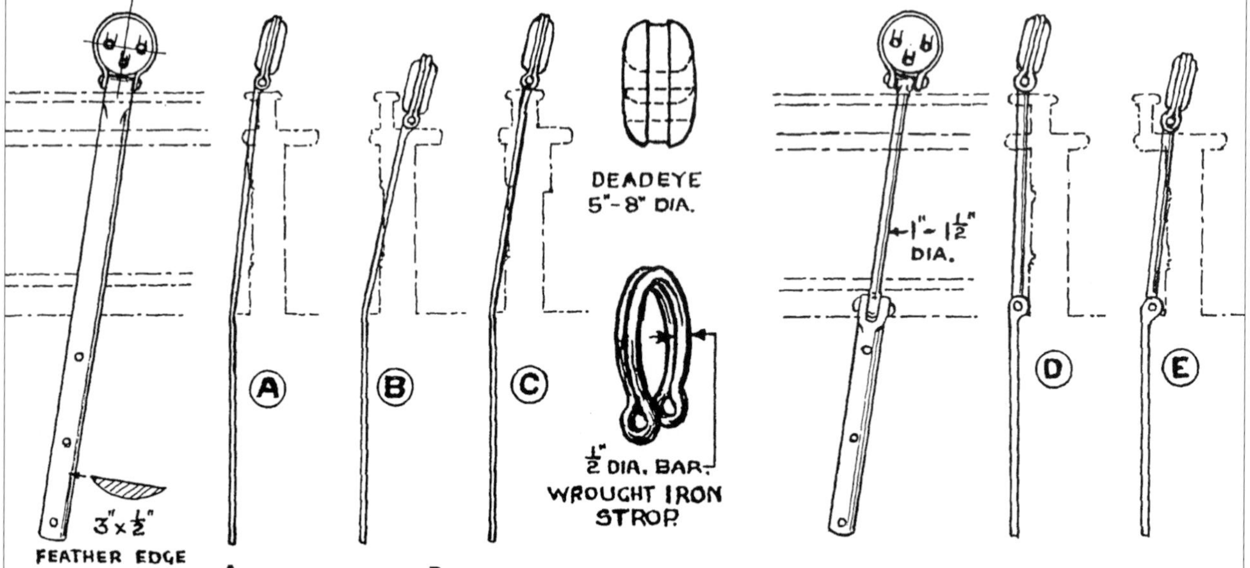

3" x ½"
FEATHER EDGE
DEADEYE 5"-8" DIA.
1"-1½" DIA.
½" DIA. BAR.
WROUGHT IRON STROP
(A) (B) (C) (D) (E)

A
Cambourne
Englishman
Fanny Crossfield
James Postlethwaite
Mary Miller
M. E. Johnson
Nellie Fleming
Ryelands
Useful

B
Ellie Park
Flying Foam
Henrietta
Irish Minstrel
Jane Banks
Katie
Kathleen & May
Lochranza Castle

C
Alert
Waterwitch

D
Minnie

E
Brooklands

Irish Minstrel coasting under full sail.

PHOTOGRAPHER UNKNOWN. TERRY BELT COLLECTION

one hinged on the forward edge and the other hinged at the top, the latter being usually larger than the others. Most vessels had an assortment of each, about three a side, but some had only the top-hinged type. The type hinged on the leading edge had the lower hinge canted outwards slightly more than the upper one, so that the weight of the door tended to keep it shut, except when the vessel was heeled well over when the function was performed by the rush of water along the lee side. Both types were restrained in their travel by ropes from eyebolts inside the bulwarks. Figure 5-7 shows a typical arrangement of bulwarks and their impedimenta. The billboards on each side of the bows were planked out flush with the hull planking and sheathed over with zinc plate. Their shape was two arcs, struck from the cathead, so that they lay square in the path of the flukes as the crown of the anchor was hauled up to the rail.

The other outside features of the bulwarks, the chainplates, were amongst the most important fittings in a wooden vessel. These appendages to the standing rigging each followed the line of the shroud or backstay to which it was attached, so that their lower ends, about 3ft [1m] below the sheerstrake, were splayed out in a fore-and-aft direction. Many builders preferred to carry them up the outside of the bulwarks where they could be seen from end to end, but this involved building bulwarks strong enough to resist the inward pull under load. Others avoided this problem by canting them inwards at deck level to come into line with the rigging, and these usually passed through the bulwarks and sometimes, as in *Alert*, through a hollow topgallant rail. Figure 5-8 shows some of the more popular variations.

Cabin and fo'c'sle (or forecastle to be literally correct) accommodation have been described frequently and fairly comprehensively, so that little more needs to be said. In all but the smallest vessels there was usually some space in the

[6] The deck crew are now but rarely accommodated in the fo'c'sle, this area being used for storage, warps, paint, etc. and as an area in which to work in shelter when not required on deck.

Minnie Fully laden and ready to depart from Newlyn, 7 June 1921.

PHOTOGRAPH BY H. OLIVER HILL. TERRY BELT COLLECTION

cabin forward of the companion and the stairs and it was here that the provisions were stored. In some schooners one or both of the chain lockers were also below this area, the other popular places being in the pump well amidships and at the after end of the fo'c'sle, below the floor. Uninhabited fo'c'sles, like empty houses, were inclined to look a bit stark, giving rise to a belief that they were far more dismal holes than they actually were. Since paraffin – rather than grease from the salt pork – was used in the lamps the light was fairly good at night, the model makers could get on with their work at the little table on the pawl-bitt, whilst those in the nearest bunks could see to read – although a plaintive cry of 'Square your yards, mate,' was sometimes heard when someone got in the way. The fo'c'sles of small vessels are much the same to this day, except that electric lighting is now almost universal.[6]

Leaky deckheads were the main sources of discomfort in either fo'c'sle or cabin, but both possessed coal stoves by which they could be heated and kept dry in the winter – the frequently carried coal cargoes ensured there was seldom a shortage of fuel at either end of the vessel.

Each man forward had a locker in which to stow his personal effects which, in the case of the older men, consisted of the small canvas bag in which the sailor kept his fid, marlinespike, serving board, palm, needles and wax, together with his kit bag and whatever clothing he saw fit to bring with him – usually not very much. Nearly all the apprentice pilots[7] had a good suit in which to go ashore – it being much easier to attract members of the opposite sex when so disguised. In *Alert* Paddy kept his suit hanging against the ceiling forward of the pawl-bitt, with a sheet of brown paper beneath it and

[7] In the final days of sail trade in coasting vessels many apprentice pilots sailed to get the necessary experience in 'square-rigged' vessels to enable them to obtain their 'pilot's ticket'. The *Waterwitch* in particular regularly took such persons to sea as a form of 'cheap crew'.

another on the outside to keep it clean. Sea-boots and oil-skins were usually deposited at the after end of the fo'c'sle, against the bulkhead.

There was no 'peggy' in schooners, the inhabitants all setting-to together to keep the fo'c'sle clean, scrubbing floor-boards, ladder, lockers, table, and everything else with tremendous thoroughness. The job was usually done on a Saturday afternoon when at anchor, while the cook was doing the same thing in the galley, as well as cleaning out the flues of the stove. Hot seawater and washing soda were used for the scrubbing, but the final wash down was with copious buckets of cold water. The constant scrubbing caused the woodwork to acquire a corrugated appearance, which will be familiar to those members of an older generation who were brought up with plain wooden kitchen tables.

Bunks aft were usually of the built-in variety, necessitating some kind of mattress or 'donkey's breakfast', both of which provided a comfortable home from which the bed bugs could sally forth to attack the sleepers. Forward there were almost invariably frame cots. These were about 6ft [1.83m] long and slightly over 2ft [0.61m] wide; the pipe frame next to the ceiling being sometimes curved to conform to the ceiling's contour. This frame was clamped to the ceiling in two places while deckhead ropes, which could be adjusted to suit the owner's preferences, supported the other side. The canvas was never stretched taught but was allowed to hang slack, giving many of the benefits of a hammock without its disadvantages. They were comfortable with or without a 'donkey's break-

Hilda of Bridgwater seen alongside the river quay at Bridgwater in April 1913.

PHOTOGRAPH BY W. A. SHARMAN. DAVID CLEMENT COLLECTION

Alert in the Mersey.

Photographer not known. David Clement Collection

fast', a blanket below the sleeper as well as one on top, being all that was necessary. One advantage that the sailing-ship seaman had over those in power-driven vessels was that, for a given state of weather, he expended far less energy in trying to stay in his bunk, the movement of his vessel being much less violent and jerky than that of a steamer.

Most men slept in their underclothes when in port, but left their shirt and trousers on when at sea. Strenuous washing and shaving were usually confined to Sundays. Some claimed that bugs did not bite them; in fact a theory had been developed that they only bit people with pure blood. This being the case a couple of men with impure blood in the fo'c'sle of a small vessel should have had the lot of them at death's door in a very short time![8] In actual fact they were always there in full force, to greet the next sailor, pure in blood if not in heart, who was unfortunate enough to join the vessel. The truth is that the impure parties were still bitten, but had obviously developed immunity to the irritation and swellings.

In some ways too much emphasis has been laid on the cottage-industry aspect of schooner building, in others too little. The early iron and steel vessels were built by methods not much better than those employed on wooden ones – frames bent and bevelled by stages on a blacksmith's hearth, plates cut by cold chisel, rivet holes drilled laboriously with ratchets, all rivets clinched by hand, and all caulking done with hand tools. It was only the economic advantage of being near the source of supply of raw materials that finally caused the concentration of iron and steel shipbuilding in the north. The Dutch carried on with these 'backyard' methods of steel shipbuilding well into the 20th century, although the plates and rolled sections they used were the products of heavy industry. As were the copper and galvanised-iron bolts used by the wooden shipbuilders, and so, too, was the iron, either wrought or cast, needed for so many parts of the hull and deck fittings. Anchors and stud-link chain were seldom produced by non-specialist firms, and it is doubtful if sail canvas was ever woven in small quantities across the British Isles. The thin copper or bronze sheets used for sheathing wooden vessels were also produced by one or two of what then would have been considered fairly large firms, the required capital outlay being too heavy to attract small-scale producers. There is a tendency to forget that behind the village shipbuilders of the 19th century stood the most heavily industrialised nation on earth, and it was this that caused all the demand for tonnage.

There was nothing 'cottage' about the outlook. The men of the day possessed one thing that we today sadly lack: a tremendous belief in themselves. They were proud of their nation and its achievements, and they set off in their cottage-built cockleshells to haul heavy commodities half way around the world. If the returns were tempting enough, they were prepared to go right around. Some of these small vessels finished up a long way from home. The *Alfred Vittery* ended her life in Australian waters leaving her sister, *Susan Vittery* at home. So did the *Lancashire Lass*[9] leaving the *Lancashire Lad*, to suffer a 'sex-change' and be re-named *Dorothy*. Many others not possessed of near relatives by whom they could be checked must have done the same. Still more, many more, left their bones on reef and shoal, and in deep water in places far away from the rain-sodden islands that sent them forth.

Although greater tonnages may since have been built (and sunk) in times of war, it is unlikely that such a tremendous burst of shipbuilding as that which took place in the second half of the 19th century had ever occurred in the world before or will ever occur again. British-built bottoms alone could not cope with the ever-increasing demand. Half the world was building and hauling for us as well. But, in spite of this, the 19th century was no more a shipbuilder's paradise than the 20th; most went broke in the end.

[8] Since writing this I have read that these bugs can steam for about 500 days without refuelling!

[9] *Next Door to Paradise – Australia's countless islands*, by Bill Beatty, Cassell Australia Ltd, 1965

VI

ANCHORS

Anchors have always loomed large in the life of the coasting seaman. They loomed larger still in the era here under consideration, because few sailing vessels were still in a fit state to fight it out at sea in the full fury of a gale, even if they had sufficient sea room in which to do so. Seldom, if ever, was there sufficient sea room for small sailing vessels working around the coasts of the British Isles. It mattered not whether a gale came from the southwest or the northeast, it was always a lee shore for someone; only the traffic in the English Channel was reasonably safe, although it could be brought to a standstill or given a glorious shove, depending upon the direction in which it was going. Even in the Channel the losses were high; elsewhere they were appalling, as a visit to any lifeboat station in the British Isles and examination of their records will rapidly confirm. The fortunate vessels were those that were blown off, either into the Atlantic or the North Sea, as they had a reasonable chance of survival as long as their crews could keep them afloat. Nature provides few really good natural harbours such as Milford, so the human race was eventually driven to set about making some of their own and, inevitably, the skippers of small vessels were forced to weigh up how far they could go with the wind in a particular direction, before putting themselves into the predicament of no shelter to which they could run. In consequence, on many coastal passages, more time was spent at anchor than at sea.

In the bows of every vessel is a device of some kind for raising the anchors from the seabed. For centuries, in merchant vessels, it consisted of a simple horizontal wooden barrel on a spindle, with rows of square holes cut into its eight sides, into which handspikes would be inserted by the crew. At the tail end of the sailing-ship era, in the big steel-hulled square riggers, it was a much more sophisticated piece of machinery, driven by worm gearing from the head capstan on the deck above it and, in some cases, capable of being worked by steam. The machine that bridged the gap between these two extremes was worked by a rocker on top of the pawl-bitt and was facetiously referred to by those who were shipmates with it as 'Armstrong's Patent Windlass'. Some said it was worked by brute force and ignorance, others claimed it was strength and stupidity that did the trick. Just when it started to oust the handspike windlass is not clear but it is interesting to note that Brunel's *Great Britain* was fitted with one, and of a far more sophisticated pattern than was being installed in schooners over fifty years later. Its popularity obviously increased rapidly as the size of crews diminished, as it had a much greater purchase than could be obtained with handspikes. Its construction is shown in Figure 6-1.

It will be noticed that the purchase could be increased, if necessary, at the expense of a shorter travel, by moving the link rods to the outer holes provided in the pawl boxes. These extra holes were primarily for use when an anchor refused to be broken out, but one suspects that in the 1860s and '70s they were frequently resorted to, in order to impart the downward curve to the jib boom that was then so much the vogue. Windlasses were supplied in endless variations; each builder seems to have had his own favourite ideas on the subject; some even had several ideas, which they tried out in a succession of vessels.

The high-water mark for complications must have been reached in the three-master *Ryelands* and the ketch *Sunshine*, both of which had their rocker on an extra 'pawl-bitt' abaft the windlass, the ratchet wheels acting also as the pinions to a pair of larger gear wheels on the windlass barrel. There was also a fore-and-aft shaft with a hand wheel, the purpose of which is now somewhat obscure. Some ratchet wheels had well-shaped teeth against which the pawls in the boxes could obviously bear, but in others the teeth were little better than rounded protuberances, from which it could be deduced that the function of the pawls was more akin to a jamming or toggle action than straight pressure. Out of all the survivors afloat in the 1930s the only British-built schooners with geared windlasses were *James Postlethwaite*, *Cymric* and *Eilian*, although nearly all the ex-Dutchmen had them.

The 'you up and me down' windlass had a sharp jerky motion that tended to take the 'puff' out of the crew; it was impossible to sing shanties to lighten the load, even if the crews of the schooners had been addicted to singing them, nor was it possible to 'sing out' as one gathers they did in the days of the handspikes. Had it not been for the fact that it

Figure 6-1
Typical windlass

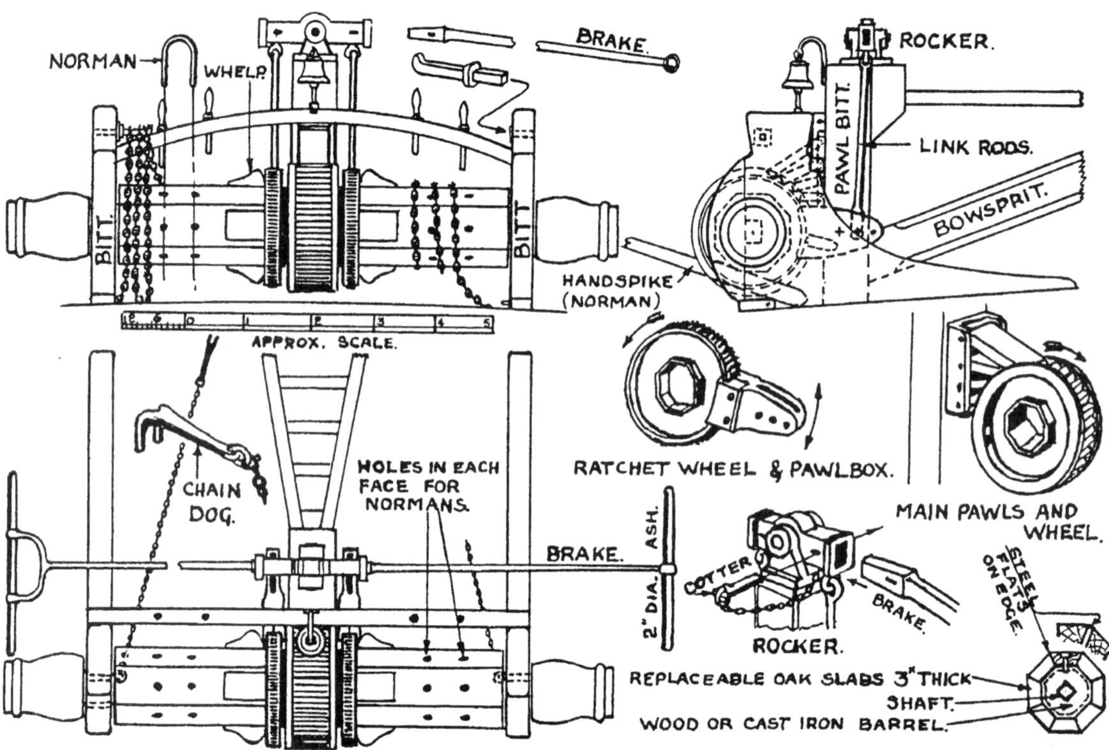

was impossible for other reasons to work it for any length of time without having to stop, it would have been considered as bad as continuous pumping, even though the actual force required to pull the brakes[1] down was quite light. The hawse pipes in schooners were invariably too close together in the bows. Where they were completely above deck level, the builders had no option but to keep them as they were so that the vessel would ride as near head to the wind as possible, but in the kind that started below deck and passed diagonally upwards, the inboard ends could have been splayed out with great advantage. What invariably happened was that as the chain was hove in it crawled slowly inwards along the windlass barrel and finally climbed partly up the whelps, where it skidded and slipped and tended to lock itself. This could be averted for a time by the mate giving the chain an occasional sideways jerk as it came off the barrel or by pulling diagonally outwards with a chain hook, as was done by the ship's boys in the past.[2] In the end, however, there was nothing for it but to stop work, dog the chain and fleet the turns back out towards the bitts.

An occupational hazard with the windlass in *Brooklands* arose because she had a pair of odd brakes, one of which was too long, and that, after years of rust and chipping hammers, their ends were such a rattling good fit in the sockets that the forward end of the wooden cross handle hit the rail before the end of the stroke. Fingers had to be kept out of the way if at all possible – failure to do so was inclined to make the nose red!

With two anchors down, one chain was dogged while the other was being hove in, the turns around the barrel being hung up loosely on the side not in use, as shown in Figure 6-1. If any length of chain had been paid out the frequent stoppages made it a long-winded job to raise the anchors; moreover, if they had managed to get foul of each other on the way down, or through swinging around, the job could sometimes take hours.

The motor winch was introduced to speed up the loading and discharging of cargo, but human ingenuity soon managed to contrive ways in which it could be harnessed to help with other jobs as well. One of them was weighing the anchors. The *Waterwitch, Mary Barrow, Alert, Donald & Doris, Irish Minstrel* and possibly some other vessels had a crank-

[1] Brake: An old-English word for a lever, which was last used in its original sense aboard small sailing vessels. The present meaning of something to arrest the movement of something or another obviously came via the farm cart.

[2] See *The Log of a Sea Waif* by Frank T. Bullen.

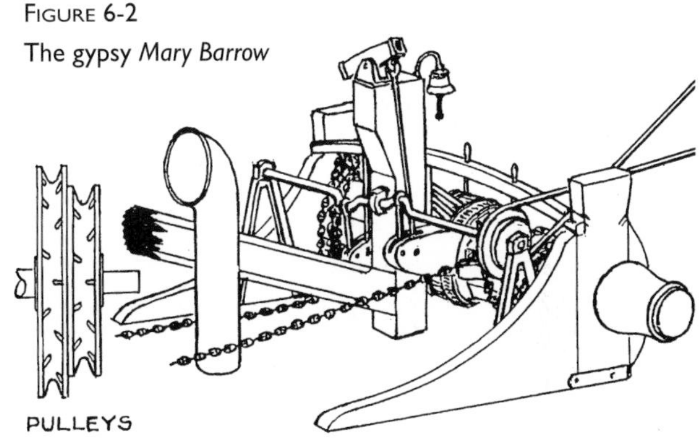

FIGURE 6-2
The gypsy *Mary Barrow*

shaft fitted on the forward side of the pawl-bitt, driven by a rope from the winch, the two cranks of which were connected to the pawl boxes by another pair of link rods in the forward set of holes[Figure 6-2]. If the brakes were being used the crankshaft wobbled backwards and forwards through half a revolution; if the crankshaft was in use the rocker danced its accompaniment. The pulley was in line with another pulley, which could be fitted to one side of the winch in place of the warping drum, and as it did not matter in which direction the crankshaft revolved, the driving rope could be arranged as fancied. The two cast-iron pulleys had a vee-shaped groove capable of taking a rope between 3in and 4in in circumference and, to give better grip, shallow ribs were cast down the groove on alternate sides. In *Alert* Frank always referred to this contrivance as 'the gypsy', and for many years I was under the impression that this was due to a fancied resemblance between these pulleys and the chain gypsy of a modern windlass. However, quite recently I discovered that North American schooners frequently had a shaft known as the gypsy, across the after end of the fo'c'sle head, with a drum at each end. This was driven from the winch in the deckhouse below[3] and could be used for warping in docks and hauling up (or down) the huge sails which these vessels set on their interminable jib-booms. In the light of this, it would seem that the expression could have been a souvenir from Frank's bootlegging adventures in the days of Prohibition. The 'gypsy' did nothing to stop the chain from riding up the whelps or locking its turns, so that one of the crew had to stand by to stop the winch when the mate let out a yell from forward. In *Alert* we managed to break the crankshaft while trying to heave up the anchor, which was foul of *Indefatigable*'s moorings and, for the rest of the passage, we resorted to what was probably the most widely used method of all.

About halfway from the mainmast to the stern, or abreast

[3] *Blue Water Coaster* by Francis E. Bowker, International Marine Publishing, Camden, Maine, 1972.

FIGURE 6-3
Anchors

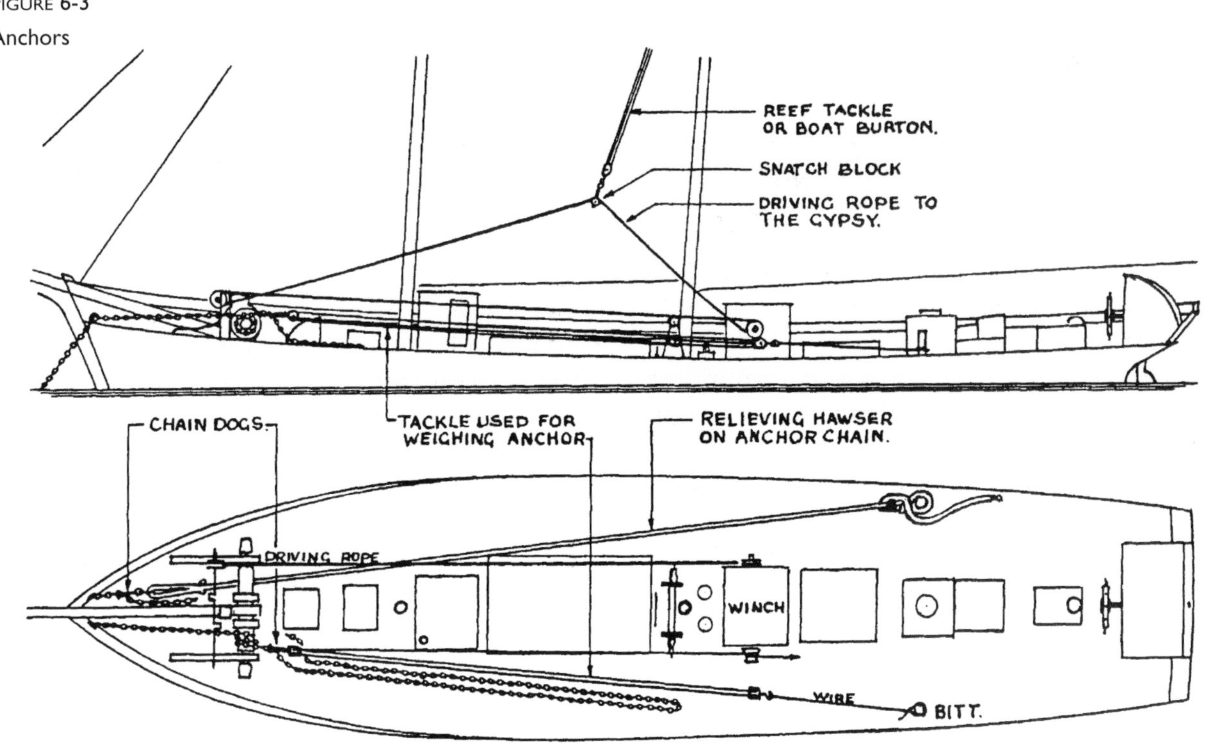

Flying Foam under full sail.

PHOTOGRAPHER UNKNOWN TERRY BELT COLLECTION

of the mizzenmast in a three-master, were a pair of heavy wooden bitts or cast-iron bollards, one on either side, which were firmly bedded into the deck beams or bolted to the cover planks. The original purpose of these fittings was to take the strain of the anchor chain off the windlass in times of extreme stress, and to provide a certain amount of elasticity to reduce the violence of the jerks on the anchor. This was done by using the heaviest ropes on board as springs, with one end made fast on the bollard aft and the other passing below the windlass barrel to a dog on the chain, as far forward as possible. In order to provide a straight pull from the bollards, the size of the forehatch, in those vessels that had one, was deliberately limited – one place at least where it had nothing to do with carrying guns! It was the motor winch that enabled these bitts and bollards to be pressed into use for weighing the anchors.

A heavy fourfold tackle was rove off with a long length of rope and a dog was removed from its chain and shackled to one of the blocks [Figure 6-3] – which block was used depended upon where the winch was situated. The standing block was made fast to the bollard and the dog was taken forward and clamped on to the chain coming off the windlass barrel. The fall was taken to the winch drum and, when the tackle came back two blocks, the dog was seized by all hands

and fleeted back along the chain for the next 'snatch'. Because the pull was diagonally outwards, there was no tendency for the chain to ride up the whelps. The windlass barrel flew around at a rate of knots, the pawls clanked like machine guns and, in spite of the crew having to heave like heroes to fleet the tackle back, the whole job could be done in half the time. One of the sources of the famous handiness of *Fanny Crossfield* was that her motor winch was just forward of the mizzenmast so that an extra long pull could be taken at her cables, with the tackle working in the five-fold direction.

The practice of using relieving hawsers on the anchor chains, as mentioned above, seems to have died a natural death in the second half of the 19th century mainly, one suspects, on account of the size which the sailing vessel had reached. It was realised that a heavier chain than was legally necessary, hanging in the long bight of a catenery, had much the same effect of damping down the jerks on the anchor. Quite a lot of the schooners had at least some of their anchor chain heavier than requirements, the general belief being summed up by the old saying that 'a light anchor on a heavy chain was a much better form of insurance than a heavy anchor on a light one'.

One schooner that did not go in for heavy chain was *Flying Foam*. While *Alert* was lying in the Sloyne we had one of our bowsprit shrouds broken by an over-enthusiastic tug, causing Frank to go rooting in his lockers for something with which to effect a repair. He came up with a length of rusty chain, which he looked at without enthusiasm and remarked that it wasn't up to much but was probably good enough for the first fifteen fathoms in *Flying Foam*. On a later occasion he passed another similar comment. At the time I thought he was laying it on a bit, but less than two years later he was proved right. In January 1936, bound south out of the River Mersey, *Flying Foam* was caught in a gale off the north Welsh coast and, being unable to reach Holyhead, made a lee under the east coast of Anglesey. Being rather low-lying, the island is not a particularly efficient windbreak. The gale rose rapidly to its full fury and the schooner started to drag. As she got further from the land she began to pitch, one of her chains parted and she dragged the other anchor all the way to Llandudno, where she went ashore and became a total loss [Figure 6-4]. According to a newspaper article at the time, the crew was taken off by the Beaumaris lifeboat and there was a young woman aboard who had a half-share in the vessel and who, despite the fact that she had been wrecked before, would not be satisfied, as the paper said, until she was once more aboard some vessel 'bounding to meet the ocean billows'. Whether the poor woman actually said all this, and a lot of other nonsense that was attributed to her, is rather doubtful. I have a feeling that, like most of her sex aboard ship in those days, she was there in pursuit of that rare and elusive commodity that is said to make the world go around!

FIGURE 6-4

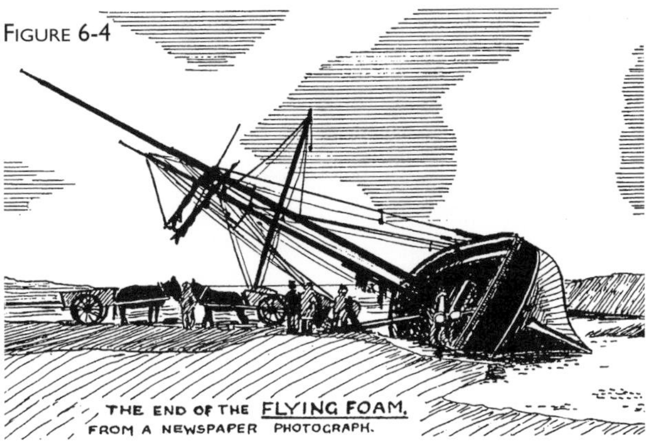

Anchors were usually left at the hawse pipes until the vessel was well outside, after which they were fished and catted. The fishing was done with a hook on the end of a chain or wire, which, either before or after hooking the catch, had to be passed below the inner bowsprit shroud or the back rope of the dolphin striker. The end was then taken to a tackle called a 'burton' [Figure 6-5] and, as the crew hauled the anchor up to the cathead, the mate paid out the chain over the windlass barrel. When the shackle of the anchor was up to the cathead the ring stopper was passed through it and made fast. The cotter of *Alert*'s ring stopper was on the end of a long chain, which passed through a hole in the shank of the cathead [Figure 6-6].

As mentioned in Chapter VI, one of the crew climbed outboard and stood on the stock of the anchor. Frank allowed a length of chain to dangle over the side and then swung it forward as though he was heaving the lead. The chain hit the inner bowsprit shroud, the end swung upwards and the cotter was fielded by the man on the anchor who passed it through the ring and sent it back again by the same method. When received by the mate, the cotter was popped into its slot and the catch shut.

The anchor was then on a double purchase of chain and, because of this and the fact that a burton, although a powerful tackle, had only a short hoist, it took two snatches to get the anchor to the cathead. The chain was blackwall hitched to the hook of the burton and, when it came up two blocks, Frank slid in the catch plate and shouted, 'Come up'. Used in this particular context the phrase meant, 'Let the fall of the tackle come up'. The hook was hauled down, the chain re-hitched and the second installment brought the ring to the cathead.

Once more we came up on the burton and hooked it into

Flying Foam the foredeck showing 'Armstrong's patent' windlass in use.

PHOTOGRAPH BY ALEX HURST. DAVID CLEMENT COLLECTION

a strop on the shank of the anchor, hoisting it up until one fluke slid inboard over the rail. Another chain, the shank painter, was then passed a couple of times around the shank of the anchor and belayed on a heavy cleat inside the rail, and this was where, on most schooners, it was left. Frank, however, was not satisfied with this; he slackened off the shank painter a little and used the handspike to prise the fluke back outboard again so that it was resting against the billboard. When the anchor was next required, all he had to do was ease out the shank painter until the anchor was hanging vertically once more. It can be deduced from Frank's insistence on this, that at some time in his career he had come up against a set of circumstances in which even the short time spent in prizing the anchor fluke over the rail could have been put to a better use.

Many schooners in the 1930s had only one burton, although the full complement was three, and some of the better equipped three-masters that carried their boat on the after hatch, even had four. They hung by short wire pennants from eyebolts in the cheeks of the lower masts and, where only one was carried, it was to starboard of the foremast. It could be shifted across to deal with either anchor, or taken abaft the galley to lift the forward end of the boat, the after end in the more poverty-stricken vessels being lifted by the main reef tackle. Anchors in docks were considered a potential menace to other vessels and, if not left hanging at the hawse pipes, were hauled up out of the way.

In the 'economy' class schooner, the burton was used for the starboard anchor, while the fore throat halyard was unhooked from the gaff and brought forward around the mast to deal with the one on the port side. An indication of the crowded conditions, which at one time must have existed in many small docks, is given by the fact that most iron catheads were secured to the bulwarks by a hinged clamp, which could be removed if necessary to allow them to be swung inboard to a position in which they, too, could cause no damage. By the mid 1930s the iron cathead was almost universal, the older wooden type being confined to one or two vessels, which included *Waterwitch*, *M.A. James*, and *Minnie*. The *Brooklands* had her wooden catheads replaced by iron at the tail

end of the 1920s.

After the anchors had been catted, the last job forward before putting the windlass to bed was to heave the bobstay taut. A couple of turns were taken around the windlass barrel, the tripping line was let go, and the bobstay was hove in as tight as possible with all hands on one brake for the last heave. The chain end was then belayed around one of the staple-shaped normans, which was inserted in its holes for the purpose. The brakes were then unshipped and their iron shafts passed down between link rods and pawl-bitt, one on each side, so that the wooden handles rested on top of the ratchet wheels.

When approaching an anchorage both anchors were prepared for letting go. After lowering the anchors so that they were hanging vertically at the catheads with the shank painters removed, sufficient chain had to be thrown forward over each side of the windlass barrel to allow the turns to be ranged along the deck [Figures 6-6 and 6-7]. It will be noticed that there were three parts of the chain lying on top of the barrel on each side and two below it. It was to guard against any fouling of chains when the anchors were let go that the normans were used to separate these turns. The staple-shaped irons were inserted on top of the windlass barrel, straddling the middle pieces of chain, while underneath them a wooden handspike was placed between the two parts of chain and lifted at its after end to lock the barrel tight. When used for this function the handspike was also referred to as 'the Norman' and, as there was only one, it had to be shifted over

FIGURE 6-5
Fish tackle

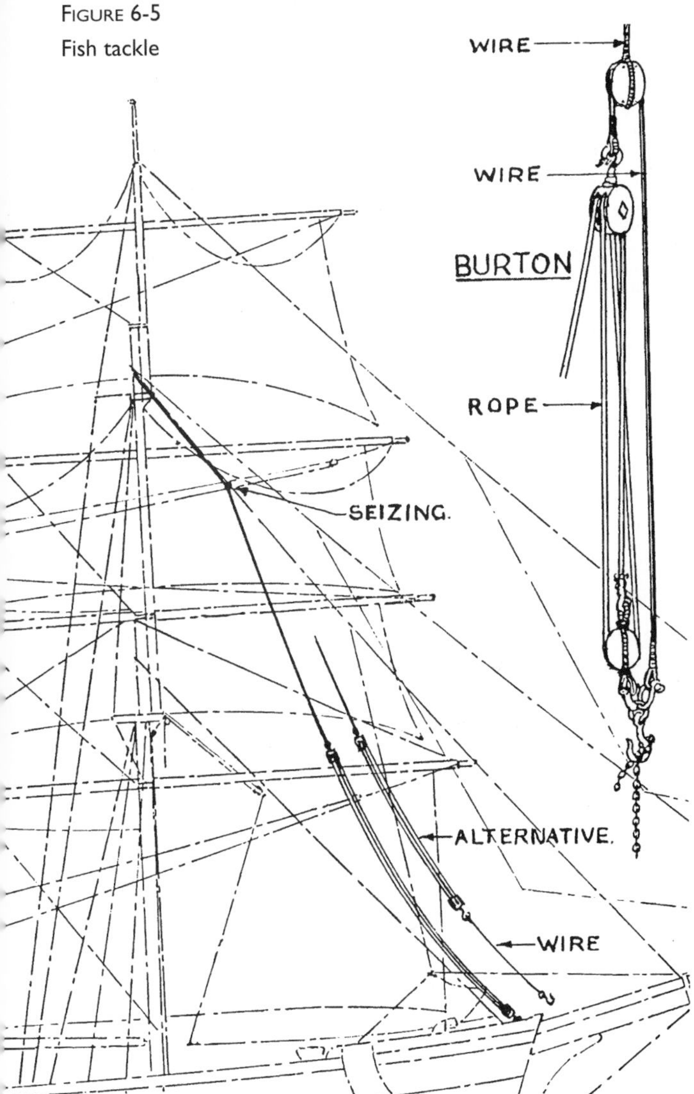

FIGURE 6-6
Cathead

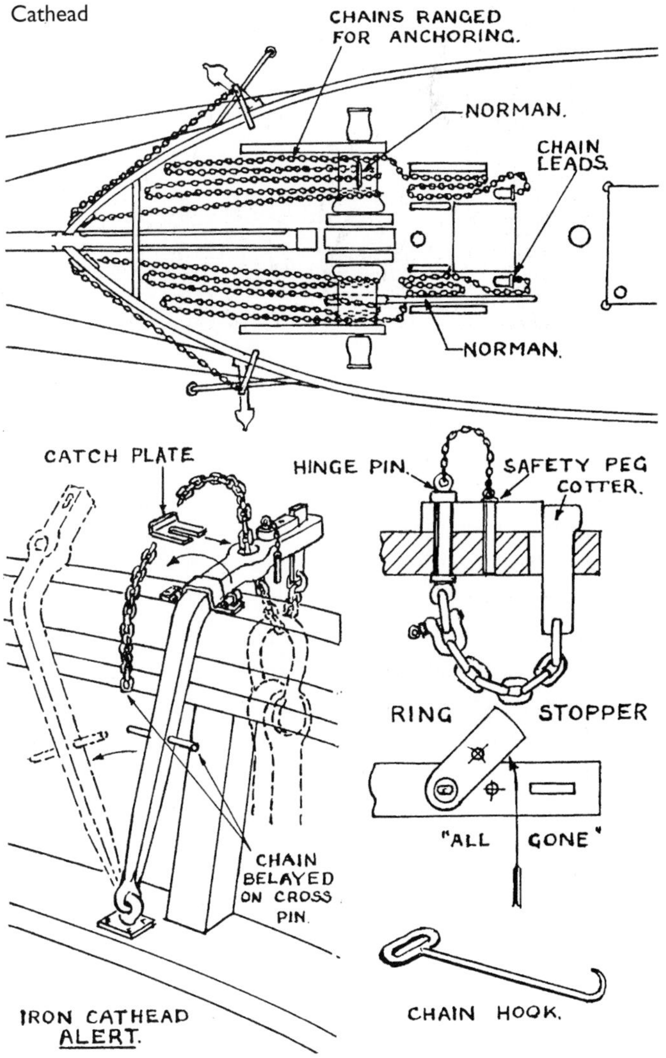

if the second anchor was to be let go. Various other things also had to be done. The jibsheets had to be removed from their pins, coiled down and dumped on the platform forward, and the staysail unshackled from its sheet horse and stowed out of the way. The bobstay had to be let go and tripped, if this had not already been done, and its inboard end hauled up and belayed on a pin to keep it in the top of the hawse pipe, well clear of the flying links of cable.

The two dogs on their chains, which normally lay forward of the bitts, had to be pulled out aft to a position well clear of the windlass. The handspike norman was inserted just before the anchor was let go, the mate removed the safety peg from the cathead and weighed up the speed of the vessel before finally knocking out the ring stopper catch. As the anchor went down there was a noisy and rather impressive clatter of flying chain – the lethal tendencies of which were only too apparent – and then, silence. The man or men not holding the norman immediately picked up the chain and flung the last turn forward over the windlass barrel, the other turn skidded out, and the process was repeated until the mate was satisfied.

FIGURE 6-7
Anchoring

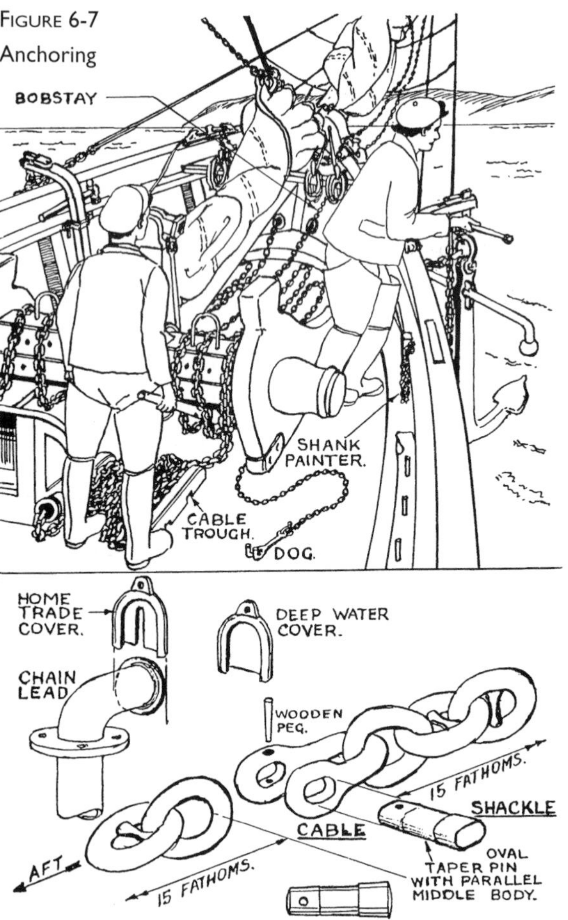

Chain lockers were normally in the forward end of the vessel, their presence in other parts being a fairly sure sign of a vessel originally intended for deep water. This was often confirmed by the possession of two sets of covers for the chain leads, one set for use in soundings and the other for when the chains were sent below [Figure 6-7]. The popularity of these separate chain lockers was due to the fact that they could be used to get the trim of the vessel if not exactly to the skipper's liking then at least to the nearest 15 fathoms of chain, which was no doubt highly satisfactory when the vessels concerned were in deep-water trades.

In the home trade they were something of a nuisance as the chains lying along the deck had to be secured to the ring bolts to prevent them finishing up in the lee scuppers in bad weather. They were also a potential cause of a fall during those hurried deck crossings when one watch was putting a schooner about, although, if he managed to avoid the chains, the careless 'Jack Tar' could still arrange to be tripped up by the wire horse on which the staysail sheet worked. Chain hooks were used to pull the anchor chains about in the normal working of the vessel but if a lot of it had to be hauled around the decks, as when it was being chipped and tarred, a hook on the end of a length of rope was used so that all hands could tail on.

The burton was the standard fish tackle for the anchors of schooners and ketches, but was not quite so suitable for brigantines and barquentines with their fully square-rigged foremasts. In these vessels both the forward boat burton and the fish tackle were hung from the fore topmast hounds but the former had to stay abaft the yards while the latter spent its life in front of them. The fish tackle was a fourfold one made of two heavy double blocks, and the wire pennant from which it hung was usually seized to the standing jib stay about 8ft or 10ft below the topmast hounds [Figure 6-5]. When not in use, the lower block was hooked into an eye in the knightheads just forward of the forestay and the tackle was allowed to hang loose, as the sheets of the standing jib had to pass outside of it. The chain pennants of the jibsheets, however, could cause considerable wear to the rope of the tackle so that, in many vessels, while at sea, the lower block was hoisted aloft on the end of a length of wire, against which the offending sheets could chafe in vain.

With only one fish tackle it was not possible for a brigantine or barquentine to haul up both anchors in dock so they were left at the hawse pipes or capsized inboard over the rail. This set-up was more or less standard for all square-rigged vessels until increasing size caused it to be superseded by the crane on the fo'c'sle head. It remained on the small ships, however, until the end.

VII

DECK FITTINGS

The last schooner in possession of the traditional arrangement of deck gear was *Snowflake*. She had no motor winch, her galley was abaft the foremast, her dolly winch was before the mainmast, and her pumps, like those of all other schooners, were just abaft the mainmast. There were four places where her decks could be crossed, abaft the fo'c'sle and cabin companions and at either end of the after hatch. The crossing place forward and the one between the pumps and the after hatch were used by the crew when putting the vessel about, but with the arrival of the motor winch the latter one disappeared and the crossing had to be made over the hatch itself or around its after end.

Cargo

In the days when cargo was discharged by hand winches, the ketch had an advantage over the schooner in being able to use her cargo gaff on the mainmast, the right way around – ie. the jaws forward – whereas the schooner, in order to deal with the main hatch out of which the bulk of the cargo was removed, had to hoist her cargo gaff on the fore side of the mainmast. This meant passing the peak and throat halyards forward around the mast and using them in a position that gave rise to more wear and tear than the orthodox one [Figure 7-1]. The only builder who seems to have thought that something better could be done was William Thomas of Amlwch, who gave *Cymric* a dolly winch at the foot of her foremast as well as one for the main [Figure 7-2].

Those bent on installing a motor winch in a schooner were faced with the alternative of either putting it abaft the mainmast and leaving the galley in its traditional position or putting the galley abaft the mainmast and the winch in its place forward. This latter arrangement had the advantages that the cargo gaff could be used on the foremast while the galley was nearer the cabin where the food was actually consumed, but these bonuses were gained at the expense of putting the galley in the wettest part of the vessel. Sometimes a different shape of galley had to be specially constructed to suit the space available – in this new position the galley could not be tucked in close to the mast as it had been when forward, because of the pumps, so it had to be given two funnels, a short one, over which the main boom could pass, for use at sea and a longer version that gave a better draught but could only be used in harbour. The winch, if installed in the same position, had to have two exhaust pipes and, as it was not thought desirable to have the foot of the mainsail scorched or covered with general smuts, the short version of pipes was usually arranged to discharge sideways instead of upwards. In the *Waterwitch*, *Jane Banks*, *Donald & Doris* and *Kathleen & May* the prob-

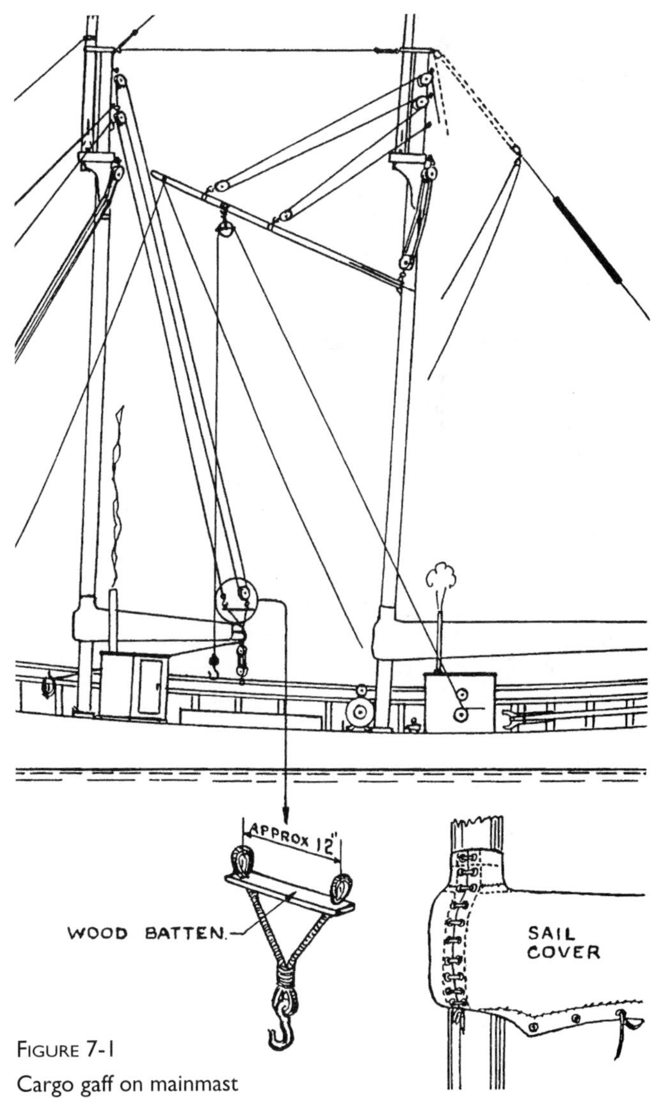

FIGURE 7-1
Cargo gaff on mainmast

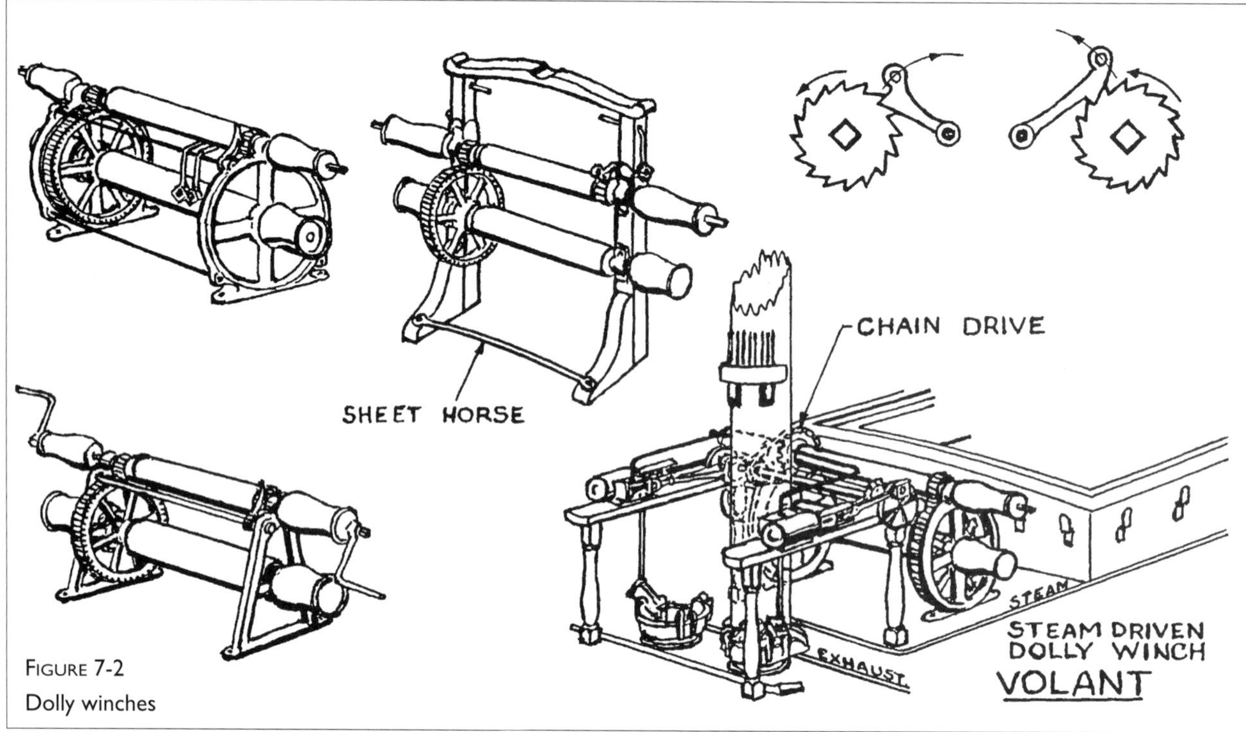

FIGURE 7-2
Dolly winches

lem was solved by leaving the galley where it was and putting the winch house on its after end, either as an extension or an appendage. This sometimes involved shifting the boat on to the after hatch, but many of the larger three-masters already carried it there. In *Alert* the winch was installed abaft the mainmast and the boat was moved forward on to the main hatch, but to get it to fit, a vee-shaped slot had to be cut in the after wall of the galley to accommodate its stem and this was covered on the inside by a trough of sheet metal.

The *Nellie Bywater* and the *J. & M. Garratt* seem to have made space to accommodate the winch abaft the foremast by transferring the cooking facilities below decks. But the most popular, as well as the most satisfactory, method was to move the galley into the space occupied by the water tank, and to provide alternative accommodation for the water in tanks of different shapes and sizes, located in different places. This was done in the ketches *Emily Barratt* and *Henrietta*, in the schooners *North Barrule* and *Ellie Park* and in the three-masters *Mary Miller*, *Mary Barrow*, *Ryelands* and *Gaelic*. It brought the galley as far aft as possible and, in a purely sailing vessel where they still ate in the cabin, it was a highly satisfactory arrangement. Not finding the smell of gas oil particularly appetising, those in auxiliary vessels had by this time, in many cases, taken to eating in the fo'c'sle.

The schooners still afloat in the 1930s had no problems in finding space to install a motor winch. The *Volant* and the *Lochranza Castle*, both owned in Northern Ireland, at some time in their careers had been fitted with steam winches, or rather with steam engines, which drove their dolly winches. The boiler was in the fo'c'sle and, when not in use, the funnel extension was removed and a cap put on it at deck level. The bottom sketch in Figure 7-2 gives some idea of what these winches were like – bearing in mind that after more than fifty years the memory is not always too reliable. I am not sure exactly what pattern of dolly winch *Volant* had, although *Lochranza Castle*'s was definitely the wooden-goal-post type, built as an integral part of the fife rail. The fife rails of both vessels frequently had ropes draped over them when in dock, so that I am unable to say whether the engines were fitted with reversing gear or, like most motor winches, they ran in one direction only. By some convention this was nearly always the same as for the dolly winches, the pawls of which dictated that the top shaft rotated clockwise and the main shaft anti-clockwise when looked at from the starboard side of the vessel. The men who worked a dolly winch stood abaft it facing forwards. These little steam engines had definitely been built to suit the fife rails and, on the face of it, Ulster would appear to be exactly the sort of heavily industrialised area where such a job could have been carried out; its steam tradition was strong. However, *Volant* still retained her original port of registry of Kirkwall, and the *Lochranza Castle* was still registered at Wick, and John Anderson[1] makes reference to yet another

[1] *Coastwise Sail* by John Anderson, Percival Marshall, London, 1934.

Emily Barratt rigged right down as a pole-masted ketch showing her deck layout. Previously she had been a topsail schooner and then a topmast ketch.

PHOTOGRAPHER UNKNOWN. TERRY BELT COLLECTION

vessel, the *Tresness of Kirkwall*, which had the same sort of steam installation. Thus, it would appear that the honours for the job must go to these far northeastern parts.[2]

That the owners, well before the era of the internal combustion engine, should think it worthwhile to cope with the periodic surveys which boilers, as well as ships, must have to keep them fully classed, says much for the bustling, outward looking attitude of the Orcadians – not exactly unexpected from an area where the Norse blood still runs strong. It was surely a tradition to which the Ulstermen who took over these little vessels, were worthy successors.

Some motor winches could be started by getting into their cabin with them and swinging the flywheel. Where this could not be done, the winch was started rather like an outboard motor, by replacing one of the warping drums with a pulley, wrapping a rope around it and heaving away. This was how it was done in *Alert* and, even on such a trivial job, the same order of precedence was observed as when we sat down to meals. Chris, as the senior AB was always at the head of the rope, then Paddy, then myself. Frank officiated at the decom-

[2] Dan McDonald advised me that Thurso was the likeliest place.

pression lever and, as the rope ran out, Chris would bawl out, 'End – Oh', so that we could brace ourselves against the wiles of Isaac Newton and at the same time let Frank know that it was time to shove the lever down. Sometimes it fired the first time. The clutch was operated from either side by a bar, which could be pushed in or out so that the shaft could be disengaged leaving the engine still running.

Three men were required to work a cargo gaff, one on the winch and two on the ropes fastened to the gaff end to swing it inboard or out as necessary. The man ashore usually had the job of tipping, so the winch man had only to hold the turns of wire on the drum whilst this was being done. When discharging ballast in *Brooklands*, Christy used to hitch the wire on the drum [Figure 7-3] before shoving the skip to the side and releasing the catch, while Tom, who controlled the gaff, timed his moves to let the rolling of the vessel assist in swinging the gaff in or out. The hitch shown is safe enough when used with rope but with wire it is inclined to be risky. The only reason that it worked in the application shown was that the wall of the winch house prevented it from unwinding itself. When working the main hatch the foresail, with its boom and gaff, had to be swung out of the way. In docks the sail covers were put on the fore and afters to prevent the all-pervading coal dust from making them even dirtier than they already were. If the cargo gaff was on the mainmast [Figure 7-1] the forepeak halyard was used to support the fore boom by means of a triangular gadget (as shown on the drawing) made of thimbles, served wire and a wooden batten, into which the hooks of the halyard blocks could be slipped. If the cargo gaff was on the foremast [Figure 7-3] the fore topping lift was used to support the boom instead. Figure 7-3 also shows how the main peak and throat halyards of a schooner or ketch were disposed of while the cover was on the sail. Bands of canvas with an eye in each end – in the more impoverished vessels, short lengths of rope – were passed under the boom and the blocks were hooked into them. If the canvas bands were white and clean they made a nice contrast to the green waterproof-canvas of the cover but, like the sails themselves, the frequent coal cargoes gave them little chance to remain clean for very long.

FIGURE 7-3 Cargo lift on mainmast

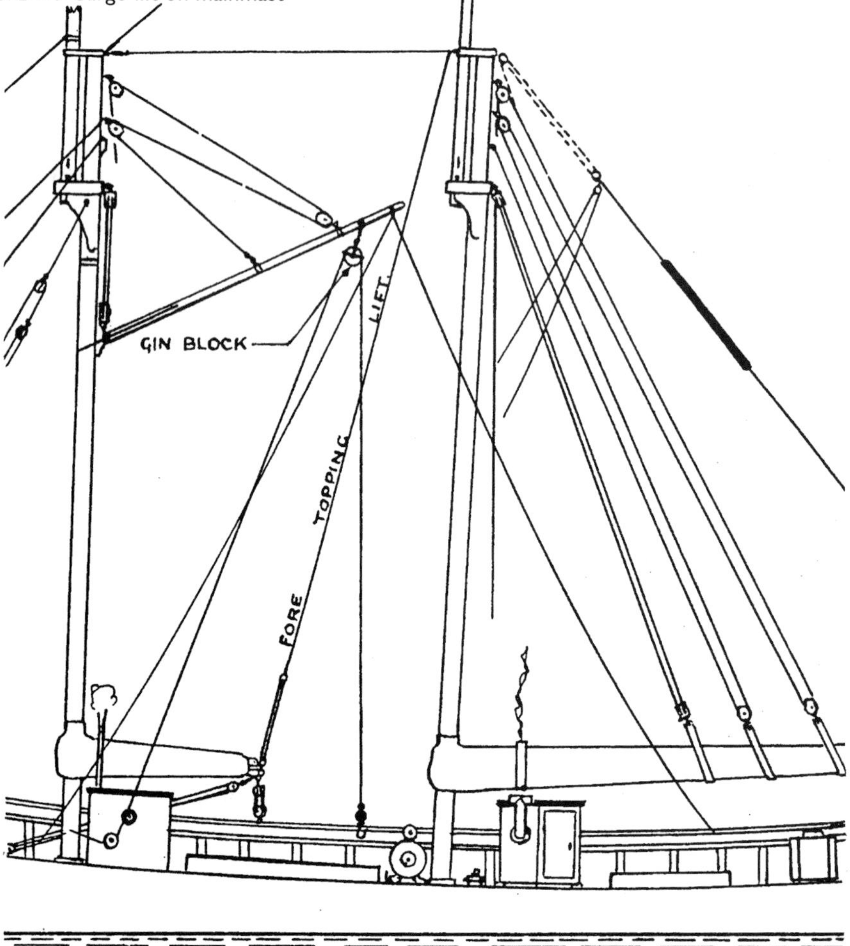

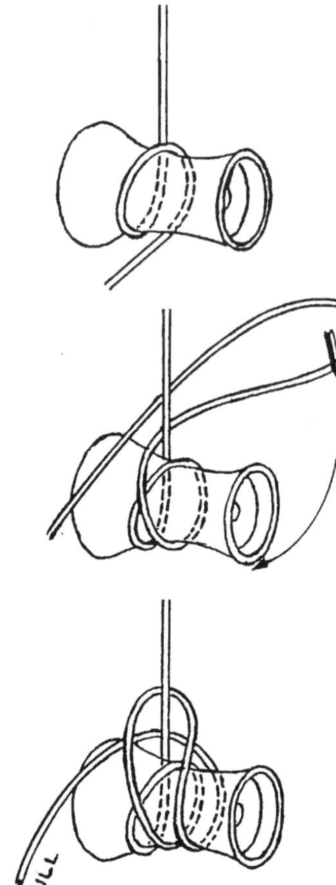

HITCH ON WINCH DRUM

Earl Cairns showing her deck layout and carving on her stern. This was prior to her having a motor installed.

THE PHOTOGRAPHER IS UNKNOWN DAVID CLEMENT COLLECTION

Ketches and schooners usually had only one cargo gaff, as befitted a vessel with only one dolly winch, although *Nellie Bywater* had two, as had most of the three-masters. When not in use they were hung in the bulwarks abaft the main rigging, secured to rings under the pinrails and in the bulwark stanchions, with their jaws forward. Like the average schooner's fore gaff they did not have wire spans on them but a couple of iron bands with rings to take the hooks of the peak-halyard blocks. From the foregoing account, one would have expected that a schooner, which used her cargo gaff on the foremast, would have possessed two anchor burtons. In fact both the *Mary Sinclair* and *Brooklands*, which were in this category, had only one each, while the *Alert*, which used hers on the main, had two.

Many schooners in the past seem to have had no cargo gaffs at all. Instead they hoisted the gin block by a halyard from each mast so that it hung over the middle of the hatch [Figure 7-4]. This would appear to be a satisfactory enough method provided the horizontal distance through which the load had to be swung was reasonably short, as when discharging into a cart alongside or on the edge of the quay. I have to thank another Society of Nautical Research member, Terry Belt, for producing so many photographs of vessels with this kind of cargo gear as to arouse a suspicion that perhaps this was the one that was normally used with the 'jump'.

Mention has been made of *Cymric*. She and her sistership *Gaelic* and the slightly smaller *Eilian* were the last survivors from William Thomas's yard. Like most iron vessels they just would not wear out. Underneath all their blarney and their 'Come day, go day' attitude, the Irish schooner owners were hard-headed businessmen who recognised good vessels when they saw them; they managed to lay their hands on the first two mentioned above, as well as collecting up as many of the ex-Dutchmen as they could. These Amlwch-built vessels were impressive. They were slightly bigger and better fitted out than the products of most other yards – the exception that immediately springs to mind being Paul Rodgers of Carrickfergus. Perhaps it was this indefinable 'something' which caused the owners of *Gaelic* to fit her with two motor winches or perhaps it was merely good business sense to get a quicker turnaround but, whatever the reason, to the best of my knowledge she was the only schooner so equipped.

Figure 7-5 shows a typical deckgear layout for a small three-master. If the mizzenmast, its dolly winch and its chainplates were removed it would stand for a two-master as well, except

FIGURE 7-4
Gin block on two halyards

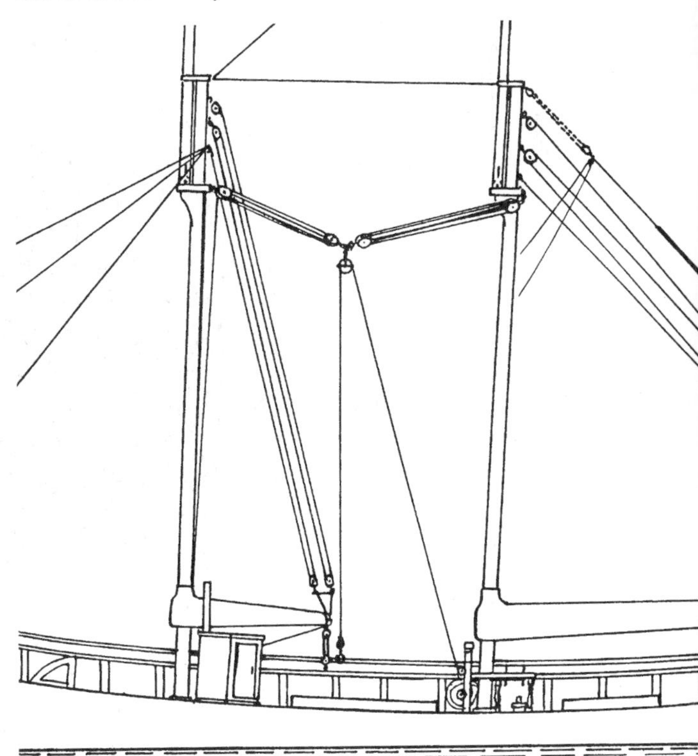

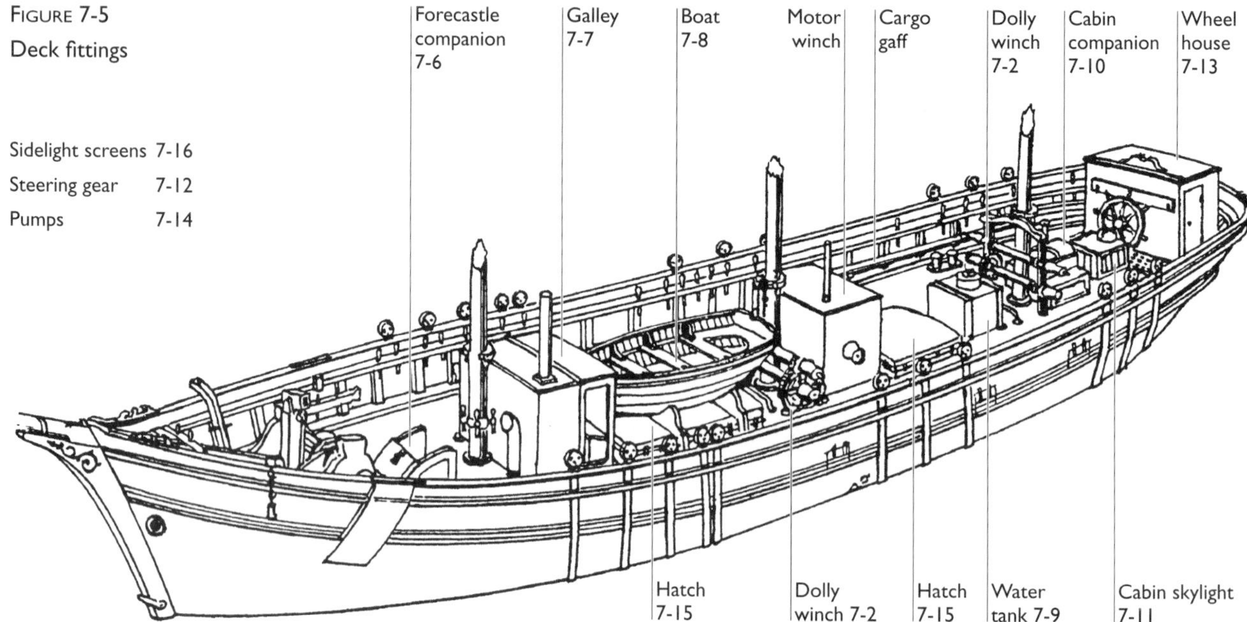

FIGURE 7-5
Deck fittings

that the bar across the top of the wheelhouse would have had three crutch positions for the boom. These were provided to meet the difficulty of pulling it to the centre of the vessel by the use of the sheet alone.

Painting Schemes

Since this chapter cannot help being little more than a long catalogue of the various pieces of equipment, it is probably as good a place as any to dispose of the question of the colours in which fittings were painted, and on which there was some degree of uniformity amongst the vessels. The popular colours were black and white, cobalt blue, a bright mid-green, light yellow ochre (known to seamen as 'mast colour' and to the landsman of yesteryear as light stone, or buff), a deeper shade of the same (hereafter referred to as deep stone), and a warm brown that was like a mixture of Indian red and burnt sienna. It was definitely nothing like the dull 'gravy brown' of which the Victorians were so fond.

If the platform in the bows was a planked-up area forward of a bar across the bowsprit it was with this brown that it was usually painted while the inboard part of the bowsprit and the pawl bitts were in mast colour. Catheads, fairleads and all ironwork on the windlass, the winches and about the decks, were painted green, although some vessels favoured black. Ironwork aloft and on the bowsprit was invariably black. If the platform was based on two bars running forward from the pawl-bitt, both it and the arched beam across the windlass, which usually accompanied it, were painted white. The working barrels of the windlass were tarred; the bitts were either brown or deep stone, whilst the warping drums were mast colour as a contrast. The inside of the bulwarks was painted white, the topgallant rail brown as far as the foremast or to the point where it gave way to the heavy solid timber topgallant bulwark which extended through to the knightheads; this was black varnished on top, but the tops of the knightheads themselves were painted white. Covering boards were mostly blue, occasionally deep stone. Deadeyes inside the rail were white, those on top of it, black, and in either case the iron strops were green. The heavy timbers in the stern were sometimes white like the rest of the bulwarks, but often mast colour or deep stone. Decks were painted with all sorts of peculiar compounds in an attempt to stop them rotting or to make them more watertight – one example was a mixture of tar and red lead boiled up together. Decks were never the beautiful holystone white of tradition.

Paint, however, was hardly plentiful in the hard times of the 1930s, and I am indebted to Dan McDonald for information on the colours used before the 1914-18 War and in the few years which followed it, while the vessels were still earning good money. Blue seems to have been the classic colour for cover planks, hatch coamings and mast coats, while the skirting boards of companions, wheelhouses and skylights were often painted in this colour as well. Out of sixty vessels upon which Dan made notes, forty conformed to this colour scheme for the first three items at least. Other colours used on the hatch coamings were red, green, brown and grey.

Topgallant rails, kevels, and the front of the main pinrail were often painted brown but, in smartly kept vessels like *Mary Miller*, *M.A. James*, and *Sunshine*, they were scraped and varnished.

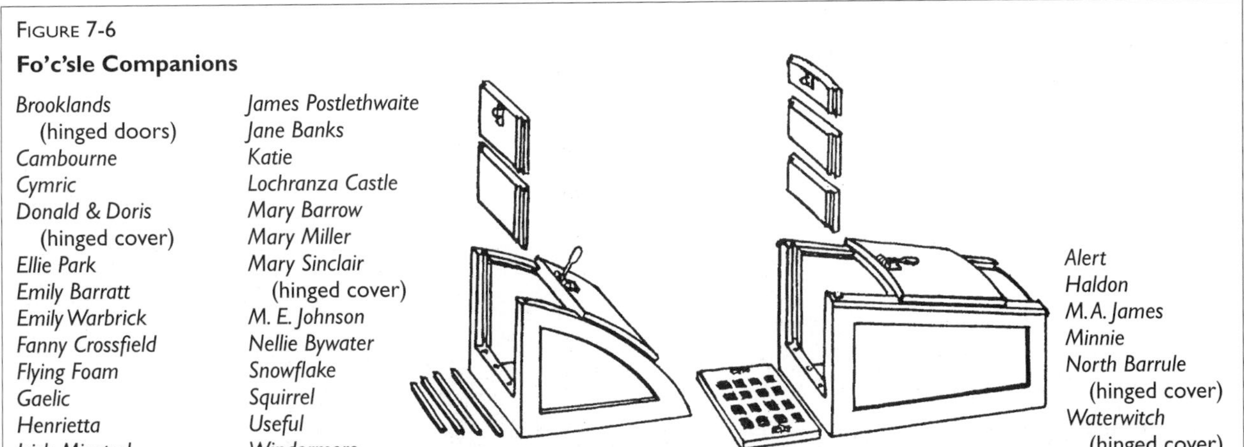

FIGURE 7-6
Fo'c'sle Companions

Brooklands (hinged doors)
Cambourne
Cymric
Donald & Doris (hinged cover)
Ellie Park
Emily Barratt
Emily Warbrick
Fanny Crossfield
Flying Foam
Gaelic
Henrietta
Irish Minstrel
James Postlethwaite
Jane Banks
Katie
Lochranza Castle
Mary Barrow
Mary Miller
Mary Sinclair (hinged cover)
M. E. Johnson
Nellie Bywater
Snowflake
Squirrel
Useful
Windermere

Alert
Haldon
M.A. James
Minnie
North Barrule (hinged cover)
Waterwitch (hinged cover)

White was almost universal for the insides of the bulwarks; the only exceptions Dan noted were in iron and steel vessels, four auxiliary schooners in which they were painted various shades of brown and the *Naiad* in which they were a pale green. There was formerly much more decoration, both carved and painted in the flat, on the outsides of the bulwarks. Both *Earl Cairns* and *Ryelands* had heraldic shields and scrollwork on their counters, and many vessels had a carved arch of rope work across it. *Volant* and *Pet* had carved fashion pieces in the quarters of their bulwarks butting on to the transom[3].

Wheel coats painted with scrolls, laurel wreaths, crossed flags and similar devices were very much in evidence, these decorations being also used on skylight tops.

Fo'c'sle Companion

Figure 7-6 shows the two basic shapes of the fo'c'sle companion. In a smart vessel the sides were white with the beading picked out in green, while the scuttle and slides were done in mast colour and deep stone. The loose sliding pieces of wood were used as washboards, the top one being left out to provide ventilation, but where the after end was fitted with doors, circular metal ventilators were provided in the sides. Possibly in the prosperous days of the 19th century, fo'c'sle companions were provided with a teak grating to prevent wear to the deck, but by the 1930s this had degenerated into a number of hardwood battens nailed to the deck with copper nails.

The Galley

The galley [Figure 7-7] was a wooden box about 5ft square [1.52m] in which the cook worked sitting down. It was painted white, its roof black, and the iron strap and two bolts, which held it down to the deck, were green. The circular wooden blocks on which it rested and which kept it raised above the camber of the deck, were usually brown. Its equipment consisted of a coal stove, some lockers and a selection of cooking utensils.

Owing to the fact that doors opening sideways would have banged about as the vessel heeled and pitched, the oven door, the fire door and the ash pit door all opened downwards in a fore-and-aft direction. The stovetop was fitted with fiddles to stop the pans from throwing themselves overboard. The cook's duties included replenishing his bunker from the peaks in the fo'c'sle, into which the crew deposited surplus coal from the cargo. If there was too much surplus it sometimes found its way into the dock, usually in the evening after everybody had gone home. The *Mary Sinclair* towed out from Runcorn on one trip with lumps of coal stacked neatly all over her decks although, of course, she was not below her marks. Doubtless she managed to dispose of it down at Rock Ferry before putting out to the deep. All other activities in the galley are best discussed under the chapter on Food.

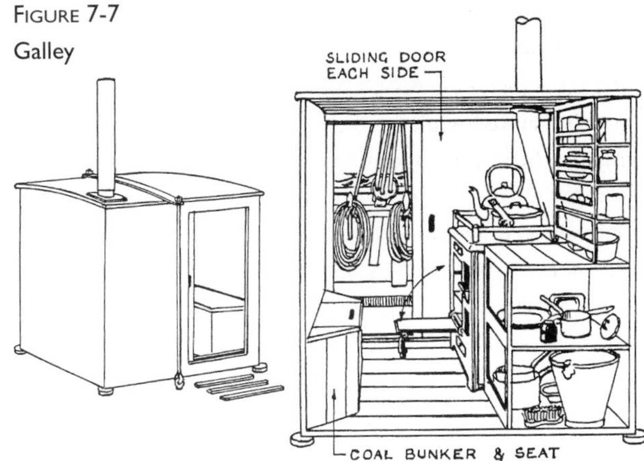

FIGURE 7-7
Galley

[3] Douglas Bennet describes the colour scheme and heraldic devices on the stern of *Brooklands* in Chapter IV.

Boats

Schooners' boats were usually between 14ft and 18ft [4.27m and 5.49m] long, with sternsheets and four thwarts, the one in the bows being rather short. Their equipment consisted of a painter, a set of gripes, two skids, chocks, a pair of rowlocks and three oars; the one for sculling being longer than the others. The boat was usually painted white, sometimes with the bottom in black, while the sheerstrake and rubbing bands were picked out in contrasting shades of brown and stone. Some boats were painted the same blue as was used on the covering boards. All boat gripes were fitted with slip hooks so that, in an emergency, a quick stroke with anything available would release each gripe, leaving the boat free to float provided, of course, her occupants could get her out from beneath the boom.

Another piece of information from Dan McDonald is that in former days most of the larger three-masters had more than one boat and that, in many of the West Country vessels, they were nicely modelled, carvel built and often fitted with a centreplate for sailing. By the mid 1930s the possession of more than one boat had become a peculiarity that seemed to follow in the wake of Captain Mørtensen and, on one occasion, the writer came across the *Mary Barrow* with no less than three! [Figure 7-8].

Before lifting the boat with the burtons, the skids were placed overside and their lanyards made fast to the pinrail. It required a good shove to get the boat's bilge clear of the rail and the general philosophy was rapidly to impart sufficient 'come-uppance' to the tackles at the end of the swing to stop it from returning inboard. After this it could be eased outwards and downwards in easy stages until it hit the water. For this reason a number of the larger vessels, whose boats tended to be on the unwieldy side, finally went in for a pair of davits. The burtons were used to extract the boat from below the boom and to dump it on the sidedeck, from which position it could be picked up by the davits' tackles and shoved outboard, one end at a time, in the normal manner.

FIGURE 7-8
Boat and sidelight

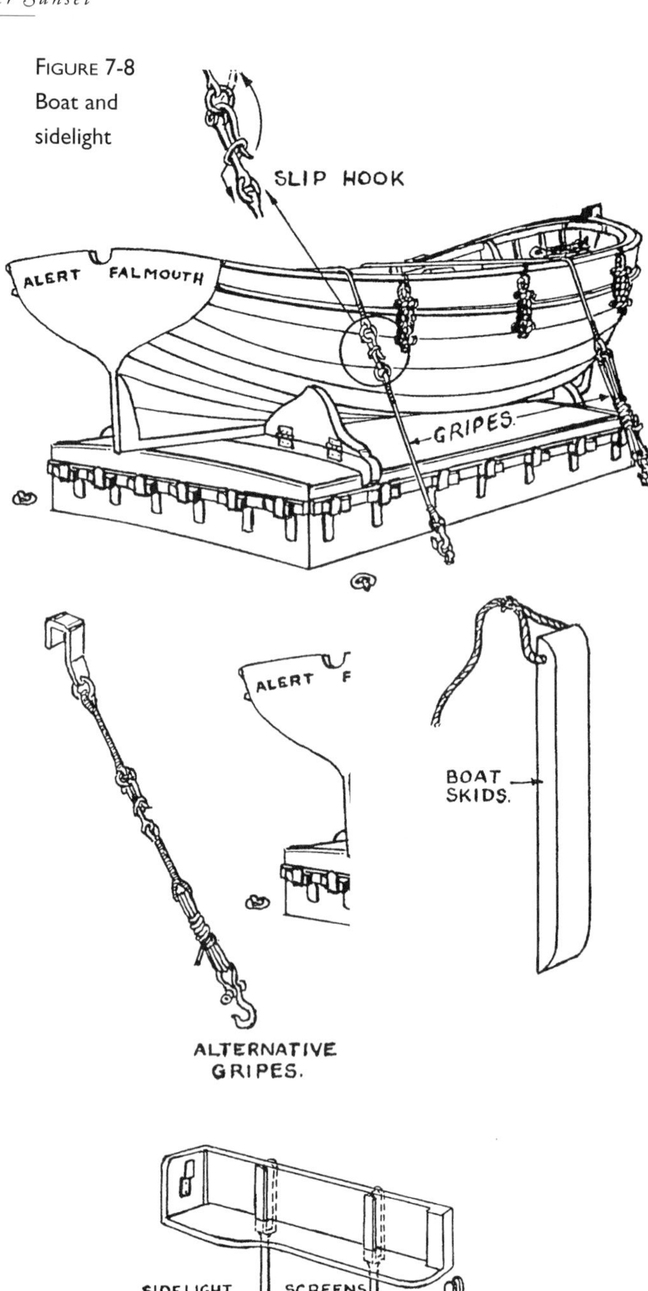

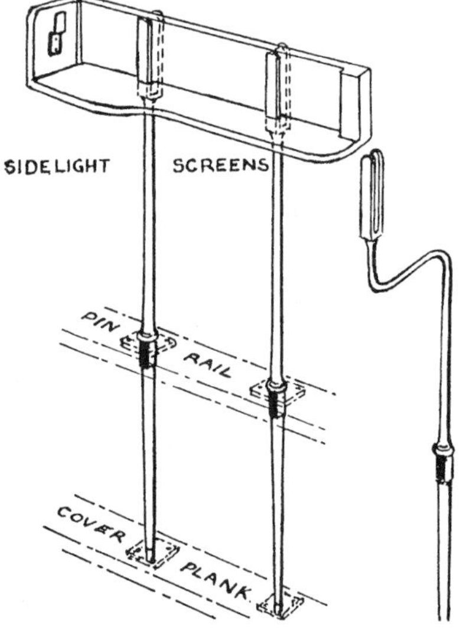

Sidelights

The stanchions for the sidelight screens [Figure 7-8] were painted green, the paint on the starboard screen itself being usually a shade lighter than that used on the ironwork. Some sidelight screens had cranked stanchions to get them further outboard so that there was less chance of their being screened from ahead by any of the sails. A lanyard was usually fastened to the wooden screen, as well as one on the lamp, to prevent either of them from floating away.

Dolly Winches

The dolly winches [Figure 7-2] had green or black ironwork,

while the wooden parts, the barrels and warping drums, were done in brown and contrasting shades of stone. Where the frame of the wooden-goal-post type was made of teak or mahogany it was usually varnished. If a dolly winch had cast-iron drums on the ends of the main barrel, they were painted in the same way as those on the motor winch – the drum black and the end white with a green rim with, sometimes, a spot of red on the boss. The days when the dolly winches were of primary importance to these small vessels ended when the motor winch took over, but they were certainly handy for use with the reef tackles, enabling two men to becket the wheel and take a roll in a sail without having to call out the watch below. They were also useful for warping in docks.

Water Tanks

The standard position for the schooner's water tank was between the after hatch and the cabin companion or mizzen-mast. The ketch also carried the tank aft, near the galley. Made of galvanised steel, these tanks, once on the market, must have rapidly replaced the barrels that had formerly been the only containers available and which could be seen in old photographs sitting on stillages in the same position. Like the galley the water tank was supported above the camber of the deck by blocks of wood beneath its corners and was held down by cross straps and bolts in much the same manner. These latter fittings were treated as ironwork, in the matter of paint, but the tank itself could be any colour the crew fancied.

Some tanks had large openings in the top, some had small ones but all had a dipper of some kind on the end of a lanyard made fast to the underside of the cover. In the ex-deep-watermen, the dipper was a pint measure so that the crew could have their allowance ladled out to them in accordance with 'The Act', 'contrary' to which, so the old song said, nothing was ever done in a 'limejuice' vessel. The capacity of the tank depended on the number of men in the crew, and varied from about 100 to 150 gallons [379-568 litres]. Figure 7-9 shows a typical tank about 3ft square [0.91m] by 2ft 6in [0.76m] high.

FIGURE 7-9
Water tanks

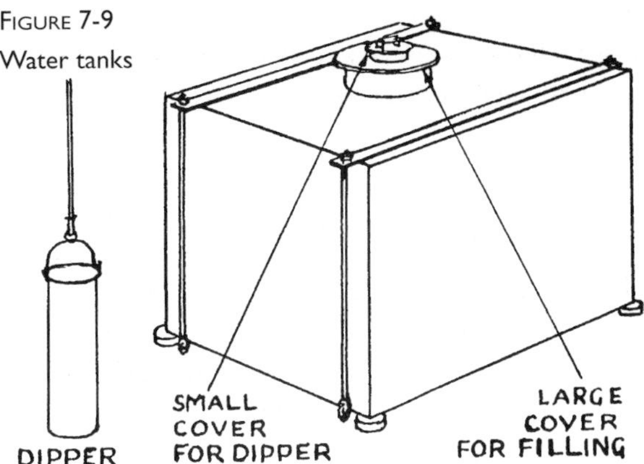

Cabin Companions

As will be seen from Figure 7-10 these were often much more ornate than the ones forward. They had to be rather higher and bigger as they gave access to a spiral stair, not a ladder, and they were more often found in varnished teak or mahogany than in oak. The 'thwartships type were space savers, as the stair turned only through a quarter of a circle, instead of a half, but they must at times have been a bit disconcerting to emerge from, when the vessel was on the port tack in a gale of wind. The spiral stair often had brass-cov-

FIGURE 7-10
Cabin companions

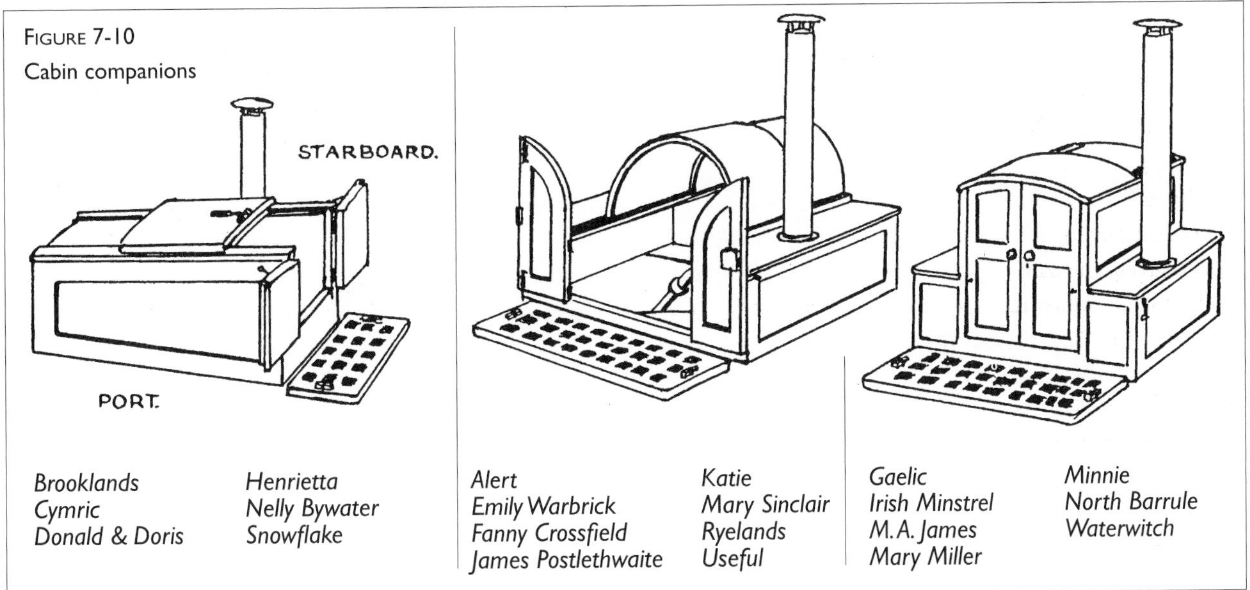

ered treads and nearly always a brass rail; there was usually a teak grating at the entrance and, through the companion to starboard, the stovepipe emerged into the light of day from the cast-iron Victorian fireplace below. All the fittings, the hinges, bolts, locks and so on were of brass.

Cabin Skylights

The typical schooner's skylight [Figure 7-11] was a rectangular box with a solid top and glass in the sides. It was difficult to say what sort of timber had been used as many were painted the usual mast colour, deep stone, brown combinations. The bars protecting the glass were nearly always of brass but many were painted green to avoid the trouble of keeping them polished. So, too, were the bells and the wheel brasswork in some vessels. In the early 1930s many schooners were in a terribly 'down-at-heel' condition, and it was only as their owners installed engines and were able to earn a little more and, finally, as the threat of war galvanised the stagnant industry of the country into life once more, that signs of pride in the appearance of these little vessels began to return.

Compass

This was either in the after end of the skylight or in a sort of binnacle on top of it and, in either case, was illuminated at night by the lamp in the forward end which also lit the cabin. Unlike the proper binnacle, there were none of the 'forlorn-hope' attempts on windy nights to get the lamps into their places without having them blown out, but the compass card

FIGURE 7-11 Cabin skylights

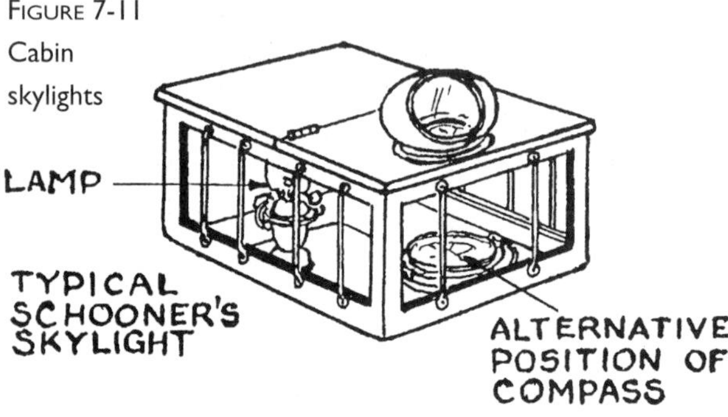

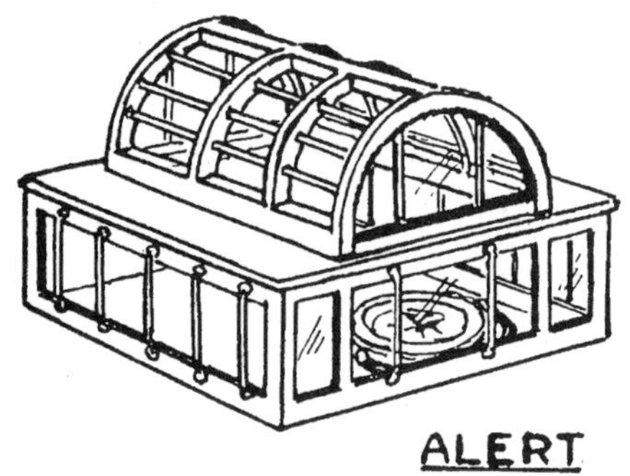

was a good 5ft to 6ft [approximately 2m] from the helmsman's eyes, the lamp had to be kept burning low to keep reflection from the glass to a minimum, and the other three sides of the skylight had to be fitted with a canvas cover at night to enable those on deck to see anything at all. The problem of 'glare' was never really solved – until electric light made it possible to direct a beam straight down on to the compass card – so that, having looked at the compass on a pitch black night, the helmsman had perforce to wait until his eyes became accustomed to the darkness once more, or to shut them in an attempt to accelerate the process.

The problem was aggravated in the odd vessel, such as the ketch *Henrietta* and the little schooner *North Barrule*, both of which had their skylight forward of the cabin companion so that the compass was about 6ft further forward as well! It was perhaps fortunate that in sailing vessels at least, steering by long tradition was seldom done by watching the compass alone – the wind, the sails, stars, lights and anything else available being used to check that the vessel was on her course. Nevertheless, the helmsman was given a compass course, since it was known, or suspected, that the gentlemen who conduct enquiries were not very partial to statements such as 'she was full and bye on the starboard tack at the time'.

Except in the odd cases, such as the *Volant* and *Brooklands*, which had binnacles, the schooner's compass invariably had glass in the top and the bottom, so that it acted as a telltale compass in the cabin as well. Unlike the majority of schooners, *Alert*, and no doubt her three sisterships also, had quite a fancy cabin skylight with curved glass in the top, built in varnished mahogany. The protecting bars were made of brass, but had been painted, although every other piece of brass in the vessel was kept polished. At night a tailored green waterproof-canvas jacket covered it with only a little square hole in the after end for the helmsman to look through and, as its extensive area of glass was considered a bit vulnerable, this was left on during the day in bad weather, making the cabin rather like the inside of an aquarium. The lamp that swung in this skylight was a big one, and it was far enough above the level of the compass for the helmsman to have few complaints.

Steering Gear

Those who, like the writer, learned the well-known rhyme on the Rule of the Road at sea prior to the year 1931, will probably admit to a tendency still to say, 'port your helm and show your red' – in 1931 it became 'starboard your helm'. The tiller, which had served the human race for thousands of years, was finally flung overboard and the wheel, which had been its rival for a hundred and more, at last came into its own. All finally was quite simple: the top of the wheel, the rudder and the ship's bows all went the same way. The people

Squirrel a decked trow seen in the docks at Bridgwater and showing clear details of her layout.

TERRY BELT COLLECTION

least impressed or troubled by the dawn of this new era were those in sailing vessels, who continued to put their helms 'up' or 'down' depending upon what they wished to achieve and the direction from which the wind was blowing. The last schooner to be steered by a tiller, the little *Ellen & Mary* of Dumfries, went to the breakers a few years later, leaving the wheel in full possession of the field.

There was nothing very sophisticated about the wheel steering of most schooners. It consisted of a wooden barrel, reinforced by iron bars, on to and off which a chain was wound, pulling the tiller on the rudder stock one way or the other. In the Irish Sea type of stern the chains came off and on to the top of the barrel while in the counter-sterned type, where the tiller was reversed, they came off the bottom. Everything was tight when the rudder was amidships but, as the wheel was put over, the chain became progressively slacker the further it went, until there was a good deal of play when it reached the limit of its travel. For this reason the middle of the chain had to be clamped to the barrel or it would have skidded around and lost the place. This slackness could have been removed by making the chain act on a quadrant on the rudder stock but, as schooners only had their helm hard over in stays

or when wearing around, the extra complication was evidently not considered worthwhile.

Quite a few counter-sterned schooners had worm steering of the single-screw, single-link-rod type – the simplest as well as the best available. It looked oddly one-sided, but the clearances of bearings, nut and rods could be kept to an absolute minimum so that when the vessel was on the wind, the helmsman could stand for hours only moving one spoke a small distance. Because of its odd appearance its works were usually kept concealed in a wheelhouse. In contrast, the double-screw, double-rod type, as favoured by the Thames barge and the Mersey and Weaver steam packet, was trying to reconcile straight line and circular movement from two directions and therefore needed quite large clearance in all bearings and pins or it would have locked itself solid after a couple of turns of the wheel. The problem could be reduced by having very long rods working on to a very short crosshead but it could never be eliminated completely and any vessel so fitted had a tendency to wander off course thanks to the play in the rudder.

This diversion into the mechanics of steering gear is necessary to explain why the Irish Sea-sterned vessels almost invariably stuck to their tiller and chains, although these could kick quite violently on occasion. The single-screw type of gear would have looked odd projecting out on one side only, whilst the double-screw type was obviously inferior to what they already had – primitive though it was, it was far less sloppy in its action when steering a straight course. A final note should be added for the benefit of the non-engineering reader. A double screw is a right-hand and left-hand screw working in tandem on the same shaft. A double-start screw is merely a means of increasing the pitch so that fewer turns are required to shift the wheel from hard over one way to hard over the other – at the expense, it may be added, of a greater effort on the part of the helmsman. Figure 7-12 shows the two popular types of gear in use aboard the schooners.

Wheelhouses

To produce the correct results with a right-handed single-screw type of steering gear, the tiller, or half crosshead, had to be on the port side of the rudder stock. This seems to be about the only likely reason for another practice that was so common it almost amounted to a tradition: the 'throne room' was nearly always on the starboard side of the wheelhouse [Figure 7-13]. Vessels with no wheelhouse, and there were quite a few, had a little hump-backed sentry box, usually in way of one of the masts. In a good many vessels its 'works' consisted of merely a bucket under a plank seat, partly filled with water, which was thrown overboard and replaced by the user.

In *Alert* there was an enamelled metal funnel below the seat, which passed down through the overhang of her counter

FIGURE 7-12
Steering gear

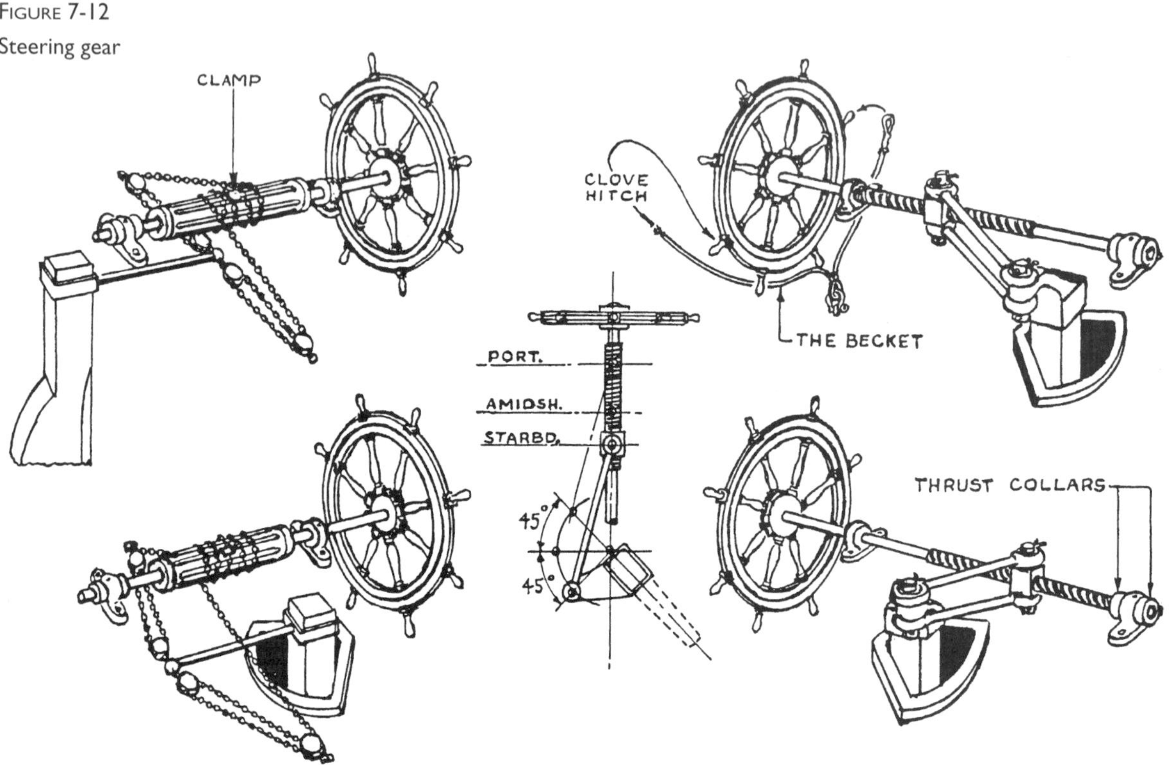

and finished well above the waterline and for this reason was not only well ventilated but, in bad weather was occasionally given a wash as well. There was a special draw bucket kept in the place for the sole purpose of flushing it out and I don't doubt that had Mrs Duddrige had seen it in any other part of the vessel, she would have had something to say.

The port side of the wheelhouse was the combined paint and lamp locker and a repository for anything else the mate thought fit to stow there. But everything was so placed and constrained that there was absolutely not chance of its shifting and jamming the steering gear. Across the front of a lot of wheelhouses were boards about 8in or 9in [approximately 22cm] wide, fitted on cleats or brackets on either side, some of which had the vessel's name and port of registry carved into the wood. One suspects that in the past these boards were lavishly painted, probably with lots of gold leaf, to act as a decoration for the vessel and that, by scratching below the layers of paint, varnished mahogany would be discovered.

White with a black roof was a popular colour for wheelhouses, although if they were the whaleback type the roof was often green. In some vessels a square of black was also painted around the latch holes of the doors, so that the dirt of constant use would not be so obvious. It can be seen in Figure 7-13 that *Brooklands* had two separate compartments in her wheelhouse, with the steering gear in the middle. The forward bearing for the wheel shaft was below a wooden bar across the front and on this Christy often used to sit when he was steering. The top of the binnacle usually being off in the daytime, he could still see the compass and he said that in winter he would open the weather door and jam it with a wedge so that it acted as a windbreak. I suspect he did this as a sort of gesture against his father, who always stood when he was at the wheel – so did everyone else.

FIGURE 7-13
Wheelhouses

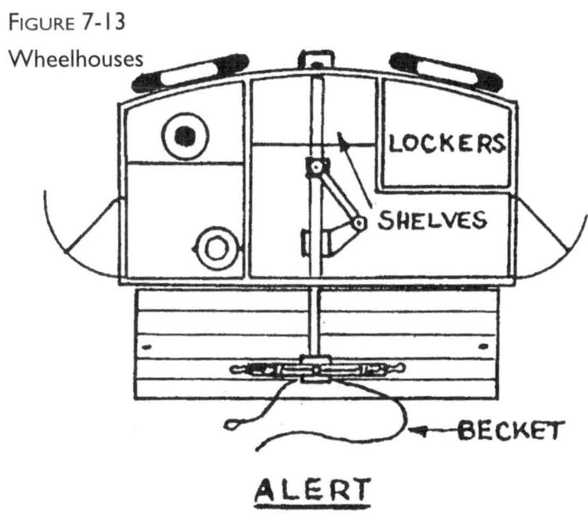

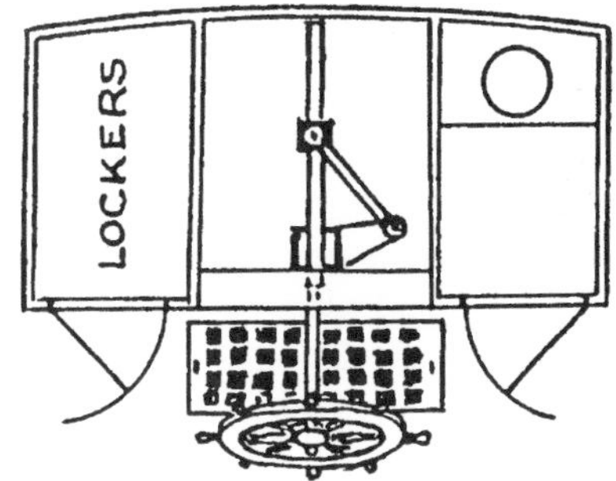

Irish Minstrel of Chester preparing to leave Penzance.

PHOTOGRAPHER H OLIVER HILL. DAVID CLEMENT COLLECTION

Pumps

Schooners' pumps were the large-bore, short-stroke type still favoured by civil engineering contractors for keeping holes in the ground free of water, although nowadays the latter are nearly always driven by a diesel engine. The suction and delivery valves were up at the top where they could be easily accessed; the strums lay between frames below the pump well and they always had about four or five sets of lugs to take the fulcrum pin of the bucket mechanism – partly as an insurance against one set breaking and partly so that they could be assembled in any way to suit the deck layout of the vessel in which they were installed. They were more tiring to work than flywheel pumps as they had no means of storing up energy to tide the operators over the fluctuations in load [Figure 7-14]. There were invariably two pumps abaft the mainmast in a schooner, or forward of the mizzen in a ketch. Some vessels had brackets on the fore side of their winch house or galley in which the brakes could be stowed; in others they were left lying on deck between the two pumps. Like all other ironwork they were painted green or black.

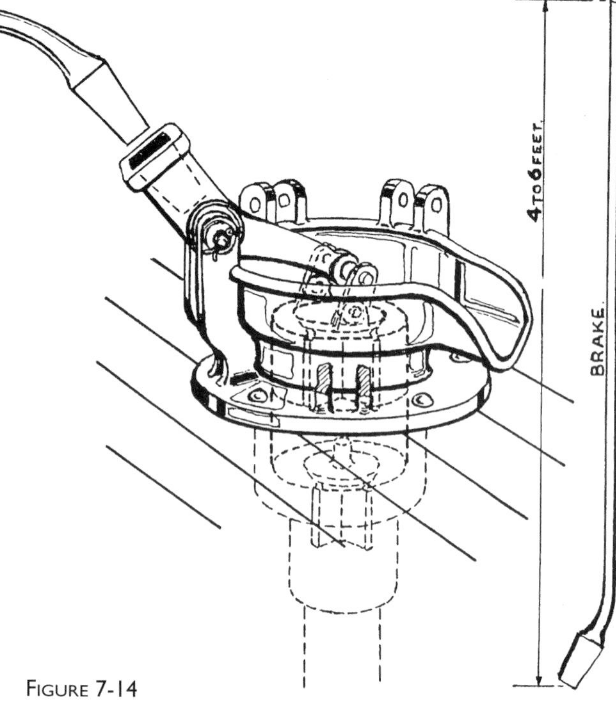

FIGURE 7-14
Pumps

Hatches

The hatches have been deliberately left to last in this catalogue of deck fittings because they deserve more attention than they usually receive. They were the most necessary, the most important and the most dangerous openings in the ship. For ninety per cent of the time they were adequate for the job they had to do; it was during the remaining ten per cent, in times of extreme stress, that their shortcomings were evident. The demise of tarpaulins, battens and wedges as a means of making a hatch watertight is now in sight, but all down the long years in which they were the only way of doing this job, there were cases of wedges being loosened in their cleats and sometimes knocked out by the ceaseless pounding of tons of moving water and the only remedy for this was for the crew to keep knocking them back in again. The cause of the trouble was the taper in the wedges, which was fairly fast, making contact with the cleat on a narrow face only [Figure 7-15] and so presenting on one side a much greater area on which the water could work than on the other. A ledge along the bottom of the batten might have helped ease this problem, but it could have been solved by using double wedges with a slower taper, which would have made full face contact with the batten, with each other and with the cleat, while at the same time presenting a balanced target for the sea. To resist the greater force exerted by the slow taper of these double wedges, the cleats would have needed to be much stronger – in small vessels at least they could be bent outwards by over-enthusiastic wedge-driving; they were, in fact, a bit too springy to get a real grip. In spite of this failing, the hatches and their covers were well conceived and designed to withstand pressures from outside, while with dry cargoes and long passages the covers could be caulked all round, to decrease the chances of water getting through.

They were not quite so successful at resisting pressures from inside, however, and there can be little doubt that it was this factor more than any other that caused small vessels laid on their beam ends by a squall, to disappear with such alarming rapidity. Compared with her total volume, the schooner's hatches were much bigger than those of a large steel square rigger; their width was a greater percentage of her total beam. There was a limit below which they could not be reduced without becoming uneconomic and, while there have been cases of big sailing vessels lying on their beam ends for days without foundering, while their crews toiled frantically to trim the cargo back up to windward, one hears very little of this sort of thing happening in schooners. On the contrary, nearly everyone has heard stories of how three schooners went into a squall together and when they came out there were two, or one, or none. Before laying the blame for this on hatches alone, it is as well to take a look at another factor, which also had a hand in these tragedies – the human one. It was not, of course, beyond the wit of man to have keyed the fore and after into position in the hatch coaming and then to have clamped the covers in such a way that no amount of

moving cargo would have shifted them, but for many centuries it had not been considered necessary and the mental change which gave rise to the problem was one which fired men's imaginations rather than caused them to sit down quietly and think.

One gathers that in the palmy days of the Honourable East India Company all sail was off the vessel about half an hour before a squall hit them and that another half hour elapsed after its passing before they started, in a leisurely sort of way, to make sail once more. The clipper-ship era changed all this. The hard-driving skipper and the hard-driving mate became the heroes of the day. It triggered off a note that found ready sympathy in many quarters. The competitive spirit was aroused and everyone wanted to make a race of it, anywhere, any time. Some have claimed that the sailing ship taught men patience but this only comes with the years. One cannot help thinking that if patience had been one of the failings of the human race, it would never have made it. It was the fast passages that men bragged about, not the slow ones, and the phrase 'more days, more dollars' was born out of philosophical resignation rather than any desire to be in the last vessel to arrive. The clipper ship disappeared almost as rapidly as she had come, her job taken over by steamers, but the tradition remained and coloured men's outlook in sailing vessels to the very end. No one liked to be thought of as being slow to carry sail; no one wanted to be the first to touch a halyard. The crews were as bad as the skippers and the mates and it mattered not that the huge crew of a clipper could have got three royals and three topgallants off her in less time than it took the miserable handful aboard a schooner to deal with their main gaff topsail and flying jib. Had our three schooners met the squall separately, with no other vessels in sight, their chances of survival would have been much greater; as it was, it was almost inevitable that sooner or later someone would hang on just that little bit too long. In defence of the men who squandered their lives and their employers' property with such reckless abandon, it can only be said that, for countless generations, our present-day preoccupation with safety would have been a luxury completely beyond their reach.

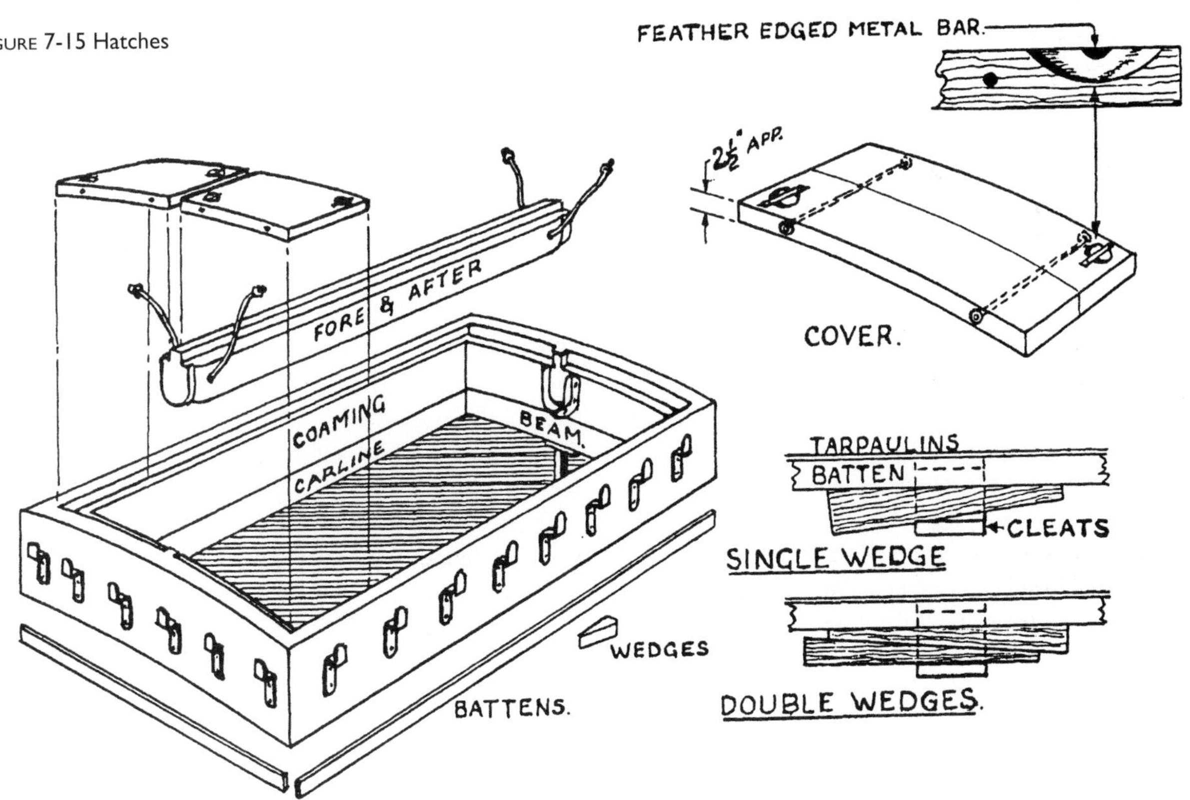

FIGURE 7-15 Hatches

VIII
VARIATIONS IN RIG

Until about halfway through the 19th century ships were classified according to the build of their hulls, but from then on the emphasis gradually changed and rig was finally considered to be of greater significance. It had not always been the case but rig was at last becoming coupled to the size of the vessel, so that to know one was to have a fair idea of the other.

At the bottom end of the scale was the cutter rig, applied to the smallest vessels only, although in the days when it was used to carry passengers and to pursue smugglers it had reached quite large proportions and often had a main boom nearly as long as the vessel's hull. Next in size came the ketch, followed by the schooner, brigantine and brig in ascending order. The barquentine rig, which for many years was entered in the registers as a three-masted brigantine, tended to be used in vessels of much the same tonnage as the brig and the snow but usually with a longer and narrower hull than the two-masted vessels; the brig and snow were finally supplanted in popularity by the barquentine. A vessel much above 300 tons or, at most, 400 tons was almost invariably rigged as a barque or a ship, the latter being the only rig considered suitable for the largest vessels.

This order of things was maintained until towards the end of the 19th century, when the four-masted barque finally supplanted the ship rig for large vessels, while at the beginning of the 20th century the Americans developed the multi-masted schooner, until it became as large as any sailing vessel ever built. The multi-masted barquentine also enjoyed a brief period of popularity.

Like many other attempts to produce order out of chaos, this new method of classification was only partially successful. It worked well enough while it was merely being used for purposes of registration, but once it had been decided to have two kinds of master's certificate – one for square-rigged and one for fore-and-aft rigged vessels – and it became necessary to put them all into one or other of these categories an element of lunacy crept into the proceedings, which denied the brigantine, with its fully square-rigged foremast, the right to be a square rigger, while allowing the barquentine to be one. The bias no doubt sprang from the fact that the barquentine was usually a larger and more expensive vessel. It is a source of regret that I am unable to acknowledge the author of the statement, but he summed the matter up by pointing out that if another fore-and-aft rigged mast was put into a vessel already classed as a fore and after, it made her into a square rigger. This may have been due to mathematical leanings on the part of the gentlemen who made the decision – minus multiplied by minus becomes plus.

However, in addition to the fairly clear-cut rigs already mentioned there were all sorts of odd vessels floating about that did not fit comfortably into any category: ketches with topsails on the mainmast (the ketch was originally a square rigger anyway), schooners with topsails on both masts, brigantines and barquentines with squaresails on the main topmast. This last was one of the few of these peculiar rigs to acquire a name – the jackass barque [Figure 8-1]. Perhaps the first vessel to carry it was of Antipodean origin, as the name could have arisen out of the ribald laughter of some conservative old seagoing gentleman who was unable to control himself when he first set eyes on it.

The brigantine had had a similar fate, for years it had been known as a hermaphrodite brig, both titles implying something that was neither one thing nor another. But there is evidence that the word 'jackass' was rooted in something older and more enduring than mere hilarity, because it cropped up partially once again in the name jack barquentine, bestowed upon a species of staysail schooner by the natives of Port-

FIGURE 8-1 Jackass barque

Marry Barrow shortly after she had been completed.

Photographer unknown. Terry Belt Collection

madoc. Once again the qualifying word indicated a hybrid rig, and once again the qualified word was the next 'squarer' vessel up the scale.

The jack barquentine[1] [Figure 8-2], as was mentioned in Chapter II, was an attempt to produce a three-masted schooner with as many of the advantages of the barquentine as possible, without actually becoming one. The yards were set lower than in a conventional schooner and, in consequence, could set a deeper standing topgallant. Instead of a boom foresail it had the three staysails of a barquentine between the foremast and mainmast – the extra work provided by these when going about was undoubtedly the reason the type never supplanted the orthodox three-masted schooner. It could be worked by a smaller crew than a normal barquentine, and it is of some significance that, when beating in confined and congested waters like the Mersey estuary, Captain Deacon always stowed his foresail and worked the old *Waterwitch* exactly as though she was a jack barquentine. It will be seen from the drawing that the jack barquentine's foremast was in two pieces only, that it had no top, merely the standard crosstrees and spreaders of the schooner. It was this feature by which the rig was classified, the possession of a top being taken as the deciding factor on whether or not the vessel was a barquentine. Sir Alan Moore made this point many years ago, in his extremely interesting and practically exhaustive catalogue of variations in rig, *Last Days of Mast and Sail*.[2]

One cannot help thinking that a more successful jack barquentine might have been produced by fitting the boom foresail with a trysail mast like a snow, so that the gaff jaws could have been hoisted above the truss of the foreyard to give a deeper sail. But no one seems to have gone in for an further

[1] There is an excellent photograph of one of these schooners on page 38 of Michael Bouquet's *Westcountry Sail.*

[2] *Last Days of Mast and Sail* by Alan Moore, Clarendon Press, Oxford, 1925.

experiments and the normal three-masted standing topgallant schooner was finally left in possession of the field.

The ceaseless experimenting to find something better slowed considerably towards the end of the 19th century. By then the steamer was in the ascendancy, the sailing ship had been ousted from the racing trades and relegated to the carrying of bulk cargoes, and the preoccupation of builders and owners was turning towards greater economy in the running of more or less standardised vessels, with the minimum number of men. Labour-saving devices came to the fore, while any further modifications to rigging and gear, not directly connected with them, came to an end. It was a world in which, at last, everyone knew what everyone else was doing. No improvement went unnoticed but was seized on eagerly, copied, and improved until it became almost universally used.

For fifty years the British Isles had stood at the centre of a ferment which embraced the whole world; in which old values ware constantly being questioned; in which progress in material matters had become measurable in miles instead of inches; and in which travel had suddenly become within the reach of all – the hungry and the hopeful of Europe swarmed out in their thousands across the face of the earth in search of land, in search of gold, in search of a better life. By the end of this tremendous burst of energy, many of the regional differences in dress, outlook, architecture and attitude, which had once added colour to the life in these islands, had been swept away, their place usurped by an overwhelming interest in the doings of the whole world, of the unruly nations and races for whom Britannia kept the peace so that trade could flourish, the rich could prosper mightily, and the poor remain much as before.

Many regional differences in shipping must have been eliminated at the same time; the steamer owed no allegiance to any town or locality and by the beginning of the 20th century the only really regional vessels still surviving were those that spent their lives wholly or partially on the inland waterways. Even here they were not entirely free from outside influences – the so very obvious Dutch origins of the narrow boat have still to be investigated and explained. Inshore fishing vessels might also be developing along lines suitable to the ports, waters and harbours they frequented, but they were being developed by men who were now in no way ignorant of what was taking place in other parts of the country.

A few isolated pockets remained. While Aberdeen still stood proudly in the van of ship design, the inhabitants of north-east Scotland no doubt felt, with some justification, that they were at the centre of the maritime world. When the increasing demand for large steam-driven iron and steel vessels caused the shipping industry to turn elsewhere for inspiration, it did not lessen by one jot their confidence in themselves, nor did it loosen the age-old ties with the Scandinavian countries – a relationship common to the whole of the British east coast but yet peculiarly intensified and direct in the country north of the Granite City, Aberdeen. It was here that the last regional variation in rig persisted, just as it was this area that clung to one of the last regional variations in hulls – variations that were also found on the far side of the North Sea.

I am indebted to the late Dan McDonald and Peterhead

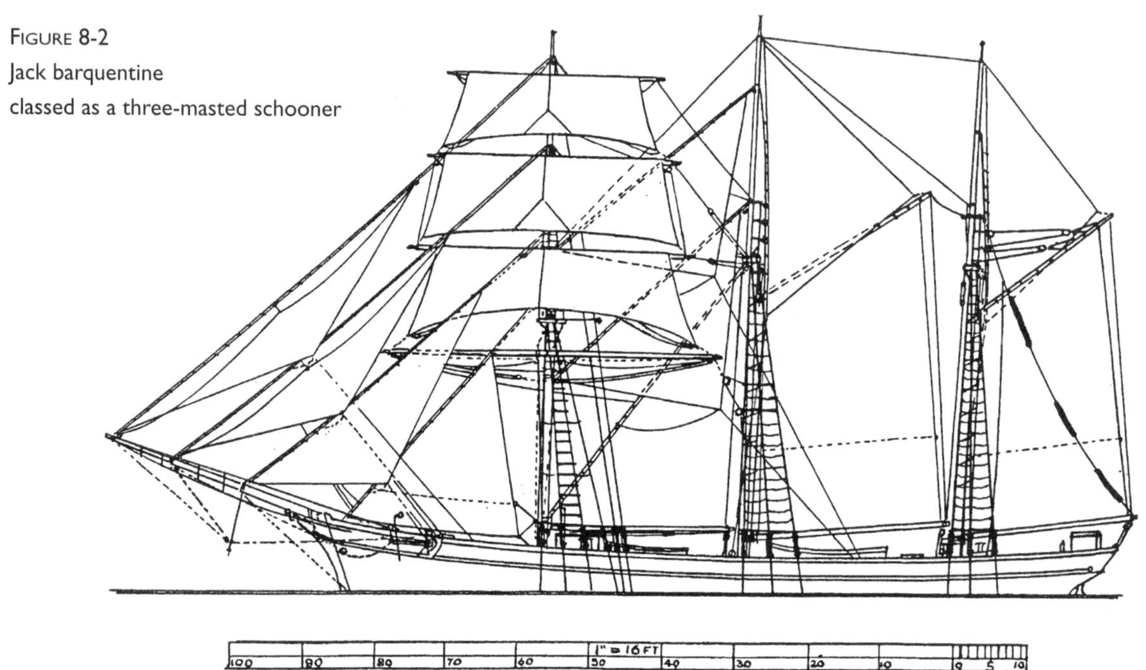

FIGURE 8-2
Jack barquentine
classed as a three-masted schooner

Mary Barrow at Penzance.

Photographer unknown but possibly H. Oliver Hill. Terry Belt Collection

Library for the evidence. Out of a dozen photographs of small vessels taken in the 1860s and 1870s, Dan found that six were of schooners (one of them the *Minnie*), each of which had a standing gaff on the fore. Five of the other six were barquentines, one of which had a standing gaff on the mizzen. Six of the twelve had roller-reefing topsails and one had what appeared to be a roller-reefing topgallant as well. These roller-reefing sails had no counterpart in Scandinavian vessels but standing gaffs were always plentiful in the Baltic and hung on there, along with point reefing, until the end. Peterhead is a far cry from Brittany (the area that most people today would associate with roller-reefing topsails) and it comes as a surprise to find that they were once strongly entrenched in this northern port. Dan puts the blame for this on the Peterhead whaling fleet.

Conducting their business in parts of the seas unfrequented by any except others in the same pursuit, the whalers were the likeliest in the world to hang on to their roller-reefing sails long after everybody else had settled for double topsails. Frozen fingers and frozen reef points do not go well together, nor do mittens and iced rigging, and the 'spouters' on many occasions probably had good cause to bless the gear which could wind up an icy sheet of canvas.

Schooners in the past were forever changing hands so that it is impossible to know whether roller topsails and standing gaffs went out of use owing to dissatisfaction with their functioning or because of a transfer of ownership to ports where they were considered as oddities. But, in the end, the Bretons had a monopoly on roller topsails, while the Scandinavians were the last to use the standing gaffs. In 1936 the Danish three-master *Merkur* [Figure 8-3] arrived in the Mersey from the West Indies, with a cargo of lignum vitae. She had a straight stem, a flat transom with the rudder out of doors and the punt slung across it on wooden davits, and she had a standing fore gaff with a vang on each side. Photographs of her appeared in the newspapers and, to a public that in the main appeared blissfully unaware that it had similar vessels of its own, she was a symbol of the past. She was also a symbol of the past to those used to sailing ships because she lay in the Sloyne with her yards squared; a practice that the rest of the working sailing ship world had long ago abandoned, being quite content to leave their yards in the position in which they had come to rest, until such time as they were driven by windy anchorages or inconvenient warehouses to adopt some other course of inaction. Although the Danish seamen aboard *Merkur* did not know it, they had a kindred spirit up the river at Runcorn, who took charge of schooners laid up in the dock there and whose first job, on taking up residence aboard, seemed to be to get the yards squared. Perhaps for too much of his life he had seen them on the backstays.

It is difficult to see why the standing gaff lasted so long in schooners. It was not 'standing' in the same manner as the square rigger's spanker, as the gaff had jaws and was fitted with peak and throat halyards, and, although the sail was furled by brailing it in to the mast, it could hardly have been reefed to work efficiently in this manner. I did not get a chance to establish whether the *Merkur* had reef points in her foresail but feel sure that they must have been there; in fact the sail must have been fitted with two sets of gear, one for reefing, the other for furling.[3]

The big square-riggers also clung to the standing gaff, although 19th century brigs and snows frequently had the lowering kind. All this could be put down to inertia, or to the foibles of shipbuilders, shipowners and captains, were it not for a peculiar incident related by Dana in *Two Years Before the Mast*[4]. It occurred with us in *Alert* during the gale that blew like fury for days out of a clear and cloudless sky, and I cannot do better than quote his exact words:

'There was no sail now on the ship but the spanker and the close reefed main topsail, which still held good. But this was too much after sail, and the order was given to furl the spanker. The brails were hauled up, and all the light hands in the starboard watch sent out on the gaff to pass the gaskets; but they could do nothing with it. The second mate swore at them for a parcel of "sogers", and sent a couple of the best men; but they could do no better and the gaff was lowered down.'

Why, in such weather, were they so reluctant to lower a gaff, which was obviously fitted with the necessary halyards? The implication would seem to be that it was considered unseamanlike to have to do so. Could this have been an attitude that had survived from the days when the gaff was not the gaff but was, rather, the long yard of the lateen mizzen? This, although little better than a shot in the dark, is not quite so unlikely as it at first seems. A tradition so deeply rooted that it lasted the full stretch of the 19th century, when changes of all kinds were an everyday occurrence, could obviously have emerged from the 18th century practically unscathed.

[3] It was Dan McDonald who put his finger on the answer to this and I may as well quote him verbatim: 'I have given some thought to this rig, and I think it must have been used in the same fashion as the spritty barges did, manoeuvring in and out of little dog-holes of ports where there were no tugs. It would be easier to brail in a sail than lower it away and have it all over the deck. With the mainsail down, a handy vessel could manage quite well with this sail and a staysail. There must have been something in it – the French and the Danes used it, and they were trading in and out of the same kind of small port.'

[4] *Two Years Before the Mast* (Chapter XXV) by Richard Dana, Rainbow Classics, London, 1946 (reprint)

FIGURE 8-3 *Merkur* 146 tons

Mary Barrow at Penzance.

Photographer unknown but possibly H. Oliver Hill Terry Belt Collection

There was nothing regional about one of the main variations in rig, which existed in schooners. Two types of topgallant sail were used, both of which were in existence before double topsails became fashionable. The earlier of the two was set semi-flying, while the later arrival had a yard with the full impedimenta – parrel, halyard, lifts, clewlines, sheets, buntlines, footropes, braces. The fact that this later sail was invariably referred to as a standing topgallant is sufficient proof that the flying sail was already in use. It is also a fair guarantee that the prefix 'flying' was not applied to its predecessor, it was just a topgallant. The expression has crept into circulation of latter years for the same reasons that now make it necessary to explain whether one is talking about a schooner with only two masts or one with a greater number. Old paintings show that some vessels as far back as 1850 had adopted the standing topgallant, so that the origins of the flying sail must have been much earlier. The two types of sail existed side by side for many years and, by one of the usual twists of fate, the last flying topgallant yard was removed from the *Useful* in 1930, many years after the standing topgallant had been dispensed with by British schooners.

The precise details of how the flying sail worked could quite easily have been lost had it not been for an excellent photograph of the *Useful's* foremast taken by Dan McDon-

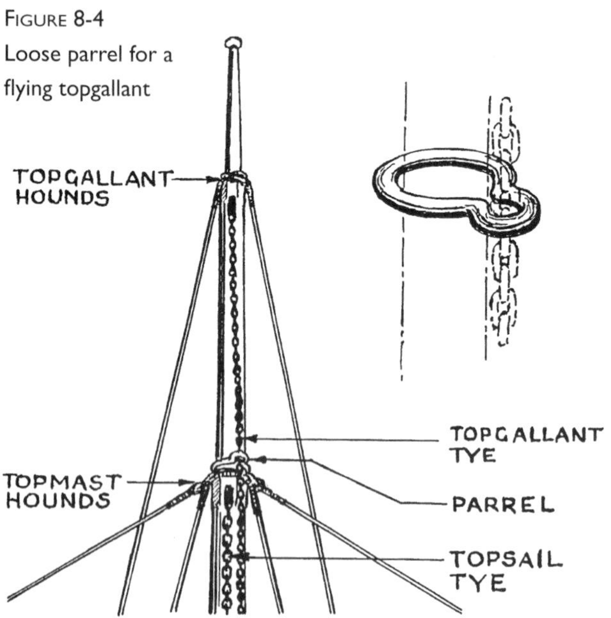

FIGURE 8-4
Loose parrel for a flying topgallant

ald in 1929, and the fact that Basil Greenhill was able to obtain a verbal description of its operation from Captain Slade. Its gear was very simple. It had a halyard, braces and a pair of downhauls, and its clews were made fast to the topsail yardarm. Those stowing the sail stood on the footropes of the topsail yard, as it had none of its own, and when the topsail was reefed or furled the topgallant yard followed it down. It was able to do this because it had a loose parrel [Figure 8-4] made like a disproportionate figure eight, the larger loop being around the topgallant mast, while the tye of the halyard passed through the smaller one. The parrel held the yard to the mast at the topmast hounds while its sail was being furled, but could not accompany it any lower, so the tye ran through the smaller loop. Above a reefed topsail the yard was restrained by its halyard, downhauls and braces but when the topsail was stowed or close reefed the topgallant braces were caught around the lifts of the topsail yard, which acted as a final steadying influence. Because of this extreme simplicity of gear the flying topgallant managed to outlast the

Mary Miller, Captain Furlong, outward bound from Weston Point for Fisherrow of 7 August 1925.
Behind her is the *Amy* of Fowey, Captain Greet, bound from Runcorn for Penryn.
PHOTOGRAPH BY DAVID E. SMITH. TERRY BELT COLLECTION

FIGURE 8-5
Flying topgallant and double topsails

standing variety. It was a small sail and by rights belonged to the tapering look of the days before steel standing rigging. The latter-day standing topgallant was much wider.

No hard and fast rules can be laid down as to where the two types of topgallant were used, but it would be broadly correct to say that the flying sail was popular in small vessels and in the home trade, while the standing was more widely used in larger vessels and on deep water. It is impossible to confuse the two in photographs of vessels at anchor or in dock but when under way the only sure indication is from the run of the boom jib stay: if it is set up from the topmast hounds, it is a sure sign that there is a standing topgallant above it but if it runs from the doubling and there is no stay from the topmast hounds, this is an equally sure indication of a flying sail. One of the drawbacks inherent in squaresails was the danger of being caught aback, putting pressure on the mast from a direction in which it was not adequately stayed to resist it. To guard against this the headstays were set up from as many points on the topmast as possible, and it was one of the minor drawbacks of the flying topgallant rig that its fore topmast could only be stayed from the topgallant hounds. This left the sheavehole of the topmast in a vulnerable position, as a weak point with no direct support from forward.

In its lack of sheets the flying topgallant foreshadowed the upper topsail. It was probably the first squaresail that had to be stowed by laying its leeches in along the yard; in all others the job had already been done by the clewlines or the clew-

FIGURE 8-6
Fore topsails and topgallants

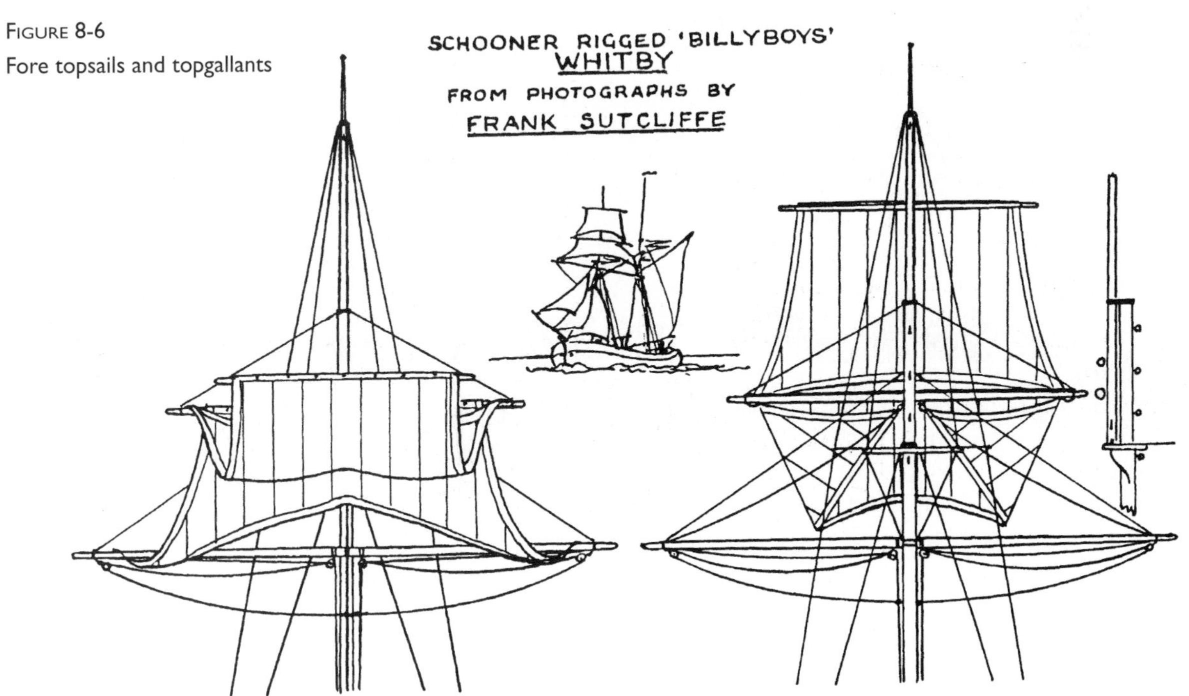

Snowflake of Runcorn seen in Mounts Bay.

PHOTOGRAPH BY H. OLIVER HILL. TERRY BELT COLLECTION

garnets. Photographs taken of ships lying at anchor in the days of single topsails, with their royal yards on deck, present a remarkably denuded appearance to those accustomed to the final multiplicity of yards but there is quite a lot of photographic evidence that the men brought up under single topsails found double topsails equally peculiar, not to say rather repugnant. Having stowed the sails they hoisted the upper topsail yards to the sheaveholes, so that there was only one yard in one place. To do this they had to provide the sails with a pair of short sheets into the top, which they did not really need – but seemingly anything was better than the horribly clumsy look aloft when both yards were together. By the time double topgallants were coming into fashion, most of these older men must have either retired or become resigned to it.

It was probably the stow of the upper topsail which gave rise to the idea of clewing all the other sails up to the yardarms, especially sensible in the wide but not very deep sails resulting from the split in which the leeches were too short to reach the bunt. Nowhere is the persistence of maritime tradition more forcibly demonstrated than in the fact that, to the end, men were still trying to make a bunt in sails pulled up evenly along the whole length of the yards by buntlines which no longer pulled to the bunt – they even went to the trouble of providing a little jigger with which to haul it up into a slightly

FIGURE 8-7
Great Lakes schooner

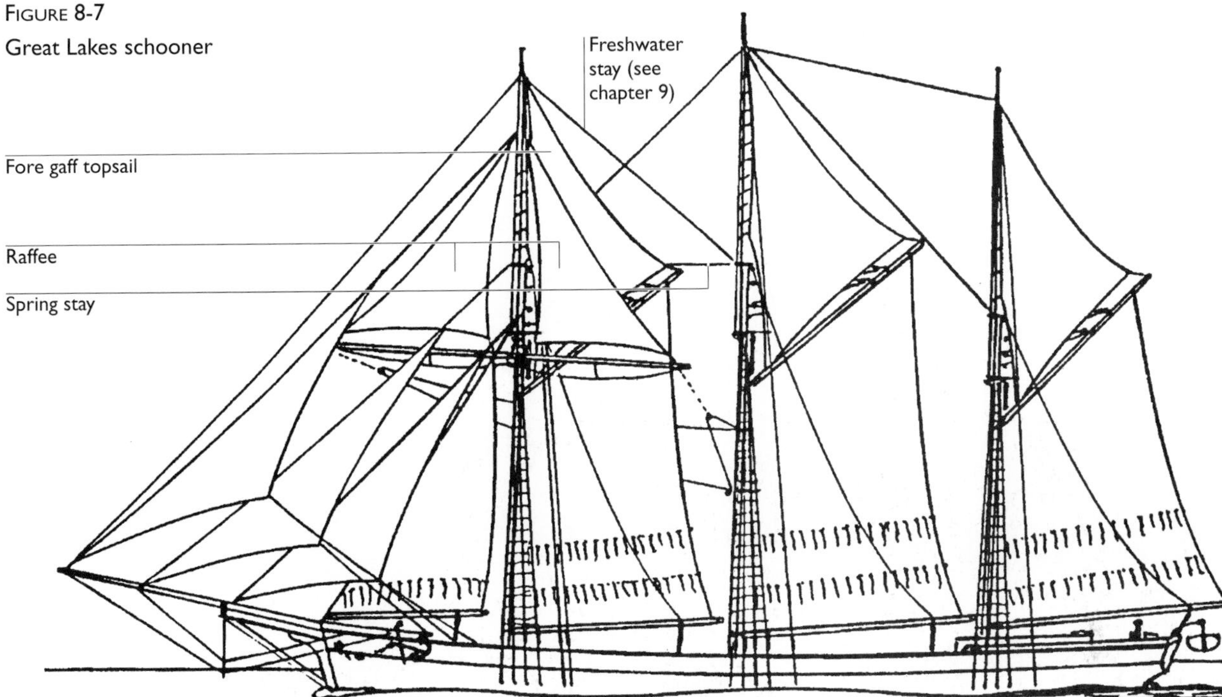

more impressive hump. Those in schooners must have found two yards together just as repulsive to their gaze as did the men in square riggers, because for many years it was customary to wrap up the flying topgallant and its yard inside the topsail to make it appear that only one yard was present. This is evident in many old photographs, from the bulky stow of the topsail, which could hardly have been produced by the amount of canvas in its sail alone. Perhaps the introduction of double topsails finally helped the flying topgallant to become respectable enough to be exhibited to the public.

The flying topgallant was almost invariably used above a single topsail, and we have to thank Henry Hughes for the information that at least there was one schooner, the *Edith Eleanor* with a flying topgallant above double topsails.[5] He points out that it was quite a handy arrangement but adds that, in spite of this, it was never generally adopted. This is hardly surprising as, when the sails were stowed, all three yards were together [Figure 8-5]. To the men of the younger generation there was one yard too many, but to the older, single topsail brigade there were two. Such things, although common in the eastern Mediterranean, never became acceptable to the seamen of northern Europe.

A peculiar arrangement of schooner topsails is frequently seen in photographs taken by Frank Sutcliffe of Whitby[6] [Figure 8-6]. The hulls of the vessels in question are apple-cheeked at both ends and are obviously none other than the famous Billyboy type, which was already a thing of the past before the 1914-18 War. Evidence of comparatively shallow draught is given by the fact that many of the vessels have no main topmast; sometimes the main lower mast is poled off and fitted with a truck, while in others the retention of the cap and crosstrees indicates that the topmast has been dispensed with. Many of the photographs were taken while the vessels were drying their sails, and the topsail yard is nearly always down on its lifts and halfway down the doubling, with the topgallant yard just above it. To finish up below the cap both of these sails must have been completely loose from the mast, or else equipped with the same kind of parrel as the flying topgallant, but just how the topsail halyard was arranged is a mystery. Many of E.W. Cooke's vessels[7] have their yards in equally peculiar places and these little vessels, which somehow managed to survive unchanged into the second half of the 19th century, would so obviously have brought joy to his heart that they give further grounds for thinking that the origins of the loose parrel lie well in the past.

A return to something very much akin to this arrangement was occasionally used in the days when topsails were nearing

[5] *Immortal Sails*, by Henry Hughes, T. Stephenson & Sons, Prescot, Lancs. 1969.
[6] *Frank Meadow Sutcliffe – A Selection of his Work* by Bill Eglon Shaw, Sutcliffe Gallery, Whitby, 1974 and *A Second Selection* by Bill Eglon Shaw, Sutcliffe Gallery, Whitby, 1978.
[7] *Shipping and Craft*, Edward William Cooke, 1829, Reproduction, Masthead Books, London, 1970

Cumberland Lassie outward bound with a ketch.

Photographer unknown. David Clement Collection

the end of the road. The topsail yard was left down on its lifts and the sail cut down in depth so that it only needed to be sheeted home like a lower topsail. The canvas removed from the topsail was incorporated in the flying topgallant so that it became a much deeper sail. Although performing the functions of an upper topsail, it probably still qualified as a topgallant since its yard went higher than the topmast hounds. Its advantage was that the topsail no longer required reef tackles or reef bands; once the topgallant was in, those on board were in the same position as in a normal double topsail schooner – the vessel was ready for the fray.

One other squaresail was carried by British schooners in the years of their decline: the raffee, the classic 'fore topsail' of the American Great Lakes [Figure 8-7]. Its use arose after an auxiliary engine had been installed and the topsail yards sent down. The schooner men were naturally reluctant to get rid of the lower yard so it seemed a logical step to use the raffee, which had an area much the same as a lower topsail, but only required one yard. Old photographs exist in which schooners can be seen with the two sails of a raffee set between truck and topgallant as a sort of flying raffee royal, so that some knowledge of it was in circulation long before it was pressed into service for its final job. It would be extremely unlikely that a Great Lakes schooner had not, at some time or other, crossed the Atlantic, and it would be even more unlikely that there were no men in British schooners who had sailed under the raffee in its home waters. There were certainly plenty who had worked in the Great Lakes steamers, those seasonal vessels in which, so they said, the pay was good, the grub was good, and they steered six-hour tricks at the wheel… sitting down. On the other hand, all that anyone really needed to know about the raffee was that it consisted of two triangular pieces of canvas fastened to hanks on the lifts of the yard. They could have sorted out the rest for themselves. But, by whatever means the necessary information arrived upon these shores, when there was a call for the raffee, the raffee appeared.

As more powerful engines were installed, the point was passed where the engine was an auxiliary to the sails and the sails became an auxiliary to the engine; the topmasts were shortened or sent down altogether so that the raffee finally dropped out of use like the topsails before it. To the best of my knowledge the last schooner to carry one was *Mary Barrow*, the runners-up being the *M.E. Johnson* and *James Postlethwaite*.

IX

MASTS, SPARS AND STANDING RIGGING

Over the years enough drawings of masts and spars have been made to overload a Norwegian timber ship, but since a book of this kind would not be complete without them, they are included here once more. In the realm of standing rigging ninety per cent of the things done in schooners were in the classic tradition of all sailing vessels. There were a few things peculiar to small fore-and-aft rigged vessels but the main justification for going over this ground is that knowledge of the classic tradition seems today to be rather thinly spread.

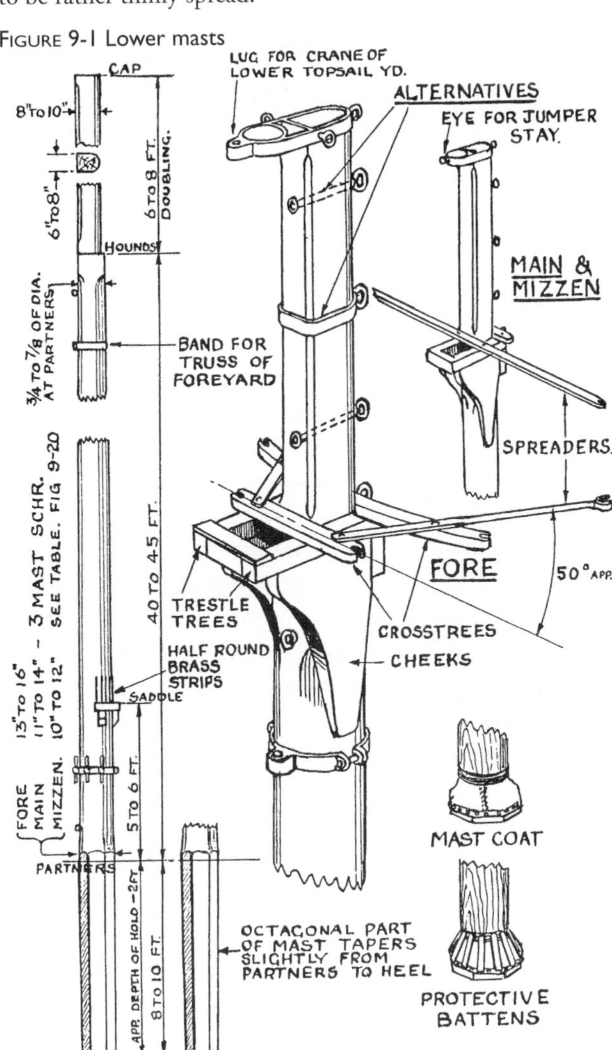

FIGURE 9-1 Lower masts

Masts

An old, fairly widely known, rule was that pitch-pine masts should have one inch of diameter for every yard of length. If applied to the foremast of the *Waterwitch* this gives results that are reasonably close to the sizes actually installed but for her main- and mizzenmasts, and for all masts in schooners and ketches, the figures obtained are too high.

Waterwitch (dimensions approximate)

Fore lower mast, heel to cap 49ft,
max. dia. 16in [14.94m & 41cm]

Fore topmast, heel to cap 31ft,
10in square at the heel [9.45m & 25cm]

Fore topgallant heel to cap 19ft,
6in square at the heel [5.79m & 15cm]

The reasons for this discrepancy are that the square-rigged mast was designed on the assumption that one day the wind would manage to blow on the wrong side of the sails and the mast would have to stand up to the load with whatever help the stays alone could give. Conversely a fore-and-aft sail reserved its foul deeds for when the wind was abaft the beam – when caught aback it merely flapped about in the breeze, endangering itself more than the mast. In consequence its mast could be made slightly thinner than a square-rigged one.

For many years I laboured under the belief that it should be possible to obtain some simple rule by which the approximate sizes of masts and spars could be ascertained and, as is usually the case, it was only after I had abandoned the struggle that I finally found out what one of the experts of his day had to say on the subject. I was loaned a copy of Robert Kipping's treatise on *Masting and Rigging*[1] which, judging from the illustrations, was probably first published in the 1860s. He has the following remarks to make:

'The rules given by different authors for determining the proportion of masts, yards &c. for merchant ships are of very little use now, for there are so many varieties in the build of these ships – some very long and narrow and others both long and broad – that it is impossible to make one rule serve in

[1] *Masting and Rigging* by Robert Kipping, Crosby, Lockwood & Son, London, 1903 (published from 1850).

Henrietta at Truro.

Photographer unknown. David Clement Collection

both cases; and it would require a great number of rules to determine the proportion of masts and yards, the way at present these ships are rigged.'

To obtain reasonable results for a fore-and-aft rigged mast, the rule first stated should be amended to three-quarters of an inch per yard, the figure obtained applying to lower masts only.

In particular the result should be thought of as the diameter of a schooner's fore lower mast at the partners, as it carried the biggest load of the various masts about to be considered. If arranged in descending order according to the area of canvas supported, the next in line would be the brigantine's mainmast, which carried a large fore and after and its gaff topsail and, in addition, took about two-thirds of the pull of the main staysails. The table in Figure 9.20 has the various lower masts arranged in this order and a coefficient allocated to each, by which one inch per yard should be multiplied to give results which approximately accord with what was done in practice. In brigantines and schooners the main lower mast was often the same thickness as the fore, or only marginally thinner, but in three-masters the difference was quite apparent, the main lower mast was thinner than the fore, the mizzen thinner than the main. In spite of this there was frequently little to choose between them as regards length.

The same descending order of thickness applied to the topmasts of three-masted schooners as well. The fore topmast, the shortest of the three, had about one inch of thickness per yard of length. It should be noted that where the fore topmast carried an extension for a topgallant this did not increase its diameter, which was based on the length from heel to topmast hounds. Neither the topgallant pole nor the length to the truck was taken into consideration. This also applied to the mizzenmasts of ketches, where the length above the hounds was often considerable. If the heel of a schooner's foretopmast were 7in square, the main would be about 6in and the mizzen 5in; these latter also had more taper. Main topmasts in barquentines, brigantines and ketches were about the same thickness as a schooner's main topmast, but it is impossible to provide them with a workable coefficient as they varied so much in length.

FIGURE 9-2 Topmasts

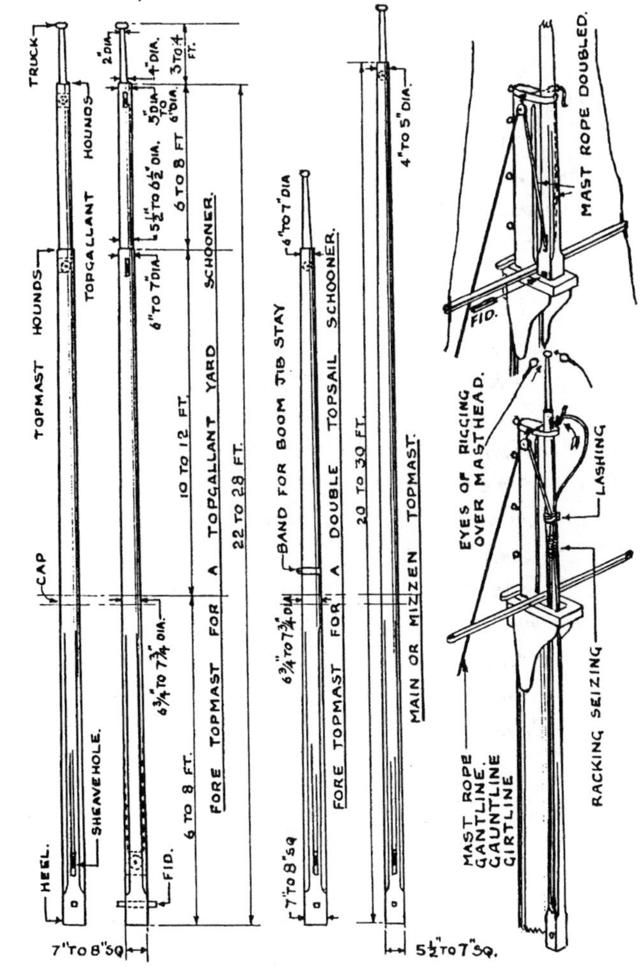

Yards etc.

The large variations in length of yards, booms and gaffs makes it impossible to fix any coefficients for them either, so that the limits of diameter and length for the vessels under consideration have been given on the various drawings. The figures can be considered as applicable to vessels varying from 75ft to about a 120ft [22.86m to 36.58m] between perpendiculars. The only rule that can be stated here with any assurance is that the diameter of a yard was not likely to exceed the diameter of that part of the mast on which it was carried.

By the mid 19th century it had been grasped that to produce a vessel with any pretensions to speed, the ratio of beam to length should be lower than it had been in the past. The reaction of the builders was not to start building narrower vessels but, rather, to increase the length of the vessels they were already accustomed to building without increasing the beam in proportion. This tendency continued throughout the rest of the century and still persists to this day. The table below shows how the schooner builders progressed in this direction:

date	*rig*	*length b.p.*	*beam*	*depth of hold*
1870	Schooner	88ft [26.82 m]	22ft [6.71 m]	9ft to 11ft [2.74m to 3.35m]
1880	Three-masted schooner	105ft [32.00m]	23ft [7.01m]	10ft to 12ft [3.05m to 3.66m]
1890	Three-masted schooner	120ft [36.58m]	24ft [7.32m]	10ft to 12ft [3.05m to 3.66m]

Although there must have been the odd exception, the wooden schooner never got much longer than 105ft [32.00m] and it

FIGURE 9-3 Spars

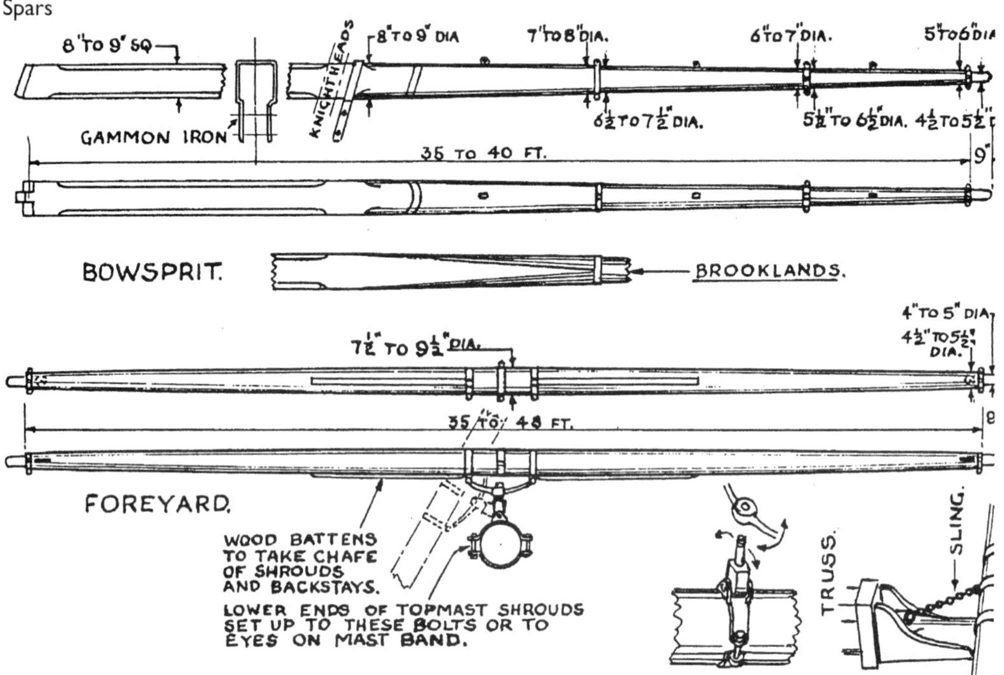

FIGURE 9-4 Spars

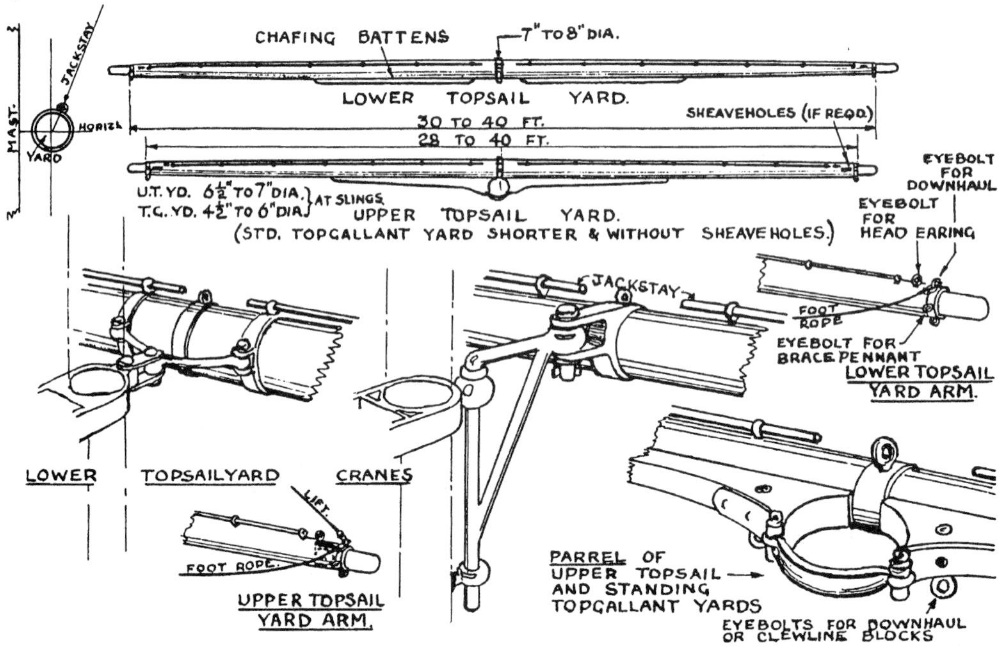

was left to the builders in iron and steel to carry the process to its conclusion. The increase in length in these latter-day three-masters was not accompanied by any increase in the length of their lower masts over and above what had already taken place because of the introduction of steel standing rigging; the vessels were saved from looking too stumpy by being fitted with longer topmasts. It would seem that some relationship existed between beam and length of lower mast and that the builders were unwilling to push matters to the limit, in case the increase should prove a source of danger in time of crisis. Robert Kipping puts this in a slightly different way: '...the extreme breadth of the ship from out to out, has been admitted by long use the best rule for determining the length of the masts, that they may have proper support by the spread of the rigging'.

So far, for the sake of convenience, reference has been made to the diameter of masts, although a bowsprit was square

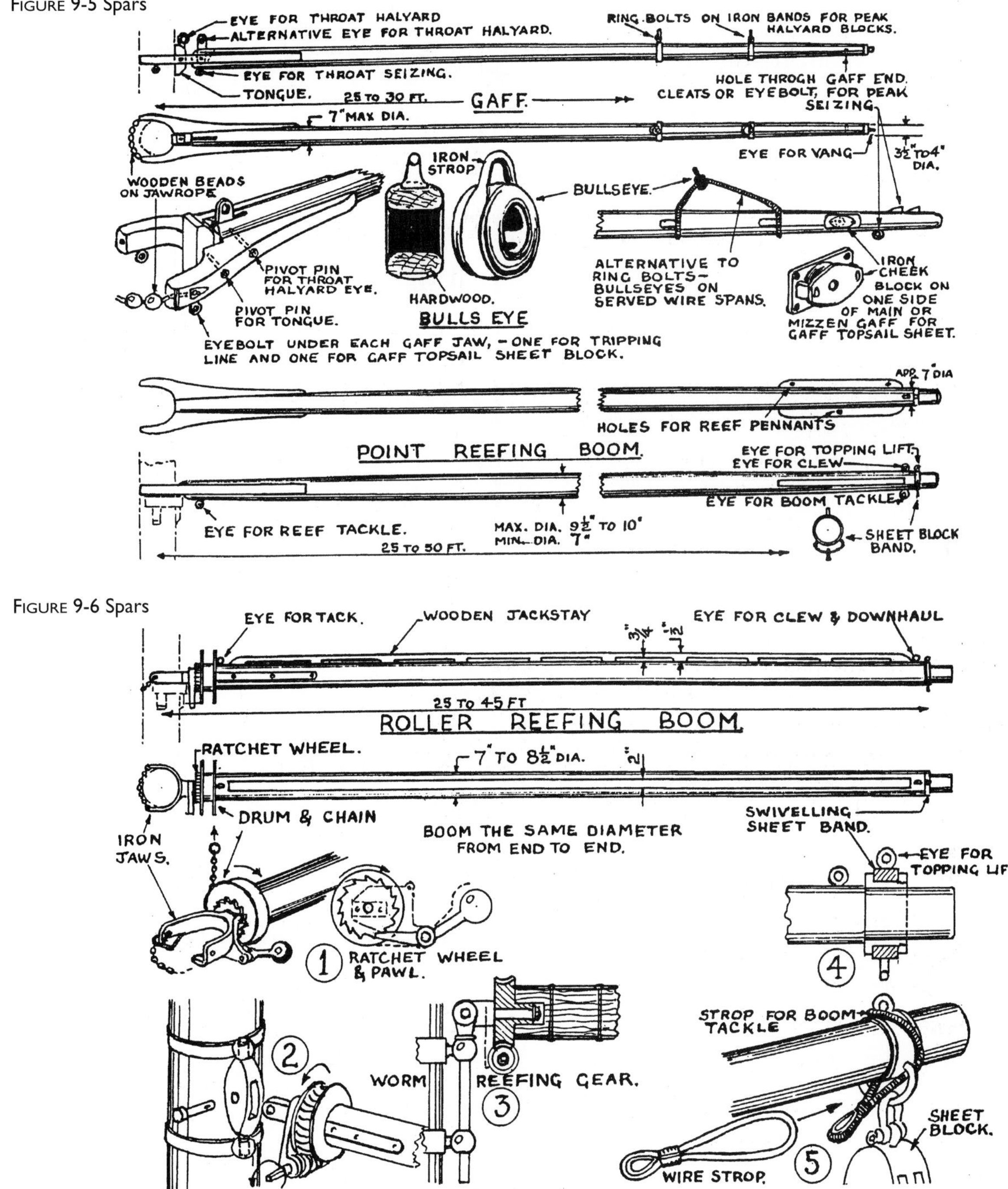

FIGURE 9-5 Spars

FIGURE 9-6 Spars

inside the knightheads, a topmast was square at its heel, and a lower mast octagonal at the partners, its point of greatest thickness, and downwards to the heel.

The partners themselves were two heavy wooden fore-and-aft pieces, between two closely-spaced deck beams, which made a square hole – filled in at the corners to make it octagonal – into which the wedges were driven to hold the mast securely in position. This area was one of the favourite places for rot in masts – a process assisted by rain far more than by seawater. Many vessels had the wedges bevelled at the sides so that, when driven home, bedded in white lead, they formed a solid block of timber, which could be painted over generously to keep out the water. Some builders preferred to leave gaps between the wedges, presumably to allow for some ventilation from below, as rot is considered to be particularly active where no fresh air circulates. For these a mast coat was required. This was a conical canvas tube with a collar sewn tightly around the mast and the coaming of the partners and lashed with spun-yarn after liberal applications of oil or tar, the whole lot being painted when dry to make it completely waterproof [Figure 9-1]. Since it was rather vulnerable it was usually protected by thin, short battens of wood, nailed to the mast and coaming by copper nails.

Standing Rigging

Nearly all wooden masts on small British sailing vessels finished up bent. The blame for this can be laid fairly and squarely on the means by which their standing rigging was set up and the use of deadeyes and lanyards. Anyone doubting this has only to look at photographs of the last survivors of the North American schooners to find that, despite their chainplates not being splayed out abaft the mast to the same extent as ours, their masts were much the same as they had been on the day they were stepped. Some of this can be put down to the fact that the Americans had an unlimited supply of first-class timber to pick and choose from and some to the fact that for the same reason they could afford to install masts with a greater diameter in proportion to length, but the main

Figure 9-7 Deadeyes and Lanyards

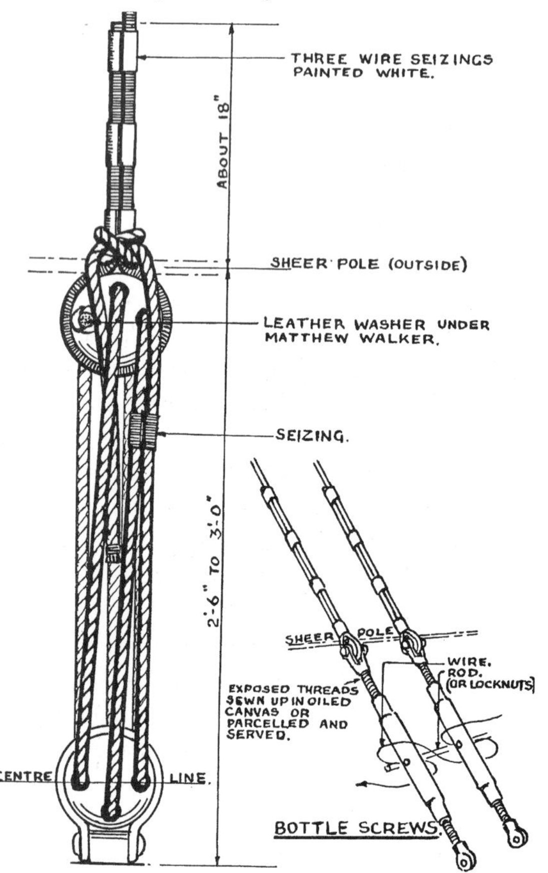

Figure 9-8 Shrouds

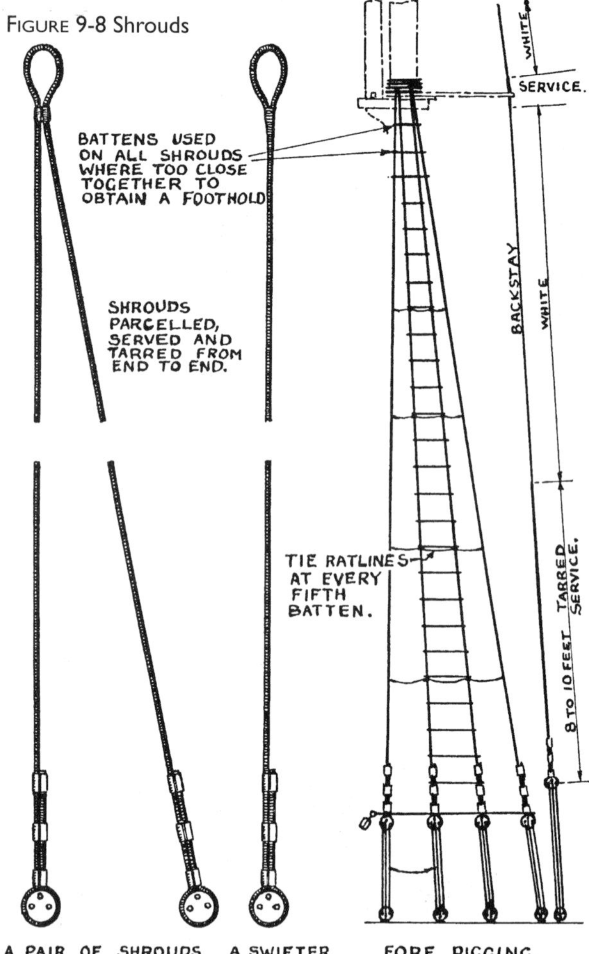

contributors to this happy state of affairs can be seen at the top of the chainplates – the Americans invariably used bottle screws to set up their standing rigging. Older North American vessels, which were fitted with deadeyes and lanyards also, exhibited the same symptoms as the British, although to a lesser degree. Length for length their schooners had more beam than ours, at least in the range in which we can compare them, but this cannot be advanced as a contributory factor because their masts, in consequence, were taller.

It has always been fashionable in some quarters to deplore the passing of the good old days and around the turn of the century someone of this mind gave utterance to the prophecy that, owing to the preponderance of large steel vessels, there would soon be no sailors left who knew how to turn in a deadeye; the implication was that only real sailors knew about such matters. The only observable difference between turning in a deadeye and turning in the steel thimble which supplanted it, is that the latter is shaped so that the process will cause less damage to the strands of the wire; but despite its manifest idiocy, the echoes of this statement are still to be heard. One cannot help feeling that had the inventor of the myth, or any

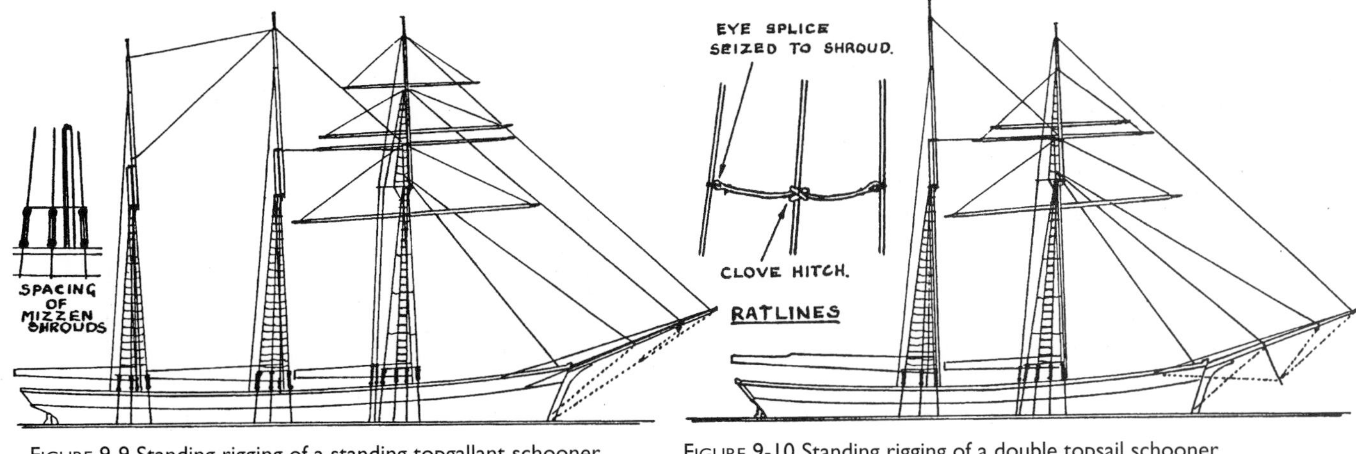

FIGURE 9-9 Standing rigging of a standing topgallant schooner

FIGURE 9-10 Standing rigging of a double topsail schooner

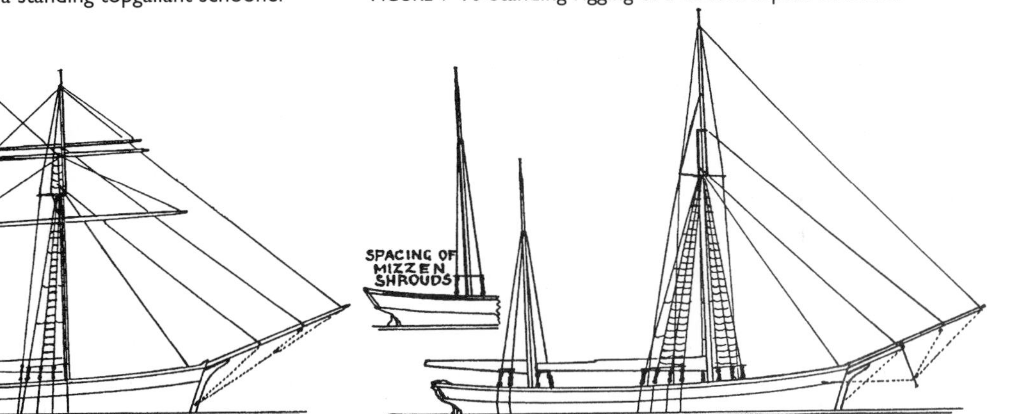

FIGURE 9-11 Standing rigging of a flying topgallant schooner

FIGURE 9-12 Standing rigging of a ketch

of those who have repeated it, ever been shipmates with deadeyes and lanyards for any length of time, they would rapidly have come to the conclusion that the sooner no one knew anything about them the happier it would be for the jack-tar industry in general.

The lanyards stretched even if the wire shrouds did not; when the poor old *Alert* was hard pressed and lay over to it in the squalls, the sheer poles on the lee side could be seen flapping about through a distance of at least 6in. It is necessary to examine the method of tightening up the lanyards to understand why they were so unsatisfactory. To do the job the clove hitch around the shroud was cast off [Figure 9-7], the seizing was cut, the lanyard was pushed back through the holes in the deadeyes so that it could be greased, and then its end was hitched to whatever tackle was available – burtons were best. The classic equipment, according to the book, was a luff tackle and a runner, to be hung from the after part of the trestletrees. In effect this was an upside-down burton, whereby it lost one fold of purchase out of the luff tackle and finished up six-fold instead of seven. The fall was swigged by the concerted efforts of everybody available but did not seem to gain much and, when the tackle was let go, the new seizing invariably pulled to some extent before taking the strain. Having dealt with a lanyard on one side, its opposite number was next tightened up and, as each successive shroud took a little more of the load, it inevitably left those already tightened taking less than they could have done. To have done the job properly it would have been necessary to go around and around all the lanyards several times, or to put a separate tackle on each lanyard and go around the lot, swigging until all shrouds and backstays would give no more. Indeed, this is what a couple of men with a set of bottle screws could do – taking up a little in each until the desired result had been obtained. When they had finished they could rest assured that neither the first gale that they encountered, nor the second, would put things back to where they started, because the barrels of the screws could be locked to prevent any slackening off.

If lanyards and deadeyes were not particularly efficient, lanyards rove through thimbles were even less so, and there were quite a number of places in the average schooner where these were to be found. One of the most important was on the upper end of the martingale on the underside of the bowsprit, where it was impossible to gain much with a tackle without losing some of it in making the lanyard fast once more. Some vessels had a screw in this position; those that did not relied upon the bobstay.

The bowsprit shrouds were another place where lanyards were often used; the outer ones, set up to the topgallant bulwark, could be dealt with reasonably well but the inner ones, with their ends down at deck level, were something of a nuisance. The worst of the lot, however, were the fore topmast shrouds, the lanyards of which were below the crosstrees, set up to rings on the mast band of the foreyard [Figures 9-16 and 9-17]. These were forever working slack because of the constant pressure of the lower topsail yard and, in the end, most schooners gave up the struggle and threw them away; the crew thereafter used the peak halyard eyebolts in the back of the doubling to climb up to the topsail yards. This made no real difference to anybody because in a double topsail schooner the ratlines had never gone any higher than the cap; they extended to the topmast hounds only in vessels with a topgallant. Anyone who had to go higher to perform such jobs as making up the gaskets shinned up the backstays.

The crew of the *Waterwitch* did not share this happy state of affairs with those in schooners. Their lanyards were also below the top because the topmast shrouds and futtock shrouds were in one piece, but they could not dispense with their services as they had no desire to shin all the way up to the topgallant yard. The result was that they were forever at it, trying to keep the lanyards tight so that they did not wobble too

Jane Banks

Photograph by Richard J. Scott. Terry Belt Collection

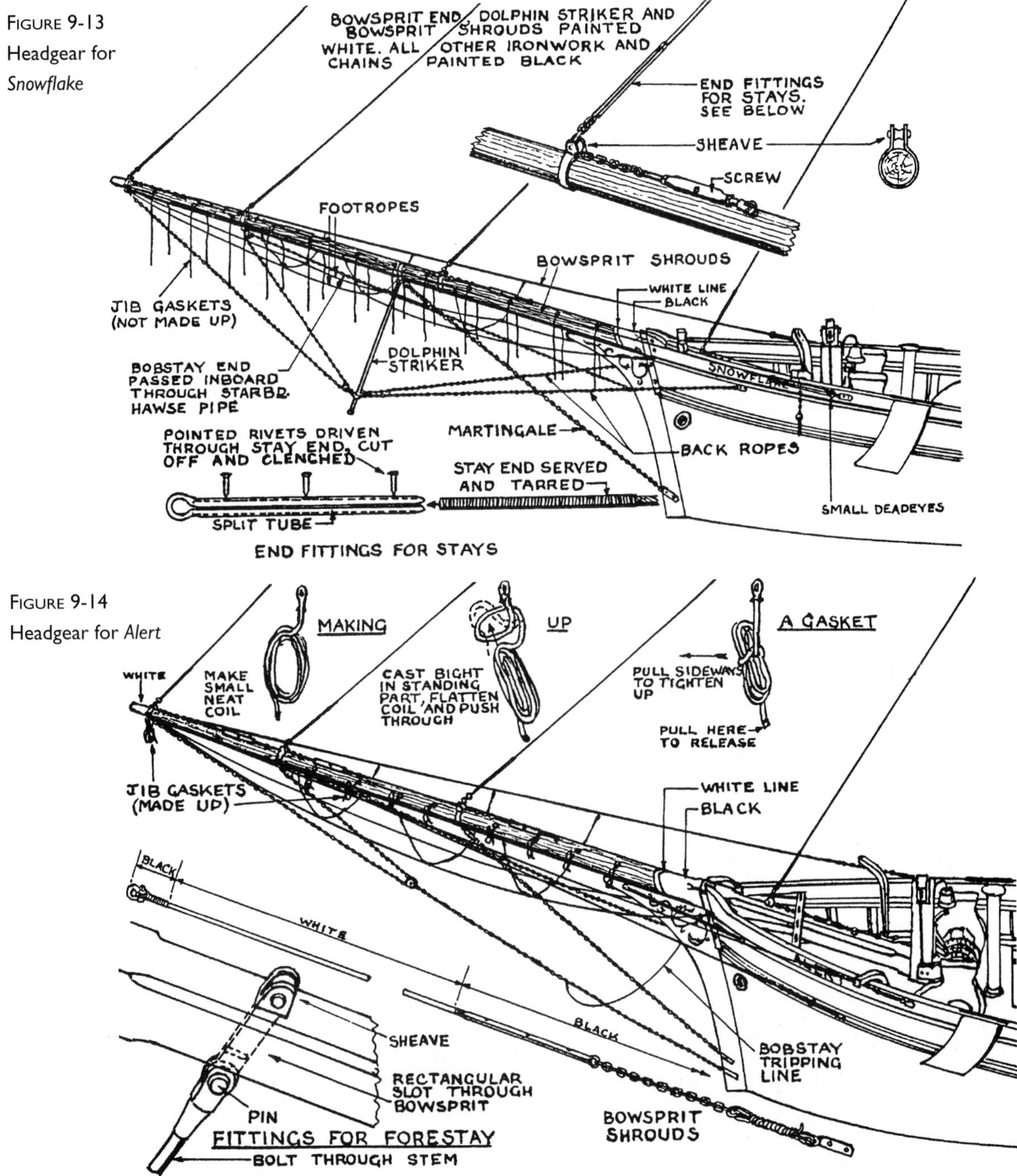

FIGURE 9-13
Headgear for *Snowflake*

FIGURE 9-14
Headgear for *Alert*

much when they went aloft. In all these places a slight investment in screws would have made a wonderful difference.

Those who have difficulty in remembering which way round the lanyards were rove in deadeyes, will find it enshrined in a hoary old nautical conundrum: 'Forrard on the starbr'd side, aft on the port side, and inside on both. What is it?' The answer is the Matthew Walker on the end of the lanyard. It will be noticed in Figure 9-7 that the end of the shroud, which was turned around the deadeye, was also on the same side as the stopper knot. This would seem to be carrying to extreme the rule that a right-hauled rope should be turned right-handed and, to my mind, the later method, in which the thimbles lay athwart ships and the ends were inside on both sides of the vessel, looked much smarter. In spite of the deficiencies of lanyards and deadeyes the occasional schooner still retained the original rake in her lower masts, the main raking aft at a slightly greater angle than the fore. One of these was the *Useful*, another was her sistership *Isabella*, although the latter had a very slight bend in her fore. Had these vessels not been related, one would have assumed that throughout their

Helena Anna coming up to anchor.

PHOTOGRAPHER UNKNOWN. DAVID CLEMENT COLLECTION

lives they had been blessed by very efficient mates or commanded by a long succession of timid skippers – evidently some builders managed from time to time to lay hands on a superior set of sticks.

But, if reasonably straight fore and main lower masts could sometimes be seen, there were very few mizzenmasts, except in ketches, which managed to escape the blight, while there were no main or mizzen topmasts that did not finish up bent forward. Inadequate staying caused most of this. The mizzenmast had three shrouds on each side [Figures 9-9 to 9-12 and 9-19] but the foremost of these were secured to chainplates some way before the line of the mast so that they could counteract the weight of the boom, gaff and sail on the topping lift. This left the other two pairs to resist the forward pull when the sail was set, although only one pair was in a position to do any really useful work. The backstays of main and mizzen topmasts were not really backstays at all; they were sidestays, the spreaders being merely the arms of one long straight crosstree. Had the spreaders raked aft in a broad 'vee', like those in American schooners, the backstays would have been able to prevent the topmasts from assuming their characteristic forward curve, as well as providing additional support to the masts below. Alone out of all the schooners and ketches left in the 1930s, the *Minnie* had a pair of chainplates abaft those of her main lower mast, which indicated that she had once worn a pair of main topmast backstays that actually could pull back

Bowsprits

Bowsprits in the 1850s were fitted with very long jib-booms, in order to produce a balanced sail plan in conjunction with a main boom, which projected out over the stern. They were a nuisance to everyone and had to be rigged-in when in dock so that other vessels could also use the facilities available; as the 19th century advanced they were gradually replaced by

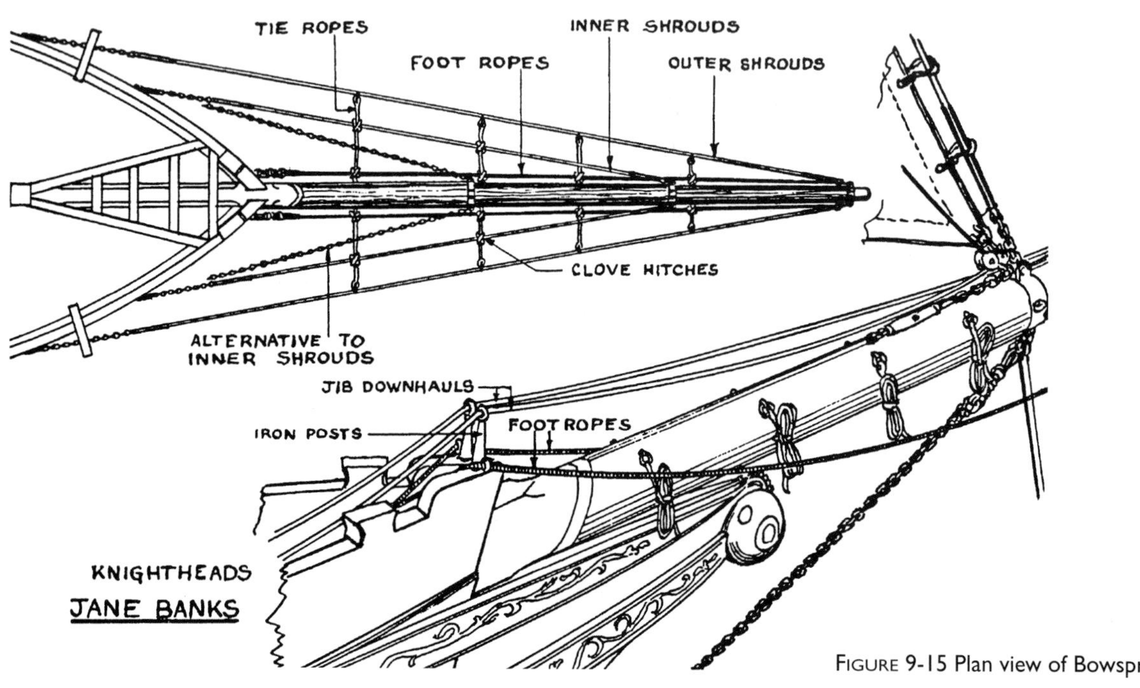

FIGURE 9-15 Plan view of Bowsprit

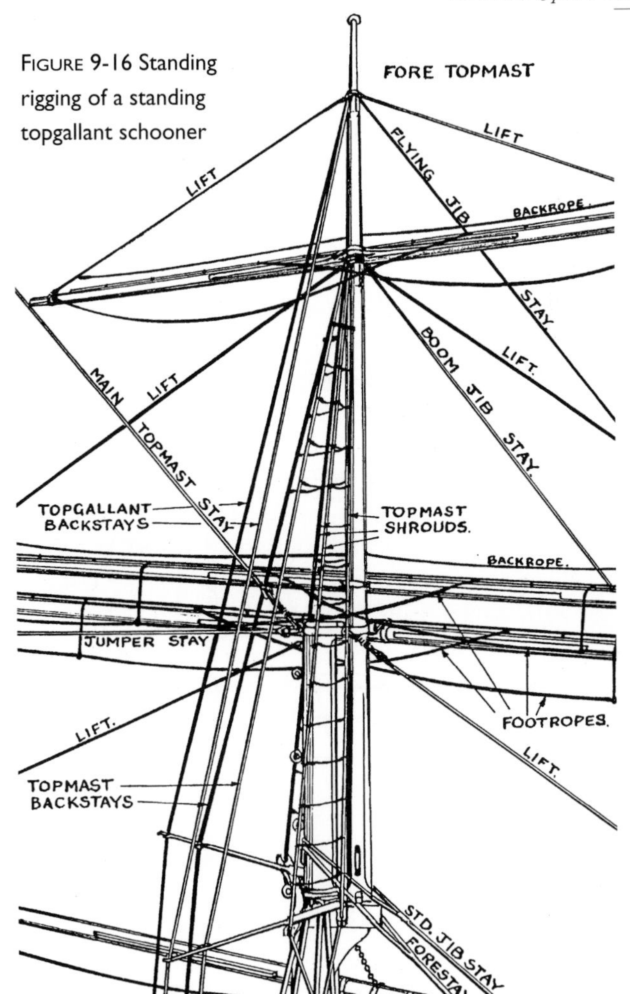

FIGURE 9-16 Standing rigging of a standing topgallant schooner

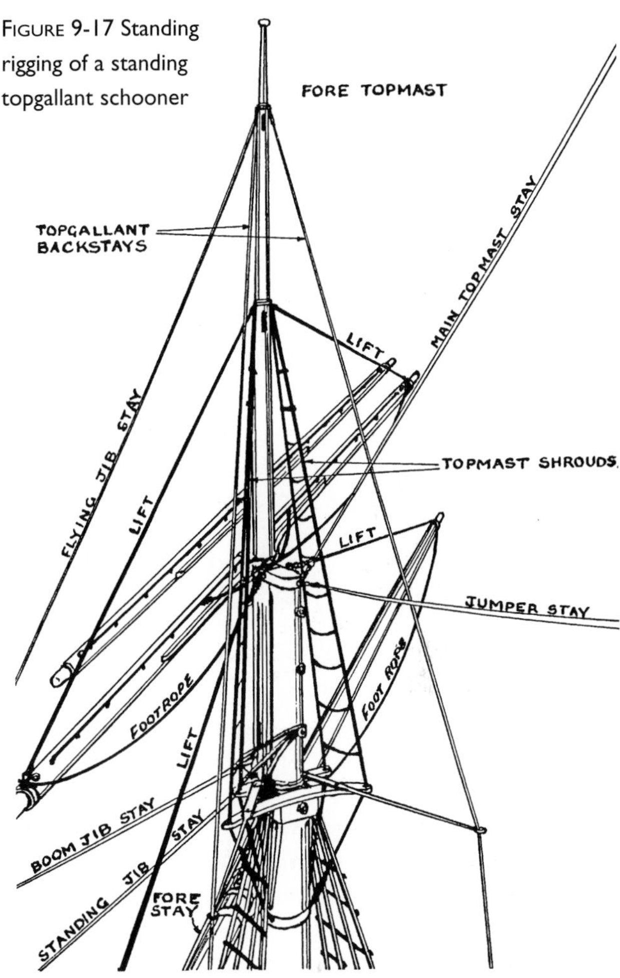

FIGURE 9-17 Standing rigging of a standing topgallant schooner

shorter spike bowsprits. This trend must have received something of a fillip when roller-reefing gear came into use as now the boom always came to an end above the counter.

At the final showing there were more ketches still with jib-booms than there were schooners, but the large original selection of bobstays and backropes had given way to a much simpler arrangement and, while the odd vessel with a spike bowsprit still had a dolphin striker, the majority made shift to manage without one.

Bowsprits were square inboard but with the corners chamfered off for neatness. They were fully square at the heel and the knightheads but once outside the latter the corners were cut down in a quick curve, so that the bowsprit became circular. For some reason this had not been done in *Brooklands* when she changed over from her original bowsprit and jib-boom; the job had been carried out using a plane alone, which can only cut in straight lines [Figure 9-14]; it only became truly circular at the standing jib band. Willy said it was an 'ugly sperr' and so it was, but it was understandable how it had come about. I am sure it was done in the refit of the 1920s. Sixty years after the building of a vessel, faced with the work of men long since dead, any shipwright worth his salt would have felt he was letting the side down if anything he put into her wasn't absolutely as strong as it could possibly be made.

Figures 9-13 and 9-14 show the two arrangements of bowsprits and headgear, which could be considered as standard. Some vessels, instead of having their inner bowsprit shrouds from the boom jib band, had a pair of chain shrouds from the standing jib band as shown in Figure 9-15, but this was a feature more frequently seen in conjunction with a bowsprit and jib-boom. Two kinds of jib gaskets were in use: long single ones, which were wrapped around and around the sail, and short gaskets in pairs, which were knotted over the top. Passing under the bowsprit, from the outer shroud on one side to the outer shroud on the other, was a series of ropes which were clove hitched around the footropes and, in places, around the inner shrouds as well [Figures 9-13 and 9-14]. These were not intended to prevent the crew from falling into the sea but to stop the jib sheets from doing so –

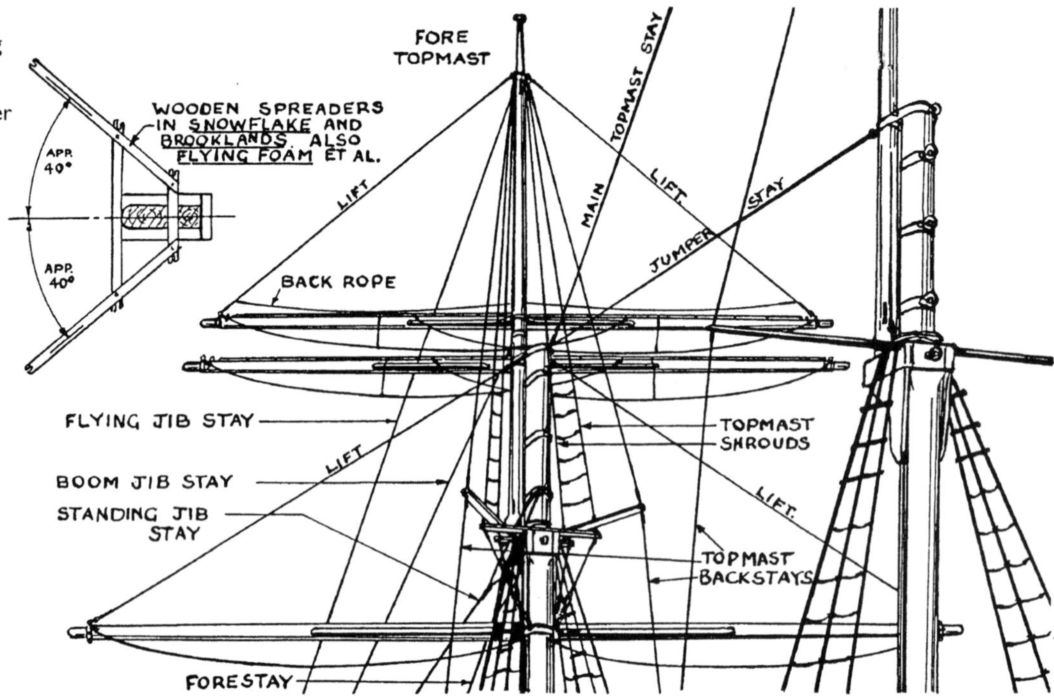

FIGURE 9-18
Standing Rigging of a Double Topsail Schooner Fore Topmast

left to themselves the weight of the chain pennants would have dragged the rest of the sheets out over the knightheads. This same tendency was the reason why a vessel without a dolphin striker had a tripping line to her bobstay.

The *Flying Foam*, *Katie*, *Jane Banks* and possibly other vessels, had a couple of short iron posts in the top of their knightheads [Figure 9-15]. *Katie* had served wires through the holes in these, with their forward ends fastened to the standing jib band and set taut by a lanyard to the foot of the forestay. They were obviously intended to be used as handrails but they also helped to make a neater stow of the standing jib. In the *Jane Banks* and *Flying Foam* they were used as leads for two of the jib downhauls, possibly with the intention of using them in the same way.

The *Jane Banks* had the after ends of her bowsprit footropes higher than in most other vessels, making some kind of hand hold almost a necessity and, although I cannot say that I noticed them doing it, I suspect that her crew used the trailboards as a first step when going out.

All the information about how, starting from scratch with nothing standing, a full-rigged ship was decked out in all her glory, can be found in a book on seamanship. The one I have is *New Seamanship*[2] by James Tait, extra master, who revised it in 1927. It is an unfortunate fact that people in possession of any technical language have a strong tendency to talk in

Lizzie at Truro with an unidentified ketch and the excursion boat *New Resolute* laden with passengers, blowing off steam and ready to depart as the tide makes, with her passengers all aboard.

PHOTOGRAPHER UNKNOWN. DAVID CLEMENT COLLECTION

[2]*New Seamanship* by James Tait, Brown, Son & Ferguson, Glasgow, 1927 rev.

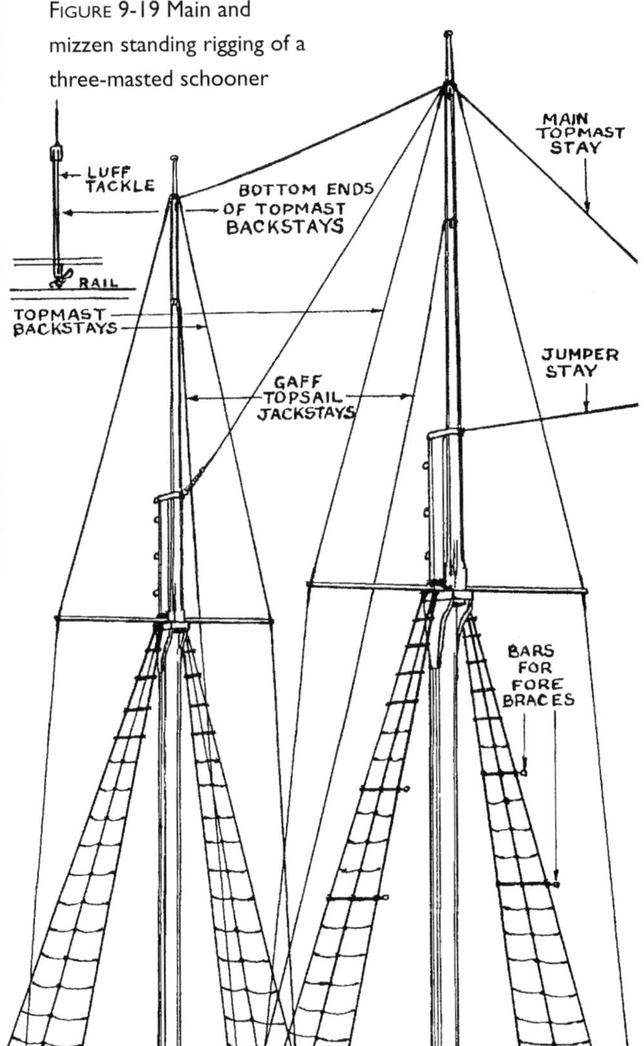

FIGURE 9-19 Main and mizzen standing rigging of a three-masted schooner

shorthand. It saves time and they do not realise they are doing it unless an outsider draws their attention to the fact. James Tait's questions and answers are based on the assumption that both questioner and respondent had actually done the job so that neither wastes his words. Most of it is easily enough understood by anyone familiar with the pieces of equipment being assembled, and the following notes, simplified to suit a schooner, are intended merely to elucidate the occasionally over-abbreviated parts of the cross-talk.

The lower masts having been parbuckled aboard and stepped by means of sheer-legs, with their crosstrees in position, the first piece of standing rigging sent aloft was the forward pair of shrouds on the starboard side of the foremast. This was followed by the forward pair to port, then the after pair to starboard, and finally the after pair to port. The forestay was then sent up, followed by the standing jib stay and, in a schooner with a flying topgallant, the boom jib stay as well, the eyes in their top ends passing over one of the eyebolts in the back of the doubling or over a wooden stop bolted in position. The forestay was set up first and adjusted until measurements taken at the partners showed that the mast was in the middle of the hole; the shrouds were then set up, after which the wedges could be driven home. The main lower mast was stayed forward by the jumper stay, the shrouds, as usual, being sent aloft first. Some schooners had four shrouds a side on the main as well as the fore but quite a lot had only three, the after ones being single shrouds with a spliced eye in the upper end [Figure 9-16]. I believe that at one time these were known as 'swifters', a term that would have become obsolete long ago had not the Merseysiders taken it to their hearts and used it as a collective expression meaning the shrouds of the lower masts only. Readers of John Masefield may have seen it used in this context.

Once the lower masts had been stayed and wedged, the topmasts could be sent up. A block was hooked into one side of the cap and a rope rove through it, down through the hole in the trestletrees, through the sheavehole in the heel of the topmast, and the two parts of the rope were fastened together with a racking seizing leaving a tail dangling at the end. Both ropes were lashed to the topmast at a point near its head, and it was them hoisted up with another rope on its heel to guide it through the hole in the trestletrees and the one above that in the cap. When the hounds of the topmast were through the cap the mast rope was belayed while the tail was made fast to the other side of the cap, then the lashing and racking seizing were both cast off [Figures 9-16, 9-17 and 9-18]. Working through the sheavehole back to the cap, the mast rope was then on a double purchase and the operation is dismissed by James Tait in a few words: 'double the mast rope and come up the racking'. Before the topmast was hoisted any higher the eyes of its standing rigging had to be put over the masthead. Most double topsail schooners had a band on the fore topmast, just above the cap, that took the end of the boom jib stay. If this was small enough to pass through the hole in the cap, it could be put on before the topmast left the deck, if not, it was the first thing over the truck. If the boom jib stay was set up from the topmast hounds, as was usual in a standing topgallant-yarder, its eye was the first thing to be put on. It was followed by the starboard topmast shrouds, then the port ones, the backstays and, finally, the strop for the upper topsail lifts. Last came the gear for the topgallant hounds, if the mast had them, flying jib stay, backstays and lift strop, if required.

All this gear would have to be sent up from the deck on another gantline, and the man aloft, whose job it was to double the mast rope and come up the racking, would stay there to see that all the eyes were well hammered down on to their respective hounds. In some vessels a final complication was caused by the fact that the crane of the lower topsail yard was partly supported by the fore topmast [Figure 9-16] and the fitting for this, unless it would pass through the trestletrees, would have to be installed after the mast was hoisted. It was quite common to see a schooner with her main or mizzen topmast housed – ie. lowered down until its hounds were just above the cap – for such jobs as scraping or replacing some item of gear, but until engines came, fore topmasts were usually left alone.

The mizzen lower masts of barquentines and three-masted schooners were probably stayed, measured and wedged by the use of the shrouds alone, unless the rake aft was such that a tackle was necessary to act as a temporary stay. It will be noticed in Figure 9-19 that the mizzen topmast was fitted with two stays to the main topmast hounds. The advantage of this arrangement was that it allowed a main gaff topsail to be set, which did not have to be clewed up and shifted over a jumper stay every time the vessel went about. Its drawback was that it relied on the main topmast to stay in one piece. The safer of the two positions in which the after end of one of these stays finished was obviously the cap of the mizzen lower mast, but as this limited the height to which the peak of the mainsail could be hoisted, it was frequently to be seen some way up the mizzen topmast. As far as I am aware these two stays between main and mizzen topmasts had no official titles. The foremasts of many sailing ships had more work to do than the others as they had not only to support their own sails but also had to resist the pull of the headsails. For this reason American and Canadian schooners had an extra pair of backstays on the fore topmast.

On the Great Lakes this does not seem to have been considered sufficient as the fore topmast had to contend with the raffee as well as a gaff topsail. Another stay was therefore added, from the fore topmast hounds down to the cap of the main lower mast. This was later copied and used in some vessels sailing the salt sea and, not unnaturally, their crews referred to it as the freshwater stay. Its introduction brought with it a slight complication in clewing up and re-setting the fore gaff topsail when going about. Anyone interested in how this problem was solved, presumably also on the Great Lakes, will find the answer in *Blue Water Coaster*[3] previously mentioned in Chapter VI.

It can be claimed that one of the two stays between the main- and mizzenmasts of British three-masters was a freshwater stay in the wrong place. There was one British schooner, and probably only one, which for a time had a real freshwater stay. She was the *Volant*, and she wore it in the years when she still set a lower topsail even though working as an auxiliary vessel. Judging by the angle at which her foremast emerged from the deck she must have had considerable rake in her masts when launched but in her later years the fore lower mast curved forward appreciably from about the truss of the foreyard upwards – so much so that the topmast, in spite of being reasonably straight itself, was out of line with the lower mast by an angle not far short of 10 degrees. It was obvious that the lower mast had been sprung and the stay was there to prevent it from getting worse. If the mast had been fished they would have been unable to carry a full foresail; the stay was dispensed with a few years later when the lower topsail yard was sent down.

Battens were used on all shrouds in places where they were too close together for a toe to be inserted – that is on the last two or three footholds to the hounds of a mast – but a smart schooner still in full possession of her sailing faculties wore battens on the shrouds of the fore lower mast only. They were set between the middle pair of shrouds and were much more serviceable than ratlines, but were not considered quite so elegant. When the job was done properly there was a tie ratline at every fifth batten. When engines were installed, some vessels gave up the struggle to maintain the appearance of their standing rigging and could be seen with widely spaced battens on one side of each mast only. Others, because of their cut-down rig, were even more determined to continue in a seamanlike manner.

Figure 9-17 shows the details of gaffs and booms, as do the detailed figures showing spars etc. in Figure 9-5 *et seq*. The roller-reefing boom was rotated in a clockwise direction when looking aft on its forward end, this being done because, by long tradition, the boltropes of a fore-and-aft sail were on the port side. If it had been rotated the other way the boltrope would have been inside, the canvas would not lie down properly on the boom and the sail would have stretched out of shape. There were two types of gear for rotating the boom: a chain wrapped around a drum that could be unwound by pulling on it with the reef tackle, and a worm-and-worm wheel. Their relative merits will be discussed along with their operation.

Roller-reefing gear brought a minor problem in its train: where to attach the boom tackle. The only parts of the boom that did not revolve were the jaws and the sheet band, but if the boom tackle had been hooked in along with the sheet it would have had to be shifted over at both ends when the vessel was gybed, or left to pull from the wrong side The problem was solved rather neatly by a wire strop looped over the swivel band [Figure 9-6 detail 5].

The standing rigging of fore topmasts and yards is shown in Figures 9-9 to 9-12. It will be noticed that the footropes of the foreyard did not cross each other in the slings; they were only necessary for access to the blocks and sheaves at the

[3] *Blue Water Coaster* by Francis E. Bowker, International Marine Publishing, Camden, Maine, 1972.

yardarms and were not even fitted with stirrups. Most upper topsail yards and, formerly, standing topgallant yards had back ropes fitted to them. These were light lines, clove-hitched around the tye and seized to the lifts so that they hung just above the yards. Their purpose was to prevent the sailors from being knocked backwards off the yard by the sail. Cynics proclaimed that they were no of earthly use and that their real name should have been 'arse ropes' but as no one seemed to fall off upper topsail yards, they would have been hard put to prove their contention.

The approximate sizes of rope, wire, and chain used for standing rigging are given in Figures 9-22 to 9-24. The gaff-topsail jackstays have been lumped in with the standing rigging for the sake of convenience, although they should properly be classed as semi-standing – when not in use their lower ends were made fast to pins in the rail so that they hung clear of the fore and afters; when in use they were set taut by a tackle at the foot of the mast. Their function will be dealt with in the next chapter.

FIGURE 9-20

Diameters of Masts

Rig	*Mast*	*Inches per Yard* *Fraction*	*Decimal*
Barquentine	Fore lower mast	1	1.0
Barquentine	Fore topmast		
Barquentine	Fore topgallant mast		
Brigantine	Fore lower mast		
Brigantine	Fore topmast		
Brigantine	Fore topgallant mast		
Schooner	Fore topmast		
Schooner	Fore lower mast	¾	.75
Brigantine	Main lower mast		
Ketch	Mizzen mast		
Barquetine	Main lower mast	¾–¹¹⁄₁₆	.75–.68
Schooner	Main lower mast		
Ketch	Main lower mast		
Barquentine	Mizzen lower mast	¹¹⁄₁₆–⅝	.68–.62
3M Schooner	Mizzen lower mast		

Approximate length of lower masts in feet: Height above deck mark plus depth of hold, minus two feet (depth of keelson)

FIGURE 9-22

Standing Rigging – Rope

Item	*Nom Dia.*	*Circ.*
Gaff jaw rope	½	1⅝
Gaskets	½	1⅝
Lanyards of lower shrouds	1–1⅛	3⅛–3½
Lanyards–miscellaneous	½–⅝	1⅜–2
Ratlines	½	1⅝
Tie ropes on bowsprit shouds	½–⅝	1⅝–2

FIGURE 9-21

Running Rigging – Wire

Item	*Nom. Dia.*	*Circ.*
Boom jib stay	¾	2⅜
Boom tackle strops	½	1⅝
Bowsprit shrouds	⅝–¾	2–2⅜
Flying jib stay	¾	2⅜
Footropes	½	1⅝
Footrope stirrups	½	1⅝
Forestay	1–1⅛	3⅛–3½
Fore topmast backstays	¾–⅞	2⅜–2¾
Fore topgallant backstays	⅝–¾	2–2⅜
Fore topmast shrouds	½–⅝	1⅝–2
Fore lifts	⅝	2
Fore topmast lifts	½	1⅝
Fore topgallant lifts	½	1⅝
'Freshwater stay'	½	1⅝
Gaff topsail jackstays	½	1⅝
Jumper stay	1½–1⅛	3⅛–3½
Mainstay (ketch)	1–1⅛	3⅛–3½
Main topmast stay	¾	2⅜
Main and mizzen topmast backstays	½–⅝	1⅝–2
Mizzen shouds (ketch)	⅝	2
Mizzen topmast stay	½	1⅝
Shrouds	1–1⅛	3⅛–3½
Standing jib stay	¾–1	2⅜–3⅛
Wire spans on gaffs	½	1⅝

FIGURE 9-23

Standing Rigging – Chain

Item	*Size in inches*
'Backropes' of dolphin striker	¼
Bobstay	¼
Bowsprit shrouds (from standing jib band)	⁵⁄₁₆
LOWER END OF HEADSTAYS	
Boom jib stay	⁵⁄₁₆
Flying jib stay	⁵⁄₁₆
Forestay	⅜
Mainstay (ketch)	⅜
Standing jib stay	⁵⁄₁₆
Martingale	⅜–⁷⁄₁₆
Sling of fore yard	⁵⁄₁₆–⅜

FIGURE 9-24

Short Link Chain

Diameter of bar	¼	⁵⁄₁₆	⅜	⁷⁄₁₆	½
Length of link	1⁷⁄₃₂	1¹⁷⁄₃₂	1²⁷⁄₃₂	1⅛	2⁷⁄₁₆
Width of link	⅞	1³⁄₃₂	1⁵⁄₁₆	1¹⁷⁄₃₂	1¾

These dimensions correspond roughly to a link 5 diameters long and 3½ diameters wide. End links to take shakles are made from bar 1.2 times the diameter of the chain and are about 6.6 diameters long and 4 diameters wide.

X

SAILS AND RUNNING RIGGING

Sails have served man for thousands of years, and countless generations must each have contributed some small improvement, if not to the sails themselves then to the way in which they were used. The invisibility of the forces being harnessed makes it certain that every one of these gains was extremely hard-won.

It is unlikely that there has ever been a shortage of people with theories about sails; they lend themselves to experts. All ages have had their keen thinkers, and all ages have had their lunatic fringe, and the full force of both has probably been at work on the sail from its very inception. Theories about it still abound, many of its mysteries are still unsolved; progress, as with our forebears, is still measurable in small fractions, and it can hardly be claimed that the application of the scientific approach has so far contributed anything that makes the long centuries of trial and error look any less impressive. Better materials are now available from which to make sails, but there are still so many deep-rooted, frequently unsubstantiated and contradictory beliefs in circulation about how they actually do their work – especially in propelling a vessel to windward – that it would be a bold man who would claim that any great progress was being made.

There is no reason to believe that before the camera came to relieve them of their obligations, the majority of artists ever considered that their job was to do anything except faithfully to portray what they saw. Even the perfervid imagination of Peter Bruegel the elder seems to have been left in abeyance when he came to dealing with ships; his treatment of them suggests that not only was he quite familiar with their gear, but also he had heard the brace blocks clatter and seen the great main yard come swinging around as the mariners 'hauled their wind' in those lumbering sea wagons of the past. From evidence left by many other artists as well, it is obvious that at one time there was a belief that the 'baggier' a sail was, the more wind it would hold – a theory that is perfectly true for a running vessel and the modem balloon spinnaker is the last word in its application. In spite of this age-old belief, someone in the latter part of the 19th century conceived the idea that, unless some means was provided to let the wind out of a sail, no more could get into it and to prove the point a square-rigger was equipped with a suit of sails that had large circular holes in them. No earth-shattering results seem to have been obtained; at least the sails were not perpetuated.

Many other theories are not so easily put to the test. Some think that overlapping sails create a kind of wind tunnel that is highly efficient, others that sails blanketed by other sails are only a drag on the vessel. In some quarters there is a theory that the luff of a sail should not only be taut to work efficiently, it should be a straight line as well – the exponents of this belief must spend a good deal of time tightening up their headstays.

While of great help when running, long ago the bagginess of a sail was discovered to be a drawback when going to windward. To prevent it from becoming too much of a handicap our ancestors used bowlines, which kept the luffs of the sails taut and enabled them to lie closer to the wind. By the middle of the 19th century, sailmakers had reduced the bagginess to a much flatter saucer than had ever been used before, and from this point bowlines rapidly went out of use. Attempts to obtain even flatter sails still continue, mainly by the use of battens, and for years there has been a growing awareness of the superiority of the Chinese junk sails over European ones. They are flatter owing to their numerous full-width battens or yards, but the issue has always been clouded by the complex system of vangs, which usually get the credit for the close-windedness of these vessels.

Alongside the attempts to produce flatter sails there has existed for many years a belief that some peculiar power resides in the curvature of a sail, that without it the results would be much poorer in some way not specified. It is impossible to produce a perfectly flat sail because the tension in the fabric would be much higher than the cloth could stand, and the nearer to complete flatness the greater the tension becomes. This process can probably be better understood by considering, in reverse, another shipboard activity – the tightening up of ropes by the method known as 'swigging', in which tremendous tension can be imparted by the application of a relatively small lateral force. In a sail, of course, as distinct from a rope, the tension works in all directions, although the direction of the maximum force is conditioned by where and how it is restrained. The procedure by which ropes were swigged can be seen in Figure 10.1. The rope to be dealt with was taken around the pin and one man hung on to the end. The others grasped the rope about head height and all threw their weight backwards in unison, pulling the rope after them and gaining a length of slack. At the end of the outward swing they sank down with knees bent, so that they could keep their full weight on the rope and prevent it from running back. At the same time they swung inwards again towards the rail, giving the slack to the 'holder-on', who took it in. To do the job properly the swiggers had to stand with one foot out behind them with which to reverse their movement although, once started, their impetus carried them on like the weight of a pendulum. On the lee side the heel of the vessel helped considerably. The first swig gave lots of slack so that the backsides of the practitioners finished up near the deck; thereafter the law of diminishing returns applied. The number of swigs, which were 'swug', depended on how tight someone, usually the mate, considered the rope ought to be. The lee braces came in for this treatment every time a schooner went about and, on one occasion in the *Alert* when Chris and I were doing it, owing to mis-timing on my part, we didn't swig the upper topsail brace as tight as Frank thought it should be. He grudgingly conceded that it would do, because it was only a short tack, but he certainly disliked things that were not done properly.

The curvature in a sail, then, is the product of necessity and it still remains to be proved that it possesses any magic powers. A survey of the laws of mechanics reveals that it is quite possible that in any sail there is only one point where it is working to optimum capacity, and that the nearer the rest of the canvas can be kept to the angle of this part, relative to the wind, then the greater would be the efficiency. There is only one drawback to the pursuit of this matter to its logical conclusion, but it is a drawback of no mean proportions and one that has been with the sailing ship since the very beginning – no wind is ever quite constant in speed or direction and in a gale this tendency becomes aggravated so that, in the squalls, it can back and veer far faster than the vessel's course can be altered to suit. For this reason, in a square-rigger the upper yards were checked in, each one a little more than the one below it and the after yards were checked in more than the forward yards so that, in the event of the upper and after sails losing the wind, the lower and forward sails would still keep drawing and provide the steerage way necessary to let the vessel go more free. The characteristic twist imparted to squaresails happened automatically in fore and afters, as the gaff sagged to leeward of the boom. The amount of sag could be controlled by the use of vangs. It is obvious from the foregoing that all sailing vessels will lie closer to the wind when shortened down, but this seldom compensates them for the increased leeway caused by the disturbance of the sea.

FIGURE 10-1 Swigging up a rope

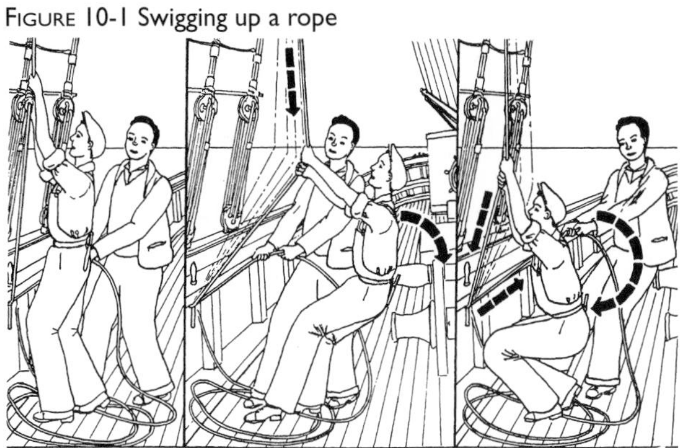

WHEN THE JOB WAS DONE BY TWO MEN ONLY, THE MAN HOLDING ON TO THE STANDING PART DID SO WITH ONE HAND AND USED THE OTHER TO ASSIST IN PULLING INWARDS.

It was racing of one kind or another which gave rise to most of the improvements which took place in the sailing ship in the latter half of the 19th century and it was racing that continued to influence the development of the commercial fore-and-after, long after the square-rigger had been driven from the racing trades. In the days of the orange trade the cargo-carrying schooner had probably carried a tremendous arsenal of flying kites of all kinds, but by the 1890s it had neither an adequate crew nor an adequate financial incentive to go as far as to cultivate the huge gaff topsails that the sporting gentlemen saw fit to set in their racing cutters. Nevertheless, many of the other theories, fashions and foibles of the day must have spilled off on to it. During the same period other sporting gentlemen were active on the far side of the Atlantic and the same processes must also have been taking place there because the two end products were slightly different.

In Europe it was thought that the foot of a gaff sail should be left free to assume its own curve so that, while the head was secured to the gaff along its full length, only the clew was made fast to the boom while the tack was fastened to a mast hoop which was left free to move up or down. The Americans were also convinced that the head should be fastened to the gaff; it had been done for so long in the square-rigger and was so much in keeping with square-rigged practice that it is doubtful anyone ever questioned it. However, they also felt that the foot of the sail should be constrained in some way so that it did not assume a bigger curve than necessary and so they fastened it to the boom at intervals with long rovings, the 'drift' of each of which was adjusted to produce the desired results. In consequence Europeans knotted their reef points under the sail, leaving it free of the boom, while the Americans crossed their points under the sail to constrain the canvas and then tied their knots below the boom [Figure 10-7]. A novel attempt of an even more complicated kind was tried in

Lochranza Castle outward bound in the Queens Channel, River Mersey, 5 July 1932.

Photograph by A. F. Dakin. Terry Belt Collection

the yacht *Endeavour*: her boom had a flat cigar-shaped top, across which little 'sheet horses' allowed the foot of the sail to assume a curve, while preventing it from lifting upwards. The sporting gentlemen were not concerned about working their yachts with a small crew but the commercial shipowner had to be, and once roller-reefing gear had been proved a practical proposition on fore-and-aft sails, their ways inevitably parted. This gear required the foot of the sail to be fastened to the boom, and fastened to the boom it was, regardless of what the current theory on the subject happened to be, as it probably enabled the bigger vessels to work a hand lighter, whilst smaller ones could manage with a boy in place of a man. For many years I was puzzled by the fact that the Americans, a nation addicted to labour-saving devices, never adopted roller-reefing gear in their huge fore-and-afters, until it dawned on me that having no squaresails they were able to luff their vessels up into the wind to take some of the pressure off the canvas while the sails were being reefed. In retrospect it strikes me that all the labour-saving devices in the world would not have enabled them to reduce their crews any further; they were down to the absolute minimum as it was. The option of luffing was also open to those in British ketches and, although it did not prevent them from being fitted with roller-reefing gear, it was often resorted to while the hooped kind of gaff topsail was being stowed. The possession of even one squaresail made it an impossibility to luff – another factor that had some bearing on the sudden disappearances of schooners in squalls.

If the first action of a schooner's crew had been to get the topsails off her, the helmsman could then have kept the vessel hung up on the wind until it was safe to put her off again to full and bye. This, too, is probably something that never crossed anyone's mind. The fathers of the men who, in the 1930s, were approaching the end of their working lives, had grown up under the full influence of the square rigger and it took more than one generation of sailing-ship seamen for such a radical alteration in outlook even to gain a foothold. It was a mental 'block' that would, and probably did, put the skipper of a Great Lakes schooner, with only a raffee, in no better position in a squall than the master of the *Preussen*. One of the lucky men was Tom Gray who told me that he was once in a schooner laid on her beam ends by a squall, which was so far over that her rudder wouldn't act. They expected the cargo to shift at any second and, in desperation, cut the mainsheet. The boom fell into the water and the sail, acting as a drag, allowed her bows to pay slowly off until she came upright once more. Fortunately all the cargo stayed where it was.

Sailmaking

Two distinct methods were, and still are, used by sailmakers to produce a saucer-shaped end product. The first was to put a taper into the overlaps of the seams so that they were narrower in the middle of the sail than they were at the edges, the second was to make the edges of the sail curve slightly outwards so that the boltrope took the strain only when the canvas had sagged inwards by the requisite amount. The first method was used in all sails, the second in some edges of some sails only. In squaresails in which the head was the only edge made fast along its whole length, it was discovered long ago that the boltropes could do their job more efficiently if the leeches were given a slight inward curve. To make the sail more baggy when running it was only necessary to ease the sheets a trifle, which had the added advantage in heavy weather of imparting a certain amount of lift to the pulling action as well as reducing the strain on the sail. The strain on a squaresail was greatest in the vertical direction so that it frequently tore across, although complete disintegration could start in the middle if the stitching failed. Loose-footed gaff and boom sails may have been under strain in a different way, but the roller-reefing variety, which were made fast to both boom and gaff, were also inclined to tear across. In this respect the modern method of cutting a Bermudan sail with the cloths running across it probably gives a better shape but at the expense of strength, as it relies purely on the stitching to keep the cloths together. In the 1930s there were quite a number of vessels sailing about with half their mast hoops missing – giving a clear indication that very little strain came on to the luff. What hoops they did have were on the upper part of the sails so that they could do their job when the stormy winds blew.

The knowledge contained in the practise of most forms of skilled manual work can be placed in one of two categories. Some of it can be transmitted to others by the spoken or written word but a good deal can only be clearly grasped by seeing it done. I am not qualified to say how much of sailmaking is in this latter category and suspect it of being quite a lot, but during my days in Runcorn I had the good fortune to share a public house with an old sailmaker, Alfred Pritchard, from whom I learned something more of the art than I could have acquired during my two brief sojourns in schooners.

Alfred's family was one of the Pritchards who had owned the little *Gleaner*; he had a quick brain and wide interests and, on the few occasions when, briefly, we had the pub to ourselves, would talk about matters vastly different from the potted idiocy with which we and the rest of the clientele strove manfully to out do each other as closing time approached. He was very good at mental arithmetic and, without doubt, it was this ability that gave rise to one of his most surprising statements. He could, so he said, cut and sew a schooner's mainsail in a pub tap-room; he didn't know why they wanted to lay it out flat because 'the damn thing wasn't flat when it was finished'. As the shape of a fore and after is fixed by the length of the diagonal, I have a suspicion that he would have had to make a scale drawing of some kind to obtain the angles at which to cut his cloths, but I am certain that he could have done the job in the manner and location specified, provided of course that he refused to listen to the call of the running beer! He probably knew a lot more about trigonometry than I suspected at the time.

Some of the West Bank shrimpers came to Alfred's family for their sails. In former days there had been in their ranks a remarkable old man who had spent the whole of his life as a fisherman, and it is with great regret that I have to admit I have forgotten his name. During his journeying to and from the fishing grounds he would bring his nobby abreast of some other boat and hold her there while they discussed the latest news and generally exchanged opinions. When all topics of conversation had been exhausted he would finally say, 'Well, I'll be leaving you now', and that was exactly what he did. He would make minute adjustments to his sheets and gear and, in no time at all, would be out ahead of them, moreover it did not matter how much they fiddled with their own equipment, they could not catch up with him again. Man and boat had obviously become as one but, underlying this, there must have been a whole lifetime's observation of all the quirks and tricks of tide and current and eddy in the upper Mersey, an estuary which someone once very aptly described as 'a raging beast of a river'.

Many of the things done in attempts to improve sails could be classed as highly debatable in their results but, in the latter part of the 19th century a tremendous improvement was made in the design of jibs and, as is often the case with such positive steps forward, it was the work of one man. Until the late 1850s, possibly later, jibs had been cut low in the foot in order to fill as much as possible of the area between the headstays. Their cloths were parallel to the leech. The sheets, pulling low down, were admirably contrived to keep the foot of the sail taut but could do little about the leech, which probably flapped about when the vessel was on a wind. A sailmaker of the kind who was not satisfied with what had been good enough for his father considered this problem and finally produced the answer. He realised that by raising the clew of the sail some of the pull going into the foot could be transferred to the leech and, carrying this train of thought further, he grasped that for the foot and leech to be in equal tension the line of the sheet would have to be at right angles to the stay. If the length of luff and the distance from luff to clew remained the same as before, there would be no loss in area. This piece of original thought might have satisfied some, but the sailmaker understood that he would still not achieve just what he wanted unless he used his canvas in such a way that the stretch in the upper and lower parts of the sail was the same. To achieve this he decided to put a seam across the line of the sheet and to cut his cloths parallel to the leech in the upper half but to the foot in the lower [Figure 10-2]. Many years ago I read somewhere, that the name of this man was Matthew Orr and, while he did not achieve the same notoriety as Matthew Walker, his way of cutting a jib is still referred to by sailmakers as the Scotch method. It was not long before all jibs were made in this way, although schooners' staysails in most cases continued to be cut in the traditional manner.

Figures 10-2 to 10-6 show the various sails used by schooners and ketches. It will be noticed that there were a number of places where they were reinforced by extra thicknesses of cloths either with the intention of strengthening them, or spreading the load, or to resist wear and tear. The horizontal cloth from the clew of a gaff topsail and the three cloths spreading out from the bunt cringle of a squaresail were in the former category, while those on the topsails were intended to withstand the wear of the buntlines, which, in the latterday schooner at

Figure 10-2
Standing jib and staysail

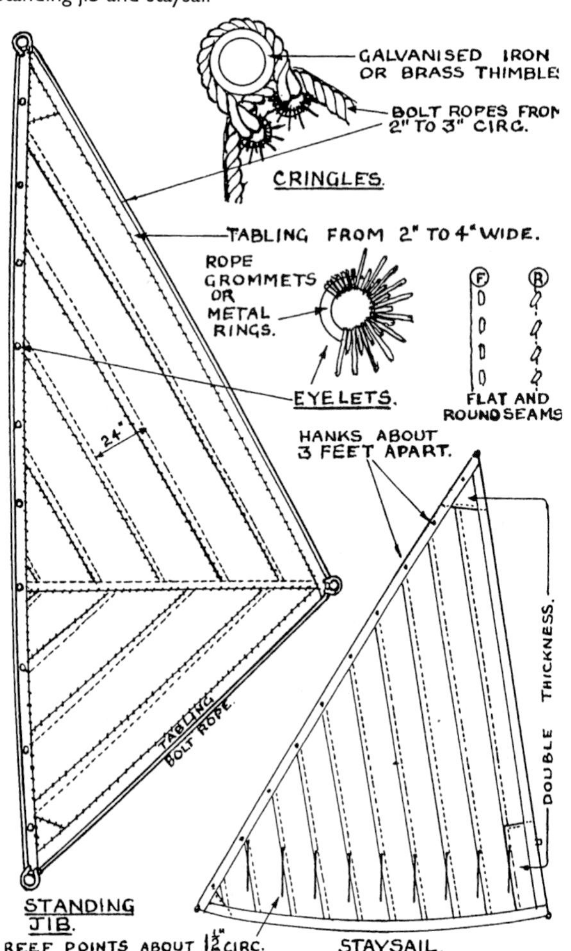

Figure 10-3
Topsails and squaresail

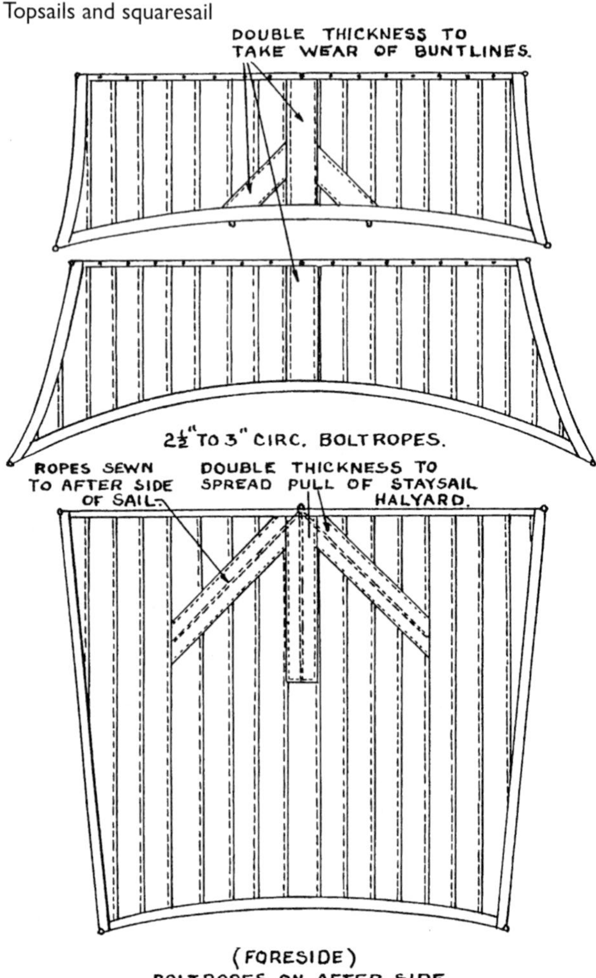

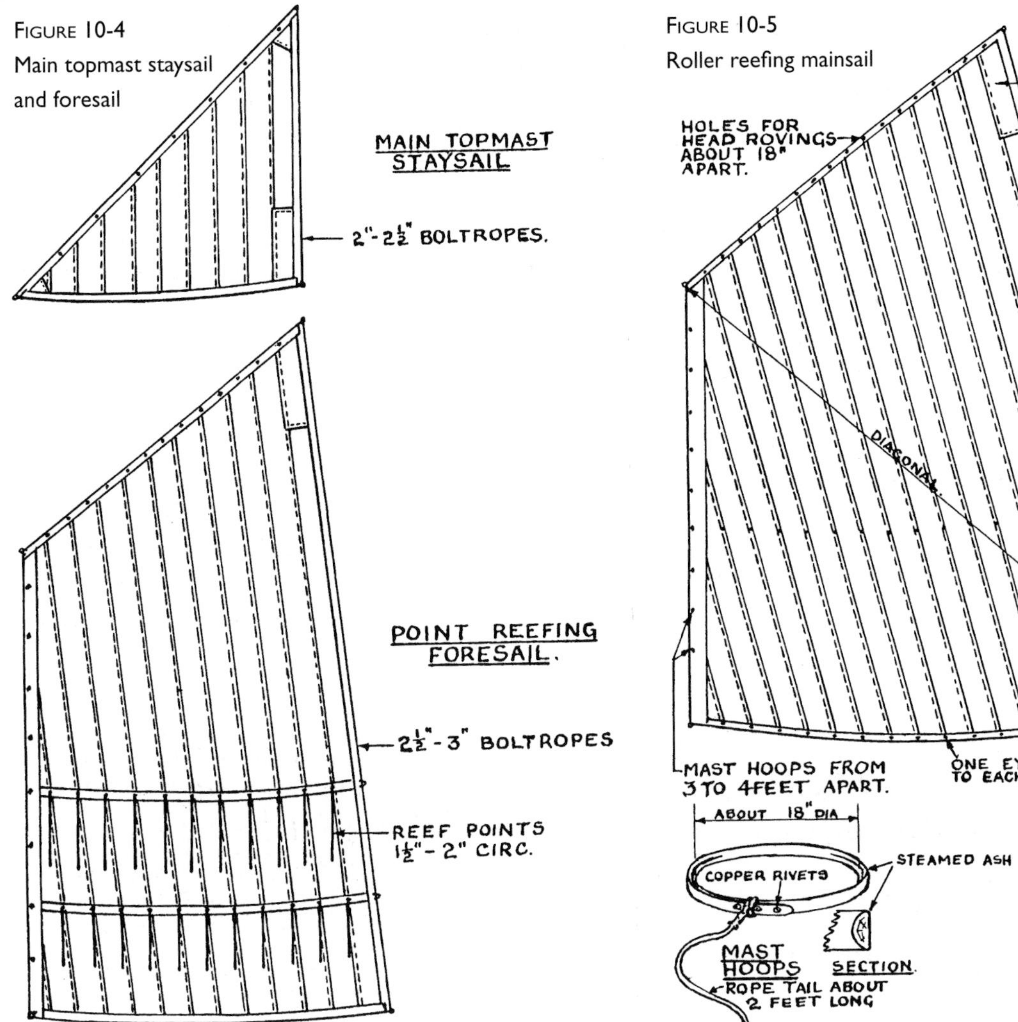

Figure 10-4
Main topmast staysail and foresail

Figure 10-5
Roller reefing mainsail

least, were never overhauled and stopped to the jackstay. The corners of sails were also reinforced because much of the strain was transmitted through them but as sailmaking is not a dying art there are now many more ways of doing this than there were in the past. Boltropes were traditionally on the after side of a squaresail and on the port side of a fore and after, the latter being a useful guide as to which end of a gaff topsail was the head and which the tack, without having to spread it all over the deck. This identification was only necessary with the kind of topsail that was sent aloft from the deck and was taken below again as soon as they came in. Jackyard gaff topsails could be set on the main topmasts of ketches, schooners and brigantines, and on the mizzenmasts of ketches and three-masters and, in the past, they frequently were but by the 1930s they had become something of a rarity. Some jackyard gaff topsails were set from the deck after the manner of a standing lug but a fair few seem to have had hoops on the topmast. These latter must have been the absolute limit to stow, as the man dealing with them would not only run the risk of being knocked out of the crosstrees by the sail but of being brained by the yard as well.

For at least a hundred years there have been two schools of thought on which spar is the jackyard. The argument has given rise to more bitter, stubborn and acrimonious correspondence in various journals than almost any other subject. One school, which belongs to the West Country and the west coast in general, calls the spar at the head of the sail the jackyard and the one at the foot, which extends the canvas beyond the peak of the gaff, the jinny-boom, jenny-boom or, in some cases, the club. The opposition states that the spar at the foot of the sail is the jackyard, and the one at the head is the topsail yard. I notice that Sir Alan Moore subscribes to this usage.[1] The fact that this school usually fails to refer to the sail in question as a gaff topsail gives rise to a suspicion that it orig-

[1] *Last Days of Mast and Sail* by Alan Moore, Clarendon Press, Oxford, 1925.

inates in the southeast, the Thames barge area, from which come other differences in nautical nomenclature.

A similar great schism applies to the two chains beneath the bowsprit. To the west coast the outer one was the bobstay and the inner one the martingale, but to their adversaries it was the other way around. Once again, Alan Moore takes the opposite view to the west coast. These differences of opinion seem doomed to go on forever, because the only fact that either side can drag out in support of its claims, is that they 'learned it from a man who was a real sailor'. Possibly some day a man will be forthcoming who can prove by integral calculus that some sailors were more real than others but until this happens it would be best for both parties to recognise that the walls of their particular Jerichos have withstood so many blasts of the trumpet that the only sensible thing left is to learn to live with each other's foibles. Provided that each party is willing to state which camp they support, no misunderstandings should arise.

A well-equipped schooner had two suits of jibs and topsails, the older of which was used in the summer. There was only one suit of fore and afters and one staysail; these were made of No.1 canvas as were the standing jib and the lower topsail. There was only one of each gaff topsail required as they were never taken very seriously in any rig except the ketch, being stowed about the same time as the flying jib and, although the main gaff topsail of a barquentine or a three-masted schooner might linger awhile after the mizzen one had come in, it was removed rapidly enough once it became obvious that dirty weather was on its way. In the poverty-stricken 1930s this lack of regard for gaff topsails was clearly evidenced by the number of old jibs, sometimes modified, sometimes not, which were sent aloft to perform the role. At rock bottom it was yet another manifestation of the persistence of the square-rigged tradition – the gaff topsails didn't matter but the square topsails must be hung on to as long as possible; they certainly pulled their weight and earned their keep.

Ketches, on the other hand, tended to hang on to their main gaff topsails until it was blowing really hard, thus making it worth carrying a summer and a winter topsail, if it could be afforded. The most likely course of action would be to carry only one,but of heavier canvas than in a schooner. The other sail of which only one was carried was the squaresail. The last ketch to cross a main yard on which a squaresail could be set was the *Lady Agnes* but by then some vessels had taken to sending yard and sail up flying.

Although popular in fishing vessels, a complete suit of tanned sails was not often seen in schooners, the only ones so equipped, to the best of my knowledge, being *James Postlethwaite* and *Lochranza Castle*. There was one sail, however, which was nearly always tanned – the staysail, possibly because it was seldom dry. In many vessels the tanning had been washed by the rain and salt spray, bleached by the sun, and blackened by the smoke from the fo'c'sle stove pipe for so many years that it was difficult to tell what its original colour had been. The staysail was referred to simply as the staysail, whether set on the forestay of a schooner or the mainstay of a ketch, but for some reason this was not its name in a barquentine or a brigantine. In these two rigs it was called the 'drum' or the 'drummer'. At one time there were some North American vessels in which it was known as the 'jumbo'. I think these were Banks fishing schooners, but would not care to swear to it after the lapse of so many years. The 'drum' in both names perhaps indicates a common ancestral word, which crossed the Atlantic and then branched in separate ways.

FIGURE 10-6 Gaff topsails

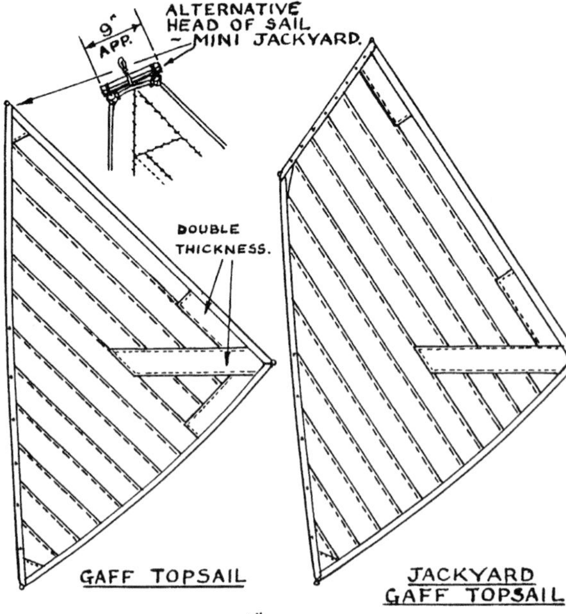

Jibs

The standing jib, the innermost of the three, was the bad-weather headsail, taken in only when it blew away – although in some vessels and in some conditions a better balance might be obtained by using the reefed staysail in its place. Staysails normally had only one reef band and, even with the reef taken in, their area was still much greater than that of the standing jib so that, if the weather deteriorated sufficiently, the latter was almost bound to be left in sole possession of the field. Some jack barquentines, but not many, had their standing jib stay set up from the band on the topmast just above the lower topsail yard so that, despite the shorter fore lower mast, a reasonable size of sail could be set. There is a painting of *Cymric* by Reuben Chappell that shows her so rigged. But if the fore topmast snapped off, the most likely place for this to happen was at the cap and, since no one had any desire to lose the services of this vital headsail, it is not surprising that long before the end of her days *Cymric*'s standing jib stay was back in the orthodox position. The boom jib, the middle sail, was marginally the largest of the three and, as its name implies, it was the sail proper of the jib-boom. The flying jib must originally have been set in some temporary manner, possibly without a stay or perhaps to a pole lashed to the jib-boom end, but this occurred so long ago that no details of how it was done seem to have survived. The jibs balanced the after sails, enabling the vessel to be steered without too much weather helm, but while the flying jib was taken in fairly early, the gaffs had to come a considerable way down the lower masts before the boom jib followed it. In this respect it had something in common with the square-rigger's topgallants; once it was in the crew felt entitled to consider the weather conditions as being a 'full gale'.

Furling Sails

Although being of all shapes and sizes, the methods used in furling sails had one feature in common: the bulk of the canvas was parcelled into a skin made from some part of the sail so that it was protected from the rain and presented a neat appearance in port. The general rule having been stated, the exceptions immediately follow. The squaresail was folded up into a long sausage, tied up with rope yarns and taken below. So were gaff topsails, which went up a jackstay, unless of course they were wet, in which case they were kept on deck until they had dried out. Sufficient has been written and said about gaff topsails set on hoops on the topmast for the statement to be made that the only intention of anyone going aloft to furl them at sea was to make the confounded things fast in any manner whatsoever, as long as they gave no further trouble. In port no doubt they could be made to look a bit more tiddly. Lubbock in the *Ross-shire*, and some others, proclaimed that all that had to be done was to ride the sail down. Tommy Gray told me that he would rather furl all the squaresails in creation than one of those unprintable affairs, and this seems to be confirmed by the experience of Alan Villiers in the *Hawk*. Everything points to the fact that this form of riding, like the bucking bronco, required a good deal of practice before proficiency was achieved.

There was a much milder hint of the same approach in the methods used to furl topsails when at sea. Any further dealings with them were to be avoided so that the turns of the gaskets were not kept together as in a harbour stow – appearance being no longer the first priority. The man, or men, doing the job got out to windward and wrapped the gaskets in a spiral round the sail so that there was a minimum of exposed canvas under which the wind could work things loose. When making a harbour stow it was the last bit of canvas near the jackstay that covered the rest, the sail being doubled and doubled again and rolled over until this part could be pulled over the top. The only way in which the operation could be clearly demonstrated would be by means of a film, but the diagrams may perhaps be of some assistance in showing roughly what was done and what was achieved in the finished job. The peculiar drawings in Figure 10-7 are an attempt to show, in a sectional manner, how the work was carried out.

Despite flapping about like so much muslin there was considerable weight in sail canvas, even when dry, so that the job of furling a squaresail was best started in the places where the

FIGURE 10-7
Furling

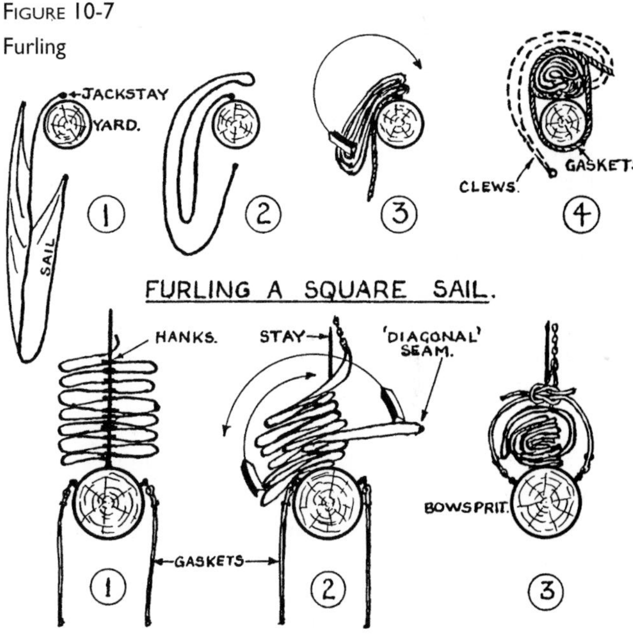

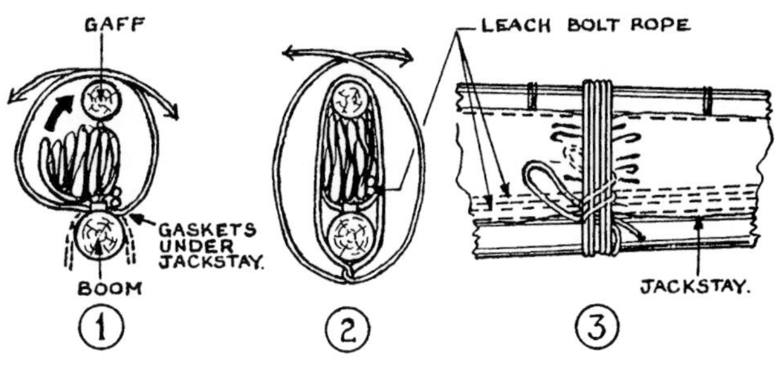

FIGURE 10-8 Furling

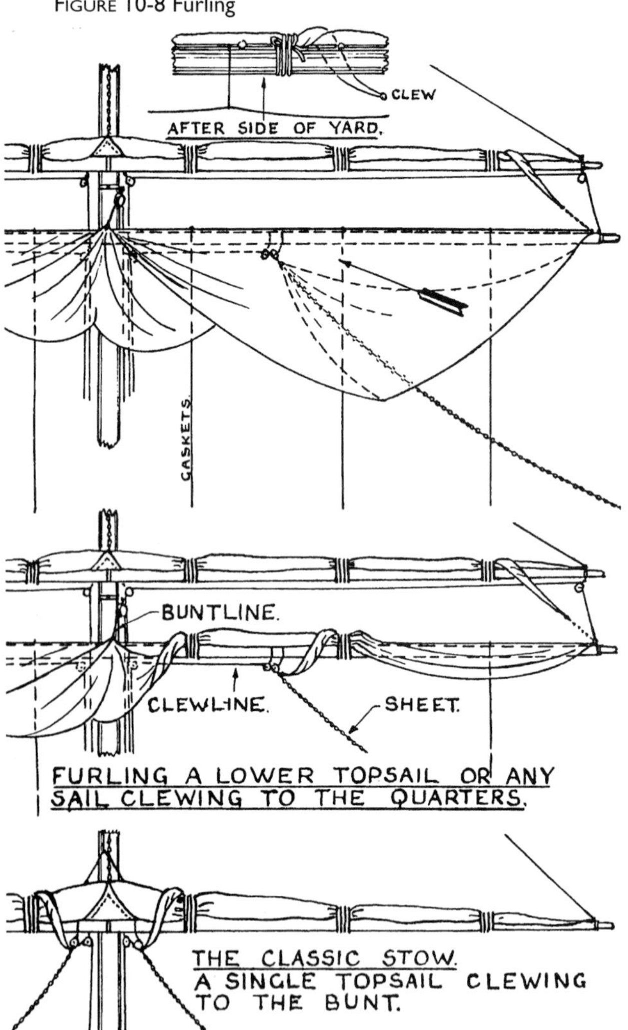

FIGURE 10-9 Furling

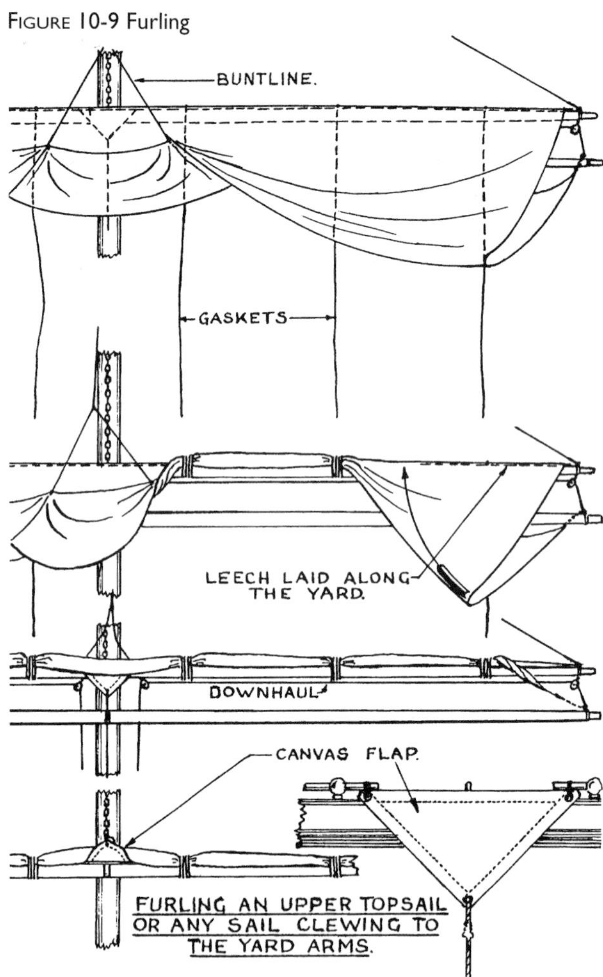

weight was already taken by the buntline or clewlines. It will be seen from Figure 10-8 that these were at the quarters or the yardarms. The hauling up and folding over tended to leave a twist in the rest of the sail still left hanging but by the time all the canvas was on top of the yard this should have been removed from everything but the clews. If it had not the mate had something to say about it. It mattered little in a schooner, except as a sort of public announcement of a change of skipper, whether a lower topsail clewed up to the yardarms or to the quarters but it was a vastly different business in a big square rigger. Clewing to the yardarms in these vessels was what today would be hailed a major breakthrough – after the lapse of centuries it finally enabled the labour force on a yard to be utilised to the full, instead of throwing the bulk of the work on to the men in the slings. As always in sail, mental processes lagged behind practice. Pride of place would have taken a fall had it been admitted that a bunt was no longer necessary, and besides, the older method of stowing had a neat, attractive and tapered look which the new one seemed bent on losing. So a bunt was still made, as far as possible, by retaining the little canvas flap shown in Figure 10-8. Although I have never heard it given a name, I take this to be the 'jigger' mentioned by Dana, which, at a signal from the mate, was let go by a hand on each yard so that the vessel could be clothed in all her canvas in an instant. The name jigger implies the one-time presence of a small tackle – a necessity, one would think, in the days when practically the full weight of the sail had to be hauled up on to the yard by the efforts of those few in the bunt who were in a position to get to grips with it.

As long as there was not too much wind, a sail would stay on top of the yard, even after all the gaskets had been cast off, until this little flap was released; this was done in schooners when setting sail in harbour, the lower topsail being let go first, followed by the upper one. It was as much as could be done to preserve the memory of an age-old practice that had its origins in the big crews and small vessels of the past. Double topsails, double topgallants and smaller and smaller crews finally brought it to an end and one suspects that if those aboard the *Preussen* had attempted to do it in the classical manner, not even the captain would have been left on deck.[2] Because the little canvas flaps stayed permanently aloft they were painted white to preserve them from the elements, causing them to stand out against the grey of the well-used sails.

Their small area made the jibs the easiest of the sails to furl, and the weight of the canvas was taken by the hanks on the stay. The first thing done by the man stowing was to heave all the canvas over to leeward, if it had not already got there on its way down. He then located the seam across the sail and hauled it out to windward, at the same time shifting it forward in order to gain some slack at the luff. The man trapped this slack piece of canvas between his stomach and the bowsprit and proceeded to pound, thump and fold the sail into the smallest possible bulk, after which the loose flap of double canvas could be folded over the top and the first gasket tied.

The job started forward and finished aft. The flying jib was the most difficult sail to stow neatly because it had the shortest length of bowsprit on which to make it fast, usually the only recourse was to fold the clew and sheets under the rest in a forward direction. The staysail often had no official gasket because it was seldom stowed when at sea. In port its sheet was unshackled from the horse and it was tied up with sennit or rope yarns and clumped on the platform over the bowsprit. An alternative frequently resorted to was to hook its own halyard into the clew and haul it up out of the way. The jibs were sometimes given the same treatment [Figure 10-10]. The advantage was that it prevented rainwater from being trapped between sail and bowsprit and, at the same time, kept the sails wrapped up against the intrusions of the all-pervading coal dust.

Fore and afters were furled rather like half an upper topsail – the leech was laid forward along the boom as the gaff was lowered. The skin in which the rest of the sail was wrapped, however, came from the foot, not the head. With a loose-footed sail, the gaskets were laid over the boom; in a roller-reefing sail they were passed through the slots in the jackstay. The first thing done after the gaff was down was to lash its peak to the boom. The crew then picked up the sail at the after end, by the part near the boom, raising it up in the form of a trough and shaking the rest of the canvas down into it before shoving the lot up towards the gaff. The gasket ends were then thrown over the gaff, pulled on simultaneously from both sides, crossed around each other below the boom and thrown back again for another pull. What was left of the gasket was then wrapped around boom and gaff and the ends were tucked in. The gaskets were about 12ft [3.66m] long and the further forward they were used, the fewer turns went around the sail as gaff and boom were slowly parted by the mast hoops.

Having dealt with the aftermost gasket, the crew moved forward to the next one. The weight of sail to be handled was at its greatest about two-thirds of the way forward; on the last lap the mast hoops were taking most of the load. It will be seen from Figure 10-11 that the process of shaking and push-

[2] I was wrong. There were forty-eight aboard her, eighteen to spare – Gustaf Erikson would have remedied that!

FIGURE 10-10
Hoisting

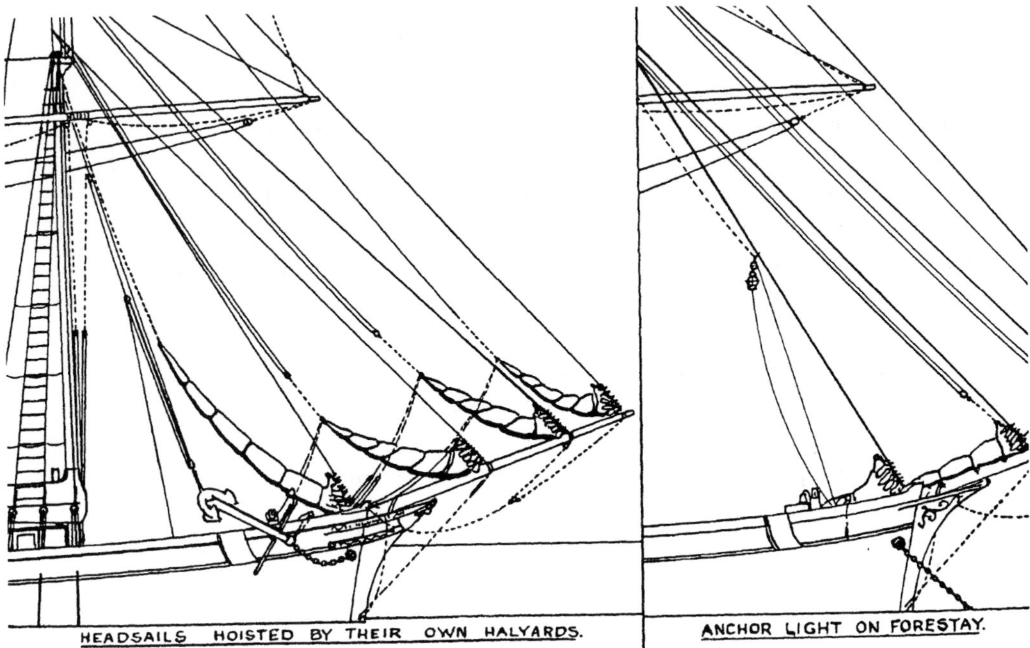

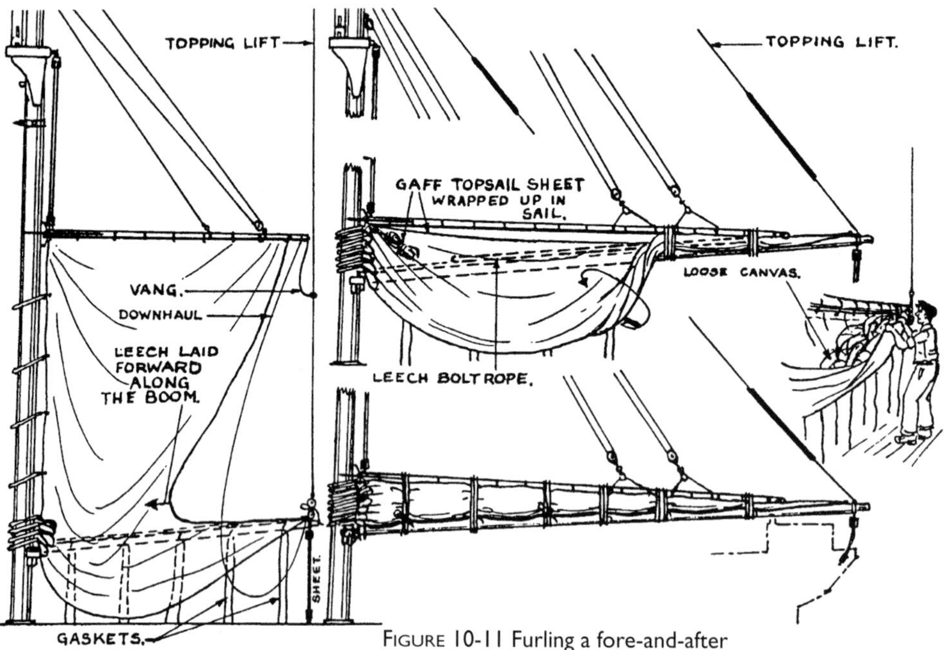

FIGURE 10-11 Furling a fore-and-after

the past that, did they but know of it, the ghosts of a million shellbacks would probably rise from their graves and cheer.

Running Rigging

Although it never reached the same high degree of organisation as it did in the square-rigger, there was a surprising uniformity about the simple running rigging of ketches and schooners and, when compared with the state of affairs in about the middle of the 19th century, there was a good deal of simplification and some sophistication as well. One

ing the canvas down to the foot produced the same twisting action on the unstowed part as was noted with the topsails.

So far no mention has been made of the topping lift, which had to be tightened before letting go the halyards. After stowing the sail the last job was to come up on the topping lift and allow the boom to drop on to its crutch. Fore and afters were not normally stowed while at sea – the exception being mizzens, which were normally stowed as a prelude to turning to run. If the sail was already rolled around the boom when it was taken in, which was usually the case, the gaskets had to go under the boom, as there was nowhere else to put them.

When stowed at sea the sails were allowed to fall to suit whichever tack the vessel happened to be on, always with the proviso that they were not allowed to come into contact with hot stovepipes. By convention, when being given a harbour stow fore and afters were brought down to port, and the leech ropes laid along the booms to starboard. This gave a uniform appearance to the finished job. On arriving at an anchorage, one of the first things done after letting go was to take the reef tackles off the booms and unwind the turns by hand, to allow the lower part of the sails to dry. The gaffs were then left standing for the rest of the day and the sails were stowed in the evening.

To a generation that knew nothing but flax and cotton, the amazing lightness and ease of handling of modern sails made from artificial fibres, comes as a tremendous surprise. In this technology a positive step forward has been taken and, although it is not likely to affect the life of the working seaman today or in the future, it would have had such an impact in

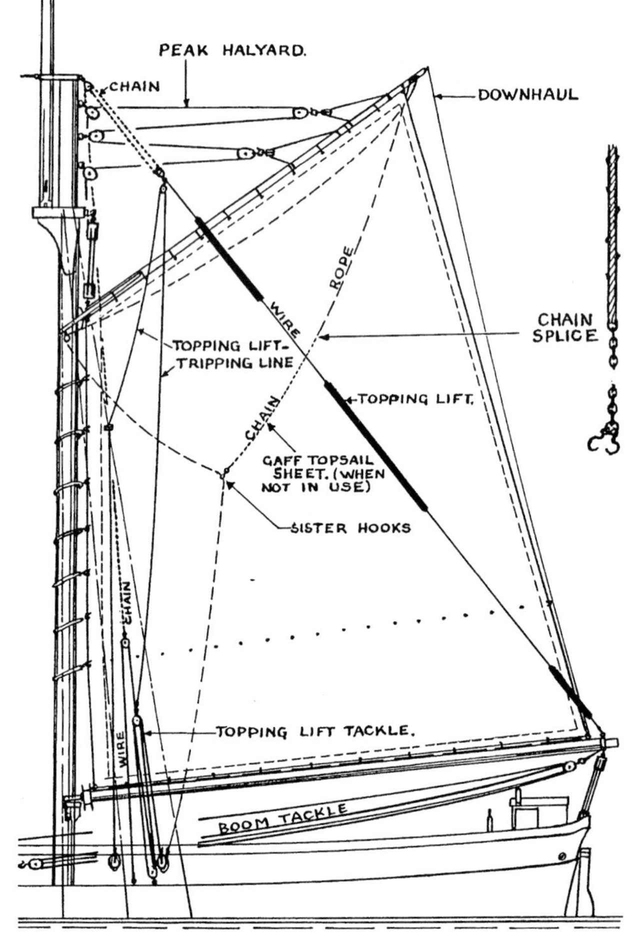

FIGURE 10-12 Running rigging of a roller reefing mainsail

FIGURE 10-13

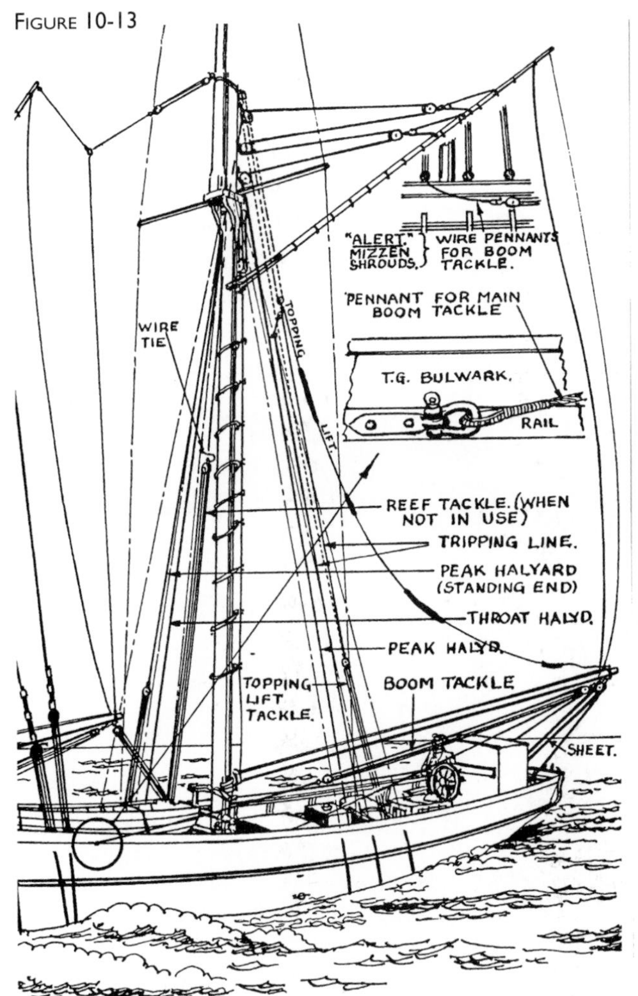

FIGURE 10-14 Running rigging of a point reefing foresail

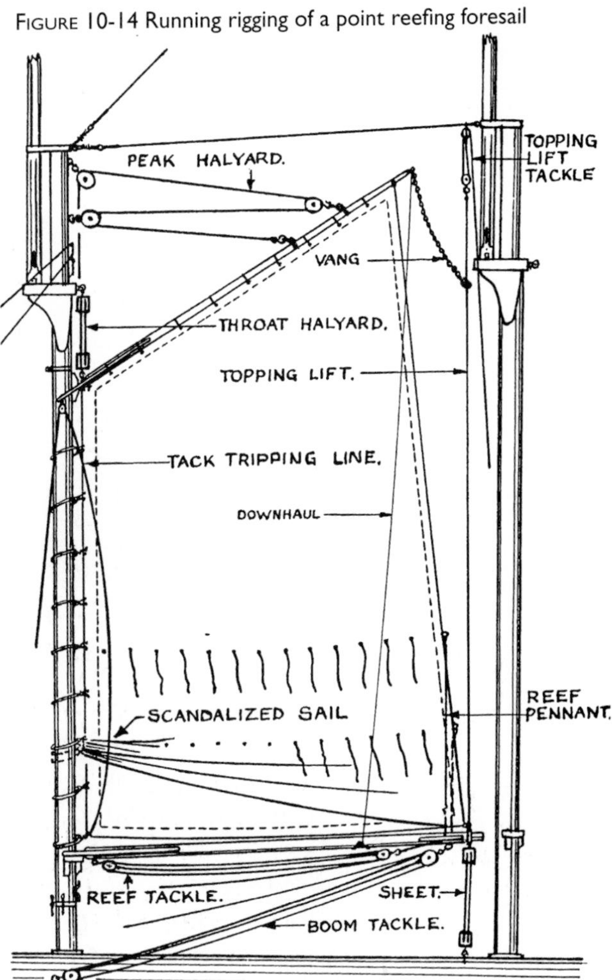

of the places where this showed up was in the topping lifts. Main topping lifts were once double affairs with a line up from each side of the boom, through blocks at the trestletrees and down to separate tackles. The advantage of this and similar arrangements was that the topping lifts exercised some control on the gaff while it was being lowered. The drawbacks were that both tackles had to be hauled together and someone had to decide when the boom was at the correct height. In the final arrangement the booms were at the correct height when no more could be taken up on the tackles, so that they arrived at their correct height in pitch darkness without anyone having to see them. The means by which this was achieved on the main booms of two-masted vessels is shown in Figure 10-12. When the tripping line was stretched taut no more could be gained on the tackle and, once the mainsail was set and the topping lift let go, the tripping line could be used to perform its other job of keeping the topping lift clear of the sail so that even the baggy wrinkle was not in constant contact with the canvas [Figure 10-13].

A similar arrangement, usually slightly simpler, was fitted to the mizzen in a three-masted vessel. The ketch had the simplest mizzen topping lift of all, while the fore-booms of schooners and the main-booms of three-masters were fitted with a length of wire and a tackle, which passed through two blocks when the boom was at the correct height. Some had the tackle aloft, others, with an eye to economy, had it down on the boom end; in either case once the sail had been set the tackle was used to control the vang, which ran up the wire and regulated the angle of the gaff [Figure 10-14].

Halyards

The staggering of halyards, which was such a feature of the square-rigger's gear, sometimes became rather mixed up in schooners, although it was still there in a modified way. For those not familiar with the principle, if the fore topsail halyard was to port (it usually was), then the main was to starboard and the mizzen to port again. Topgallant halyards were the other way around – fore and mizzen to starboard, main

My Lady outward bound on the Mersey from Runcorn to Padstow on 6th. April 1928.

PHOTOGRAPH BY DAVID E. SMITH. TERRY BELT COLLECTION

to port; while the royal halyards were on the same side as the topsail halyards.

This went on alternately for as many square-rigged masts as the vessel carried. It was done so that if she were laid on her beam-ends on either tack, there would always be something that could be let go. The reason why it tended to go astray in schooners was because they were originally a two-masted rig only. The almost standard arrangement for a schooner's foremast was to have the topsail and throat halyards to port and the topgallant and peak halyards to starboard. The main peak halyard however was double-ended, as it was in the ketch and brigantine, and the standing end was fitted with a tackle by means of which the last bit could be sweated out of the peak. Because of this it could be let go from either side of the vessel, at least as far as to leave only half the sail still drawing. The normal arrangement dictated by the rule was to have the standing end and throat halyard to starboard and the running end to port – the opposite way to the boom foresail. The brigantine, apart from having no fore peak and throat halyards, had the same set-up as the schooner [Figure 10-15].

For some reason, now lost in the past, the main topping lift, once it had stopped being a double affair, managed to get itself so firmly entrenched on the port side that, in the end, it almost exercised the same time-honoured rights as the fore topsail halyard. When main gaff topsails started to be sent aloft on wire jackstays, it was found best to do this on the starboard side, away from the topping lift and its appurtenances, so that this too became part of the tradition. Gaff topsail halyards were not included in the staggering arrangements as they were made fast at the foot of the mast where they could be got at whichever side of the vessel was under water. Into this state of affairs the introduction of the three-masted schooner and the barquentine produced an element of discord. It was the claim of the topping lift to be on the port side that now caused the trouble, and it was the three-

FIGURE 10-15
Halyards

1 Flying jib halyard
2 Boom jib halyard
3 Standing jib halyard
4 Staysail halyard
5 Fore throat halyard
6 Fore peak halyard
7 Main peak halyard, starboard end tackle
8 Main peak halyard, standing end
9 Main peak halyard
10 Fore topsail halyard, tye
11 Fore topsail halyard, runner
12 Fore topsail halyard, tackle
13 Main throat halyard
14 Main gaff topsail, halyard
15 Main gaff topsail, tack
16 Main gaff topsail, Sheet
17 Main topping lift
18 Main topgallant lift tackle
19 Signal halyard

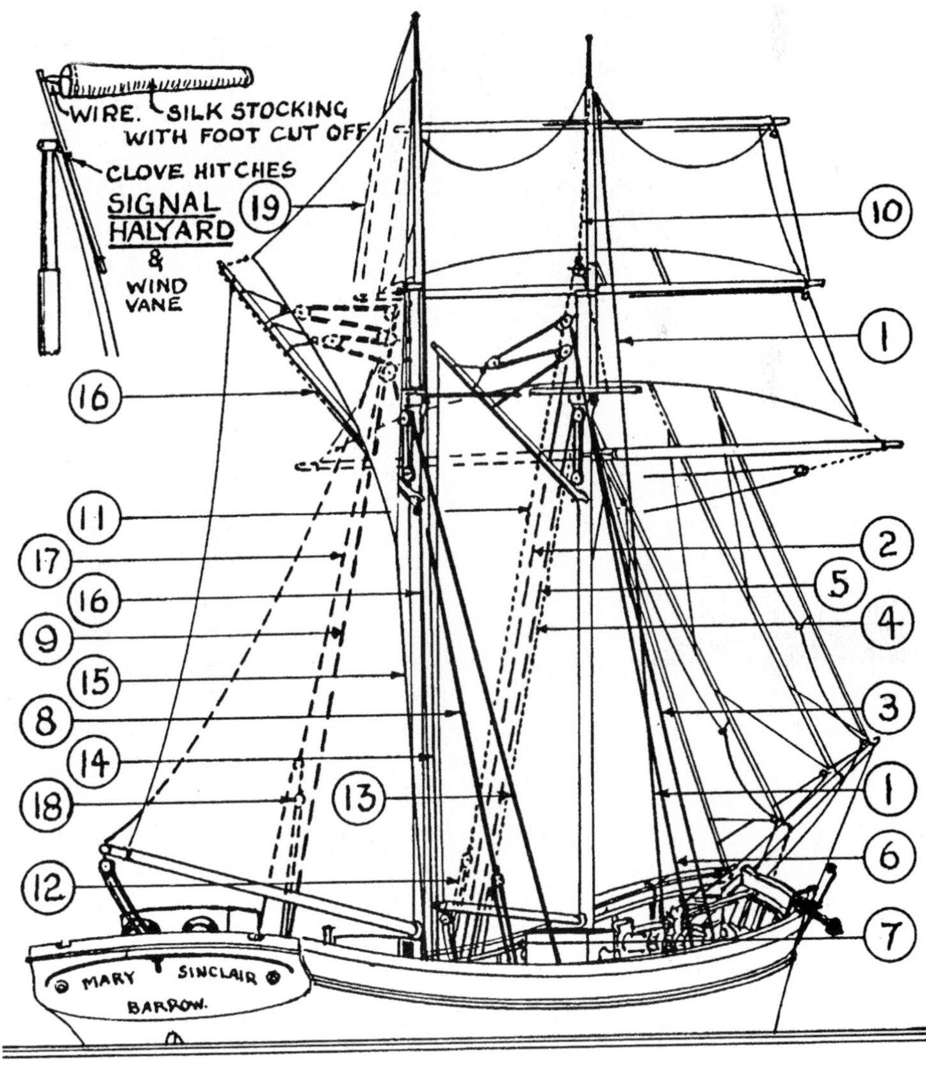

Mary Miller under sail.

PHOTOGRAPHER UNKNOWN. TERRY BELT COLLECTION

masted pair that received it. In these rigs the main peak halyard was usually single ended, as befitting a smaller sail, and the main boom had the same kind of topping lift as the schooner's foresail, the fancy topping lift being transferred to the mizzen. In British schooners there was no shifting over of gaff topsails when the vessels went about – although some sent their tack down between peak-halyard and gaff in the North American manner – but the tradition of staggering was strong enough to dictate that both gaff topsails should not be set on the same side.

On this basis, the mizzen topping lift should have gone over to starboard leaving the port side to the gaff topsail and this, with the mizzen throat halyard to port and peak halyard to starboard would have conformed to the long-standing tradition. In the *Alert* the main gaff topsail was set on the port side and the mizzen gaff topsail on the starboard side but she had all three peak halyards to starboard and all three throat halyards to port. The *Brooklands* had her fore topsail halyard to starboard, as did the *Jane Banks* and the *Flying Foam*. Her fore and mizzen peak halyards were to port, her main to starboard, but both her gaff topsails were set on the starboard side. The *Waterwitch* managed to remain semi-orthodox as her mainsail was big enough to warrant a double-ended peak halyard.

Ketches also had their main topping lifts to port, although occasionally one could be seen with it on the other side but the only three-masted schooner that I can recollect defying convention and having her mizzen topping lift on the starboard side was *Mary Miller*.

None of the vessels mentioned were handicapped in their normal functions by these oddities in their gear, but it would be interesting to know how and why a piece of running rigging that could have functioned just as effectively on either side of the vessel, was allowed, in the end, to upset a centuries-old tradition. Did the mate grab it as his private property, or did the skipper repudiate the custom?

The kind of incident which seems to occur in yachts from

time to time, in which someone loosed a rope that is subsequently pulled from his grasp by the force of the wind and either unreeves itself or finishes up with its business end at the masthead, very seldom, if ever, happened in schooners. Every piece of running rigging, except the peak and throat halyards, had its end permanently hitched to the pin. The hitch might be removed on the odd occasion to take a kink out of the rope but it was replaced again as soon as the job was done; in the case of the peak and throat halyards they were removed from the pins for the purpose of taking them to the drums of the motor winch. The hitch used was a kind of figure eight and is shown in Figure 10-16 (left) as well as appearing in some of the pinrail diagrams.

There was another very simple hitch also found in conjunction with belaying pins, which I first saw in the *Alert* ,but five years were to elapse before I found out its full story. At some time in her career *Alert* had sustained a fairly heavy bump in way of the starboard fore rigging, which had forced inwards the topgallant bulwark so that there was not enough space between the pin and the bulwark to accommodate the coils of the upper topsail downhaul. To overcome this the hitch shown in Figure 10-16 (top) was used in which the standing end of the rope was pulled through the coil, capsized over itself and the loop thus formed dropped back on to the pin. It was a neat, quick way of doing the job, and it seemed to me to have advantages over the method normally used. It prevented the running rigging from being washed off the pins one bight at a time – either it all stayed where it was or it all went. Later I noticed that it was used on practically all coils of running rigging in the big Scandinavian four-masters, and to my mind gave them a much neater appearance than I was accustomed to seeing.

Five years later, while in the *Brooklands*, I made the mistake of coiling a rope into rather small loops, so that there were more turns than the stumpy pin would accommodate comfortably. I could have re-coiled it in larger bights but it seemed easier to make the hitch mentioned, and to pass on to other things. About a quarter of an hour later Christy, wandering around the deck, suddenly let out a loud bellow, 'Who deh hell's done dat, dat's a bloody German hitch'. I turned to find that he was regarding my handiwork with disfavour. In a flash of enlightenment I realised that I had never seen it in any of

FIGURE 10-16 Belaying pins

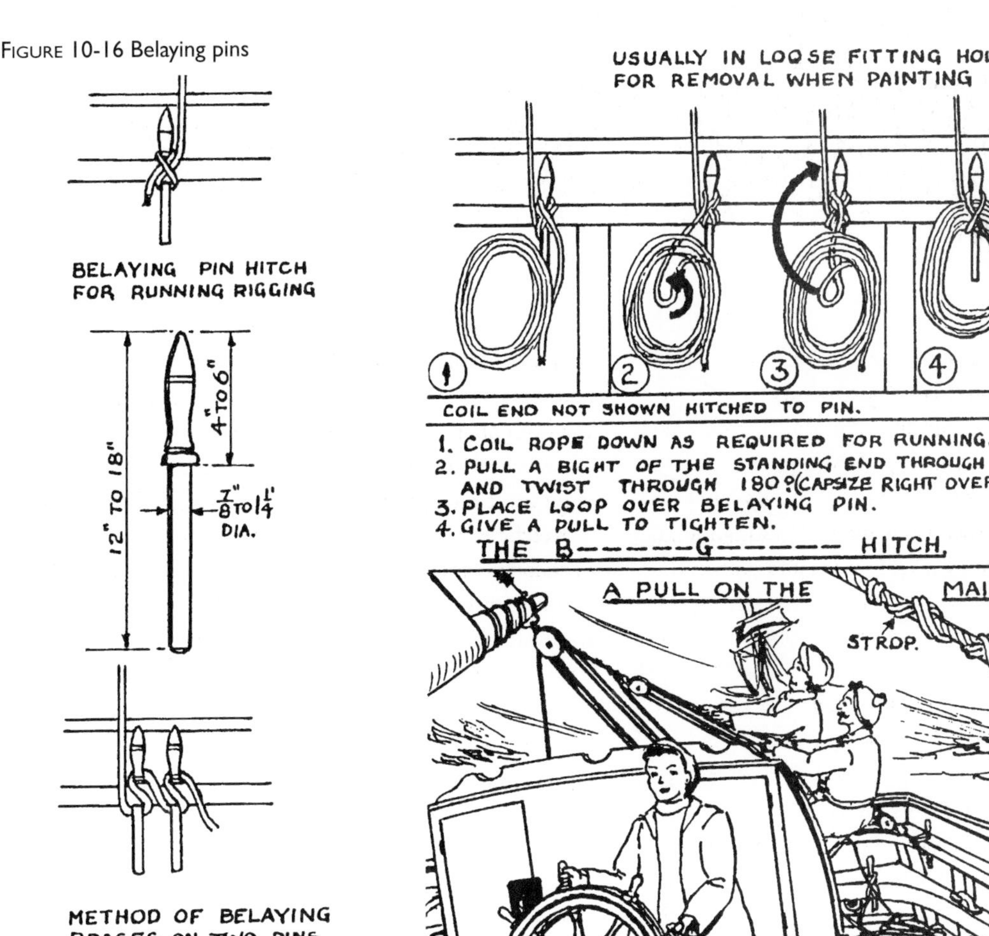

our own vessels except for that one pin in the *Alert*. So at last I knew. I apologised in triplicate and restored the coil to a state of British purity. It may be that at the time the doings of Adolf Hitler had some bearing on Christy's asperity, but I thought then, and still think, that to discard a good idea simply because it was invented by some nation with which one has a difference of opinion, was carrying matters to the point of absurdity. But, what surprised me most of all was that it should be Christy, an Irishman, who was so British about it.

Running Rigging of Headsails

The downhauls of the four headsails were made fast to a set of pins located in the after edge of the platform in the knightheads or on the curved beam across the fore side of the windlass and, for obvious reasons, they were to be found on the same side as the halyard of the sail they served. According to the book, the correct procedure if a jib downhaul carried away was to put the vessel before the wind and send out a couple of men to downhaul the sail.

In coasting vessels the first part could frequently not be complied with for lack of men, thus the method was for a man to go aloft and slide down the stay. The helmsman would have to becket the wheel so that he could let go the sheet when the upper part of the sail was down to the diagonal seam. This was the one drawback to Matthew Orr's jibs but it was a trifling price to pay for a sail that set so well. About the only advantage ever derived from strong headwinds was that, after a jib had been repaired, in situ, without unbending it, the man on the bowsprit had only to bawl out to someone to cast off the downhaul, after which he could lift the head about a foot or so up the stay and the wind would send it aloft like an express train. The weight of the fall would ensure that the halyard came down on deck. The man who let go the downhaul had to haul the sheet in rather rapidly before the full blast got into the sail or it would have taken a handy billy to flatten it. An obvious point, but nevertheless one worth mentioning, is that jib downhauls and jib halyards were not shackled separately to the sails, they were fastened together permanently, end to end, and the sails shackled to the combination at the point of junction. The same was true of lower topsail sheets and clewlines.

The running rigging of the headsails is shown in Figure 10-17 and it will be noticed that the flying jib was the only one with single-line halyard and sheets. The runner of the staysail halyard was made of chain mainly because it was also used when setting the squaresail, in which function it took the lion's share of the load. The staysail sheet worked on a wire horse across the foredeck. When not in use one end of this was unshackled and it was laid along the scuppers or tied up in the shrouds to keep it out of the way. The staysail bowline was a length of rope spliced into the reef cringle in the leech of the sail; to set it up it was passed through a bullseye on the forward end of the sheer pole, back through another at the clew and then to a pin in the rail.

The pattern thus formed possibly bore some resemblance to the old-fashioned 'crow's foot' by which bowlines in the past were secured to the leeches of square sails and its functions were much the same as those of its ancestors, although its pull was applied in the opposite direction. The other type of bowline sometimes used was a luff tackle, which could be hooked into an eye in the cover plank. It was not very frequently met with, possibly because when it was let go, after the schooner had passed through the wind's eye, it clattered

FIGURE 10-17
Headsails

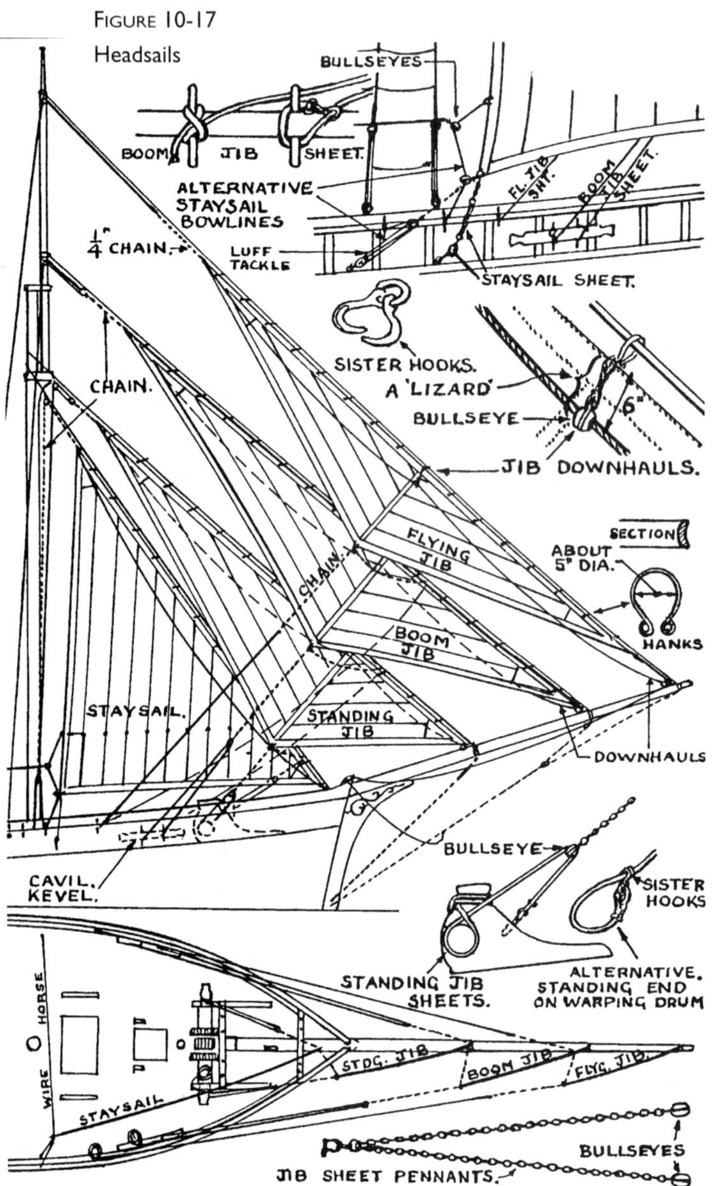

North Barrule at Princes Dock, Glasgow 14 August 1929 having brought a cargo of scrap iron from Douglas, Isle of Man. In November 1936 she dragged ashore near Menai Bridge carrying a cargo of pig iron. Refloated in May 1937 she was taken to Caernarfon and sold for scrap. Broken up near Port Dinorwic in August 1937.

PHOTOGRAPH BY DAN MCDONALD. TERRY BELT COLLECTION

and clonked across the deck as the sail slammed over to leeward and was probably more prone to catching on something than was the plain rope tail.

Running Rigging of Square Sails

Hanging from the ends of the foreyard were a pair of gun tackles, the yard ropes, which were used in conjunction with the staysail halyard for hoisting the square foresail. The staysail halyard was shackled to the centre cringle, and the yard ropes and their falls were made fast to the two head cringles, the falls to act as downhauls when the sail was taken in. In *Brooklands* the yard ropes were single lines that were too short for the job so a couple of gaskets from the fore and afters had to be bent on to their ends to remedy the deficiency. The sail was partly hoisted by the staysail halyard alone before the sheets were made fast, after which it was hauled up and out to windward as far as possible to reduce to a minimum the area blanketed by the boom foresail. It was a sail that could be used to good effect on a reach, with its tack boarded on the cathead, but its main use was when the wind was abaft the beam [Figure 10-18].

Figures 10-19 and 10-20 show front and back views of the running rigging for double topsails and standing topgallant. In a schooner there was only one buntline to each sail. It usually had a bridle at its lower end to pick up the foot of the sail at two points and this would seem to explain why no attempt was ever made to pass it through a bullseye or a block fastened to the jackstay. To some extent, therefore, the sail

was free to flap about even when pulled up. The nearest approach to the big-ship method was to take a single line from the foot of a lower topsail, through a block on the mast at the boom jib stay band and thence down to the deck. The *Alert*'s lower topsail buntline was, at the and of her career, rove off in this way but, to the best of my knowledge, when the *Jane Banks* sailed for Estonia her lower topsail buntline still passed upwards outside the upper topsail to the topmast hounds, before starting its descent – just as it had done in other vessels for centuries before double topsails were invented.

Upper topsail and topgallant buntlines were standing ones with their top ends made fast to their respective hounds so that they merely held the foot of the sail where it was, as the yard came down. The standing topgallant functioned in the same way as a square-rigger's royals; like them it was on an extension to the mast below it, so that it had the same short distance through which it was sheeted home before being hoisted to the masthead. Figure 10-21 shows the running rigging for double topsails and gives an indication of the kind of leads provided for the gear. They were much more thinly spread in schooners than in square-riggers.

The upper topsail downhauls performed two functions: they hauled the yard down and also steadied the lower topsail yard, which was not equipped with lifts. The upper topsail yard had to be hauled down – its own weight, even when aided by the force of the wind on the sail, was not usually sufficient to bring it down under its own steam. Part of the resistance was caused by the pull of the parrel against the mast but the main contributor was the friction of the tackle rope in the blocks. In the days of single topsails this function was performed by the clewlines and was equally necessary. The sheets were held fast until the yard had been pulled down on to its lifts, after which the sail could be pulled up to the yard.

All this sort of work required little coordination when performed in daylight as everyone could see what was going on but at night with half a gale blowing it was a slightly different proposition. Then the proceedings were punctuated by shouts of 'All gone', a password which obviously started from

FIGURE 10-18 Yardropes

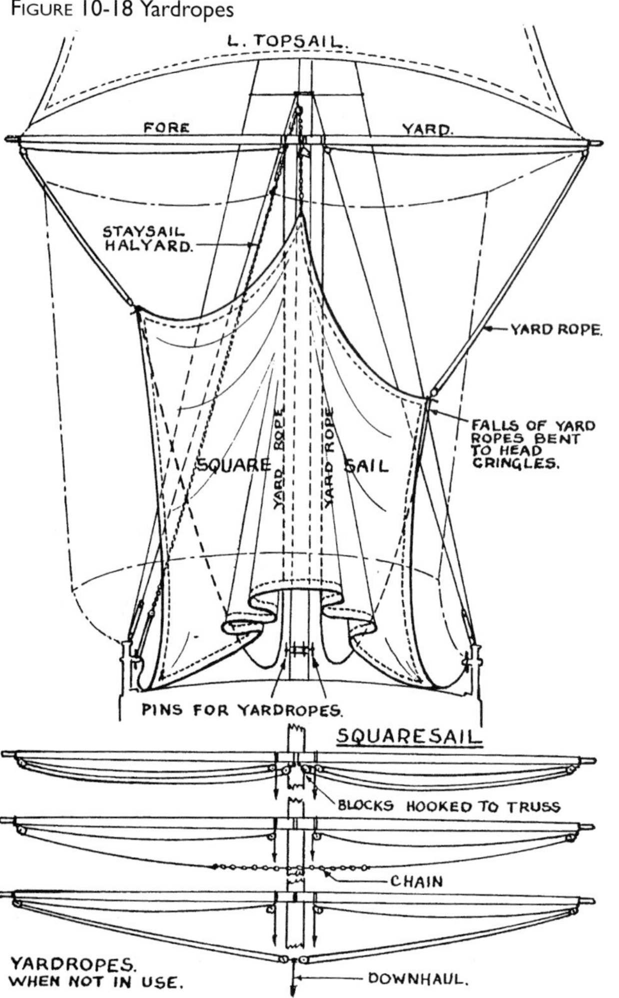

FIGURE 10-19 Running rigging

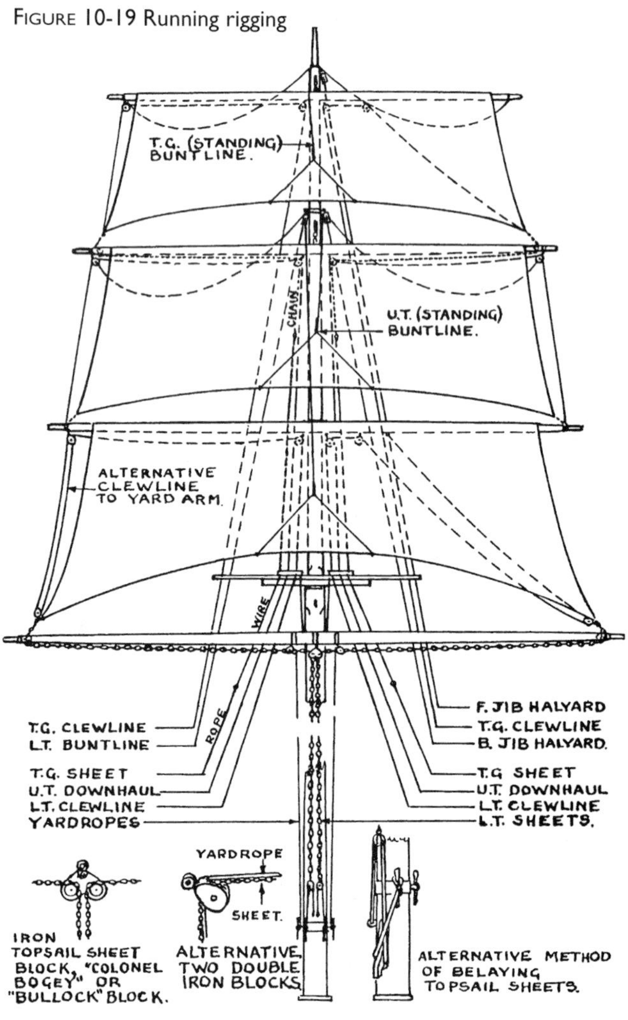

the casting off of mooring lines, and finished up as the height of nautical correctness even when only one rope was let go. The mate, for instance, would shout 'All gone', when he let go the upper topsail halyard so that the men on the downhauls could heave together. If they did not do so and the yard became canted it had then to be ascertained which side was low before it could be persuaded to move another inch. In contrast, when taking in a lower topsail, when the deckside parties worked quickly and independently to prevent the sail from flogging itself to pieces, the mate would shout 'All gone a weather' and 'All gone a lee' as each sheet was let go, so that the men could spring into action without further ado. In this case the mate would also shout in daylight as he was concealed by the galley – regardless of necessity the shout was so much part of the ritual that everyone shouted it at all times.

The man who belayed a halyard was expected to bawl 'All fast' to those still hanging on to it so that they would know it was safe to release their grasp on the rope. Finally, to coordinate their own and each other's efforts, the whole crew at times indulged in a process known as 'singing out', in which noises like 'Ayeoop', 'Ahigh', 'Aho' and so on were bellowed so that everyone's heave could be timed to a nicety. As would be expected this sort of thing fell far short of the musical perfection that it achieved in Disney's Snow White and the Seven Dwarfs!

The running rigging for a single topsail and flying topgallant is shown in Figure 10-22. As an alternative to this example, the topsail buntline could have been taken through a block at the topgallant hounds so that it could act as a restraint to the topgallant, which had no buntline of its own. Figure 10-23 shows the gear for a single topsail and standing topgallant. The last square 'topsail' used in schooners, the raffee, is shown in Figure 10-24. This was like a couple of jibs set on the lifts of the yard and, as with proper jibs, the 'sheets' had to be let go when the sails were halfway down or they would descend no further. No doubt the men on the Great Lakes, many years ago made up their minds what these two ropes were to be called, but to the unenlightened they were like the appendages of the sail known as a 'course' and should

FIGURE 10-20 Typical arrangement of leads for gear

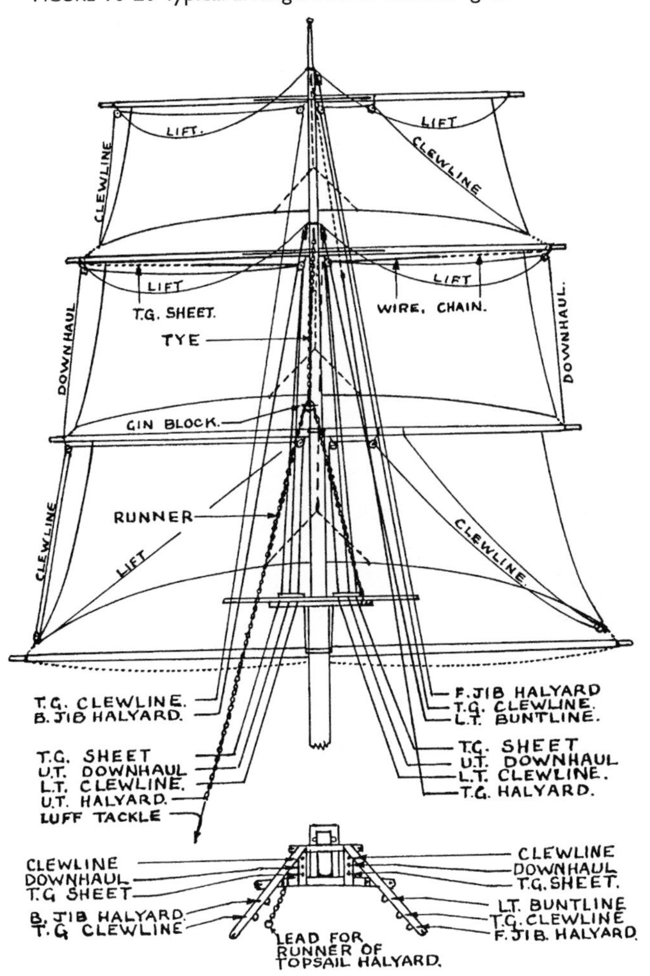

FIGURE 10-21 Running rigging for double topsails

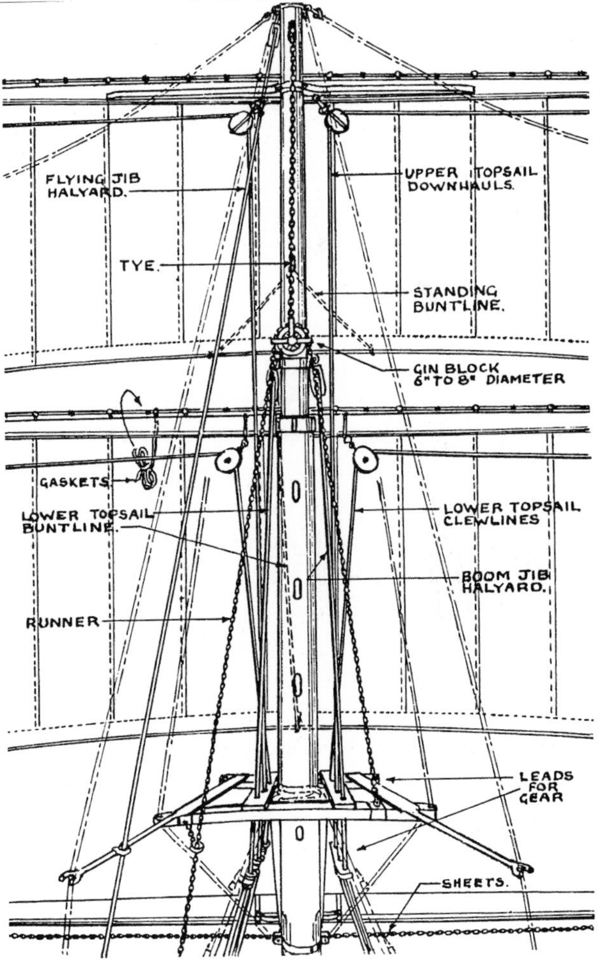

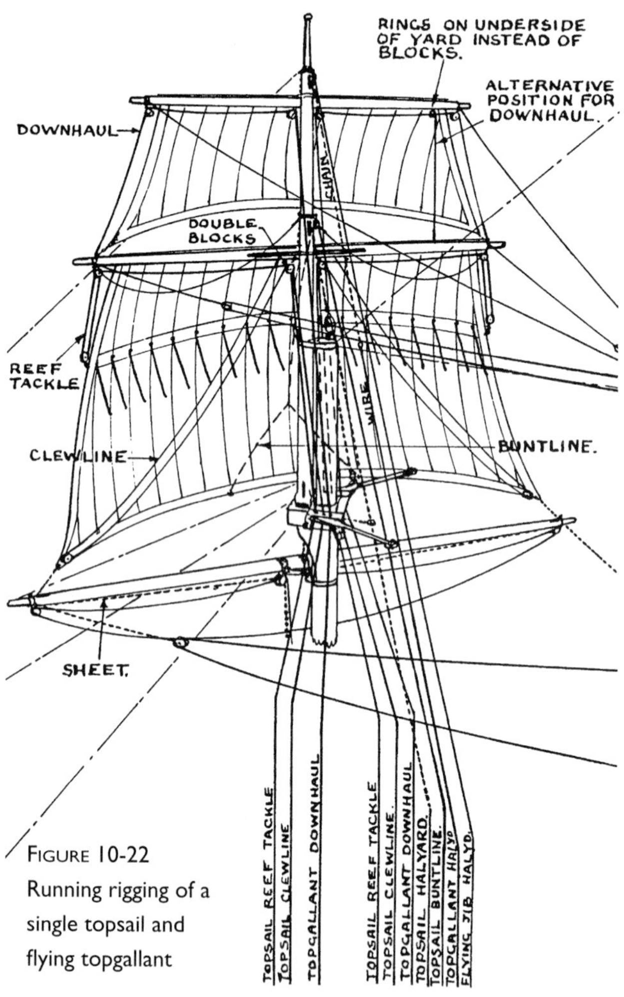

Figure 10-22
Running rigging of a single topsail and flying topgallant

have changed their names every time the yard was swung.

Pictures of schooners painted in the 1850s show that the fore braces were then nearly always taken through blocks at the hounds of the main lower mast and that, in the few cases where the brace blocks were secured to the shrouds, they were well up, near to the crosstrees. This arrangement was the best that could be done with hemp standing rigging, which would soon have worked slack from the constant pull if the blocks had been as low down as they were later to become. Figure 10-25 shows the arrangement that was finally adopted. Topgallant braces were invariably single lines but all the others were double. Each brace had its own pin but the braces of the lower yard were made fast to the after member of a pair of oversized pins set in the rails about 6in apart; there was one pair on each side of the vessel. When the wind was abaft the beam the braces were all on their own pins but when the schooner was on the wind all the braces were belayed together on these two large pins so that they could all be cast off at one move when going about.

Braces

In spite of the fact that it was done without any apparent concern, the coiling of ropes in sailing vessels was carried out with due care so that when the time came for them to run out they did so without kinks or other entanglements. When the yards had been braced up once more, the lower and topsail braces were coiled down, all three together, starting from the standing ends, and the large coil thus formed was lifted off the deck and hung on the topsail brace pins. In bad weather the coil was sometimes hung from the sheer pole but it was more usual to put it on the drum end of the dolly winch, as this reduced its chances of going out through the wash ports.

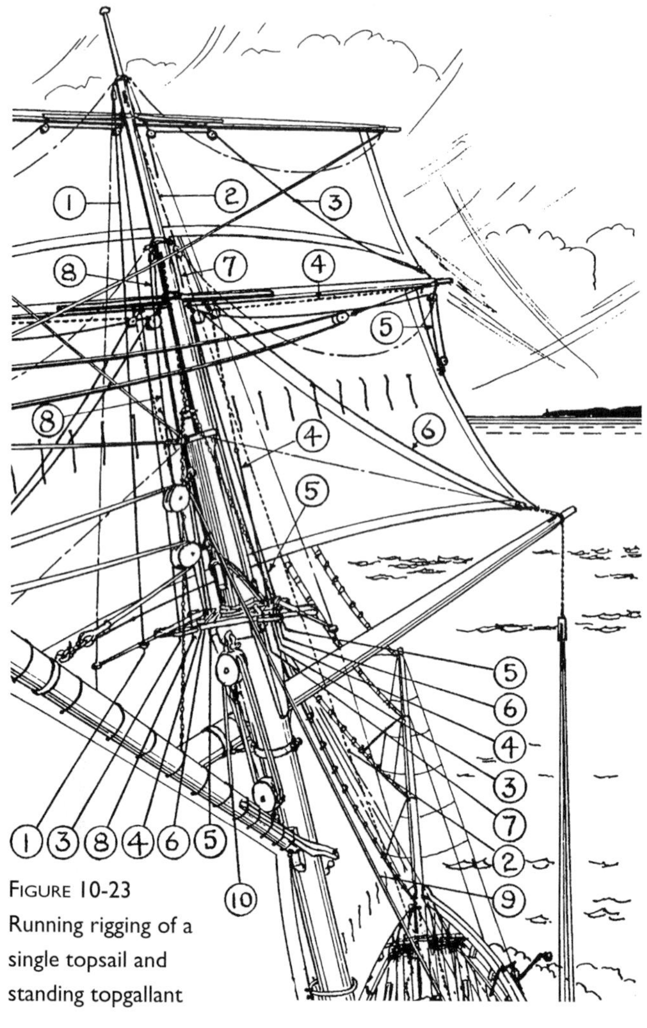

Figure 10-23
Running rigging of a single topsail and standing topgallant

1 Flying jib halyard
2 Topgallant halyard
3 Topgallant clewline
4 Topgallant sheet
5 Topsail reefing tackle
6 Topsail clewline
7 Bm. jib halyard
8 Topsail buntline
9 Peak halyard
10 Throat halyard

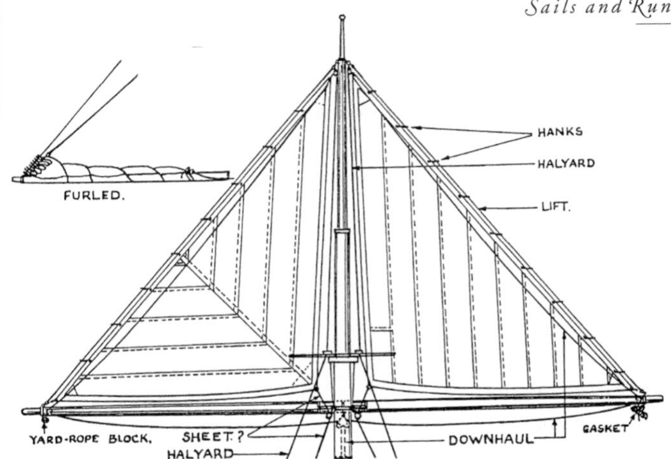

FIGURE 10-24 Running rigging of a raffee

When the dolly winch was required for reefing, the coil was given a temporary home on the corner of the hatch.

The topgallant braces paid out or came in at only half the rate of the others. For this reason they could not be coiled down along with the rest but had to have a separate coil of their own, which also had to be dropped to the deck, clear of the main coil, before going about. For the same reason they could not be hauled on with the other three when swinging the yards, and the topgallant yard was perforce left to find its own way around; when the sail was set the wind saw it safely home, with yardarm clewlines it was dragged around by the upper topsail yard and with clewlines to the quarters it might expect a little assistance on its way. So far the process has been described as hauling on the braces but in reality it was more like seeing them safely down on deck because, once the yards were started, they came flying around without further effort from the crew, who were hard put to keep pace with the rate that the ropes were being delivered to them. It was this phenomenon that made brace winches a possibility. The *Alert* had a couple of double leads on the foremost main shrouds, through which her topsail braces were led, making it easier to keep all three ropes together; but *Brooklands*, with her long wire pennants and the whips up and down the shrouds, had to do without them as the lee blocks finished not very far above the rail.

As might be expected, the jack barquentine did not have quite the same arrangement of braces as the orthodox schooner. Her short fore lower mast made it possible to lead the lower topsail braces to the hounds of the main lower mast. The last schooner afloat to carry them in this position was the *Jane Banks* [Figure 10-26]. She was also, I am sure, the last schooner to continue yet another souvenir from her youth on deep water – a studding sail boom, which wasn't used for anything but which her crew were obviously reluctant to throw overboard or chop up for firewood. With one of these out on each side, the spread on her foremast must have seemed nearly as wide as it was high.

One of the practises in 'round the land' schooners, used to avoid calling out the sleepers below, was to put the vessel about, whenever possible, at the change of the watch. However, the job could be done, and frequently was, by only two

FIGURE 10-25 Braces

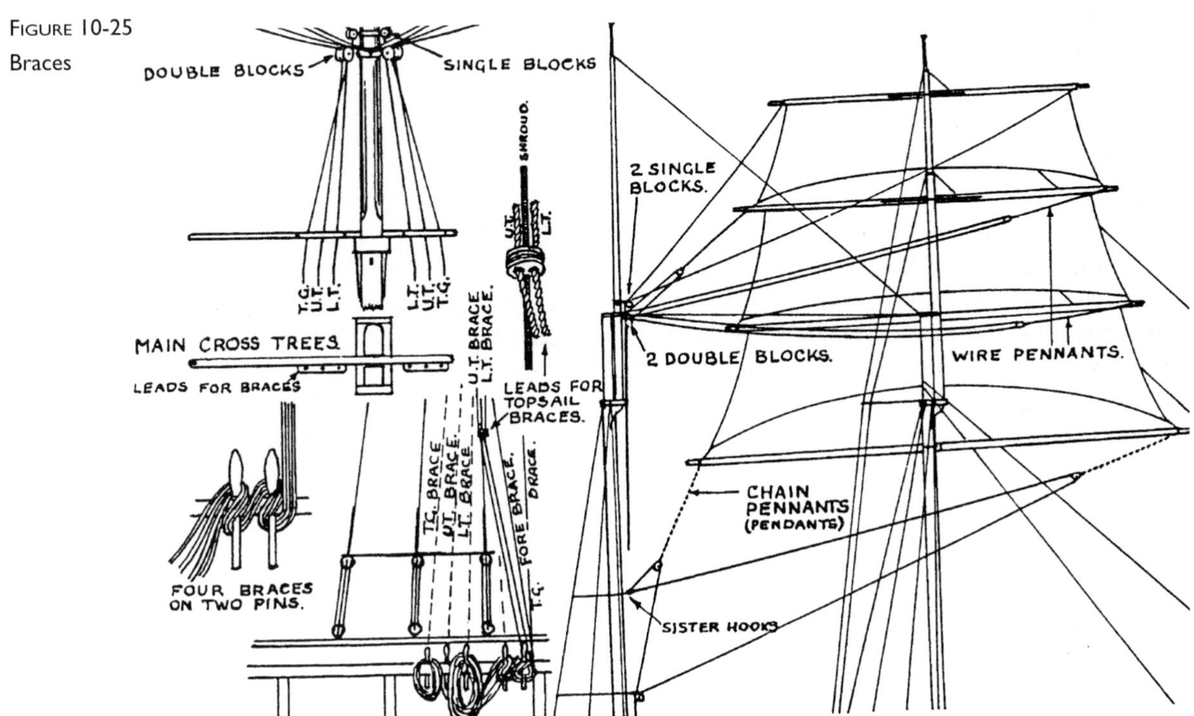

men. It was only the larger three-masters that carried a crew of five and, for this reason, as a complete greenhorn I would never have managed obtained a job in a two-master – both men on deck had to know what they were doing.

When the job was done by two, the skipper or mate took the wheel and put the vessel off the wind a bit to allow her to gather more speed while the other man set off forward on the lee side, laying the coil of braces down on the deck before passing on to deal with the jib sheets. He stood forward on the lee side as the helm was put down and the schooner started to come up into the wind. As soon as she was near enough to the wind's eye for the jibs to stop drawing, he had to let go the three sheets, charge over to the other side and haul the clews over the stays, swigging each one as tightly as possible, flying jib first, standing jib last. By the time he had done this, the topsails had been aback for some time, so that the way was off the vessel and she was rolling about with her gaffs and booms slamming from side to side.

Also by this time the helmsman had straightened up the wheel and was on his way forward. He let go the braces about the same time as the man forward was casting off the staysail bowline and the pair of them set off at a gallop for the lee braces, the man forward having a straight run, but the helmsman having to double back in his tracks to somewhere abaft the mainmast – it was definitely not safe to squeeze past the foresheet even if the first careless frenzy of the boom had about spent its force; in most schooners there was insufficient space between sheet and boat for it to be even attempted. Both men arrived at the braces together and, grabbing all three, gave them a hearty heave to start them on their way. When the yards were around the fore brace was seized, swigged on the forward member of the twin pins and turned around both as shown in Figures 10-16 and 10-25.

The lower and upper topsail braces were given the same treatment in rapid succession and, in the days when there was one, the topgallant as well. In bad weather it did not seem to matter how fast the job was done, before the third brace was finished with, the schooner had heeled again to the blast, taken her preliminary lunge forward on the new tack and the water had come cascading inboard along the length of the lee rail. But it was not for this reason that the job was done in such haste, rather it was to release the helmsman so that he could race back to the wheel and get the vessel properly on to her course. While he was doing that, the other man went forward to set up the staysail bowline, after which he had the jib sheets and braces to coil down for the next occasion, the latter being in the middle of the swimming bath amidships! When the vessel was on the wind again they could, if they thought it necessary, becket the wheel and attend to anything that was not to their satisfaction.

When the job was done by the whole crew the skipper took the wheel, the mate stood to leeward to let go the jib sheets, after which he let go the staysail bowline and started aft on the new weather side about the same time as the rest of the crew set off for the lee braces. It was the mate who passed each brace below the pin, leaving the rest of the crew to do the swigging, and it was the mate who turned each one up as it was swigged taut. After that the watch due to beat a retreat did so. The hitches, which secured the brace ends to their pins, were positioned so that, on either tack, the yards were trimmed and checked in properly by merely swigging the lee braces taut. This meant that when the upper topsail was stowed, its yard came around slightly more than it did when it was at the masthead.

In the ketch, schooner and brigantine the mainsheet was one of the heaviest ropes aboard, although the standing jib-sheet and the staysail bowline sometimes ran it a close second. It was rove through a three-sheave block on the boom and a two-sheave block at the bottom, and was usually double-ended – ie. it could be hauled on from either side. This was done with a strop and a handy billy [Figure 10-16, bottom] and, in anything like a breeze, it took the combined efforts of the crew, heaving like Trojans at the end of a roll, to gain anything from it. The ketch was the handiest vessel for this job as its mainsheet was in the body of the vessel; the old-fashioned transom stern provided a comfortable little corner in which the crew could congregate in the execution of the work; on the elliptical counter it was every man for himself – half the effort was wasted in trying to maintain some sort of balance and the other half because the men at the tail end of the rope were, of necessity, pulling around the bend. The aftermost sail in all rigs had no sheet horse; in the ketch the mainsheet often had none either, as its mizzenmast was too short and light to take a vang from the main gaff.

After the sheets the next ropes in degree of importance were the peak and throat halyards and a schooner with long splices in these could be considered as being on the bones of her financial backside. They were turned end for end from time to time, to spread the wear, but it would have been folly to carry this too far, as the failure of just one could lead to dire trouble. When the sails were set the halyards were not belayed directly on the pins but were first taken around half cleats on the bulwark stanchions, crossing over the standing part as shown in Figure 10-16, and then to the belaying pin. Their coils were too big and heavy to be accommodated on a pin, so they were hung from the sheer pole by a lanyard. From this position they had to be dropped to the deck when reefing was about to take place.

Figure 10-26
Braces of *Jane Banks*

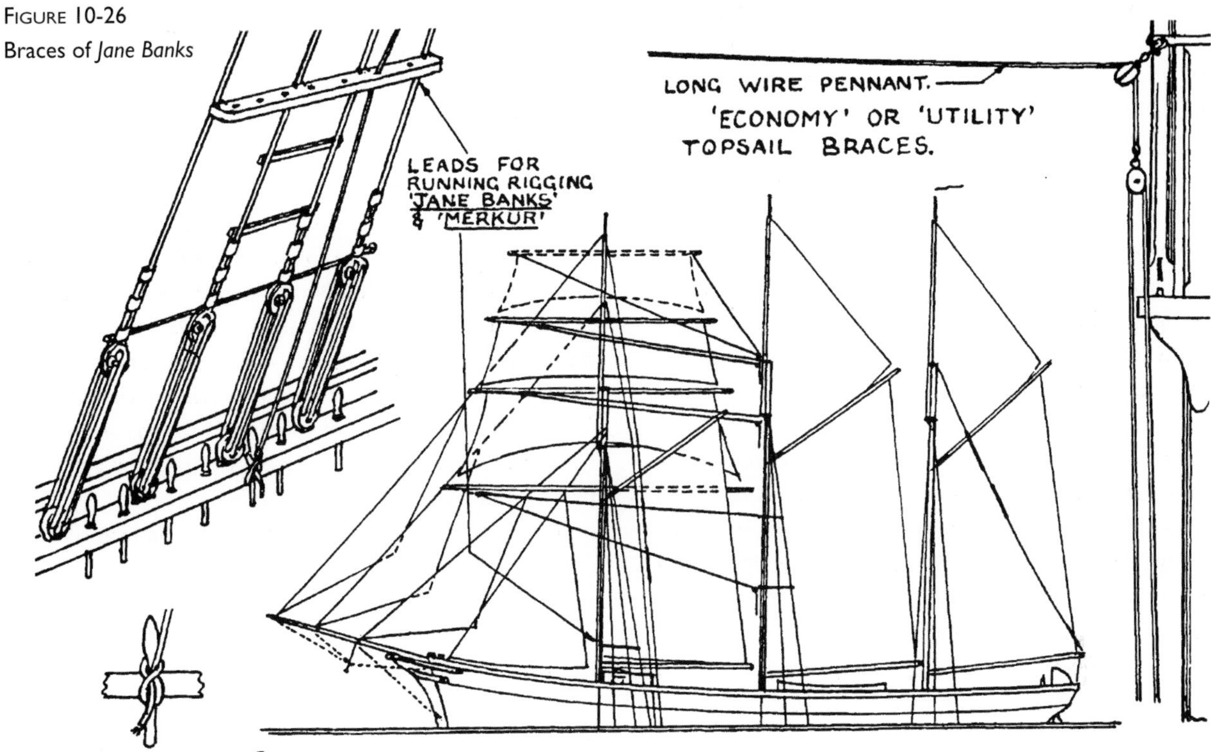

Reefing Gear

Point reefing [Figure 10-14] for obvious reasons hung on longer on schooners' foresails than on any others. To get at the reef tackle, lash the cringle to the boom and knot the points, it was only necessary to climb into the boat, which made an admirable platform for this purpose and gave easy access to the roof of the galley from which the forward end could be dealt with. Other sails were not always quite so handy and those with booms over the stern were the worst. The mainsails of schooners and brigantines are therefore the most likely ones to have had roller-reefing gear first. Not that it seems at all probable that these vessels were the first to which the gear was fitted, the honour of which must surely go to the famous Bristol Channel pilot cutters.

The pilot having been deposited aboard some inward-bound vessel, the cutter was sailed home by one man – one resolute and hardworking man who was capable of retrieving and getting back aboard his vessel a boat that had to be big enough to be used in all sorts of dirty weather and strong enough to stand being thumped against the sides of much larger ships. But, however resolute the man, to point reef singlehanded a mainsail with a boom of between 20ft and 30ft long [6.10m to9.14m] must have been hard graft and the newfangled innovation was probably welcomed with open arms.

The worm gear shown in Figure 9-6, detail 3 (page 99), was ideal for singlehanded operation. All that had to be done was to ship the same kind of handle as was used on a dolly winch, and turn it. This raised the boom and, by so doing, tightened up the sheet. The boom was raised usually no more than 6in [15cm] at a time. The throat halyard was eased out so that the boom could drop back to its normal position and the peak halyard was also paid out a little but not so much as the throat. This was done to guard against two tendencies: for the luff of the sail to creep aft along the boom, and for the after end of the boom to sag as the leech moved forward. This latter tendency was most marked in the mainsails of two-masters where the leech had more slope than in other sails. In all rigs there came a time, if the sails were shortened down far enough, when the weight of the main boom had to be taken by the topping lift, to prevent an intolerable strain being placed on the after part of the sail; some support was provided by the downhaul from the peak of the gaff because it too was rolled around the boom as it rotated. Thus, taken in by small instalments the sails were gradually reduced in area, a full turn on an 8in-diameter [20cm] boom removing about 2ft [60cm] of canvas.

The drift between the luff of the sail and the mast was greater near the boom than it was higher up where it was secured to the mast hoops and, for this reason, in unreefed condition, the first hoop was usually about 4ft [1.22m] above the boom jaws. This, then, was where the hoops were kept as the sail came down the mast, being removed one by one and hung from the next higher hoop still in business. The pitch of the worm was kept low so that it had no tendency to run back when the handle was released. A ratchet wheel and pawl were not necessary and the gear ratio was more than adequate for one man to do the job on his own. The double gooseneck and long bar enabled the boom to rise so that the man could leave the handle, slacken off his halyards and return to the job without needing any assistance. In a pilot cutter the singlehander would doubtless have had his tiller lashed and his vessel hove-to while he was reefing, but one of the advantages of roller-reefing gear was that there was no need to get the wind out of the sail while the job was being done.

The kind of worm gear shown in Figure 9-6, detail 2 (page 98) had to be worked by two men because the boom would not lift. Thus, the throat halyard had to be paid out as the boom was rotated. The drum-and-chain type of reefing gear [Figure 9-6, detail 1] was the simplest as well as the cheapest and was therefore the one most commonly met with in schooners. The reef tackle was fourfold, with two double blocks, and was hung by a length of wire from an eyebolt in the starboard cheek of the lower mast. When not in use the lower block was hooked into an eyebolt in the rail. Most examples of this type of gear were fitted with a ratchet wheel and pawl, not normally used but there in case of need. If the reef tackle was let go with the pawl engaged, the iron boom jaws would twist around until they locked on the mast, grinding with good effect on the brass strips. For this reason the fall of the tackle was belayed after reefing and the pawl kept permanently tied off with a length of spun yarn.

One of the drawbacks to this type of gear manifested itself in the *Alert* at the midnight hour. On the port tack, with boom, gaff and sail all over to starboard there was a danger of one of the descending mast hoops falling foul of the rising hook of the lower reef tackle block, and this was what happened, bringing the business to a standstill. A bellowed conversation ensued between Frank, Chris and Paddy in the pitch dark, in which they eliminated other possibilities; then Paddy climbed on top of the dolly winch and felt around until he had located the offending hoop. By coming up slightly on the reef tackle the restraint was removed without any further trouble. It was to guard against such an occurrence that the upper block of the reef tackle was usually tied back to one of the shrouds by a short length of wire. In this particular case it had failed to do its job.

The drum-and-chain reefing gear also needed two men to work it, although one man might conceivably have done so by holding the fall of the reef tackle onto the dolly winch with one hand and heaving on the handle with the other – stopping frequently to shift his grip – and then having to belay the rope while he attended to the halyards. Where there was no dolly winch – ie. on nearly every schooner's foresail – the job needed two men at least to swig the reef tackle. Here, therefore, the obvious answer was to becket the wheel and get the whole job over and done with as quickly as possible [Figure 10-27].

By the 1930s all two-masted vessels had roller-reefing mainsails. Some ketches had roller-reefing gear on their mizzens as well, and some schooners had their boom foresails so equipped. The majority of three-masted schooners had roller-reefing gear on all three fore and afters, the *Jane Banks* being one of the few that still retained point reefing on the fore. Usually each sail was fitted with the same kind of gear but it seems fitting that the little *Mary Miller*, one of the last to cross topsail yards, should have been a floating exhibition of all the different types. She had point reefing on her foresail, drum-and-chain gear on her main, and worm gear on the mizzen.

Running Rigging of Fore and Afters

Every gaff and boom was fitted with peak and throat halyards, a sheet, a topping lift, a reef tackle and a boom tackle. Some had vangs, some had tripping lines and some carried gaff topsails above them. The gaff had a downhaul from its peak to keep it under control while it was being lowered. All throat halyards were fourfold tackles with two double blocks. Peak halyards were usually made up from single blocks only, although the odd ketch sported a double block on her mizzenmast. Main peak halyards were always fourfold; foresails and mizzens were sometimes four, sometimes three. Regional variations in schooners' running rigging was practically non-existent, the only one I can call to mind being in *Lochranza Castle*, a frequent visitor to the Mersey, which had a Mersey flat's peak and throat halyards on her mainsail. These were made of chain and passed through single blocks on the mast to a pair of fourfold tackles working vertically [Figure 10-29].

The tack tripping line or tricing line [Figure 10-14] was a feature found in point reefing sails only and was quite unusual in the 1930s. This was a line from the tack of the sail (and its bottom masthoop), up through a block on the underside of one of the gaff jaws and then back down to the deck. It was used to haul up the tack to spill some of the wind out of the sail, and was resorted to when towing, as it allowed the crew to get the fore and afters on the vessel without over-running the tug. It was also used when hove-to, for instance when waiting for a pilot, as it reduced the lack of balance between the forward shove of the fore and afters, and the backed topsails that were resisting them. Finally it could be used to reduce further the area of close-reefed sails when hove-to at the height

FIGURE 10-27 Reefing

of a gale [Figure 10-28, detail 4]. This process of hauling up the tack was known as 'scandalising'. If a Victorian lady had hoisted up the hem of her skirt so that her ankles were revealed, the members of her own sex would have been absolutely scandalised, while propriety would have forced the gentlemen, at least, to go through the motions of being so moved; there is, therefore, a strong possibility that the expression arose out of some real or imaginary incident along these lines. Roller-reefing gear put an end to these scandalous goings-on, bringing British schooners into line with American ones, in having only one method with which to spill the wind: taking up the slack in the topping lift and easing out the peak halyard until the area of canvas abaft the diagonal was no longer drawing.

Boom tackles, those highly necessary curbs to the frivolity of fore and afters, have been mentioned many times in this book. They were heavy fourfold tackles and, when set up from the fore booms of all schooners and the main booms of three-masters, the forward block was hooked into an eyebolt in the cover plank. The long main booms of schooner and brigantine were too far outboard for this and their boom tackles were hooked into wire pennants secured at their forward ends to plates on the outside of the bulwarks, usually just abaft the fore rigging [Figure 10-12 to 14]. Not having sailed in a ketch, I have no precise information on what they did with their main boom tackle but would fancy they would use a similar pennant from some point forward of the main shrouds. The narrowness of the after part of a vessel caused the same sort of problem with the mizzens of three-masters and ketches and, as very few vessels seem to have been fitted with outside plates for the purpose, the boom tackles were provided with an improvised pennant. The ends of all these pennants, when not in use, were kept inboard. One or two schooners, including *Ellie Park* and *North Barrule* had no wheelhouses to support their main booms or, as on the *Useful*, were only provided with one at the eleventh hour. These vessels had a small luff tackle for use when at anchor; it would pull against the mainsheet and stop the boom from eternally creaking its jaws against the mast. It was hooked into the rail abreast of the cabin skylight. They also had, of course, the full-sized article for use when running.

No schooner in the 1930s still set a main topmast staysail. Photographic evidence points to the fact that, before they were entirely dispensed with, the vessels that carried them did so purely for 'showing off' because they had only one sheet and that was led back to the main cap, on the centreline of the vessel. A sail sheeted in this way could hardly have been anything but a drag when going to windward, although it might have contributed some useful work when the wind was on the quarter and its sheet well eased. In the days when it was taken seriously its sheets were led through blocks on the main spreader, about half way out, so that it could be flattened to do its work in the proper manner [Figure 10-29, bottom].

Running Rigging of Gaff Topsails

The minimum number of ropes required by a gaff topsail was three: a halyard, a sheet, and a tack. Gaff topsails fastened to hoops on the topmast also required a clewline and this could be a simple or quite complicated affair depending on what was expected of it. In most cases it functioned as a combined clewline and downhaul and in its simplest form was a line from the clew passing through a block or bullseye at the head of the sail and then down to the deck [Figure 10-31, left]. To clew up the sail, the halyard was let go and the clewline hauled in until the hoops were down on the cap, then the sheet was released and more pulling brought the clew in to join them. It was not necessary to touch the tack, or tack rope, as it was sometimes called, as the load came off it when the halyard was let go. It was at this point that whoever was going to furl the sail set off up the rigging and, judging by the amount of blasphemy that even the memory of it brought forth, the clewing was a trifle inadequate – the sail was probably little better than a canvas balloon banging about the doubling.

Some North American schooners had the clewline passing through a hole in the sail, or perhaps through a thimble seized into a length of rope that was stitched to the canvas, and this may be the reason they were able to cope with much larger gaff topsails than were ever used on this side of the Atlantic. They certainly had more in the way of crosstrees to stand on than did British vessels, as well as having topmast shrouds rattled as high as the cap. But perhaps when it came to stowing them it required more than one man to deal with each sail.

North American clewlines, however, were usually even more complicated than the type just mentioned as they had to be capable of getting the sail bunched up above the cap, so that the tack and sheet could be shifted over when the schooner went about. One version is shown on the right hand side of Figure 10-31. I suspect that the halyard was slackened off to provide a more direct pull on the clew and this would have been augmented if the second rope to be let go were the tack. The result would then have been a double-purchase pull

FIGURE 10-28 A schooner going about

1 Vessel has been put off to clean full and the helm put down. She is now coming up into the wind.
2 In stays. Staysail and topsails are aback and vessel's head is paying off to port. The jibs have been pulled over the stays. The man forward is about to let go the staysail bowline, while the helmsman is waiting until he starts aft before letting go the braces.
3 Yards round and vessel on the starboard tack. Staysail bowline set up.
4 A schooner under reefed and scandalized fore and afters.

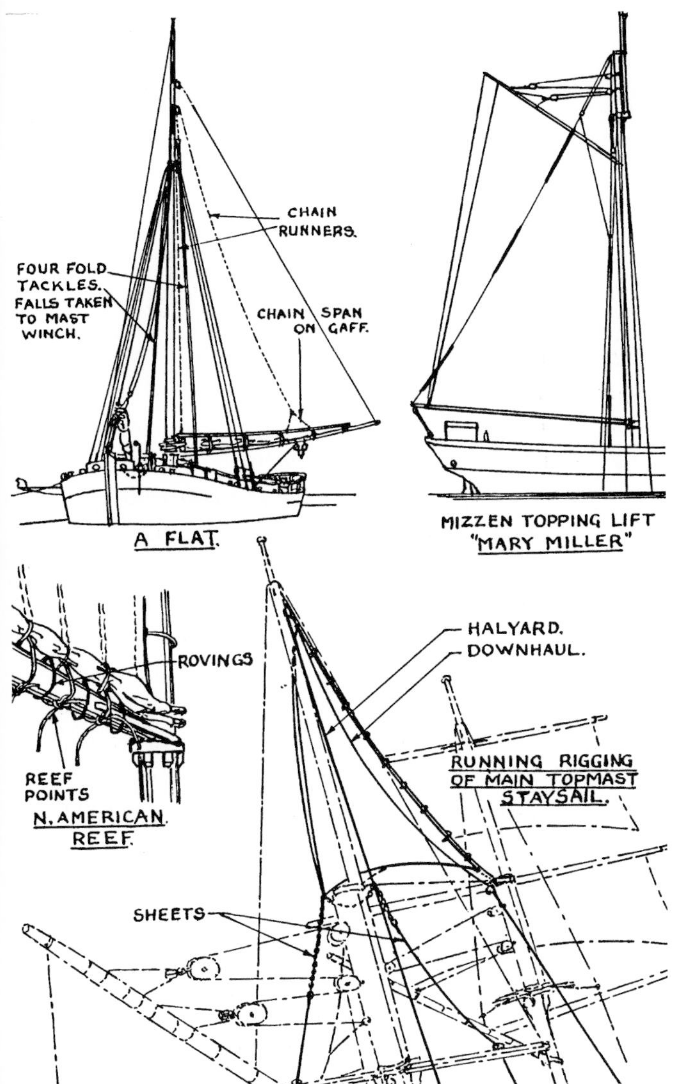

FIGURE 10-29

to haul the chain sheet in towards the mast. The above conjectures were made many years ago after looking at a model of the Grand Banks' fishing schooner *Bluenose*; they may not be correct, and anyone seriously interested in the matter would be well advised to apply to the land of the free and the home of the brave, or its next-door neighbour to the north, for further enlightenment on the subject.

In British schooners the problems of gaff topsails were finally sorted out by sending the sails up on a jackstay – a length of wire from a point on the topmast above the line of the sheet, which was set up to the deck at the foot of the mast. The hanks were permanently fastened to the sail, and the end of the jackstay was threaded through them before being bowsed taut with a lanyard or tackle. The sheet and halyard were then made fast, usually by moused sister hooks, and the sail was hoisted aloft. When the head was up to the sheavehole the clew was hauled out and the tack tackle set up to stretch the luff taut. At the foot of their masts many schooners had the rusty remnants of what had been permanent iron snatch blocks for this duty but, after becoming a constructive total loss, their job had been taken over by ringbolts. In some vessels the dolly-winch drums were used to belay the falls, while Captain William Slade seems to have thought up quite an ingenious method of taking the jackstay through a ring and using the tack tackle to tighten the luff of the sail and the jackstay together [Figure 10-30].

The business part of a gaff topsail halyard – the part abaft the mast when the sail was not set – was made of wire to reduce the amount of stretch that took place in a long rope. The end passed through the sheavehole at the topmast head and a thimble was eye-spliced into it, to which the rope was fastened. With the larger gaff topsails, the two-masters usually had a single block and whip at this point so that, when the sail was aloft, there was a fair-sized coil of rope on deck. Gaff topsail sheets invariably had a length of chain at the end, which worked in the cheek block on the side of the gaff. It could be anything from 5ft to 10ft [1.52m to 3.05m] in length, and the rope was fastened to its end by a chain splice to allow it to run through the block [Figure 10.31, left].

The job was better suited to a four-strand rope than a three-strand one but could be done with either. With a four-strand rope two strands were cut off, the other two were passed through the end link and laid back In the track of the cut-off strands, as in a long splice, the job was finished 'whatever way you fancy.' With a three-strand rope, one strand was cut off and the remaining two were passed through the link. One strand only could be laid back down the rope, leaving the other to be disposed of in some other way. The easiest way was to tuck it under and over like a short splice; the neatest was to divide it into three parts and dispose of them down the line, either with or against the lay and with their ends spaced out. When not in use at sea the gaff topsail sheets had their sister hooks fastened around the fall [Figure 10-23], which was then hauled in several feet so that the hooks were well above head height. The fall was made fast to the pinrail so the whole lot hung clear of the sail on either tack. Halyards and jackstays were also made fast to the rail in the same way when not in use. When the sheet was needed again the weight of the chain on its end ensured that a few flicks of the rope would bring its end sliding down until the sister hooks were within reach.

Figure 10-32 gives the range of sizes for the various pieces of running rigging. The dimensions of the short-link chain used in running rigging were the same as that used for standing rigging and are given in Figure 9-23 of the previous chapter.

Figure 10-31 Going about

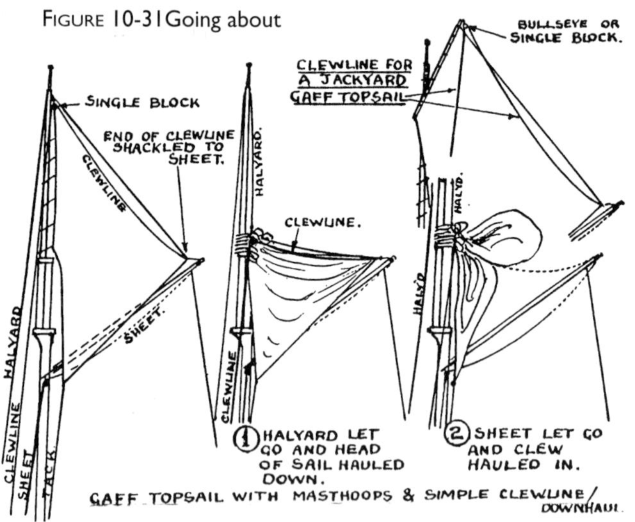

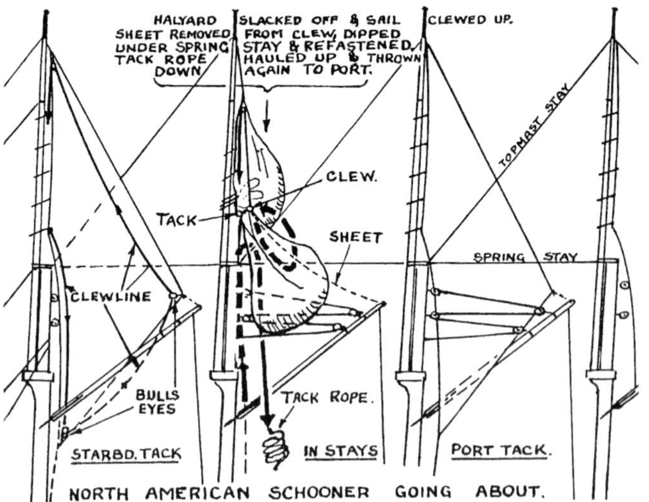

Figure 10-30 Jackstays

Only large main gaff topsails fitted with double purchase halyard. Sheet not usually fitted with a tackle as the luff of the sail could be set taut by the jackstay and tack tackle, No downhaul or clewline required. After letting go halyard and sheet, the sail was hauled down by the tack.

JACKYARD GAFF TOPSAIL

JIB HEADED GAFF TOPSAIL.

SHEET.

HANKS.

HALYARD

(WIRE)

ROPE

SHEET

JACKSTAY

TACK

JACKSTAY

IRON SNATCH BLOCK.

JACKSTAY

TACK TACKLE

TACK

CAPT. SLADE'S METHOD.

Figure 10.32

Running Rigging

Item		*Bar Dia.*	*Dia.*	*Circ.Rig*
Bowline (Staysail) *Rope pennant*				3–4
Bowline (Staysail) *Luff tackle*				2
Bobstay tripping line				1½–2
Boom tackles			3–3½	
Boom tackle pennants (Main booms two-masters)			½	
Brace pennants *Lower yard*		¼		
Brace pennants *Topsail yards*			½	
Braces *Topgallant yard (single line)*				1½–2½
Braces *Lower yard*				3–3½
Braces *Topsail yard*				2–2½
Clewlines *Lower topsail*				2–2½
Clewlines *Topgallant*				1½–2½
Clewlines *Gaff topsail*				1½
Downhauls *Jib and staysail*				2–2½
Downhauls *Upper topsail*				2–2½
Downhauls *Gaff*			2½	
Gaskets			1½–2	
Halyards *Peak and throat*				3–4
Halyards *Jib*			2–2½	
Halyards *Staysail*			2–2½	
Halyards *Upper topsail tye*		⅜		
Halyards *Upper topsail runner*		¼–5⁄16		
Halyards *Upper topsail tackle*				2–3
Halyards *Gaff topsail*			½	2–3
Mast hood lanyards				1½
Reef tackles			3	
Sheets	Jib (Flying and boom)	¼		2½–3
Sheets	Jib (Standing)	¼		3–4
Sheets	Fore and afters			3½–4½
Sheets	Lower topsail	¼–5⁄16		2–3
Sheets	Topgallant	¼		1½–2
Sheets	Gaff topsail	¼		1½–2½
Topping lifts		¼	⅜–½	1½–2½
Tack ropes	Gaff topsail			2½
Yard ropes				2½–3

XI

ENGINES

The economic drawbacks of wind-driven vessels have received far less attention than they deserve, comments on them being usually confined to mention of slow passages and unpredictable arrival dates. These factors were worse in the Home Trade than on deep water, even in the days when the schooners were in their prime, and the repercussions that they had on the businesses served by them, are seldom mentioned. The uncertainty of delivery dates forced these businesses to stockpile, which in turn tied up considerable amounts of capital earning nothing. The problem went further because when the wind-bound schooners finally got a slant, the whole fleet frequently arrived within hours of each other and, in spite of limited discharging facilities, their bills would have to be met almost one after the other. For this more money had to be available in the bank and, although it was at least earning interest, it could probably have been put to good use in many other ways. In consequence the men in charge of these businesses had to be sure they had sufficient money available before taking any step towards an increase in turnover. Thus, expansion, although steady, tended to be slow.

Stockpiling was not a bad thing for the country as a whole because it enabled it to ride over minor emergencies without undue trouble, but it pressed hard on small firms, which could find themselves in financial difficulties while still in possession of considerable assets. For these reasons as the years passed the schooners were gradually relegated to the handling of low-priced bulk commodities but, while they were in competition with only steam vessels, they remained an economic proposition and provided a living for their owners and crews.

The internal-combustion engine brought this phase to an end. Whereas the smallest steamer needed at least two men to attend constantly to fires and engine, the internal-combustion engine could be started up by anyone and left to run for hours without attention. No fuel was used in port to maintain a head of steam for the winches, as the motor-driven winch could be started and stopped as required. As the number of small motor vessels began to increase, the steamers became uneconomic, while the schooner was left with its back almost to the wall. That it did not disappear overnight is probably due to old-fashioned businessmen who saw no reason to take their custom away from men whom they had known and respected for many years; nevertheless, the end was in sight. Not being able to beat the motor vessels, the schooner owners were forced to join them. The first machines to come aboard were small engines to drive winches so that the loading and discharging of cargo could be expedited and, in many cases, additional labour from ashore could be dispensed with.

The first auxiliary engines were also small and were mainly intended to push the vessels through a calm and thus to dispense with tugs but it was soon found that they were a great help when the schooners were under sail, as they prevented them from making as much leeway; enabled them to catch their tides and be generally much more predictable in their times of arrival. Once this stage had been reached and clearly grasped, what followed was inevitable.

Topsail yards were sent down, flying jibs dispensed with, bowsprits cut short and topmasts, when not removed altogether, cut down to short stumps so that many of the vessels rapidly became a travesty of what they had once been. The men who did this were not unmindful of the symmetry and gracefulness that they were destroying, and their outlook was well summed up in the comment of one of the Irish skippers: 'It's no use starting the job unless you're prepared to make an absolute "Colonel Bogey" of it". He was right, but many did not have the necessary brutality to carry things to their logical conclusion. Some preferred to leave the bowsprit as it was, although they set no flying jib on it; others left their full-length topmasts aloft, whether they set gaff topsails on them or not, while others only shortened them a little and left them in position for ornamental purposes. Nearly all, however, were determined to get the topsail yards down at the earliest opportunity, some possibly because they felt the engine was an adequate replacement, others in order to remove the necessity of keeping an eye, or at night an ear, on the luff of the upper topsail when on a wind, so that the wheel could be enclosed in a house, and shelter obtained from the wintry winds.

One vessel that did not have her topsail yards removed right away was the *Mary Barrow*. Peter Mørtensen had a

wheelhouse built with the glass in the upper front sufficiently high that, from its shelter, the helmsman could see whether the sails were drawing properly or not. She retained her topsail yards for perhaps two or three more years before they were replaced by a raffee.

The general reluctance to dispose of the foreyard has already been mentioned but what to do with it while under sail posed something of a problem. The square-rigged tradition was too strongly ingrained for anyone to think of going to windward with it squared and, since they considered they would have to swing it anyway, some opted for the raffee while others preferred still to set a lower topsail. Who came up with the answer will never be known but it was very simple and, in the end, was universally adopted. The yard was cock-billed as high as it would go, the lifts being taken through blocks at the cap and down to the deck for this purpose. It still offered the same windage as before but looked less obtrusive and everyone was quite content to beat to windward with it in this position. There were one or two non-conformists who sent the yard and squaresail up flying, and the *Eilian*, a vessel well-endowed with power, shortened her yard, cut the sail down to suit and, since the braces would have fallen foul of the boom foresail, led them out to the bowsprit end and back inboard, as was done in the 18th-century ketch.

One or two more things had to be done; one or two more regulations complied with. In the 1930s sailing vessels were already rare enough for a whole generation to assume that the absence of white lights indicated that there were no ships about – the schooner men were only too pleased to have the right to carry a masthead light when under power. At first it was probably taken aloft up the shrouds, but a contrivance of wire and thimbles was soon produced, in imitation of the two bars on the foreside of a steamer's mast, so that it could be hauled up from the deck [Figure 11-1]. In busy estuaries a sailing vessel under power as well as sail was required to indicate this by displaying in a rigging a black ball 2ft in diameter. This was the same sign as was used to indicate that a vessel was at anchor. A lot of schooners used a pudding fender for this latter purpose, although it was smaller than the regulation demanded, and after conversion to auxiliary vessels simply used it for its new role as well. The black ball was originally the day mark of a steam vessel proceeding under sail alone. One or two vessels, including *Donald and Doris*, had a ball of the proper size made of two circular sheets of plywood that could be slotted into each other at right angles when in use [Figure 11-1] but others who had an equal desire that there should be no doubt about what they were doing (in case of an enquiry), thought it best to lower their sails well

FIGURE 11-1

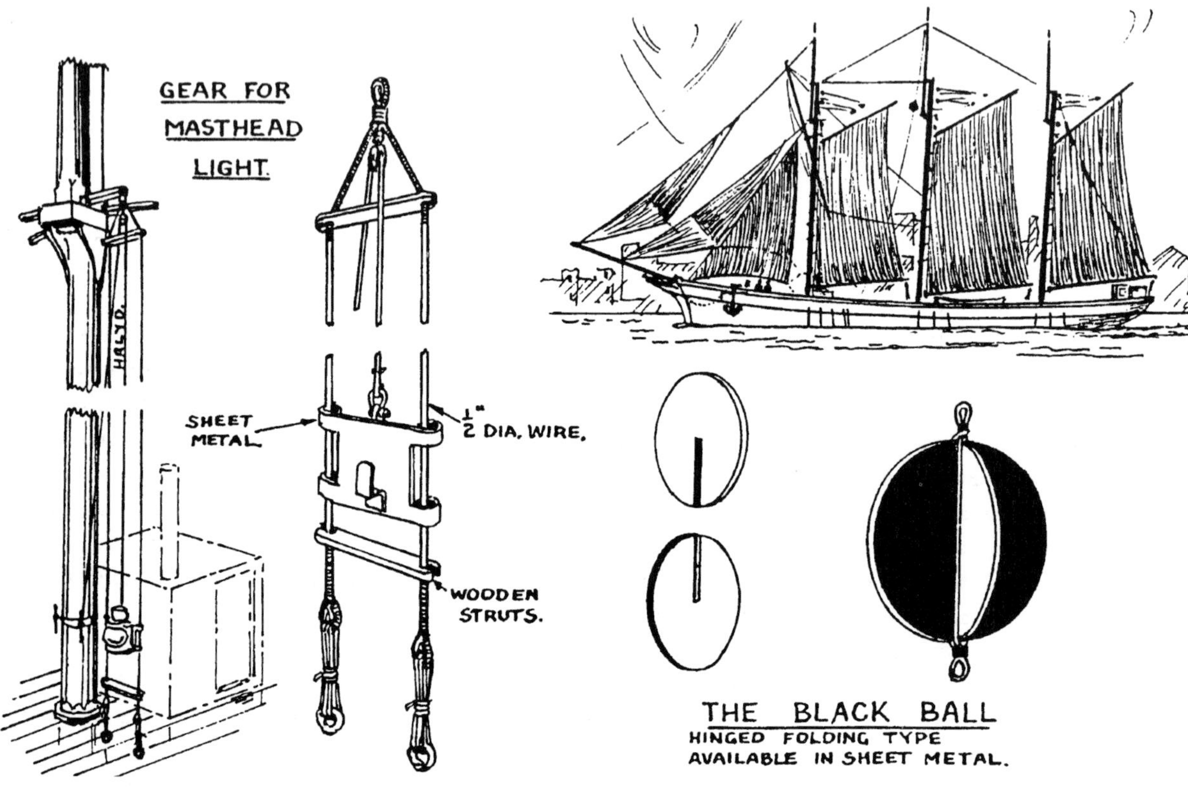

before they got into the thick of the traffic.

There were tremendous variations in the horsepower of the engines installed. The ketch and the three-masted schooner had the least space, abaft the mizzenmast, into which to fit the machinery. In some cases it was adequate for the size of the vessel, in others not. The *Mary Barrow*, after having various engines in her, finished up with a handed pair of diesels abreast of her mizzenmast. For obvious reasons there was a marked reluctance to encroach on the hold space, but where this had to be done to accommodate the desired horsepower the schooners had the best of it. As well as sufficient space for the engine, the fuel tanks had also to be accommodated, while still leaving enough space to dismantle the engine when necessary, and a good many vessels finished up with a reduction in their net tonnage. In some cases the main cabin was left intact and the engine installed forward of it but in many others the skipper and the mate folded up their tents and stole silently forward, leaving their noisy, smelly shipmate in full possession of the after end. Those vessels that were converted late in the day had a much wider choice of machinery than did the pioneers of the movement as they were able to take advantage of the smaller high-speed multi-cylinder engines that were originally developed for use on road vehicles.

These engines were geared down to the propeller, which was smaller than that used by the old slow-running semi-diesels; there was more slip but when under sail alone there was less drag on the vessel. These latterday engines developed far more horsepower for their size but at the expense of a much shorter life.

The petrol/paraffin engine was another type used in some of the early conversions. One of its drawbacks was its higher-priced fuel; the other was the damp salt-laden atmosphere in which it had to function failed to bring out the best in its electrical system. In the main it was confined to small machines, which were probably used much more as real auxiliaries than some of the later engines; it was never a very serious competitor to the diesels.

The Semi-diesel

Doctor Rudolph Diesel would have disclaimed all responsibility for the 'semi' had he been accused of it, and would have passed the blame on to a Yorkshireman called Ackroyd. Its compression ratio was not high enough to start combustion without pre-heating, and a blow-lamp was played on a bulb in the cylinder head until it was hot enough to fire. This usually took about 20 minutes. The blowlamps used paraffin and compressed air and, when opened full out, they let out a snarl like a cage full of hungry tigers, so that conversation tended to languish. The compressed air was supplied by the engine itself, blown back through an adjustable spring-loaded valve – usually the one by which the engine was started – into two receivers, one for the blowlamps and the other for kicking the engine over when it was hot enough to fire. Cartridges were also available for this purpose in the event of a complete loss of compressed air in which case, of course, hand blowlamps would have had to be used. They were two-stroke engines with a firing stroke every revolution and it was discovered early on in their career that if splash lubrication was used they would send enough oil up through the transfer port to keep the engine running even if the fuel supply was turned off and frequently did so until drip-feed lubrication was adopted. Before this there was no stopping them. They also had another disconcerting propensity: they did not care which way they ran and in the 1930s this caused much consternation to motor cyclists, when they shot backwards after letting in the clutch. Early marine engines of this type often had reversing propellers so that, if the machine set off the wrong way, it was definitely not safe to leave it running without attempting to trip it back to the right direction. Before this was attempted it was prudent to blow up both air receivers, after which the injection pumps could be held off until the machine slowed right down, a mark on the flywheel arrived at a certain position, and a couple of jerks on the pump levers sent it back in the proper direction.

Frequently it would stall and had then to be barred around to the starting position before another attempt could be made. Many semi-diesels were also fitted with water-injection pumps. This kept the bulb temperature rather lower, reducing the danger of cracking, and also pushed up the mean effective pressure so that the engine developed more power but woe betide the engineer if he forgot to disengage the water pumps before slowing down or manoeuvring. Sooner or later the engine would stall. Another drawback to water injection was that it required yet another tank. The engine in the *Squirrel* drank more water than gas oil, and she had a rare old collection of drums, tanks, and water barrels at her stern end. A typical Semi-diesel is shown in Figure 11-2. They were relatively slow-running engines built in the tradition of steam-reciprocating machinery, the basic assumption being that they would be started up in Southampton and stopped in Singapore. In their old age many showed signs that this had been done not once but numerous times and some people seemed surprised and positively pained when they finally refused to function any longer.

I was shipmate for a time with a semi-diesel in this condition in 1944. It was a two-cylinder engine built by a Danish firm and installed in an ex-Lowestoft fishing vessel, which had been converted to a cargo carrier and was registered in

FIGURE 11-2
A semi-diesel marine engine

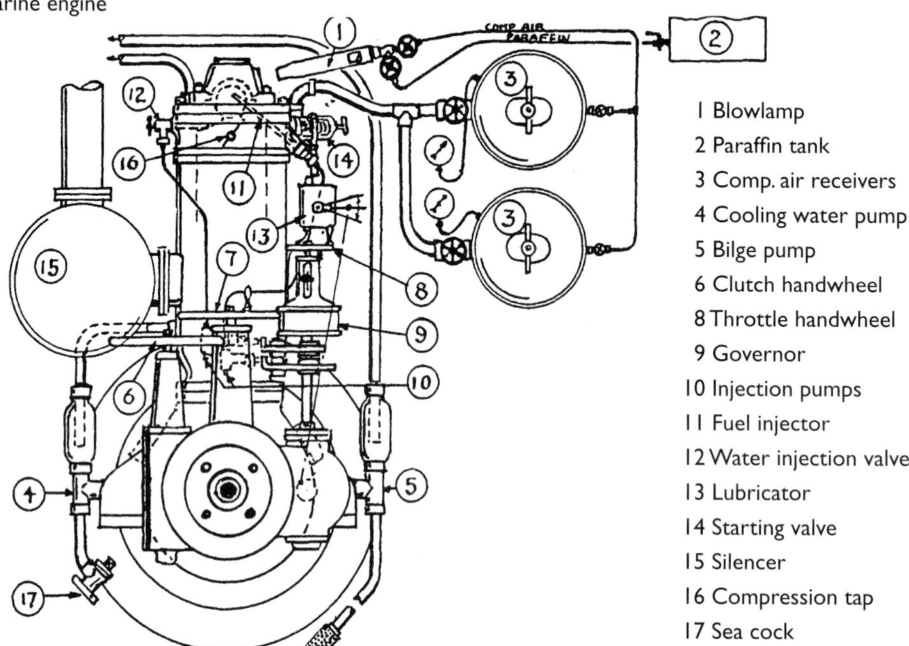

Mäløy, Norway. It must have been a fine upstanding engine in its youth. An eccentric on the shaft between crank-case and flywheel worked two ram pumps, one for the cooling water and one for the bilge, both of which were so worn that they ran on packing and consumed it in large quantities. When the bilge pump had pumped the vessel dry it lost its prime and would pump no more and, if the engineer was away for any length of time, the steady stream coming in through the stern tube caused the water level to rise until it came up to the bottom of the flywheel, creating a watery Catherine Wheel in the forepart of the engine room. It was right in line with the ladder so that, when he returned, the engineer was well moistened before his feet even touched the plates. The drill on these occasions was to slacken off and remove a union nut on top of the air vessel, pour in some water and clap the nut back on before a watery Vesuvius had time to join the dreadful revelry, thereafter retreating to the after end of the engine room to await results. The gland of the stern tube also consumed packing at an alarming rate and when the engine was stopped the grease gun that served it had to be screwed down a considerable way before the trickling came to an end.

There are shades of lunacy in practically all human occupations, each with its own peculiar flavour, and in this vessel it contained an element of surrealism. One night in Gosport the mate and I turned out to warp our vessel out of the way so that another lying inside us could go about her business. We had an energetic time of it, heaving in and letting go and shifting ropes from one place to another, and about an hour later, having finished the job, we were about to go below when we noticed a chink of light coming from the galley door. It was long past midnight, and we opened the top part to find a member of the crew standing facing us and brushing his teeth. Closing the door rapidly we retired to our bunks. In the morning, at breakfast, he proclaimed that during the night the vessel had been over-run by Norwegians.

The wheelhouse in this vessel was about 6ft square and housed the binnacle, wheel and engine controls; anyone dealing with the latter invariably banged the well-worn clutch home while the engine was going at full speed. My remonstrations produced results on only one occasion. I had started the engine and for some reason the skipper did not wait for any intimation that all was in order but cast off right away. When I turned the blowlamps off I discovered that it was only firing on one cylinder so I hurriedly set about relighting the other. Suddenly there was a lot of shouting up above and we rocked about considerably. This disturbed the paraffin in the tank feeding the blowlamps, the level in which was rather low, and the dirt came down the pipe and put out the blowlamp. While I was clearing the nipple someone in the wheelhouse threw the clutch out and slowed the engine down and it stalled immediately. I relit the blowlamp, started to bar the engine around to the starting position, and it went out again. I lit it again and gave the engine the starting sniff of compressed air, after winding the throttle up with a spanner and this time I thought it was firing in both pots but, being reluctant to turn off the blowlamp until I was quite sure, I climbed the ladder to listen to the exhaust, and was immediately assailed by loud shouts of 'give us a hand'. We were alongside the ferry, *Ulster Monarch*. To be precise, she was about 5ft away and our mizzenmast was lying between two of her davits, which were not the old-fashioned swivelling kind. We were going slowly astern with the tide, and the entire crew, with the exception of the skipper, were pushing like mad on our over-sized boat hook to get us clear. Eventually the two items cleared each other by a midge's whisker. I found out later that we had narrowly avoided a collision and that each of the skippers involved was convinced that it was the other man's fault. They started bellowing rude remarks at each other and even when the engine conked out and everyone else on board was working with might and main and mizzen to push the vessel clear, our skipper was standing in the wheelhouse like some Nautical Nero, torch in hand, transmitting his last thoughts on the matter in Morse. The crew said he was drunk with power.

Our vessel's original name was *Silver Wave* and it was still cut into the timbers on her bows. Her Norwegian name, in its own environment, may have been quite innocuous, but in plain English it was that of a well-known laxative, 'Exlax', so that we were at a disadvantage from outset when dealing with other vessels.

But it was the winch engine aboard this packet that in the end gave the finest performance, although the diameter of its piston was only about 4in, whilst that of its flywheel could not have been much more than 2ft. Its origins were lost in the mists of antiquity, at least its maker's nameplate had long ago disappeared, but it had a hit-and-miss governor of considerable ingenuity. An eccentric on the shaft worked the fuel-injection pump through a rod and crosshead guide, and between a pair of lugs on the crosshead was pivoted a block of metal with its centre of gravity outboard of the two pivot pins. If the engine ran too fast, the block swung outwards and its striker missed the pump ram, the speed at which this took place being controlled by an adjustable spiral spring and hand nut. This engine was also a semi-diesel and its blowlamp was an over-sized version of the kind used by plumbers and was fitted, when in use, onto a bicycle headlamp bracket on the upper part of the cylinder. It was completely without shelter of any kind and stood abaft the mainmast on the port side of the deck.

One cold, wet, gusty morning the vessel was chugging down the Solent in search of a landing ship (tank) and the thought crossed my mind that some time might be saved if I got the winch engine going before we came alongside. This decision turned out to be very much in keeping with the tradition that we had already established aboard. I tried to rig up a tarpaulin to protect the blowlamp from the worst of the wind, but there was nothing to which it could conveniently be anchored and it kept blowing out of place. The blowlamp was also being frequently extinguished by the gusts and I had to take it into the lee of the bulwarks and hurriedly relight it before it had time to cool off. After about fifteen minutes the engine got to the exasperating stage where it appeared to be on the point of firing and, between bouts of relighting the blowlamp and dragging the tarpaulin back, I made repeated attempts at spinning the flywheel. Every time I did this some fuel was injected into the cylinder. This went on for about an hour, and then the landing ship came in sight, and I left things to their own devices and went aft to attend to the main engine. The LST was partly tide-rode and as we came alongside and were in her lee the wind seemed to lose its force and the sun came out.

Once we were fast I left the main engine to tick over until it had cooled down and hurried forward to the winch. The blowlamp was still alight and was as calm and peaceful in the lee of the landing ship as in the brick-walled rose garden of some country seat. It was just what the winch engine needed. Seizing the flywheel I turned it back until it started to compress and then flung it forward. There was a bang and the piston shot down with tremendous rapidity, the speed rose alarmingly in a few seconds until by the sound of the exhaust beat the thing must have been doing close on a thousand revs. It was going too fast for me to see what the hit-and-miss governor had done, but wherever it was it must have stayed there, it had had no time in which to do anything else. After a brief period the exhaust pipe began to glow and soon became red-hot, the heat travelling along a 12in length of pipe until it came to the silencer. When it reached the silencer all the carbon and half-used fuel of ages was set in motion, and a shower of sparks shot up as high as the hounds of the mainmast. In the dark it would have been wonderful and we should probably have been prosecuted for trying to get in touch with the enemy. I warned the rest of the crew to keep out of the line of the flywheel as without recourse to a measuring device, a tachometer and a slide rule I didn't care to advance any theories as to how long it was liable to remain in one piece, but they hung about the galley door, as far aft as possible and evinced not the slightest desire to examine the phenomenon at closer quarters. For what seemed like half an hour, but may perhaps have been much less, that engine tore at the flywheel as though it was trying to break the record. I expected it to get so hot that it would seize up and wreck itself, but nothing of the sort happened.

Perhaps the air passing through the crank case kept it cool enough to continue its outrageous behaviour but at long last it began to falter in its stride, and slowly, very slowly, it reduced its mad gallop until finally it was idling over, hitting and missing in the approved manner, as though butter wouldn't melt in its cylinder. The crew of the landing ship had lost interest in us as soon as they discovered we had nothing to do with the NAAFI but on hearing the horrible racket overside they returned to the rail. They lingered, I think, in the hope that it would blow up and bring a ray of sunshine into their drab and cheerless lives, but when it began to slow down they slouched sadly away once more and soon our crew were knocking out the wedges and lifting the hatch covers and were ready to discharge the cargo.

For many years I felt that I could safely write the obituary for the semi-diesel. I intended to say that with it passed the sporting engineer of the late 19th and early 20th centuries, a man fearless enough to chance everything on the spin of a flywheel, and that Messrs Bolinders of Stockholm, a name synonymous with these machines pretty well all over the world, had moved on to higher things, in fact to the production of full-blown diesels. In 1977, however, I was aboard a small ex-Danish ketch, the *J.P. Thorsøe* (always these Danes), in which I discovered to my great surprise that the Bolinder semi-diesel was still in our midst and going strong and, according to her skipper, still very popular with Danish fishermen. This one was a single-cylinder machine and had most of the old foibles; if someone shifted his chewing gum it would drift off the starting position, just over top dead centre; too much air and it was lost up the exhaust pipe, too little and it would kick back and start off the wrong way, so that winding the reversing propeller from one position to the other would have produced the opposite result to what was expected. One obvious difference that this engine had was that there was no blowlamp to warm it up, instead there was a cylinder-heating plug, and as soon as this glowed red the engine would fire. It continued to fire when the current was switched off, indicating that the compression ratio had been increased until it was functioning as a true diesel.

I am at a loss now to know why I went in this vessel. I had long harboured a notion that if there was anything I wanted to do, I should get it done around the age of sixty, before it was too late. I was attracted by the appearance of the ketch, and forgetting all about my own luck and the British climate, I let my imagination run riot. I would have my last fling in her and, in so doing, would experience something which had eluded me all my life. I would have some carefree cruising. The only solid fact upon which this flight of fancy was based was that the ketch carried no cargo so that she did not have to get anywhere in particular. I imagined myself in the company of a bunch of congenial shipmates being wafted along by balmy breezes, while we pottered about gently with paintbrushes, fids, marline-spikes and serving boards, and went sculling ashore in the evenings to talk rubbish to the locals in village pubs. We certainly managed to talk quite a lot of rubbish in quite a lot of pubs, the company was congenial enough, but the balmy breezes failed to materialise. It was bitterly cold most of the time and we were four days windbound while a gale blew itself out in the Channel. Crossing Torbay we were beset by squalls with rain, but the biggest, best and blackest of the lot deposited on us a load of hailstones, which carpeted the deck and showed not the least sign of melting and running overboard. While sending them on their way with the draw bucket, we discovered that a poor old pigeon had landed on the deck. Perhaps he was on his way home after being dumped out of his basket in some corner of a foreign field, or he may have been making an overland passage and got blown off the church but whatever the story, it was evident that he had been fighting hard to stay airborne and was just about all in. The skipper's wife gave the resident cat and dog a clout on the ear apiece to draw their attention to the fact that the pigeon was entitled to his bit of deck, and fitted him up in the knightheads with a cardboard box and some food. The ketch was light forward, so although her bows went up and clown like a yo-yo the bird was in no danger of being washed out. He displayed very little interest in anything for several days and when we got back to Dartmouth he took off, flew around the mizzenmast and straight back to his home in the bows. He was still there when I left her.

The semi-diesel has been given the lion's share of this chapter because, in spite of the fearlessness of the Danes, it too will pass like the little vessels that it served. For the benefit of posterity there are still one or two small ones on the inland waterways of this country, looked after with loving care by their owners who are well aware that they are the custodians of museum pieces. It was the forerunner of the true diesel engine but for all its extreme simplicity it was no match for the compact modern machines that have taken its place.

When converted to an auxiliary vessel the schooner's earning power was considerably increased and the general trend was to continue to reduce the sail area and to install more powerful engines. Somewhere along this road there lay a hidden danger, which probably had some bearing on the losses of vessels in their later years. Many of them had inadequate power to function as true motor ships and with their reduced sail area they were no longer able to perform the feats that

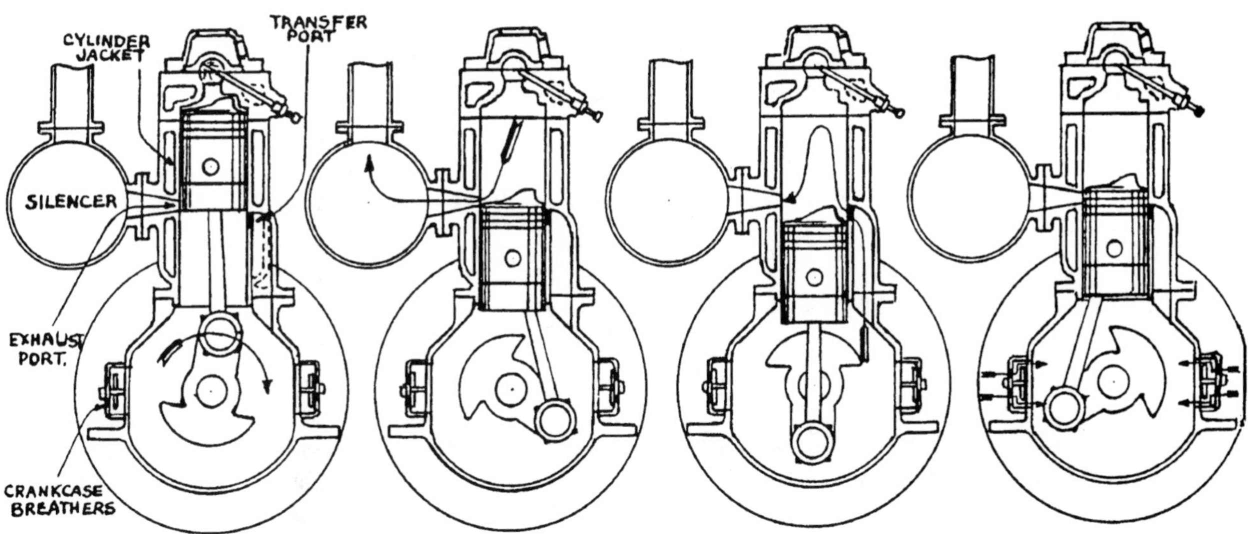

FIGURE 6-3 A two-stroke semi-diesel

As the crank passes over top dead centre, fuel is injected into the cylinder. The explosion drives the piston down. This causes the crank case breathers to close and the air trapped in the crankcase becomes slightly compressed.

The piston descends until it uncovers the exhaust port and gases escape through the silencer.

At the bottom of the stroke the piston uncovers the transfer port and the air compressed in the crankcase passes through into the cylinder. The lip on top of the piston deflects the air upwards so that it scavenges out as much of the exhaust gas as possible.

The piston begins to rise under the energy stored in the flywheel closing the transfer port and the exhaust port and compressing the air in the cylinder. At the same time the breathers open and more air is drawn into the crankcase.

could be expected of the fully rigged vessel. All was well while the two forms of motive power were both given sufficient attention but there was obviously a tendency to neglect one at the expense of the other. The possession of the engine encouraged the handling of the schooner as though she were a motor vessel but if it failed in some precarious position, the sails alone might not be able to extricate the vessel from danger. Had another generation of schooner men followed their fathers, their vessels would inevitably have been fully powered motor ships, without any sails at all. The split allegiance between two forms of motive power would hardly have held any attraction for them. The wind may be free – although canvas and rope cost money – but the factor that would have weighed most heavily in favour of their decision would have been the endlessness of the business of keeping a sailing vessel in running order. There could be no letting up or, sooner or later, the wind and the sea would win.

The account given in this chapter of the various changes in modes of transport is not quite complete. From their inception the railways were strong competitors for the coastwise traffic and remained so until the era of the motor vessel. With the latter came the motor lorry, which had a tremendous advantage over the railways in that it did not have to maintain its own tracks, as these were built and kept in a state of repair out of public funds. The arrival of the motor lorry finally cast to the four winds the stockpiling mentality of our 19th-century predecessors. Now, because of the rapidity of delivery, it is the fashion to wait until supplies run out before telephoning for an 'urgent delivery yesterday'. As well as burning up the miles, the lorries burn up the fuel at a tremendous rate but sea transport is now so much out of fashion that many things are sent by road over distances which may be three or four times as long as the route by water. From the modern standpoint, the drawback associated with ships would seem to be that when they reach their destination their cargoes have to be dug out of them whereas the lorry, by mounting a ramp, can tip its load directly into a bunker. Of course, the problem can be overcome by the use of containers. Maybe when we have squandered a good deal more of our shrinking supplies of fuel, ships will come into their own once more, as they use up far less fuel per ton-mile than any other form of transport.

XII
FOOD

Before the days of canneries and refrigerators there were two methods by which food could be preserved: by drying and by salting. Strong alcohol could also have been used, but history seems remarkably silent on the subject, giving rise to a suspicion that in the past people held much the same opinions as they do today – that it would have been an appalling waste of good alcohol.

Food preserved by drying was confined to vegetables and fruit, the most common being peas, beans, prunes, apples, apricots, raisins and currants. The last three were not often met with in schooners but another form of preserved fruit, jam, was not entirely unheard of. Beef and pork were preserved by pickling in strong brine, and usually had a rather wizened look when removed from the cask. Some of the saltiness could be taken out by putting them into hot fresh water and more by boiling, but whatever was done neither recovered much of the original flavour. Herring and other fish could also be preserved by keeping them in salt or brine but the most popular and widely-used was stockfish, ie. cod, salted and dried in Newfoundland and Labrador, the same commodity that had provided the schooners with a living in their youth and which, at the height of the trade, was shipped across the Atlantic at the rate of hundreds of tons per year.

The finished article was covered in crystalline salt and was available in flat slabs that were as hard as boards and would last indefinitely as long as they were kept dry. When cut the fish had the colour of light mahogany and could have been worked by the usual joiner's tools – sawn, planed, dovetailed and possibly even sanded and varnished. Other food, which had to be kept dry on shipboard, included flour, biscuits, and ordinary bread. The latter tended to develop a green mould after a time, but this could be cut out and the rest eaten.

The preparation of stockfish started at least twenty-four hours before it was due to appear on the table. The first step was to put it into a bucketful of seawater to remove some of the salt. Had a model ship been placed in the bucket along with the fish it would have been lifted to its Winter North Atlantic marks in no time at all and by the end of one watch the water had to be changed. The second bucketful was allowed about eight hours to do its stuff and then the fish was transferred to fresh water. It was cooked by boiling in fresh water until it arrived at the flaky consistency of normal cooked fish. It could be dried and browned off in a frying pan to make it look slightly more appetising, but was usually eaten boiled, and although it still tasted strongly of salt, a certain fishiness could also be detected. It was nutritious food, if not particularly mouth-watering, and in the 1920s and '30s was eaten by many people ashore who had the advantage of unlimited supplies of fresh water available to deal with it.

These three items, beef, pork and stockfish, together with ship's biscuits were the cornerstones of the sailing ship's menu. I feel something of an impostor in having to state that the only 'ship's bread' or biscuits with which I have had any dealings, looked and tasted like large water biscuits and did not require hitting with a belaying pin before conveying them to the mouth. The cement and other mysterious ingredients had obviously been left out and a final point, which seems to confirm that these were not the genuine article: there were no weevils in them.

The problem with all dried foods at sea was how to keep them dry. It was a problem that was only solved in the latter part of the 19th century, when tins with air-tight lids became available. Before this, barrels must have been used. These are excellent for the storage of liquids, which keep the wood damp and any leakage can be easily detected, but they give no indication that damp air is passing inwards and, on long passages in the past, quite a lot of food must have been ruined owing to this happening.

The problem with a menu confined to so few basic commodities was how to make it interesting. As no one ever found a way of doing this, it is not surprising that the crews of sailing ships were keen fishermen to a man. In a reasonably fed vessel, however, this state of affairs only arose towards the end of a passage, and in the home trade there was no real reason why it should have arisen at all. The limiting factor on the amounts of potatoes, carrots, swedes, onions and so on that could be taken aboard, was obviously the number of weeks they could be kept before going bad. No stories have ever been heard of crews having to eat their way through huge mounds of them to prevent this happening, but it is fairly

The after cabin of *Waterwitch*. Tea's made and the well lived-in space is illuminated from the companion and skylight. The painting, of 1930, is by Arthur Bradbury who sailed for long periods in *Waterwitch*.

COLLECTION OF BASIL GREENHILL

certain that the majority of deep-water schooners started off with a reasonable supply. They could hardly have kept their crews voyage after voyage if the parsimony of their owners had been on the same level as that of the owners of the big square-riggers.

Captain Duddridge of the *Alert* was fond of his food, so the crew fared reasonably well. In port there was bacon and egg for Sunday breakfast and also at odd times during the week. On other days it was sausages or bacon alone, with bread, plain or fried. Sufficient potatoes were frequently boiled for dinner to provide not only for the evening meal but also to allow some surplus, which could be chased around the frying pan in the morning. Burgoo (porridge) was a frequent alternative. When she towed out of Runcorn, the schooner had four large hunks of beef hanging from her mizzen boom, which seemed to come to no harm in spite of the heat. Perhaps the salty atmosphere prevented any bacteria from getting aboard, or perhaps with six people and a dog all going at it, it didn't last long enough for the bacteria to get into their stride. There were also some cabbages and beetroot, a couple of cauliflowers and a fair supply of the less transient vegetables already mentioned, as well as a pile of fresh bread. At meals the skipper sawed slices off the loaf as requested, and he did so with none of the reluctance that characterised others of his calling, whose reactions to such requests, according to the forecastle, were 'What! Another slice of bread? You young fellows must have worms!' The bread lasted until we got to Holyhead, after which we were on biscuits.

For a brief period we had fresh meat one day, salt meat the next and salt pork on the third. The pork was always boiled perhaps because it didn't lend itself to roasting. The water in which it was cooked was used as stock for pea soup, which was simmered for hours until the peas became mushy. There were several dishes that could be produced with either fresh or salt meat. One of the most popular was 'schooner on the rocks'. This was a piece of meat roasted on top of potatoes, with plenty of turning over and basting, so that everything became nicely browned. Before serving, the gravy was decanted and thickened with flour and water.

There were two kinds of hash, wet and dry, both made with the same ingredients. In both cases the meat was cut up small, preferably with an onion, and put into a roasting tin to about half its depth. With wet hash, potatoes were cut into slices and placed on top of the meat until the tin was full. Water was then poured in to about three-quarters of the depth, the tin was covered with some kind of a lid, usually an enamelled plate, and put into the oven, where it simmered slowly without losing too much liquid. The plate was removed for the last half hour, so that the potatoes on top became browned, giving the dish a more appetising appearance. With dry hash the meat was covered to its own depth with water. The potatoes were boiled the day before, or dealt with in the early part of the watch. They were mashed and put on top, and the dish cooked without a lid until brown on top. In both dishes vegetables, such as carrots, turnips or swedes, could be cut up and mixed with the meat or, of course, cooked separately, the former being less troublesome to the cook. Conjured up in a variety of receptacles and masquerading under various names such as hot pot, scouse or taterash, these dishes, or variations of them, were well-known in most homes in those days, the percentage of meat being dependent on how much the exchequer would run to.

The fresh meat, of course, could never be much more than a gesture and, once it was finished, the menu settled down to the standard pattern – salt meat one day, salt pork the next. The end of the fresh meat was followed closely by that of the fresh vegetables, leaving dried peas and beans in possession of the field. Finally the potatoes became a thing of the past, their place being taken by ship's biscuits. Meat and biscuits cooked together were known as Cracker Hash. It was in preparation of this dish that the cook resorted to the use of a belaying pin, not because the biscuits were hard to break, but because the job could be done much more quickly by this means. The biscuits were softened by steam and water and browned to some extent, and, although monotonous, it was nourishing food and was gulped down avidly.

One thing that the restricted diet tended to promote was a desire for fresh fruit. There were none available, but there were dried apples and prunes, both of which could be bought very cheaply. The apples were dried in rings, and could be re-hydrated with boiling water and simmered until they went soft. They were not intended for use with the pork, and I never heard of anyone making an apple duff with them. It would probably have used too many. The real standby for dessert were the prunes, which were trotted out from time to time, perhaps in case the crew became constipated through lack of exercise.

But the dish considered the high-water mark of haute cuisine in these vessels, was duff, which was served on Sundays only. In its original form the agency by which the flour was made to rise must have been fat from the salt pork, but in the 1930s suet was becoming available in an already chopped-up state, dusted with flour and packed in grease-proof cartons, a handy form for use ashore, but doubly so at sea. The mixture of flour, suet and water was wrapped in a cloth and boiled in the time-honoured manner and, like all other puddings produced by this method, it did not come out in the wonderful spherical shape beloved by illustrators, but like the planet on which it found itself – slightly flattened at the poles. It was considered unsafe to let the water go off the boil, because it would then penetrate the duff and make it soggy – but this risk could not have lasted long, as the outside part, next to the cloth, rapidly became covered with a layer of white slime that was impervious to water but added nothing to the taste of the finished article. The slime could be avoided by cooking the duff in a basin and covering the top with grease-proof paper from a block of margarine, but this method had few adherents in schooners. When brought to the table it was cut by the skipper into slices about half an inch thick. He deposited approximately equal portions on each plate, together with a spoonful of syrup to give it some taste. The remains of it, if any, could be warmed up in the oven for tea.

It is difficult to explain the tremendous reluctance to change over to corned beef, which in the 1930s was quite cheap and obtainable in tins of various sizes. With this meat it was possible to produce food that was much more tasty than any made with salt beef. In some cases it was probably parsimony, in others it may have been conservatism. There were many people at the time who were convinced that tinned food could not possibly contain the same nourishment as the fresh variety, that by some mysterious means it had had the 'goodness' boiled out of it. This may well be true of fruit but can hardly apply to beef. Since many people ashore held these views, it would not be very surprising if those in sailing vessels, cut off as they were from the main stream of progress for much of their lives, did not take an even more conservative view of any proposed alteration to their traditional diet.

Like everyone else on board, the cook worked watch and watch. He prepared the food during his time on deck and, if he was below when the time came for it to be put on to cook, this was done by the AB in the port watch. It was not the AB's job to have any more dealing with the food than was

absolutely necessary, so it was customary to have Burgoo, boiled stockfish or fried-up potatoes for breakfast on the days when he was in charge. Those coming on watch helped to carry the food aft, and when the meal was over the watch going below lent a hand in taking the dishes forward again for washing up. Seating at meals was in order of seniority, the skipper to starboard, then the mate and the ABs in order of age, with the cook at the tail end, to port, where he was handy for the stairs. Except in the case of things like the duff, which had to be cut up, each man helped himself in the same order, and each man tried scrupulously to see that it was whacked out reasonably evenly, knowing that if he still felt hungry when he had finished, he could come back for more.

When the dish arrived back with the cook, and he had taken out his own portion, he took the rest back to the galley and put it in the oven so that it would keep warm for the helmsman. When he returned aft he brought with him the teapot, a large enamelled one that held about six pints. The tea was good strong stuff, with condensed milk and syrup added to it, and was drunk out of pint mugs. When the cook took the teapot off the stove, he replaced it with a bucket of seawater, which had already been heated up, and was to be used for the washing up. After breakfast and dinner the tea was swigged off fairly rapidly, so that the helmsman could be relieved to get his food and the watch going below could beat a retreat. If the cook was going off watch he washed up before he went and returned to the cabin all the utensils that belonged there, by rights.

About six bells in the afternoon (nobody struck them in schooners), the food left over from dinner was put into the oven to warm up for tea. This was augmented by bread and margarine and sometimes there was jam as well. Tea-time marked the beginning of the dog watches, so instead of consuming their beverage on the premises, ie. in the cabin, the crew took their mugs on deck and sat on the bulwarks abreast of the wheel, while they extracted what humour they could from the situation; at least they did so when the weather was reasonable. When it was not, there was no choice but for the off-duty watch to return forward, where they could smoke, talk or have a two-hour nap. The cook joined whatever was going on after he had washed up.

To deal with greasy plates. the bucket of seawater had to be on, or very near to the boil. Some washing soda was added to it, to pay lip service to the idea of soap, but whether it did any good is open to doubt. The cook dipped each article separately into the water, causing the grease to melt, and then pulled it out and wiped it on a cloth. Naturally he dealt with the non-greasy articles first. The bulk of the grease was left floating on the water and what remained on the plate was transferred to the cloth. Like all jobs in the galley it had to be done sitting down and, inevitably, some of the grease finished up on the cook's trousers. It was not long before the dishcloth and the cook's trousers were black, and precious fresh water and soap had to be used to restore them to cleanliness. It would have taken a lot of soap to get the dishcloths really clean so the cook's trousers, which followed into the bucket after the cloths had been removed, were put in more as a gesture than anything else, in the faint hope that some of the dirt might float to the top of the boiling water. It was hardly a state of affairs to please the fastidious, but the only person aboard the *Alert* in that category was Mrs Duddridge, who probably preferred not to know – the rest simply didn't care.

Other duties that the cook performed were to scrub the woodwork in the galley once a week, replenish the coal bunker under the seat from the peaks in the fo'c'sle and, from time to time, give the stove a good clean out so that it would work efficiently. It was also his job to polish the bell and the brasswork on the wheel but this was only done in good weather or while in harbour. When the cook was at work the lee galley door was normally left open and operations such as peeling potatoes were performed whilst sitting on the corner of the bunker with the bucket out on deck. On the odd occasion there was a point of sailing that caused the foresail to downdraught the stovepipe and when this occurred the only remedy was to close the lee door and partially open the weather one, giving the stove the benefits of forced draught.

Too much has already been written about the food in sailing ships for any more to be added here. It was a monotonous diet and it was an inadequate one also. Until lime juice was included in it, in many cases neither the quality nor the quantity of the food were what they could have been, as it seems to have crossed few people's minds that men who, for much of their working lives, were deprived of the tremendous variety of food ashore, were at least entitled to the best of what could be taken to sea.

Despite its shortcomings, salt food must have had a long and not entirely undistinguished history. The Norsemen who pushed off to the west in search of other lands could hardly have entertained such an idea without it, or without the barrel in which it and fresh water could be kept for fairly long periods. Neither could Columbus have crossed the ocean, and the exploration of this planet would have been restricted to the coast-hopping methods, that are still attributed in some quarters to the ancient Mediterranean voyagers. Now that it is a thing of the past and will, hopefully, never rear its head again, we can afford to refrain from sneering at its memory. It served its turn and served it to the best of its ability.

XIII

SCHOONER MODELS:
THEIR LINES AND DESIGN

In contrast to those whose interest lies in large and famous vessels, the maker of schooner models is faced with an almost complete lack of drawings or any other information, apart from what can be obtained from photographs. It is true that, thanks to the efforts of a few determined men, the lines and sail plans of *Alert, Clara May, Hobah, Lady of Avenel, M.A. James, Result, Rhoda Mary, Waterwitch* and *William Ashburner* have been put on paper, but if the chosen vessel does not happen to be among this handful, the only recourse open to the model-maker is to squeeze out of any available photographs of the schooner in question the last drop of information which he can extract.

Fortunately there are plenty of photographs. In the 1930s those who wandered around docks taking snaps of schooners and ketches must, like the writer, have often felt very much alone in their interests but now it would appear there were literally hundreds of them – at least the quantity of film that they used turns out to have been quite phenomenal. Many of these men were and are members of the Society for Nautical Research, and many of them, in correspondence with others, have amassed amazing collections of prints, so that it would be very surprising if nothing at all could be obtained for any particular vessel. This chapter is concerned with methods by which drawings of reasonable accuracy can be produced, based in the main on photographic evidence.

Contrary to what might be expected, it is not necessary to have a great deal of information on offsets to fix a vessel's lines. Anyone who cares to try it out will discover that one waterline and the midship section, in conjunction with the deck profile, will dictate what the shape of the hull has to be and to produce any radical alteration it will be found necessary to modify at least one of them. The best photographs from which to obtain the required information are obviously those taken when the vessel was light. A waterline halfway down the hull has the least chance of creating any great inaccuracies. With a fully loaded vessel there is very little indication of how the buttock lines are likely to run, while the waterline below the counter is often shrouded in darkness. Wooden vessels with no cargo or ballast aboard floated at about half their full draught, while steel ones were usually slightly higher. The exact depth and trim depended on the vessel's lines but this information need only be resorted to in rare cases as, even if the depth marks and load line are not visible, there are other means by which the whereabouts of a waterline can be established. Unless a photograph was taken in very poor light there is usually little difficulty in seeing where the entry merges into the middle body, and where the run begins, while the disposition of light and shade will often give some indication of how the buttock lines are likely to slope.

The shape of a vessel's midship section is governed by her stability, her cargo-carrying capacity and the beam and draught, and if it had to be a matter of pure guesswork it would still be guesswork within well-established limits. However, some hint of what it is like can often be obtained by studying the official information about her, ie. from her vital statistics as given in *Lloyd's Register.*[1] If a survey is made of the dimensions of a sufficient number of schooners, it becomes apparent that the builders had certain fixed proportions in their heads, from which they all deviated but of which they never completely lost sight. A two-masted vessel, it would seem, should have a length of four times her beam and a depth of hold of half her beam. This proportion of depth to beam seems to have been of long standing. Implicit in the old Thames Measurement for yachts it was the factor that provided the loophole that allowed the 'plank on edge' cutter to be developed.

As the survey of dimensions proceeds it emerges that there were two popular sizes for two-masted vessels, the larger of which could be put down as 88ft × 22ft × 11ft [26.82m × 6.71m. × 3.35m], and the smaller as 76ft × 19ft × 9.5ft [23.16m. × 5.79m. × 2.90m]. The smaller size was used indiscriminately for both schooners and ketches. The larger one

[1] It will be appreciated that generally only vessels in excess of 100 gross tons were included in *Lloyd's Register* unless they were classed. There are other avenues where the details of the measurements can be obtained, including the Survey Reports and the Ship's Documents, many of which are available at the National Maritime Museum. Other maritime museums, including those in Glasgow and the Liverpool Maritime Museum on Merseyside, also hold details of some of the vessels.

Jane Banks at Looe discharging coal.

PHOTOGRAPHER UNKNOWN. TERRY BELT COLLECTION

was confined in the main to schooners. The survey also shows that beam and depth could vary by about a foot either way but that length was probably stipulated by the customer, as schooners with about 22ft [6.71m] beam were built with a length which could vary from 80ft to 90ft [24.38m to 27.43m]. The latter-day wooden three-master was produced by pushing the length up to about 105ft [32m] without proportional alteration to beam or depth and this process was completed by the builders in iron and steel who increased the length to about 120ft [36.58m]. Between 90ft and 100ft [27.43m and 30.48m] was common ground for the classic two-master and the later three-master; both rigs being found

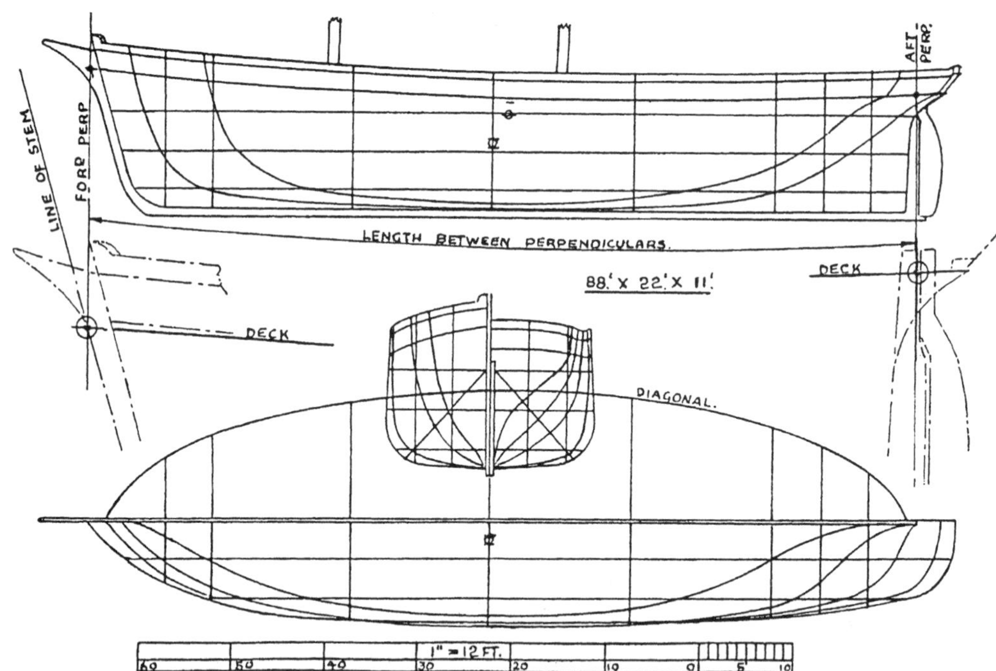

FIGURE 13-1
Full-lined schooner

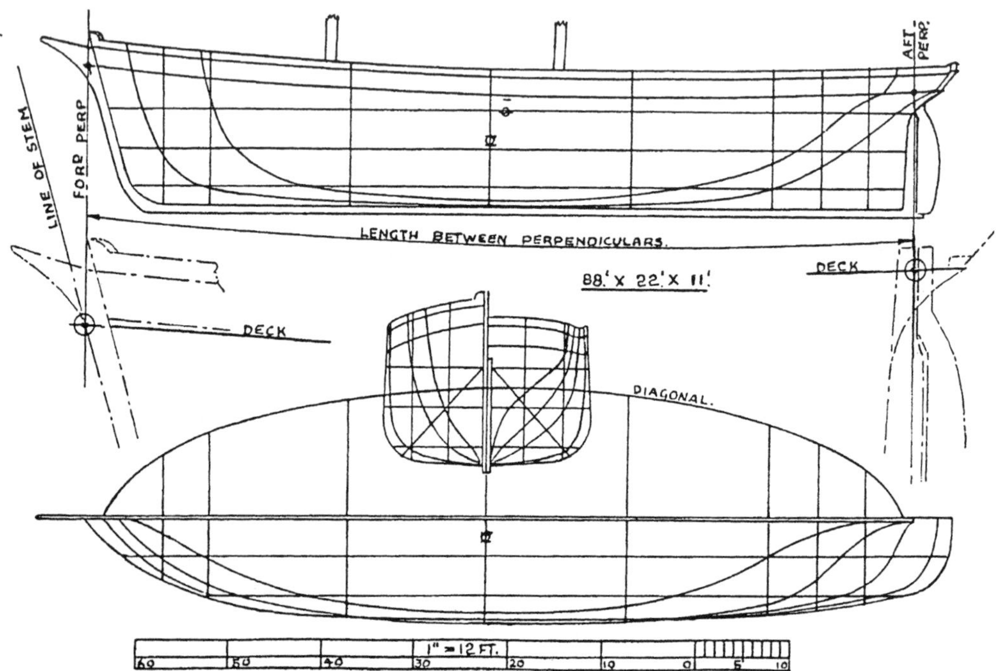

FIGURE 13-2
Fine-lined schooner

Mary B. Mitchell seen as a "Q" ship during the First World Way.

PHOTOGRAPHER UNKNOWN. TERRY BELT COLLECTION

in this range in equal numbers.

Underlying these basic but bendable proportions was another factor, which had considerable effect. There seems to have lurked in the minds of many shipowners a strong desire to keep the draught of their vessels down to something below 11ft [3.35m], no doubt because they felt this would not debar them from using many of the smaller ports. As small ports exist all over the world this tendency often had as much bearing on vessels built for deep water as on those destined for the home trade. Certainly there were far more vessels under 90ft long with a depth of hold of less than 11ft than there were with draught deeper than 11ft. According to some, this limitation was particularly prevalent in the Irish Sea area, although by no means confined to it. During the years when the West Country was predominantly concerned with the carriage of fruit, its vessels were in many ways quite different from those built in other parts and it must be emphasised that most of the statements made in this chapter do not apply to the survivors of that once famous trade. They were in a class by themselves. By 1870, however, the racing was over, and schooners built after this date, whether West Country or not, were inevitably intended to load a reasonable cargo of some lowly commodity, thereby earning for their owners a modest income. Not that the builders or the owners surrendered by one iota their hopes that a new vessel would turn out to be a fast one, but any chances of getting rich by means of speed had disappeared for ever.

Much has been written about fast vessels but most of the evidence points to the fact that the speed belonged to the men aft, not to the ship. This has been proved to the hilt by the

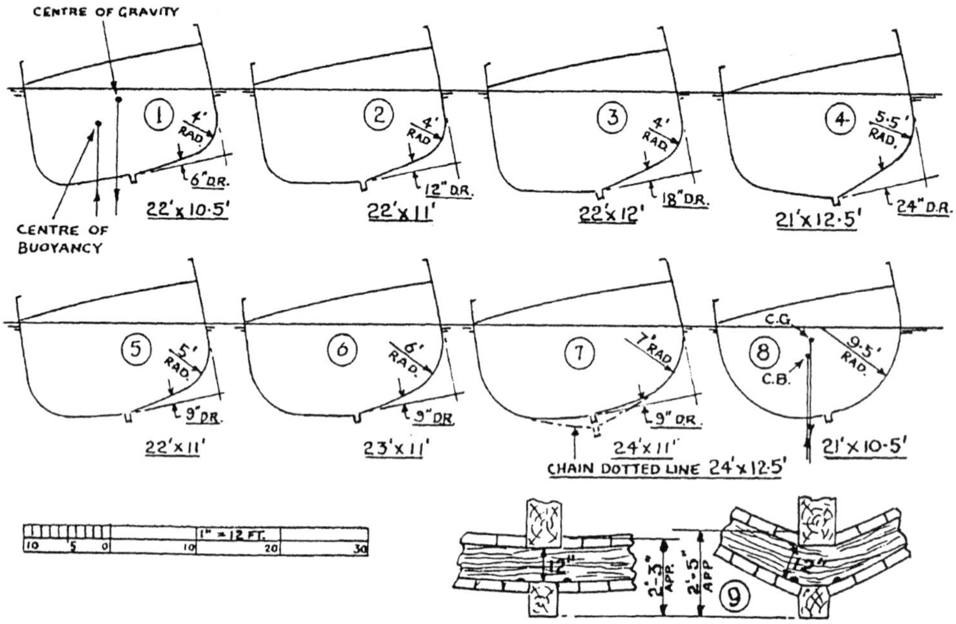

Figure 13-3
Midship sections

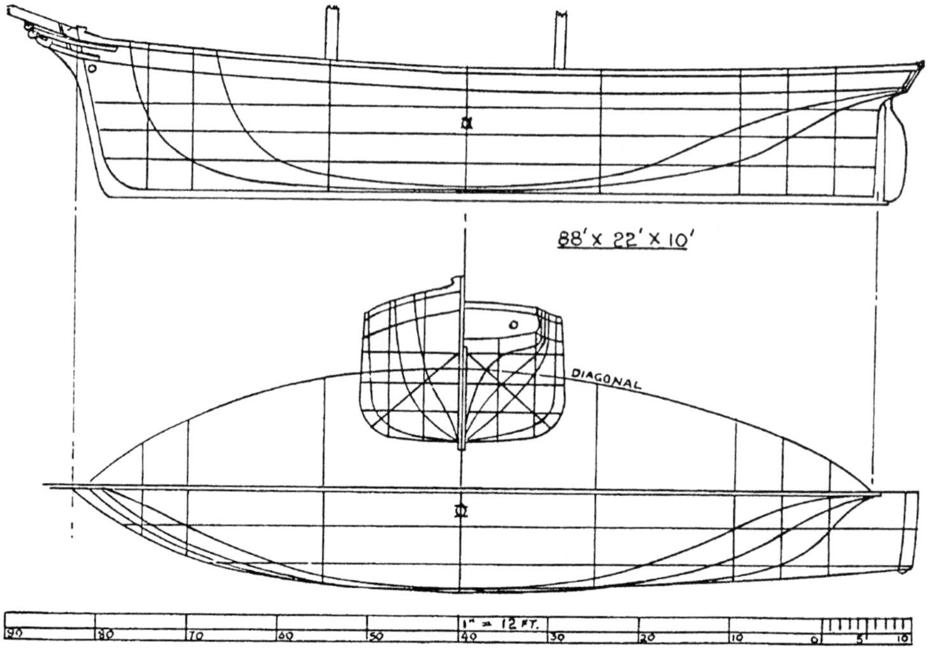

Figure 13-4
Moderate-lined schooner

many cases that have existed of vessels of all sorts and sizes that drifted around for years without doing anything spectacular but which suddenly wakened up on a change of skipper and dashed off a series of fast passages that left everyone who knew them gasping with amazement. The point has been mentioned here as it shows that a vessel with a reputation for speed did not have to have narrow beam and a big deadrise – she might just as easily have been built with flat floors and a hard bilge.

The designer and builder of sailing ships was always on the horns of a dilemma. For a vessel to carry a reasonable cargo she needed a full midship section and this helped her to stand up to her sail. Beyond a certain point it also prevented her from having a shape that could be driven easily through the water, because full sections carried too far inevitably produced bluff bows and a short run. This can be seen in Figure 13-1 and shows the limits to which this treatment was carried in the second half of the 19th century. Figure 13-2 shows a schooner with the same dimensions, deck profile and midship section, which has been fined away to the limit usually met with in practice. Any further fining would inevitably carry the hollowness in the lower part of the entry higher up the bows. The *James Baines* had a much-elongated version of a hull developed on these lines. The general objection to hollow entries has always been that, because the angles of incidence and reflection are the same, the type would throw the displaced water sideways far more than a convex curve, thereby causing greater drag on the vessel. Donald McKay seems to have been one of the first to grasp clearly that the main factor governing the speed of a ship was the length of its waterline.

The more usual approaches to producing a fine-lined vessel were to give the floors more deadrise or to soften the turn of the bilge, ie. to give it a greater radius of curvature. There were limits to these options, too, as they had an adverse effect on the stability. Figure 13-3, detail 1, shows the midship section of a vessel, which is heeled. The centre of gravity has moved outward on the lee side but the greater submerged volume on that side has shifted the centre of buoyancy even more, producing a righting force, which balances the pressure of the wind on the sails. It should be borne in mind that only about one third of the vessel's length produced this force – the ends were too cut away to have any effect. This flat-floored, hard-bilged, midship section had a lot to recommend it and was one of the most popular. It produced a really stiff vessel and provided, on the minimum draught, a hull that could take a fair-sized cargo and could also sail without ballast. When heeled it drew more water than when upright, thus keeping leeway to a minimum. Figure 13-4 shows a schooner with moderate lines, based on this midship section but with the draught reduced to 10ft. Giving it slightly more deadrise or a slightly easier bilge could vary it but the two could not be used together without some increase in depth or beam. There are obviously numerous variations that can be produced in this way, some of which are shown in Figure 13-3. The sections shown on the top row are based on increased deadrise while those below are based on a softer bilge.

It can be taken as a rough and ready rule that the former is favoured by an increase in draught and the latter by an increase in beam. The first two modified sections, N^O^s 2 and 5, both produce roughly the same result; thereafter the two schools go their separate ways. The two sections on the right are the extreme cases. N^O^ 4 is a fruiter's midship section, with 1ft less than the alleged standard beam and 18in more on the draught and this, coupled with 2ft of deadrise at half floor is enough to inform anyone that in this case everything else was subservient to the production of a hull that could be driven easily through the water. It should be remembered that the real racing for the orange schooners was when they were homeward bound and that, for most of the time, they could rely on having a southwesterly wind well abaft the beam. N^O^ 8 represents a pitfall for the unwary: on the face of it, it would seem to have advantages in giving an easy set of lines in all directions; its drawback is that no amount of heel produces any great shift in the centre of buoyancy and the nearer it approaches a complete semi-circle the less the shift becomes. A cylinder placed in water can be rotated without effort and has absolutely no stability in a lateral direction – there has to be some semblance of a bilge somewhere to produce results and the nearest approach to this type of hull is N^O^ 7.

Taking 22ft [6.71m] beam and 11ft [3.35m] draught as the point of departure for vessels between 80ft [24.38m] and 90ft [27.43m] length, it can be seen that some indication of what was in the builder's mind can be gathered from the way in which he modified these two dimensions. From 90ft to 100ft [30.48m] the beam to be departed from can be taken as 23ft [7.01m] and over 100ft as 24ft [7.32m]. Vessels with draught that was greater than 12ft 6in [3.81m] were nearly always larger than those discussed here, and were almost invariably rigged as barquentines. A study of a few of the schooners still afloat in the 1930s will perhaps help to make some of the points a bit clearer.

There were two vessels both 99ft long, which were the absolute antithesis of each other. The one thing they had in common was that both started life with two masts and both finished up as three-masted schooners. Their dimensions were as follows:

Brooklands 99.5ft × 21.4ft × 11.8ft
[30.33m × 6.52m × 3.60]

Irish Minstrel 99.1ft × 25.0ft × 11.4ft
[30.21m × 7.62m × 3.48m]

There is no mistaking what trade *Brooklands* was built for. Her narrow beam and deep draught proclaim the racer, even without knowledge of her deadrise, which was like N^O^ 4 in Figure 13-3. Even in the days when she carried a topgallant she could hardly have been a particularly lofty vessel and when cut down to a plain double topsail schooner she was quite low in her rig. She had as much sail as her wedge-shaped hull would stand; possibly on many occasions in her youth she had more than enough. The *Irish Minstrel* was built to the standard proportions of a two-master, with the usual reduction in draught, but was 10ft longer than normal. She was probably built more with an eye to carrying than to breaking records but her lines were moderate, something similar

Isabella of Barrow laid up at Par 29 July 1934. This photograph clearly shows lines and body shape of a traditional sailing coaster.

Photographer believed to be H. Oliver Hill.

Terry Belt Collection

to that detailed in Figure 13-4. She was originally rigged as a brigantine and was then probably a much loftier vessel than when converted to a three-masted schooner.

Under this latter rig *Irish Minstrel* was stiff enough to have carried a standing topgallant and the long main and mizzen topmasts that went with it, and she would obviously have been much more successful if she had been converted to a barquentine. As it was she was under-canvassed for her big hull; she had a reputation for being a bit of a slow-coach and, according to those who had sailed in her, it took half a gale to really get her moving. The *Emily Warbrick*, also launched as a brigantine, was 6ft longer than the *Irish Minstrel*, had slightly more draught and over 18in less beam. Having the proportions of a three-master she was more of a success. Her original rig is a fair guarantee that she was flat in the floors. It is hardly fair to compare the *Irish Minstrel* with *Brooklands* without sandwiching between them an average three-master.

The *James Postlethwaite*, 99.7ft × 23.0ft × 10.0ft [30.39m × 7.01 × 3.05m], was not notorious for anything in particular. Like many other ships and human beings she went about her business and did her share of work without ever hitting the headlines. She and her sistership, *M.E. Johnson*, and the smaller two-masted pair from the same yard, *Useful* and *Isabella*, all had slightly more rake to their stems than the average British schooner, but to offset this they were all originally rigged as single-topsail, flying-topgallant vessels, a much more tapered sail plan than the standing topgallant set up.

There were three surviving wooden three-masters over 100ft long [30.48m], each of which had been in the Newfoundland trade, and each of which had originally crossed a standing topgallant yard above their double topsails.

Alert	103.8ft × 23.6ft × 11.1ft [31.64m × 7.19m × 3.38m]
Jane Banks	102.0ft × 24.3ft × 12.6ft [31.09m × 7.41m × 3.90m]
Mary Barrow	103.0ft × 24.0ft × 10.8ft [31.39m × 7.31m × 3.29m]

Each of these represented a different approach to the problem of building a sailing vessel. These three vessels were usually to be found together, they were well matched and it would be difficult to say that any of the three builders was any more right in his answer than the others. Two of them were products of the Irish Sea area, and the one with the least draught came from the West Country. The *Jane Banks* was the stiffest of the three. Her beam and draught, both in excess of average, more or less guaranteed this, while still allowing her builder to give her an easy bilge and a reasonable amount of deadrise. Her midship section was probably something like that shown in N°7 complete with the chain-dotted part shown at the bottom. In spite of her beam she was no *Irish Minstrel* but a highly successful attempt to produce a vessel that would be in her element in hard winds. The fact that Bert Carrivick, her last British skipper, usually managed to keep up with *Waterwitch* says much for her, and for him.

The ability to stand up to her sail must have been a gratifying attribute in the Newfoundland trade during the hard beat westward. Her long yards ensured that she had adequate sail area under which to run. Her bows were high and powerful and not particularly sharp but her appearance was marred by a rather heavy looking counter stern. She was not particularly happy in balmy breezes but did not come to a full stop.

The *Alert* had even more sheer forward than the *Jane Banks*, and much the same sort of entry, but slightly finer. Her run was a delight to the eye. She had little deadrise to her floors but the turn of her bilge was easier than the average. Her midship section was fairly near to that detailed in N°6. She was a lofty schooner and was considered to be a trifle tender; some went so far as to say she was a bit cranky. She had the least beam of the three.

The *Mary Barrow* was the most extreme and, when light, there was a hint of hollowness showing in her entry. She had a run that was really lovely and a beautifully proportioned counter stern with a long overhang. It had a slight edge on the *Alert*'s, which was on the same lines. Her beam was 1ft over the standard but her draught was light for her size. She had to have it somewhere so her bilge must have been hard and her midship floors nearly flat. The hollowness forward would seem to bear this out.

One final comparison is worthwhile to get the whole picture into its correct perspective. The following three vessels have been deliberately chosen as they were built as far apart as possible. The *Volant* was built in northeast of Scotland and bore signs of the long association with the Scandinavian countries. The *Mary Sinclair* was a product of the upper Irish Sea and *My Lady* was a West Country vessel.

Volant	86.8ft × 21.7ft × 10.3ft [26.46m × 6.614m × 3.14m] 113 tons gross
Mary Sinclair	88.8ft × 21.4ft × 10.5ft [26.46m × 6.52m × 3.20m] 118 tons gross
My Lady	84.5ft × 21.3ft × 10.6ft [25.76m × 6.49m × 3.23m] 110 tons gross

Doubtless the men who sailed in each of these vessels were convinced that their own was the fastest but there could have been little to choose between them. In the 1930s there were at least another twenty still afloat, of roughly the same size and in their heyday there must have been hundreds which, apart from the oddities that sailors were quick to observe and remember, must have been all so very much alike as to be absolutely monotonous.

There was one sure guide to the fineness of a schooner's lines, which shows up even in the poorest photograph. This was the distance from the knightheads to the foremast. The reader may have noticed in the three line drawings [Figures 13-1,13-2 and 13-4] that as the lines become finer the masts move aft. The reason for this was the large area of sail hanging on the foremast, which, as the support below it was removed, had to be shifted further aft to prevent the forward part of the vessel from becoming like a half-tide rock. Mention has already been made of the 'Barrow flats' *Useful*, *James Postlethwaite*, and company in this connection – their raking stems tended to undermine the foremast – but the problem was most acute in the latter-day standing topgallant yarders, a great many of which had plenty of sheer forward and full, if by no means bluff, bows to give adequate reserve buoyancy to counteract this tendency. A writer in *Sea Breezes* in the 1930s cited the case of a schooner called *Hilda* that had an out-of-doors rudder. She turned out to be so wet that they were forced to take her foremast out and re-step it 3ft further aft, which did, indeed, bring a slight improvement. Two vessels that had their foremasts noticeably further aft than normal and were still afloat in the 1930s were the *Brooklands* and the little *North Barrule*. This clear-cut guide to the lines of the vessel is, itself, a strong incentive for the model-maker to wish to establish the spacing of the masts as accurately as possible.

It is unfortunate that very few photographs of schooners have been taken with the camera exactly amidships and square on to the vessel. Even the man determined to get such a shot for the sole purpose of making a sail plan, was often thwarted by the configuration of docks, the disposition of other vessels, and so forth and it is a matter of pure good luck if the model-maker manages to lay his hands on one. Nevertheless there are plenty of photographs that are nearly in this category and the following studies can be used on these with reasonable confidence.

Before embarking on a detailed description of the procedure a few explanations and definitions are necessary. The dimensions in *Lloyd's Register* have already been referred to. They are in feet and decimals of a foot as was decreed in 1855.

The first figure is the length between perpendiculars, (BP), ie. from the fore side of the stem to the afterside of the sternpost measured on the main deck. Where the stem is curved out into the clipper type of bow, the forward perpendicular is taken as passing through the point of intersection of the main line of the stem with the line of the deck. This is shown in Figure 13-1 and, unless the rake of the stem is greater than normal this point can be considered as directly beneath the forward points of the knightheads, a very convenient place as these show up well on most photographs. Where the two do not quite coincide it is helpful to treat them as though they do, during the preliminaries, as it helps to put down the length BP in a straight line – the necessary corrections can be made after the line of the sheer has been drawn in. The position of the after perpendicular is not quite so clear cut except in those vessels with their rudder out of doors. In the counter stern it can be safely assumed that the rudder stock is joggled forward by about 6in before entering the trunk, so that the afterside of the sternpost must retreat forward by the same amount but, owing to the darkness that usually prevails below the counter, the exact point where one starts and the other finishes is often a matter of guesswork.

The second figure in *Lloyd's Register* is the maximum beam over the planking. The point at which this occurs is well below deck level, but it is a figure that is useful without deduction of the tumble home, which is not likely to be more than 6in at each side.

The third figure is the depth of hold, measured from the underside of the amidships deck planking to the top of the ceiling alongside the keelson.

So far in this chapter depth of hold and loaded draught have been bandied about as though they were one and the same thing, which, indeed they were, to within reasonably close limits, in all vessels except those with a big deadrise. One of the contributory reasons for the discrepancy in the latter case can be seen in the two diagrams at the bottom of Figure 13-3, N^O 9; the other was that large deadrise was frequently found in conjunction with a deep keel, the outward and visible sign of which was a raking sternpost and steering wheel.

Three sources of measurement are available in schooner photographs. The first is the load line, the circle of which is 12in outside diameter and the line through it 18in long. The second is the depth marks, 1ft apart, on the posts at either end. But the real standbys, which are always available, are the ratlines and battens on the shrouds. These are 15in apart and can be relied upon, because the human eye is capable of detecting quite small differences in dimensions and, if they were not up to standard, the men who put them there would have heard from the mate. Eight pitches give a length of 10ft and this can be used to produce a tapering scale by means of which dimensions of greater accuracy can be obtained than from

Isabella of Barrow. Stern of vessel showing lines, at Par 29 July 1934.

Photographer believed to be H. Oliver Hill. Terry Belt Collection

FIGURE 13-5
Tapered scales

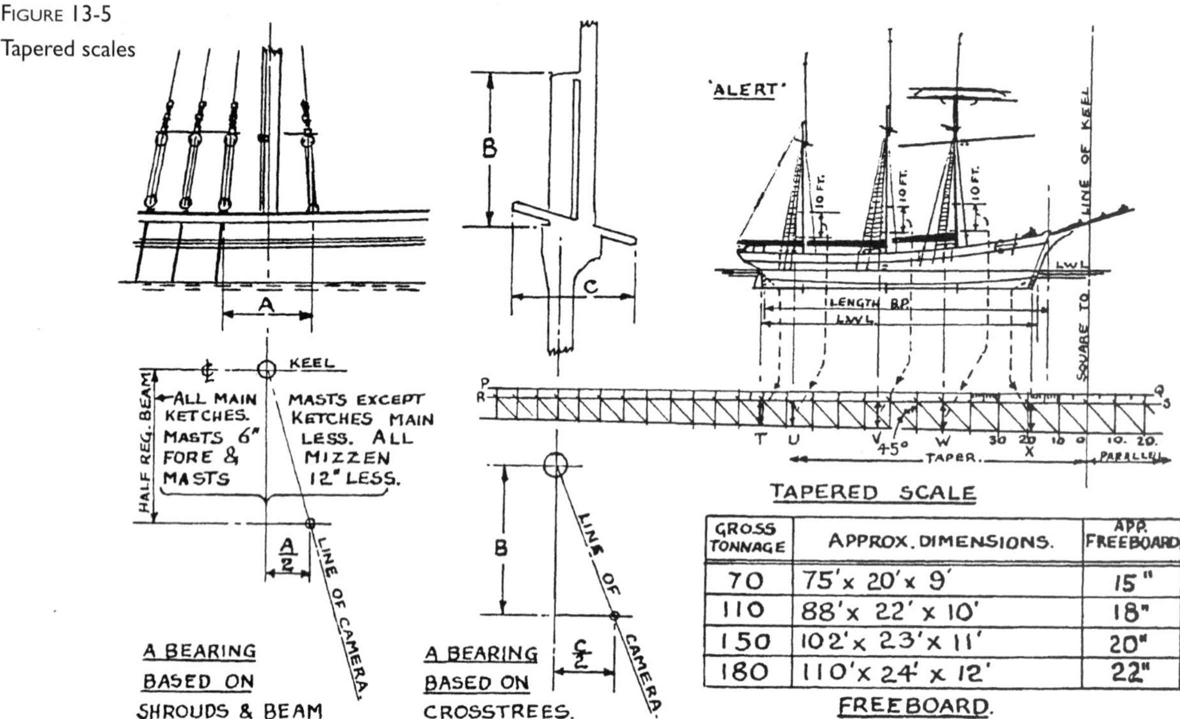

GROSS TONNAGE	APPROX. DIMENSIONS.	APP. FREEBOARD
70	75'x 20'x 9'	15"
110	88'x 22' x 10'	18"
150	102'x 23'x 11'	20"
180	110'x 24' x 12'	22"

straightforward division of the length between perpendiculars as shown on the photograph. The limitations of this method of calculation will be discussed after the procedure has been outlined.

The job is started by mounting the photograph on a board of some kind with a piece of paper below it on which two horizontal lines P-Q and R-S [Figure 13-5] have been drawn to act as a basis for the scale. On to this should be projected the lines of the shrouds from which the measurements are to be taken, the lines of the posts and, in cases of dire necessity, the Plimsoll mark as well. Lengths of 10ft are extracted from the photograph with a pair of dividers and are marked off vertically below line R-S on their own base line. In the case of the depth marks on the posts, two or more snatches will have to be made and for this the centre screw type of dividers is the handiest. The likely error introduced by ten shifts of the dividers is why the load line should only be resorted to when absolutely necessary. A straight line should then be drawn through the points T, U, V, W, and X, or whatever number is available – this will slope upwards as it recedes from the camera.

Then, starting at the nearest shroud as being the most reliable, a straight-edge and 45-degrees set square should be used to mark in diagonals and perpendiculars in both directions until more than the length of the vessel has been covered. On the diagram it will be seen that the diagonals run from northwest to southeast. If the picture diminishes in the other direction they should be from northeast to southwest. When put in the wrong way around the scale diminishes too rapidly. The squares below the knightheads and sternpost should now be divided into feet. The length should be halved with a pair of dividers and, with a little practice, it will be found that four ticks can be placed fairly quickly, freehand, with reasonable accuracy on each side of the mid-point. This is not strictly accurate but any error introduced is well within the limits to which the job can be done. These divisions are used to check whether the scale corresponds roughly to the length between perpendiculars. It would be little short of miraculous if it did, and a second one should be drawn, below it, with the amount of slope increased or decreased very slightly to remedy the discrepancy.

Before cutting the second scale loose it should be continued towards the camera sufficiently far to cover whatever needs to be measured at the near end – in the case shown this is the bowsprit – and away from the camera enough to cover the height of the most remote mast. It will also save a good deal of frustration and irritation if all divisions are split up into feet (or centimetres), as the scale can only be used by placing that part from which the original dimension was taken onto the place from which it came. In order to measure the height of the foremast in the case shown the scale should be applied vertically to the photograph, big end down, and with point W in the middle of the 10ft length in the fore shrouds. Some assistance in using the scale can be obtained by mark-

ing, with a red pencil and suitable initials, the positions of masts, posts, counter, knightheads, etc.

There is a possibility that if the photograph was enlarged, a greater degree of accuracy might be obtained, but the evidence seems to point to the fact that the camera itself introduces far greater errors than those caused by dealing with microscopic dimensions. Whatever the cause, there is a definite 'falling off' in size in those parts that are remote from the camera, which could only be remedied by a rising curve instead of a straight line. The shape of this curve would be pure guesswork. This source of error is not quite so bad in the case shown, as the worst effects of it are only felt in the mizzenmast and its topmast. With the stern nearest to the camera things are much more unsatisfactory. The important dimension from knightheads to foremast is diminished by an amount that can only be guessed at, and the bowsprit beyond it will be even more foreshortened.

In spite of this drawback the scale gives better results than equal division of the length and can be used to establish the line of the sheer and the whereabouts of the waterline, which in turn, will be used to develop the lines drawing. The reader may have noticed that no mention has been made of correcting the pitch of the ratlines for the slope of the shrouds. This is one means by which the general foreshortening can be counteracted; better results for a mast height are obtained if a 10ft length is taken from the shrouds as high up as possible and developed into a straightforward scale with equal divisions to be used on this one mast alone. Two photographs, one taken from each end of the vessel, would also help to solve the problem of the masts, but it should be remembered that it is not the average that should be taken as there is no evidence to prove that the camera makes things oversize – the longest dimension found for each mast will be the correct one.

(There is another method that can be used for establishing mast height and this will be mentioned later – its is inextricably tied up with the ketch rig for which it is a necessity not an alternative.)

The limitations of the tapered scale led to a search for another method of dealing with the spacing of the masts, and eventually one was arrived at which is based on no firm scientific principles that can be detected, but seems to produce slightly better results. In its simplest form it relies on the fact that by law the load line (Plimsoll mark) has to be at the middle of the load waterline as measured from the fore side of the stem to the after side of the stern post or as near thereto as is practicable. Anyone who suspects that there may a considerable difference between this and the results obtained by bisecting the distance as measured on a straight line, can check it by stepping it out with dividers on as many drawings as possible. He will find that the error is seldom very great.

Another factor that might conceivably affect the position of the load line, is the spacing of the masts and their chainplates but, as the British schooner normally had her main-

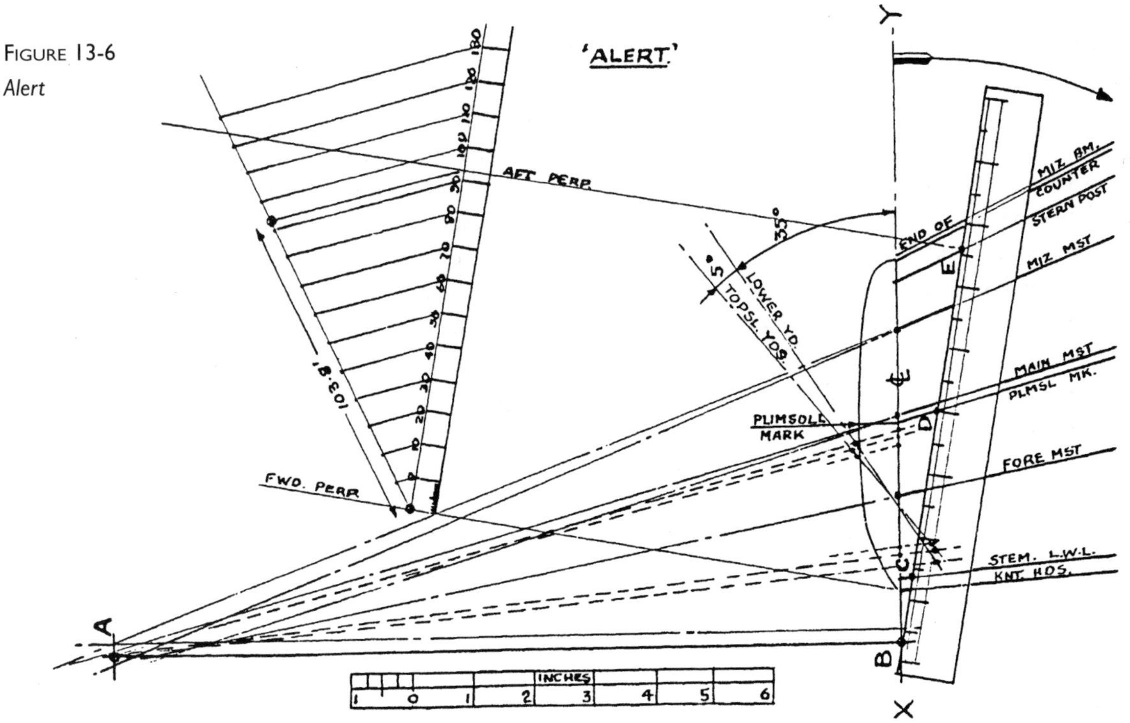

FIGURE 13-6
Alert

mast slightly abaft the half-way mark, this can usually be ignored. In those cases where some doubt may exist as to whether the loadline has been forced further forward by the position of the main chainplates a certain amount of latitude, inherent in the method used, can be resorted to, in order to get around the difficulty. The method involves an attempt to establish roughly where the camera was relative to the vessel when the photograph was taken and it is started in the usual way by drawing a straight line on a piece of paper and marking on it all the points of interest [Figure 13-6].

Two things can be used to take 'bearings' on the camera: the shrouds and the crosstrees of the fore and aft masts – ie. all mainmasts and the mizzens of three-masters. An examination of photographs taken bow- or stern-on will show that the length of the spreaders, from one side to the other, is about twice the length of the doubling of the mast that carries them. A line drawn from the top of the spreader to the cap would be at 45-degrees. Figure 13-5 shows how this and the shrouds can be used. The spreader, which is really an elongated crosstree, should not be used unless both ends of it are visible. When using the shrouds a certain amount of guesswork is necessary regarding the beam of the vessel at the point where they are situated. If possible the forward shrouds on each mast should be used as they are in line with the mast, except in the case of the mizzen, where they are usually 12-18in forward of it. If both shrouds are not visible another opposite pair should be taken and it seems to make little difference whether the correct jumping-off point is taken or whether it is done from the mast. The practitioner of this method will rapidly discover that no great accuracy of 'fix' is possible, owing to the shortness of the baseline; some of the lines may go a bit wide of the mark. For this reason it is of little use to indulge in any great nicety of dimensions and it has been found that half the registered beam is good enough for the mainmasts of all but ketches, without bothering about the amount of tumblehome. For all fore- and mizzenmasts this figure less 1ft should be used while for the mainmast of a ketch half the beam less 6in seems to be about right. These figures are based on the assumption that the broadest part of the deck is amidships and that the tapering off each way is fairly evenly matched.

This may not always be quite correct, but the writer can confirm that he has never seen a vessel with a deck plan in the shape of a tadpole, with the greatest beam well forward and a narrow stern end. Sufficient spread of the shrouds to give the masts adequate support was one good reason why this was not done.

Having obtained a bearing from each mast a guess is made at where, either inside or outside the vessel, the camera was at right angles to the line of the keel. Out of the hodgepodge of intersecting lines a point A [Figure 13-6] has to be chosen as the likeliest position for the camera but as this does not seem to be very critical no undue head scratching need be indulged in. If the point chosen necessitates the dropping of a new perpendicular to the line of the keel X-Y, this should be done and the point of intersection clearly marked. The position of the Plimsoll mark should be projected inward on to the line of the keel.

Three lines radiating from point A should now be drawn; the first one through the fore side of the stem on the load waterline; the second through the load line as marked on the centreline of the vessel; the third through the after side of the sternpost, again on the load waterline. A scale is placed on line X-Y and with one end pivoted on point B, the other is moved away from the vessel in the direction of the arrow until the two distances, C-D and D-E, are equal. A line is then drawn in this position and on to it is projected everything of importance starting with the two perpendiculars that give the end points of the vessel's registered length. A scale is then made to suit this length so that all fore-and-aft dimensions can be taken off. This scale is, of course, not valid on any but its own line and cannot be used for any other purpose.

One drawback to this, which may have already crossed the reader's mind, is that in many photographs the load line is not visible. In these circumstances there are several other factors that can be taken into consideration. In three-masted schooners the mainmast is seldom very far abaft the mid point of the load water line. It will never be found before it. The mizzen boom was slightly longer than the fore boom, the main boom being the one with the greatest variation in length. In all schooners, except those built well before 1850, the distance from the knightheads to the foremast will never be less than the distance from the foremast to the main. In some cases it may be only microscopically greater, in others it can be quite a lot. All these aspects of the case should be taken into consideration when using the second method, before finally drawing the line, whether the Plimsoll mark is visible or not. If there is any chance of increasing the distance from the knightheads to the foremast, without prejudice to the other factors, it should be taken. The first rule when dealing with the British schooner should be: 'the foremast is always further aft than you think it is'.

Model-makers would do well to treat the works of marine artists with caution until satisfied that they, too, were aware of this rule. One of the worst offenders in this respect was Reuben Chappell. I can speak with authority and some feeling on this as it was a trap into which I fell headlong in my youth and for many years wondered why the resulting picture was not quite as it should be. When dealing with ketches by the second method there is only one guide that can be relied upon. The scale should be swung until the distance from the stem to the mainmast is at least one third of the length of the load water line, taken as a straight line. If anything gives rise to the least suspicion that the vessel had finer lines than average, the mast should be shifted further aft.

Few ketches, if any, had ratlines or battens on their mizzen shrouds so the model-maker is faced with the problem of finding some other way to ascertain the height of the mast. If the sails are set one way out of the difficulty would be to use the pitch of the mast hoops as a means of comparison, so that the height of the mizzenmast can be referred back to the mainmast. If nothing else is available the bulwarks should be pressed into service. The same procedure is adopted as was used to make the tapered scale, except that about five or six pitches of bulwark height should be transferred to the vertical lines, as shown in Figure 13-7. The intention is to find the vanishing point – the point at which parallel lines appear to meet. When dealing with a seascape this point is on the horizon; on land it is taken to be at the eye level of the beholder. The problem can be dealt with by drawing but usually requires a piece of paper several feet long. It can also be solved algebraically but, as the long flat triangles being used

FIGURE 13-7
Ketches

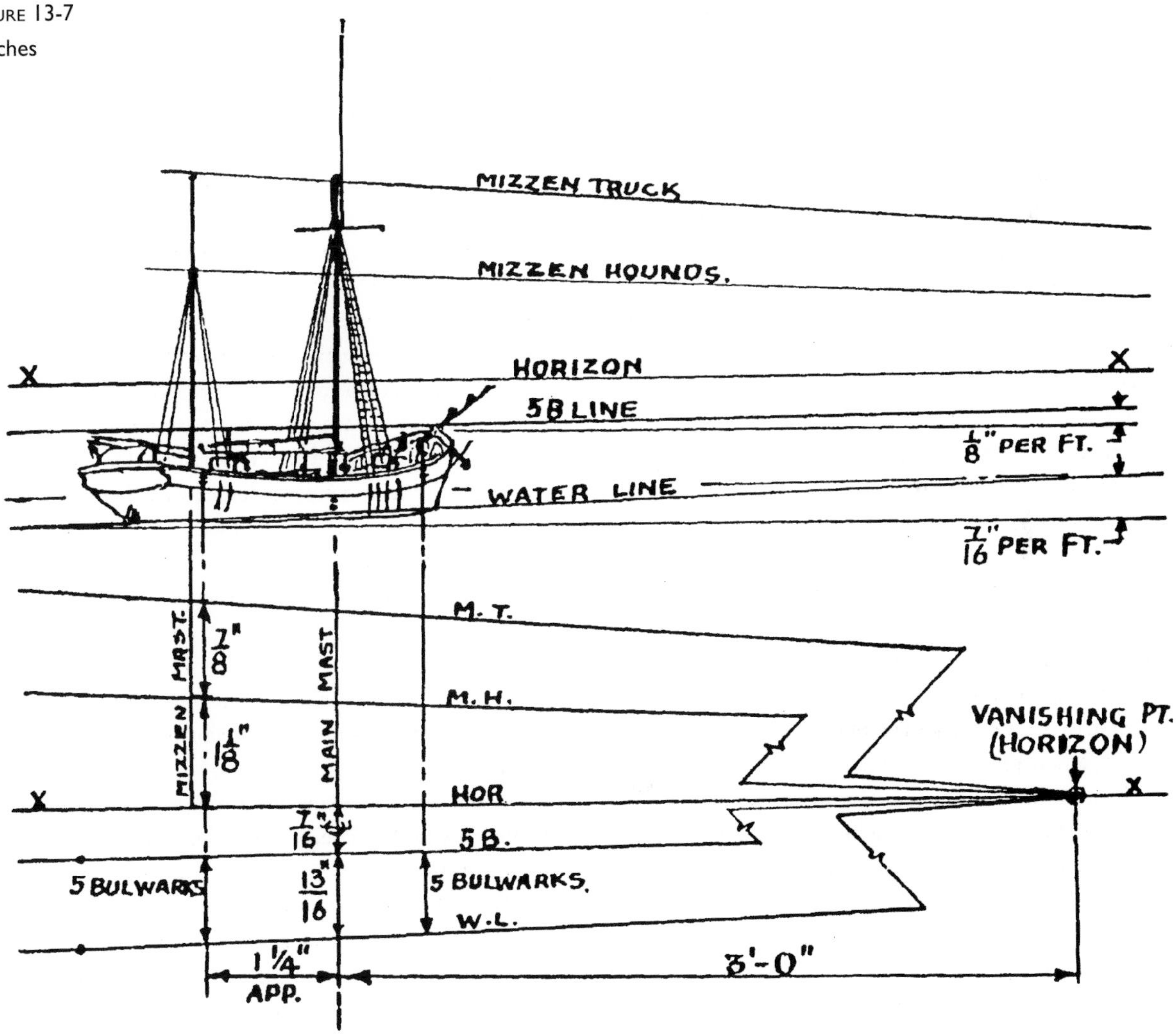

Waterline rises at 7/16″ per foot
5B line rises at 1/8″ per foot
W.L. and 5B.L. converge at the rate of 5/16″ per foot.
Distance apart at mainmast = 13/16″ they intersect at a point 2.6ft from mainmast.

Total rise in waterline 2.6 x 7/16″ = 1 1/8″
Total rise in 5B line 2.6 x 1/8″ = 5/16″ add 13/16″ = 1 1/8″
1 1/8″ = height of horizon above waterline at line of mainmast.
Mizzen hounds 1 1/8″ above horizon. slope of line 7/16″/ft.
Mizzen truck 2″ above horizon. Slope of line 3/4″ /ft.

produce very little error, it is hardly worth the trouble; the rate of convergence of the lines can be taken off with a scale, and the distance to the vanishing point worked out quite simply. The height of the vanishing point is also required so that the slope can be worked out for lines from the mizzen hounds and truck.

By means of these lines the height of the mizzenmast can be referred to the mainmast and taken off with an uncorrected batten scale as previously mentioned. Cases where sixteenths of an inch and so on do not lend themselves to easy division can sometimes be sorted out by changing to millimetres.

After ploughing through as much or as little of the foregoing as he feels inclined to, the model-maker is at last in a position to make a start on his drawings; the hull lines for obvious reasons being dealt with first. It is not worthwhile in the preliminary stages to work on a large drawing and it pays to use as few sections, waterlines and buttocks as possible until some of the unknown quantities have been resolved. As many straight lines as possible should be put in, in permanent ink as this makes them proof against the frequent alterations. The job should be approached from the standpoint that the waterline, which starts things off, is based on fact, however approximate, while the midship section is based on conjecture.

As the work proceeds the truth of the conjecture should show up, but at the same time an unlikely midship section should not be accepted if reasonable alterations to waterlines and buttocks can produce something more probable. Before doing any fairing the diagonal should be drawn, as this is the real check that things are in order and, having got the lines reasonably correct, the rest of the work may as well be carried out on the full-sized drawing.

One point that has not yet been dealt with is how to establish the length of a schooner's yards if they are braced up, end on to the camera. The only thing which can be done is to assume that the lower yard will be slightly longer between the yardarm bands than twice the beam of the vessel. This is a fairly reliable assumption, but the topsail yards above it can vary quite considerably in length and, if at all possible, a photograph should be obtained with the yards the other way around. The apparent length of the yards should be marked in on the line of the keel as shown in Figure 13-6 and it can be assumed that in dock or at anchor they will lie at the angles shown. It should be checked that the braces are reasonably tight on, what at sea, would be the lee side. The real length of the yards should be taken with the scale used for the foremast, as the part nearest the camera should compensate reasonably well for the diminution of the other side – at times this may not be quite correct owing to the position of the camera. Under sail and on a wind the upper topsail yard will be checked in by a further 5 degrees from the lower topsail yard, but all three yards will be at about 3 degrees less than the angles given – ie. 32 degrees, 37 degrees and 42 degrees with the keel, in ascending order. If the model-maker has his proportions correct, this will cause the foreyard and lower topsail yard to press the lee backstay inwards with a visible kink in both places.

An aspect of wooden masts that has not been mentioned is that they all had two rakes, the one they were installed with and the one they finished up with. When installed they were never quite vertical, all had a slight rake aft, the mainmast a little more than the fore, and the mizzen a little more than the main. After thirty, forty or fifty years of constant strain nearly all finished up permanently bent forward, and the degree of bend was in the same order as before, the main being bent forward more than the fore, and the mizzen more than the main. The *Alert*'s mizzen truck finished up about 3ft forward of the place where it started life. The model-maker has the option of installing the masts to their original rake or of putting in bent ones to show the appearance of the vessel in her later years. What seems to be getting the worst of both worlds is to install a straight mast from the deck to the place where the truck finished up, but some drawings show that this is exactly what has been done. It imparts to the vessel something of the appearance of a medieval carrack, whose foremast seemed always in imminent danger of falling over the bows.

The question might well be asked whether all this long-winded drawing and calculating is worthwhile, and the answer must obviously depend a great deal on the temperament of the model-maker. Sailors' models were guessed, and were none the worse for it, but the sailors had the advantage of knowing their subject matter inside out. Today their work seems to be dismissed in bulk as being correct in the rigging but otherwise rough – a sweeping generalisation, which is often a long way from the truth. The standard of model-making nowadays is high but, as in many other fields, an element of lunacy seems to have crept in here and there. One way in which this manifests itself is in the belief that a wooden ship should have a matt finish to her hull. This might perhaps have some foundation in fact if the hulls had been painted with tar, which does dry out to a matt finish, but the material used was black varnish, which dries out in a glossy state. There seems little basis for the belief that a glossy finish when scaled down would become matt – as the roughness and irregularities become smaller the surface should finish even shinier. This chapter, however, is not concerned with finish so much as what is to be finished and how that is arrived at.

To those who prefer to guess the information here given should be of some assistance to their guessing, while the meticulous, who wish to go through the full procedure, can feel that they have reduced the element of error as much as possible.

The methods outlined arose out of a long correspondence with a member of the Society of Nautical Research, Owen Wicksteed of Darlington, who, for some years worked on a set of drawings of the *Alert*. Shortly after he started, two more members, Dan McDonald of Glasgow and Terry Belt of Winchester were also drawn into the vortex, where they remained. The *Alert* was the guinea pig on which the various methods were tried out. The workpiece was a beautifully clear photograph taken by Owen Wicksteed at Fisherrow, the check print an enlargement of a photograph taken by the writer when she was lying in the Mersey about half a mile offshore – although only a grey silhouette this image showed *Alert* absolutely square on and clear enough to show the trucks of the masts. It was the *Alert*, which provided confirmation of my assumptions on the angles of the yards when close hauled – evidence of this was gleaned from the second of a pair of snaps of the ship entering Newlyn. A good deal of energy, spread over many months, was wasted in the preliminary attempts but after various snags had been ironed out the procedure was applied to *Brooklands* and *Jane Banks*, followed finally by *Mary Barrow* for which no check print was available, but for which there were a large number of photographs from all other angles.

None of the methods outlined are without pitfalls, and the intending practitioner is warned that on the least sign of anything fishy, the best he can do is to sit down and take stock. The *Brooklands* was dealt with from a well-known photograph taken at a time when she was painted light grey. It also happened to be one of her more poverty-stricken periods when there were a minimum number of battens on her main and mizzen shrouds, pitched out much wider than normal and impossible to check. The line of demarcation between her bulwarks and sheerstrake was not clear and I was only able to do the job from the knowledge that the cap of her main lower mast was from 12-15in higher than the fore. This enabled me to establish a second horizontal line by which the 'Lost Horizon' method could be used, and the height of the main- and mizzenmast referred back to the fore. For a long time I was baffled by the fact that the results gave a slightly greater height of masts than that obtained from what I considered to be the check print. The reason for this finally came to me: the so-called check print was taken from her own boat from about 200 yards away, and the camera could not have been more than 4ft above the water. The grey-painted photograph was obviously taken from a much larger, or at least higher, vessel towards which she was heeling so that any foreshortening of the masts was at an absolute minimum. It was the check print that was inaccurate.

In my preliminary dealings with the *Jane Banks* I was unable to obtain by use of the second method any place where the two lengths of load water line evened themselves out, and concluded that it was unworkable, at any camera angle less than 70-degrees to the midship point of the vessel. I finally discovered that I had not projected the load line back on to the line of the keel and once this was done the whole thing fell into place. The angle at which this method becomes unworkable has therefore still to be established.

When I had made the scale to measure the spacing of the masts, I discovered that the distance from fore to main was greater than that from main to mizzen. This did not seem right and I went carefully over everything to see where I had slipped up. I also tried various other angles of straight-edge, and found that a reduced angle made things worse while an increased one put the Plimsoll mark too far out of position. After looking in vain for some reason for this peculiarity, I rooted out a couple of small but reasonably square-on photographs of her and discovered that this was actually the case, although in a slightly less exaggerated form than I had arrived at. With *Brooklands* in mind, I then concluded that the two small square-on prints were not square-on after all. I laid the whole thing aside and several hours later it popped into my head that she was originally rigged as a jack barquentine. This spacing was normal for the barquentine rig.

It is hoped that if others join in, some of the more tedious parts of the procedure may perhaps be made a bit shorter or easier; the limits to which the various methods can be used may be established and, in the fullness of time, the whole thing may become less of an art and more of a plain straightforward set of well-defined steps, which will help the modelmaker to produce reasonably accurate drawings. The large number of cameras in use in the past, as well as the present, and the wide variations in the lenses fitted to them, make it quite certain that none of the methods outlined will ever become an exact science.

XIV

THE VESSELS

INTRODUCTION

The production of this book has been accompanied throughout by a good deal of exchange of ideas between the members of the 'Schooner Circle'. This is particularly true of this chapter, concerned as it is with hard facts, and it can be looked upon as a combined project to which all have contributed. It is an attempt to leave sufficient record of a number of schooners to give the intending model-maker the satisfaction of being able to work on a particular vessel instead of merely a type. The choice of vessels has been influenced by several factors, mostly of a haphazard nature. In the first place I have tried to limit the vessels to those that I have actually seen myself – some could be classed as old friends, others were no more than casual acquaintances. This in itself cuts heavily into what can be made available as I only managed to set eyes on about one third of the vessels mentioned by John Anderson in his handy little reference book, *Coastwise Sail*[1]. However, to some extent this has been compensated for by the inclusion of some vessels not mentioned in that work. The selection available has been further reduced by insufficient information on hull lines, deck gear or original lengths of masts and spars, without any of which the job cannot be completed. The final offering is, therefore, something of a lucky dip.

The schedule, which follows immediately after this introduction and is accompanied by his own explanatory text, is the work of another enthusiast, David Clement.

By sheer chance David's list includes two schooners, *Volant* and *Minnie*, built in northeast Scotland, one, *Flying Foam*, built in France, and two, *Brooklands* and *Mary Barrow*, from the West Country. Neither of these latter two could be classed as an average vessel for the area; both in their own way were extreme cases and, to redress this lack of balance, it has been necessary to draw in *My Lady*, a much more representative vessel.

Chance has little to do with the rest of the vessels included here. Practically to the last one they were the products of the same area: the upper Irish Sea, that stretch of water from North Wales to the Firth of Clyde and the North Channel, bounded on the west by the upper part of Ireland and on the east by the serrated coastline of northern England and southern Scotland and, for good measure, having the Isle of Man in its middle. This may seem quite a large area until it is compared with the whole coastline of the British Isles, and, it must be stressed that the vessels dealt with here are but a small fraction of the total number built in these parts that were still afloat in the 1930s. It would be presumptuous to think that the products of this area were more strongly-built or more durable than those from other quarters and it can only be concluded that sheer weight of numbers resulted in such a heavy concentration among the final survivors. The economic reasons for this tremendous outburst of localised shipbuilding are not hard to find, but are beyond the scope of this book.

The reader will probably be aware that, by some long-standing convention, drawings of ships are made with the vessel proceeding from the left-hand side of the paper to the right – ie. they are viewed on the starboard side – and he may well wonder why most of the writer's vessels are going in the opposite direction. This has been done in order to show the complications of the main or mizzen topping lift, clearly, in full lines, instead of dotted lines behind the sail, but it has become such a habit that in the odd case that treatment has been meted out to vessels with topping lifts on the starboard side. The drawings vary tremendously in regard to the amount of available information from which to produce them and this applies particularly to the lines; it has, therefore, been necessary to classify them in order to prevent the intending model-maker from being misled by the more fully detailed treatment of the deck gear into believing the lines are equally detailed. It is obvious that a 'four star' set of lines could only be obtained from the vessel herself, from the builder's drawing or tables of offsets, or from a half mode. None are in this category, although one or two, such as *Brooklands*, *Cymric* and *Gaelic* come very close.

In some cases I have attempted to give the reader a brief description of the problems involved, but it would be impossible to recount all the doubts and uncertainties, which must of necessity beset those working with such intangible material. In general it can be said that 'three star' lines have only been produced where there has been some concrete information on the shape of the midship section and, in a great

[1] *Coastwise Sail* by John Anderson, Percival Marshall & Co., London, 1934, revised 1948.

many cases, this evidence has been produced by Terry Belt. The lack of this vital information has caused a number of vessels to be placed in the lower categories, as any conclusions on the shape of the hull have had to be deduced from other factors. The whole process of dealing with these little vessels has finished up as a search, usually a vain one, for some excuse to depart from the small deadrise and hard bilge that is so monotonously common. Vessels like *Jane Banks*, whose dimensions positively shout that here is something out of the ordinary, do not crop up very often.

There is another factor that should be taken into consideration. Every man has, in the dim recesses of his mind, a set of blockages, biases and peculiar mental twists with which he was either born or that he has acquired on his way through life, and which act like railway tracks to keep him ploughing on in the same endless groove. This point has been raised to reassure anyone in possession of evidence that does not tally with the results given here – he should feel free to modify and amend things until he obtains a more satisfactory result. It has also been raised for the future as, one by one, the photographers come to the end of the road, the pictures of these little vessels taken between the two Wars are slowly finding their way into libraries, museums and similar institutions; but it will be many years yet before it is possible for the model-maker to lay hands on all the available evidence for one particular vessel. When that day arrives the drawings given here may have to be modified. The ship model-makers of the future, however, will find no shortage of evidence in the narrow field with which we are dealing.

The one aspect of schooners that does not show up well on photographs is their deck gear, but a perusal of the drawings will reveal that it was very much according to a pattern. It is not always possible to say what modifications were carried out when a motor winch or auxiliary engine was installed but everyone can be reasonably certain of what was on the deck and where it was when she left her builder's yard. Water barrels were probably being replaced by galvanised steel tanks in the 1890s – having served ships well for thousands of years – and wheelhouses at the stern were putting in an appearance about the same time, but apart from these, there are only three areas where the model-maker may find himself in doubt. It has already been mentioned in the chapter on deck gear that there were two basic types of platform in the bows, two patterns of fo'c'sle companion, and two patterns of cabin companion, and that this last was sometimes installed athwartships. If all else is proportioned as correctly as possible, failure to guess the right pattern for these pieces of equipment does not seem to me to be of so great enough importance as to invalidate the rest of the work. If it is, then all the replicas and models of the *Santa Maria*, *Golden Hind*, *Mayflower* and so on would also be invalidated, however much careful research had gone into their building.

Camborne at Gloucester 2 October 1934 loaded with 180 tons of salt and ready to depart for Cork.

PHOTOGRAPHER UNKNOWN. DAVID CLEMENT COLLECTION

In the main the deck-gear drawings have been reproduced from rough sketches made forty years ago and more, sometimes from memory, and no attempt was then made to assess dimensions, unless they were a great deal above or below average practice; thus, is possible to give or take perhaps as much as 18in in some places. As far as possibly they have been checked against available photographic evidence, without, I suspect, any great improvement in dimensional accuracy. In spite of this, if the model-maker bears in mind such simple facts as the deck had to be crossed when going about and hatches had to have reasonable access on all four sides to knock in the wedges, he will find that the spacing of the masts prevents him from going very far wrong. The day when these basic principles tended to be pushed aside was when motor winches and auxiliary engines began to be installed. It will be found that, on some of the deck gear, no indication is given of the smaller items such as bollards, bitts and hold ventilators. This does not mean that they were not there, they almost certainly were, but as they are not shown on my original sketches I feel that, after the lapse of so many years, it is only fair to draw the attention of the reader to those places where guesswork will be required.

Another feature that frequently does not appear on the drawings is the position of the vessel's name on the bows. At the time when I was making the sketches, I relied on this showing up on photographs but was often disappointed to find it was concealed by the anchors, catheads or bowsprit shrouds and, in some cases, had not been picked out in white paint for a considerable time. At the stern it can be safely assumed that the name and port of registry were cut into the timber of the topgallant bulwark across the counter, unless some evidence is given to the contrary. Iron and steel vessels did not normally have topgallant bulwarks, and the name was usually above the port of registry on the stern, both frequently done on arcs of a circle.

The Schedule

The drawings included by Douglas Bennet in his original manuscript represented only a selection of the last remaining British schooners and omitted some well-known vessels. For completeness the opportunity has been taken to schedule all those schooner-rigged sailing vessels still operational and registered with Lloyd's or in the *Mercantile Navy List*. By this means an overview of the situation in the years prior to the outbreak of war in 1939 is given. Of necessity, the details are brief but nonetheless important as a survey of the final years of sail in Britain. In his text Douglas also commented on ketches and for that reason they are also included here. The spritsail rig, by and large confined to the waters of the Thames, the Medway and the East Coast – albeit passages were made around the British coastline and to the near continent during this period by such vessels as *Will Everard*, *Alf Everard* and others – is not generally included as that type of vessel was generally unique in its construction and of a differing form of rig. A hermaphrodite type, rigged as a schooner or ketch, but flat-bottomed and using leeboards is included for those few examples that survived into 1934-35.

Whilst this list is as complete as possible, some vessels continued to trade that, for one reason or another, were not listed by either *Lloyd's Register* or the *Mercantile Navy List*; other vessels that were listed were no longer trading and in some cases no longer extant. The listings used are principally those of the two aforementioned publications but it will be appreciated that vessels under 100-tons gross that did not hold their Class under Lloyd's Rules would not have been included in that *Lloyd's Register*.

British Register was also open to debate as some vessels registered with United Kingdom ports never visited the United Kingdom and, indeed, traded (or were laid up) at ports overseas. As far as possible the list published here details only those working in the coastal and short-sea trades around the islands known as the British Isles, but also includes the country of Eire.

Measurements are those detailed in the records and in some cases it will be found that they are marginally different from those recorded by Douglas Bennet within his meticulously researched drawings. Where appropriate both measurements are given but as those within the drawings are generally the result of actual physical measurement I suspect that these are possibly the more correct – albeit the differences are extremely marginal.

There could be a few, very few, additional British- and Irish-owned and -operated sailing vessels which have been omitted but as all vessels over 1 ton were supposed to be included within the *Mercantile Navy List*, I do not anticipate those numbers being more than one or two. However, a word of caution: the well-known ketch, *Emily Barratt*, appeared in neither publication in 1933/4 although she was very much in trade. Similar comments can be made for other vessels included in this listing. It is remarkable fact that as late as 1934 the schedule of British Registered sailing vessels in the *Mercantile Navy List* ran for some 377 pages – with an appendix of a further nineteen late entries!

The list included all types from all corners of the then wide-flung British Empire and its Dominions – the Far East, the Indian sub-continent to Africa, Australasia; the Pacific and south Atlantic territories; the Caribbean, Canada and the North American British Territories. Some vessels, registered in London, formed a part of the Irrawaddy River Company flotilla in Burma, for example and, although built in the UK, never saw home waters; the Hudson's Bay Company and other similar examples can be found elsewhere. Such vessels have been excluded as have those four or five sailing schooners and ketches acquired by the Ministry of War Transport from foreign owners and operated by the government for the duration of the 1939-45 War by the government.

In mid-1930s Britain commercial sail was still to be seen along the East Coast and beyond in the guise of the spritsail barge of the Thames and East Coast rivers, and the occasional wherry, keel, and flat on the Yorkshire rivers and estuaries, and in the Mersey. A few pilot vessels still operated under sail. In the Bristol Channel a handful of the once vast fleet of open-decked sailing trows still plied, many of them, however, by then cut down to humble un-rigged towing barges. The last of the sailing trawlers were reaching their 'Valhalla' and some smaller fishing vessels still used sail. In Carrick Roads the Falmouth oyster dredgers continue the sailing tradition and are now the last commercial sailing vessels operating in the United Kingdom following a traditional trade. They have survived primarily as a way of preventing the over-fishing of the oyster beds but their activity is now threatened by pollution in the estuary.

Finally, I accept that some restorations and reproductions still sail – but with the object of carrying fare-paying passengers, not cargoes. Generally speaking, however, such vessels are not a part of Douglas Bennet's book and in preparing my list for this schedule they have been disregarded. What follows therefore is a brief but reasonably complete listing of

Camborne arriving at Truro on 26 July 1934.

Photograph taken by H. Oliver Hill. Terry Belt Collection

The wreck of the *Mary Peers*. Sadly, a great majority of the hundreds of coastwise sailing vessels built through the years came to grief. The *Mary Peers* of Fowey was wrecked on 8 December 1932 1½ miles from Port Wrinckle whilst she was on passage from Torquay to Fowey in ballast. Despite having an engine she was blown ashore in Whitsand Bay when her motor proved inadequate against a strong wind and tide. Captain Henry Jones of Connah's Quay and three crew were saved by breeches buoy.

PHOTOGRAPHER NOT KNOWN. DAVID CLEMENT COLLECTION

those schooners and ketches that were the survivors of a huge fleet of 'maids of all work'. Generally carrying low-value bulk cargoes such as coal, grain, sand, cement, china clay etc., they plied the coasts of Britain, Ireland, and the near-continent through the swansong of sail – the lorries of yesteryear, distributing the wants and needs of communities from the small settlement to the larger urban areas.

Where the information is known the schedule gives the vessel's rig as at 1934/5, her port of registry, date and place of build and shipbuilder, measurements in feet, and the tonnage, gross and net. Last, her official number and flag hoist are given as recorded. The flag hoist would change dependent upon when allocated but it is that which is recorded by the two principle sources that has been used; in those instances where Douglas Bennet has provided drawings of the vessel a brief descriptive comment is included as well.

My connection with the schooners began in the 1950s when, as a small boy, I was allowed to join the *Kathleen & May* under Captain Tommy Jewell, sailing from Pembroke to Appledore and back to Spillers Mill at Pembroke. In 1960 I was involved in the insurers' enquiries into the cause and responsibilities following the fatal accident involving the *P.K. Harris* and the *A.C.M.*, both original sailing barges loading gravel from the sandbars at the entrance to the Taw and Torridge. With such connections and a family background in shipping circles from Kidwelly, Llanelli and Swansea grew a love of the subject that has remained ever since.

The rapidity of the decline in sail is readily apparent when we look at those vessels still listed by *Lloyd's Register* ten years later, in 1945, which vessels are identified here by * beside their names. Within that one decade the majority of those listed had become a faint shadow of their former selves; many were laid up following work as barrage balloon vessels or as lighters or barges with the armed forces. By 1960 just three vessels still plied commercially. They all operated out of Appledore and were the *Irene*, *Kathleen & May* and the *Result*, all substantially cut down in rig and primarily operating as small motor-vessels assisted with sail on occasions. A very few endeavoured to continue as charter vessels carrying passengers on 'experience' holidays but the age of commercial sail was effectively over, lingering only in the memories of those men who sailed them until they, too, pass from the scene. It is, however, fitting that through the pages of Douglas's book, we get a feel of what was required to sail these last ladies of British commercial sail and how it was done – although nothing could ever replace the experience of the 'real thing', warts and all.

Around the United Kingdom, for the vast fleet of schooners, the sun had finally and irrevocably set.

SCHEDULE

(Vessels marked* were still listed in 1945)

Acacia Wood Ketch, Barnstaple, built 1880 by Banks, Plymouth.
60.3 × 18.6 × 7.4ft.
60 tons gross, 40 tons net.
Official Number: 81036.
Signal Hoist: MFSM.

Ada Wood ketch, Gloucester, built 1869, Bristol.
67 tons gross.
Official Number: 62742.
Signal Hoist: MFPT

Ada (ex-*Annie Christian*) Wood ketch, Bideford, built 1881, Barnstaple, W. Westacott & Sons. 76.5 × 20.5 × 9ft.
77 tons gross, 52 tons net,
Official Number: 76819.
Signal Hoist: MDXF

Adelaide Wood two-masted schooner, Falmouth, built 1869, Tredwen, Padstow.
106 × 24.3 × 12.7ft.
180 tons gross,138 tons net.
Official Number: 58295.
Signal Hoist: MDLX

Advance* Steel three-masted schooner, Stornaway, built 1898, T. Turnbull & Son, Whitby. 125 × 25 × 9.7ft.
278 tons gross, 232 tons net.
Official Number: 108364,
Signal Hoist: None advised

Aeolus Wood two-masted schooner, Portsmouth, built 1896, Brixham. 66 tons net.
Official Number: 108001.
Signal Hoist: None advised

Agnes* Wood ketch, Bideford, built 1904, Henry Stapleton, Bude. 70.6 × 18.5 × 8ft.
67 tons gross, 54 tons net.
Official Number: 105246.
Signal Hoist: MLGV.
Rebuilt on the hull of an older worn-out vessel, the *Lady Acland*. Originally built in 1835, this vessel was eventually purchased for use as a yacht in 1958 and was wrecked in the West Indies the same year – effectively 123 years old!

Agnes Craig* Wood auxiliary three-masted schooner, Dublin, built 1884, Ferguson & Baird, Connah's Quay, Cheshire.
94.7 × 23 × 10.4ft.
128 tons gross, 85 tons net.
Official Number: 88705.
Signal Hoist: EICX.

Agnes & Constance Wood ketch, Rochester, built 1889, Curel, Frindsbury, Kent.
63 tons net.
Official Number: 97711.
Signal Hoist: MJCP.

Albatross Wood ketch, Southampton, built 1894, Southampton. 41 tons net.
Official Number: 104037.
Signal Hoist: None.

Alert Iron three-masted schooner (ex-steamer), Liverpool, built 1865, Laird Bros., Birkenhead.
117.8 × 21 × 10.7ft.
189 tons gross, 186 tons net.
Official Number: 29992.
Signal Hoist: JGVW.

Alert Wood ketch, Portsmouth, built 1903, Portsmouth.
46 tons net.
Official Number: 116192.
Signal Hoist: None

Alert Wood three-masted schooner, Falmouth, built 1885, Brundrit & Co., Runcorn.
103.8 × 23.6 × 11.1ft.
163 tons gross, 133 tons net.
Official Number: 83511.
Signal Hoist: MJBK.
Alone among the vessels dealt with in this book, *Alert* needs no scaling up of her drawings, nor the fairing up which must needs follow it, as the originals have been done to 3/16in : 1ft and are here reduced to one-third of their size to conform with the rest.

Owen Wicksteed chose this

Sail plan of *Alert*

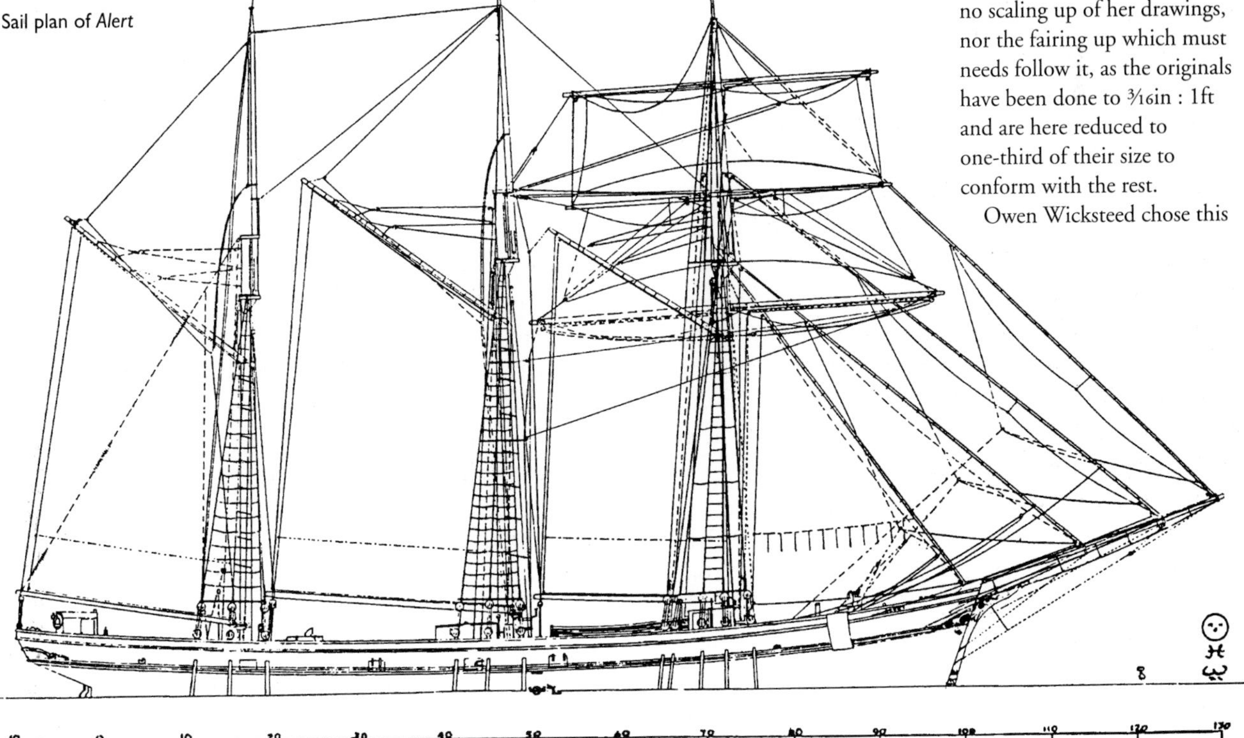

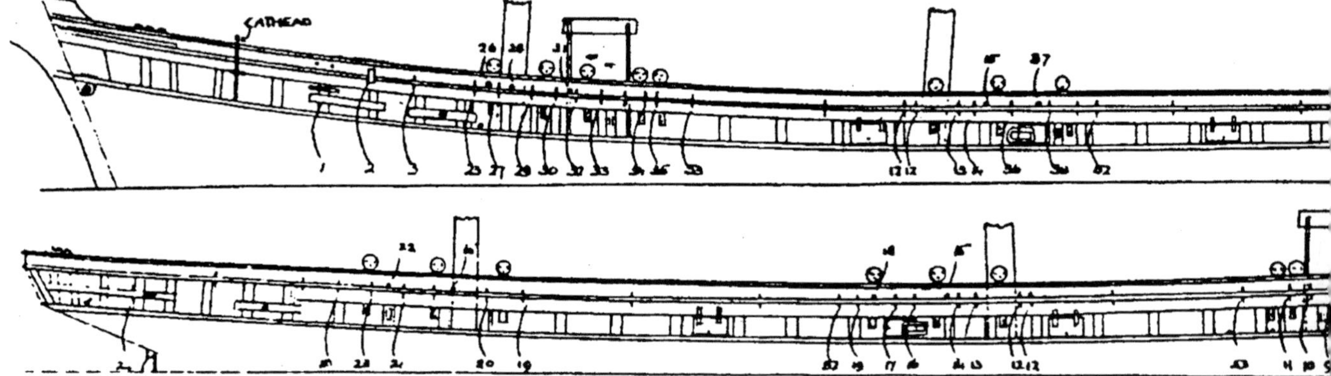

1 Boom jib sheets
2 Shank painters
3 Flying jib sheets
4 Starboard jib halyard
5 Lower topsail clewline halyard
6 Upper topsail downhaul halyard
7 Eye for burton
8 Pin for port burton
9 Fore throat halyard
10 Lower topsail buntline
11 Upper topsail halyard
12 Fore braces
13 Lower topsail braces
14 Upper topsail braces
15 Eyes for main and mizzen topmast downhauls
16 Rope topping lift
17 Main throat halyard
18 Main gaff topsail jackstay
19 Main gaff topsail halyard
20 Main topping lift
21 Mizzen throat halyard
22 Eye for mizzen topping lift
23 Pin for mizzen topping lift
24 Mizzen sheet
25 Fore staysail halyard
26 Eye for standing end staysail sheet
27 Burton (starboard)
28 Eye for starboard burton
29 Starboard lower topsail clewline
30 Starboard upper topsail clewline
31 Eye for rope reef tackle
32 Pin for rope reef tackle
33 Fore peak halyard
34 Inner jib halyard
35 Flying jib halyard
36 Main sheet tackle
37 Eye for main sheet tackle
38 Main peak halyard
39 Eye for mizzen reef tackle
40 Pin for mizzen reef tackle
41 Mizzen peak halyard
42 Mizzen gaff topsail jackstay
43 Inner jib downhaul
44 Boom jib downhaul
45 Staysail downhaul
46 Starboard jib downhaul
47 Lower topsail sheets
48 Yard ropes
49 Main gaff topsail halyard
50 Eye for fore staysail bowline
51 Mizzen boom guy tackle
52 Main boom guy tackle
53 Fore boom guy tackle
54 Eyes for main boom guy tackle
55 Eyes for fore boom guy tackle

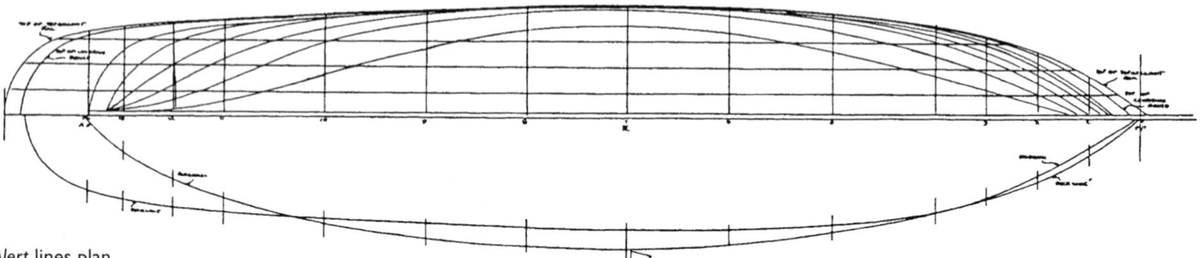

Alert lines plan

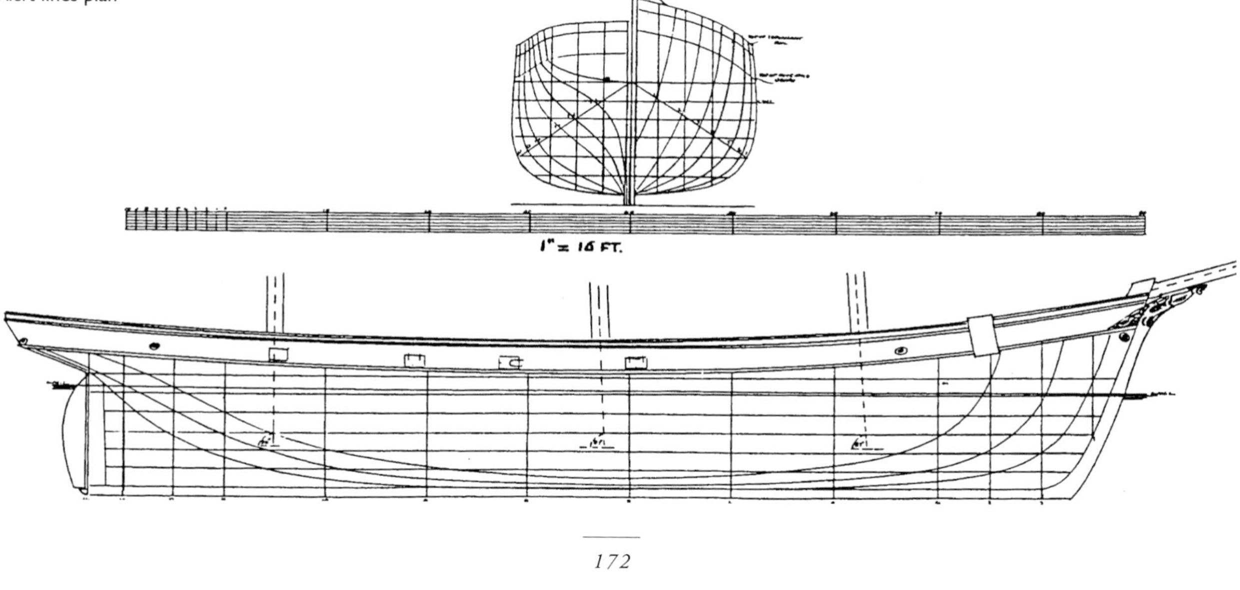

1" = 16 FT.

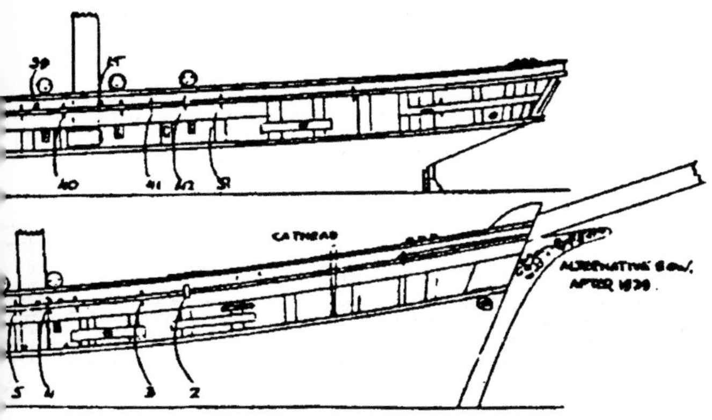

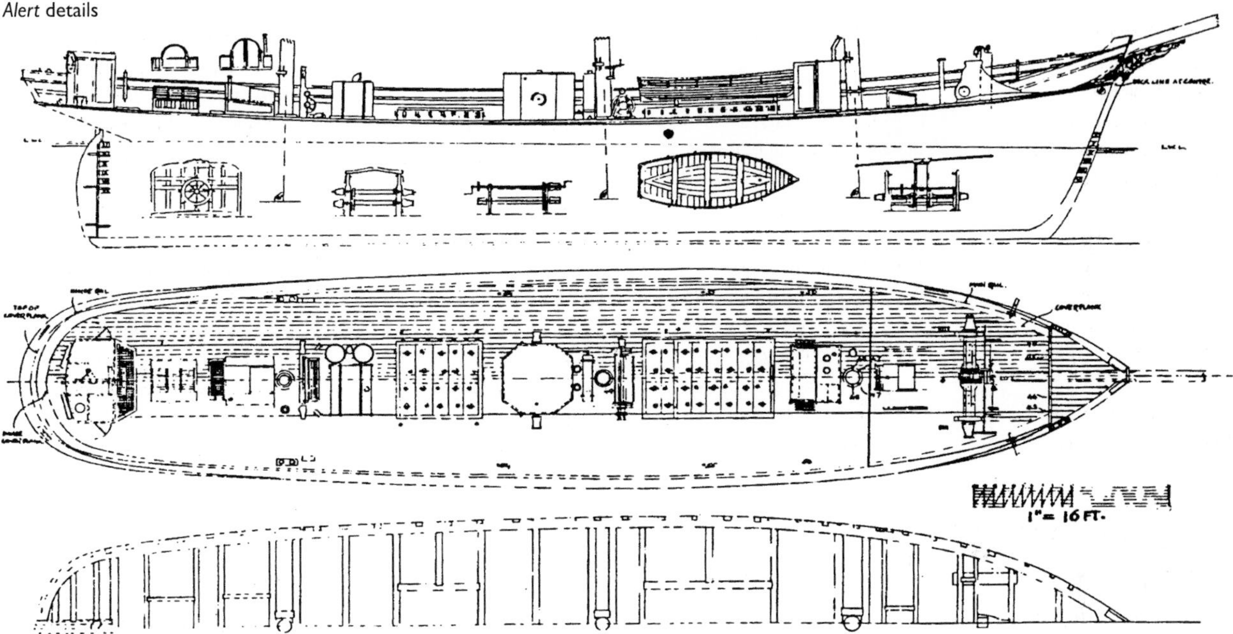

Alert details

scale because it permits a fair amount of detail without making the finished model too large to be accommodated in the average modern home. *Alert* is also unique in having full photographic coverage of her deck gear. This was achieved by the late Dan McDonald when she was in Glasgow on two separate occasions and his photographs tell the model-maker practically everything that he could possibly want to know. Copies have found their way into the National Maritime Museum. Dan's propensity to photograph the deck gear as well as taking a portrait of the ship has been of tremendous help. Without it I should have been unable to deal adequately with either *My Lady* or *Mary B. Mitchell*, and Owen Wicksteed would have had more difficulty in producing his drawings of the *Alert*. She was a well-photographed vessel in the last years of her life, but few of the results so far seem to have come into the hands of the publishers of 'coffee table' books, so handy for quick references to all sorts of detail. Indeed, the only well-known shot of *Alert* is the first of a pair taken by H.O. Hill as she was entering Newlyn.

This deficiency was remedied for 'Wicky' by Terry Belt who managed, as usual, to haul up an amazing collection from his bottomless pit. Most of us tend to build up in our minds a nice tidy little world in which everything can be coiled down neatly and hung on its proper pin, but Terry's collection contains photographs of vessels with such unlikely oddities of rigging and gear that one is left with the impression that the Victorians must have tried out practically every variation imaginable. One of the most staggering is a photograph of a vessel that could only be classified as a 'brigantooner'. She has a top and a standing gaff on the square-rigged foremast, as well as a full set of main staysails and, as though this wasn't enough, she was built of iron to carry tar in bulk, and was equipped with a boiler in a house on deck to keep the tar, or render it, molten while being discharged – presumably by steam pumps through some sort of flexible pipe. This peculiar mixture of ancient and modern must have been quite common in the latter part of the 19th century. The first cargo of New Zealand mutton to arrive on these shores came around Cape Horn in a sailing vessel, with its refrigerator compressor, driven by steam, hammering away day and night for something approaching 100 days at least. The feasibility of the project having been proved, the steamers were quick to snatch the trade away.

Alfred Rooker Wood ketch, Plymouth, built 1876, Darton, Plymouth. 71 × 19.5 × 9.2ft. 76 tons gross, 59 tons net.
Official Number: 68350.
Signal Hoist: MQWK.

Alice May* Wood ketch barge, Ipswich, built 1899, McLearon, Harwich.
Official Number: 109205.
Signal Hoist: None.

Alma Wood ketch, Bristol, built 1854, Gloucester (rebuilt 1916). 77 × 17 × 6ft. 41 tons net.
Official Number: 11684.
Signal Hoist: MNPB.

Altje Wood ketch, London (operated out of Topsham), built 1905, Nordloh.

Bessie

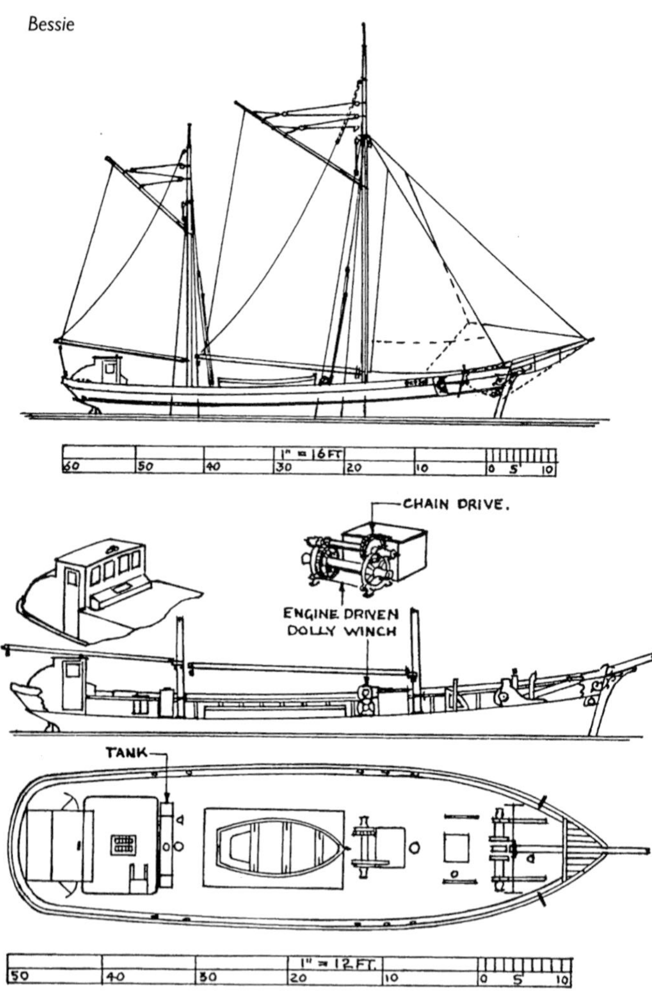

Susan Vittery
conjectural original
sail plan

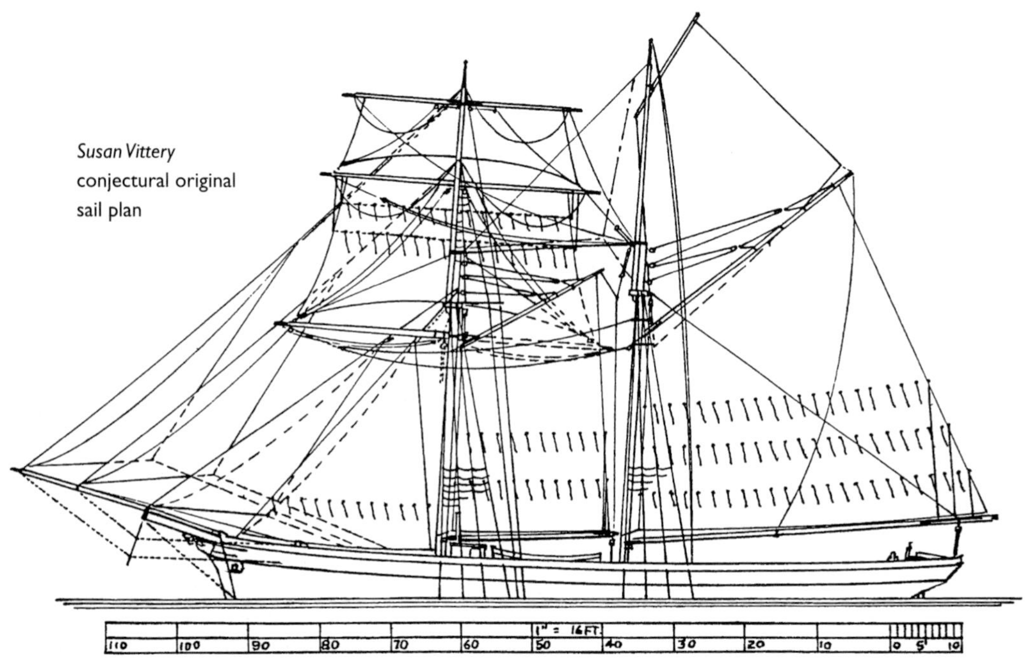

33 tons net.
Official Number: 139069.
Signal Hoist: MFXK.

Amanda Wood two-masted schooner, Padstow, built 1867, Willmet, Padstow.
82.7 × 21.3 × 10.1ft.
97 tons gross, 80 tons net.
Official Number: 58243.
Signal Hoist: MQRK.

Amazon Wood ketch, Barnstaple, built 1866, D. Le Seuer, Jersey; lengthened 1870. 65.5 × 16.3 × 8.2ft.
50 tons gross, 38 tons net.
Official Number: 55266.
Signal Hoist: None.

Ann Auxiliary wood ketch, Salcombe, built 1889, W. Date & Sons, Kingsbridge.
47 tons gross, 33 tons net.
Official Number: 86469.
Signal Hoist: None.

Annie Wood ketch, Cardigan, built 1895, J. & W. Francis, Milford Haven.
64.5 × 18.1 × 7ft.
46 tons gross, 38 tons net.
Official Number: 104117.
Signal Hoist: None.

Antelope* Wood auxiliary two-masted schooner, Wexford. Built 1885, The Dockyard Co., Wexford. 91.5 × 24.7 × 10.2ft.
129 tons gross, 88 tons net.
Official Number: 70153.
Signal Hoist: EIFB.

A.T. Wood ketch, Barnstaple, built 1894, J. & W. Francis, Milford Haven. 62 × 18 × 7ft.
42 tons gross, 30 tons net.
Official Number 104112.
Signal Hoist: None.

Azariah Wood ketch, Ipswich, built 1878, W. Bayley, Ipswich.
79.7 × 17.9 × 6.3ft.
64 tons gross, 53 tons net.
Official Number: 79054.
Signal Hoist: MGRX.

Belmont Wood ketch-barge, Faversham, built 1895, Whitstable Shipbuilding Co., Whitstable. 104 × 24.1 × 9.6ft.
149 tons gross.
Official Number: 104933.
Signal Hoist: None.

Bessie Wood auxiliary ketch, Barnstaple, built 1900, J. & W. Francis, Milford Haven. 59.4 × 18 × 6.6ft.
41 tons gross, 28 tons net.
Official Number: 112455.
Signal Hoist: None.
It will be noted from Figure 14-4 that the measurements from the actual survey carried out by Douglas Bennet vary slightly from her registered dimensions given above.

This tiny ketch, the smallest vessel dealt with in this random selection of drawings, was referred to with obvious affection by the natives of Barnstaple as *Little Besseye.* After the war she was bought by two ex-Royal Navy men who, together with an anonymous Irishman, sailed her to the Mediterranean, where they had endless fun with her ancient and decrepit semi-diesel. Her inclusion here should, in some small measure,

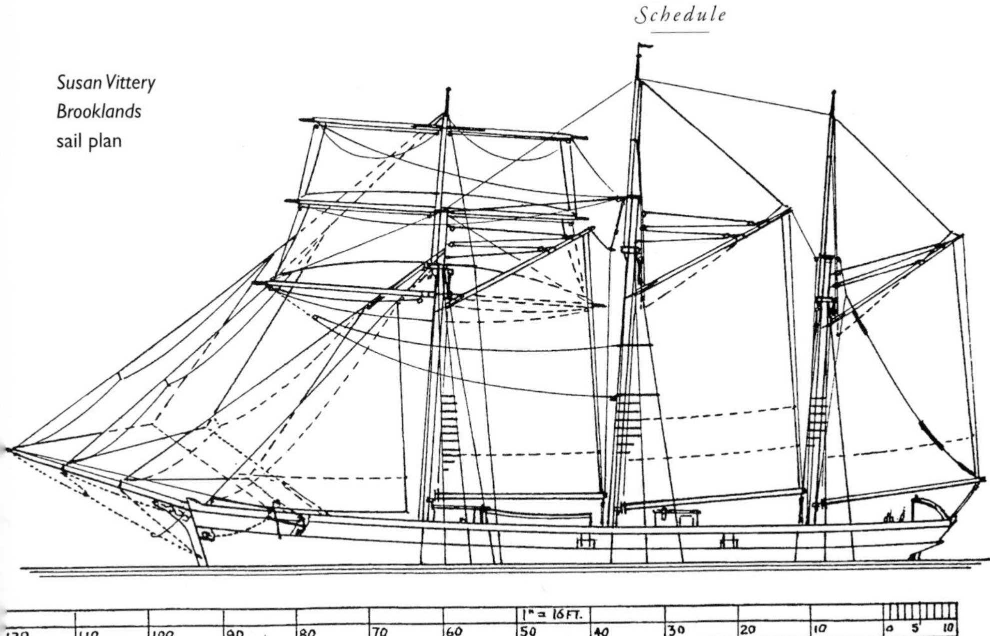

Susan Vittery
Brooklands
sail plan

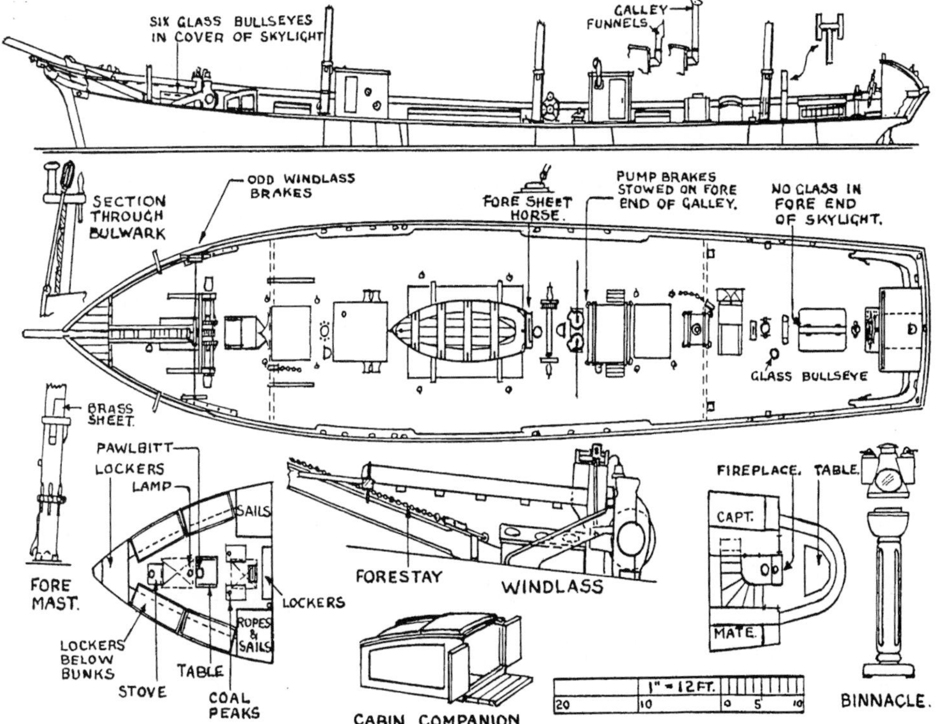

Brooklands details

placate those living in South Wales – with justification they could claim that North Wales had been given the lion's share of the publicity. She was an attractive little vessel and I regret that I am unable to give her deck equipment in greater detail.

Bessie Clark Wood ketch, Barnstaple, built 1881 by H.M. Restarick, Bideford.
59.1 × 18.2 × 7.5ft.
44 tons gross, 40 tons net.
Official Number: 84471.
Signal Hoist: None.

Bessie Ellen* Wood ketch, Barnstaple, built 1907, W.S. Kelly, Plymouth.
77.4 × 20.1 × 9.5ft.
78 tons gross, 57 tons net.
Official Number: 120098
Signal Hoist: MCPN.
She is still sailing and can be seen, stump rigged in the Cattewater, Plymouth.

Bessie Gould Wood ketch, Barnstaple, built 1872, W. Westacott, Barnstaple.
65 × 20.5 × 8.2ft.
44 tons gross, 42 tons net.
Official Number: 69928.
Signal Hoist: None.

B.I. (ex-*Sarah Ann*) Wood two-masted schooner, London, built 1874, May, Shoreham.
87.1 × 21.4 × 10.2 ft.
108 tons gross, 79 tons net.
Official Number: 69928.
Signal Hoist: MQRJ.

Bonita Wood ketch, Barnstaple, built: 1881, D. Le Seuer, Jersey.
57.9 × 16.1 × 7.5ft.
37 tons gross and net.
Official Number: 76278.
Signal Hoist: MJGM.

British Queen Iron three-masted schooner, Barrow, built: 1864, W. Allsup, Preston.
106 × 21.2 × 10.3ft.
164 tons gross, 133 tons net.
Official Number: 51083.
Signal Hoist: MCGW.

Britomart Wood ketch, Plymouth, built 1898, Brixham. 25 tons net.
Official Number: 109306.
Signal Hoist: None.

Brooklands (ex-*Susan Vittery*) Wood three-masted schooner, Cork, built 1859, W. Kelly, Dartmouth; rebuilt 1918.
99.5 × 21.4 × 11.8ft.
138 tons gross, 106 tons net.
Official Number: 27753.
Signal Hoist: EIFX.
Built in Dartmouth as the fruit schooner *Susan Vittery* for the Vittery family of Brixham, this vessel had a full life, participating in the deep-sea trades to the Azores and Caribbean and later in the Newfoundland trade, before becoming a lowly coaster around the British and Irish coasts. Because of being designed for her original trade

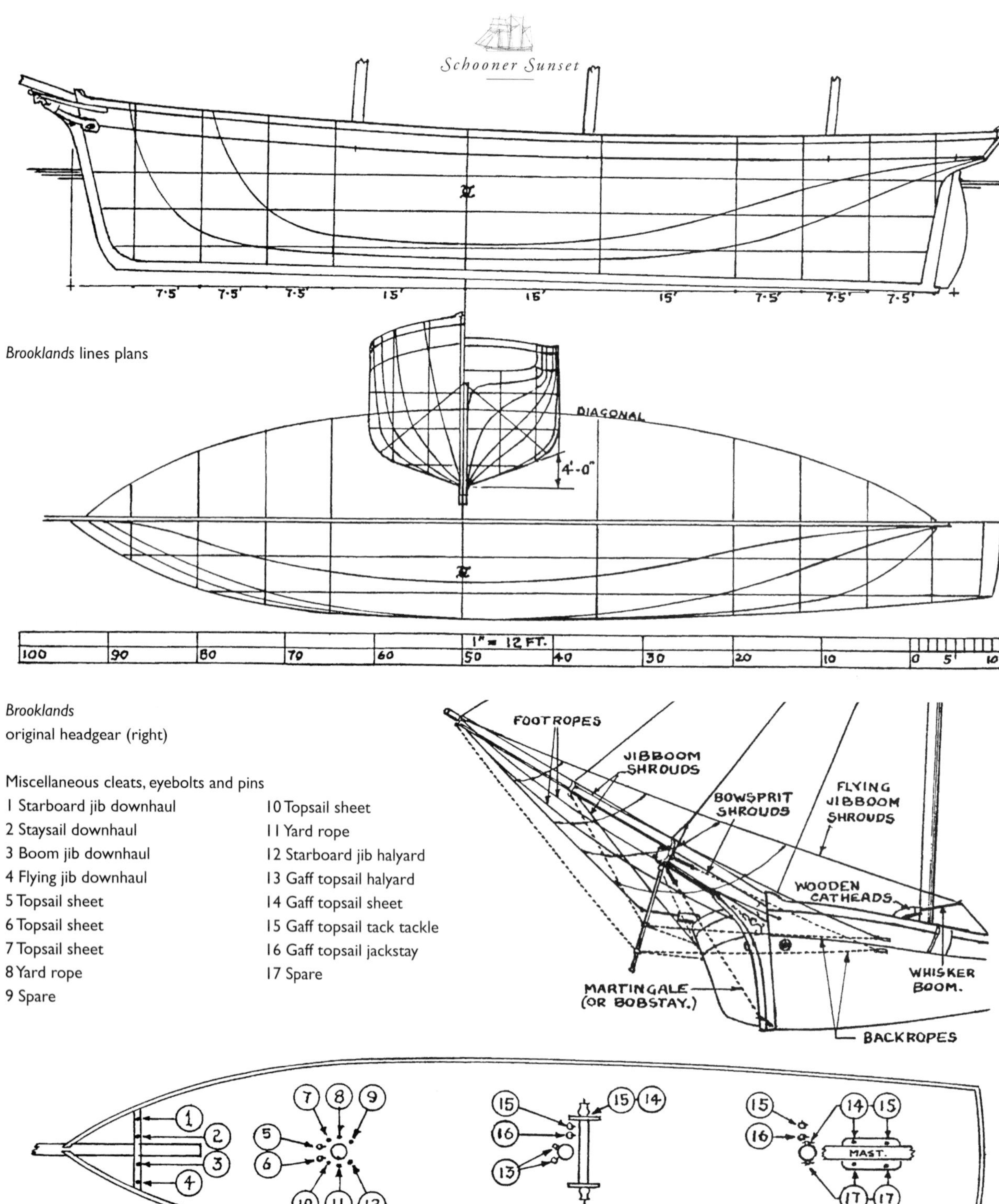

Brooklands lines plans

Brooklands
original headgear (right)

Miscellaneous cleats, eyebolts and pins

1 Starboard jib downhaul
2 Staysail downhaul
3 Boom jib downhaul
4 Flying jib downhaul
5 Topsail sheet
6 Topsail sheet
7 Topsail sheet
8 Yard rope
9 Spare
10 Topsail sheet
11 Yard rope
12 Starboard jib halyard
13 Gaff topsail halyard
14 Gaff topsail sheet
15 Gaff topsail tack tackle
16 Gaff topsail jackstay
17 Spare

in fruit she was not best suited to coastal trades where low-value bulk cargoes were moved often to local ports and harbours where facilities were rudimentary and drying out could be a problem because of her underwater shape. Her shape also placed constrictions on her cargo capability as discussed earlier.

She has been fully covered in the general text from the experiences of Douglas Bennet. The sail plan on page 174, shows the sail plan it is thought she would have carried during her days as a fruiter, when she was rigged with two masts. The sail plan on page 175 shows her with her rig changed to three masts but with her fore topmast shortened. The lines plan above show her lines taken by the method discussed in the previous chapter, whilst the drawing on page 175 gives details of her deck arrangements taken from sketches drawn by Douglas Bennet when he was aboard her.

The three sets of drawings on the opposite page give an excellent representation of the use of her pinrails for her three masts, both port and starboard,

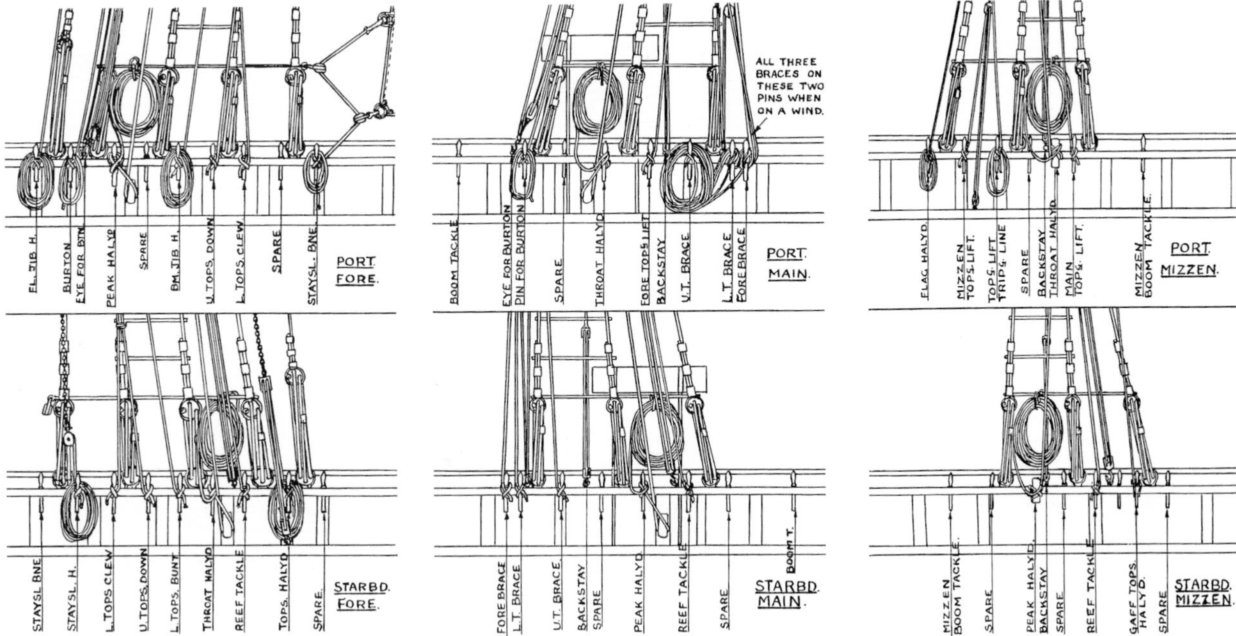

Brooklands pinrails

and could be of considerable assistance to a model-maker who wished to recreate the running, and for that matter the standing, rigging in an authentic manner

Last, the positions of the fastenings for the running rigging that led to the mast and/or deck are shown opposite. The headgear is that believed to have been carried during her days as a fruiter.

Brothers Wood ketch, Gloucester, built 1847, Brimscombe. 53 tons net. *Official Number:* 10808. *Signal Hoist:* MLSP.

C.F.H.* (ex-*Yolande*, ex-*C.F.H.*) Wood auxiliary ketch, Barnstaple, built 1892, James Goss, Calstock. 74 × 20.4 × 9.3ft. 76 tons gross, 56 tons net. *Official Number:* 99268. *Signal Hoist:* MVHK.

C. & F. Nurse Steel three-masted schooner, Falmouth, built 1900, W. H. Lean, Falmouth. 89.7 × 21.8 × 9.9ft. 119 tons gross. 98 tons net. *Official Number:* 109222. *Signal Hoist:* MDML.

Camborne* Wood auxiliary three-masted schooner, Swansea, built 1884, W. C. Paynter & Co., Amlwch, Anglesey. 93.2 × 22.5 × 10.1ft. 118 tons gross, 79 tons net. *Official Number:* 87234. *Signal Hoist:* MJVS.
This three-master was well known in her later years through her captain and owner, Hugh Shaw, whose book, *Schooner Captain*[2], is well worth hunting down. Before being converted to an auxiliary vessel she was evidently rigged as a plain double topsail schooner but a photograph taken in the harbour at Amlwch shows that she was originally fitted with a single topsail and flying topgallant. It is under this original rig that she has been drawn, although her deck gear has, of necessity, been shown as it was in her final years. I have insufficient information to attempt a drawing of her lines. The two posts of her dolly winch, which stand without benefit of either

Camborne sail plan

1" = 16 FT.

[2] *Schooner Captain* by Norah Ayland, D. Bradford Barton Ltd., 1972.

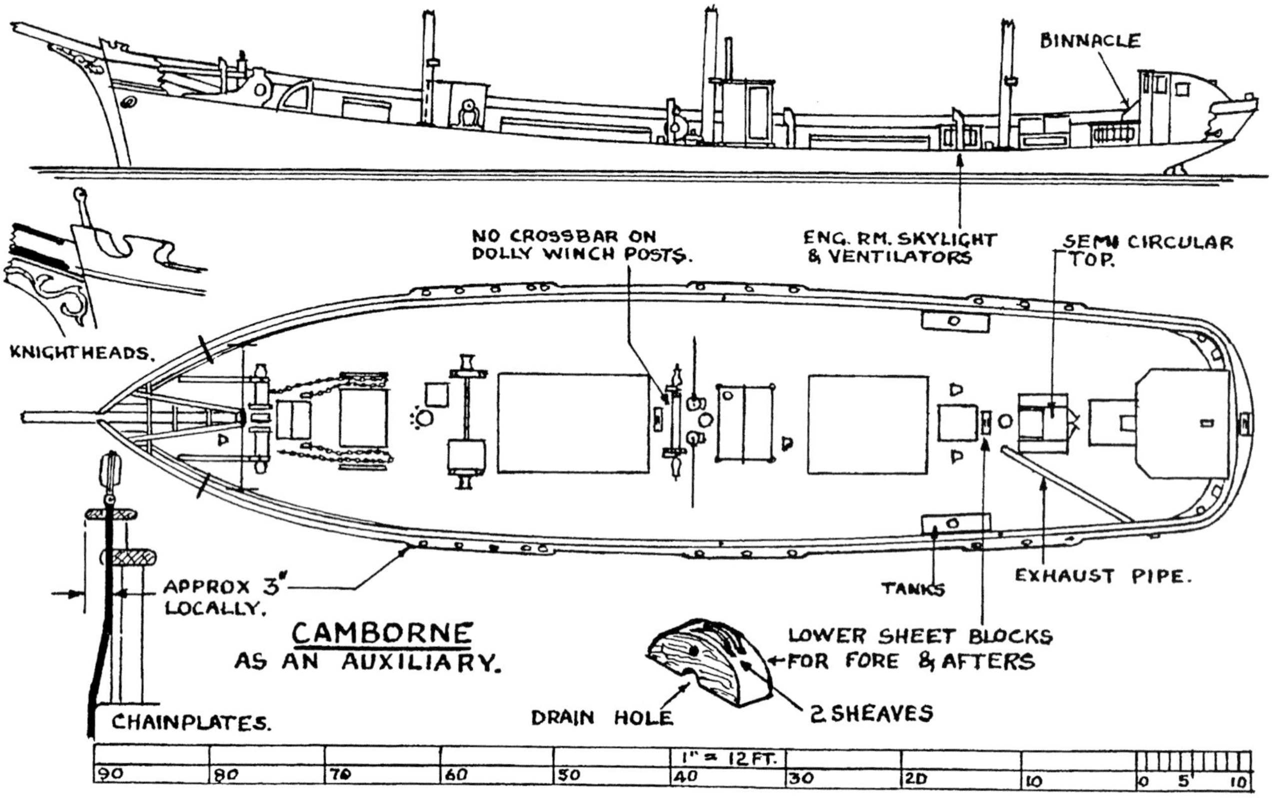

Camborne details

knees or crossbar, are obviously the forward corner posts of the pump well carried upwards through the deck. She probably had a crossbar on them previously and they would have provided a convenient crutch for the fore boom.

Cantick Head Wood ketch, Kirkwall, built 1903, Portknockie. 51 tons net.
Official Number: 132499.
Signal Hoist: None.

Carbid (ex-*Butterfly*) Wood ketch, London, built 1878 H.M. Restarick, Bideford; lengthened Gorleston, 1887. 78 tons gross, 53 tons net.
Official Number: 77060.
Signal Hoist: None.

Ceres Wood ketch, Padstow (Bude), built 1811, Salcombe. 65.2 × 17.7 × 17.2ft.
32 tons net.
Official Number: 15560.
Signal Hoist: MQGC.

Champion Wood ketch, Bridgwater, built 1853, Bristol. 82.7 × 19.2 × 7.9ft. 68 tons net.
Official Number: 10814.
Signal Hoist: None

Cicelia Wood auxiliary ketch, Barnstaple, built 1867, D. Le Seuer, Jersey. 78.3 × 19 × 8.8ft. 79 tons gross, 53 tons net.
Official Number: 55289.
Signal Hoist: MCZJ.

Clara May* Wood ketch, Plymouth, built 1891, Watson & Fox, Plymouth. 75.8 × 19.6 × 8.9ft.
73 tons gross, 53 tons net.
Official Number: 99255.
Signal Hoist: MDCD.

Clymping Wood ketch, Littlehampton, built 1909, J. & W.B. Harvey, Littlehampton.
93 × 23.4 × 8.3ft.
121 tons gross, 99 tons net.
Official Number: 105598.
Signal Hoist: MCZP.

Cristal Wood ketch, Milford Haven, built 1863, Jersey; rebuilt 1910. 30 tons net.
Official Number: 47081.
Signal Hoist: None.

Crown of Denmark* (ex-*Auto*, ex-*Afienda Marchiena*) Steel ketch (formerly schooner), London; operated out of Braunton and Topsham, built 1918 Stadskanaal, Netherlands.
101.6 × 19.1 × 8.5ft.
136 tons gross.
Official Number: 145111.
Signal Hoist: MKNC.

Cymric* Iron auxiliary twin-screw three-masted barquentine, Dublin, built: 1893, W. Thomas & Sons, Amlwch. 123 × 24 × 10.8ft.
228 tons gross, 114 tons net.
Official Number: 101751.
Signal Hoist: EIFP.
The *Cymric* and her sistership, *Gaelic*, fine iron three-masters were the final survivors of a number of vessels built to the same model by William Thomas of Amlwch in the last ten years of the 19th century. The 1890s can be said to have ushered in the final phase for the sailing vessel. The steamers had won the day, but there was still a place for the wind-driven ship in the carriage of bulk cargoes for which there was no particular urgency of delivery. The extreme clippers of the 1870s had given way to the intermediate clippers – larger iron vessels with greater cargo-carrying capacity but still with some pretensions to speed. To many these ship-rigged vessels, with their classical Greek names, were the real high-water mark of the sailing vessel incorporating a much better balance between speed and cargo capacity than the out-and-out racers that preceded them.

They were followed by the full-lined vessels of the 1890s;

by four-masted barques, which became more and more akin to floating warehouses. As lines became fuller, foremasts started to move forward once more but they were never again to reach the point from which they had departed. It was in the '90s, one suspects, that the phrase 'built by the mile and cut off in lengths' was first coined, with 'wall-sided and flat-bottomed' thrown in for good measure. Nevertheless, in spite of the sneers of those who had known the racers of the past, length still counted, and, in the hands of men who understood them, some of these latter-day steel tanks could put up performances that were in no way unworthy of their sleeker-lined predecessors. They were immensely strong compared with all that had gone before, with steel masts, steel yards, steel standing rigging, backstays galore, and steel-wire bolt ropes to their sails; if they bruised their way through the sea instead of slicing into it, they did so with a grand defiance.

To return to *Cymric* and *Gaelic*, however, one of the earliest of their sisterships was the barquentine *Detlef Wagner*, built in 1891. There is a photograph of her, taken when ready for launching, that is reproduced in *Ships and Seamen of Anglesey*.[3] This book also contains the specification for one of these vessels, complete with a profile drawing and sail plan, and anyone intending to model either will find in it a good deal of useful information, which will also be of great assistance in sorting out which items of deck gear were in them originally and which were added later.

It is seldom that the schooner model-maker gets such a bountiful handout as *Ships and Seamen of Anglesey* provides. The freshly painted hull of the *Detlef Wagner* in the photograph gives two beautiful waterlines, the only remaining area of doubt being in the entry, which in any case must have been in keeping with the run. The hull is that of a typical carrier of the 1890s and were it not for this photograph I should not have felt justified in giving these vessels such full lines. In the realm of shipbuilding at least, there seems to have been precious little village mentality in Amlwch. The builders were right up to date with the latest fashion, and the natives, had they so wished, had every reason to consider their little town as one of the more important suburbs of Liverpool, which, in essence was then and remains the capital of North Wales.

The specification given is for a vessel that was to have been built on the same lines as the others, but only 116ft long compared with the average of about 125ft. It would seem that the order for her was never placed, which is a pity, because she had several features that were a radical departure from the other vessels. The drawing shows the foremast well forward and indicates the builder had had second thoughts about the main and mizzen masts and intended to move them forward as well. This was in keeping with the contemporary practice in four-masted barques but, as though to compensate for it at least slightly, the fore yard is a mere 42ft long as against the standard 48ft (twice the beam) of *Cymric* and *Gaelic*.

The square foresail was obviously intended to be bent to the yard – it is fitted with clewgarnets – and she was to have had a deep upper topsail and an even deeper standing topgallant. But, most surprising of all, on the bowsprit she was to have had two jibs only, both of tremendous size, with a big overlap, and an area that dwarfed the staysail. The overall height from her load water line to the main truck was to have been slightly over 100ft. One is left with the suspicion that the builder was eager to try out these modifications, that he was confident that even in this shortened version his hull could stand up to the sail plan without showing any bad habits but that the customer was rather more conservative and preferred to stick to what had already been tried and proved. At any rate, the next vessel off the slip was *Cymric*, 123ft long, with three jibs and the foremast in its normal position. There is a possibility that the vessel in the printed specification may have been intended for a gentleman's yacht, as this would have been quite common in the 1890s – the oddities in the gear point to a larger crew than would normally be carried in a working vessel.

It is possible that 100ft from the waterline to the truck was the standard height of mainmast for all these vessels but I have been unable to discover any evidence that justifies going beyond 94ft for either of the

[3] *Ships and Seaman of Anglesey* Aled Eames, The Anglesey Antiquarian Society, 1973.

Cymric and *Gaelic* sail plan

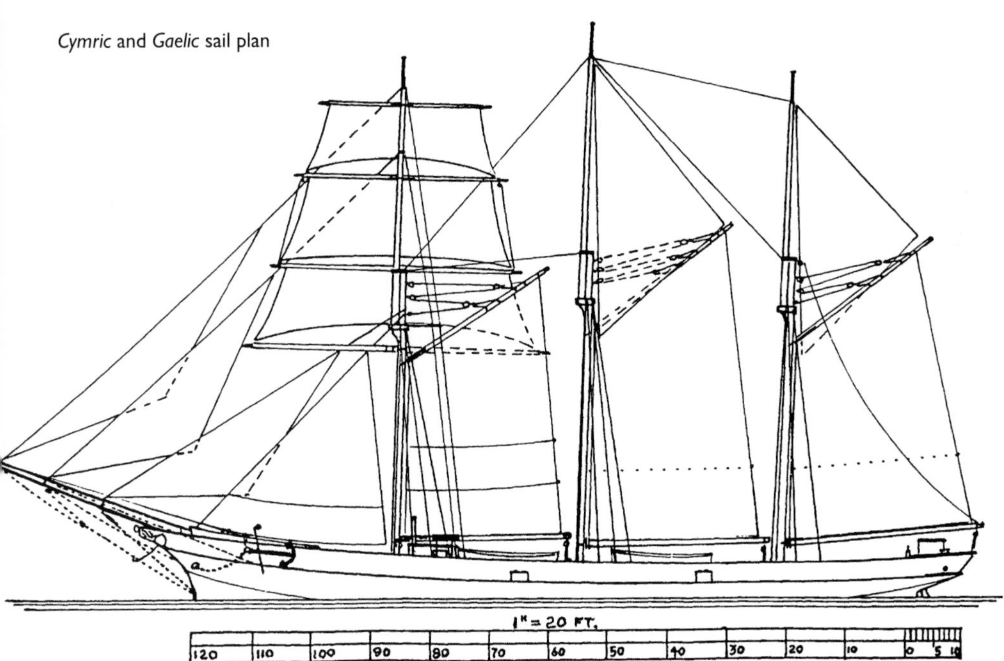

two survivors of the 1930s. There are good reasons for taking this attitude. The first is that after thirty years of battling with the sea, there is too great a possibility that some of their spars, at least, were not the ones originally put into them. The second reason is rather less direct but gives rise to the same conclusion. In the 1930s, from time to time, various people made the statement that one or other of the sisterships had once been rigged as a barquentine. Others contended equally strongly that they had not. The only conclusion that could be drawn from this was that, for reasons that were not very apparent, some people had difficulty in telling the difference between a barquentine and a three-masted standing topgallant schooner. The answer to all this was provided many years later by Terry Belt. Out of his collection of photographs he produced one of the *Gaelic*, anchored in Nantes Roads in 1920, taken by P.A. Vicary of Cromer, Norfolk. In this photograph the vessel had a bowsprit and a jib-boom, a fully square-rigged foremast complete with royal yard, and a topgallant bulwark – an oddity in a lot of steel vessels, which extended from the counter to the main rigging. Obviously this was at the end of her period as an Admiralty 'Q' ship and before she had been restored to her normal rig and returned to her owners. Having removed her spike bowsprit, fore lower mast and topmast, it is hardly likely that would have labelled them neatly and stored them carefully away. They probably went straight into some other decoy vessel that had had the sticks shot out of her, which then proceeded to sea and got them shot out again. Thus, it is highly unlikely that any of these vessels were refitted with their original masts at the end of the war.

Some of the deckhouses that *Cymric* and *Gaelic* finished up with may also have been installed during their period as 'Q' ships, as this would have been another way of disguising the fact that they had been encountered by the enemy on some previous occasion. William Thomas's specification refers to two houses only: 'a wheelhouse over the steering gear forming paint locker and W.C' and 'an iron galley of approved dimensions floored with neat tiles, well lighted, provided with range, locker, seat and shelves' .

Cymric's galley, moved aft, answered this description. It had two brass-rimmed glass ports in its forward end but could not have been used for cooking in the 1930s because it then had no funnel. (Brass ports and a tiled floor! – 'There's posh for you, Blodwen'.)

The peculiar arrangement of companion and skylights in her after hatch is an indication of how far *Cymric's* engine room extended forward of the mizzenmast. Both vessels were originally provided with two boats and one pair of davits but as the specification states that the boats could be removed from the hatches on either side of the vessel there must have been four sets of brackets and footsteps in the bulwarks. In the 1930s *Cymric* had her davits in the port, forward position while *Gaelic* carried hers to starboard, aft. The two schooners were distinguishable from a distance by the fact that *Gaelic* had a shortened bowsprit and only set two jibs and even more so by virtue of *Gaelic's* mizzenmast, which had an abominable rake forward.

I am unable to give any detailed information on the functioning of the windlass that was installed in these vessels and which was also to be found in both the *James Postlethwaite* and the ketch, *Emily Barratt.* I was never fortunate enough to come across any of them when there was someone on board. William Thomas's specification describes it as a 'Patent Friction Windlass', so there is a possibility that some information may still be in existence in the archives of the Patent Office, but unless a model is being constructed to a much larger scale than normal, the small details of such things can hardly be entertained – any more than the exact features and fashion of dress can be imparted to a minute figurehead.

The side frames or 'bitts' of the windlass were of cast iron and, in the *Emily Barratt* there were three sets of bearings on the forward side that must at one time have carried a train of shafts and gears.

What remained on all four vessels was a large central gear wheel flanked on either side by a gypsy, and with the usual warping drums outside the bitts. There is a possibility that the 'patent friction windlass' consisted of a pair of cone clutches that could be eased out to act as brakes when an anchor was let go, and forced in again when it was being hove up. I am indebted to Dick Scott and Captain Frank Forde of the British & Commonwealth Line for what information I have been able to obtain on the latter-day usage of these pieces of machinery. Captain Forde recalls with, I suspect, a touch of envy that, unlike the

Gaelic lines plans

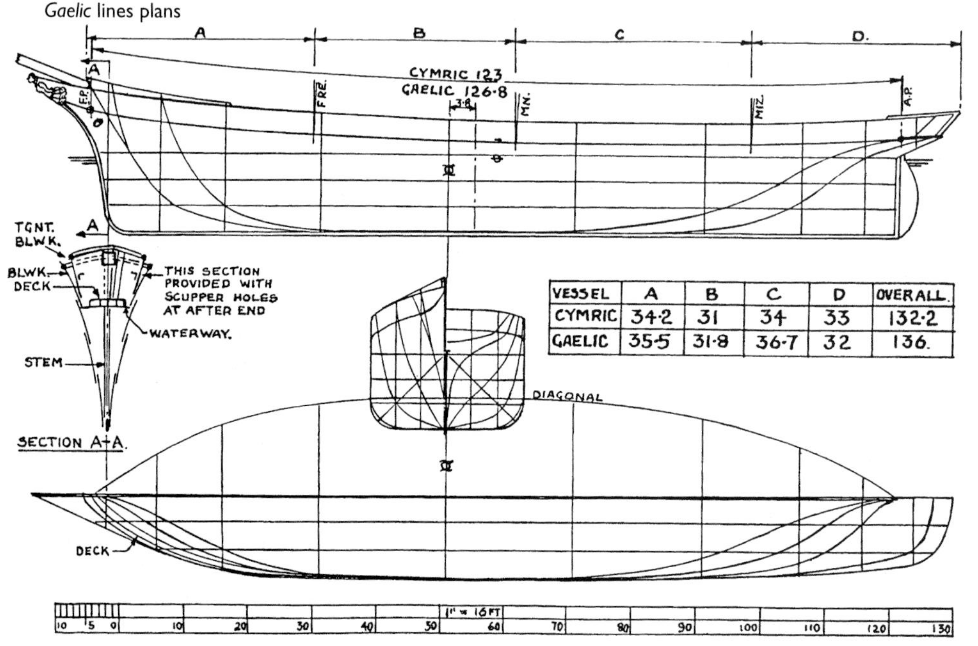

VESSEL	A	B	C	D	OVERALL
CYMRIC	34·2	31	34	33	132·2
GAELIC	35·5	31·8	36·7	32	136.

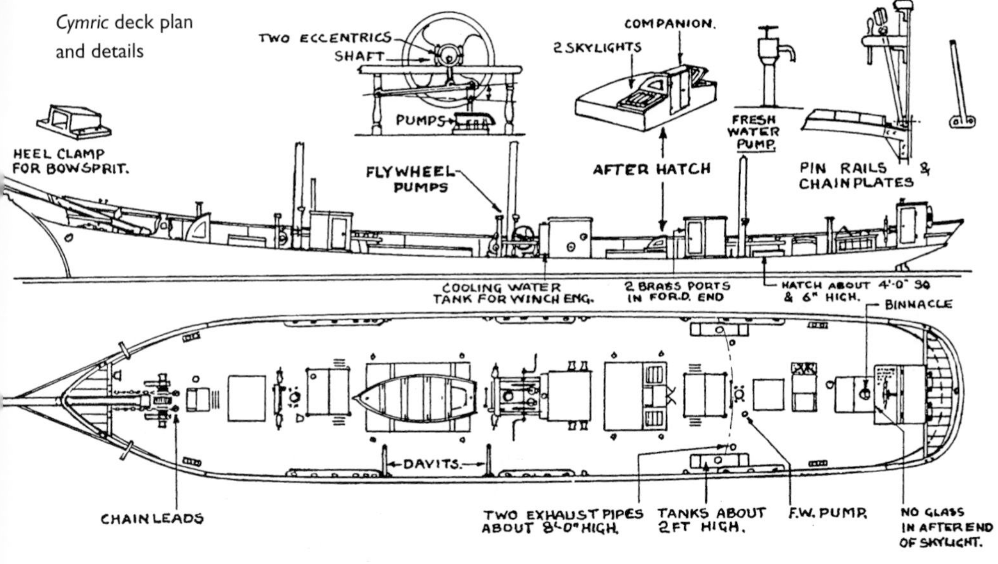

Cymric deck plan and details

ex-Dutchmen *De Wadden* and *Venturer*, the *Gaelic*, in which he started his seagoing career, had no endless chain by which the motion of the winch could be transmitted to the windlass. Thus, the job of weighing an anchor was done by the 'dog and tackle' method in much the same way as it was in vessels with the old 'Armstrong's Patent'. There was, however, one difference. The anchor chain coming off the gypsy was fed down the pipe straight into the chain locker. Thus, instead of putting the dog on to the chain abaft the windlass, it had to be done forward of it, right in the bows of the vessel. Captain Forde recalls that the boy – himself for the first twelve months – had to crawl under the platform in the bows to hook the dog on to the cable. When the dog reached the windlass it was unhooked by an AB and flung back again for another snatch. He remembers one incident in a heavy swell at the mouth of Lough Swilly, in which he became remarkably damp in consequence. The *Gaelic* disappeared with all hands on passage from Dublin to Lisbon in February, 1944.

Dannebrog* Wood ketch-barge, Harwich, built 1901, McLearon, Harwich.
71 tons gross.
Official Number: 109881.
Signal Hoist: MFFZ.

Davenport Wood ketch-barge, Ipswich, built 1877, W. Colchester, Ipswich.
86 × 19 × 6ft. 86 tons gross.
Official Number: 65379.
Signal Hoist: MJFB.

De Wadden* Steel auxiliary twin-screw three-masted schooner, Dublin, built 1917, Gebr. Van Diepen, Waterhuizen, Netherlands.
116.8 × 24.4 × 10.3ft.
239 tons gross, 159 tons net.
Official Number: 144980
Signal Hoist: EIKF.
Now preserved at Liverpool's Merseyside Maritime Museum.

Democrat* Auxiliary wood ketch, Barnstaple, built 1909, J. & W. Francis, Milford Haven. 71.2 × 19 × 7.7ft.
64 tons gross. 43 tons net.
Official Number: 120099.
Signal Hoist: None.

Despatch Iron ketch, Goole, built 1876, H.M. Dockyard, Plymouth. 116 × 22.3 × 10.7ft.
202 tons gross, 155 tons net.
Official Number: 122961.
Signal Hoist: None.

Diamond Wood ketch, Portsmouth, built 1879, J.T. Crampton, Portsmouth.
49 tons gross, 47 tons net.
Official Number: 81011.
Signal Hoist: None.

Dido C* (ex-*Jules Claes*) Auxiliary wood ketch, Barnstaple, built 1921, Lysckil, Sweden. 74.7 × 20.9 × 7.4ft.
68 tons gross, 41 tons net.
Official Number: 148211.
Signal Hoist: None.

Diolinda (ex-*Annie Reece*) Steel twin-screw auxiliary three-masted schooner, Wexford, built R. Cock & Sons, Appledore.
99.1 × 22.7 × 9.4ft.
150 tons gross, 88 tons net.
Official Number: 119636.
Signal Hoist: EIBX.

Dispatch Wood two-masted schooner, Inverness, built 1888, James Geddie, Garmouth, Scotland.
90.1 × 21.5 × 10.3ft.
120 tons gross, 100 tons net.
Official Number: 95741.
Signal Hoist: MGQK.

Donald & Doris* Wood auxiliary three-masted schooner, Bideford, built 1897, W.C. Paynter & Co., Amlwch.
96.7 × 23.1 10.5ft.
149 tons gross, 99 tons net.
Official Number: 102465.
Signal Hoist: MFTP.

Dorjoy (ex-*Uranus*) Wood three-masted schooner, Lerwick, built 1908, J. Wiln, Kaleten. 118 × 29.3 × 12.7ft.
275 tons gross, 246 tons net.
Official Number: 128455.
Signal Hoist: None.

Duras Iron auxiliary schooner, Belfast, built 1893, J.P. Rennoldson & Sons, South Shields. 95.5 × 18.1 × 9.7ft.
Official Number: 71844
Signal Hoist: None

E.R.A. Wood ketch, Liverpool, built St. Helens but date not known; rebuilt Liverpool 1895, on the hull of an earlier differently named vessel.
47 net tons.
Official Number: 106889.
Signal Hoist: None

Earl Cairns* Wood auxiliary three-masted schooner, Bideford, built 1883, Ferguson & Baird, Connah's Quay.
93.2 × 23.8 × 10.4ft.
131 tons gross. 82 tons net.
Official Number: 87826.
Signal Hoist: MCTB.

Eclipse Wood ketch, Plymouth, built 1892, Penryn.
32 tons net.
Official Number: 99259.
Signal Hoist: None.

Edith May Wood auxiliary two-masted schooner, Wexford, built 1877, Lund, Tarleton, Lancashire. 80.9 × 21.1 × 9.4ft.
93 tons gross. 57 tons net.
Official Number: 73476.
Signal Hoist: None.

Effort Wood ketch, Bristol, built 1856, Stroud. 74.7 × 18.5 × 9ft. 49 tons net. *Official Number:* 17892. *Signal Hoist:* None.

Effort* Wood ketch, Salcombe, built 1880, W. Date, Kingsbridge. 67.7 × 18.6 × 8.2ft. 66 tons gross, 31 tons net. *Official Number:* 81757. *Signal Hoist:* MFZX.

Eilian* Steel auxiliary three-masted schooner, Barnstaple, built 1908, W. Thomas & Sons, Amlwch. 102.6 × 21.9 × 9.4ft. 140 tons gross, 77 tons net. *Official Number:* 127943. *Signal Hoist:* MCWQ.

Eliza Wood ketch, Gloucester, built 1864, Bristol. 57 tons net. *Official Number:* 51203. *Signal Hoist:* None.

Eliza Jane Wood ketch, Bristol, built 1873, Bridgwater. 89.5 × 22.6 × 10.1ft. 135 tons gross, 98 tons net. *Official Number:* 67226. *Signal Hoist:* MGNC.

Elizabeth Ellen Fisher Wood auxiliary two-masted schooner, Dublin, built 1871, McLea, Rothesay. 86.3 × 21.2 × 10.2ft. 110 tons gross, 83 tons net. *Official Number:* 63934. Signal Letters: None.

Ella Wood ketch, Portsmouth, built 1900, Emsworth. 32 tons net. *Official Number:* 110230. *Signal Hoist:* None.

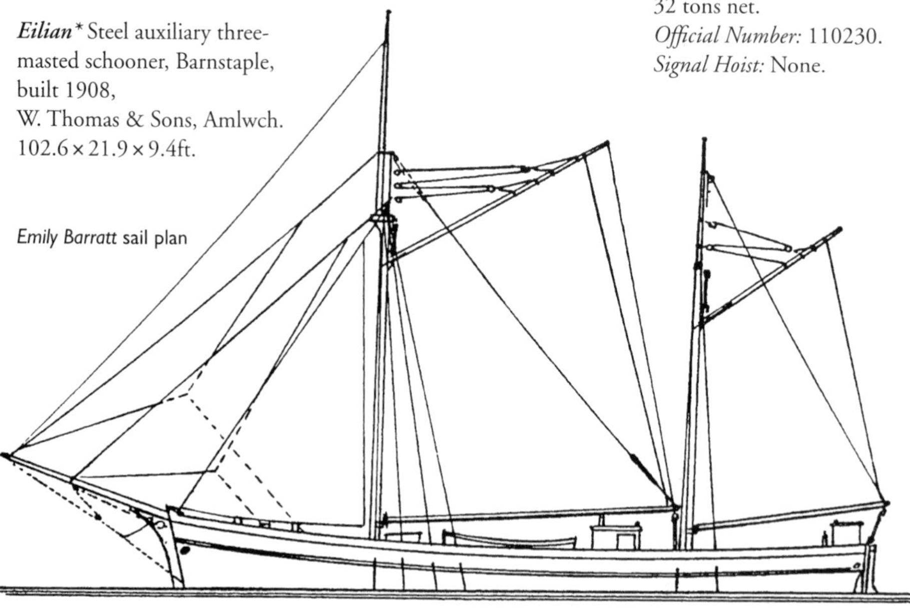

Emily Barratt sail plan

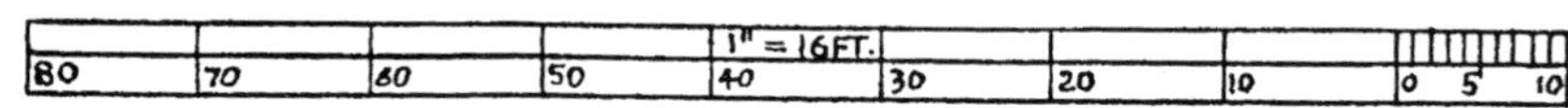

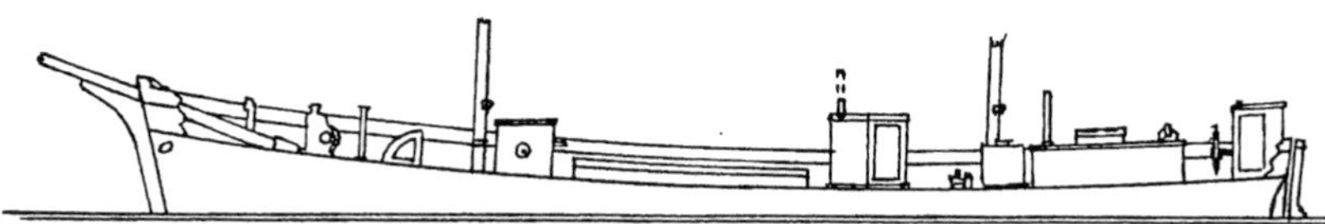

Emily Barratt profile and deck plan

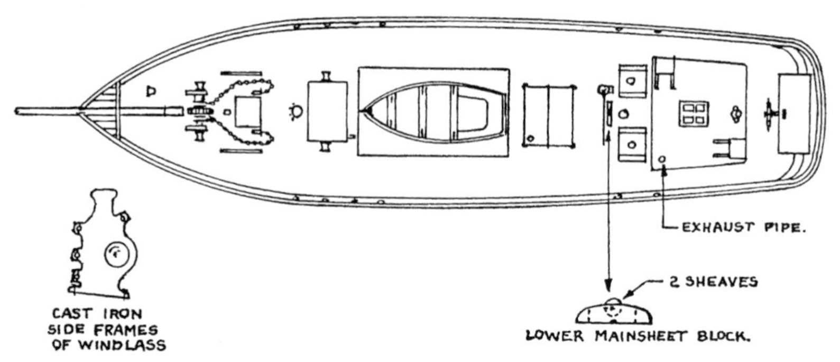

Ellen Wood two-masted schooner, Wexford, built 1882, J. Prosser, Bridgwater. 79.3 × 20.9 × 9.3ft. 98 tons gross, 76 tons net. *Official Number:* 81530. *Signal Hoist:* EIJZ. Laid up Arklow.

Elvy* (ex-*Moucheron*) Steel auxiliary ketch, Cardiff, built 1913, Gebr. Van de Meer, Vlaardingen, Netherlands; lengthened 1936. 109.3 × 21.7 × 10.9ft. 199 tons gross, 99 tons net. *Official Number:* 167817. *Signal Hoist:* MLBR. Operated during the Second World War by the Ministry of War Transport and returned to her French owner in 1945.

Ely Wood ketch, Bristol, built 1895, Chepstow. 69 tons net. *Official Number:* 102490. *Signal Hoist:* None.

Emilly Barratt* Wood ketch, Barnstaple, built 1913, Duddon Shipbuilding Co., Millom. 76.8 × 20 × 8.1ft. 71 tons gross, 59 tons net. *Official Number:* 125907. *Signal Hoist:* JVBP. This vessel was built for the Hodbarrow Mining Company of Millom and was the last vessel of her type constructed on the northwest coast of Cumbria. Two features point to the fact that she was originally rigged as a schooner. The first is her place of build, Millom; very few ketches, if any, were built so far north and, although her sail plan as seen here is reminiscent of that of the 'Flat', the fidded topmast, bowsprit and schooner bow are definitely not the appendages of that rig. The second feature is the position of the mainmast. It is slightly further forward than was normally found in a ketch and is in exactly the position one would expect to find the foremast of a schooner with this type of hull. It can be safely assumed that the change in rig took place when she came under west country ownership. She is still afloat and there are plans to preserve her.

Emily Warbrick Wood brigantine, Fleetwood, built 1872, Gibson, Fleetwood. 105.6 × 23.3 × 12ft. 167 tons gross, 142 tons net. *Official Number:* 67128. *Signal Hoist:* MNTW.

Emma Ernest Wood three-masted schooner, Faversham, built 1867, Jones, Milford Haven. 109.2 × 23.7 × 12.7ft. 216 tons gross. 163 tons net. *Official Number:* 70555. *Signal Hoist:* MQWV.

Emma Louise* Wood auxiliary ketch, Barnstaple, built 1883, W. Westacott, Barnstaple. 75.4 × 19.8 × 8.3ft. 66 tons net. *Official Number:* 84475. *Signal Hoist:* None.

Emperor* Wood auxiliary ketch, Bristol, built 1906, G.H. Down, Chepstow. 83.9 × 18.2 × 7.9ft. 97 tons gross, 63 tons net. *Official Number:* 117727. *Signal Hoist:* None

Empress Wood two-masted schooner, Dublin, built 1855, Jersey. 82.8 × 20.5 × 10.4ft. 93 tons gross. 80 tons net. *Official Number:* 10087. *Signal Hoist:* None

Enid* Wood ketch, Barnstaple, built 1898, J. & W. Francis, Pembroke Dock, Milford Haven. 61.4 × 18.1 × 7.1ft. 43 tons gross, 30 tons net. *Official Number:* 108435. *Signal Hoist:* None.

Epney Lass Wood ketch, Gloucester, built 1860 Saul, Gloucester. 64 tons net. *Official Number:* 27875. *Signal Hoist:* MQYK.

Ethel Edith* Wood ketch, Faversham, built 1892, Robert Peck, Ipswich. 88.5 × 23 × 7.9ft. 114 tons gross, 94 tons net. *Official Number:* 97684. *Signal Hoist:* MRQZ.

Eva Wood ketch, Portsmouth, built 1896, Emsworth. 29 tons net. *Official Number:* 95103. *Signal Hoist:* None.

Evolution Wood ketch, Portsmouth, built 1888, Emsworth. 55 tons net. *Official Number:* 95103. *Signal Hoist:* None.

Excelsior Wood ketch, Gloucester, built 1891, Brimscombe. 36 tons net. *Official Number:* 93400. *Signal Hoist:* None.

Express Wood ketch, Bridgwater, built 1861, Meagor, Swansea. 58 × 18.2 × 7.9ft. 45 tons gross. 40 tons net. *Official Number:* 27880. *Signal Hoist:* MQYL.

Fanny Crossfield Wood three-masted schooner, Barrow, built 1880, Paul Rodgers, Carrickfergus. 95.6 × 22.1 × 9.8ft. 119 tons gross. 93 tons net. *Official Number:* 76898. *Signal Hoist:* MFLJ.
Fanny Crossfield, Mary Miller and others from the same yard were handy little three-masters and have already been mentioned frequently. They were well liked by the men who sailed in them and it would be surprising if the four known to the writer were the only ones produced.

The *Mary Miller*, Irish-built, was the last English-owned schooner to cross topsail yards and, for this reason far more photographs of her will ultimately become available to the model-maker than there will be for any other vessel mentioned in this book. The reader will notice the dimensional variations in the vessels. These should not be attributed to the demands of customers but rather to the limitations in accuracy, which were to be expected in wooden shipbuilding. For the rest there are one or two oddities about the *Mary Miller*, which deserve a mention. The man who produced the curved bar across her windlass was obviously out to show what he could do because, when looked at in elevation, it was a perfect arc of a circle but in plan it was akin to a cupid's bow. I have never been sure whether it was cut from one piece of timber, or from two, but suspect the former as being the more difficult. It may have been the same man who fashioned the curved piece of timber behind the heel of the bowsprit but why it was put there is something of a mystery. Perhaps the heel was found to be going rotten or someone may have thought that another foot of bowsprit outboard would in some way be beneficial. It could have been done to increase the steeve of the spar slightly so that it carried through the run of the sheer. But it may have been done for no valid reason at all – it could have been such a

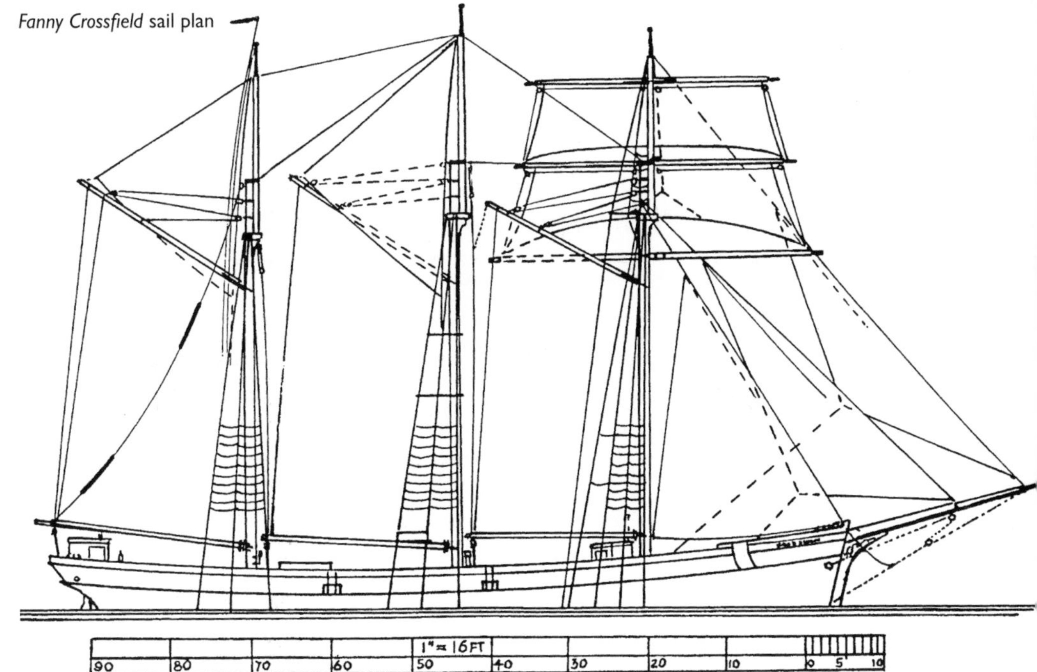

Fanny Crossfield sail plan

Fanny Crossfield and her sisterships lines plans

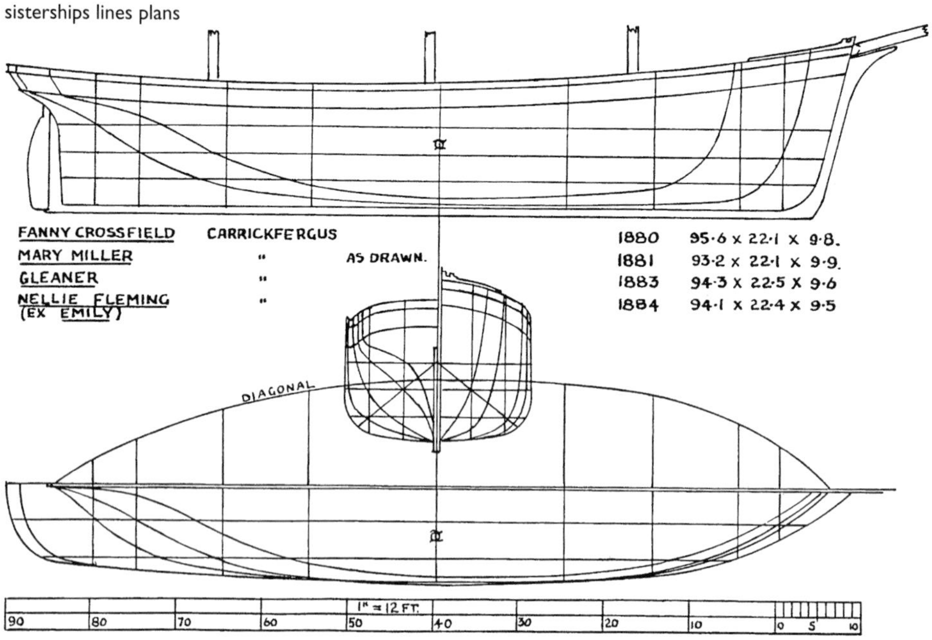

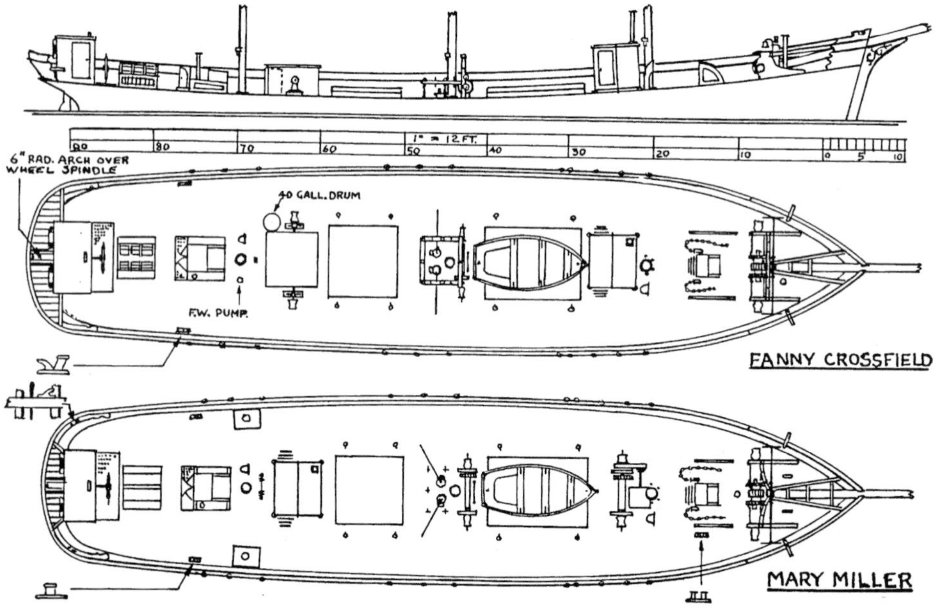

Profile and deck plans demonstating the differences between *Fanny Crossfield* and *Mary Miller*

beautifully-grained piece of naturally curved wood, that the shipwright, whoever he was, went around for weeks scratching his head until he finally found a place where he could put it to use. It would have shown up to advantage in the days when varnish was more liberally used than in the poverty-stricken 1920s and 30s.

Anyone extracting dimensions from the *Mary Miller* as she was in the last few years of her working life would do well to avoid using the battens on her shrouds as they were spaced rather wider than the 15in, which was once the standard pitch.

Fanny Jane* Wood ketch, Bridgwater, built 1858, Gough, Bridgwater. 77 × 18.2 × 6.9ft. 62 tons gross, 60 tons net. *Official Number:* 10941. *Signal Hoist:* MLVZ.

Florette* (ex-*Inski*, ex-*The Moto* ketch) Steel auxiliary ketch, Chester, built 1910, Edwards & Co., Millwall, London. 78 × 20.2 × 9ft. 110 tons gross, 77 tons net. *Official Number:* 127083. *Signal Hoist:* MLBF.

Flower of the Severn Wood ketch, Bristol, built 1841, Lydney. 45 tons net. *Official Number:* 3897. *Signal Hoist:* MDSW.

Flying Foam (ex-*Marie*) Wood two-masted schooner, Bridgwater, built 1861, Asplet, St. Malo, France. 85.2 × 18.9 × 10.5ft. 98 tons gross, 82 tons net. *Official Number:* 43846. *Signal Hoist:* MFMR. Some writers have stated that this vessel was built at St. Malo while others have argued that she was built in Jersey. I am indebted to Terry Belt and Dan McDonald for the answer to the mystery. There were two vessels with this name. The first was built at St. Malo in 1861, for Jersey owners. She was sold to French owners in 1879, renamed *Marie* and reregistered at Treguier. This was to make way for a new *Flying Foam*, built in Jersey in 1879. This new vessel was eventually lost in a collision in the Channel some time in 1899 or 1900. About the same time the *Marie* was bought by E. Perkins of Porlock Weir, given back her old name, and registered at Bridgwater. She was damaged in a collision in 1906 and rebuilt at Cardiff in 1919. In correspondence on this subject published in *Sea Breezes* in April 1954 it was established by Commander H.O. Hill that this was the vessel that was lost at Llandudno in January 1936. This timely information saved me from starting the drawings to the wrong set of dimensions. To avoid any further misunderstanding, the dimensions of both are given here:

Flying Foam (ex-*Marie*)
built St. Malo 1861.
85.21 × 18.91 × 10.5ft.

Flying Foam built Jersey by
Le Huquet, 1879.
88.4 × 20.4 × 10.5ft.

The *Flying Foam* of 1861, with which we are concerned, was rather low in her rig, a feature not surprising in view of her narrow beam. After spending most of her life without a dolphin striker, she finally blossomed out with one in her last few years – a fair indication that some weakness had been detected in her bowsprit. This may well have been the reason why she slackened off her bowsprit shrouds and hung them up from the fore rigging while in dock or being towed. Seventy-five years is not a bad working life for a schooner. Some of this can be attributed to pure luck, some to the rebuild in Cardiff, and some to the boys in Brittany who selected her timber and drove her bolts. If her chains had been stronger, her life might well have been longer.

Forward Wood three-masted schooner, London, built 1876, Stephen & Co., Peterhead.
85.3 × 22 × 10.4ft.
113 tons gross, 99 tons net.
Official Number: 75248.
Signal Hoist: None.

Frances & Jane Wood three-masted schooner, Plymouth, built 1878, Vaux & Co., Harwich. 110.8 × 25.7 × 12.6ft.
213 tons gross, 171 tons net.
Official Number: 78979.
Signal Hoist: MJLJ.

Francis* Wood three-masted schooner, Lancaster, built 1861, Reay, Hindpool, Barrow.
89 × 21.2 × 11ft.
130 tons gross, 127 tons net.
Official Number: 28007.
Signal Hoist: MQYR.

Flying Foam sail plan

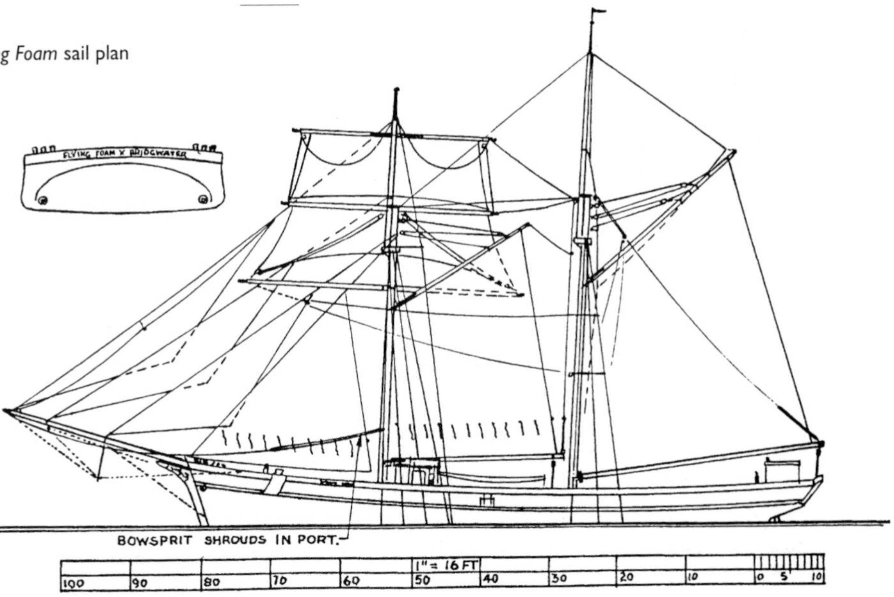

Flying Foam lines plans

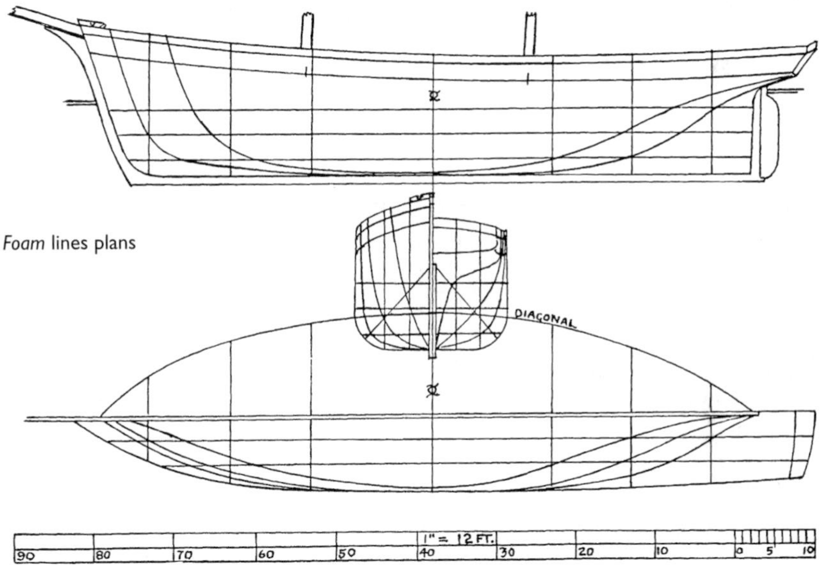

Flying Foam details

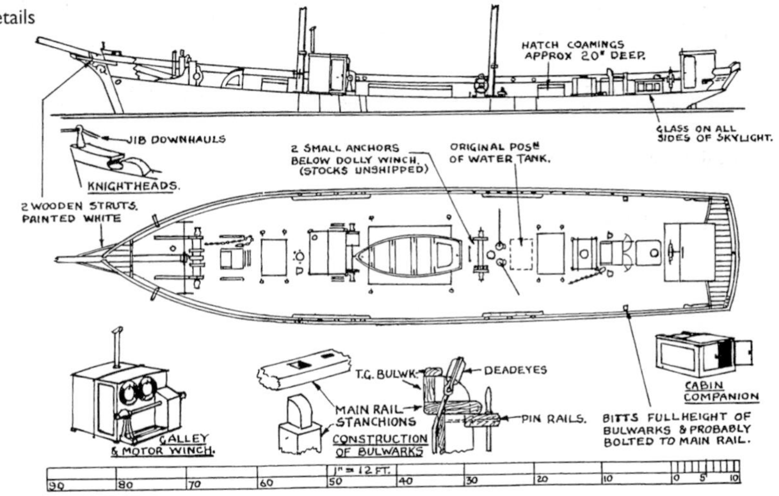

Gaelic* Iron auxiliary barquentine, Dublin, built 1898, W. Thomas & Sons, Amlwch. 126.8 × 24 × 10.8ft. *Official Number:* 101760. *Signal Hoist:* EIGB. For further information see *Cymric.*

Garlandstone* Wood ketch, Milford, built 1909, J. Goss, Calstock. 76 × 20.2 × 9ft. 76 tons gross 62 tons net. *Official Number:* 128746. *Signal Hoist:* None. Recently refitted and now in full sailing trim as an exhibit at Morwhelham Quay, near Tavistock.

George* Wood ketch, Gloucester, built 1839, Gloucester. 64 tons net. *Official Number:* 11638. *Signal Hoist:* None.

George Henry Wood two-masted schooner, Carnarvon, built 1864, Owens, Pwllheli. 75.7 × 20 × 10.7ft. 100 tons gross. 80 tons net. *Official Number:* 47758. *Signal Hoist:* MGRG.

Gertrude Wood ketch, Gloucester, built 1875 Saul, Gloucester. 35 tons net. *Official Number:* 69912. *Signal Hoist:* None.

Gipsy Queen Wood ketch, Portsmouth, built 1855, Jersey. 37 tons net. *Official Number:* 9649. *Signal Hoist:* None.

Glenmore Wood ketch, Rochester, built 1902, Rochester. 61 tons net. *Official Number:* 113710. *Signal Hoist:* MGJS.

Glenrosa Wood auxiliary ketch-barge, Harwich, built 1884, Parsons & Cann, Harwich. 87 × 20 × 6ft. 70 tons gross, 46 tons net. *Official Number:* 84037. *Signal Hoist:* MGSY.

Goldfinch* Wood two-masted schooner-barge, Faversham, built 1894, J.M. Goldfinch, Faversham. 98.5 × 22.8 × 9ft. 144 tons gross. 117 tons net. *Official Number:* 89869. Signal Letters: PNVS.

Gold Seeker Wood two-masted schooner, Douglas, Isle of Man, built 1873, Douglas. 56 tons net. *Official Number:* 67283. *Signal Hoist:* None.

Halcyon* Steel auxiliary ketch, Hull, built 1903, H. Scarr, Hessle. 84.3 × 20 × 7.8ft. 101 tons gross. 57 tons net. *Official Number:* 116167. *Signal Hoist:* MGGP.

Haldon* Wood auxiliary ketch, Bideford, built 1893, Hawke Bros., Plymouth. 88 × 21.6 × 9.9ft. 113 tons gross, 77 tons net. *Official Number:* 85958. *Signal Hoist:* MQKS.

Hanna* Steel auxiliary two-masted schooner, Poole, built 1915, J.J. Patje & Zoom, Waterhuizen, Netherlands. 91.3 × 21.1 × 7.9ft. 120 tons gross, 81 tons net. *Official Number:* 144984. *Signal Hoist:* None.

Hannah* Wood auxiliary ketch, Gloucester, built 1872, Framilode, Gloucester. 58 tons gross. 40 tons net. *Official Number:* 63098. *Signal Hoist:* None.

Happy Harry* Wood auxiliary three-masted schooner, Whitehaven, built 1894, Duddon Shipbuilding Co., Duddon, Lancs. 101.2 × 23 × 10.3ft. 142 tons gross, 115 tons net. *Official Number:* 102462. Signal Letters: EIMZ.

Hare Bell Wood three-masted schooner, Lerwick, built 1864, Hutchinson, Newcastle-on-Tyne. 102.2 × 26 × 14.6ft. 231 tons gross, 194 tons net. *Official Number:* 80290. *Signal Hoist:* None.

Harvest King* Wood auxiliary three-masted schooner, Londonderry, built 1879, Brundrit & Co., Runcorn. 91.3 × 21.7 × 10.5ft. 119 tons gross. 81 tons net. Official Number 80290. *Signal Hoist:* EIGN.

Hawarden Castle (ex-*Columbus*, ex-*Emma Linneman*) Steel auxiliary three-masted schooner, Chester, built 1907, C. Lühring, Hammelwarden, Germany. 115.5 × 24.1 × 9.4ft. 210 tons gross, 147 tons net. *Official Number:* 146400. *Signal Letters:* MNDJ.

Heartsease (ex-*Adela*) Wood auxiliary two-masted schooner, Southampton, built 1903, Southampton. 122 tons net. *Official Number:* 114585. *Signal Hoist:* MGFM.

Hector Cundy (ex-*Cecil Brindley*) Wood two-masted schooner, Plymouth, built 1871, Aberdovey. 87 tons net. *Official Number:* 56416. *Signal Letters:* MLQK.

Helena Anna Wood three-masted schooner, Fowey, built 1870, Axel Drenthe, Perkela, Netherlands. 106.2 × 25.2 × 11.7ft. 179 tons gross. 134 tons net. *Official Number:* 85257. *Signal Hoist:* MQRT.

Gaelic details

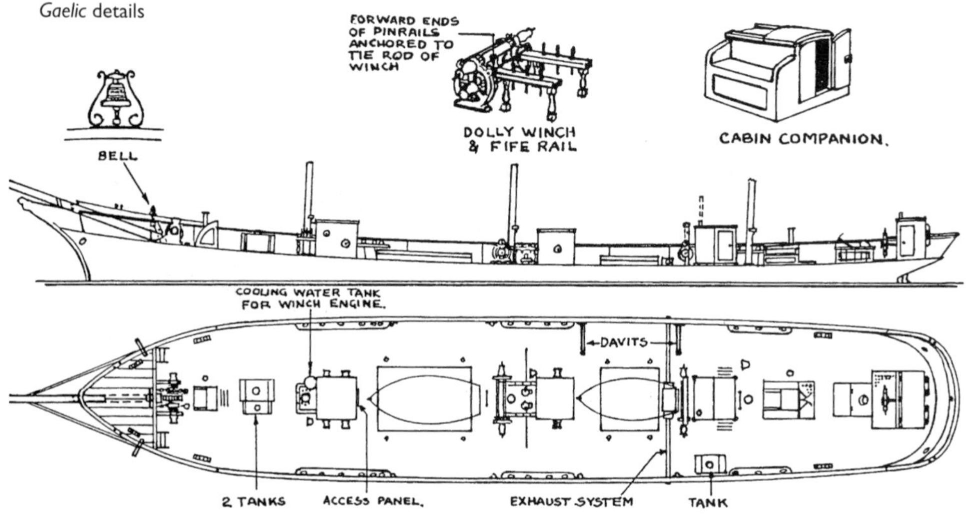

Henrietta sail plan

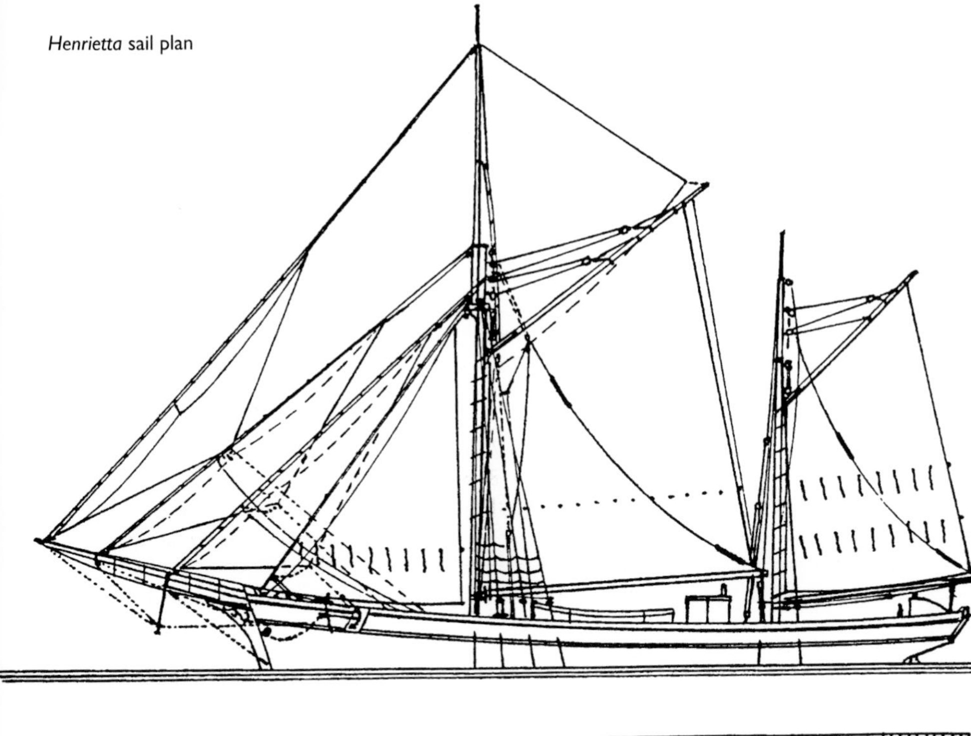

Helen Bate Wood two-masted schooner, Liverpool, built 1906, Runcorn. 68 tons net. *Official Number:* 145946. *Signal Hoist:* None.

Henrietta Wood two-masted ketch, Truro, built 1898, Stephens, Malpas. 74.9 × 19.9 × 9.4ft. 65 tons net. *Official Number:* 78963. *Signal Letters:* MJJV. This little ketch has several claims to fame. I first came across her in Canning Dock, Liverpool, where most of the County Down vessels used to discharge granite kerbstones before proceeding upriver to Garston to load coal for the return passage. However, it was only in recent years that I discovered anything of her subsequent history. She was purchased in 1937 by Mr. Herbert Ward, in Kilkeel, on behalf of Gordonstoun School, and was sailed from that port through the Caledonian Canal, by Ward, Godfrey Wicksteed

Henrietta details

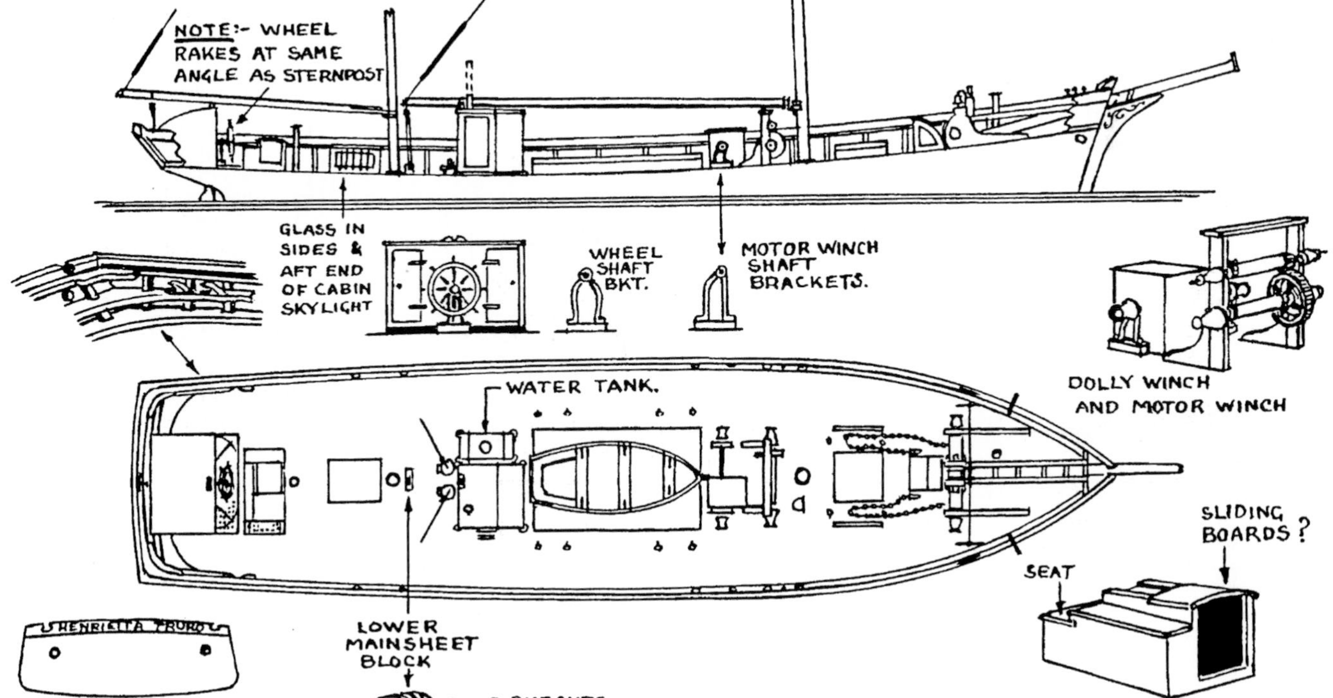

(Owen Wicksteed's cousin), and others, to Hopeman on the Moray Firth, where she was fitted with a diesel engine. Messrs Wicksteed and Ward, who were old shipmates from Alan Villiers's *Joseph Conrad*, then took her to Norway and back with a crew that included a young man then known as Prince Philip of Greece. After her return she passed back into Ward's hands. He had her re-rigged as a single topsail standing topgallant schooner, and she was eventually lost to fire. I am indebted to Herbert Ward and Godfrey Wicksteed for the loan of photographs from which her lines and some general information were extracted. Her deck gear is given as it was in her working days. The pinrail diagrams owe

DIAGONAL
1" = 12 FT.
80
70
60
50
40
30
20
10
0
5'
10

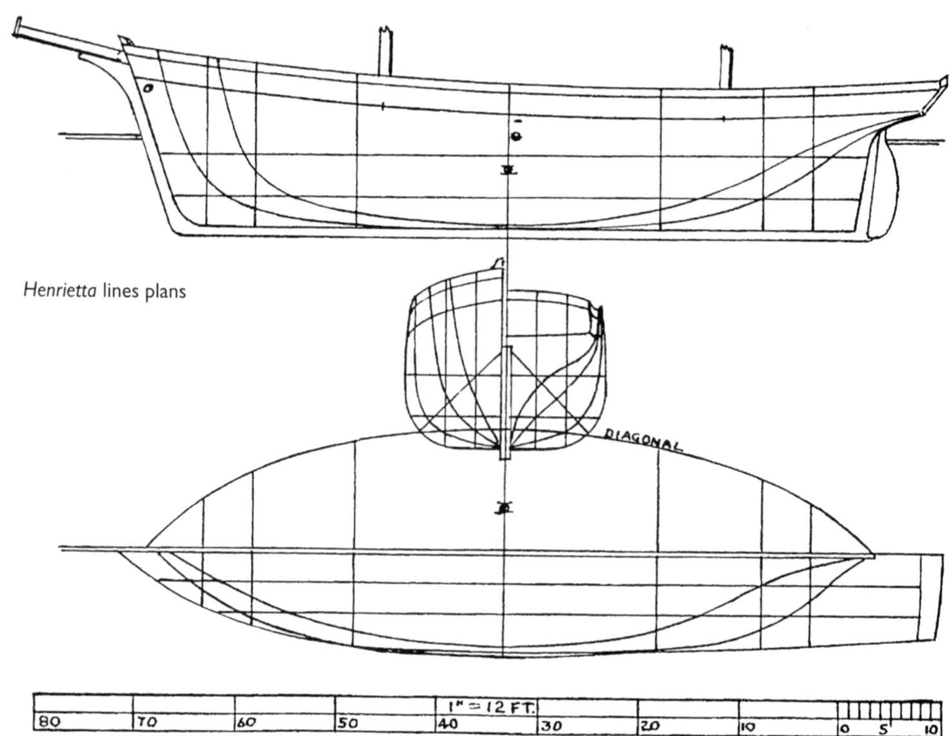

Henrietta lines plans

Henrietta pinrails

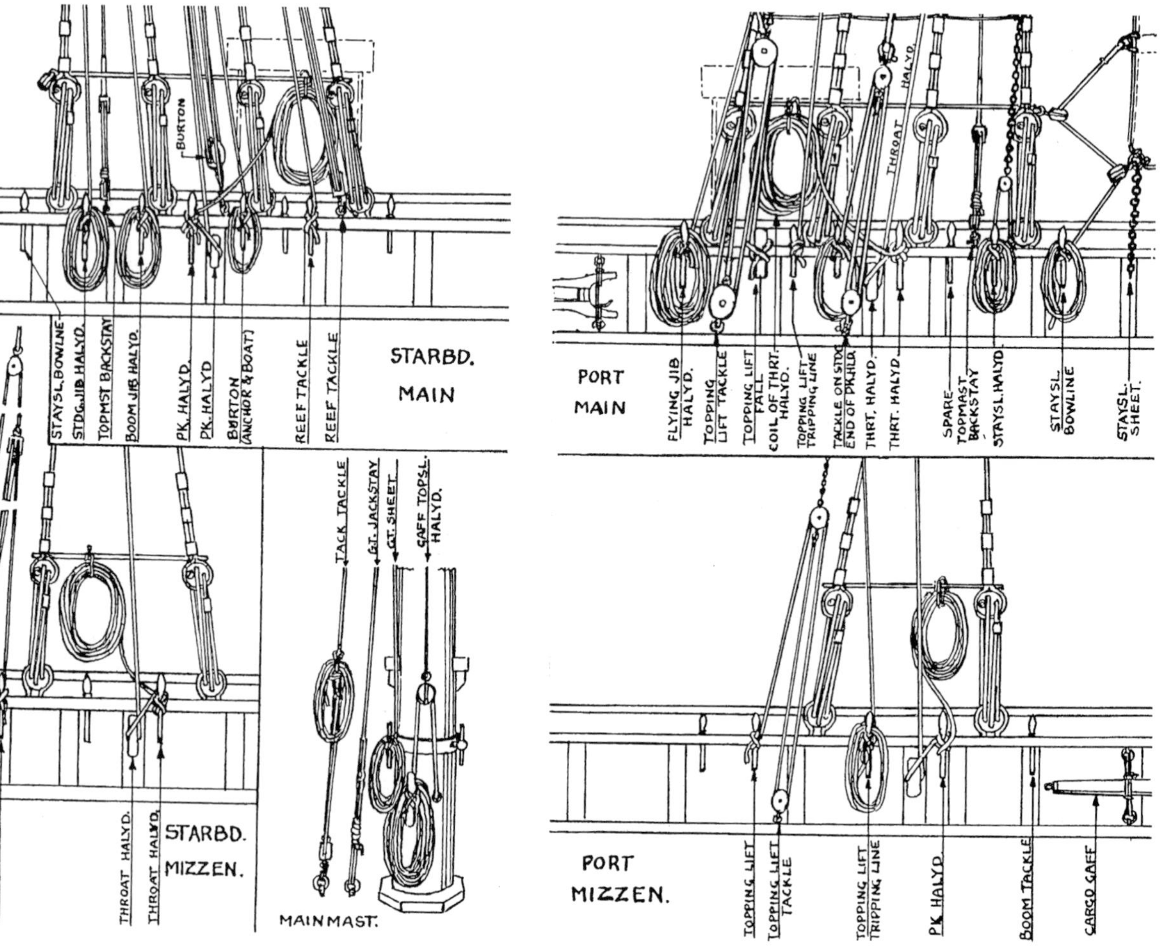

BURTON
STAYSL.BOWLNE
STDG.JIB HALYD.
TOPMST BACKSTAY
BOOM JIB HALYD.
PK. HALYD.
PK. HALYD
BURTON (ANCHOR & BOAT)
REEF TACKLE
REEF TACKLE
STARBD. MAIN
THROAT
HALYD.
PORT MAIN
FLYING JIB HALYD.
TOPPING LIFT TACKLE
TOPPING LIFT FALL
COIL OF THRT. HALYD.
TOPPING LIFT TRIPPING LINE
TACKLE ON STAY END OF PK.HLD
THRT. HALYD.
THRT. HALYD.
SPARE TOPMAST BACKSTAY
STAYSL.HALYD.
STAYSL. BOWLINE
STAYSL. SHEET.
BOAT BURTON
BOAT BURTON
THROAT HALYD.
THROAT HALYD.
STARBD. MIZZEN.
TACK TACKLE
G.T. JACKSTAY
G.T. SHEET
GAFF TOPSL. HALYD.
MAINMAST.
PORT MIZZEN.
TOPPING LIFT
TOPPING LIFT TACKLE
TOPPING LIFT TRIPPING LINE
PK HALYD
BOOM TACKLE
CARGO GAFF

Hilda sail plan

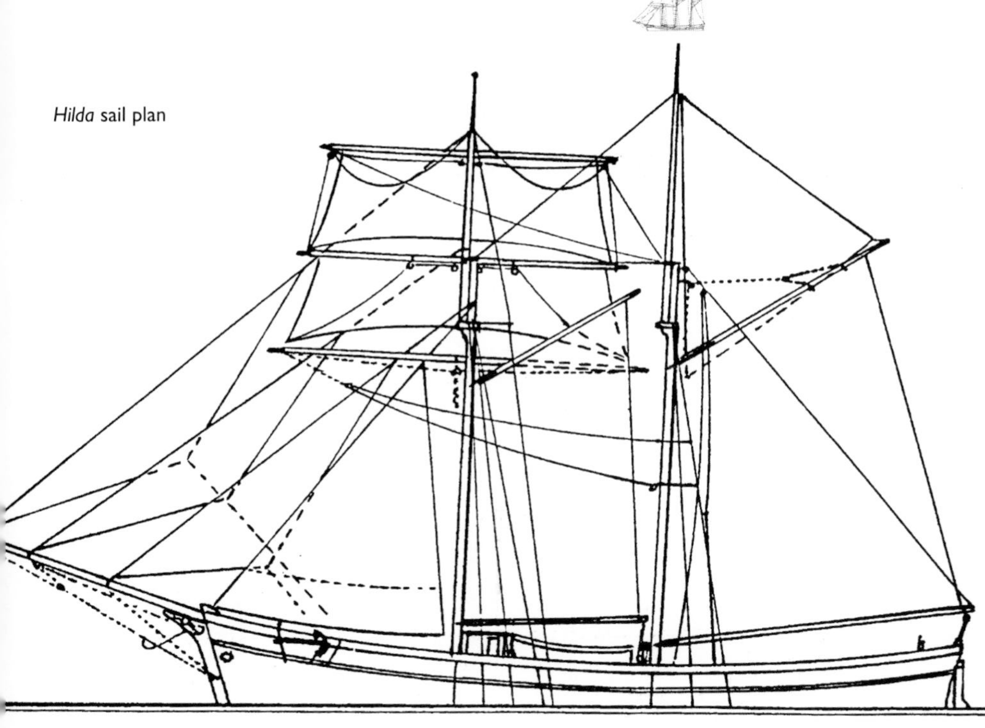

something to these photographs but in the main have been based on general practice.

Hetty* Wood auxiliary two-masted schooner, Falmouth, built 1877, John Stephens, Feock, Truro. 87.2 × 20.7 × 11.2ft. 107 tons gross. 67 tons net. *Official Number:* 74428. *Signal Hoist:* MJKK.

H. F. Bolt* Wood ketch, Bideford, built 1876, J. Johnson, Bideford. 71.6 × 19.6 × 8.7ft. 62 tons gross, 51 tons net. *Official Number:* 76713. *Signal Hoist:* MJKJ.

Hilda Wood two-masted schooner, St. Ives, built 1867, Widnes. 79.3 × 19.7 × 9.2ft. 72 tons net. *Official Number:* 56589. *Signal Hoist:* MQDK. As with a number of vessels in this schedule, the *Hilda* is not listed in either *Lloyd's Register* or the *Mercantile Navy List* for 1935. However, we do know she was operational in 1935, as were others in the schedule, some of whom were also working actively after the 1939-1945 War.

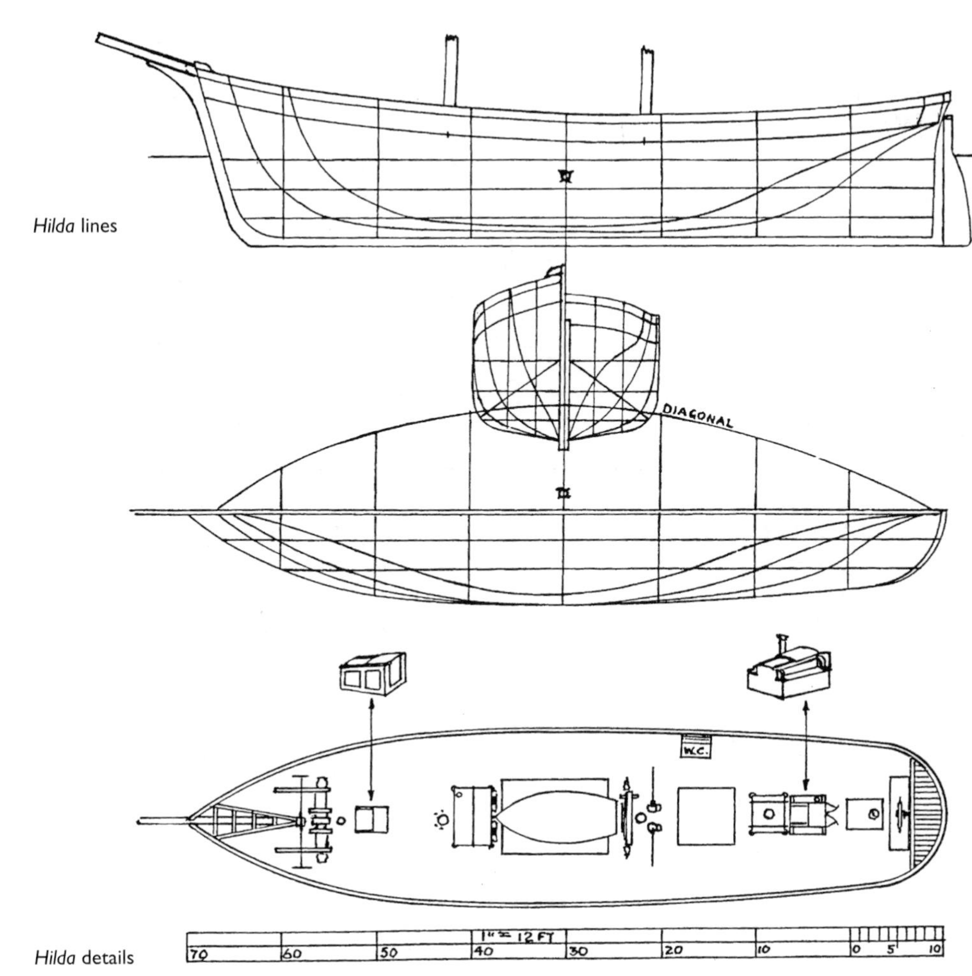

Hilda lines

Hilda details

Hobah Wood auxiliary ketch, Bideford, built 1879, T. Gray, Trellew Creek, Mylor. 78.6 × 19.9 × 9ft. 77 tons gross, 55 tons net. *Official Number:* 81154. *Signal Hoist:* MGFD.

Hope Wood ketch, Plymouth, built 1891, Plymouth. 20 tons net. *Official Number:* 97479. *Signal Hoist:* None.

Houton Head Wood ketch, Kirkwall, built 1900, St. Monance, Fife. 47 tons net. *Official Number:* 132497. *Signal Hoist:* None.

Hydrogen Wood ketch, London, built 1906, G. Gill & Sons, Rochester. 94.8 × 22 × 7.3ft. 98 tons net. *Official Number:* 123640. *Signal Hoist:* MDLF.

Independent Wood ketch, Bristol, built 1823, Brimscombe, Gloucester. 46 tons net. *Official Number:* 3926. *Signal Hoist:* None.

Invermore* Wood auxiliary three-masted schooner, built 1921, J. Tyrrell & Sons, Arklow. 92 × 22.4 × 11ft. 146 tons gross, 78 tons net. *Official Number:* 144972. *Signal Hoist:* EINC.

Irene Wood auxiliary ketch, Bridgwater, built 1907, Carver, Bridgwater. 85.5 × 21.1 × 9.1ft. 97 tons gross, 67 tons net. *Official Number:* 111394. *Signal Hoist:* MCQW. This vessel, the last of her kind built at Bridgwater, remains in a seagoing condition having been carefully maintained as a charter vessel. She has been much altered from her trading days with a large deckhouse forward of her wheel, which does nothing to assist the helmsman! Of the old trading schooners and ketches, however, she is the only one in a suitable condition to enable her to continue passage making. At the time of writing she is understood to be engaged on the Venezuelan coast.

Irish Minstrel Wood auxiliary three-masted schooner, Chester, built 1879, Connick & Co., Dundalk. 99.1 × 25 × 11.4ft. 154 tons gross, 126 tons net. *Official Number:* 76253. *Signal Hoist:* MFPM. This vessel's reputation for slow passages has been mentioned several times and, in an attempt to prove my contention that she was underpowered for her size, I decided to compare her with another schooner, and chose the *Mary Sinclair* as an average vessel of roughly the same proportions and with nothing about her that could be considered as extreme. For the purpose of the comparison I assumed that both vessels had the same block coefficient, which I took as 0.7, although I am sure that neither of them had so high a figure. The *Mary Sinclair* probably had the finer lines of the two, but to work on a lower block coefficient would have been to load the dice too heavily in her favour. It turned out that each square foot of canvas she possessed had to push 3.7 cubic feet of hull through the water, whereas in *Irish Minstrel* the figure was 4.2 cubic feet. The final comparison was made with *Irish Minstrel* under her

Irish Minstrel sai plan rigged as a brigantine

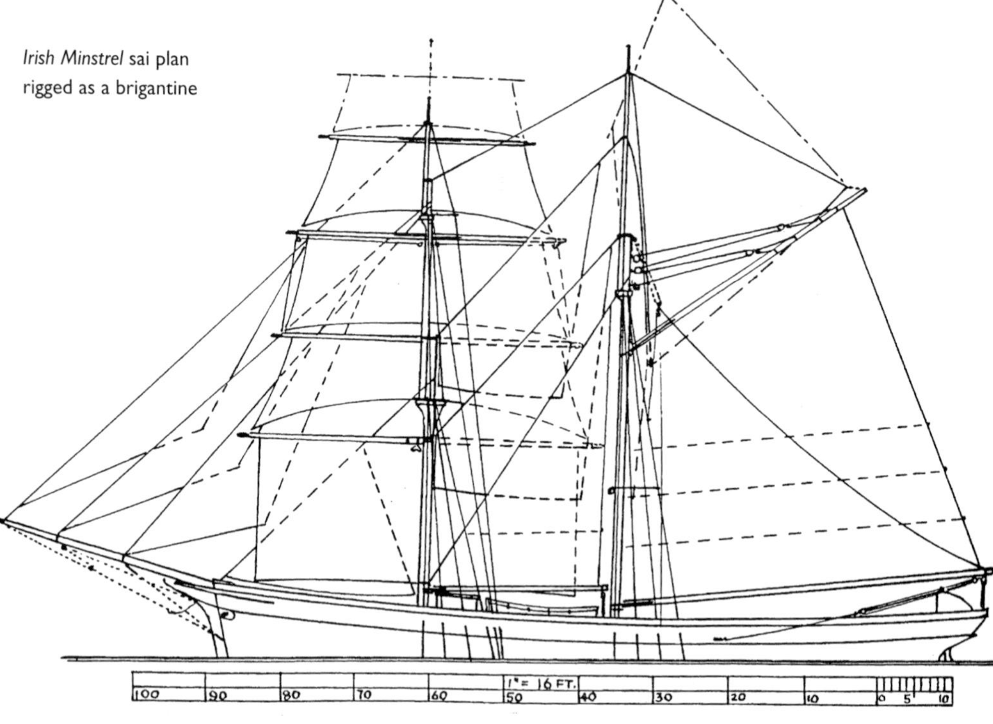

Irish Minstrel sail plan

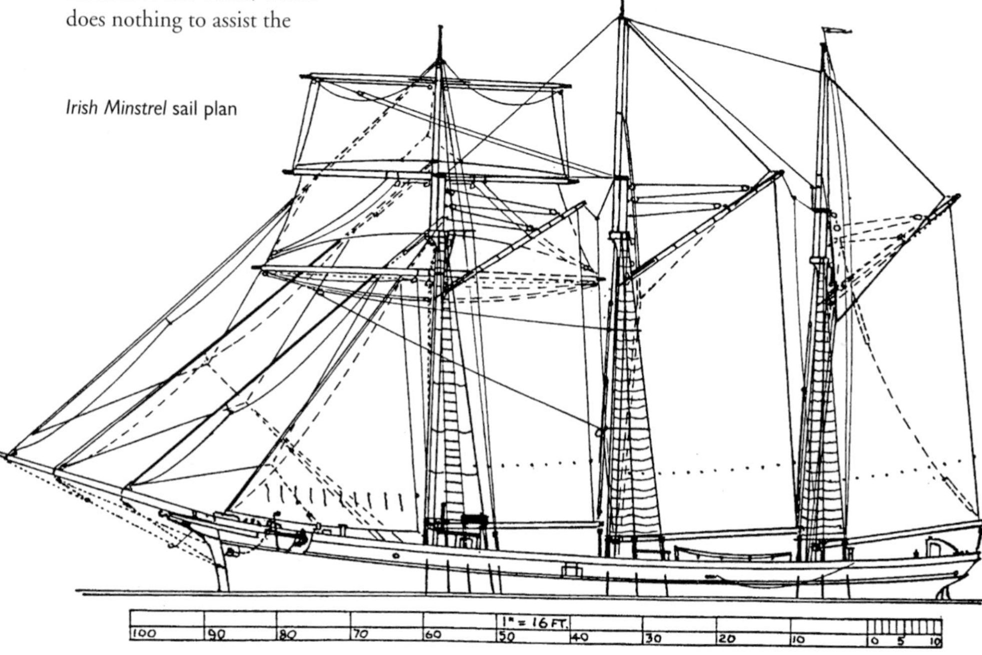

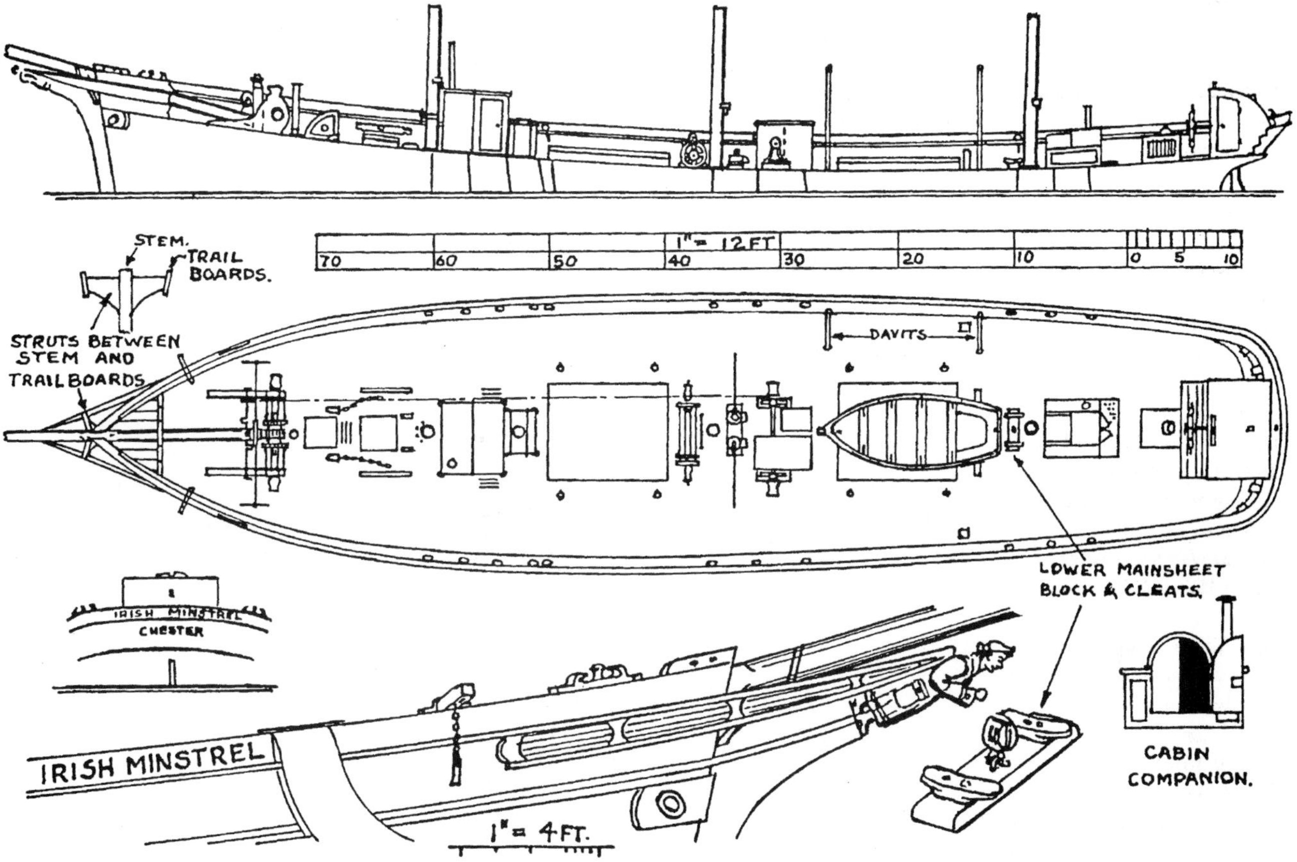

STEM.
TRAIL BOARDS.
STRUTS BETWEEN STEM AND TRAILBOARDS
1" = 12 FT
70 60 50 40 30 20 10 0 5 10
DAVITS
LOWER MAINSHEET BLOCK & CLEATS.
IRISH MINSTREL
CHESTER
IRISH MINSTREL
1" = 4 FT.
CABIN COMPANION.

Irish Minstrel details

original rig as a brigantine. This reconstruction was based on the assumption that her fore- and mainmasts were in their original position and that she was in possession of her original bowsprit, yards, main lowermast, and main topmast. This brought the figure down to 3.5 cubic feet; slightly in her favour – a result obtained without having to postulate the presence of a royal yard or an over-sized jackyard gaff-topsail. In all probability she had both in her original state. Against her own background she was hardly to be classed as a small or unimportant vessel. Drawing her as a brigantine brought out another of the few things she had in common with *Brooklands* – she too had carried a main boom 50ft long. These big mainsails must have performed like Trojans in a

DIAGONAL.
1" = 12 FT.
80 70 60 50 40 30 20 10 0 5 10

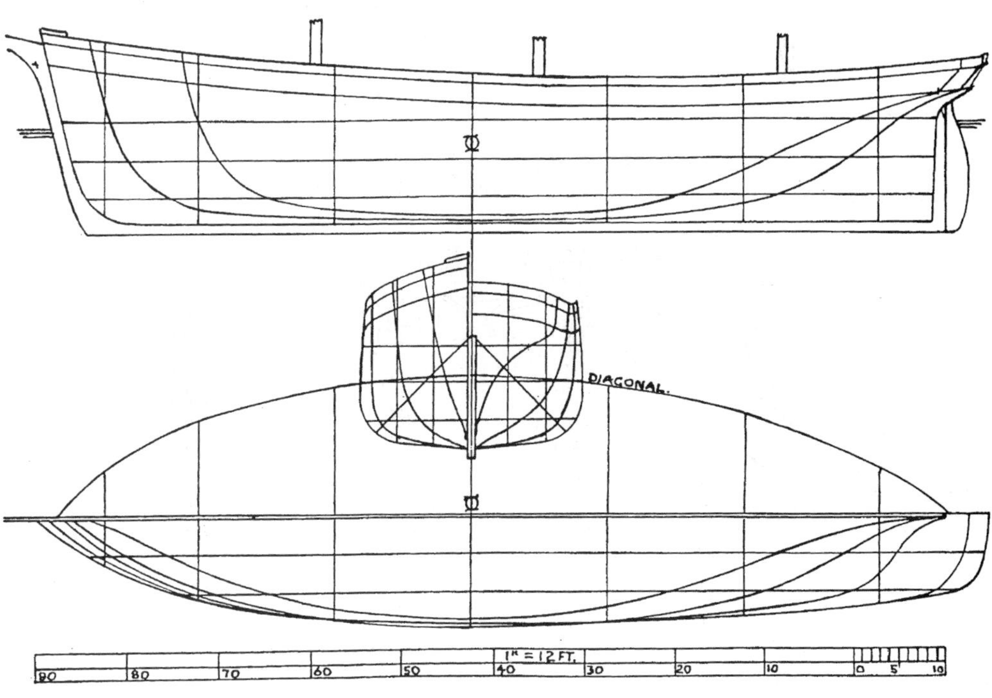

Irish Minstrel lines plans

hard thrash to windward but were undoubtedly a bit too much of a good thing when it came to shortening down.

Irishman Wood ketch, Galway, built 1879, Arklow. 33 tons net.
Official Number: 89019.
Signal Hoist: None.

Isabel Wood auxiliary ketch, Fowey, built 1897, J. & W. Francis, Milford Haven.
63 × 18.1 × 6.9ft.
52 tons gross, 32 tons net.
Official Number: 108427.
Signal Letters: None.

Isabel* Wood auxiliary fore-and-aft schooner, Dublin, built 1857, Murray Harbour, Prince Edward Island.
88 × 21.4 × 9.7ft.
118 tons gross, 52 tons net.
Official Number: 39204.
Signal Hoist: EIGM.

Isabel* Wood auxiliary ketch, Bideford, built 1878, Sunderland. 81 tons net.
Official Number: 79029.
Signal Hoist: MFCH.

Isabella* Wood auxiliary ketch, Gloucester, built 1872, Freckleton, Gloucester.
72 tons net.
Official Number: 62772.
Signal Hoist: MCFC.

Isabella* Wood two-masted schooner, Barrow, built 1879, William Ashburner, Barrow.
88.5 × 21.2 × 9ft.
97 tons gross, 75 tons net.
Official Number: 76889.
Signal Hoist: None.

Looking at the sisterships, *Isabella*, *Useful*, *James Postlethwaite* and *M.E. Johnson*, it can be seen that the larger and later of these two sets of twins were a stretched versions of the smaller pair. In common with many other similar jobs, the increase in length was accompanied by an increase in beam and, in this case, an increase in depth of hold as well. It is obvious that someone was quite impressed by the two-masted pair and wanted a larger three-master on much the same model. The proof that this was the case lies in the length of the two sizes between perpendiculars, 88ft and 99ft respectively, both divisible by 11.

To achieve the required result the builder, William Ashburner of Barrow, would have had to put down a new set of lines on the floor of his loft and produce a new set of templates for the broader part of the middle body at least. However, a good deal of work could be saved by spacing out the 66 pitches of frames at 16in centres, which the first two undoubtedly had, to 66 pitches at 18in centres for the new vessel. With timber sided at 9in instead of 8in this would have worked out very well. Anyone who doubts whether a 19th-century

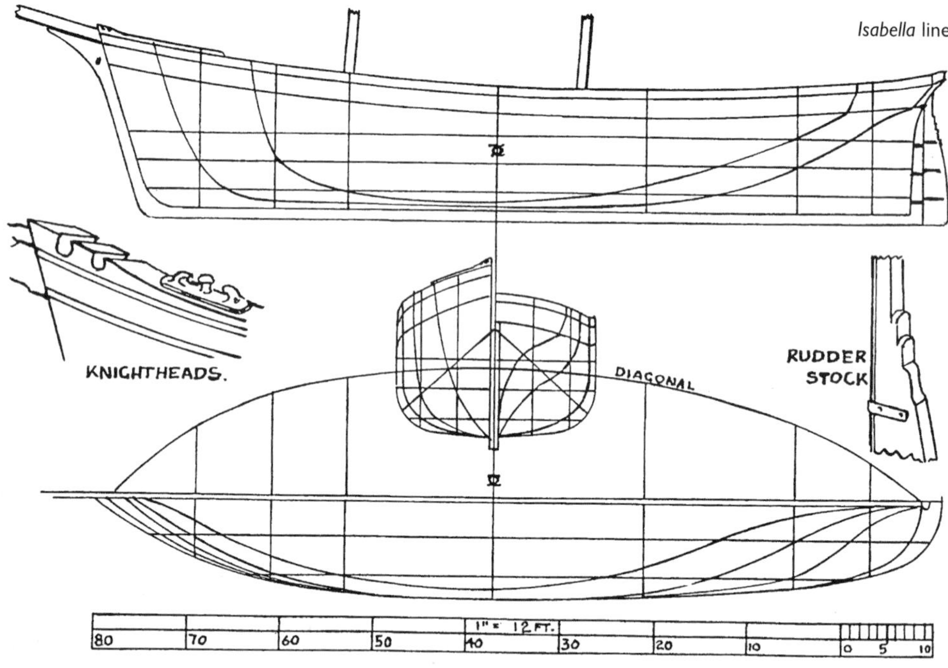

Isabella lines

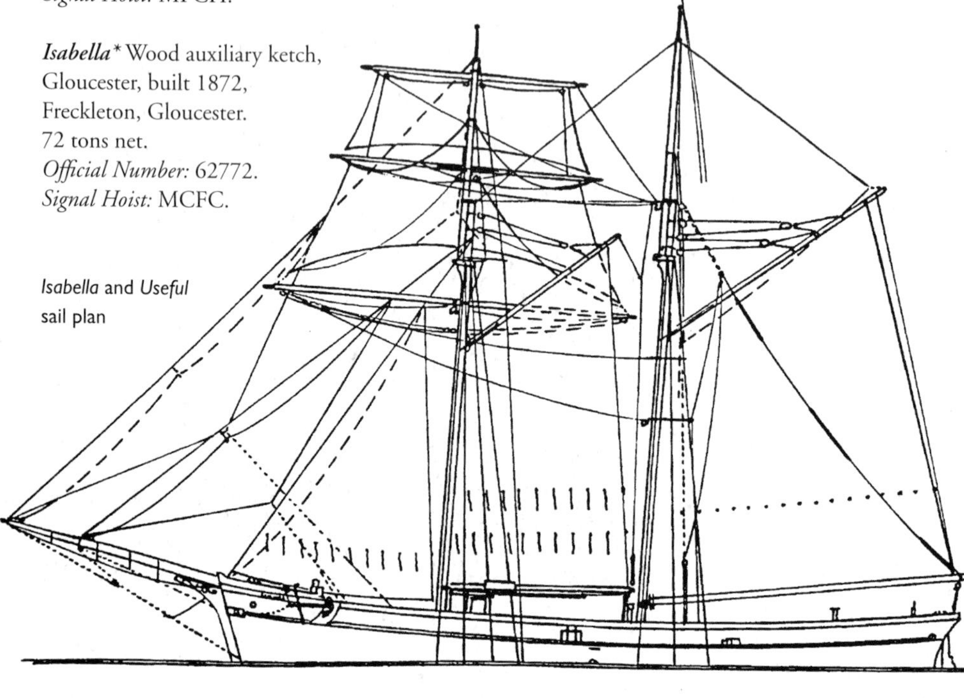

Isabella and *Useful* sail plan

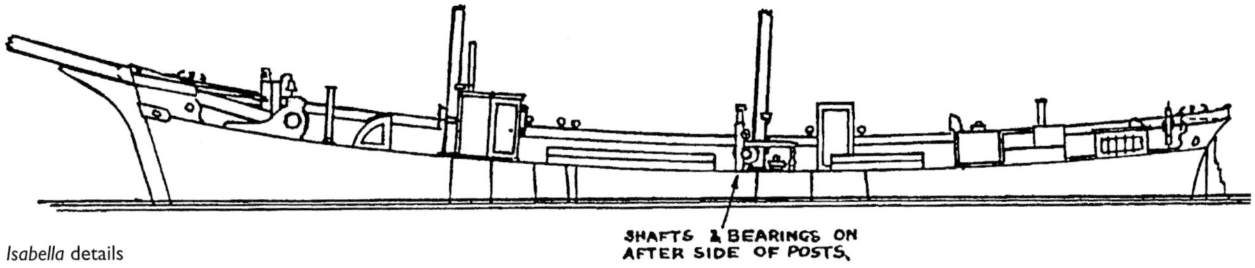

SHAFTS & BEARINGS ON AFTER SIDE OF POSTS.

WC

SEMI-CIRCULAR TOP ON CABIN COMPANION.

FLAT BAR

CHAIN PLATES "HALF ROUND" OR "FEATHER EDGE"

1" = 12 FT

80 70 60 50 40 30 20 10 0 5 10

Isabella details

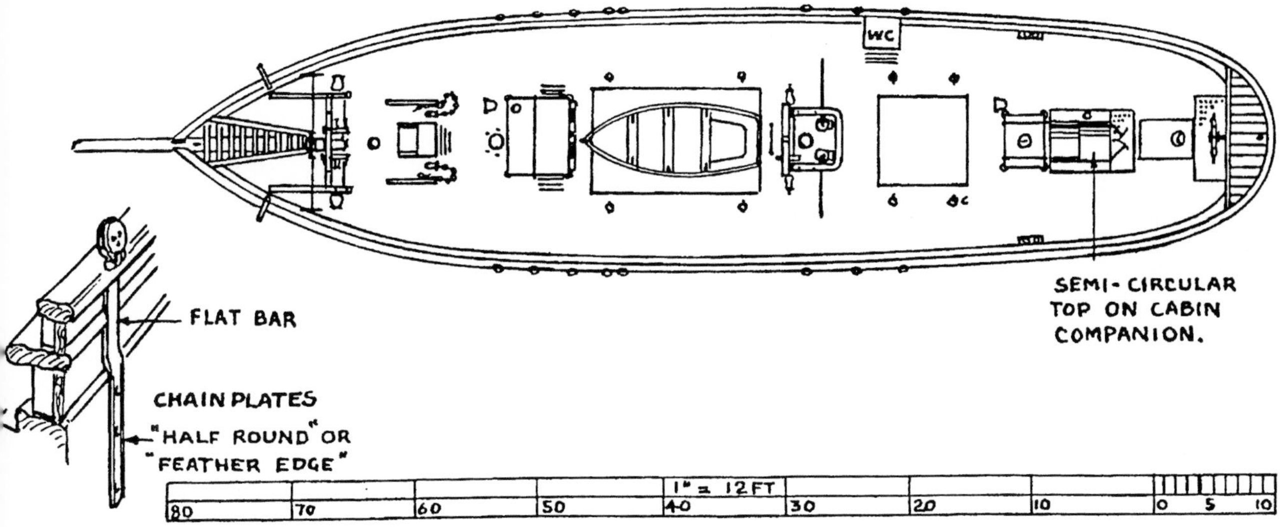

shipbuilder would go in for this sort of thing should take note that the ketch *New Design* of Bridgwater was built with doubled frames, each sided at 8in and spaced out at 32in centres,[4] obviously with no loss in strength; although what particular result was hoped for from this departure from standard practice is anyone's guess.

There were one or two odd points at which these vessels differed. *James Postlethwaite* and *M.E. Johnson* both had very wide topgallant rails, 8in or 9in at least, and, as a result, their pinrails were short lengths of timber set inwards from the main rail. Both vessels probably started life with main fife rails, like the smaller pair, but I cannot say that I ever thought to look for evidence to that effect. Three of them dispensed with the reef band in the topsail by the standard method of leaving the yard down on its lifts and deepening the topgallant; only the *Isabella* found another way out of the difficulty. Here only half the total hoist available to the yard was used but to keep its area small, the foot of the sail was given much more gore than usual. *Useful* also retained her topsail halyard, but only to give support to the middle of the yard. In the larger pair I suspect that the lifts were lengthened to allow the parrel to rest on the cap, which would have produced the same result.

The sterns of these four schooners were slightly more elegant than those of the average vessel with an 'out of doors' rudder and closely resembled those of Donald McKay's *Lightning* and *James Baines* in their extreme shortness of overhang. The fine upstanding masts of *Useful* and *Isabella* have already been mentioned and these allow a reasonably reliable check to be made in the amount of bend in the masts of the other two, which, one would assume, were put in with the same angle of rake. The results shown in Figure 14-45 (see *James Postlethwaite*) are quite surprising – the amount of bend does not seem excessive until the original line of the mast is drawn in.

Isallt Wood auxiliary three-masted schooner, Skibbereen, built 1909, David Williams, Portmadoc. 94.3 × 23 × 10.6ft. 134 tons gross, 84 tons net. *Official Number:* 122816. *Signal Hoist:* EICF.

Ivy P. Wood ketch, Dublin, built 1893, Peck, Ipswich. 79 tons gross, 66 tons net. *Official Number:* 97690. *Signal Hoist:* EIDC.

J. & A.R. Wood ketch, Gloucester, built 1894, Saul, Gloucester. 66 tons net. *Official Number:* 99535. *Signal Hoist:* None.

J. & M. Garrett Wood auxiliary three-masted schooner, Chester, built 1884, Barrow. 92.4 × 21.5 × 9.2ft. 104 tons gross, 75 tons net. *Official Number:* 88702. *Signal Hoist:* MFTC.

James Wood ketch, Cardigan, built 1864, Cardigan. 25 tons net. *Official Number:* 29670. *Signal Hoist:* MCPC.

[4] This information was obtained from an article in *Sea Breezes* published in the 1930s.

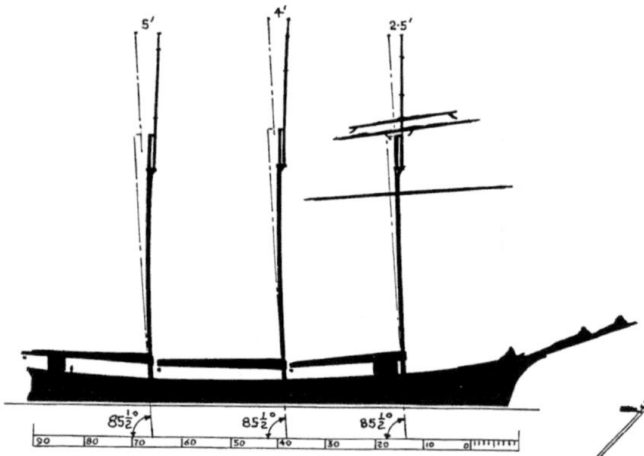
5'
4'
2·5'
85½°
85½°
85½°
90
80
70
60
50
40
30
20
10
0

James Postlethwaithe masting diagram

James Postlethwaithe and *M.E. Johnson* sail plan

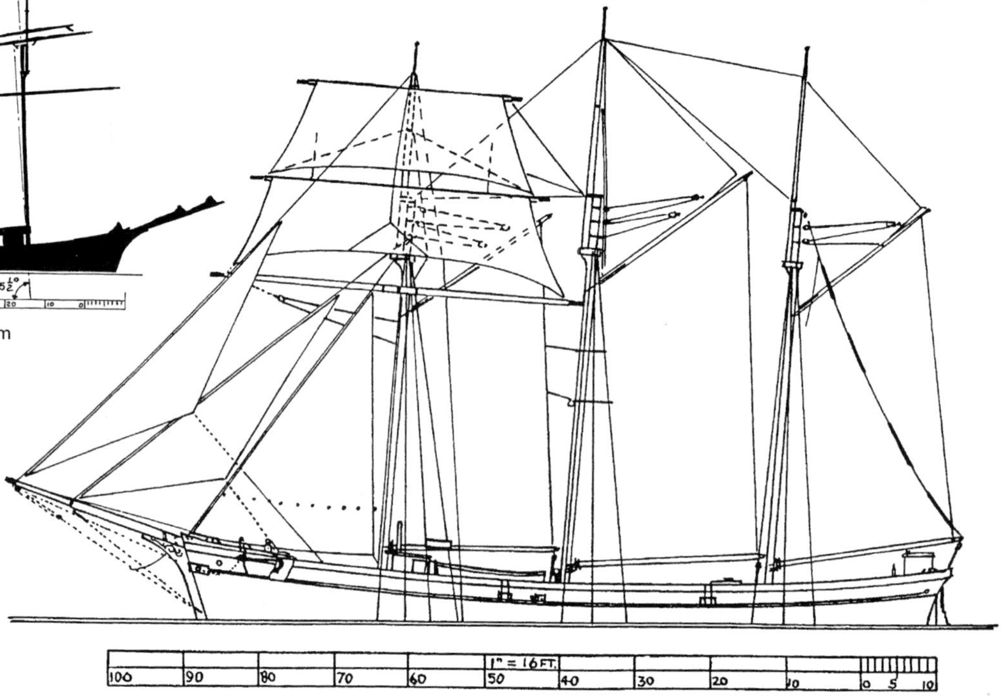
1" = 16 FT.
100
90
80
70
60
50
40
30
20
10
0
5
10

*James Postlewaite** Wood auxiliary three-masted schooner, Dublin, built 1881, William Ashburner, Barrow. 99.7 × 23 × 10.1ft. 134 tons gross, 87 tons net. *Official Number:* 83976. *Signal Hoist:* EIDR. For further information see *Isabella* of Barrow.

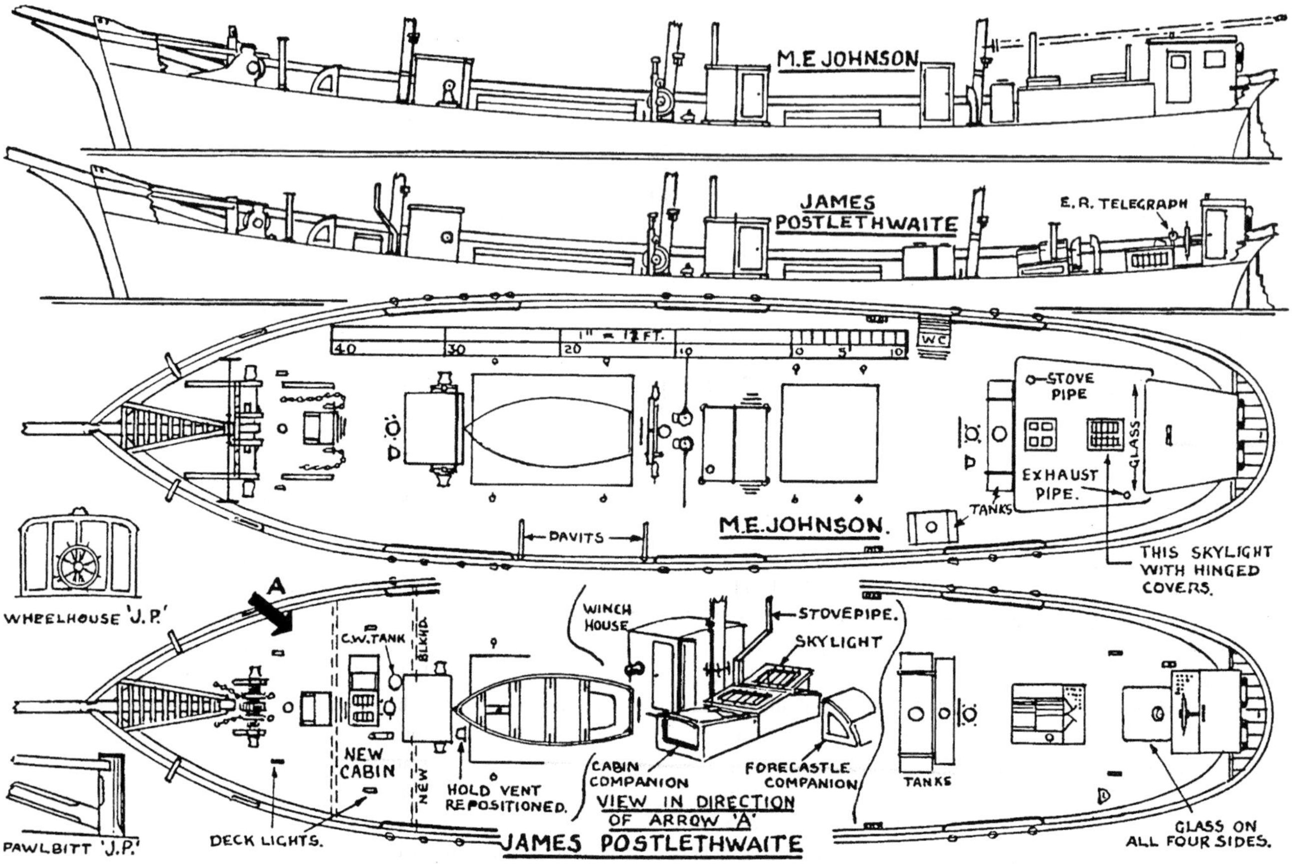
M.E JOHNSON
JAMES
POSTLETHWAITE
E. R. TELEGRAPH
1" = 12 FT.
40
30
20
10
0
5
10
WC
STOVE
PIPE
GLASS
EXHAUST
PIPE.
TANKS
DAVITS
M.E.JOHNSON.
THIS SKYLIGHT
WITH HINGED
COVERS.
WHEELHOUSE 'J.P.'
A
C.W. TANK
BLKHD.
WINCH
HOUSE
STOVEPIPE.
SKYLIGHT
NEW
CABIN
NEW
HOLD VENT
REPOSITIONED.
CABIN
COMPANION
FORECASTLE
COMPANION
VIEW IN DIRECTION
OF ARROW 'A'
TANKS
PAWLBITT 'J.P.'
DECK LIGHTS.
JAMES POSTLETHWAITE
GLASS ON
ALL FOUR SIDES.

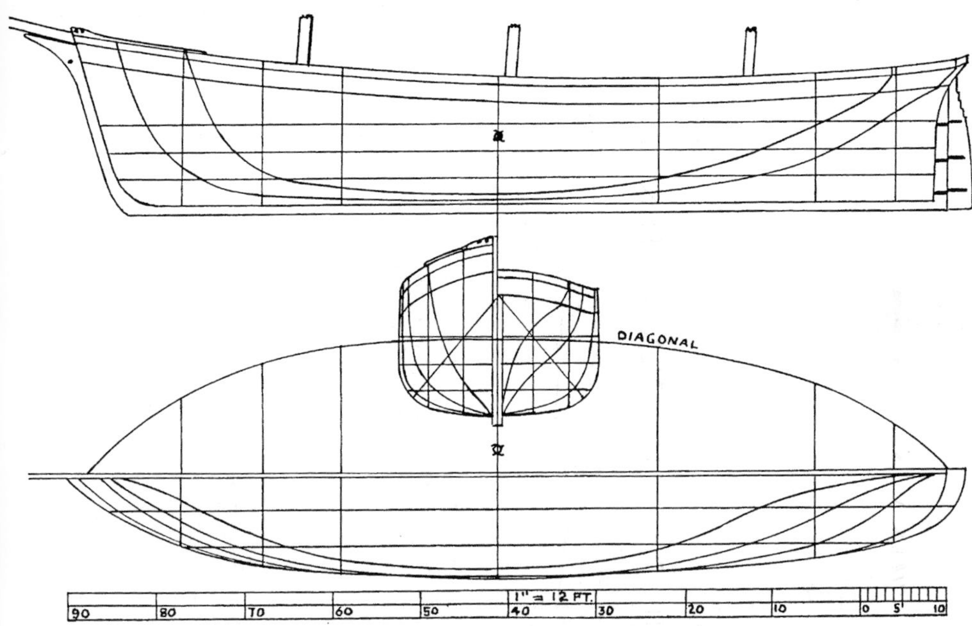

James Postlethwaithe lines plans

onslaught. I have examined every available photograph for signs of it – its presence would be visible on the outside of the bulwarks as well as on the deck – but without any success.

After completing the sail plan of this vessel I received a photograph of her from Dick Scott, in which her yards were absolutely square to the camera. This has proved that her upper topsail yard, as drawn, is 2ft shorter than it should be.

Janie Wood two-masted schooner, Truro, built 1876, Scoble, Malpas, Truro.
92.9 × 22.7 × 11.6ft.
135 tons gross, 105 tons net.
Official Number: 77425.
Signal Hoist: MQYP.

James & Ann Wood two-masted schooner, Belfast, built 1852, Tyrone. 40 tons net.
Official Number: 8203.
Signal Hoist: None

Jane Banks (ex-*Frau Minna Petersen*) Wood three-masted schooner, Fowey, built 1878, Jones, Portmadoc.
102 × 24.3 × 12.6ft.
176 tons gross. 142 tons net.
Official Number: 77428.
Signal Hoist: MJTS.
Two points about this vessel elude me. They are the raised quarter-deck and the 'Simon Jones Flare', both mentioned by Henry Hughes.[5] I have a photograph taken from her bowsprit end and the flare does not seem to be anything out of the ordinary. The flat – the ancestral type for the upper Irish Sea – was a vessel completely devoid of flare and Portmadoc can be considered as marginally inside its sphere of influence. But it is difficult to believe that until 1878 no one there had modified its lines to make it slightly less wet on the foredeck. This is especially the case when one considers that the *Englishman* built at Glasson in the heart of the 'Flat area', fourteen years before the *Frau Minna Peterson* was launched, had far more flare to her bows than any other British schooner that the writer has seen.

The raised quarter-deck is perhaps not quite so mysterious. By the time they were reaching the end of their working lives, most of the schooners were old enough to have had at least one really heavy overhaul, and this feature is one that could have been removed during one such

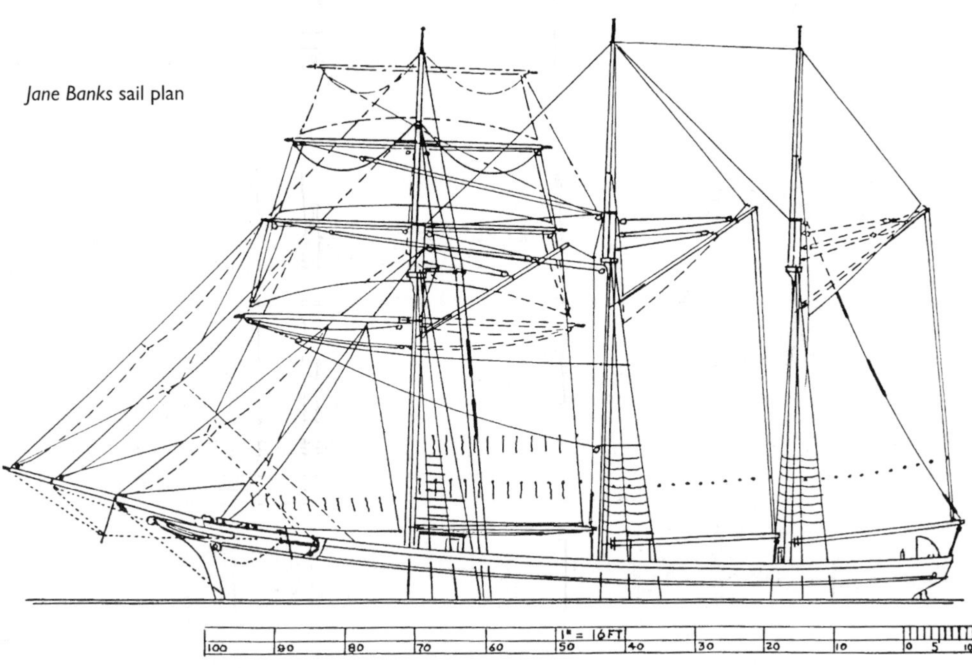

Jane Banks sail plan

J. Milton* Wood ketch, Bridgwater, built 1872, Saul, Gloucester. 84.5 × 22 × 9.5ft.
91 tons net.
Official Number: 65317.
Signal Hoist: None.

John Hannah Wood barquentine, Ramsgate, built 1868, Hannah, Garlieston.
91.6 × 22 × 11.5ft.

[5] *Immortal Sails* by Henry Hughes (Chapter 18, 'The Phosphate Carriers'), T. Stephenson & Sons Ltd, Prescot, Lancs. 1969

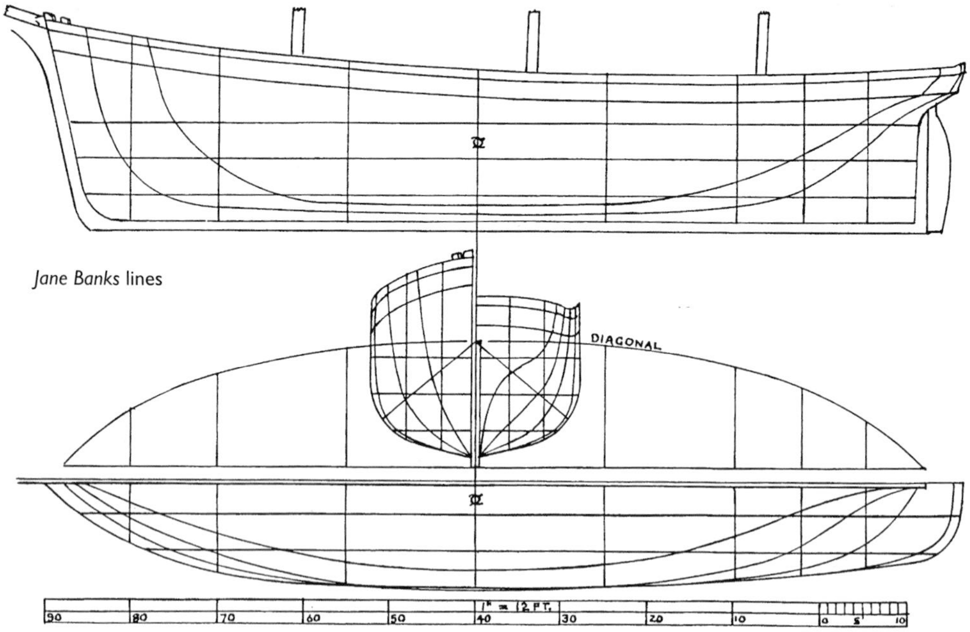

Jane Banks lines

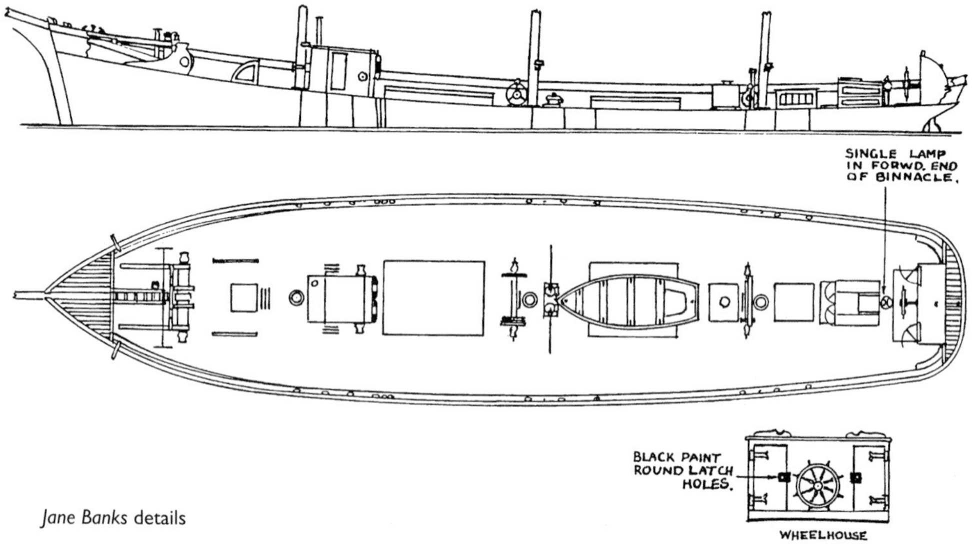

Jane Banks details

135 tons net.
Official Number: 62261.
Signal Hoist: None.

John Morrison Wood three-masted schooner, Dublin, built 1874, Tracey, Arklow. 105.5 × 25 × 12.4ft. 202 tons gross. 172 tons net. *Official Number:* 67774. *Signal Hoist:* None.

John Sims Wood two-masted schooner, Gloucester, built 1873, Trethowen, Falmouth. 89.9 × 21.4 × 10.8ft. *Official Number:* 68328. *Signal Hoist:* MCTM.

Jonadeb* Wood ketch, Bristol, built 1848, Newport. Rebuilt 1894. 68 tons net. *Official Number:* 26731. *Signal Hoist:* MQWD.

J. T. & S.* Wood auxiliary three-masted schooner, built 1918/20, John Tyrrell, Arklow. 85.3 × 21.8 × 10.6ft. 129 tons gross, 83 tons net. *Official Number:* 140457. Signal letters: EIMV.

Julie Wood ketch, Barnstaple, built 1889, Scoble, Malpas; operated by William R. Voysey, Topsham. 26 tons net. *Official Number:* 84514. *Signal Hoist:* MFPR.

Kate Wood auxiliary two-masted schooner, Barrow, built 1874, White, Ulverston. 82.8 × 20.8 × 9.7ft. 104 tons gross, 75 tons net. *Official Number:* 70473 *Signal Hoist:* None

Kate Wood ketch, Gloucester, built 1863, Waterford. 64 tons net. *Official Number:* 45357. *Signal Hoist:* MGGK.

Kathleen & May* (ex-*Lizzie May*) Wood auxiliary three-masted schooner, Bideford, built 1900, Ferguson & Baird, Connah's Quay, Cheshire. 98.4 × 23.2 × 10.1ft. 139 tons gross, 95 tons net. *Official Number:* 104473. *Signal Hoist:* MDNN. This vessel has been completely restored and was re-launched in March 2001; she will be re-rigged as a traditional topsail schooner at Bideford, which will remain her home port. In August 2001 she sailed for Youghal.

Katie* Wood auxiliary two-masted schooner, Padstow, built 1871, Cowl & Sons, Padstow. 88.5 × 23 × 10.9ft. 116 tons gross, 76 tons net. *Official Number:* 80410. *Signal Hoist:* MJFJ.

Ketch* Wood ketch, Bideford, built 1894, W. Fife & Son, Fairlie. 69 × 19.7 × 8.5ft. 56 tons net. *Official Number:* 99732. *Signal Hoist:* None.

Kindly Light* Wood ketch-barge, Ipswich, built 1904, J.W. & B. Harvey, Littlehampton. 91.4 × 22.3 × 7.8ft. 111 tons gross, 90 tons net. *Official Number:* 120780. *Signal Hoist:* MCFT.

K.T. Wood schooner, Dublin, built 1900, J. Tyrrell & Co., Arklow. 86 × 23 × 8ft. 76 tons net. *Official Number:* 111028. *Signal Hoist:* None.

Lady Agnes Wood ketch, Carnarvon, built 1877, St. Agnes. 70 tons net.

Official Number: 68865.
Signal Hoist: MCWN.

Lady Margaret Wood ketch, Greenock, built 1893, Fairlie. 40 tons net.
Official Number: 65343.
Signal Hoist: None.

Lady of Avenel (ex-*Virgo*, ex-*Island*) Wood auxiliary two-masted schooner, Falmouth, built 1874, H.S. Trethowan, Falmouth. 99.2 × 23 × 12.2ft. 163 tons gross, 139 tons net.
Official Number: 65343.
Signal Hoist: MKFZ.
Converted to a yacht.

Lady Quirk* (ex-*Raymond*) Wood three-masted schooner, Douglas, Isle of Man, built 1876, Lefurgey, Prince Edward Island. 104.8 × 24.3 × 12.9ft. 201 tons gross, 85 tons net.
Official Number: 74196.
Signal Hoist: MCSM.

Leading Light* Wood ketch barge, Ipswich, built 1906, J.W. & B. Harvey, Littlehampton. 92.3 × 22.6 × 7.8ft. 114 tons gross, 95 tons net.
Official Number: 122973.
Signal Hoist: MCTJ.

Lewisman Wood auxiliary ketch, Bideford, built 1878, Stornaway. 70.1 × 18.5 × 8.1ft. 66 tons gross, 46 tons net.
Official Number: 79131.
Signal Hoist: None.

Lily Wood ketch, Faversham, built 1873, Millwall, London. 85 tons net.
Official Number: 67256.
Signal Hoist: MJNW.

Linette (ex-*Drel Geschwister*) Steel three-masted schooner, King's Lynn, built 1908, Waterhuizen, Netherlands. 65 tons net.
Official Number: 139084.
Signal Hoist: MFYD.

Lisette Wood auxiliary two-masted schooner, Cowes, built 1873, Cowes. 69 tons net.
Official Number: 67582.
Signal Hoist: None.

Loch Ryan (ex-*Vlaardingen*, ex-*Catharina*) Steel auxiliary two-masted schooner, Skibbereen, built 1913, J.G. van der Werff, Hoogezand, Netherlands. 111.2 × 22.5 × 9ft. 210 tons gross, 166 tons net.
Official Number: 144585.
Signal Hoist: EIDS.

Lochranza Castle Wood two-masted schooner, Wick, built 1876, Ardrossen. 84.6 × 20.5 × 9.5ft. 75 tons net.
Official Number: 73463.
Signal Hoist: MFMC.
For additional information see *Mary Sinclair*.

London Premier (ex-*Oranje*) Steel auxiliary schooner, London, built 1905, Netherlands. 82 × 16.4 × 6.7ft. 92 tons gross, 51 tons net.
Official Number: 162498.
Signal Hoist: None.

Lord Churchill Wood ketch barge, Faversham, built 1888, J.W. Harvey, Littlehampton. 84.5 × 20.1 × 6.8ft. 76 tons gross, 60 tons net.
Official Number: 94389.
Signal Hoist: MNBQ.

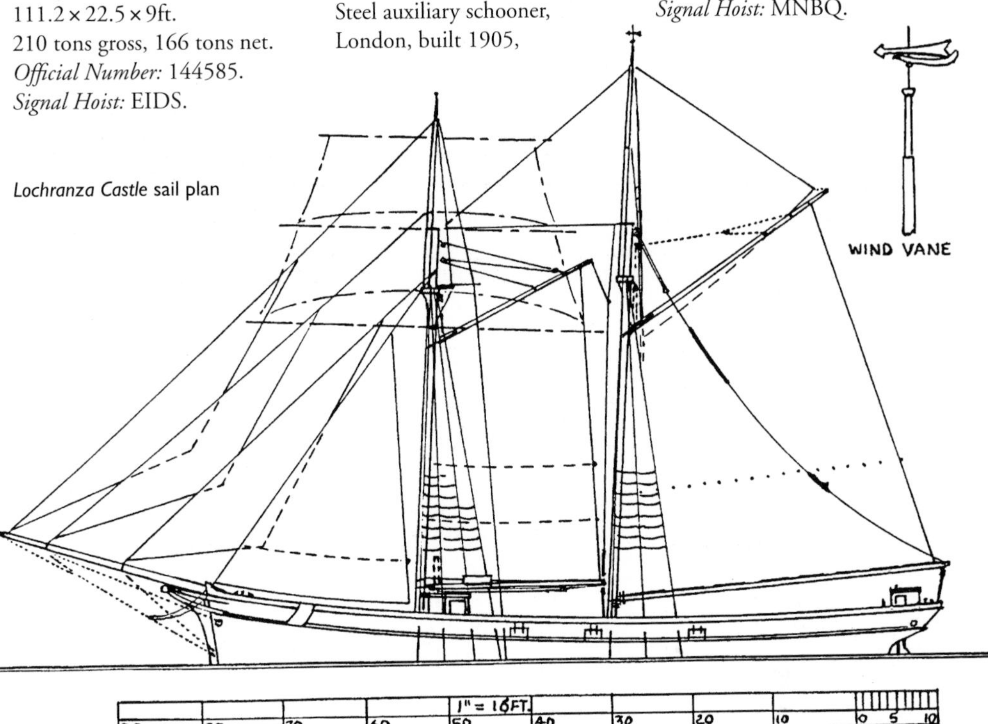

Lochranza Castle sail plan

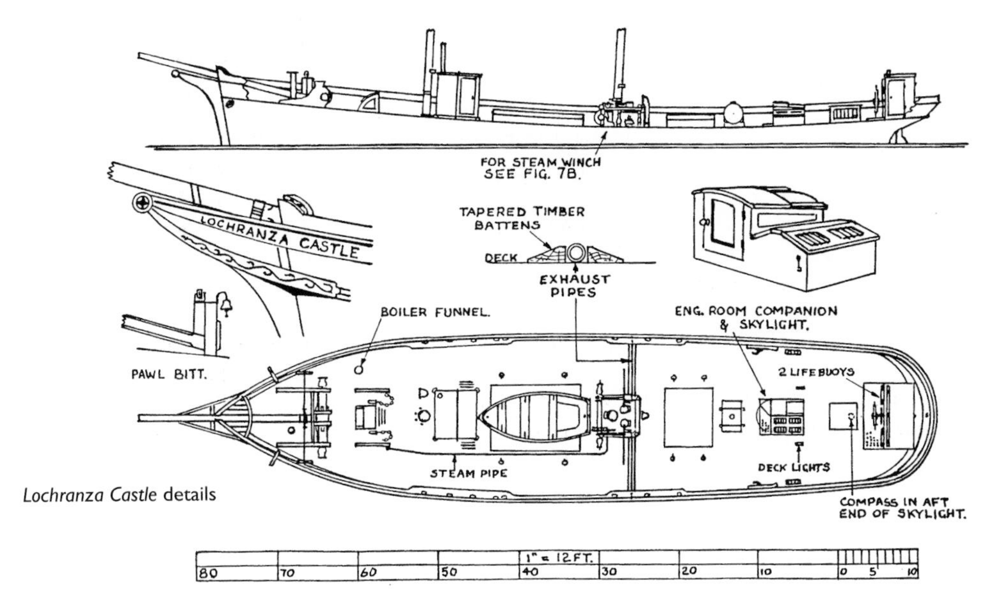

Lochranza Castle details

Lord Landsdowne Wood ketch barge, London, built 1890, J.W. Harvey, Littlehampton. 101 × 23.9 × 8.8ft. 144 tons gross, 109 tons net. *Official Number:* 98099. *Signal Hoist:* MQFT.

Lord Roseberry Wood ketch barge, Rochester, built 1893, William Ellis, Upnor, Kent. 72 tons net. *Official Number:* 99922. *Signal Hoist:* MQVD.

Louise Wood two-masted schooner, Padstow, built 1877, T.& J. Clemens, Gannel Yard, Newquay. 87.4 × 22.9 × 11ft. 114 tons gross, 93 tons net. *Official Number:* 70478. *Signal Hoist:* MCTC.

Lucie Wood auxiliary two-masted schooner, Dundalk, built 1881, Dundalk. 52 tons net. *Official Number:* 76254. *Signal Letters:* None.

Lucy Richmond Wood three-masted schooner, London, built 1875, Robertson, Ipswich. 106.7 × 24.4 × 8.6ft. 148 tons gross, 128 tons net. *Official Number:* 68313. *Signal Hoist:* MQVK.

M. A. James* Wood three-masted auxiliary schooner, Bideford, built 1900, David Williams, Portmadoc. 89.6 × 22.7 × 10.6ft. 125 tons gross, 88 tons net. *Official Number:* 109732. *Signal Hoist:* MDKK.

Maggie Annie Wood auxiliary ketch, Barnstaple, built 1881, Bridgwater. 76.5 × 20.2 × 9ft. 83 tons gross, 51 tons net. *Official Number:* 78706. *Signal Hoist:* MJJJ.

Major* Wood ketch barge, Harwich, built 1897, McLearon, Harwich. 67 tons net. *Official Number:* 105424. *Signal Hoist:* MQZB.

Margaret Garton Wood auxiliary two-masted schooner, Castleton, Isle of Man, built 1877, Port St. Mary, Isle of Man. 75.6 × 19.7 × 9.6ft. 83 tons gross, 59 tons net. *Official Number:* 63921. *Signal Hoist:* None.

Margaret Hobley* Wood auxiliary two-masted schooner, London, built 1868, J.D. Warlow, Pembroke Dock. 86.6 × 22.2 × 10.8ft. 119 tons gross. 82 tons net. *Official Number:* 55374. *Signal Hoist:* MFZR.

Margaret Mitchell Wood two-masted schooner, Campbeltown, built 1868, Rothesay. 39 tons net. *Official Number:* 55462. *Signal Hoist:* None.

Marie Celine Wood ketch, Drogheda, built 1892, Nantes. 75 tons net. *Official Number:* 114921. *Signal Hoist:* None.

Martinet Wood ketch-barge, Goole, built 1912, G. & T. Smith, Rye. 95.2 × 22.8 × 8ft. 126 tons gross, 99 tons net. *Official Number:* 128880. *Signal Hoist:* MDVN.

Mary Wood ketch, Gloucester, built 1872, Brimscombe, Gloucester. 50 tons net. *Official Number:* 63097. *Signal Hoist:* None.

Mary and Effie Wood auxiliary ketch, Greenock, built 1896, Fraserburgh. 27 tons net. *Official Number:* 143764. *Signal Hoist:* None.

Mary and Gertrude Wood two-masted schooner, Wexford, built 1897, Connah's Quay, Cheshire. 70 tons net. *Official Number:* 58203. *Signal Hoist:* EIFT.

Mary Barrow Wood twin-screw auxiliary three-masted schooner, Truro, built 1891, W.H. Lean, Falmouth. 103 × 24 × 10.8ft. 164 tons gross, 128 tons net. *Official Number:* 93424. *Signal Hoist:* MNGC.
In her later days as a plain double topsail schooner the *Mary Barrow* had as much width of sail on her upper topsail yard as could possibly be accommodated between the two lift bands, giving her a rather square look, which accentuated the loss of her topgallant. Nevertheless, she was still a fine-looking vessel. So many cameras were levelled at her on so many occasions that she became one of the most difficult vessels for which to produce a set of drawings – not through lack of information, but through a surfeit of it; the details of one photograph inevitably being contradicted by those from another, until the best one could do was go for a happy medium between all the conflicting information. Even so, such results are likely to be slightly more accurate than those gleaned from only one source of information.

Her lines have been given two stars only because of a lack of any concrete evidence on the turn of her bilge, notwithstanding the fact that she was a bit too fine to be anything other than fairly flat in the floors. I fancy that the coaming of her after hatch was raised after she became an auxiliary vessel, to compensate,

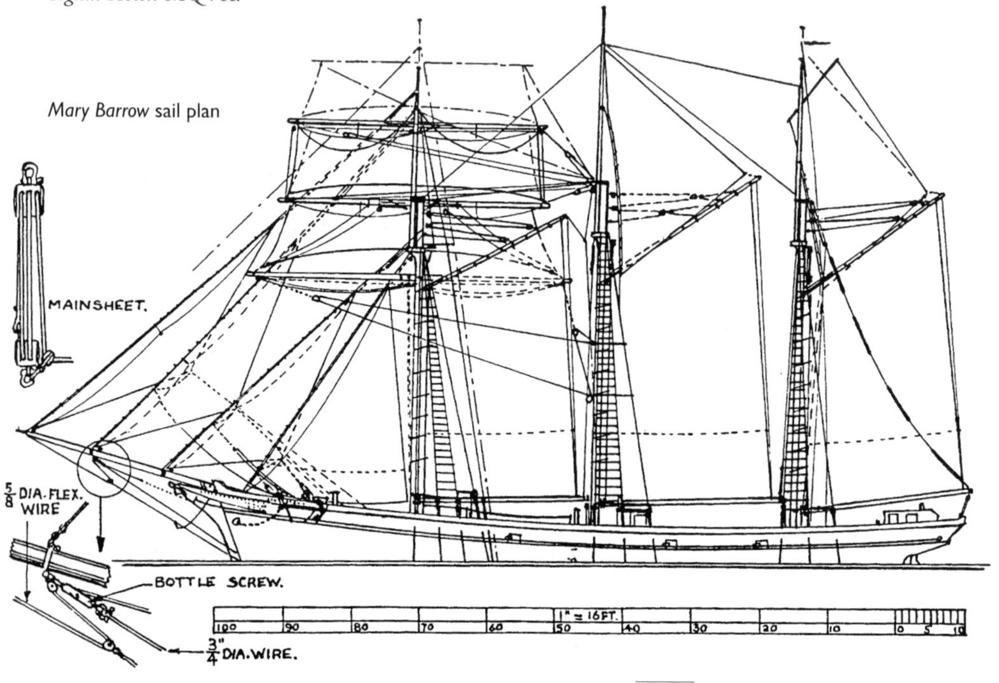

Mary Barrow sail plan

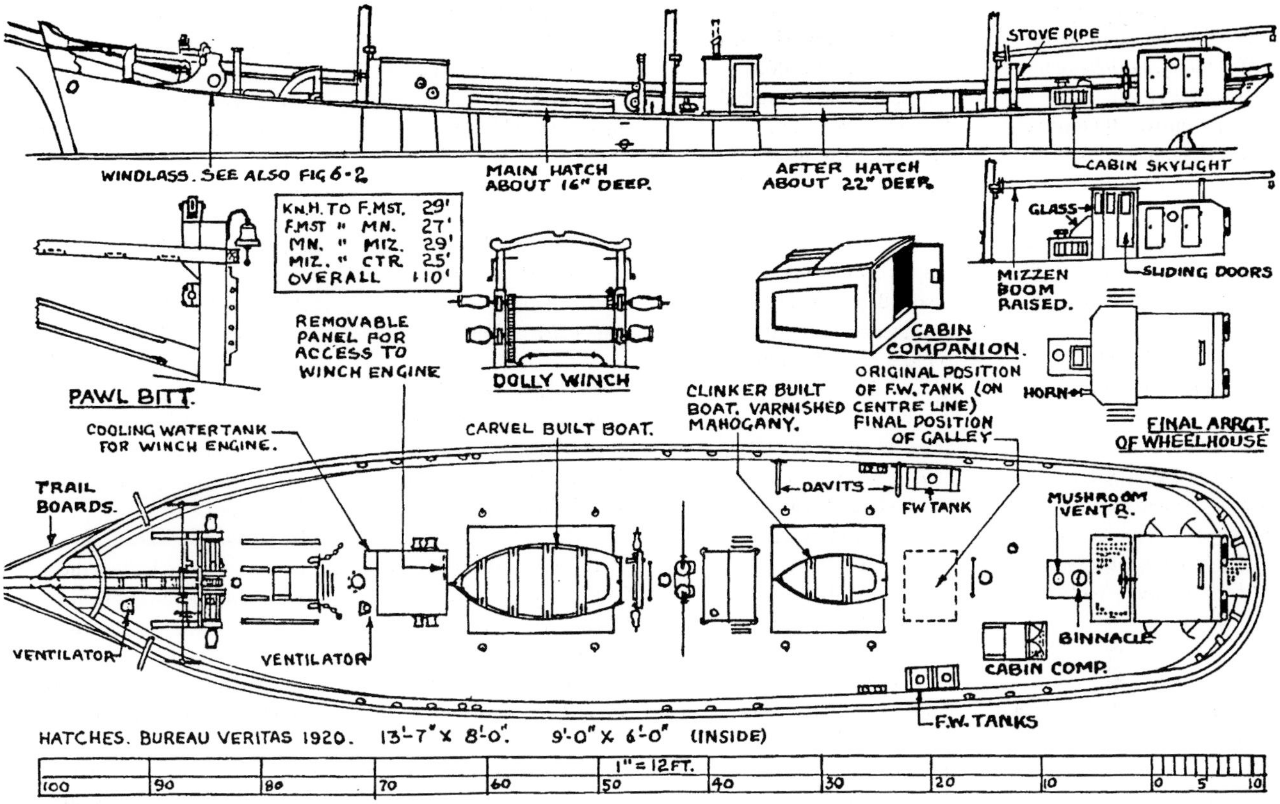

Mary Barrow details

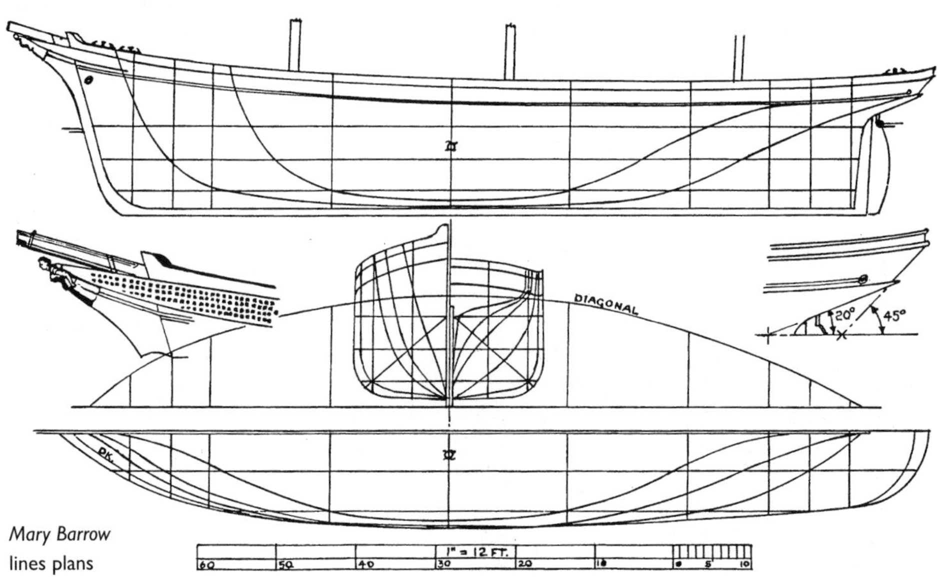

Mary Barrow lines plans

however slightly, for the encroachment on the hold space.

It is a pity that she was lost on the Calf of Man, as she would have been a fine vessel for the preservationists, even though their efforts are often doomed to failure unless some means can be found to completely inhibit rot. With our present technical knowledge it would probably be a good deal cheaper to build reinforced concrete or fibreglass replicas, as, once the hidden and unprotected wooden frames are attacked, the end is inevitable.

Mary Barrow's loss in fog on 28 September 1938 should not be taken as a reflection of Captain Mørtensen's seamanship. It should be remembered that for most of his life he was a sailing-ship skipper… had his vessel been without engine in such conditions she would have been at a standstill, admittedly a sitting duck for any power-driven vessel in a hurry, but capable of making enough noise to ward off disaster. To conduct a fine lined, heavily powered vessel in thick fog, it is necessary to know the exact point from which she took her departure, and the exact time, her exact speed through the water and exactly what the tides are doing with her. Naturally the schooner skipper was concerned with all these things but not to four decimal places, and with a smooth sea the *Mary Barrow* was probably eating up the miles far faster than anyone on board realised. The final contribution to her loss was probably the machinery itself – but for the beat of her powerful diesels her crew might have heard distant foghorns or the wash of water on rocks in time to take evasive action. I am aware that Alan Villiers has written about Captain Reuben de Cloux, but I feel strongly that no slur should be cast upon the memory of the dashing Dane; mad he may have been, but a sailor he certainly was. Others, far better qualified to judge than I am, have said so. At the time of her loss *Mary Barrow* was bound for Truro with a cargo of coal from Point of Ayr colliery.

The Bureau Veritas dimensions for the size of or her after hatch are suspect as it was deepened in the mid 1930s, when her final pair of

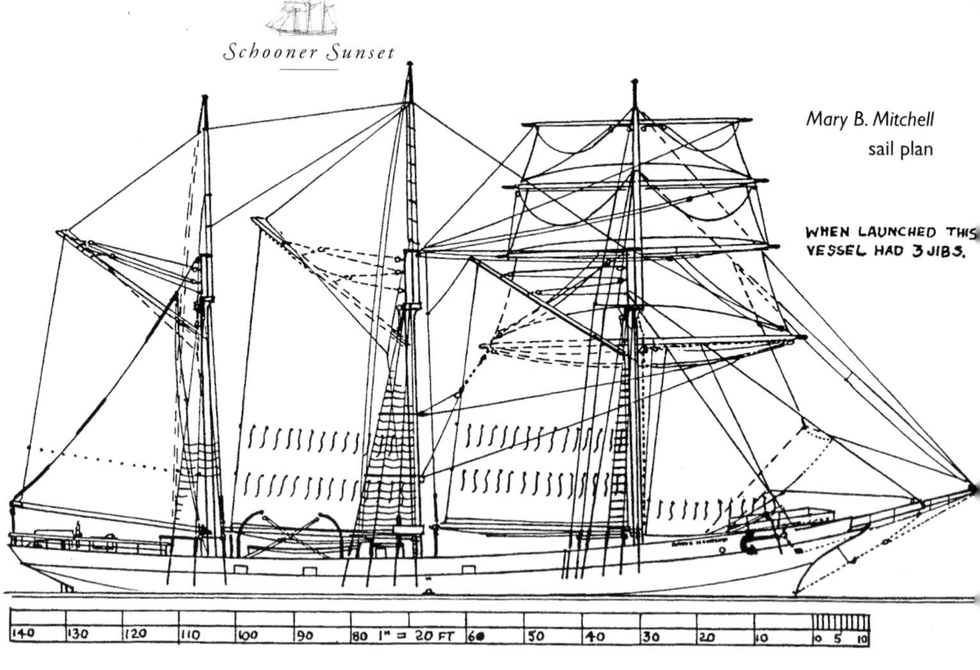

Mary B. Mitchell sail plan

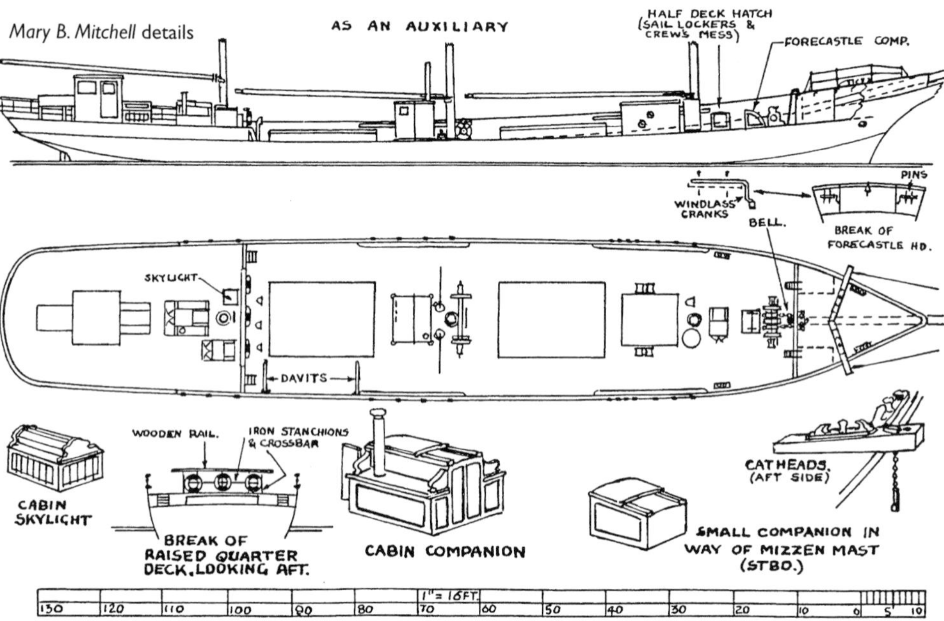

Mary B. Mitchell details

engines was installed. The dimensions were taken from the 1920 register and also point to the fact that it was enlarged (pre-1920 as well as in the 1930s or does he mean that the dimensions are such that the hatch must have been enlarged in the 1930s as these measurements would not have accommodated the engines?). The last time I had a close look at *Mary Barrow* was in 1935, and both hatches were then the same width.

*Mary B. Mitchell**
Steel auxiliary twin-screw three-masted schooner, Dublin, built 1892, Paul Rodgers & Co., Carrickfergus.
129.7 × 24.4 × 10.8ft.
227 tons gross, 133 tons net.
Official Number: 97575.
Signal Hoist: EIFN.

If the reputation of Paul Rodgers had to rest on his little wooden three-masters alone, it would be secure enough, and yet they were anything but typical products of his yard, which was well known for much larger iron and steel vessels, many of which were built to the order of James Fisher & Sons of Barrow. The last of his steel schooners still in commission was the *Mary B. Mitchell* and, although in her later years I considered her to be far from attractive, I decided that I could produce a reasonably accurate sail platform what the available photographs. This I felt was the least, and the most, I could do to keep Rodgers in correct perspective.

Before I had finished I received four good shots of her deck gear from Dan McDonald, a pile from Dick Scott – including at the end of her life, wrecked at Kirkcudbright, which gave a sure guide to the lines of her hull – and a number of useful comments from Jim Tyrrell of Arklow, her final owner. Paul Rodgers, I feel, should rest in peace.

I had not got far with her sail plan before making the discovery that the distance from fore- to mainmast was greater than that from main to mizzen, a sure sign of a barquentine. That she was intended to be just that was clinched by my own notes and one of Dick Scott's photographs, which showed that she had seven chainplates per side in way of the foremast, indicating that she was meant to carry a pair of royal backstays. An eleventh-hour change of mind probably had something to do with the square-rigged ticket problem, and her launch photograph shows her as a three-masted standing topgallant schooner.

Many considered Paul Rodgers's steel schooners to be as wet as Niagara Falls. Even the one he did not design himself, the *Result*, was well up to

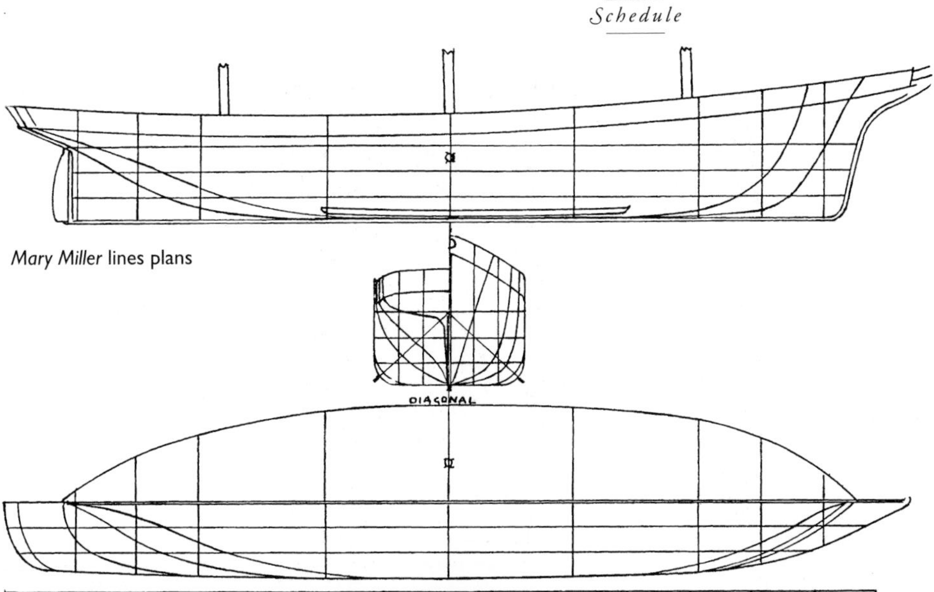

Mary Miller lines plans

before and during the 1914-18 War – than she finished up with, and it is this later one that is shown on her sail plan. The original was lost on 8 January 1917 off Berry Head, South Devon, during a gale that saw the loss of both her foremast, with spars, and the mainmast.

Mary Catharine Wood ketch, Beaumaris, built 1858, Amlwch. 62 tons net.
Official Number: 21269.
Signal Hoist: None.

Mary Edwards Wood ketch, Beaumaris, built 1863, Bangor. 50 tons net.
Official Number: 43875.
Signal Hoist: None.

Mary Eliezer* Steel auxiliary ketch, Hull, built 1904, Hammelwarder, Germany.
81.6 × 18 × 7.7ft.
66 tons gross, 58 tons net.
Official Number: 118818.
Signal Hoist: MCBR.

Mary Miller* Wood three-masted schooner, Dublin, built 1881, Paul Rodgers & Co., Carrickfergus,
93.2 × 22.1 × 9.9ft.
119 tons gross, 93 tons net.

specification on this score. But before going any further it must be said that to the generation that grew up with wooden vessels, all iron and steel schooners were wet. This was not a conclusion arrived at out of prejudice – the lack of constant pumping was a feature on the credit side that did much to redress the balance of opinion – they actually were wetter, a phenomenon that is not easy to explain. If two vessels were built to the same model and dimensions, one in steel and one in wood, the steel one would float higher than the wooden one when empty, even before the timbers of the latter had become properly waterlogged. The steel vessel would also have a slightly bigger hold space, because the distance from the outside of the ceiling was, in most places, only about half that in the wooden vessel. From this it follows that when both vessels were down to their marks, both would be exactly the same weight, but the steel vessel would be carrying a larger cargo than the wooden one. It seems that this must be the single factor that causes the difference. If a vessel pitching into a sea is considered as two weights on a see-saw, one forward and one abaft the centre of buoyancy, the greater weight in the steel ship, once set in motion, must cause the ends to plunge deeper into the water before the movement is arrested and reversed. It would take a set of extremely long-winded calculations, akin to finding the real metacentric height, to establish whether this hypothesis is correct.

It should be noted that the deck gear drawing for the *Mary B. Mitchell* shows the arrangement in her final years. The skylight and companion abreast of the mizzenmast were put in when her engines were installed during her 'Q' Ship days of the First World War. The galley was originally abaft the foremast and she had flywheel pumps and the fife rail, which went with them, abaft her mainmast. The wheel and steering gear were originally exposed to the elements. Finally she had a slightly longer lower mast –

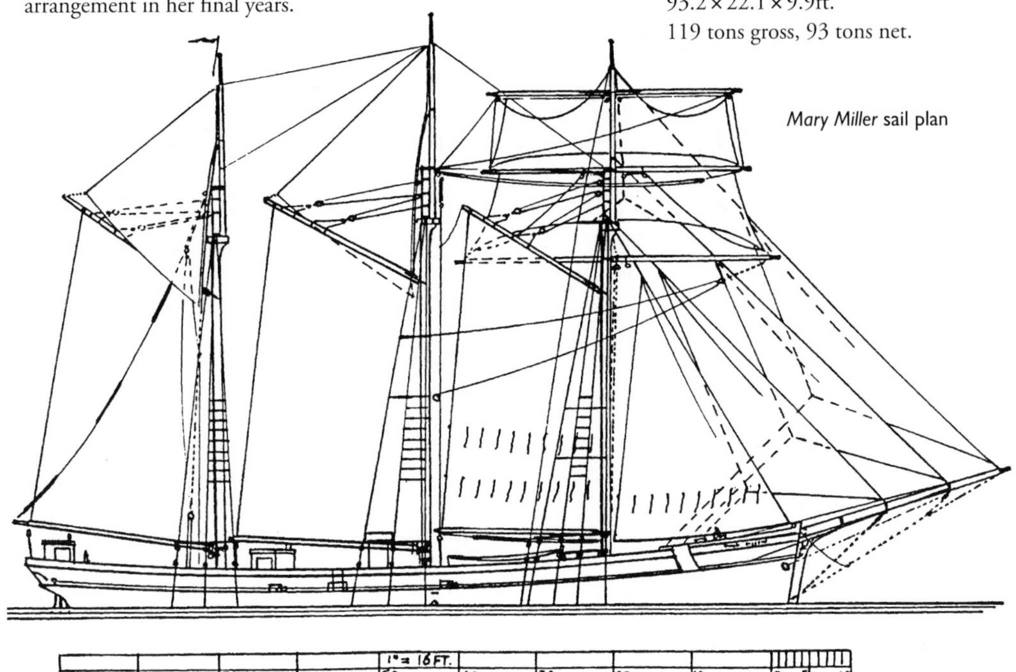

Mary Miller sail plan

Mary Miller details

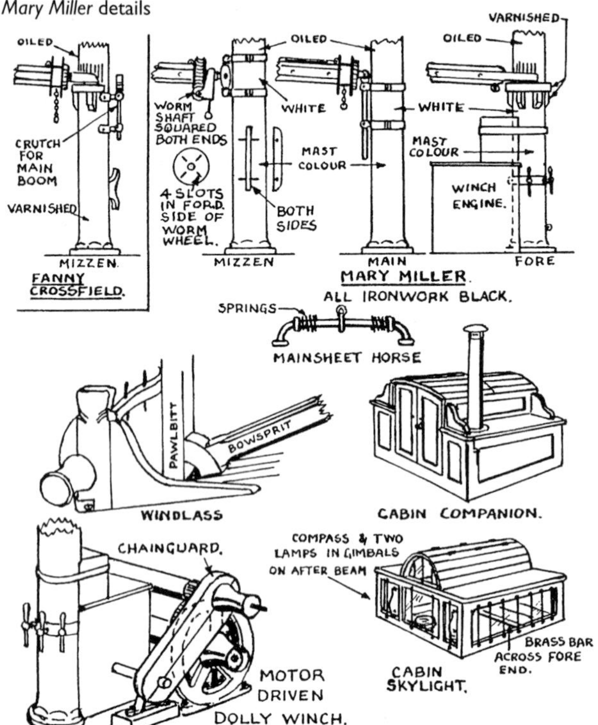

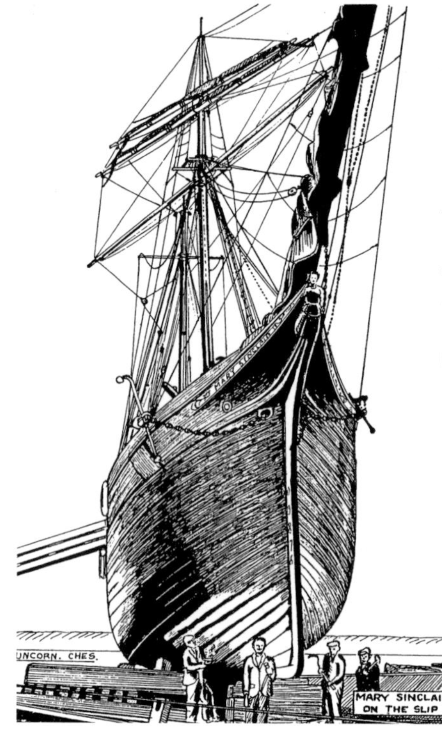

Mary Sinclair drawn on the slip from which it will be seen she is supported on one side only, relying upon her underwater shape to prevent her falling over and when read in conjunction with her lines she can be seen to have a relatively 'flat' bottom.

Official Number: 83974.
Signal Hoist: EICN.
For further information see *Fanny Crossfield.*

Mary Sinclair* Wood three-masted schooner, Barrow, built 1876, Barclay, Ardrossen.
88.8 × 21.4 × 10.5ft.
118 tons gross, 91 tons net.
Official Number: 70478.
*Signal Hoist:*MQVX.
The *Mary Sinclair* and *Lochranza Castle* were both launched at Ardrossan by the same yard, in the year 1876, and for this reason have been dealt with together. While there is an abundance of photographic evidence for the *Mary Sinclair* lines I have nothing on the *Lochranza Castle* except a scribbled note from the 1930s, which states that they were about average, and three free-hand waterlines giving my assessment of her run. Their dimensional differences are not sufficiently great to support any theories that the two were based on quite different models and, though the *Lochranza Castle*'s foremast is proportionately further aft than the *Mary Sinclair*'s, she could easily have carried a longer foretopmast with a greater area of sail than is shown on the drawing, as this, for lack of any evidence, has been based on the latter vessel.

Both of these schooners have already received more than a passing mention and what remains to be said concerns the *Mary Sinclair* alone. She was one of a number of vessels that came through the worst of the slump with a crew of only three men. At the time someone put forward the theory that the mate stood his watches alone and for many years I accepted this without question, assuming that in the event of any trouble he could stamp on the deck until the skipper came up from below. At the same time I could not

Mary Sinclair sail plan

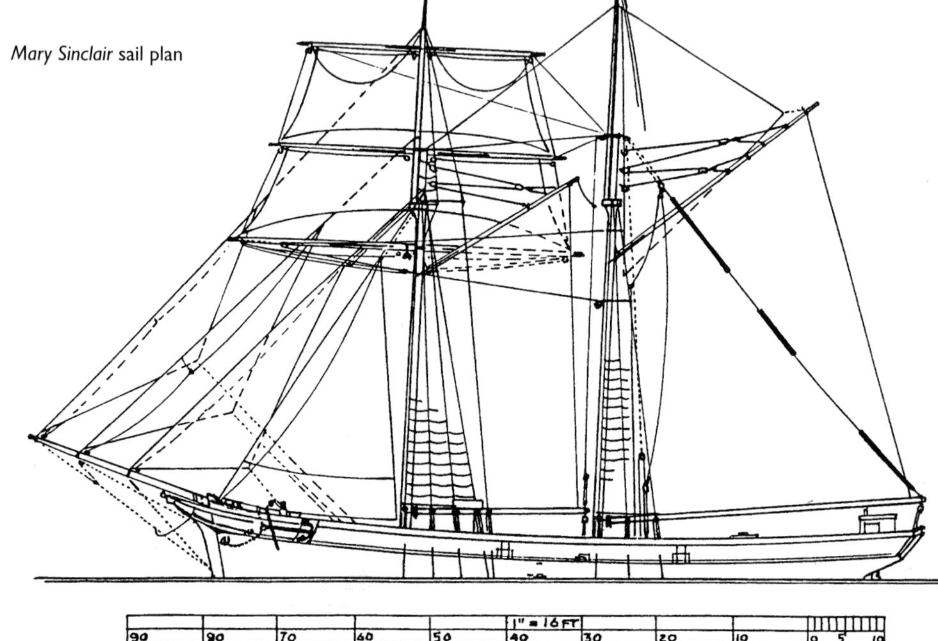

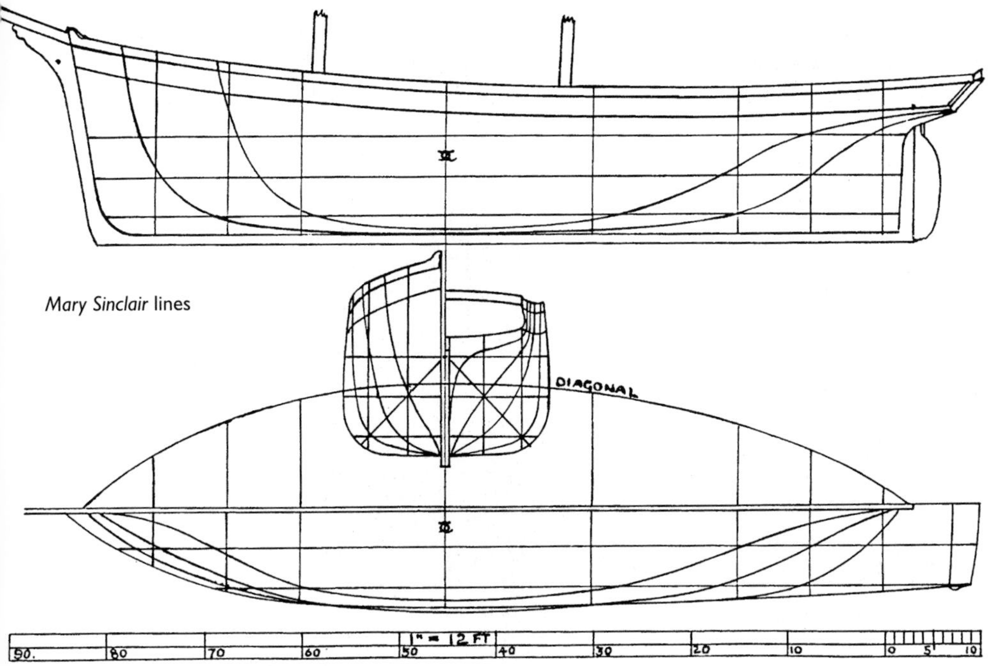

DIAGONAL

1" = 12 FT

50. 80 70 60 50 40 30 20 10 0 5' 10

Mary Sinclair lines

Mary Sinclair details

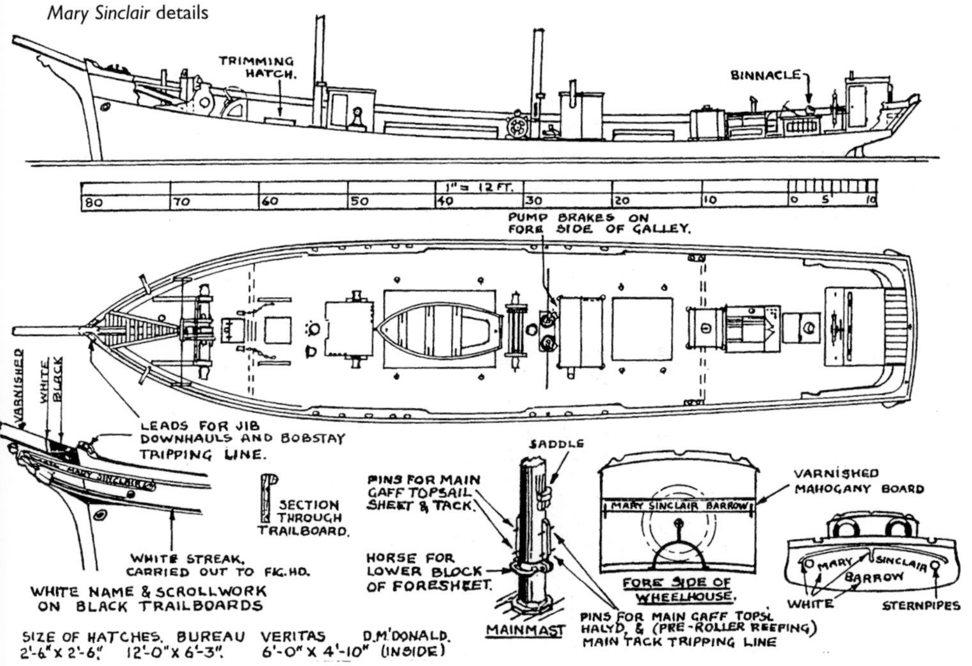

TRIMMING HATCH.

BINNACLE

1" = 12 FT.

80 70 60 50 40 30 20 10 0 5' 10

PUMP BRAKES ON FORE SIDE OF GALLEY.

VARNISHED

WHITE

BLACK

LEADS FOR JIB DOWNHAULS AND BOBSTAY TRIPPING LINE.

MARY SINCLAIR

SECTION THROUGH TRAILBOARD.

WHITE STREAK, CARRIED OUT TO FIG. HD.

WHITE NAME & SCROLLWORK ON BLACK TRAILBOARDS

SADDLE

PINS FOR MAIN GAFF TOPSAIL SHEET & TACK.

HORSE FOR LOWER BLOCK OF FORESHEET.

MAINMAST

PINS FOR MAIN GAFF TOPSL HALYD, & (PRE-ROLLER REEFING) MAIN TACK TRIPPING LINE

MARY SINCLAIR BARROW

FORE SIDE OF WHEELHOUSE.

VARNISHED MAHOGANY BOARD

MARY SINCLAIR BARROW

WHITE

STERNPIPES

SIZE OF HATCHES. BUREAU VERITAS D.M'DONALD.
2'-6" X 2'-6". 12'-0" X 6'-3". 6'-0" X 4'-10" (INSIDE)

help thinking that it was a bit risky during the night. Finally it dawned on me that the whole business really had to revolve around the preparation and consumption of food and if the wind happened to be abaft the beam there would be no possibility of the mate lashing the wheel while he peeled potatoes or did anything else. Some sort of rota for the skipper and the mate, the mate and the AB, and the AB and skipper would have to be worked out. The crew of the *Lochranza Castle*, however few, were not concerned with such issues as their vessel was normally engaged on short-passage work between the Mersey and Ulster, whereas the *Mary Sinclair* normally worked 'round the land'.

I had finished the drawings of the deck gear for the *Mary Sinclair* when I received a set of dimensions for her three hatches that Dan McDonald had extracted from the Bureau Veritas Register – on which, he said, a fair number of British schooners were to be found. He was of the opinion that it would require an Underwriter to explain why they were there, but thought that it must have been due to the fact that Lloyds would only grant 100 A1 classification for a set number of years, after which heavy repairs would have to be carried out to obtain re-classification. The dimensions given were in metres and I converted them to Imperial measure and added to the drawing. In all three cases I have taken the first dimension to be the fore and aft one and that all are the inside measurements of the hatchway. A minimum of 8in should be added to each to obtain the outside measurements. The reader will note similar dimensions, from the same source, in the case of the *Mary Barrow*.

Mary Stewart* Iron auxiliary ketch, Greenock, built 1876, Montrose. 72 .6 × 19.5 × 8.3ft. 83 tons gross, 39 tons net.
Official Number: 72414.
Signal Hoist: MFTJ.

Mary Stewart Wood two-masted schooner, Ardrossen, built 1868, Ardrossen.
43 tons net.
Official Number: 60618.
Signal Hoist: None.

Maude Wood auxiliary ketch, Bideford, built 1869, Widness.
47 tons net.
Official Number: 62010.
Signal Hoist: None.

Maudianne Wood two-masted schooner, Penzance, built 1864, J. Johnson, Bideford.
92.5 × 21.1 × 11.5ft.
138 tons gross, 116 tons net.
Official Number: 47152.

Signal Hoist: MJTC.
In 1934 was operated under sail having previously operated as a motor vessel.

Maud Mary Wood auxiliary two-masted schooner, Bideford, built 1889, Howden Dyke. 77.2 × 20.6 × 9.4ft. 79 tons gross, 62 tons net.
Official Number: 91320.
Signal Hoist: MPBX.

Mavis Wood auxiliary ketch, Hull, built 1896, Beverley. 50 tons net.
Official Number: 105088.
Signal Hoist: MQTX.

M. E. Johnson* Wood auxiliary three-masted schooner, Dublin, built 1879, William Ashburner, Barrow. 98.3 × 23 × 9.9ft. 131 tons gross, 81 tons net.
Official Number: 76895.
Signal Hoist: EINB.
For further information see *James Postlethwaite.*

Mermaid Wood two-masted schooner, Wexford, built 1869, Wexford. 77 tons net.
Official Number: 49510.
Signal Hoist: None.

Millbay Wood auxiliary ketch, Plymouth, built 1880, Stonehouse, Plymouth. 45 tons net.
Official Number: 83941.
Signal Hoist: MFYF.

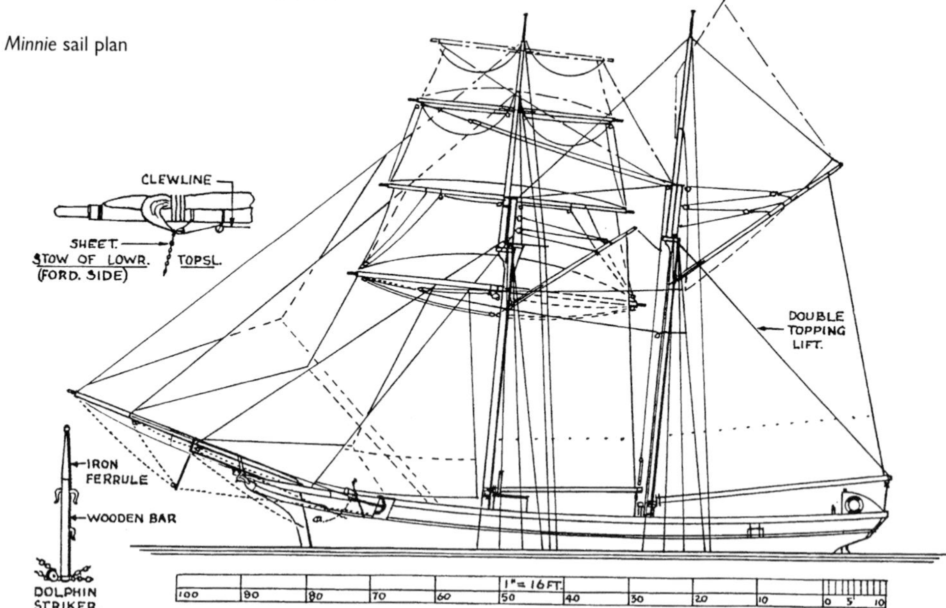

Minnie sail plan

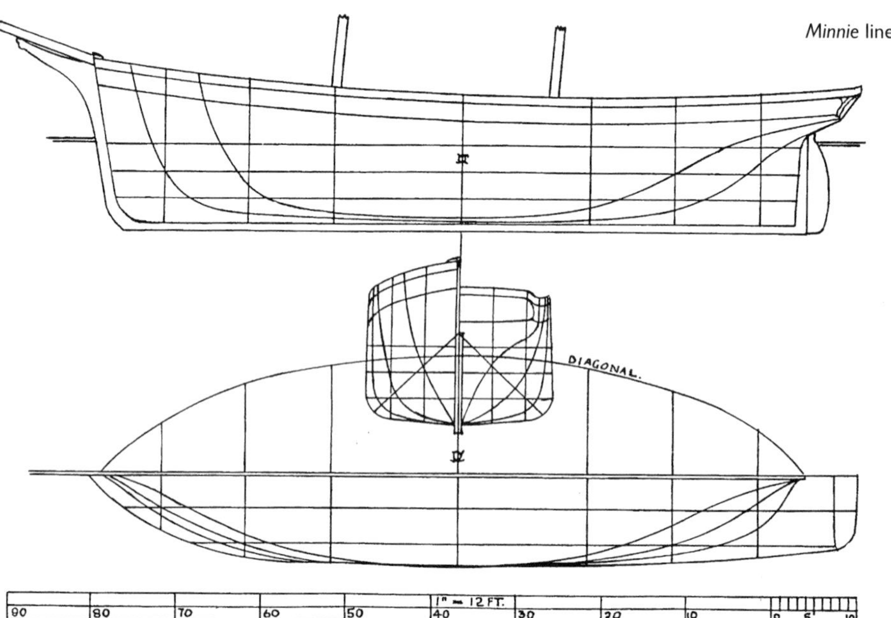

Minnie lines

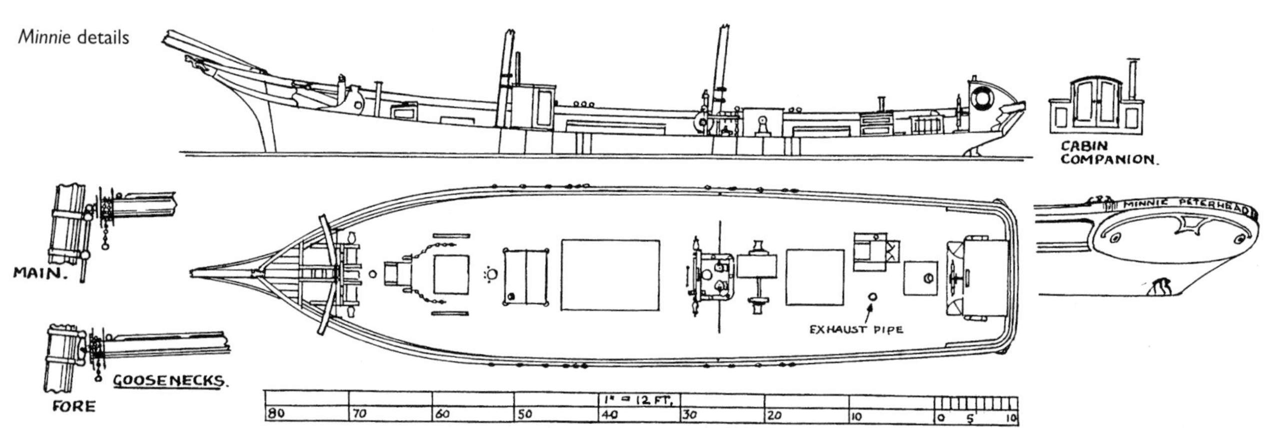

Minnie details

Minnie Wood two-masted schooner, Peterhead, built 1878, Peterhead.
84.2 × 21.3 × 10.3ft.
79 tons net.
Official Number: 75253.
Signal Hoist: MDQQ.

Minnie Flossie* Wood auxiliary ketch, Bideford, built 1879, Davis, Milford Haven.
61.5 × 18 × 7.7ft.
54 tons gross. 22 tons net.
Official Number: 78475.
Signal Hoist: None.

Miss Beck Wood two-masted schooner, Carnarvon, built Portinllaen, Carnarvon.
82.4 × 22 × 11.5ft.
124 tons gross, 101 tons net.
Official Number: 20000.
Signal Letters: MQJN.

Mistletoe Wood auxiliary ketch, Exeter, built 1890, Plymouth. 59 × 18.2 × 7.4ft.
46 tons gross. 23 tons net.
Signal Hoist: None.
Sailed out of Topsham.

Mizpah Wood auxiliary ketch, Plymouth, built 1898, William Date, Kingsbridge.
68.4 × 18.7 × 7.1ft.
54 tons gross, 33 tons net.
Official Number: 108556.
Signal Hoist: None.

Monarch Wood ketch, Gloucester, built 1890, Gloucester. 76 tons net.
Official Number: 105409.
Signal Hoist: None.

Mose Rose Wood ketch, Ramsgate, built 1890, Margate. 43 tons net.
Official Number: 97695.
Signal Hoist: None.
(The spelling of her name is as per *Mercantile Navy List*, 1935.)

Moultonian* Wood auxiliary ketch barge, Littlehampton, built 1919, J. & W. Harvey, Littlehampton.
99.6 × 23.8 × 8.5ft.
164 tons gross, 94 tons net.
Official Number: 131979.
Signal Hoist: MPGD.

My Lady Wood two-masted schooner, Plymouth, built 1889, William Date & Son, Kingsbridge.
84.5 × 21.3 × 10.6ft.
110 tons gross, 93 tons net.
Official Number: 95134.
Signal Hoist: MPJL.
This vessel has been dealt with from photographs taken by Dan McDonald. She was similar in appearance to *Mary Sinclair* but could be distinguished from that vessel by her hump-backed wheelhouse and slightly longer bowsprit. Her two chain lockers, one forward and one aft, indicate that she was built for deep water. Her lines were abstracted from a photograph showing her sitting high and dry on a sandbank, which

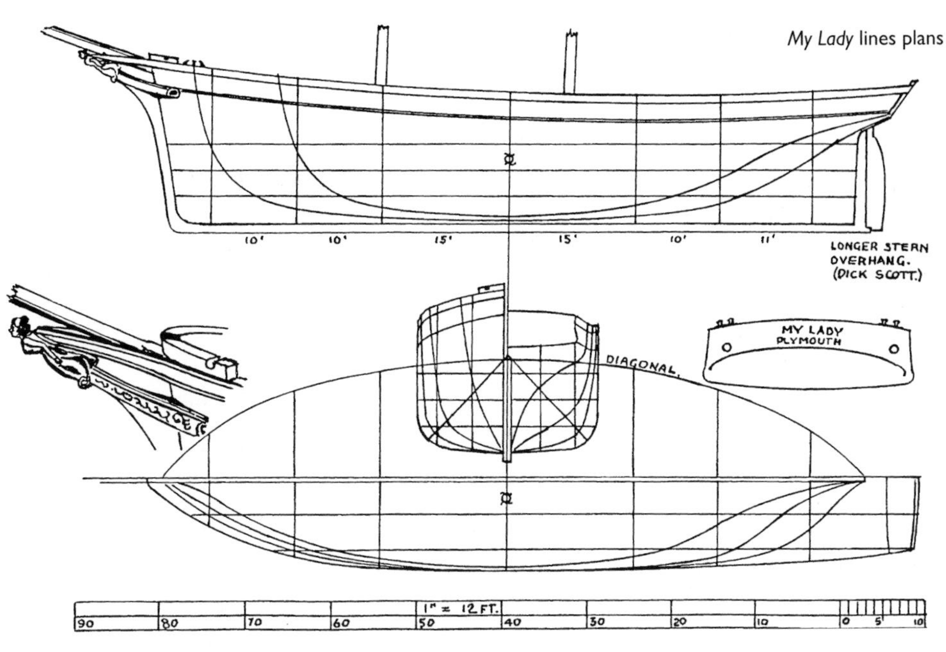

My Lady lines plans

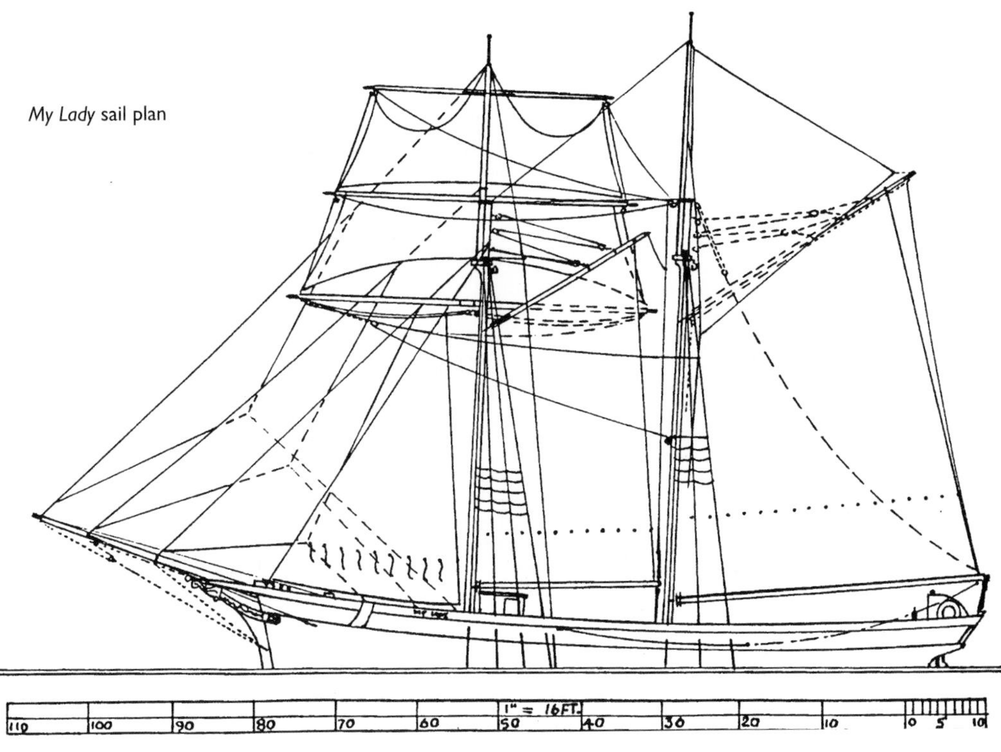

My Lady sail plan

My Lady details

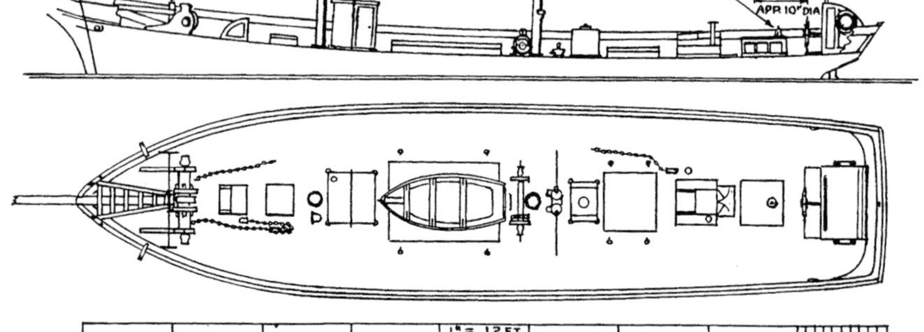

END FRAMES OF DOLLY WINCH.

A song, not to be taken too seriously, probably written during the 1914-18 War but possibly earlier, proclaimed that:

'You can talk aboot your King's
Guards, Scots Greys an' a',
You can sing aboot your kilties
and your Gallant Forty Twa',
And any other regiment, under
the King's command,
But the South Down Militia are
the terrors of the land.'

appeared in *Sea Breezes* many years ago.

Myrtle Wood ketch, Portsmouth, built 1898, Emsworth. 45 tons net. *Official Number:* 109388. *Signal Hoist:* None.

Mystery Wood ketch barge, Faversham, built 1875, Shrubshall, Milton, Kent. 61 tons net. *Official Number:* 73253, *Signal Hoist:* MGSZ.

Narcissus (ex-*Eleanor Maria M*) Wood ketch, Kirkwall, built 1885, Hull. 70 tons net. *Official Number:* 91542. *Signal Letters:* MJGZ.

Native Queen Wood ketch, Lerwick, built 1901, Sandwick. 46 tons net. *Official Number:* 128456. *Signal Letters:* None.

Nell Jess Wood ketch, Ipswich, built 1902, J. & W. Harvey, Littlehampton. 91.4 × 22 × 7.7ft. 115 tons gross, 96 tons net. *Official Number:* 113754. *Signal Hoist:* None.

Nellie Bywater* Wood auxiliary two-masted schooner, Newry, built 1873, Thomas, Duddon. 89.7 × 22.2 × 10.1ft. 115 tons gross, 76 tons net. *Official Number:* 69715. *Signal Hoist:* MQJC.

Nellie Bywater sail plan

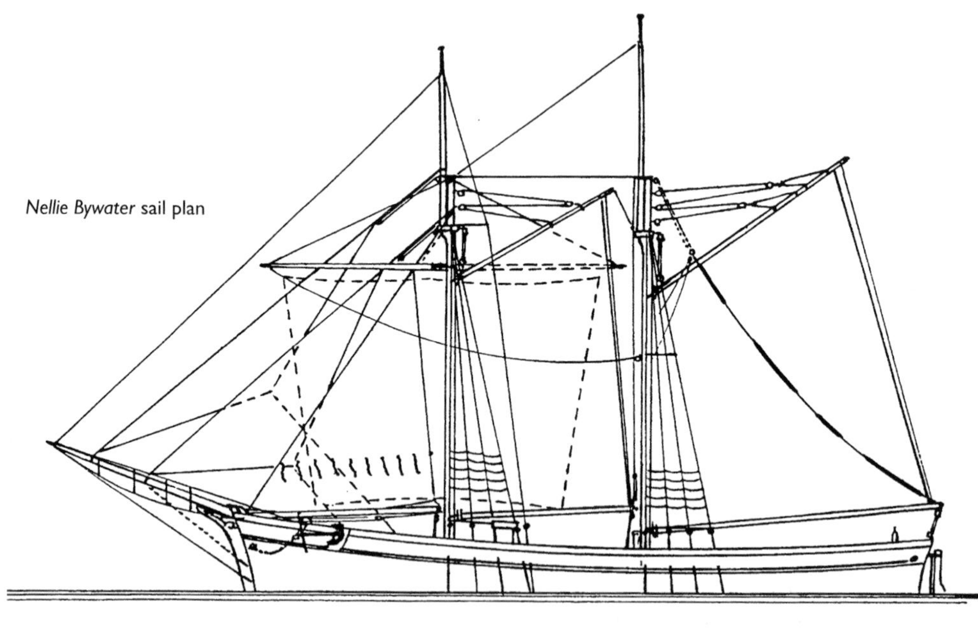

Nellie Bywater details

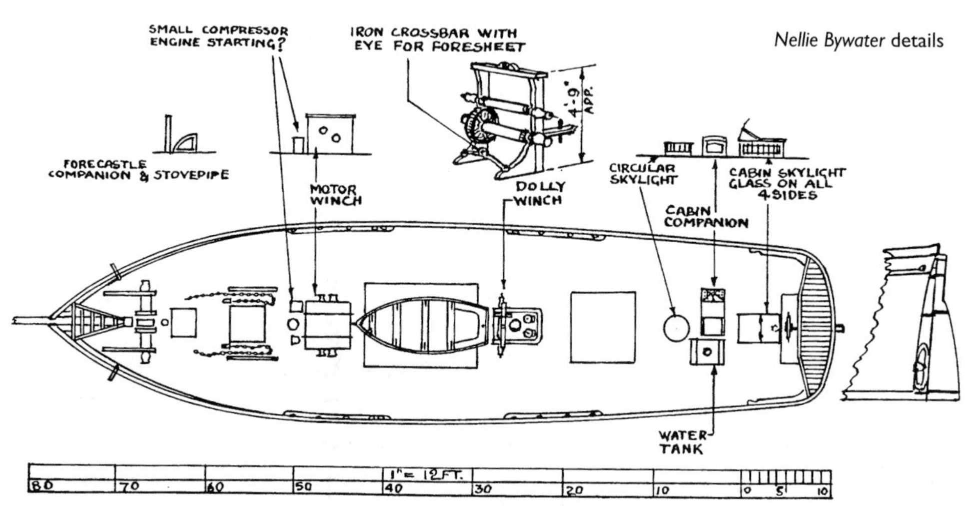

In their heyday, and judging by the number afloat in the 1930s, it may well be that the Jolly Jack Tars of this little corner of the Emerald Isle were the terrors of the sea. Certainly it deserves a mention as one of the last strongholds of sail, and some years ago a booklet entitled *Sailing Ships of Mourne* was published that came across with a direct homespun simplicity that endeared it to its readers. The vessels from these parts were often referred to collectively as 'The Annalong Schooners' – although they came from all over – and of the survivors only the *Goldseeker* cannot be included here, owing to a complete lack of information. I have insufficient evidence on which to base a set of lines for *Nellie Bywater*, nor have I any guide as to her original sail plan. There is a good chance, however, that most of this missing information will ultimately come to light. The details provided show her as she was during the 1930s.

Nellie Fleming (ex-*Emily*) Wood three-masted schooner, Cork, built 1884, Paul Rodgers & Co., Carrickfergus. 94.1 × 22.4 × 9.5ft. 119 tons gross, 94 tons net.
Official Number: 83510.
Signal Hoist: EICS.

Nellie Wood ketch, Portsmouth, built 1876, Emsworth. 22 tons net.
Official Number: 109388.
Signal Hoist: None.

New Design (II) Wood two-masted schooner, Bridgwater, built 1871, Carver & Co., Bridgwater. 50 tons net.
Official Number: 62979.
Signal Hoist: MLCV.

New Providence Wood two-masted schooner, Falmouth, built 1841, Falmouth. 32 tons net.
Official Number: 13422.
Signal Hoist: None.

Nonpareil Wood ketch, Portsmouth, built 1893, Emsworth. 69 tons net.
Official Number: 104445
Signal Hoist: None.

North Barrule Wood auxiliary two-masted schooner, Dumfries, built 1880, Ramsey, Isle of Man. 76.8 × 19.3 × 8.4ft. 52 tons net.
Official Number: 109388.
Signal Hoist: None.

Like many other stretches of water, the upper part of the Irish Sea can be an extremely unpleasant place at times, but it would be even more so were it not for the providential presence, right in the middle of it, of 'Ellen Vannen', with its green hills by the sea – better known to most as the Isle of Man. When the west wind begins to kick up dirty weather the island provides shelter for shipping and, as far as small vessels are concerned, there are two popular places to which they can beat a retreat. Those to the west can make a dash for Peel where a rocky promontory, complete with haunted castle, has been augmented by a breakwater to provide a commodious harbour with a wide entrance. Those too far east to reach Peel can come to an anchor off the town of Ramsey under the shelter of Maughold[6] Head, which breaks the force of wind and sea. This headland is at the seaward end of a region of hilly country, that rises inland until culminating due south of the town, at the peak known as North Barrule. It is for this hill that the last Manx-built schooner to remain afloat was named. The islanders, and the people of Ramsey in particular, were the builders of an iron barque that is still afloat and, from time to time, sailing, in San Diego, California. The town is also the birthplace of this little schooner, and they have every right to feel equally proud of her, although her remains have long since gone the way of all wooden vessels. She also had the distinction of being the last sailing vessel to carry, in succession, the names of two ancient ports, Dumfries and Chester, which today have little left to bear witness to long centuries of bustling maritime activity.

To the model-maker and the man searching for a hint of her lines, *North Barrule* turns out to be something of an enigma. For her size she was a tall vessel, and this may have had something to do with her name. By all the rules she should have had flat floors, a hard bilge and full lines. But the long distance from knightheads to foremast suggests the exact opposite – a fine entry and run.[7] Her profile and mast heights were taken from four sources: a sketch made at Connah's Quay in 1935; a very small photograph taken in Moelfre Bay –

[6] Pronounced "Mackle" with a short 'a'.

[7] Corroborated by Dan McDonald.

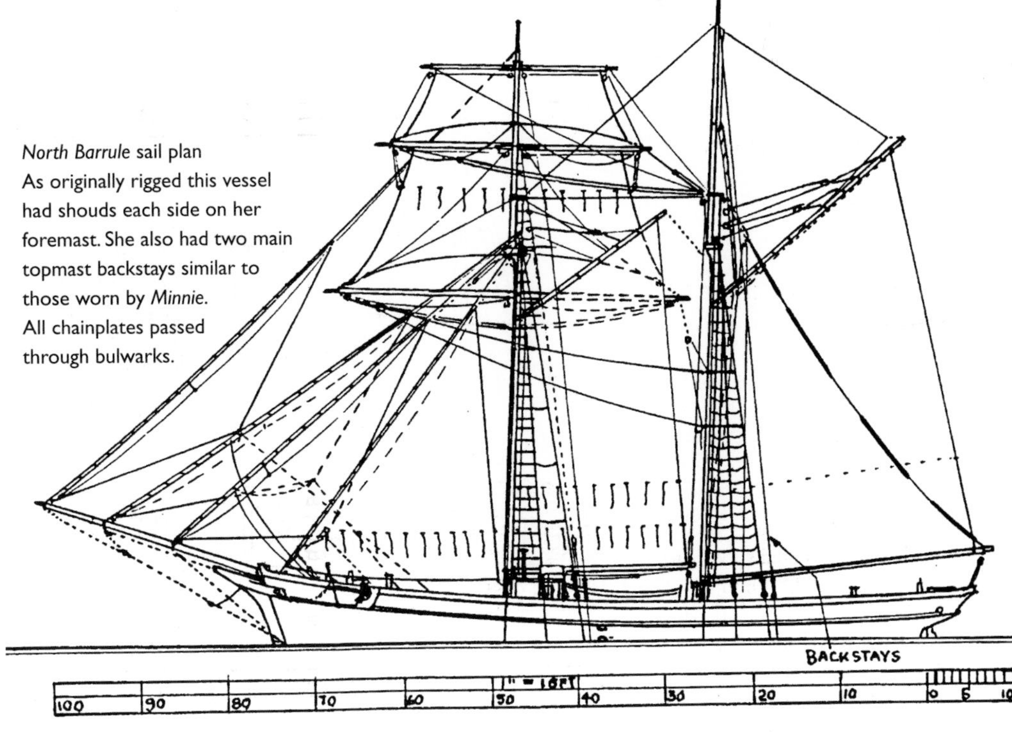

North Barrule sail plan
As originally rigged this vessel had shouds each side on her foremast. She also had two main topmast backstays similar to those worn by *Minnie*. All chainplates passed through bulwarks.

DIAGONAL
1" = 12 FT.
70
60
50
40
30
20
10
0 5 10

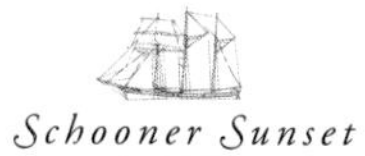

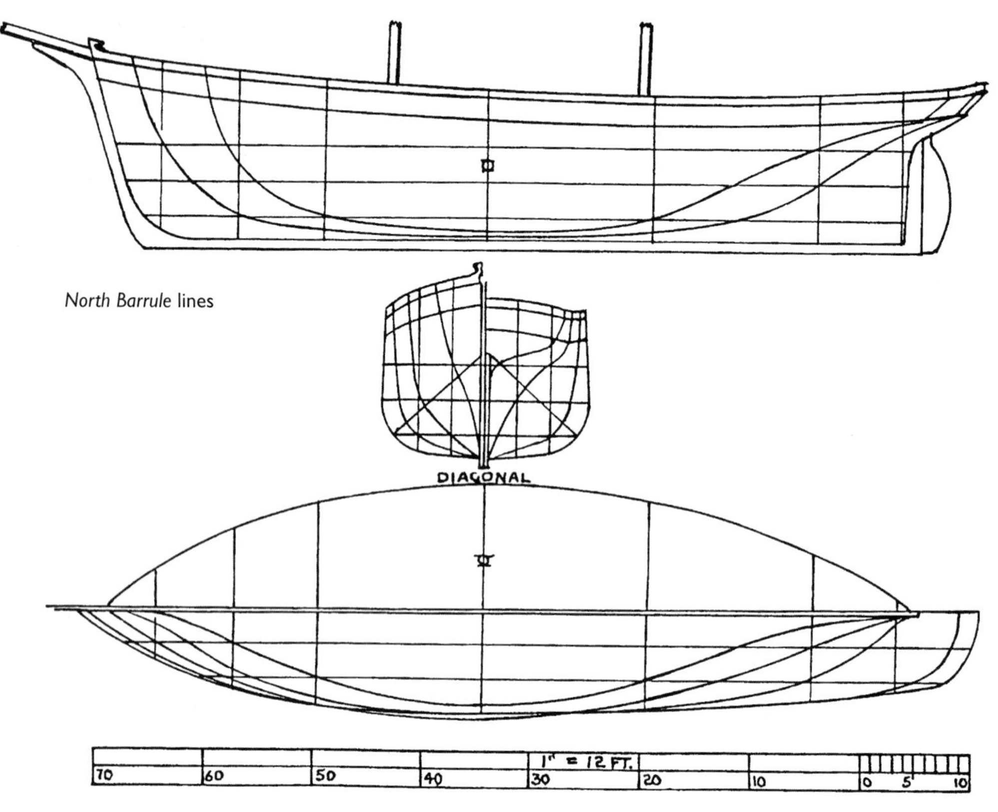

North Barrule lines

the negative of which has been lost for many years; and two photographs loaned by Terry Belt, one almost stern-on, from which I extracted the length of her yards. When I saw her at Connah's Quay she was loaded and her waterline gave no indication of anything out of the ordinary in the hull below. Before making any serious attempt on her lines I looked for some justification for reducing the height of the masts, or pushing them further forward, but found insufficient evidence for doing either.

The results, therefore, must be considered little more than a guess. On reflection, however, there is no real reason why she should not have been built with all these features. The handy mainsail produced by the position of her masts was not fully compensated for by the increased size of staysail so that,

North Barrule details

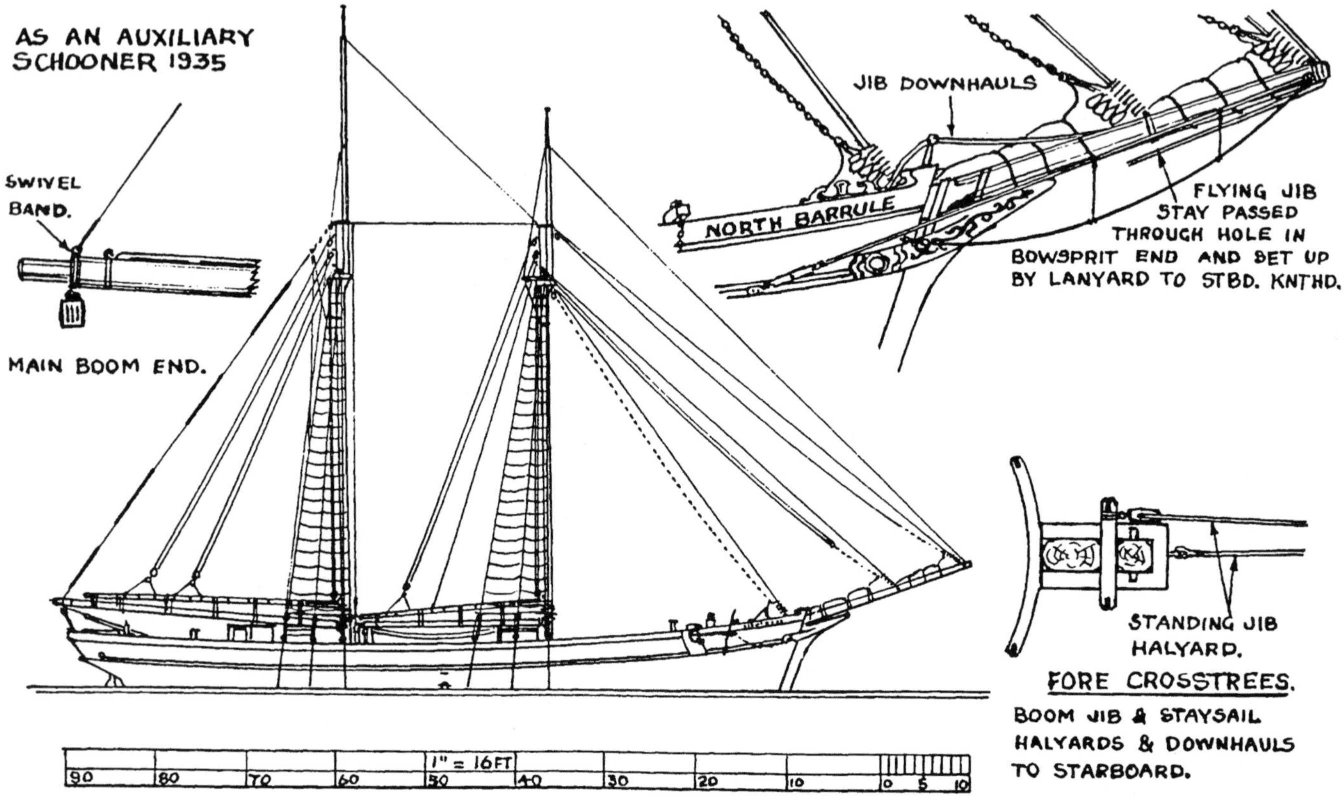

AS AN AUXILIARY SCHOONER 1935
SWIVEL BAND.
MAIN BOOM END.
JIB DOWNHAULS
NORTH BARRULE
FLYING JIB STAY PASSED THROUGH HOLE IN BOWSPRIT END AND SET UP BY LANYARD TO STBD. KNTHD.
STANDING JIB HALYARD.
FORE CROSSTREES.
BOOM JIB & STAYSAIL HALYARDS & DOWNHAULS TO STARBOARD.
1" = 16FT
90
80
70
60
50
40
30
20
10
0 5 10

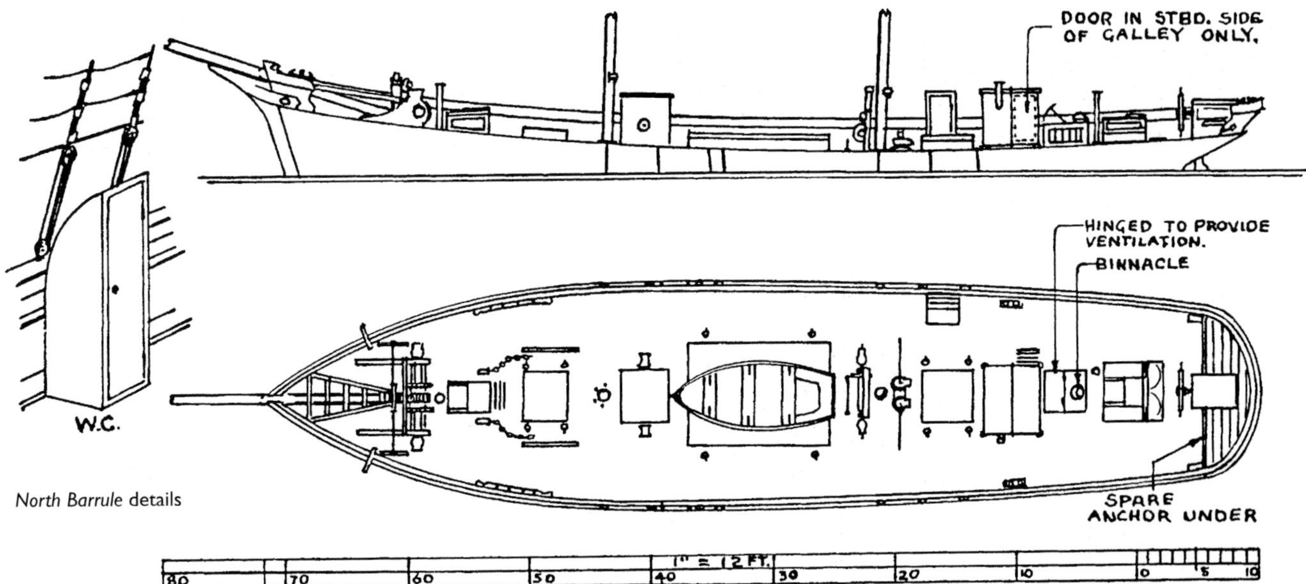

North Barrule details

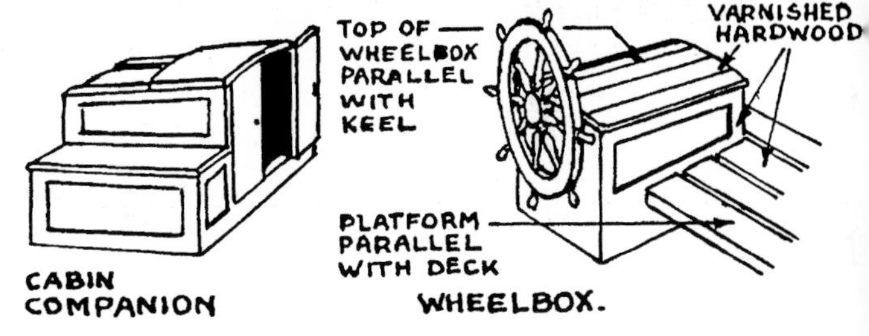

once her flying jib, gaff topsail and fore topgallant were set, she would not have been very over-canvassed. Obviously she would have to start shortening down before stiffer and stumpier vessels did so, but there is no reason to assume that her speed would be decreased by so doing. With her foremast so far aft, her headgear appears to stick out a mile but this is based on a point I noted at Connah's Quay – the distance from from knightheads to boom jib stop was about the same length as the fore boom.

North Barrule seems to have been a schooner that was always well maintained. It was often said that she had linoleum on the floor of her fo'c'sle – the last word in gentility in those days. When her engine was installed the mate moved forward but the skipper stayed aft, so perhaps the fancy fo'c'sle dated from her conversion. When her yards were sent down the crew seem to have seized the opportunity to discard the serviceable but unsightly battens in the fore rigging and to replace them once more with ratlines. Her mainsail was definitely fitted with roller-reefing gear but I have no note on her foresail[8]. The position of the binnacle suggests that at she was once steered by a tiller but, if so, the cabin companion would have had to be athwartships, with more space between it and the skylight. After the lapse of so many years I should be inclined to think that the presence of the stovepipe between the companion and the skylight was a mistake on my part, were it not for the fact that the ketch *Henrietta* had an almost identical set-up. In both vessels it may have been so arranged when their engines were installed.

Nyassa (ex-*June*) Wood auxiliary ketch, Cowes, built 1904, Emsworth. 36 tons net. *Official Number:* 120391. *Signal Hoist:* None.

Ocean Gem Wood auxiliary two-masted schooner, Barnstaple, built 1864, Castleton, Isle of Man, Rebuilt: 1882. 44 tons net. *Official Number:* 47281. *Signal Hoist:* MJZN.

[8] Dan McDonald stated that it was point reefed in 1929.

Olive Annie (ex-*Emma & Ellen*) Wood auxiliary ketch, Bideford, built 1872, Chepstow. 74 × 19.5 × 7.5ft. 85 tons gross, 59 tons net. *Official Number:* 69221. *Signal Hoist:* None.

Olive Branch Wood auxiliary ketch, Barnstaple, built 1878, Duncan, Kingston-on-Spey. 78.3 × 19.5 × 8.4ft. 66 tons gross, 56 tons net. *Official Number:* 76578. *Signal Hoist:* MQFJ.

Orestes* Wood ketch, Bridgwater, built 1885, D. Banks, Plymouth. 64.7 × 19 × 8.1ft. 49 tons net. *Official Number:* 91802. *Signal Hoist:* MJPV.

Ostrea Wood ketch, Portsmouth, built 1890, Emsworth. 35 tons net. *Official Number:* 95120. *Signal Hoist:* None.

Palace Wood ketch, built 1827, William Close, Brimscombe, Gloucester. 43 tons net. *Official Number:* 10887. *Signal Hoist:* None.

Parton Wood two-masted schooner, Whitehaven, built 1866, Nicholson, Annan. 81.9 × 20.7 × 10.6ft. 115 tons gross, 93 tons net. *Official Number:* 53139. *Signal Hoist:* None.

Pearl Wood ketch, Ipswich, built 1889, Orvis & Fuller, Ipswich. 85.4 × 21.4 × 7.2ft. 88 tons gross, 76 tons net. *Official Number:* 95309. *Signal Hoist:* MFQB.

Penryn Wood auxiliary ketch, built 1880, Falmouth. 74.1 × 20.3 × 9.2ft. 77 tons gross. 56 tons net.

Official Number: 83853.
Signal Hoist: MJJD.

Pilot Wood auxiliary ketch, Liverpool, built 1894, I. Pimlott, Northwich. 78.9 × 21.1 × 8.6ft. 103 tons gross, 77 tons net.
Official Number: 105389.
Signal Hoist: None.

Pooldoy (ex-*Iris*) Wood three-masted auxiliary schooner, Sligo, built 1904, Sixten Grath, Sjötorp, Sweden. 100 × 22.4 × 9.5ft. 180 tons gross. 96 tons net.
Official Number: 136475.
Signal Hoist: None.

Pride of Mourne Wood auxiliary ketch, Newry, built 1870, Appledore. 49 tons net.
Official Number: 62897.
Signal Hoist: None.

Progress* Wood auxiliary ketch, Bideford, built 1866, William Date & Sons, Kingsbridge. 80.2 × 19.2 × 9.2ft. 84 tons gross, 59 tons net.
Official Number: 86466.
Signal Hoist: MGJZ.

Progress Wood two-masted schooner, Castletown, Isle of Man, built 1878, Castleton. 69 tons net.
Official Number: 78217.
Signal Hoist: None.

Queen of the West* Wood two-masted schooner, Milford Haven, built 1849, Vivien, Salcombe; rebuilt 1876. 85.2 × 21 × 12ft. 120 tons gross. 98 tons net.
Official Number: 5496.
Signal Hoist: MFSV.

Rambler Wood ketch, Galway, built 1880, Peel, Isle of Man. 42 tons net.
Official Number: 104691.
Signal Hoist: None.

Raycreek (ex-*Kubo*) Steel auxiliary two-masted schooner, London, built 1932, NV Sheepswerk, Delfzjl, Netherlands. 102.2 × 20.8 × 7.6ft. 181 tons gross. 91 tons net.
Official Number: 163578.
Signal Hoist: MBFN.

Regina Wood ketch, Milford Haven, built 1897, Milford Haven. 65.7 × 18.4 × 7.3ft. 51 tons gross, 39 tons net.
Official Number: 108423.
Signal Letters: None.

Result* Steel auxiliary three-masted schooner, Barnstaple, built 1893, Paul Rodgers & Co., Carrickfergus and R. Kent & Co. 102 × 21.7 × 9.1ft. 130 tons gross. 86 tons net.
Official Number: 99937.
Signal Hoist: MQSG.

Rhoda Mary* Wood three-masted schooner, Falmouth, built 1868, John Stephens, Point, Feock. 101.2 × 21.9 × 11.5ft. 130 tons gross. 86 tons net.
Official Number: 62036.
Signal Hoist: MQKJ.

Rhodesia* (ex-*Semper Spero*) Steel ketch, Faversham, built 1909, Gebr. Niestern, Delfzjl, Netherlands. 97.4 × 19.4 × 6.8ft. 141 tons gross, 118 tons net.
Official Number: 124364.
Signal Hoist: MKJD.

Richard Cobden Wood two-masted schooner, Swansea, built 1868, McDonald, Prince Edward Island. 83.7 × 22.3 × 9.5ft. 107 tons gross, 92 tons net.
Official Number: 60632.
Signal Hoist: None.

Rigdin (ex-*Ingrid*) Wood auxiliary three-masted schooner, Southampton, built 1907, E. Soderström, Geta, Netherlands. 141.2 × 29.9 × 13.2ft. 397 tons gross, 311 tons net.
Official Number: 145353.
Signal Hoist: MKRZ.

Ripple* Wood ketch, Gloucester, built 1895, Gloucester. 30 tons net.
Official Number: 105406.
Signal Hoist: None.

Rival Wood ketch, Gloucester, built 1887, Evans, Saul, Gloucester. 47 tons gross, 32 tons net.
Official Number: 93454.
Signal Hoist: None.

Robert Elsie Wood auxiliary ketch, Newry, built 1905, Peel, Isle of Man. 22 tons net.
Official Number: 120859.
Signal Hoist: None.

Roger Wood auxiliary ketch, Galway (no building information but Official Number indicates a date of about 1921-2). 73 tons net.
Official Number: 146015.
Signal Hoist: None.

Rollo Wood ketch, Portsmouth, built 1895, Emsworth, 45 tons net.
Official Number: 105942.
Signal Hoist: None.

Roselyne* Iron auxiliary ketch, London, built 1918, Gouda, Netherlands. 94.2 × 21.8 × 9.3ft. 138 tons gross, 90 tons net.
Official Number: 160352.
Signal Hoist: None.

Rosetta* Wood auxiliary ketch, Aberystwyth, built 1890, Plymouth. 76.3 × 19.5 × 8.7ft. 74 tons gross, 46 tons net.
Official Number: 79402.
Signal Hoist: MCKK.

Rosie Wood auxiliary ketch, Bideford, built 1885, Robert Cock, Appledore. 83 × 21 × 9.9ft. 101 tons gross. 80 tons net.
Official Number: 79358.
Signal Hoist: MJST.

Roska Steel auxiliary ketch, Greenock, built 1930, Port Banatyne, 36 tons net.
Official Number: 161783.
Signal Hoist: MPTV.

Rothersand Steel two-masted schooner, London, built 1907, J. Pattje, Waterhuizen, Netherlands. 93.8 × 21.4 × 9.5ft. 140 tons gross. 114 tons net.
Official Number: 136840.
Signal Letters: MFVP.

R. Passmore Wood ketch, Dundee, built 1890, T. Garside, Burton Stather. 81.3 × 20.3 × 9.5ft. 79 tons net.
Official Number: 96418.
Signal Hoist: MBSQ.

Ryelands* Wood auxiliary three-masted schooner, Lancaster, built 1887, Nicholson & Marsh, Glasson Dock, Liverpool. 102.2 × 22 × 10.8ft. 151 tons gross, 110 tons net.
Official Number: 84964.
Signal Hoist: MKTD.

S. F. Pearce (ex-*Weser*, ex-*Marie Linnemann*) Steel auxiliary three-masted schooner, Fowey, built 1908, C. Lühring, Hammelwarden, Germany. 117.7 × 24.1 × 9.5ft. 213 tons gross, 159 tons net.
Official Number: 136824.
Signal Hoist: MVFK.

Sabrina Wood ketch, Gloucester, built 1893, Gloucester. 89 tons net.
Official Number: 99533.
Signal Hoist: None.

Sadie R. (ex-*Procellaris*) Wood auxiliary three-masted schooner, Bideford, built 1894, L. Minier, Binic, France. 101.2 × 23.7 × 11.9ft. 159 tons gross. 96 tons net.
Official Number: 143981.
Signal Hoist: None.

Safety Wood auxiliary ketch,

Gloucester, built 1838, Thomas Drew, Stourport. 63.4 × 13.0 × 7.5ft. 45 tons net. *Official Number:* 11118. *Signal Hoist:* None.

Saint Austell Wood auxiliary ketch, Barnstaple, built 1873, Portreath; rebuilt 1917, Appledore. 74 × 19.6 × 9.3ft. 77 tons gross, 49 tons net. *Official Number:* 69841. *Signal Hoist:* None.

Salacia Wood brigantine, Faversham, built 1867, W. H. Pearson, Sunderland. 104.6 × 25.4 × 15.3ft. 227 tons net. *Official Number:* 58087. *Signal Hoist:* None.

Sarah Wood ketch, Gloucester, built 1862, Gloucester. 48 tons net. *Official Number:* 43674. *Signal Hoist:* None.

Sarah Anne Wood ketch, Liverpool, built 1859, Northwich. 52 tons net. *Official Number:* 27948. *Signal Hoist:* None.

Snowflake sail plan

Sarah Bridget Wood three-masted schooner, Carnarvon, built 1858, Bangor. 99 tons net. *Official Number:* 21672. *Signal Hoist:* MQNW.

Sarah Latham Wood auxiliary ketch, Chester, built 1903, Ferguson & Baird, Connah's Quay. 80.7 × 21.5 × 8ft. 87 tons gross, 63 tons net. *Official Number:* 104478. *Signal Hoist:* MJGK.

Sea Lass Wood auxiliary ketch, Dover, built 1909, Lossiemouth. 81.1 × 20.1 × 8.6ft. 64 tons gross. 39 tons net. *Official Number:* 137758. *Signal Hoist:* None.

Shamrock* Wood ketch, Plymouth, built 1899, F. Hawke, Stonehouse, Plymouth. 57.6 × 18.1 × 5.4ft. 31.7 tons gross, 25 tons net. *Official Number:* 111344. *Signal Hoist:* None. *Shamrock* is still floating, preserved by the National Trust/National Maritime Museum at Cotehele on the River Tamar, Cornwall.

Snowflake details

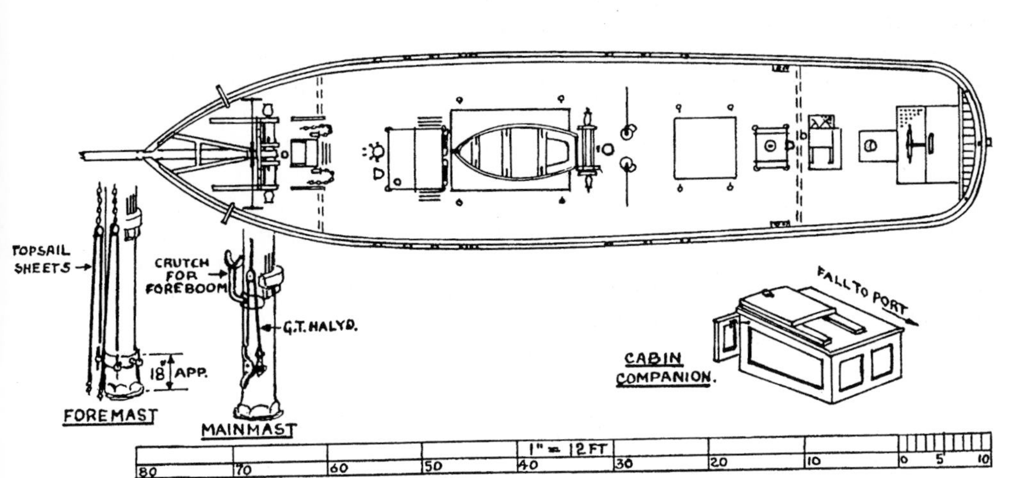

Sibyl Wood ketch, Portsmouth, built 1890, Emsworth. 25 tons net. *Official Number:* 95117. *Signal Hoist:* None.

Six Sisters* (ex-*Sigrid*, ex-*Jens*, ex-*Ryving*, ex-*Yrsa*, ex-*Linnea*) Wood auxiliary three-masted schooner, Hull, built 1902, F.A. Demar, Saltvik, Kalmar, Sweden. 114.4 × 25.9 × 9.1ft. 169 tons gross, 131 tons net. *Official Number:* 163144. *Signal Hoist:* None.

Snow Flake Wood two-masted schooner, Runcorn, built 1880, Brundritt & Co., Runcorn. 88.2 × 21.8 × 9.7ft. 109 tons gross, 88 tons net. *Official Number:* 80298.

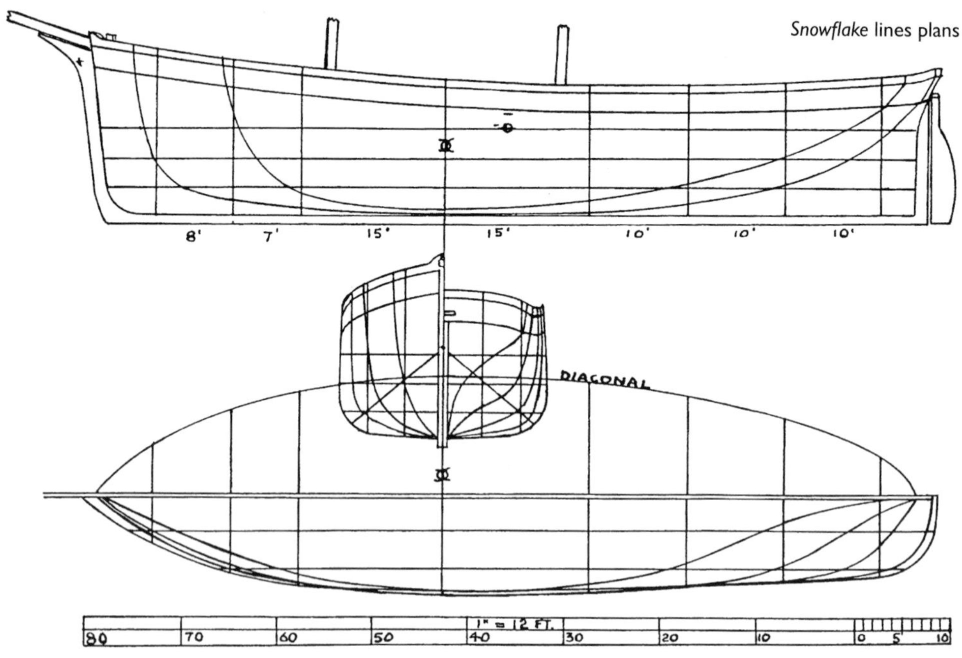

Snowflake lines plans

Signal Hoist: MDMJ.

As originally rigged *Snowflake* had a bowsprit and jib-boom that were probably replaced, as the result of a collision, by the long spike bowsprit that she carried at the end of her career. Like all the other 'Flats' she had her masts further forward than was normal in vessels with a counter stern. This was so that a reasonable size of mainsail could be obtained but the sailing qualities of the vessels did not seem to be in any way better or worse than those with the more expensive appendage. As would be expected they tended to be rather more full in the bows than the counter-sterned vessels and it was probably this feature which prevented their sail plan from being out of balance. In the 1930s a theory was put forward that the weather helm carried by most sailing vessels was caused, not by pressure of wind on the sails, but by pressure of water on the lee bow. The exponents of this theory claimed that this was similar to the wing of an aeroplane, which was not lifted by air pressure underneath it but by lack of pressure on top – in some way this made things much more scientific and, therefore, impressive. Without wishing to get too involved with this game of carts and horses, it is fairly obvious that in a heeled vessel the amount of water being thrown sideways by the lee bow must be much greater than on the weather side, and the bluffer the bows, the more this disparity would show up. It was this, one suspects, that caused bluff bows and foremasts stepped right in the eyes of the vessel, to hang on for thousands of years but as the vicious circle was finally broken in about the middle of the 19th century, it is not surprising that these theorists of the 20th century were unable to point the way to any outstanding improvement.

Solway Lass (ex-*Adolf*)
Steel auxiliary two-masted schooner, Dumfries, built 1902, Gebr. G. & H. Bodewes, Martenshoeck, Netherlands.
80.4 × 19.3 × 7.7ft.
100 tons gross, 76 tons net.
Official Number: 139003.
Signal Hoist: MFXB.

Spry* Wood ketch, Bristol, built 1894, W. Hurd, Chepstow.
71 × 9 × 8ft. 41 tons net.
Official Number: 99538.
Signal Hoist: None.
Spry is preserved at the Ironbridge Industrial Museum.

Squirrel Wood auxiliary ketch, Cardiff, built 1882, Bridgwater.
74.6 × 19.7 × 7ft. 51 tons net.
Official Number: 84671.
Signal Hoist: None.

For many years I suspected that this vessel had originally been a Severn Trow, until informed, by Dan McDonald, that she was built at Bridgwater. The factors pointing to the vessel working in the inland navigation were her shallow draught, originally only 6ft depth of hold, and her rather wide hatches, although these latter could have come into being when the middle section of her deck was raised by about 1ft. It is not impossible that

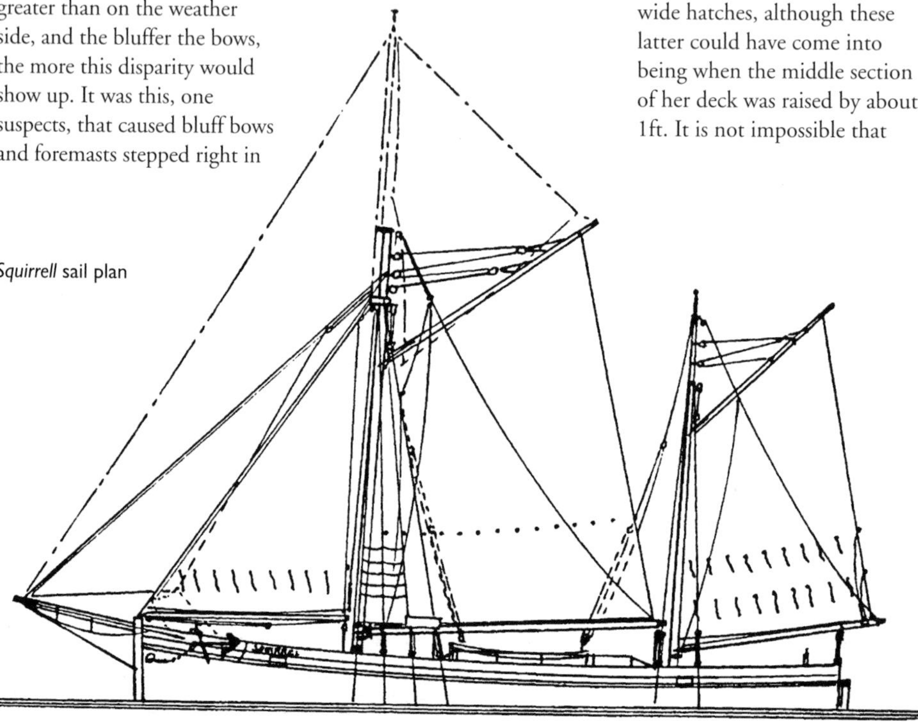

Squirrell sail plan

she was built like this but it seems far more probable that it was a later modification intended to increase the cargo capacity. Her cooking facilities were in the fo'c'sle so I am at a loss to know what purpose was served by the other stove in the starboard bulwarks, abreast of the mainmast. It may have come out of the cabin when the engine was installed.

Star Wood ketch, Colchester, built 1868, Aldous, Brightlingsea. 100 × 23.2 × 8ft. 118 tons gross, 53 tons net. *Official Number:* 58160. *Signal Hoist:* MDZT.

Stucley Wood ketch, Padstow, built 1839, Fowey. 58.2 × 16.2 × 6.3ft. 32 tons net. *Official Number:* 22387. *Signal Hoist:* None.

Sunbeam Wood ketch, Bridgwater, built 1893, Chepstow. 54 tons net. *Official Number:* 99532. *Signal Hoist:* Nil.

Sunshine* Wood auxiliary ketch, Bridgwater, built 1900, Falmouth. 88 × 22.3 × 8.8ft. 76 tons net. *Official Number:* 111391. *Signal Hoist:* None.

Sunshine Wood ketch, Faversham, built 1890, The Whitstable Shipbuilding Co., Whitstable. 95.8 × 23.3 × 9ft. 133 tons gross, 118 tons net. *Official Number:* 89864. *Signal Hoist:* MKWS.

Tarragona Wood auxiliary brigantine, Dublin, built 1863, Kennedy, Whitehaven. 92.2 × 21.6 × 12.2ft. 145 tons gross. 107 tons net. *Official Number:* 44230. *Signal Hoist:* None.

Squirrell lines plans

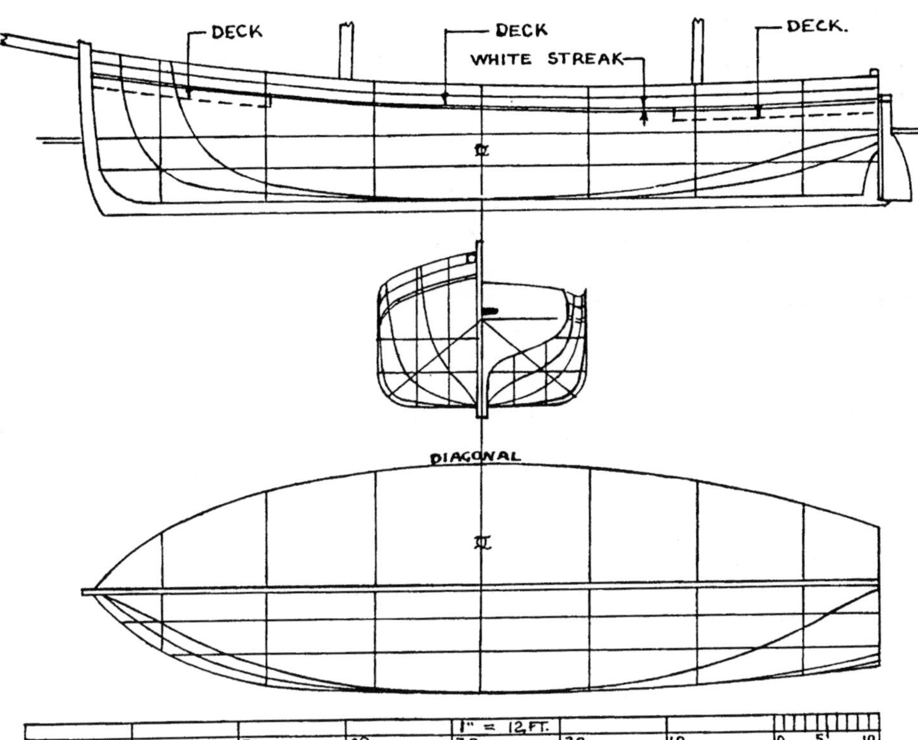

Squirrell details

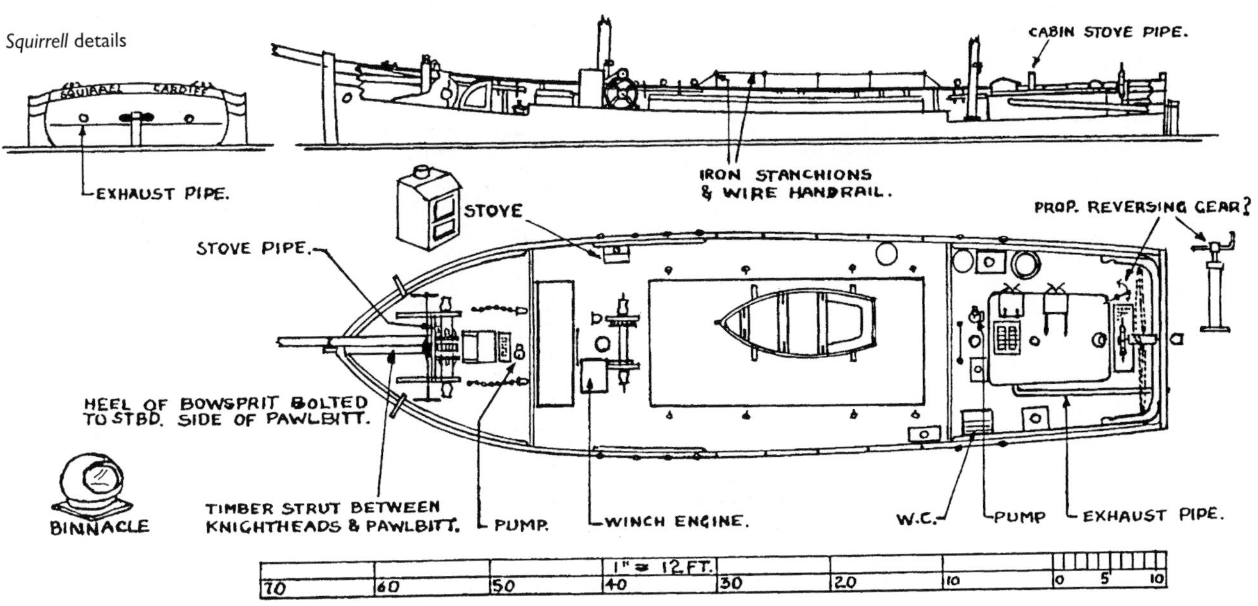

Teresa Wood ketch-barge, London, built 1892, Alfred White, Sittingbourne. 93 tons not. *Official Number:* 10193. *Signal Hoist:* MQJF.

Thistle Steel ketch, London, built 1895, Port Glasgow. 79 tons net. *Official Number:* 105727. *Signal Hoist:* MGJN.

Thistle Wood two-masted schooner, Plymouth, built 1863, Scott & Co., Bowling, Glasgow. 86 × 20 × 11ft. 122 tons gross, 100 tons net. *Official Number:* 45249. *Signal Hoist:* None.

Thomas Aylan Wood three-masted schooner, Fowey, built 1860, Polruan. 97 tons net. *Official Number:* 20600. *Signal Hoist:* MQLC.

Thor Wood ketch, Gloucester, built 1864, Gloucester. 35 tons net. *Official Number:* 51202. *Signal Hoist:* None.

Topsham* (ex-*Oliver*) Wood ketch, Exeter, built 1871, Hempstead, Gloucester. 63 tons net. *Official Number:* 63087. *Signal Hoist:* None.

Traly* Steel auxiliary ketch, Barnstaple, built 1912, Edwards & Co., Millwall, London. 79.7 × 20.1 × 9ft. 108 tons gross, 70 tons net. *Official Number:* 128846. *Signal Hoist:* MDVG.

Trio Wood auxiliary ketch, Bridgwater, built 1876, Le Seuer, Jersey. 77.6 × 19.6 × 9.2ft. 81 tons gross. 77 tons net. *Official Number:* 72564. *Signal Hoist:* None.

Two Sisters* Wood auxiliary ketch, Barnstaple, built 1865, Thomas Waters, Bideford. 70.8 × 19.4 × 9.5ft 79 tons gross, 62 tons net. *Official Number:* 47889. *Signal Hoist:* None.

Two Sisters Wood auxiliary ketch, Bideford, built 1882, T. Smart, Bosham. 94.8 × 21.8 × 9.7ft. 124 tons gross, 100 tons net. *Official Number:* 84246. *Signal Hoist:* MDRY.

Uncle Ned* Wood auxiliary two-masted schooner, Dublin, built 1867, Robertson, Ipswich. 116.5 × 23.8 × 12ft. 188 tons gross. 130 tons net. *Official Number:* 66644. *Signal Hoist:* EIBZ.

Useful* Wood auxiliary two-masted schooner, Barrow, built 1879, William Ashburner, Barrow. 89.3 × 21.3 × 9.1ft. 77 tons net. *Official Number:* 76892. *Signal Hoist:* None. (For drawings see under *Isabella*).

Venturer* Steel auxiliary two-masted schooner, Dublin, built 1920, NV Sheveningsche Schpsb. Mij., Scheveningen, Netherlands. 112 × 22.6 × 10.3ft. 210 tons gross, 159 tons net. *Official Number:* 144599. *Signal Hoist:* EIDT.

Vernon Wood two-masted schooner, Dublin, built 1857, Dorchester, New Brunswick. 79 tons net. *Official Number:* 35232. *Signal Hoist:* EIGK.

Vernona (ex-*Xarifa*) Wood auxiliary ketch, London, built 1912, Gosport 147 tons net. *Official Number:* 146143. *Signal Hoist:* GMTP (radio).

Victor (ex-*Concordia*) Wood barquentine, Youghal, (no building information but Official Number indicates a date of about 1859/60). 141 tons net. *Official Number:* 39473. *Signal Hoist:* None.

Victory Wood ketch, Gloucester, built 1877, Gloucester. 37 tons net. *Official Number:* 69918. *Signal Hoist:* None.

Vivian Wood auxiliary ketch, Portsmouth, built 1895, Portsmouth. 54 tons net. *Official Number:* 104449. *Signal Hoist:* None.

Volant* Wood auxiliary two-masted schooner, Kirkwall, built 1877, J. & W. Geddie, Banff. 86.8 × 21.7 × 10.3ft. 113 tons gross, 77 tons net. *Official Number:* 70520. *Signal Hoist:* MQSY.
The *Volant* and *Minnie* were built in the same area and for many years I believed that they would have a lot in common. I tackled *Volant*'s sail plan several years before I turned my attention to *Minnie* and, having only seen the latter vessel in the days when she mooched rather sedately about the Irish Sea, with stump topmasts and an auxiliary engine, I was unprepared for the revelations of one of Dan McDonald's photographs. *Volant* could perhaps be described as the 'Gentle Maiden' of the schooner world, whereas, in her youth, *Minnie* must have been a real 'tearaway'. By a strange chance

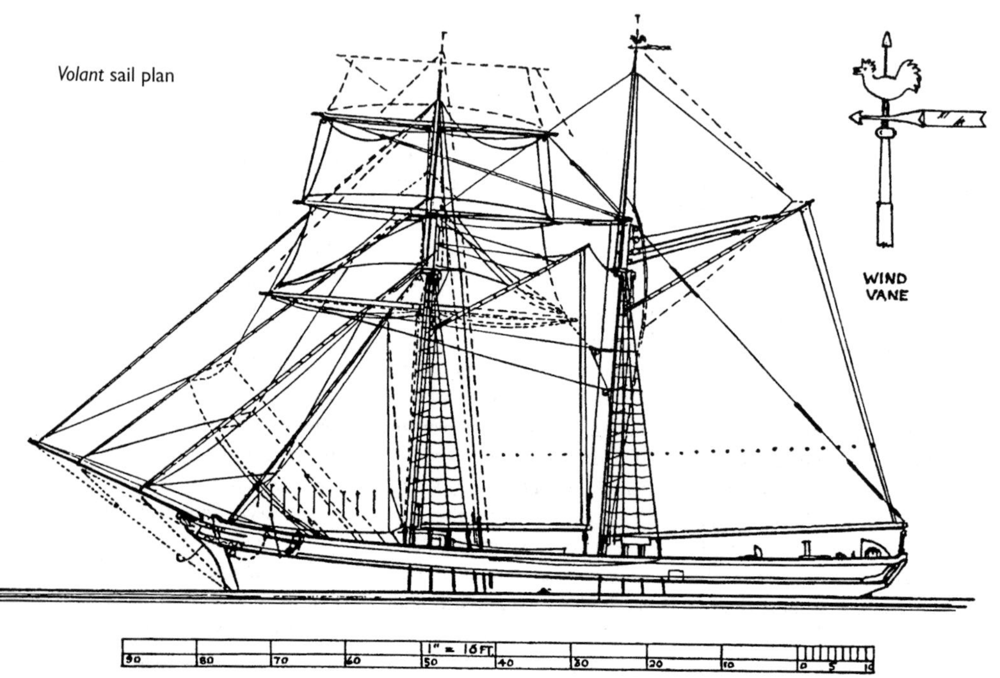

Volant sail plan

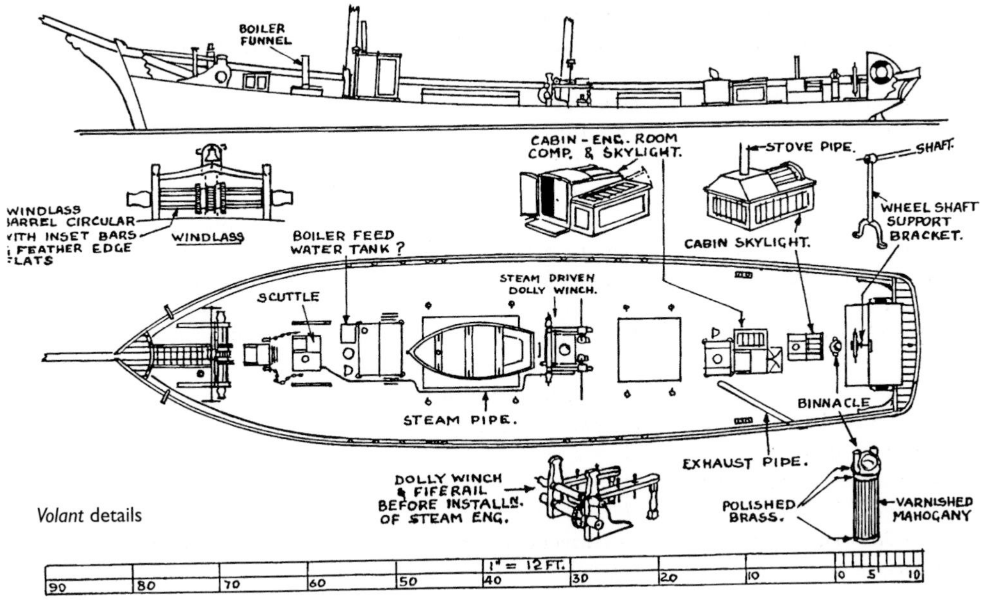

Volant details

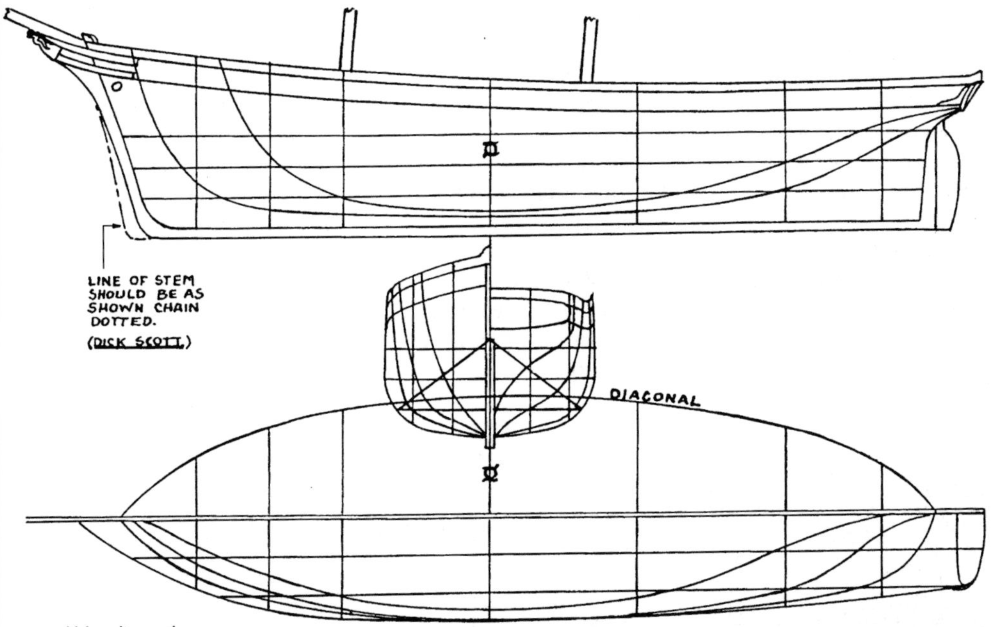

Volant lines plans

I could have made this discovery many years before, merely by looking at their figureheads: 'Miss Volant' was a nice cuddly little armful of talent, but 'Minnie' was a big buxom lass with something of a 'no nonsense' look about her. The vessels that had carried these ladies, had but two things in common: they both had the same kind of stern and both originally carried standing topgallants. There the similarity ended.

In spite of being 2ft 6in longer than *Minnie* between perpendiculars, *Volant* looked both a smaller and daintier vessel. Some of this was caused by *Minnie*'s figurehead, which stuck out a long way forward of the knightheads. She also had a long jib-boom and a pair of tall masts with a rake to that would have turned a Baltimore clipper captain green with envy. Everything pointed to the fact that before she was fitted with roller-reefing gear, her main boom must have stuck out a long way abaft the counter. She must have been a stiff vessel to stand up to such a sail plan and I feel quite justified in giving her a really full midship section. Perhaps it would put things into better perspective if this statement were reversed. She was built with a full-lined hull to carry plenty of cargo, and was given a sail plan that would drive it through the water at a reasonable speed. Her two extra main topmast backstays indicate that neither the gaff topsail nor the main topmast staysail were intended to be treated as flying kites, to be taken in on the first hard puff of wind. Altogether she was such a rakish little packet that I am sure more than one person will want to make a model of her. The marks of the 'old timer', the wooden catheads and dolphin striker, and the double topping lifts on the main boom, surely all add to the attraction. The position of the lower topsail clewlines must be unique, mid way between quarters and yardarms – almost as though the men who put them there liked the neat stow of the former but had to concede that the latter had its advantages and, not being able to resolve these conflicting desires, finished up half way between heaven and earth. [Drawings of *Minnie* appeared earlier in this chapter].

In contrast to *Minnie, Volant* had a much lower sail plan and the easier lines that went with it. It has already been mentioned that both she and the *Lochranza Castle* had steam driven winches; of the two, *Volant*'s boiler was in the better position, directly below the trimming hatch forward, which must have been partitioned off from the hold. In this position the boiler could be easily hoisted on deck for survey and repairs and would leave the f'o'csle rather cooler in summer. The scuttle on the starboard side of the hatch may have been for ventilation purposes but could also have been used to get the boiler fuel below decks without having to get it down the ladder.

It has already been stated that long before the 19th century came to an end there was precious little of a regional nature left in British shipbuilding; that from one end of these islands to the other, everyone had a clear idea of what the other fellow was up to. The fact that two such dissimilar vessels as *Volant* and *Minnie* could be built a mere three years and thirty miles apart, drives this home with peculiar intensity. The customer could have any kind of schooner he liked, just as long as he coughed up the money. Of the two, *Volant* had much more in common with Scandinavian vessels, with their rounded bilges and easy lines, and she was perhaps the last British sailing vessel to bear the signs of the ancient ties of commerce and culture, which stretch back into the past across the North Sea and are epitomised in the ballad of Sir Patrick Spens:

Oh wha has done this fell, fell deed
And tauld the king o' me
To send us oot at this time o' year
To sail upon the sea?
To Noroway to Noroway,
To Noroway ower the faem
The king's daughter o' Noroway,
'tis thou maun bring her hame.

Volunteer Wood ketch, Gloucester, built 1871, Gloucester. 30 tons net. *Official Number:* 63092. *Signal Hoist:* None.

Walter J. Cummins Wood brigantine, Irvine, built 1865, Brown, Mirimichi, Welford, New Brunswick. 91.3 × 23.1 × 11.6ft. 154 tons gross, 151 tons net. *Official Number:* 50850. *Signal Hoist:* MGVS.

Wasp Wood ketch, Gloucester, built 1895, Saul, Gloucester. 36 tons net. *Official Number:* 119633. *Signal Hoist:* None.

Welcome Wood auxiliary ketch, Gloucester, built 1885, P Rawstrone, Freckleton, Gloucester. 94 × 22.4 9.6ft. 119 tons gross. 79 tons net. *Official Number:* 88713. *Signal Hoist:* MJWL.

Welcome Home Wood schooner, Gloucester, built 1881, Stornaway. 94 tons net. *Official Number:* 79955. *Signal Hoist:* MJFM.

Wessex Wood ketch-barge, Littlehampton, built 1918, J. & W. Harvey, Littlehampton. 100.7 × 24.2 × 8.4ft. 84 tons net. *Official Number:* 131977. *Signal Hoist:* MJGV.

Whiteriggs Wood two-masted schooner, Gloucester, built 1856, Liverpool. 71 tons net. *Official Number:* 15191. *Signal Hoist:* None.

Wild Wave Wood two-masted schooner, Dublin, built 1873, Falmouth. 58 tons net. *Official Number:* 67766. *Signal Hoist:* EIFQ.

Wildflower Wood two-masted schooner, Wexford, built 1860, Fairlie, Ayr. 28 tons net. *Official Number:* 27927. *Signal Hoist:* EIFZ.

William Wood ketch, Bristol, built 1809, Bower Yard, Shropshire. 50 tons net. *Official Number:* 3912. *Signal Hoist:* MDJB.

William Ashburner* Wood auxiliary three-masted schooner, Barrow, built 1876, William Ashburner, Barrow. 115.1 × 25.1 × 12.8ft. 205 tons gross, 128 tons net. *Official Number:* 70843. *Signal Hoist:* MJJZ.

Willie Wood ketch, Gloucester, built 1893, Gloucester. 38 tons net. *Official Number:* 99531. *Signal Hoist:* None.

Windemere* Wood auxiliary three-masted schooner, Dublin, built 1890, Ferguson & Baird, Connah's Quay. 104.2 × 24.3 × 11.2ft. 179 tons gross, 127 tons net. *Official Number:* 93420. *Signal Hoist:* EIFK.

Winifred Wood auxiliary ketch, Liverpool, built 1898, Ferguson & Baird, Connah's Quay. 81.7 × 20.8 × 8.5ft. 89 tons gross, 69 tons net. *Official Number:* 104472. *Signal Hoist:* None.

Winifred* Wood auxiliary ketch, Plymouth, built 1897, Falmouth. 64 × 19.3 × 7.5ft. 53 tons gross, 38 tons net. *Official Number:* 108553. *Signal Hoist:* None.

Woodcock Wood auxiliary ketch, Barnstaple, built 1895, W.S. Kelly, Plymouth. 61.3 × 17.5 × 6.7ft. 43 tons gross, 28 tons net. *Official Number:* 105768. *Signal Hoist:* None.

Wye Wood ketch, Bristol, built 1860, Bristol. 57 tons net. *Official Number:* 28503. *Signal Hoist:* None.

Yarra* Wood ketch, Cardiff, built 1880, Bristol. 56 tons net. *Official Number:* 83802. *Signal Hoist:* None.

Zebina* Wood auxiliary three-masted schooner-barge, Cardiff, built 1873, Gann, Ipswich. 109.1 × 24.5 × 9.9ft. 189 tons gross, 142 tons net. *Official Number:* 60245. *Signal Hoist:* MGCS.

Zebrina* (ex-*Anna Jensen*) Steel auxiliary two-masted schooner, London, built 1921, Schiffswerk AG, Hamburg. 112.3 × 23 × 9.6ft. 237 tons gross, 165 tons net. *Official Number:* 148588. *Signal Hoist:* None.

Zenobia Wood ketch-barge, London, built 1886, Bayley, Ipswich. 85.6 × 20.6 × 6.9ft. 78 tons gross. 68 tons net. *Official Number:* 91903. *Signal Hoist:* MJXG.

XV

CONCLUSION

It is already apparent that in the foreseeable future we shall be driven to seeking energy in sources other than the hydrocarbons, which we are using up at a tremendous speed. Fortunately there are plenty of other power options available. Wind and falling water have been used since the dawn of time but, thus far, the heat of the sun and the energy in the tides have barely been touched, while miles below our feet is a vast reservoir of tremendous heat that we are currently only able to use in odd places where, by some freak of nature, water gets into it and steam rushes up through the earth's surface.

The time will come when the wind-driven ship will be with us once more and, whatever form she may take, at our present level of technology, there will be at least one piece of equipment found aboard her: a wind-driven turbo-generator, possibly of no great size but capable of keeping a set of electrical batteries charged. These batteries may possibly be used to give the vessel a modest shove through the doldrums and horse latitudes, but their real function will probably be to keep the refrigerator operating so that the crew can enjoy the same wide variety of food as those living ashore.

There are plenty of enthusiasts eager to point the way to the sailing ship of the future and, although their ideas vary tremendously, there already exists a strong lobby that believes the Flettner Rotor ship should be one of the first to be given a fair trial. Another group would like to build an oversized *Potosi*, taking up the big square rigger at the point where the Germans left off – although why this latter group does not go the whole hog and settle for a larger *Preussen* is something of a mystery. However, one factor that all these people may have overlooked is, just as there was at the 'tall' end of the 19th century, there will be a need for a fleet of powerful sea-going tugs to pick up these sailing giants as they approach the narrow waters of their destination and to see them safely into port. The tugs would obviously use up fuel, but they would use far less than a powered vessel bringing the cargo the whole way. The belief that a low-powered auxiliary engine could sufficiently enable the tugs is a fallacy – no large sailing vessel would be safe in soundings if she was not controlled by the same size of engines as a fully powered ship.

One school of thought on the future sailing ship seems bent on using an aerofoil. This, I take it is, akin to an aeroplane wing but I have no information on how it would propel a ship's hull through the water. Its present use is to lift a comparatively light load off the ground by the creation of a vacuum above its upper surface and, while it may well have points in common with the sail, it would take a tremendous amount of research, carried out in a wind tunnel designed for no other purpose, to establish the best method by which it could be harnessed to this new job. To be successful this sort of project would need government backing, which is not likely to be forthcoming for many years yet*.

The surprising thing that emerges from all these proposals is that there are so many people who seem to think it necessary to build bigger vessels than ever before, in spite of the fact that the huge unit ashore is already somewhat discredited as far as its much vaunted efficiency is concerned, while the huge unit at sea frequently conveys the impression that the entire crew are convinced that somewhere there is a man aboard who is keeping a good lookout. And, when the supertanker breaks up at sea, the cost to everyone for hundreds of miles around is so immense that they all wish the tanker owners would put their eggs into smaller baskets.

It is a strange fact that so far no one has come forward with a proposal to build a fourteen-masted *Thomas W. Lawson*, although by the yardstick of the number of men required to work her, she would win hands down against the square riggers. It is generally accepted that the fore-and-aft rig is not ideal for running the easting down in high latitudes but enough of these big schooners must have done just that to prove they were capable. If, some day, the records of their westward-bound performances, either around Cape Horn or across the North Atlantic, are dragged out, there is a strong

* Since writing this book the Walker Windsail has, of course, been tried, albeit on only a few yachts. Whilst it was not entirely unsuccessful, acceptance was a long time coming and the company failed. The possible commercial use of this form of wind-power is still some time away. There have also been experiments with the use of wind-power elsewhere in the world but results thus far have been of limited benefit. However, as the cost of hydrocarbons escalate, the economic benefit of wind-power may one day again become a realistic consideration.

chance that they will reveal a fair amount of eyebrow-lifting evidence.

There was nothing wrong with the *Thomas W. Lawson*, despite her untimely end. She was no great beauty – the *Wyoming* was a much nicer looking vessel – but she was one of thousands, all through the centuries, that came to grief in the same trap. 'From Ushant to Scilly is thirty-five leagues' says the old song and, on the face of it, this hundred-mile gap would seem wide enough for any number of ships to pass through in safety. But for a vessel 1,000 miles out in the Atlantic with a southwest gale behind her and no sight of the sun for days on end to give an exact position, it was little better than running blind at a hole in a wall. Those vessels that made their landfall during the night were fortunate – the lights of the 19th century would give them far more accurate information than grey smudges of land would do in daylight. It was inevitable that ship after ship – before they knew exactly where they were – landed into trouble of one kind or another and, when they turned to fight their way clear, their sails blew out of the bolt ropes, leaving them at the mercy of the wind and the sea. The losses were bad enough in the 19th century, but in all other centuries they must have been appalling – making this, the front door of northern Europe, the most wreck-strewn area in the world. Unless we can manufacture sailcloth that is capable of standing up to winds of above 100-miles per hour and which deteriorates reasonably slowly, the conventional sailing ship would appear to be a doubtful starter for the future. The losses would still be too high, especially against a background that is far more safety-conscious than any previous generations could ever afford to be.

One way in which really strong sails could perhaps be produced would be by using fine-mesh steel-wire cloth of the kind commonly in use for screening materials in milling processes. The seams would have to be welded together and the finished sail welded to its steel-wire bolt-ropes, after which the whole fabrication could be coated with plastic material to render it wind and rust proof. The increased tensile strength of this material would enable a flatter sail to be produced than with orthodox canvas but whether this would give increased efficiency to windward would remain to be seen. Obviously such a sail could not possibly be stowed by conventional methods so that some kind of roller reefing and furling gear would have to be used.

If this new canvas proved a practical proposition there would be no necessity to go mad and replace every sail in the ship; only those on which the vessel would have to rely in extremity would need to be changed, leaving the rest to be made, handled and furled in the time-honoured way. For a square rigger this would mean the inner jib, topmast staysails, spanker, courses and lower topsails would be high-tech with the fore upper topsail as an optional extra. In a schooner the necessary sails would be the standing jib, staysail and the fore and afters.

The schooner would be the ideal rig in which to test these sails because the gear for roller-reefing her sails has already been in existence and proved to be a success. To avoid having a triangle of unstowable canvas the gaffs would have to lie parallel to the booms, the main gaff topsail would have to be cut deeper to fill the extra space, and a neater stow could be produced on the furled sail if the mast booms could be removed from the mast one by one as they arrived at deck level. The two headsails could be furled on rollers on their respective stays, the gear for which has been in use on yachts for many years. No doubt this would make a mess of the vessel's appearance but, in the end, a generation would arrive that had never known anything else.

The square rigger would not be quite as simple to deal with as the schooner. Its fore-and-aft sails would present no problems since they would be dealt with by the same type of gear as described above, except, of course, that it would be bigger and heavier. In the past, several methods of roller-reefing or furling squaresails were tried, all of which had some drawbacks and all of which finally gave way to double topsails – although the Bretons hung on to one version right to the end. This was the 'Colling and Pinkney's' method in which the topsail yard was fitted with a roller below, on to which the sail was wrapped by pulling on chains wound around drums at each end. The roller was not heavy enough to stand with no other support than the bearings at each end and to remedy this two metal hooks were fitted to the quarters of the yard to prevent it from bending under load. Photographic evidence points to the fact that these hooks were the cause of a certain amount of wear and tear on the sail and, as more and more canvas was wrapped around the roller, the friction must have increased considerably. Another method, 'Cunningham's patent', used the yard itself to wrap the sail around. To do this there had to be a slot up the middle of the sail; this was closed by a cloth called the bonnet which was laced or unlaced to the body of the sail, and the canvas was paid out or rolled in. Another method of closing the gap was by means of wooden cross battens with claw ends that slid up and down the slot on doubled bolt ropes carrying a strip of canvas which, when the sail was close-reefed, was left bunched up at the bunt. This would not be possible with the kind of new sailcloth being discussed and it might be asked whether it was really necessary to close this gap at all.

If the gap was left open it would certainly not be the first time a sail had been split into two separate pieces. It is generally believed that a large single area of canvas is more efficient than a number of smaller ones but time and again ease of handling seems to have won the day. The lateen mizzen must have been a grand sail for shoving a vessel to windward but, in spite of this, it finished up as two separate sails, a staysail forward of the mast and a gaff-and-boom sail abaft it. The raffee was probably conceived from the lateen as two staysails hanked on to the lifts, although its gear would have been much simpler if it had been made as a single triangle of canvas with a halyard and a downhaul fastened to its head cringle. Everyone is familiar with the case of double topsails and, after them, double topgallants. If after each of these innovations there had been a really marked decrease in efficiency, history would surely not have been so silent on the subject. The famous holes in the sails of the *Invercauld* probably did not do any good, but obviously they did no great harm either.

In the main the roller-reefing and furling patents of the 19th century were concerned with topsails; when double topsails were introduced and it became possible to pass from full topsails to close-reefed sails by the mere letting go of a halyard and pulling on a couple of downhauls, everyone was satisfied. The case under discussion, however, is the production of a sailing vessel capable of clawing her way to windward against gales of tremendous force and, for this, the courses are far more suitable than the topsails. They give the greatest pulling power and yet possess the least tendency to put the vessel on her beam ends. Here the roller reefing gear is dictated by the construction of the sails and, if the slots down the middle gave the slightest indication of impairing the efficiency of the braced-up courses, they would definitely have to be covered up. This could be done by a separate cloth attached to the bolt rope at the foot of the sail only, perhaps four or five times the width of the slot, which could be wound on or off a separate short roller mounted above the yard by brackets from the truss. This could be operated from either end.

The writer envisages the roller-reefing yard as having a worm wheel or chain drum at its centre, flanked on either side by a ball race in which it can rotate, and fitted at the yardarms with swivel bands to take the lifts, topsail sheets, braces and clewgarnet blocks. These last would still be needed when going about, although topsail clewlines could conceivably become a thing of the past. There would have to be a bar of some kind on the after side of the yard, from which to hang the footropes so that the swivel bands could be periodically inspected to see if they were adequately lubricated. The chain-and-drum method of working the reefing gear would obviously be more in keeping with nautical tradition, as the fall of the tackle could be taken to a deck capstan in much the same way as the schooner men used the dolly winches.

It seems fairly certain that another hundred years will pass before the problem of dwindling fuel supplies becomes so acute that those who, from folly or greed, wish to continue to exploit fossil fuels will finally be forced to desist and even the politicians will have to take the problem seriously. Perhaps, therefore, it would be as well if those nations that still support government-owned or -sponsored sail-training vessels, were encouraged to carry on if only to sustain the necessary sailing ship skills and information that will be needed by a future generation. These vessels, usually naval training ships, have an advantage over the many amateur-rigged vessels that today masquerade as 'Tall Ships' in that they still persist in doing everything strictly according to the book.

There can be no argument that the sailing ship of the future definitely needs stronger sails but, apart from this, tinkering with it will yield very little in the way of progress. The sailing ship took so many thousands of years to evolve and each part so interacted with everything else that to alter even one small item would disrupt the balance of the whole. In spite of this, many of the 'Tall Ships' can be seen sporting radical departures from the practise of the past. And such things appear to have no adverse effect on the vessels concerned because the sails are no longer used to get to windward – such arduous labour is left to the engine. As long as the engine is an old worn-out semi-diesel this is considered legitimate, even praiseworthy.

From the foregoing it is almost certain that, sooner or later, a school of thought will appear to examine the whole problem in the light of modern technology and re-design a sailing vessel from scratch. This will particularly be the case if the Flettner Rotor ship does not come up to expectations and, as long as the designers keep firmly before them the hard-won knowledge of past generations of seamen, there is no real reason why they should not be successful.

A hypothetical vessel in this category might have tubular steel masts – cantilevered up from the deck and capable of standing without stays of any kind would be an obvious choice. These would be capable of revolving through at least 130 degrees and would be fitted with brake drums at deck level and stops in various positions, such as for beating or running. The sails would be of metal, preferably duralumin, and would be capable of a certain amount of lateral movement to impart the 'twist' so necessary when close-hauled in a gale. Trimming in small vessels would be done from the deck by means of handwheels, and in larger vessels by a hydraulic system, the electrical power for which would be kept topped up by a wind-turbine-driven pump. All sorts of safeguards would be incorporated. The most important of these would be a centreline bulkhead and removable shifting

boards in the way of the hatches, such as have been used for years in bulk grain carriers. The centre of effort of the sails would be offset from their pivot bar so that, in the event of too much wind pressure, a slipping clutch would allow the sail to flip around to something approaching a right angle to its normal working position. The load at which this occurred would be greatest for the courses and least for the royals. Hand gear would be provided to turn the sails to the completely 'furled' position, parallel to the sea. If the angle of heel exceeded a certain figure the stops on the masts would be released to allow them to swing head to wind. The sort of mechanism by which some of these things would be accomplished could be executed using the common equipment of the heavy engineering industry with the final product no doubt being far more sophisticated.

If we are still suffering from the belief that civilisation is about computers and machines, not men, when this sort of vessel makes its debut, then messages will be fed into a computer from anemometers, chronometers, barometers, thermometers and sextants so that no one on board will have to think until, of course, something goes wrong with the works and they are left thumbing frantically through the handbook to find out where to start. (It does not seem likely that a computer will ever be able to know what a bygone generation of seamen achieved with a lifetime's observation of the wind and the sea and the sky.) Finally, on a vessel such as this, going aloft would be up the inside of the masts with an oil can, and life aboard would be very similar to a normal seagoing engineer's job. There would be no struggling with wildly thrashing canvas – those who have a desire to fight the elemental forces of nature would probably give up the sea and take up mountaineering instead.

In spite of hoping that sail-training vessels continue to carry on the traditions of the past, I have to confess that I have always been one of their lukewarm supporters. The cost of the vessel and the expense of running her make it necessary to cram in as many trainees as possible. The presence of a crew far bigger than that needed to work the vessel makes it imperative to find or invent all sorts of jobs to keen them fully occupied and to place them with a small army of bawling petty officers who can herd them around like sheep and keep them constantly on the move. The real sailoring will generally be done by bosuns. The sail- training ship is in exactly the same position as are the armed forces in times of peace – having to keep a large number of personnel fully occupied by whatever means they can lay their hands on. As these vessels carry no cargo the only reason for keeping them at sea in bad weather can be to accustom the trainees to seasickness. The whole thing can be summed up in a phrase well-known to service personnel: 'If in doubt, bugger them about a bit.'

The bogus nature of a good deal of such training is not lost on young people and does much to undo any good that the experience might otherwise bestow on them. The tendency is for the noisy extrovert to push his way to the front and, as the trainees are only in the vessel for a short period, any latent ability that the less vocal may possess has little chance to show up. I cannot claim that I care a damn what happens to the noisy extrovert – he can be relied upon to shove his way into a better position than his abilities usually merit. It is the quieter sort of lad in whom my interest is centred. Of course, given time the sea itself will sort out the wheat from the chaff, but I suspect the process will happen with much greater speed in a small under-manned vessel. This was one of the unsung services performed by the schooners of the 19th century, quietly and without fuss, and the men they trained knew plenty about the sea long before their training was finished – they lived too damn close to it not to. For years there has been a lot of vague rubbish talked about sail training being a 'character building' experience, but all observation points to the fact that a man's character is something he was born with and remains shackled to for life, although environment may modify it slightly. When the schooners were in their heyday, or any other kind of sailing vessel for that matter, it would have been possible to collect out of them such a set of characters as would have frightened any would-be sail trainee ashore for the rest of his life.

It might well be asked whether there is any aspect of sail training or sailing-ship experience in general, that might be of use to those who do not intend to make the sea their career, or to those who must, of necessity, go to sea in power-driven vessels. To my mind the answer is a decided 'No' except for one thing – and that happens to be worthwhile for anybody.

It did not take long for a young man in a sailing vessel to realise that anything he worked on about the ship, especially aloft, might be grabbed by himself or his shipmates, not only in daylight but in the wild blackness of a dirty night – for this reason alone he learned to do everything to the absolute best of his ability. Following on from this came the realisation that the failure of one small item, such as a lashing, could throw more strain on to something else, which might then also give way, so that the ship, like the kingdom, might ultimately be lost for the want of a nail. If this message did not come through very clearly from personal experience it could be deduced from the careful, almost careworn, way in which the older men finished off even the smallest job, lingering to see that all was in order before coiling up little pieces of spunyarn and putting their tools away in their little canvas bags. One real gale would be enough to tell the young man why.

However vaguely grasped, this lesson surely could not fail to have its effect on anything that the young man was called upon to do in later life.

To learn this kind of thing it was not necessary to be a character. There was nothing subtle about the way the wind and the sea hammered their message home, all that was asked of those wishing to ship in a schooner was that they have two arms and two legs and the ability to work. The thing which strained the newcomer's credulity to the limit was that the crew were supposed to be jolly jack tars, not a handful of rather disgruntled individuals getting on with a job.

It is a sad fact that the men who worked before the mast in schooners were not considered of any great standing in the communities of their home towns. They probably never were, even when the schooners were in their balmy days, but as steam vessels came more and more to the fore their position steadily deteriorated until, by the 1930s, it was at its lowest ebb. A schooner skipper might just about scrape into respectability if he attended church regularly while in port and avoided over-indulgence in alcoholic beverages but the really solid citizens were the steady-going men who worked in tugs, weekly steamers, dredgers and similar vessels, who came home at fairly regular intervals so that their children did not think they were the 'gas man'. Without anything being directly said on the subject, the impression was conveyed that the schooner hand was little better than a seagoing deadbeat whose only saving grace was that he disappeared for long intervals, showed his face briefly and, if he got drunk too often, would be departing soon. In short it was not an occupation that anyone in those days would have bragged about. In my own case I rapidly discovered that I had even more reason than most to keep quiet about it: at the mere mention of schooners I was immediately assailed with the question, 'What's an engineer doing to get himself involved with such an antiquated form of transport?' There didn't seem to be any answer except the rather lame one that I was interested in them. In time I learned to keep my mouth shut and to avoid letting drop any back-chat that might inform a listener that I knew more about schooners than I should. I had no desire to be classed as a 'low tar'.

Which brings us back to the problem already postulated – why one form of receptacle rather than another; why the sailing vessel rather than the steamer? Among the tremendously varied works of man are some that can be set in motion and imbued with a life of their own – they are classified under the general heading of 'machines'. Until the Industrial Revolution really got into its stride, the sailing ship was by far the most complicated machine that man had ever evolved. Compared to the sailing ship, the clock, the windmill and the water-wheel were relatively simple, their methods of functioning much easier to grasp. For centuries the ship floated about encrusted with shields, castles, tusks, galleries, battlements, lanterns and countless other peculiar pieces of equipment, but in its last few years it shed most of these and at last achieved a streamlined look, a smoothness, a sleekness, a fitness of purpose akin to that which is so marked in animals, birds and fishes. It has since been surpassed by only the aeroplane and it is in this that much of the tremendous attraction must lie.

The sea, of course, has never been without other attractions, other reasons to tempt people to venture forth upon it. It has always been a vast repository for those who, for one reason or another, have found it too difficult to cope with the greater complexities of life ashore; to some it has promised wealth, and to others distant scenes and far horizons. The reader will no doubt be familiar with Joseph Conrad's famous summing up of just how far it goes towards implementing all these promises. Some restless souls would seem to be attracted to it because only in its greater restlessness can they find the peace that they so much desire. Finally, for those who long for struggle, for the opportunity to win their spurs, to demonstrate their courage or their skill, the sea has always provided challenge enough to satisfy anybody. (It says much for the ferocity of the human race that its members were not satisfied, have never been satisfied. Not content to fight against the wind and the waves, they hurl lime pots and fire arrows at each other, attempt to puncture each other's vessels by ramming and, when they became available, mount guns with which to achieve the same result. The struggle with the sea has often had to take second place, although when Father Neptune finally cries 'Enough', and releases the full fury of a gale upon them, they still have to put their guns away.)

Most of the lures, wiles and will o' the wisps so far discussed apply as much to the power-driven vessel as to the sailing ship. But the latter had one attraction that the other did not possess and which was all the more gratifying because it was completely unexpected – the rigging. It did not surface in bad weather – at such times no one went aloft with any other intention than of returning to the deck at the earliest possible moment – but in fine weather to be up in the rigging gave a feeling of light, space and airiness that was in marked contrast to the deck below and helped to put the petty grievances and frictions of life into their correct perspective. Possibly it was not a factor that struck forcibly at those in big square riggers and North American fore and afters, whose decks were wide and spacious enough, but in the little ships of northern Europe, cluttered from end to end with gear, no one, I think, could set foot outside the knightheads or above the sheer-pole without a feeling of having escaped some kind of prison. By modern standards it would probably be considered as a poor and not particularly satisfactory substitute for flying. Of course it was nothing to be compared with the view from a high hill as there was only miles of water to stare at, but I suspect that in the small overcrowded naval vessels of the past many a man must have gone aloft for no other reason than to get away from the welter of packed humanity on and below the deck.

In my Runcorn days I rubbed shoulders at infrequent intervals with a man who was well qualified to pronounce the final judgement on the schooner and its entire works. His name was Tom, a native of Anglesey, and he had obtained his first command, a 530-ton coasting steamer while still in his early thirties, after having been a mate since about the age of twenty-four. This was in the depths of the 'slump' when there were plenty of good, well-qualified men out of a job. There was nothing out of the ordinary about his appearance or stature but he gave the impression of hidden reserves of power and energy that would only show up in a crisis. Later, when I met Christy Creenan, I was forcibly reminded of the Welshman.

About twelve months after our first meeting I learned from his shipmates that he was a good man to be with in a tight hole; a man with a lively mind who took an interest in all that was going on around him, with a strong tendency to get involved rather than stand about as an interested spectator. He was not, as far as I know, a dreamer, a romantic or a visionary, he seemed to have his feet firmly enough on the deck. His father was a schooner skipper and, in his childhood, Tom spent his summer holidays along with his sisters and his mother, aboard his father's vessel. It was the only time the whole family could be together for anything more than a few hours. It was inevitable that, sooner or later, the subject of schooners would crop up between us.

He told me that when he was fourteen he was sent off by train to join his first vessel at Connah's Quay. Along with various other things to be cooked for dinner the skipper gave him a large swede. He cut the skin off, as he had no doubt seen his mother do on many occasions, and put it into a pan of water to boil. When the meal was ready he carried it aft in the pan.

The skipper lifted the lid, jabbed at the swede with a fork and swore at him in Welsh and English, but mostly in English – I gather the Welsh language is remarkably deficient in the sort of high-power expletives that the skipper seemed to think were fitting to the occasion. Having by this means worked himself up into a frenzy the skipper finished his tirade by hurling the offending vegetable at young Tom.

On a much later occasion he was in a schooner that was left by her crew at Menai Bridge at noon on Saturday, with a clean-swept hold. When they returned on Monday morning after brief visits to their families they found she had 4ft of water in her above the ceiling. I do not now remember what astronomical length of time he said it took them to pump her out, but as he spoke I could see in his eyes that the memory of those endless weary hours of bitter, boring, back-breaking toil had come flooding back to him with peculiar intensity. Had his youthful footsteps been taken in places where big ships congregated I don't doubt for one minute that he would have risen to command them; as it was I am equally sure that, long before his seagoing career came to an end, he would have stood on the bridges of much larger and more imposing vessels than the humble 500-tonner that was his first command Society owes such men a hearing, for upon their capable shoulders rests much of the responsibility for seeing that the humdrum, day-to-day and highly necessary work of the world is carried out.

His verdict on schooners was pungent and to the point: *'Somebody ought to set fire to the whole bloody lot.'*

INDEX

The *Schedule of Ships* on pages 171-216 is not indexed. Page numbers in italic refer to illustrations.